Collins
EUROPE H

Conte

2 – 5	Factfile and motoring information
6	Country web site addresses
7	International country identification
8 – 9	Distance map and chart
10 – 11	International road signs
12	The European Union and Euro currency
13	Key to route planning maps
14 – 27	Route planning maps 1:5 833 000
28	Legend for road maps
29	Key to road maps
2	
9	...ugh-route maps
90	Amsterdam, Athina
91	Barcelona, Belfast
92	Berlin, Bern
93	Bordeaux, Bratislava
94	Bruxelles, București
95	Budapest, Cardiff
96	Dublin, Edinburgh
97	Firenze, Göteborg
98	Den Haag, Helsinki
99	København, Lisboa
100	Ljubljana, London
101	Madrid, Napoli
102	Oslo, Paris
103	Praha, Roma
104	Stockholm, Venezia
105	Warszawa, Wien
106 – 152	Index to place names

Published by Collins
An imprint of HarperCollins Publishers
Westerhill Road
Bishopbriggs
Glasgow G64 2QT
www.harpercollins.co.uk

First published 2009

Fourth edition 2014

A catalogue record for this book is available from the British Library

ISBN 978-0-00-758116-0

10 9 8 7 6 5 4 3 2 1

Printed in China by South China Printing Co. Ltd

All mapping in this atlas is generated from Collins Bartholomew digital databases.
Collins Bartholomew, the UK's leading independent geographical information supplier, can provide a digital, custom, and premium mapping service to a variety of markets.
For further information:
Tel: +44 (0)208 307 4515
e-mail: collinsbartholomew@harpercollins.co.uk
or visit our website at: www.collinsbartholomew.com

If you would like to comment on any aspect of this book, please contact us at the above address or online.
e-mail: collinsmaps@harpercollins.co.uk
facebook.com/collinsmaps  @collinsmaps

Country Capital city Country identification National flag	Official language	Currency	Speed limits Motorway Dual carriageway Rural Town	Emergency numbers Police Fire + Ambulance	Motoring Organisations
Austria Wien A	German	Euro = 100 cents	Motorway 130 km/h Rural 100 km/h Town 50 km/h	Police 112 Fire 112 + 112	**ÖAMTC** Österreichischer Automobil-, Motorrad- und Touring Club www.oeamtc.at **ARBÖ** Auto-, Motor- und Radfahrerbund Österreichs http://www.arboe.at/home
Albania Tiranë AL	Albanian	Lek = 100 qindarka	Motorway 110 km/h Rural 80/90 km/h Town 40 km/h	Police 19 Fire 18 + 17	**ACA** Klubi i Automobilit te Shqipërisë http://aca.al/
Andorra Andorra la Vella AND	Catalan	Euro = 100 cents	Rural 70 km/h Town 40 km/h	Police 110 Fire 118 + 116	**ACA** Automòbil Club d'Andorra www.aca.ad/
Belgium Bruxelles B	French Dutch Flemish	Euro = 100 cents	Motorway 120 km/h Dual carriageway 120 km/h Rural 90 km/h Town 50 km/h	Police 112 Fire 112 + 112	**RACB** Royal Automobile Club of Belgium www.racb.com **TCB** Touring Club Belgium www.touring.be
Bulgaria Sofiya BG	Bulgarian	Lev	Motorway 130 km/h Rural 90 km/h Town 50 km/h	Police 166 Fire 160 + 150	**UAB** Union of Bulgarian Motorists www.uab.org
Bosnia and Herzogovina Sarajevo BIH	Bosnian Serbian Croatian	Konvertibilna Marka = 100 pfennig	Motorway 130 km/h Rural 80 km/h Town 50 km/h	Police 122 Fire 123 + 124	**BIHAMK** Bosanskohercegovački auto-moto klub www.bihamk.ba
Belarus Minsk BY	Belarussian Russian	Belarus Rouble	Motorway 110/120 km/h Rural 90 km/h Town 60 km/h	Police 02 Fire 01 + 03	**BKA** Belarussian Auto Moto Touring Club www.bka.by
Switzerland Bern CH	German French Italian	Swiss Franc = 100 rappen/ centimes	Motorway 120 km/h Dual carriageway 100 km/h Rural 80 km/h Town 50 km/h	Police 117/112 Fire 118/112 + 144/112	**TCS** Touring Club Suisse/Schweiz/Svizzero www.tcs.ch **ACS** Automobil Club der Schweiz/Automobil club de Suisse www.acs.ch
Cyprus Lefkosia (Nicosia) CY	Greek Turkish (North Cyprus)	Euro = 100 cents North Cyprus New Lira = 100 new kurus	Motorway 100 km/h Rural 80 km/h Town 50 km/h	Police 199/112 Fire 199/112 + 199/112 (N Cyprus): Police 155/112 Fire 199/112 + 112	**CAA** Cyprus Automobile Association www.caa.com.cy
Czech Republic Praha CZ	Czech	Koruna = 100 hellers	Motorway 130 km/h Rural 90 km/h Town 50 km/h	Police 112 Fire 112 + 112	**ÚAMK** Ústřední automotoklub České republiky www.uamk.cz **ACCR** Autoklub České Republiky www.autoklub.cz
Germany Berlin D	German	Euro = 100 cents	Motorway 130 km/h Rural 100 km/h Town 50 km/h	Police 110 Fire 112 + 110	**ADAC** Allgemeiner Deutscher Automobil Club www.adac.de **AVD** Automobilclub von Deutschland www.avd.de
Denmark København DK	Danish	Krone = 100 øre	Motorway 110/130 km/h Rural 90 km/h Town 50 km/h	Police 112 Fire 112 + 112	**FDM** Forenede Danske Motorejere www.fdm.dk

Country Capital city Country identification National flag	Official language	Currency	Speed limits Motorway Dual carriageway Rural Town	Emergency numbers Police Fire + Ambulance	Motoring Organisations
Spain Madrid E	Spanish Catalan Galician Basque	Euro = 100 cents	120 km/h 100 km/h 90 km/h 50 km/h	112 112 + 112	**RACE** Real Automóvil Club de España www.race.es
Estonia Tallinn EST	Estonian	Euro = 100 cents	110 km/h 90 km/h 50 km/h	112 112 + 112	**Eesti Autoklubi** www.autoclub.ee
France Paris F	French	Euro = 100 cents	130 km/h 110 km/h 90 km/h 50 km/h	17/112 18/112 + 15/112	**Automobile Club Association** Association Française des Automobilistes www.automobile-club.org
Finland Helsinki FIN	Finnish Swedish	Euro = 100 cents	120 km/h 100 km/h 80 km/h 50 km/h	112 112 + 112	**AL** Autoliitto www.autoliitto.fi
Liechtenstein Vaduz FL	German	Swiss Franc = 100 rappen	80 km/h 50 km/h	112 112 + 112	**ACFL** Automobil Club Fürstentum Liechtenstein www.acfl.li
United Kingdom London GB	English	Pound = 100 pence	70 mph 70 mph 60 mph 30 mph	999/112 999/112 + 999/112	**AA** Automobile Association www.theaa.com **RAC** Royal Automobile Club www2.rac.co.uk
Greece Athina GR	Greek	Euro = 100 cents	130 km/h 80/110 km/h 50 km/h	112 112 + 112	**ELPA** Automobile and Touring Club of Greece www.elpa.gr
Hungary Budapest H	Hungarian	Forint = 100 fillér	130 km/h 110 km/h 90 km/h 50 km/h	107 112 + 104	**Magyar Autóklub** www.autoklub.hu
Croatia (Hvratska) Zagreb HR	Croat	Kuna = 100 Lipa	130 km/h 110 km/h 90 km/h 50 km/h	192 193 + 194	**HAK** Hrvatski Autoklub www.hak.hr
Italy Roma I	Italian	Euro = 100 cents	130 km/h 110 km/h 90 km/h 50 km/h	112 115/112 + 118/112	**ACI** Automobile Club d'Italia www.aci.it
Ireland Dublin IRL	Irish English	Euro = 100 cents	120 km/h 80/100 km/h 50 km/h	999/112 999/112 + 999/112	**AA Ireland** The Automobile Association Ireland Limited www.aaireland.ie
Iceland Rekyavik IS	Icelandic	Krona = 100 aura	90 km/h (tarmac) 80 km/h (untarred) 50 km/h	112 112 + 112	**FIB** Félag íslenskra bifreiðaeigenda www.fib.is

Country Capital city Country identification National flag	Official language	Currency	Speed limits Motorway Dual carriageway Rural Town	Emergency numbers Police Fire + Ambulance	Motoring Organisations
Luxembourg Luxembourg L	Luxembourgish French German	Euro = 100 cents	130 km/h 90 km/h 50 km/h	113 112 + 112	**ACL** Automobile Club du Grand-Duché de Luxembourg www.acl.lu
Lithuania Vilnius LT	Lithuanian	Litas = 100 centas	130 km/h 110 km/h 90 km/h 50 km/h	112 112 + 112	**LAS** Lietuvos automobilininkų sąjunga www.las.lt
Latvia Rīga LV	Latvian	Euro = 100 cents	110 km/h 90/100 km/h 50 km/h	02/112 01/112 + 03/112	**LAMB** Latvijas Automoto Biedrība www.lamb.lv
Malta Valletta M	Maltese English	Euro = 100 cents	80 km/h 50 km/h	112 112 + 112	**TCM** Touring Club Malta www.touringclubmalta.org
Monaco Monaco MC	French	Euro = 100 cents	130 km/h 110 km/h 90 km/h 50 km/h	112 112 + 112	**ACM** Automobile Club de Monaco www.acm.mc
Moldova Chişinău MD	Romanian Ukranian	Leu = 100 bani	110 km/h 80 km/h 50 km/h	902 901 + 903	**ACM** Automobil Club din Moldova www.acm.md
Macedonia (F.Y.R.O.M.) Skopje MK	Macedonian Albanian	Macedonian Denar	120 km/h 100 km/h 80 km/h 50 km/h	192 193 + 194	**AMSM** Avto Moto Sojuz na Makedonija www.amsm.com.mk
Montenegro Podgorica MNE	Serbian (Montenegrin) Albanian	Euro = 100 cents	120 km/h 100 km/h 80 km/h 50 km/h	92 93 + 94	**AMSCG** Auto-moto savez Crne Gore www.amscg.org
Norway Oslo N	Norwegian	Norwegian Krone = 100 øre	100 km/h 80/90 km/h 50 km/h	112 110 + 113	**KNA** Kongelig Norsk Automobilklub www.kna.no
The Netherlands Amsterdam NL	Dutch	Euro = 100 cents	120 km/h 100 km/h 80 km/h 50 km/h	112 112 + 112	**ANWB** Koninklijke Nederlandse Toeristenbond ANWB www.anwb.nl **KNAC** Koninklijke Nederlandsche Automobiel Club www.knac.nl
Portugal Lisboa P	Portuguese	Euro = 100 cents	120 km/h 100 km/h 90 km/h 50 km/h	112 112 + 112	**ACP** Automóvel Club de Portugal www.acp.pt

Country Capital city Country identification National flag	Official language	Currency	Speed limits Motorway Dual carriageway Rural Town	Emergency numbers Police Fire + Ambulance	Motoring Organisations
Poland Warszawa PL	Polish	Złoty = 100 groszy	140 km/h 120 km/h 90 km/h 50/60 km/h	997/112 998/112 + 999/112	**PZM** Polski Związek Motorowy www.pzm.pl
Kosovo Prishtinë RKS	Albanian Serbian	Euro = 100 cents	130 km/h 100 km/h 50 km/h	92/112 93/112 + 94/112	
Romania Bucureşti RO	Romanian	New Romanian Leu = 100 new bani	130 km/h 90/100 km/h 50 km/h	112 112 + 112	**ACR** Automobil Clubul Roman www.acr.ro
San Marino San Marino RSM	Italian	Euro = 100 cents	130 km/h 110 km/h 90 km/h 50 km/h	112 887777 + 118	**ACS** Automobile Club San Marino
Russia Moskva RUS	Russian	Rouble = 100 kopeck	110 km/h 90 km/h 60 km/h	02 01 + 03	**VOA** All-Russian Society of Motorists www.voa.ru
Sweden Stockholm S	Swedish	Krona = 100 öre	110/120 km/h 70-100 km/h 70-100 km/h 30-60 km/h	112 112 + 112	**M** Motormännens Riksförbund www.motormannen.se
Slovakia Bratislava SK	Slovak	Euro = 100 cents	130 km/h 90 km/h 50 km/h	158/112 150/112 + 155/112	**SATC** Slovenský Autoturist Klub www.satc.sk
Slovenia Ljubljana SLO	Slovene	Euro = 100 cents	130 km/h 100 km/h 90 km/h 50 km/h	113 112 + 112	**AMZS** Avto-Moto Zveza Slovenije www.amzs.si
Serbia Beograd SRB	Serbian Albanian Hungarian	Serbian Dinar = 100 paras Euro = 100 cents	120 km/h 100 km/h 80 km/h 50 km/h	92 93 + 94	**AMSS** Auto-moto savez Srbije www.amss.org.rs
Turkey Ankara TR	Turkish	New Turkish Lira = 100 kuru	120 km/h 110 km/h 90 km/h 50 km/h	155 110 + 112	**TTOK** Türkiye Turıng ve Otomobıl Kurumu www.turing.org.tr
Ukraine Kyiv UA	Ukrainian	Hryvnya = 100 kopiyok	130 km/h 110 km/h 90 km/h 60 km/h	02 01 + 03	**FAU** Federation Automobile d'Ukraine www.fau.ua

Country	Official website	Tourism website
Albania	www.km.gov.al	www.albaniantourism.com
Andorra	www.govern.ad	www.andorra.ad
Austria	www.bundeskanzleramt.at	www.austria.info
Belarus	www.belarus.by	http://eng.belarustourism.by
Belgium	www.belgium.be/en	Flanders: www.visitflanders.com Wallonia: www.opt.be www.eastbelgium.com
Bosnia and Herzegovina	www.fbihvlada.gov.ba	www.bhtourism.ba
Bulgaria	www.government.bg	http://bulgariatravel.org
Croatia	www.vlada.hr	www.croatia.hr
Cyprus	www.cyprus.gov.cy	www.visitcyprus.com
Czech Republic	www.czech.cz www.vlada.cz/en/	www.czechtourism.com
Denmark	www.denmark.dk	www.visitdenmark.com
Estonia	www.valitsus.ee	www.visitestonia.com
Finland	www.valtioneuvosto.fi	www.visitfinland.com
France	www.gouvernement.fr	www.uk.franceguide.com
Germany	www.deutschland.de	www.germany.travel
Greece	www.primeminister.gr	www.visitgreece.gr
Hungary	www.magyarorszag.hu	http://gotohungary.com
Iceland	www.iceland.is	www.visiticeland.com
Ireland	www.gov.ie	www.discoverireland.ie
Italy	www.governo.it	www.italia.it
Kosovo	www.rks-gov.net/en-US	www.kosovotourismcenter.com
Latvia	www.saeima.lv	www.latvia.travel/en
Liechtenstein	www.liechtenstein.li	www.tourismus.li
Lithuania	www.lrv.lt	www.travel.lt
Luxembourg	www.gouvernement.lu	www.visitluxembourg.com
Macedonia (F.Y.R.O.M.)	www.vlada.mk	www.exploringmacedonia.com
Malta	www.gov.mt	www.visitmalta.com
Moldova	www.moldova.md	www.turism.gov.md
Monaco	www.monaco.gouv.mc	www.visitmonaco.com
Montenegro	www.gov.me	www.visit-montenegro.com
Netherlands	www.overheid.nl	www.holland.com
Norway	www.norway.info	www.visitnorway.com
Poland	www.poland.gov.pl	www.poland.travel
Portugal	www.portugal.gov.pt	www.visitportugal.com
Romania	www.guv.ro	www.romaniatourism.com
Russia	www.gov.ru	www.russiatourism.ru
San Marino	www.consigliograndeegenerale.sm	www.visitsanmarino.com
Serbia	www.srbija.gov.rs	www.serbia.travel
Slovakia	www.government.gov.sk	www.slovakia.travel
Slovenia	www.gov.si	www.slovenia.info
Spain	www.la-moncloa.es	www.spain.info
Sweden	www.sweden.se	www.visitsweden.com
Switzerland	www.swissworld.org	www.myswitzerland.com
Turkey	www.mfa.gov.tr	www.goturkey.com
Ukraine	www.kmu.gov.ua	www.traveltoukraine.org
United Kingdom	www.direct.gov.uk	www.visitbritain.com
Vatican City	www.vaticanstate.va	www.vaticanstate.va

International country identification

Code	English	Français	Deutsch
A	Austria	Autriche	Österreich
AL	Albania	Albanie	Albanien
AND	Andorra	Andorre	Andorra
B	Belgium	Belgique	Belgien
BG	Bulgaria	Bulgarie	Bulgarien
BIH	Bosnia and Herzegovina	Bosnie-et-Herzégovine	Bosnien und Herzegowina
BY	Belarus	Bélarus	Belarus
CH	Switzerland	Suisse	Schweiz
CY	Cyprus	la Chypre	Zypern
CZ	Czech Republic	République tchèque	Tschechische Republik
D	Germany	Allemagne	Deutschland
DK	Denmark	Danemark	Dänemark
DZ	Algeria	Algérie	Algerien
E	Spain	Espagne	Spanien
EST	Estonia	Estonie	Estland
F	France	France	Frankreich
FIN	Finland	Finlande	Finnland
FL	Liechtenstein	Liechtenstein	Liechtenstein
FO	Faroe Islands	Iles Féroé	Färöer-Inseln
GB	United Kingdom GB & NI	Grande-Bretagne	Grossbritannien
GBA	Alderney	Alderney	Alderney
GBG	Guernsey	Guernsey	Guernsey
GBJ	Jersey	Jersey	Jersey
GBM	Isle of Man	île de Man	Insel Man
GBZ	Gibraltar	Gibraltar	Gibraltar
GR	Greece	Grèce	Griechenland
H	Hungary	Hongrie	Ungarn
HR	Croatia	Croatie	Kroatien
I	Italy	Italie	Italien
IRL	Ireland	Irlande	Irland
IS	Iceland	Islande	Island
L	Luxembourg	Luxembourg	Luxemburg
LT	Lithuania	Lituanie	Litauen
LV	Latvia	Lettonie	Lettland
M	Malta	Malte	Malta
MA	Morocco	Maroc	Marokko
MC	Monaco	Monaco	Monaco
MD	Moldova	Moldavie	Moldawien
MK	Macedonia (F.Y.R.O.M.)	Ancienne République yougoslave de Macédoine	Ehemalige jugoslawische Republik Mazedonien
MNE	Montenegro	Monténégro	Montenegro
N	Norway	Norvège	Norwegen
NL	Netherlands	Pays-Bas	Niederlande
P	Portugal	Portugal	Portugal
PL	Poland	Pologne	Polen
RKS	Kosovo	Kosovo	Kosovo
RO	Romania	Roumanie	Rumänien
RSM	San Marino	Saint-Marin	San Marino
RUS	Russia	Russie	Russland
S	Sweden	Suède	Schweden
SK	Slovakia	République slovaque	Slowakei
SLO	Slovenia	Slovénie	Slowenien
SRB	Serbia	Sérbie	Serbien
TN	Tunisia	Tunisie	Tunisien
TR	Turkey	Turquie	Türkei
UA	Ukraine	Ukraine	Ukraine

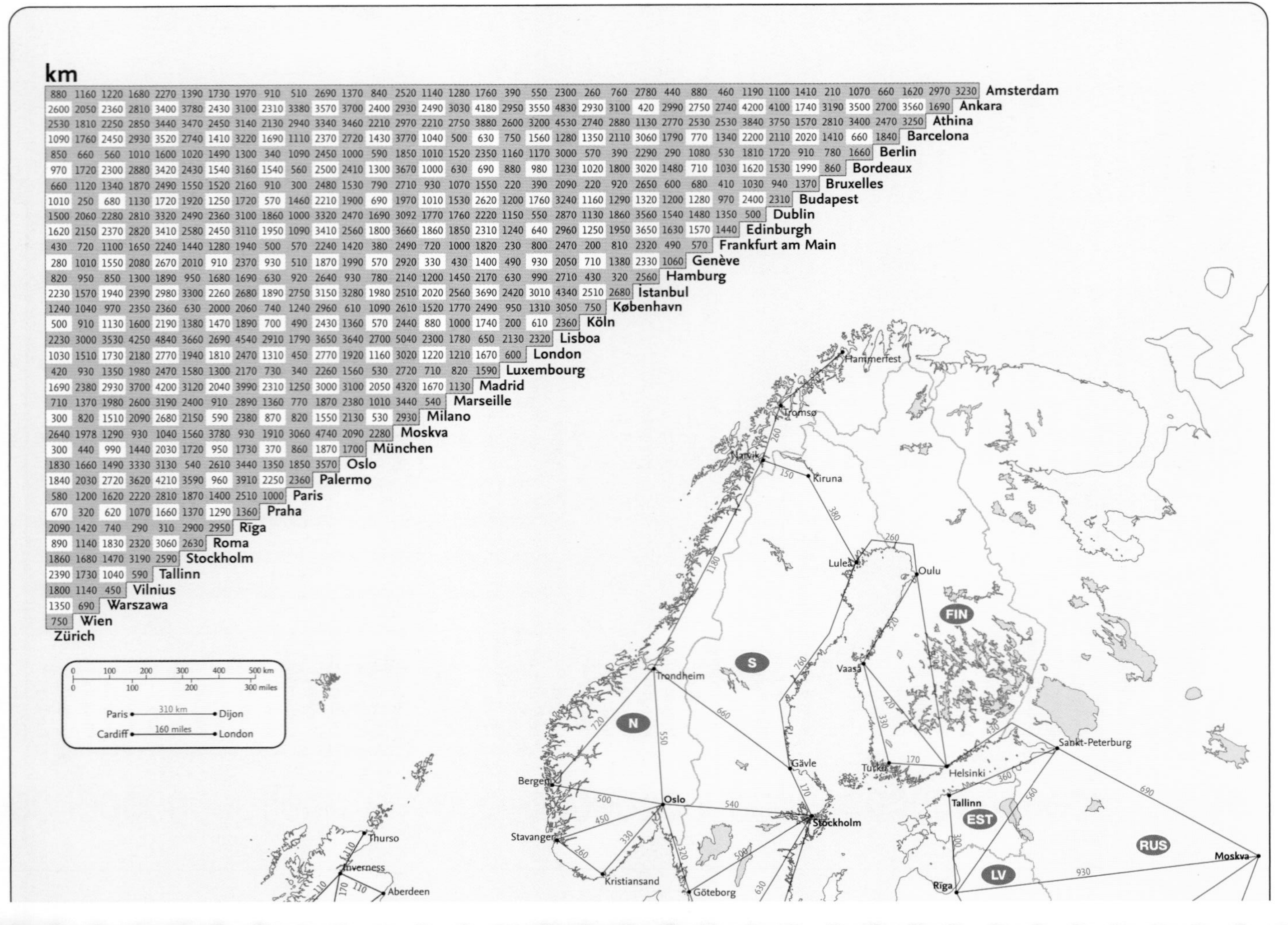

km

	Zürich	Wien	Warszawa	Vilnius	Tallinn	Stockholm	Roma	Rīga	Praha	Paris	Palermo	Oslo	München	Moskva	Milano	Marseille	Madrid	Luxembourg	London	Lisboa	Köln	København	İstanbul	Hamburg	Genève	Frankfurt am Main	Edinburgh	Dublin	Budapest	Bruxelles	Bordeaux	Berlin	Barcelona	Athina	Ankara
Amsterdam	880	1160	1220	1680	2270	1390	1730	1970	910	510	2690	1370	840	2520	1140	1280	1760	390	550	2300	260	760	2780	440	880	460	1190	1100	1410	210	1070	660	1620	2970	3230
Ankara	2600	2050	2360	2810	3400	3780	2430	3100	2310	3380	3570	3700	2400	2930	2490	3030	4180	2950	3550	4830	2930	3100	420	2990	2750	2740	4200	4100	1740	3190	3500	2700	3560	1690	
Athina	2530	1810	2250	2850	3440	3470	2450	3140	2130	2940	3340	3460	2210	2970	2210	2750	3880	2600	3200	4530	2740	2880	1130	2770	2530	2530	3840	3750	1570	2810	3400	2470	3250		
Barcelona	1090	1760	2450	2930	3520	2740	1410	3220	1690	1110	2370	2720	1430	3770	1040	500	630	750	1560	1280	1350	2110	3060	1790	770	1340	2200	2110	2020	1410	660	1840			
Berlin	850	660	560	1010	1600	1020	1490	1300	340	1090	2450	1000	590	1850	1010	1520	2350	1160	1170	3000	570	390	2290	290	1080	530	1810	1720	910	780	1660				
Bordeaux	970	1720	2300	2880	3420	2430	1540	3160	1540	560	2500	2410	1300	3670	1000	630	690	880	980	1230	1020	1800	3020	1480	710	1030	1620	1530	1990	860					
Bruxelles	660	1120	1340	1870	2490	1550	1520	2160	910	300	2480	1530	790	2710	930	1070	1550	220	390	2090	220	920	2650	600	680	410	1030	940	1370						
Budapest	1010	250	680	1130	1720	1920	1250	1720	570	1460	2210	1900	690	1970	1010	1530	2620	1200	1760	3240	1160	1290	1320	1200	1280	970	2400	2310							
Dublin	1500	2060	2280	2810	3320	2490	2360	3100	1860	1000	3320	2470	1690	3092	1770	1760	2220	1150	550	2870	1130	1860	3560	1540	1480	1350	500								
Edinburgh	1620	2150	2370	2820	3410	2580	2450	3110	1950	1090	3410	2560	1800	3660	1860	1850	2310	1240	640	2960	1250	1950	3650	1630	1570	1440									
Frankfurt am Main	430	720	1100	1650	2240	1440	1280	1940	500	570	2240	1420	380	2490	720	1000	1820	230	800	2470	200	810	2320	490	570										
Genève	280	1010	1550	2080	2670	2010	910	2370	930	510	1870	1990	570	2920	330	430	1400	490	930	2050	710	1380	2330	1060											
Hamburg	820	950	850	1300	1890	950	1680	1690	630	920	2640	930	780	2140	1200	1450	2170	630	990	2710	430	320	2560												
İstanbul	2230	1570	1940	2390	2980	3300	2260	2680	1890	2750	3150	3280	1980	2510	2020	2560	3690	2420	3010	4340	2510	2680													
København	1240	1040	970	2350	2360	630	2000	2060	740	1240	2960	610	1090	2610	1520	1770	2490	950	1310	3050	750														
Köln	500	910	1130	1600	2190	1380	1470	1890	700	490	2430	1360	570	2440	880	1000	1740	200	610	2360															
Lisboa	2230	3000	3530	4250	4840	3660	2690	4540	2910	1790	3650	3640	2700	5040	2300	1780	650	2130	2320																
London	1030	1510	1730	2180	2770	1940	1810	2470	1310	450	2770	1920	1160	3020	1220	1210	1670	600																	
Luxembourg	420	930	1350	1980	2470	1580	1300	2170	730	340	2260	1560	530	2720	710	820	1590																		
Madrid	1690	2380	2930	3700	4200	3120	2040	3990	2310	1250	3000	3100	2050	4320	1670	1130																			
Marseille	710	1370	1980	2600	3190	2400	910	2890	1360	770	1870	2380	1010	3440	540																				
Milano	300	820	1510	2090	2680	2150	590	2380	870	820	1550	2130	530	2930																					
Moskva	2640	1978	1290	930	1040	1560	3780	930	1910	3060	4740	2090	2280																						
München	300	440	990	1440	2030	1720	950	1730	370	860	1870	1700																							
Oslo	1830	1660	1490	3330	3130	540	2610	3440	1350	1850	3570																								
Palermo	1840	2030	2720	3620	4210	3590	960	3910	2250	2360																									
Paris	580	1200	1620	2220	2810	1870	1400	2510	1000																										
Praha	670	320	620	1070	1660	1370	1290	1360																											
Rīga	2090	1420	740	290	310	2900	2950																												
Roma	890	1140	1830	2320	3060	2630																													
Stockholm	1860	1680	1470	3190	2590																														
Tallinn	2390	1730	1040	590																															
Vilnius	1800	1140	450																																
Warszawa	1350	690																																	
Wien	750																																		

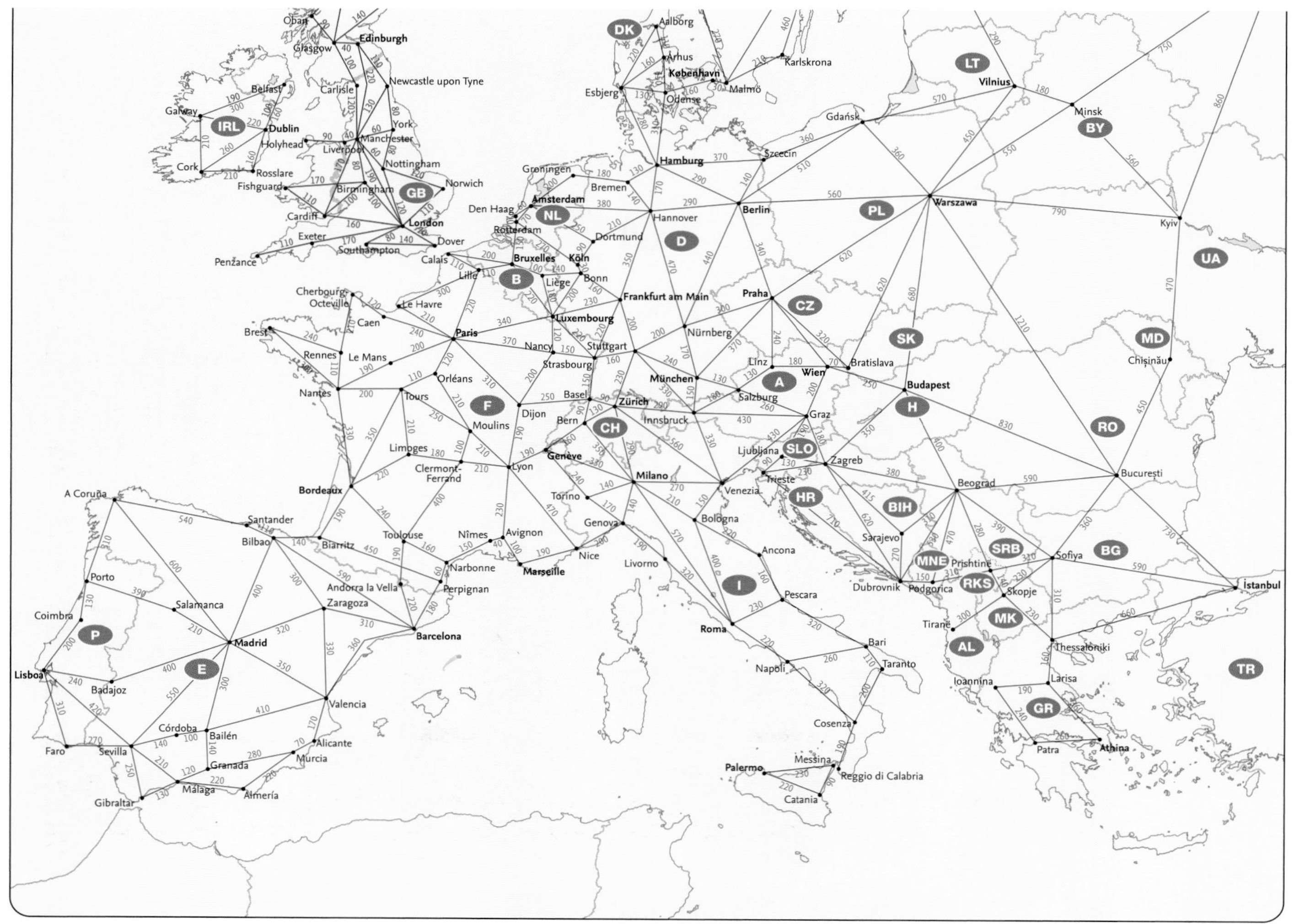

Oban
Edinburgh
Glasgow
Newcastle upon Tyne
Carlisle
Belfast
Galway
IRL
Dublin
Holyhead
York
Manchester
Liverpool
Cork
Rosslare
Nottingham
Fishguard
Birmingham
GB
Norwich
Cardiff
London
Exeter
Dover
Southampton
Penzance
DK
Aalborg
Århus
København
Odense
Esbjerg
Malmö
Karlskrona
LT
Vilnius
Minsk
BY
Gdańsk
Szczecin
Hamburg
Groningen
Bremen
Amsterdam
NL
Den Haag
Rotterdam
Hannover
Berlin
PL
Warszawa
Kyiv
UA
Dortmund
D
Calais
Bruxelles
Köln
Lille
B
Liège
Bonn
Frankfurt am Main
Praha
CZ
Cherbourg-Octeville
Le Havre
Caen
Luxembourg
Brest
Paris
Nancy
Stuttgart
Strasbourg
Nürnberg
SK
MD
Chişinău
Rennes
Le Mans
Linz
Wien
Bratislava
Nantes
Orléans
München
A
Budapest
Tours
F
Basel
Zürich
Salzburg
Dijon
Moulins
Bern
CH
Innsbruck
Graz
H
RO
Limoges
Clermont-Ferrand
Lyon
Genève
Ljubljana
SLO
Zagreb
Milano
Trieste
Beograd
Bucureşti
A Coruña
Bordeaux
Torino
Venezia
HR
BIH
Santander
Bilbao
Biarritz
Toulouse
Nîmes
Avignon
Genova
Bologna
Sarajevo
MNE
SRB
Sofiya
BG
Narbonne
Marseille
Nice
Livorno
Ancona
Prishtinë
RKS
Porto
Andorra la Vella
Perpignan
Dubrovnik
Podgorica
Skopje
İstanbul
Salamanca
Zaragoza
I
Pescara
MK
Coimbra
P
Madrid
Barcelona
Roma
Tiranë
AL
Thessaloniki
Bari
Napoli
Taranto
TR
Lisboa
Badajoz
E
Ioannina
Larisa
Valencia
GR
Córdoba
Bailén
Alicante
Cosenza
Faro
Sevilla
Granada
Murcia
Patra
Athina
Messina
Palermo
Reggio di Calabria
Málaga
Almería
Catania
Gibraltar

Motorway
Autoroute
Autobahn

Motorway
Autoroute
Autobahn

End of motorway
Fin d'autoroute
Ende der Autobahn

End of motorway
Fin d'autoroute
Ende der Autobahn

Lane for slow vehicles
Voie pour véhicules lents
Fahrsspur für langsam fahrende Fahrzeuge

'Semi motorway'
Route pour automobiles
Kraftfahrstraße

End of 'Semi motorway'
Fin de route pour automobiles
Ende der Kraftfahrstraße

European route number
Numéro européen de route
Nummernschild für Europastraßen

Priority road
Route prioritaire
Vorfahrtstraße

End of priority road
Fin de route prioritaire
Ende der Vorfahrtstraße

Priority over oncoming vehicles
Priorité par rapport aux véhicules venant en sens inverse
Gegenverkehr muss warten

One way street
Rue à sens unique
Einbahnstraße

One way street
Rue à sens unique
Einbahnstraße

No through road
Route sans issue
Sackgasse

Hospital
Hôpital
Krankenhaus

Parking
Parking
Parkplatz

Pedestrian crossing
Passage pour piétons
Fußgängerüberweg

First aid post
Premiers secours
Erste Hilfe

Information
Informations
Fremdenverkehrsbüro oder Auskunftsstelle

Hotel/Motel
Hôtel
Autobahnhotel

Restaurant
Restaurant
Autobahngasthaus

Mechanical help
Assistance mécanique
Pannenhilfe

Filling station
Station essence
Tankstelle

Telephone
Téléphone
Fernsprecher

Camping site
Zone de camping pour tentes
Zeltplatz

Caravan site
Zone de camping pour caravanes
Wohnwagenplatz

Youth hostel
Auberge de jeunesse
Jugendherberge

Right bend
Virage à droite
Kurve (rechts)

Left bend
Virage à gauche
Kurve (links)

Double bend
Succession de virages
Doppelkurve

Roundabout
Circulation en sens giratoire
Kreisverkehr

Intersection with non-priority road
Intersection avec une route non-prioritaire
Vorfahrt

Traffic merges from left
Rétrécissement sur la gauche
Verkehr ordnet sich von links ein

Traffic merges from right
Rétrécissement sur la droite
Verkehr ordnet sich von rechts ein

Road narrows
Chaussée rétrécie
Verengte Fahrbahn

Road narrows at left
Chaussée rétrécie à gauche
Einseitig (links) verengte Fahrbahn

Road narrows at right
Chaussée rétrécie à droite
Einseitig (rechts) verengte Fahrbahn

Give way
Cédez le passage
Vorfahrt gewähren

Slippery road
Chaussée glissante
Schleudergefahr

Uneven road
Cassis
Unebene Fahrbahn

Steep hill – descent
Descente ou montée à forte inclinaison
Gefälle

Tunnel
Tunnel
Tunnel

Opening bridge
Pont mobile
Bewegliche Brücke

Road works
Travaux
Baustelle

Loose chippings
Projection de gravillons
Splitt, Schotter

Level crossing with barrier
Passage à niveau avec barrière
Bahnübergang mit Schranken oder Halbschranken

Level crossing without barrier
Passage à niveau sans barrière
Unbeschrankter Bahnübergang

Tram
Tramway
Straßenbahn

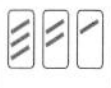
'Count down' posts
Balises pour passage à niveau
Bake vor Autobahnausfahrt

'Danger' level crossing
Attention au train !
Achtung Bahnübergang

Low flying aircraft
Avions volant à basse altitude
Flugbetrieb

Falling rocks
Chutes de pierre
Steinschlag

Cross wind
Vents contraires
Seitenwind

Quayside or river bank
Débouché sur un quai ou une berge
Ufer

Two-way traffic
Circulation dans les deux sens
Gegenverkehr

Traffic signals ahead
Annonce de feux tricolores
Lichtzeichenanlage

Pedestrians
Piétons
Fußgänger

Children
Endroit fréquenté par les enfants
Kinder

Animals
Passages d'animaux
Viehtrieb, Tiere

Wild animals
Passage d'animaux sauvages
Wildwechsel

Other dangers
Autres dangers
Gefahrstelle

Beginning of regulation
Début de prescription
Anfang

Repetition sign
Panneau de rappel
Wiederholung

End of regulation
Fin de prescription
Ende

End of all restrictions
Fin de toutes les limitations
Ende sämtlicher Streckenverbote

Halt sign
Stop
Halt! Vorfahrt gewähren!

Customs
Douanes
Zollstelle

No stopping ("clearway")
Arrêt interdit
Halteverbot

No parking/waiting
Arrêt et stationnement interdits
Eingeschränktes Halteverbot

Priority to oncoming vehicles
Priorité aux vehicules venant en sens inverse
Dem Gegenverkehr Vorrang gewähren!

Use of horns prohibited
Avertisseur sonore interdit
Hupverbot

Roundabout
Circulation en sens giratoire
Kreisverkehr

Direction to be followed
Obligation de suivre la direction indiquée par la flèche
Vorgeschriebene Fahrtrichtung

Pass this side
Obligation de suivre la direction indiquée par la flèche
Rechts/Links vorbei

Minimum speed limit
Vitesse minimum autorisée
Vorgeschriebene Mindestgeschwindigkeit

End of minimum speed limit
Fin de vitesse minimum
Ende der vorgeschriebenen Mindestgeschwindigkeit

All vehicles prohibited
Interdit à tous les véhicules
Verbot für Fahrzeuge aller Art

No entry for all vehicles
Interdiction d'entrer pour tous les véhicules
Verbot der Einfahrt

No right turn
Interdiction de tourner à droite
Rechtsabbiegen verboten

No u-turns
Interdiction de faire demi-tour
Wendeverbot

No entry for motor cars
Accès interdit aux automobiles motorisées
Verbot für Kraftwagen

No entry for all motor vehicles
Accès interdit à tous les véhicules motorisés
Verbot für Kraftfahrzeuge und Kraftwagen

Motorcycles prohibited
Interdit aux motocycles
Verbot für Krafträder

Mopeds prohibited
Interdit aux motocylettes
Verbot für Mofas

No overtaking
Interdiction de dépasser
Überholverbot für Kraftfahrzeuge aller Art

End of no overtaking
Fin d'interdiction de dépasser
Ende des Überholverbots für Kraftfahrzeuge aller Art

Maximum speed limit
Vitesse maximum
Zulässige Höchstgeschwindigkeit

End of speed limit
Fin de limitation de vitesse
Ende der zulässigen Höchstgeschwindigkeit

12 The European Union and Euro currency

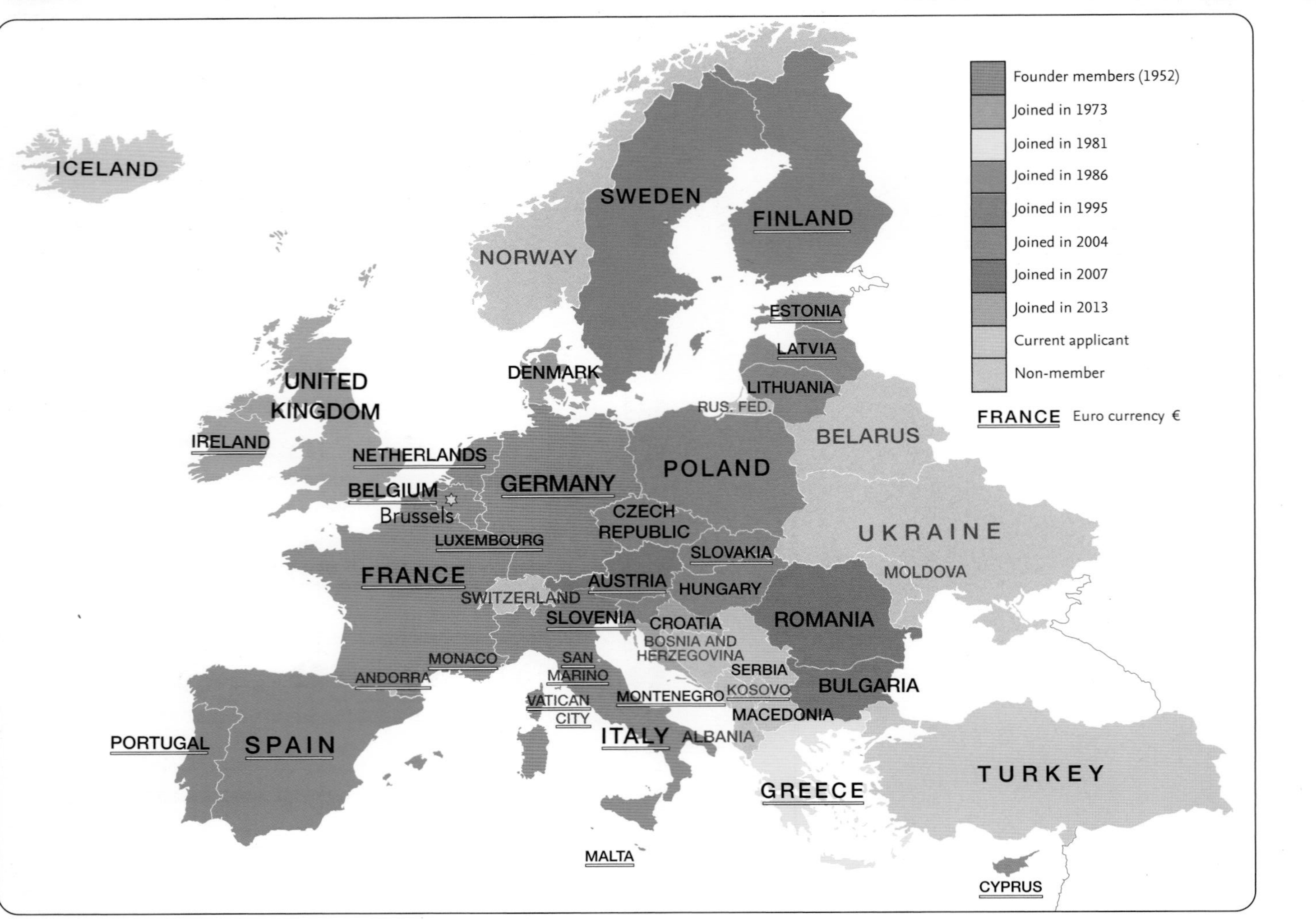

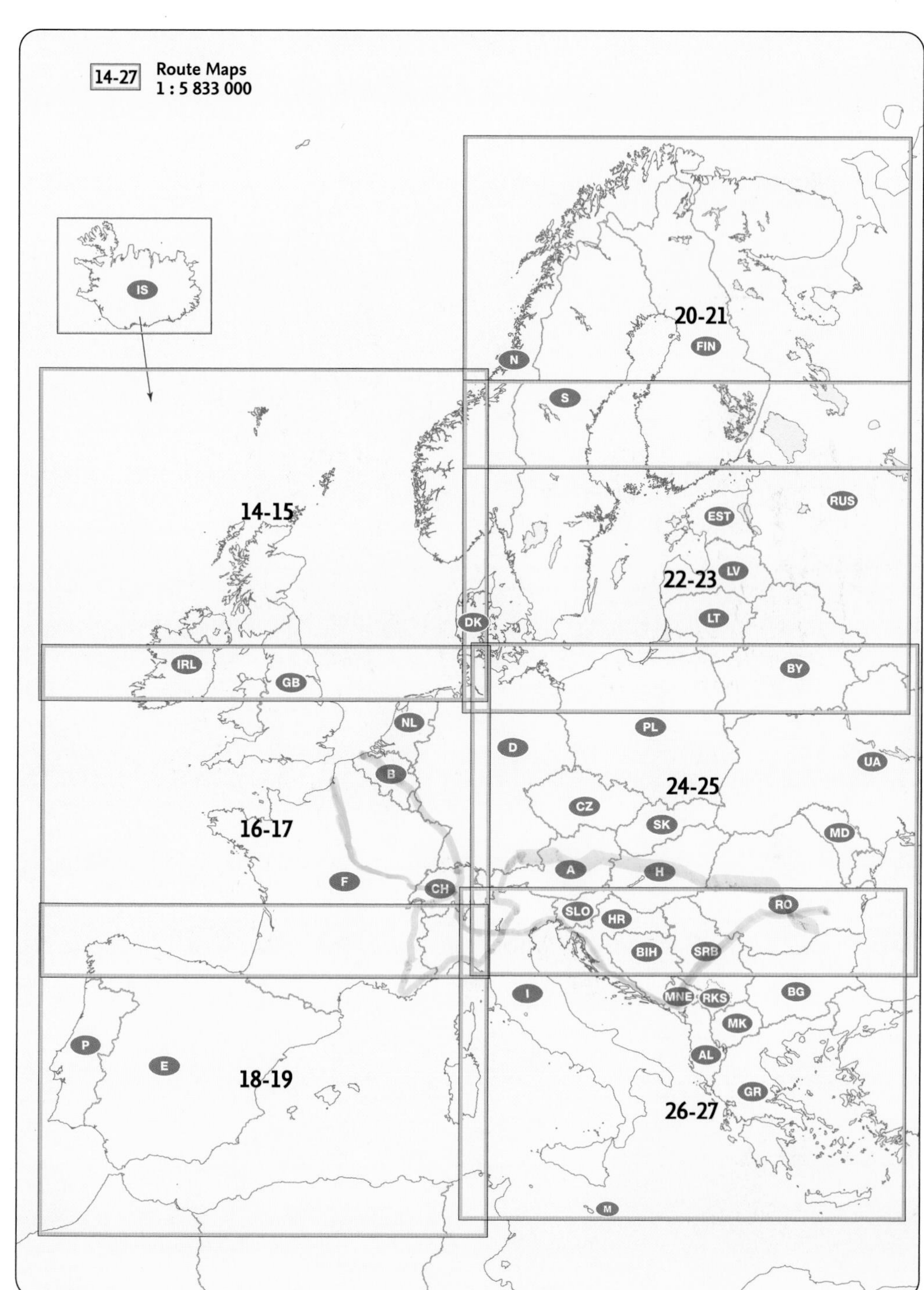
14-27
Route Maps
1 : 5 833 000
IS
N
FIN
20-21
S
14-15
RUS
EST
LV
22-23
DK
LT
IRL
GB
BY
NL
PL
D
B
UA
24-25
CZ
16-17
SK
MD
A
H
F
CH
RO
SLO
HR
BIH
SRB
I
MNE
RKS
BG
MK
P
E
18-19
AL
GR
26-27
M

66° 24° 22° 20° 18° 16°
Straumnes
Horn
Ísafjörður
Bjargtangar
Grímsey
Reiphólsfjöll
881
Húnaflói
Eyjafjörður
Breiðafjörður
Sauðárkrókur
Rifstangi
Öxarfjörður
Arctic Circle
Hafursfjörður
Faxaflói
Fontur
Akureyri
Borgarnes
REYKJAVÍK
64°
66°
Keflavík
Reykjanesta
1763
Ódáðahraun
IS
Bárðarbunga 2009
Egilsstaðir
Borgarfjörður
Seyðisfjörður
1491
Grímsvötn
Sviahnúkar 1719
Snæfell 1833
Vestmannaeyjar
Vestmannaeyjar
Surtsey
Vík
Kötlutangi
Hvannadalshnúkur 2119
Skaftárós
Breiðdalsvík
Vesturhorn
20° 18° 16° 14°

10° 8°
62°
FO
FAROE ISLANDS (FØROYAR)
DK
Eysturoy
Vágar
Sandoy
Gluggarnir 610
Suðuroy
60°

56° 16° 14° 12° 10° 58°
Lewis
Cape Wrath
Stornoway
St Kilda
Western Isles
Clisham 799
South Harris
North Uist
Benbecula
South Uist
Barra
Little Minch
The Minch
Ullapool
A835
Portree
Skye
993
Carn Eighe 1183
A87
A82
Rum
Coll
Tiree
Fort William
Ben Nevis 1344
A82
Grampian
Mull
966
Ben Lawers
Oban
A85
A85
Colonsay
A82
A84
Jura
Loch Lomond
Stirling
Islay
Greenock
Glasgow
Paisley
873
Kintyre
Arran
Campbeltown
Kilmarnock
Ayr
A77
Merrick 843
Stranraer
Dumfries
A75
Solway Firth
Workington
Scafell Pike

ATLANTIC OCEAN

54°
Tory Island
Malin Head
Errigal 752
Letterkenny
Coleraine
A2
A26
Ballymoney
Londonderry (Derry)
A6
Donegal
N15
A5
Magherafelt
Ballymena
Donegal Bay
Lough Neagh
Larne
Achill Island
Sligo
N15
Enniskillen
Omagh
M1
Belfast
Bangor
Nephin 806
A4
A4
A29
Lisburn
Newtownards
N17
N4
Lower Lough Erne
Armagh
765
Castlebar
Lough Mask
Carrick-on-Shannon
Cavan
Monaghan
852
Slieve Donard
N5
Roscommon
Longford
N2
Dundalk
Dundalk B.
Peel
Snaefell 621
Isle of Man
DOUGLAS
Barrow-in-Furness
N17
Galway
Athlone
Mullingar
Navan
M1
Drogheda
Galway Bay
M6
M3
E01
52°
Lough Ree
IRISH SEA
Lancaster
Blackpool
Preston
N18
Tullamore
M4
Ennis
L. Derg
IRL
Naas
M50
DUBLIN
Southport
Loop Head
M18
M7
E20
M7
Dun Laoghaire
Anglesey
Colwyn Bay
St Helens
Limerick
Wicklow Mts
926
Wicklow
Holyhead
A55
A55
Liverpool
Slea Head
953
Tralee
N21
16
N24
Carlow
M9
N11
Chester
Dingle Bay
N20
920
M8
Kilkenny
Snowdon (Yr Wyddfa) 1085
Bangor
A5
1041
Killarney
Clonmel
E01
Penygadair
A470
Crewe
N22
E30
Waterford
N25
Wexford
Cardigan
Shrewsbury
14° 12° 10° 8° 6°

0 100 200 km
0 50 100 miles

Shetland Islands
Unst
Yell
Lerwick
Foula
Fair Isle
Orkney Islands
Kirkwall
Hoy
Tórshavn
Thurso
Moray Firth
Elgin
Inverness
Peterhead
Aberdeen
Ben Macdui
1309
Arbroath
Dundee
Perth
Kirkcaldy
Firth of Forth
Edinburgh
Berwick-upon-Tweed
Galashiels
Hawick
Morpeth
Newcastle upon Tyne
South Shields
Sunderland
Durham
Hartlepool
Middlesbrough
Darlington
Kendal
Northallerton
GB
York
Scarborough
Bridlington
Bradford
Leeds
Selby
Kingston upon Hull
Huddersfield
Scunthorpe
Manchester
Stockport
Sheffield
Doncaster
Grimsby
Chesterfield
Matlock
Stoke-on-Trent
Mansfield
Lincoln
NORTH SEA
SKAGERRAK
Hellesvik
Frøya
Smøla
Hitra
Kristiansund
Molde
Ålesund
Åndalsnes
Storskrymten
1985
Stranda
Volda
Måløy
Sandane
Florø
Førde
N
Galdhøpiggen
2470
Sula
Høyanger
Bergen
Hardangervidda
Harteigan
1690
Numedal
Møsvatnet
Bømlo
Haugesund
Karmøy
Setesdal
1443
Stavanger
Sandnes
Egersund
Arendal
Kristiansand
Lindesnes
Skien
Hirtshals
Hjørring
Hanstholm
Brønderslev
Thisted
Aalborg
Struer
Skive
Holstebro
Viborg
Herning
Silkeborg
Ringkøbing
Ikast
DK
Vejle
Varde
Fredericia
Esbjerg
Kolding
Ribe
Odense
Rømø
Haderslev
Aabenraa
Sønderborg
Sylt
Flensburg
Nordfriesische Inseln
Husum
Schleswig
Eckernförde
Rendsburg
Heide
Helgoland
Helgoländer Bucht
Neumünster
Kiel
Itzehoe
Elmshorn
Cuxhaven
Ostfriesische Inseln
Norden
17
22
64°
62°
60°
58°
56°
54°
6°
4°
2°
0°
8°

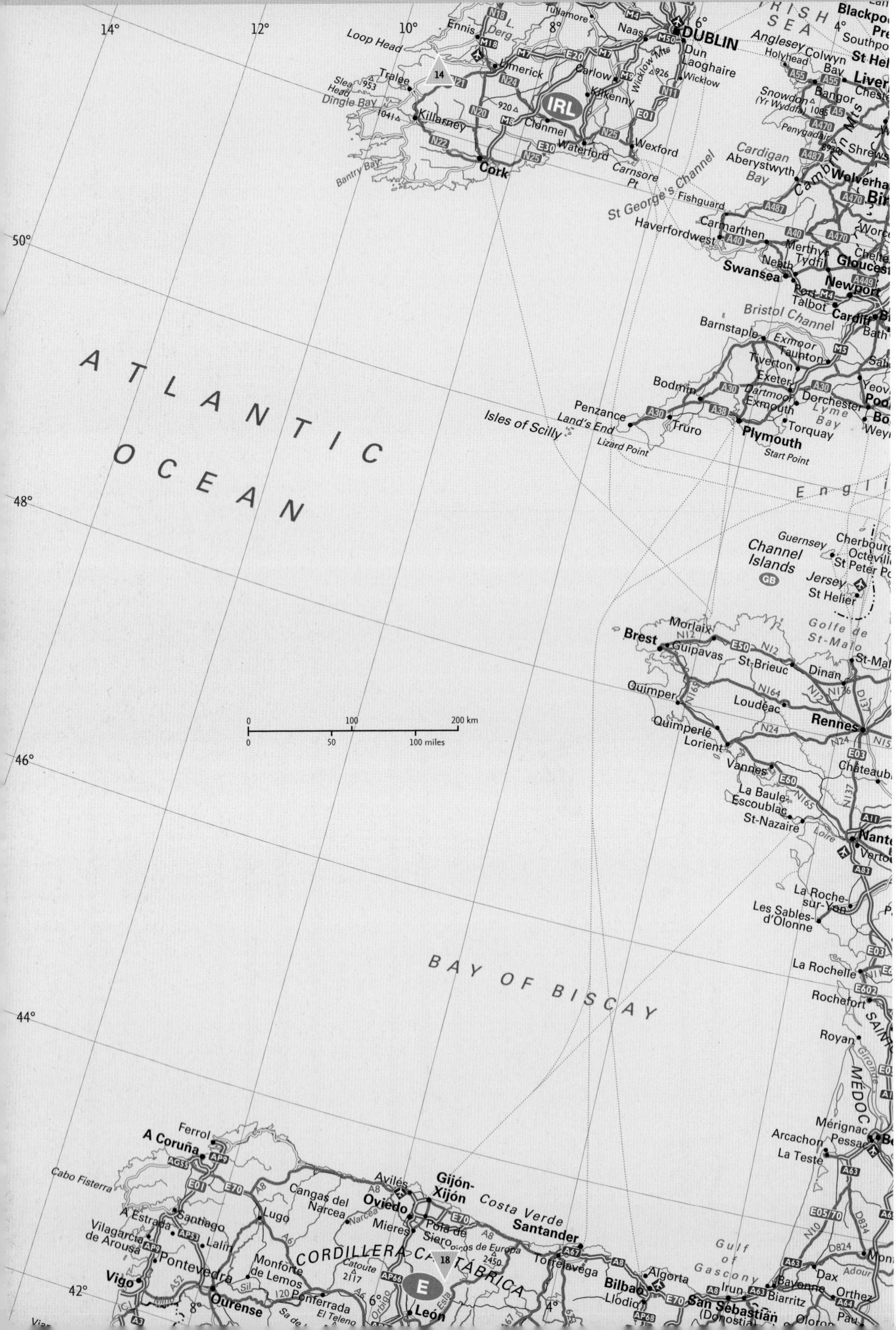

ATLANTIC OCEAN

BAY OF BISCAY

IRISH SEA

DUBLIN
Tullamore
Naas
Ennis
Loop Head
Limerick
Carlow
Wicklow Mts
Dun Laoghaire
Wicklow
Tralee
Slea Head
Dingle Bay
Killarney
Kilkenny
IRL
Clonmel
Waterford
Wexford
Carnsore Pt
Cork
Bantry Bay
St George's Channel
Fishguard
Haverfordwest
Carmarthen
Swansea
Neath
Port Talbot
Merthyr Tydfil
Cardiff
Newport
Gloucester
Cardigan Bay
Aberystwyth
Cambrian Mts
Anglesey
Holyhead
Colwyn Bay
Bangor
Snowdon (Yr Wyddfa)
Penygadair
Blackpool
Southport
St Helens
Liverpool
Chester
Shrewsbury
Wolverhampton
Bristol Channel
Barnstaple
Exmoor
Taunton
Tiverton
Exeter
Dartmoor
Exmouth
Bodmin
Penzance
Land's End
Isles of Scilly
Lizard Point
Truro
Plymouth
Start Point
Torquay
Dorchester
Lyme Bay
English Channel
Guernsey
Channel Islands
GB
Jersey
St Helier
St Peter Port
Cherbourg-Octeville
Golfe de St-Malo
St-Malo
Morlaix
Brest
Guipavas
St-Brieuc
Dinan
Quimper
Loudéac
Rennes
Quimperlé
Lorient
Vannes
Châteaubriant
La Baule-Escoublac
St-Nazaire
Loire
Nantes
La Roche-sur-Yon
Les Sables-d'Olonne
La Rochelle
Rochefort
Royan
Gironde
MÉDOC
Mérignac
Pessac
Arcachon
La Teste
Adour
Dax
Bayonne
Biarritz
Orthez
Pau
Gulf of Gascony
Irun
San Sebastián (Donostia)
Bilbao
Algorta
Llodio
Santander
Torrelavega
Costa Verde
Picos de Europa
CORDILLERA CANTÁBRICA
Gijón-Xixón
Avilés
Oviedo
Mieres
Pola de Siero
Cangas del Narcea
León
Ponferrada
El Teleno
Catoute
Monforte de Lemos
Lugo
Ferrol
A Coruña
Cabo Fisterra
Santiago
A Estrada
Lalín
Vilagarcía de Arousa
Pontevedra
Vigo
Ourense
E

14° 12° 10° 8° 6° 4°
50° 48° 46° 44° 42°

0 100 200 km
0 50 100 miles

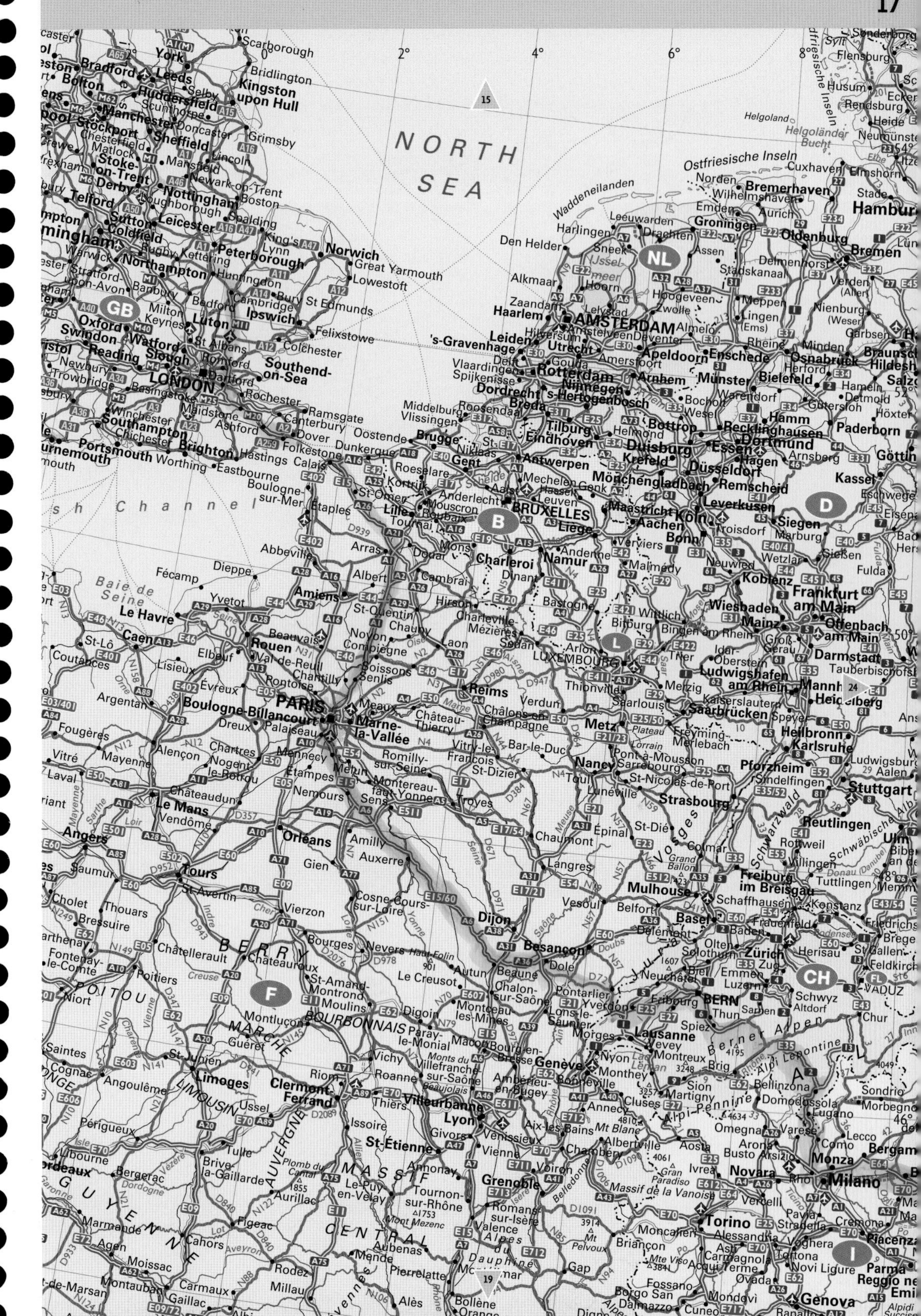
NORTH SEA
English Channel
GB
NL
B
L
D
F
CH
I
LONDON
PARIS
BRUXELLES
AMSTERDAM
LUXEMBOURG
Milano
Torino
Genova
Lyon
Marseille
Frankfurt am Main
Hamburg
Bremen
Köln
Düsseldorf
Dortmund
Essen
Stuttgart
Zürich
Basel
Bern
Genève
Strasbourg
Dijon
Reims
Rouen
Lille
Birmingham
Manchester
Leeds
Sheffield
Norwich
Southampton
Portsmouth
Brighton
BERRY
POITOU
LIMOUSIN
AUVERGNE
GUYENNE
MASSIF CENTRAL
BOURBONNAIS
MARCHE
Vosges
Schwarzwald
Berner Alpen
Alpi Pennine
Waddeneilanden
Ostfriesische Inseln

10°
8°
6°
4°
2°
16
BAY OF BISCAY
ATLANTIC OCEAN
Ferrol
A Coruña
Cabo Fisterra
A Estrada
Santiago
Vilagarcía de Arousa
Lalín
Pontevedra
Vigo
Lugo
Cangas del Narcea
Avilés
Gijón-Xijón
Oviedo
Mieres
Pola de Siero
Costa Verde
Santander
Picos de Europa 2450
Torrelavega
CORDILLERA CANTÁBRICA
Monforte de Lemos
Catoute 2117
Ourense
Ponferrada
El Teleno 2188
Sa de la Cabrera
León
Bilbao
Algorta
Llodio
Gulf of Gascony
Irun
San Sebastián (Donostia)
Bayonne
Biarritz
Arcachon
La Teste
Miranda de Ebro
Vitoria-Gasteiz
Pamplona
Logroño
Burgos
Viana do Castelo
Póvoa de Varzim
Braga
Guimarães
Chaves
Bragança
Sierra de la Culebra
Matosinhos
Porto
Vila Real
Palencia
Zamora
Valladolid
Sierra de la Demanda
Tudela
Ovar
São João da Madeira
Aveiro
Ria de Aveiro
Viseu
Embalse de Almendra
Salamanca
Aranda de Duero
Soria
Alto del Moncayo 2313
Figueira da Foz
Coimbra
Serra da Estrela
Torre 1993
Guarda
Covilhã
Segovia
Sierra de Guadarrama
E
Calatayud
Zaragoza
Marinha Grande
Leiria
P
Ávila
San Sebastián de los Reyes
Colmenar Viejo
Peniche
Torres Novas
Tomar
Plasencia
Almanzor 2592
MADRID
Guadalajara
Alcalá de Henares
Torres Vedras
Caldas da Rainha
Castelo Branco
Valle de Tiétar
Fuenlabrada
Sierra de Gredos
Talavera de la Reina
Aranjuez
Arganda del Rey
Embalse de Buendía
Serranía de Cuenca
Santarém
Amadora
Cascais
Almada
LISBOA
Vila Franca de Xira
Cáceres
Portalegre
Sierra de San Pedro
Embalse de Valdecañas
Las Villuercas 1601
Montes de Toledo
Corral de Cantos 1410
Toledo
Cuenca
Teruel
Baia de Setúbal
Setúbal
Elvas
Évora
Badajoz
Mérida
Sierra de Guadalupe
Villanueva de la Serena
Don Benito
Embalse de Cíjara
Alcázar de San Juan
LA MANCHA
Embalse de Alarcón
La Vall d'Uixó
Barragem de Alqueva
Almendralejo
Tomelloso
Ciudad Real
La Roda
Requena
Torrent
Valencia
Beja
Albacete
Algemesí
Catarroja
Peñarroya-Pueblonuevo
Puertollano
Valdepeñas
Molatón 1242
Carcaixent
Sueca
Cullera
Almansa
Gandia
Oliva
ALGARVE
SIERRA MORENA
VALENCIA
Lagos
Portimão
Cabo de São Vicente
Faro
Olhão
Linares
Hellín
Alcoy-Alcoi
Villena
Jumilla
Novelda
Elda
Benidorm
Villajoyosa
Huelva
Las Marismas
Costa de la Luz
Sevilla
Guadalquivir
Carmona
Córdoba
Andújar
Úbeda
Caravaca de la Cruz
Cieza
Alicante
Écija
Martos
Jaén
Orihuela
Elche-Elx
GULF OF CÁDIZ
Lebrija
Utrera
Montilla
Lucena
Puente-Genil
Alcalá la Real
Murcia
Costa Blanca
Jeréz de la Frontera
Sanlúcar de Barrameda
Morón de la Frontera
Antequera
Loja
Lorca
Cádiz
El Puerto de Santa María
Ronda
Coín
Granada
Guadix
Cartagena
Cabo de Palos
Chiclana de la Frontera
San Fernando
Vélez-Málaga
Mulhacén 3482
Sierra Nevada
Águilas
Barbate de Franco
Cabo Trafalgar
Málaga
Marbella
Estepona
Costa del Sol
Motril
El Ejido
Almería
Algeciras
La Línea de la Concepción
Gibraltar
GBZ
Golfo de Almería
Strait of Gibraltar
Tanger
Ceuta
E
MED
Larache
Tétouan
Isla de Alborán
E
Ksar el Kebir
Souk el Arbaâ du Rharb
Chaouèn
Al Hoceima
Baie d'Al Hoceima
Melilla
E
Nador
Sidi Ali
Aïn Tédélès
Arzew
Oran
Mostaganem
Beni-Saf
Mohammadia
Kénitra
Oued Beht
MA
Ghazaouet
Aïn Temouchent
Zemmora
RABAT
Sidi Kacem
Oued Sebou
Taounate
Berkane
Nédroma
Mascara
Khemisset
Fès
Taza
Maghnia
Tlemcen
Sidi Bel Abbès
Tiaret
Casablanca
Meknès
Taourirt
Oujda
Télagh
Sebdou
Saïda
42°
40°
38°
36°
34°
6°
4°
2°
0°

Angoulême
Limoges
Clermont-Ferrand
Riom
Roanne
Villeurbanne
Lyon
Ambérieu-en-Bugey
Bonneville
Monthey
Sion
Martigny
Bellinzona
Domodossola
LIMOUSIN
MÉDOC
Ussel
Thiers
Annecy
Cluses
Aix-les-Bains
Mt Blanc
4810
4634
Omegna
Varese
Périgueux
Issoire
St-Étienne
17
Givors
Vénissieux
Vienne
Chambéry
Albertville
Aosta
Arona
Busto Arsizio
Mérignac
Pessac
Bordeaux
Libourne
Brive-la-Gaillarde
AUVERGNE
Plomb du Cantal
1855
Aurillac
Le-Puy-en-Velay
MASSIF
Annonay
Tournon-sur-Rhône
1753
Mont Mezenc
Grenoble
Voiron
4061
Gran Paradiso
Ivrea
Novara
Massif de la Vanoise
Vercelli
GUYENNE
Bergerac
Dordogne
Romans-sur-Isère
Valence
Alpes du Dauphiné
D1091
3914
Mt Pelvoux
Torino
Stradella
Pavia
Marmande
Figeac
CENTRAL
Moncalieri
Briançon
Alessandria
Asti
Carmagnola
Voghera
Tortona
Agen
Cahors
Moissac
Montauban
Aubenas
Mende
Pierrelatte
Montélimar
Gap
Mte Viso
3841
Acqui Terme
Novi Ligure
Ovada
Mont-de-Marsan
Dax
Orthez
Carmaux
Gaillac
Rodez
Millau
Cévennes
Alès
Bollène
Orange
Borgo San Dalmazzo
Fossano
Mondovi
Cuneo
Genova
Rapallo
Savona
Auch
Albi
Toulouse
Colomiers
Muret
Pau
Tarbes
Lourdes
F
Nîmes
Avignon
Cavaillon
Arles
Digne-les-Bains
Alpes Maritimes
3297
Cima dell'Argentera
Albenga
La Spezia
Montpellier
Mazamet
LANGUEDOC
CAMARGUE
Manosque
Verdon
Nice
Imperia
Golfo di Genova
San Remo
MONTE CARLO
44°
PYRENEES
St-Gaudens
Pamiers
Carcassonne
Béziers
Sète
Agde
Salon-de-Provence
Aix-en-Provence
Grasse
Antibes
Cannes
Marignane
Pic Long
3192
Foix
Narbonne
Durban-Corbières
Golfe du Lion
Marseille
Aubagne
Brignoles
St-Raphaël
La Ciotat
Toulon
Côte d'Azur
LIGURIAN SEA
Îles d'Hyères
Cotiella
2912
Pic d'Estats
3141
AND
ANDORRA LA VELLA
Étang de Leucate ou de Salses
Perpignan
Port-Vendres
Huesca
Puigmal
2910
Figueres
Cap Corse
Monte Stello
1307
Monzón
Olot
Costa Brava
Monte Padro
2393
Zaragoza
Lleida
Manresa
Vic
Girona
CORSE (CORSICA)
Monte Rotondo
2622
Igualada
Sabadell
Blanes
Golfe de Sagone
Ebro
El Prat de Llobregat
Reus
Mataró
Barcelona
Ajaccio
42°
Tarragona
Vilanova i la Geltrú
Pnte l'Ovace
1339
Porto-Vecchio
Tortosa
Golf de Sant Jordi
Capo Pertusato
Strait of Bonifacio
Golfo dell'Asinara
Porto Torres
26
Tempio Pausania
Castellón de la Plana
Burriana
Sagunto
Golfo de Valencia
Valencia
MALLORCA (MAJORCA)
Cap de Formentor
Menorca (Minorca)
Ciutadella
Mahón
Sassari
Alghero
Ozieri
SARDEGNA (SARDINIA)
Macomer
Nuoro
Puig Major
1436
Inca
Palma de Mallorca
Manacor
E
40°
Oristano
Terralba
Guspini
Villacidro
San Gavino Monreale
Iglesias
Carbonia
Cagliari
Quartu S. Elena
Sant' Antioco
Golfo di Cagliari
Eivissa (Ibiza)
Denia
Cabo de la Nao
Illa de Cabrera
ISLAS BALEARES (BALEARIC ISLANDS)
Formentera
La Vila Joiosa
0
100
200 km
50
100 miles
MEDITERRANEAN SEA
38°
ALGER
Aïn Taya
Dellys
Boumerdes
Collo
Skikda
Annaba
Mateur
Ténès
Gouraya
Tipasa
Koléa
Blida
Cherchell
Larba
Tizi Ouzou
Bejaïa
Jijel
El Milia
El Hadjar
El Tarf
El Kala
Tébourba
Kerba
Aïn Defla
Ech Chélif
Miliana
Médéa
Bouira
Akbou
Tazmalt
Bougaa
Chelghoum el Aïd
Mila
El Arrouch
Azzaba
Dréan
Béja
Jendouba
Relizane
Tissemsilt
Theniet El Had
Berrouaghia
Sour el Ghozlane
Sétif
Constantine
Guelma
DZ
Ksar el Boukhari
Sidi Aïssa
Bordj Bou Arreridj
El Eulma
Oued Zénati
Souk Ahras
Le Kef
TN
Sedrata
Chahbounia
Mahdia
Aïn el Hadjel
M'Sila
Aïn Oulmene
Aïn Azel
Aïn-M'Lila
Oum el Bouaghi
M'Daourouch
El Aouinet
Siliana
36°
Tiaret
Aïn Oussera
Atlas Tellien
Zenzach
Chott el Hodna
Batna
Aïn Beïda
Morsott
Sougueur
Frenda
Ksar Chellala
Barika
Bou Saâda
Khenchela
Tébessa

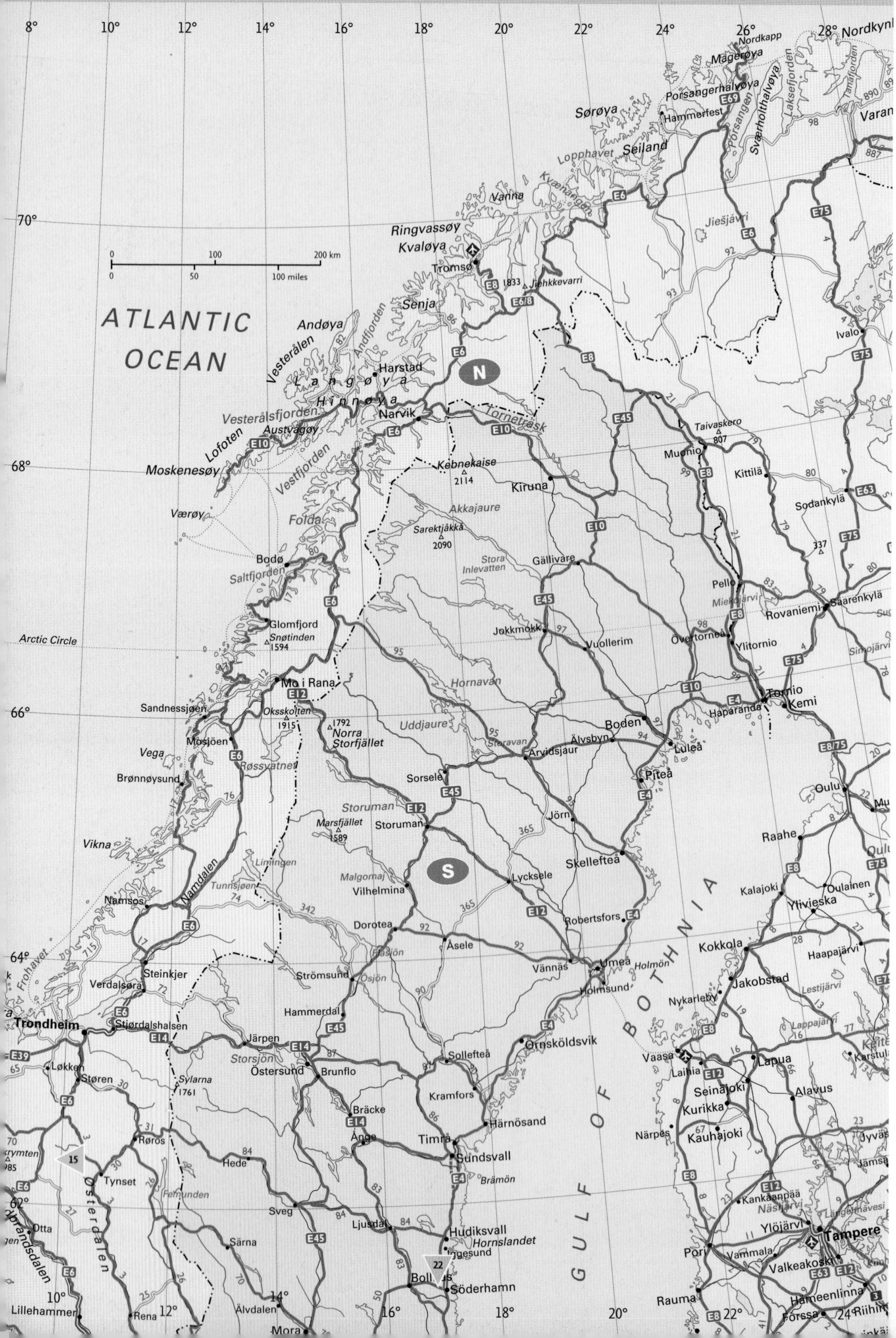

8° 10° 12° 14° 16° 18° 20° 22° 24° 26° 28°

Nordkapp
Nordkynl
Magerøya
Porsangerhalvøya
E69
Porsangen
Sværholthalvøya
Laksefjorden
Tanafjorden
890
Hammerfest
Sørøya
98
Varan
Loppahavet
Seiland
887
Kvænangen
Vanna
E6
Jiešjávri
E75
70°
Ringvassøy
Kvaløya
E6
Tromsø
92
0 100 200 km
0 50 100 miles
E8
1833 Jiehkkevarri
E6/8
93
Senja
ATLANTIC OCEAN
Andøya
Andfjorden
Vesterålen
82
86
E6
N
Ivalo
Harstad
Langøya
E75
E8
Hinnøya
Vesterålsfjorden
Narvik
Torneträsk
E45
21
Austvågøy
E10
E6
E10
Taivaskero 807
79
Lofoten
Vestfjorden
Muonio
Kebnekaise 2114
99
E8
Kittilä
80
68°
Moskenesøy
Kiruna
E63
Sodankylä
Akkajaure
Værøy
Folda
79
Sarektjåkkå 2090
E10
E75
337
Bodø
80
Stora Inlevatten
Gällivare
21
Saltfjorden
Pello
83
80
17
E6
E45
Miekojärvi
79
Rovaniemi
Saarenkylä
Glomfjord
E8
Jokkmokk
97
98
Arctic Circle
Snøtinden 1594
Vuollerim
Övertorneå
Ylitornio
Simojärvi
4
95
E75
78
Hornavan
Mo i Rana
12
E12
E10
E4
Tornio
Kemi
66°
Sandnessjøen
Oksskolten 1915
1792 Norra Storfjället
Uddjaure
Boden
Haparanda
95
Storavan
Älvsbyn
94
Luleå
Mosjöen
Arvidsjaur
E8/75
Vega
E6
Røssvatnet
Piteå
20
Brønnøysund
Sorsele
E45
E4
Oulu
22
76
Storuman
E12
Mu
Jörn
Marsfjället 1589
Storuman
365
Raahe
Vikna
Limingen
Skellefteå
Oulu
E8
E75
S
Namdalen
Tunnsjøen
Malgomaj
Vilhelmina
Lycksele
Oulainen
Kalajoki
74
GULF OF BOTHNIA
Ylivieska
Namsos
342
365
E12
E6
Robertsfors
E4
715
17
Dorotea
92
27
Flåsjön
Åsele
92
Kokkola
28
Haapajärvi
64°
Frohavet
Steinkjer
Vännäs
Umeå
Holmön
Strömsund
Ösjön
Jakobstad
Verdalsøra
72
90
Holmsund
Lestijärvi
Nykarleby
13
E6
Hammerdal
19
Lappajärvi
77
Trondheim
Stjørdalshalsen
E45
E4
Kälte
E39
E14
Järpen
E14
87
Örnsköldsvik
16
Storsjön
Vaasa
Lapua
Karstula
65
Løkken
Støren
Sylarna 1761
Östersund
Brunflo
Sollefteå
Laihia
E12
30
Seinäjoki
Alavus
E6
Kramfors
8
Bräcke
86
Kurikka
23
31
Røros
E14
Härnösand
Närpes
67
Kauhajoki
Jyväs
Trolheimen
Ånge
Timrå
15
Hede
84
Sundsvall
Tynset
Jämsä
E6
E4
Brämön
E8
Østerdalen
Femunden
83
E12
Kankaanpää
62°
Nåsijärvi
Längelmävesi
Sveg
84
Otta
Ljusdal
84
Hudiksvall
Hornslandet
Ylöjärvi
Tampere
Särna
E45
Iggesund
Pori
Vammala
Gudbrandsdalen
E6
26
22
Valkeakoski
70
Bollnäs
E63
E12
3
25
Söderhamn
Rauma
Hämeenlinna
10°
14°
16°
18°
20°
E8
22°
24°
Riihimä
Lillehammer
Rena
12°
Älvdalen
50
Forssa
Mora

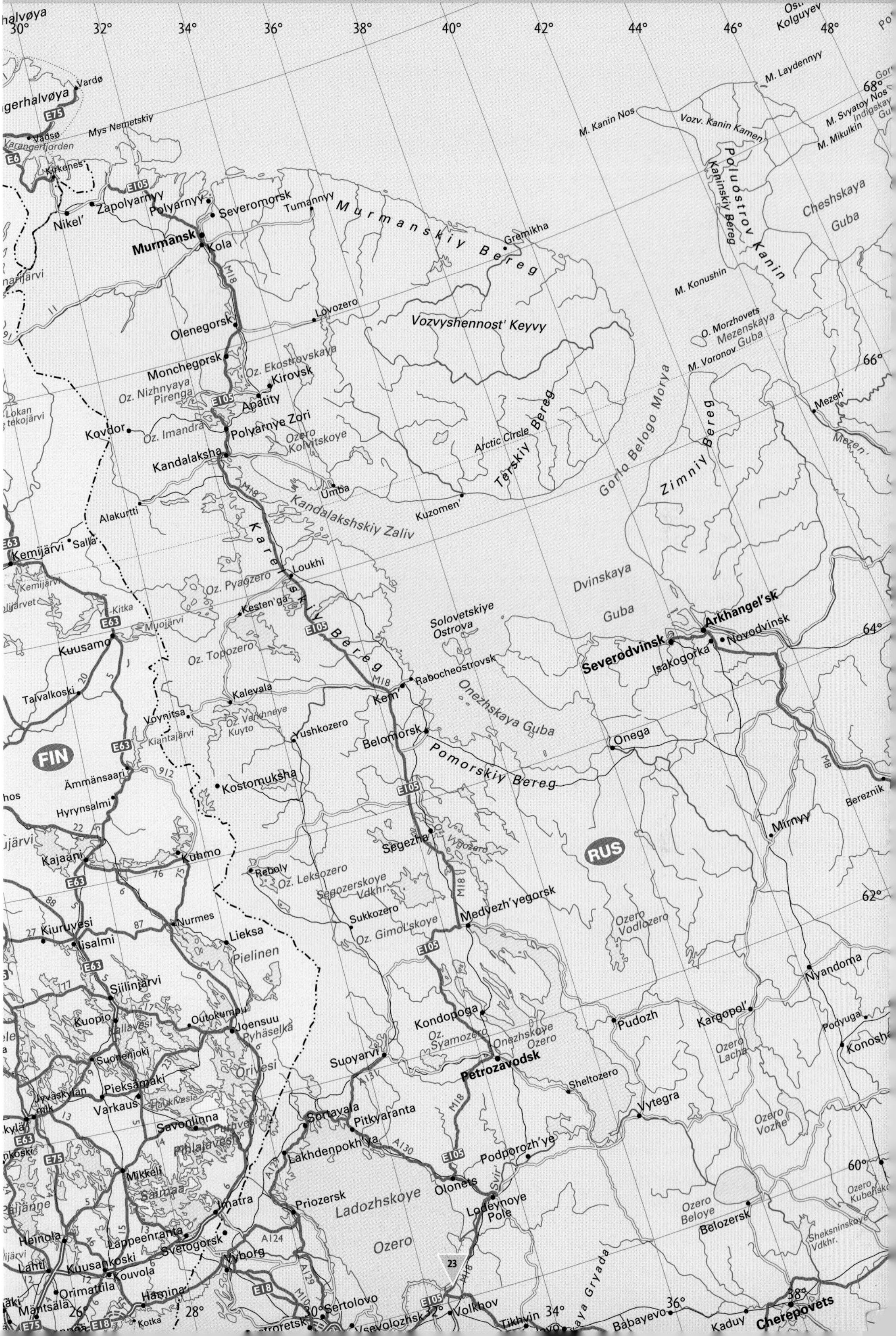

Murmansk
Kola
Severomorsk
Polyarnyy
Zapolyarnyy
Nikel'
Kirkenes
Vadsø
Vardø
Mys Nemetskiy
Murmanskiy Bereg
Gremikha
Tumannyy
Lovozero
Olenegorsk
Monchegorsk
Kirovsk
Apatity
Polyarnye Zori
Kandalaksha
Kovdor
Alakurtti
Salla
Kemijärvi
Umba
Kuzomen'
Kandalakshskiy Zaliv
Terskiy Bereg
Arctic Circle
Vozvyshennost' Keyvy
Gorlo Belogo Morya
Zimniy Bereg
Poluostrov Kanin
Kaninskiy Bereg
M. Kanin Nos
Vozv. Kanin Kamen
M. Laydennyy
M. Konushin
O. Morzhovets
Mezenskaya Guba
M. Voronov
Cheshskaya Guba
Mezen'
Kolguyev
Loukhi
Kesten'ga
Karel'skiy Bereg
Oz. Pyaozero
Oz. Topozero
Kuusamo
Taivalkoski
Kalevala
Voynitsa
Yushkozero
Kem'
Rabocheostrovsk
Solovetskiye Ostrova
Dvinskaya Guba
Arkhangel'sk
Severodvinsk
Novodvinsk
Isakogorka
Onezhskaya Guba
Belomorsk
Pomorskiy Bereg
Onega
Kostomuksha
Ämmänsaari
Hyrynsalmi
Kajaani
Kuhmo
Segezha
Reboly
Oz. Leksozero
Medvezh'yegorsk
Sukkozero
Oz. Gimol'skoye
Mirnyy
Bereznik
RUS
FIN
Ozero Vodlozero
Nyandoma
Kiuruvesi
Iisalmi
Nurmes
Lieksa
Pielinen
Siilinjärvi
Kuopio
Outokumpu
Joensuu
Kondopoga
Pudozh
Kargopol'
Konosha
Podyuga
Onezhskoye Ozero
Petrozavodsk
Suoyarvi
Sheltozero
Vytegra
Ozero Lacha
Ozero Vozhe
Suonenjoki
Pieksämäki
Varkaus
Jyväskylä
Savonlinna
Sortavala
Pitkyaranta
Lakhdenpokh'ya
Podporozh'ye
Olonets
Lodeynoye Pole
Mikkeli
Saimaa
Priozersk
Ladozhskoye Ozero
Ozero Beloye
Belozersk
Sheksninskoye Vdkhr.
Imatra
Lappeenranta
Svetogorsk
Heinola
Lahti
Kuusankoski
Kouvola
Vyborg
Orimattila
Hamina
Mäntsälä
Kotka
Sertolovo
Vsevolozhsk
Volkhov
Tikhvin
Babayevo
Kaduy
Cherepovets
Svir'
23
30° 32° 34° 36° 38° 40° 42° 44° 46° 48°
68° 66° 64° 62° 60°
26° 28° 30° 32° 34° 36° 38°

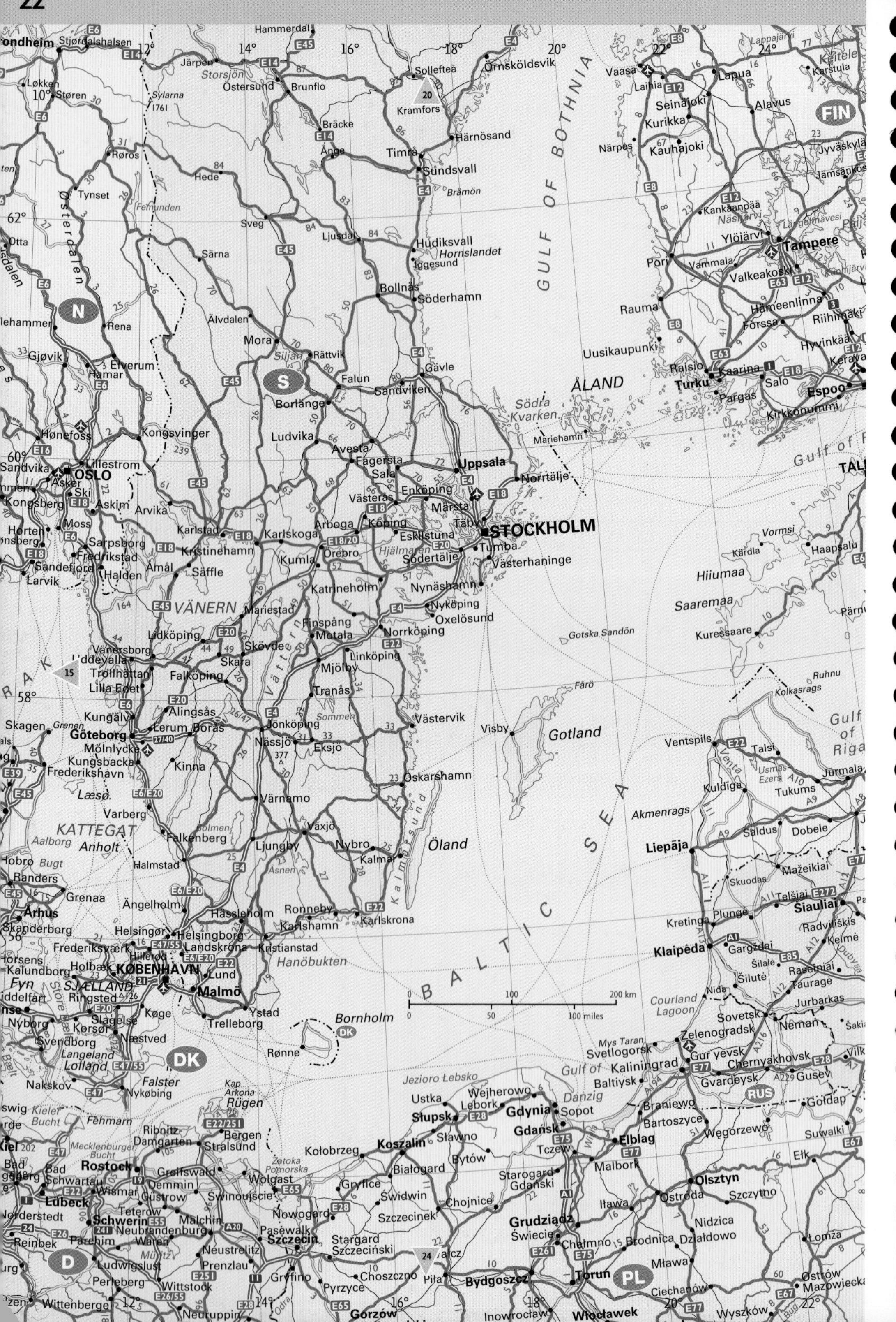
GULF OF BOTHNIA
BALTIC SEA
ÅLAND
Södra Kvarken
Gulf of Riga
Gulf of Finland
KATTEGAT
Hanöbukten
Gulf of Danzig
Courland Lagoon
Kieler Bucht
Mecklenburger Bucht
VÄNERN
Vättern
Siljan
Storsjön
Hjälmaren
Sommen
Bolmen
Åsnen
Kalmarsund
Femunden
Österdalen
Gotland
Öland
Bornholm
Hiiumaa
Saaremaa
Vormsi
Ruhnu
Fårö
Gotska Sandön
Rügen
Fyn
SJÆLLAND
Lolland
Falster
Fehmarn
Læsø
Anholt
N
S
FIN
DK
D
PL
RUS
STOCKHOLM
OSLO
KØBENHAVN
Trondheim
Stjørdalshalsen
Løkken
Støren
Røros
Tynset
Otta
Lillehammer
Gjøvik
Hamar
Elverum
Rena
Hønefoss
Kongsvinger
Lillestrom
Sandvika
Asker
Ski
Askim
Kongsberg
Moss
Horten
Sarpsborg
Fredrikstad
Sandefjord
Larvik
Halden
Hammerdal
Järpen
Östersund
Brunflo
Sylarna
Sollefteå
Örnsköldsvik
Kramfors
Härnösand
Bräcke
Ånge
Timrå
Sundsvall
Brämön
Hede
Sveg
Ljusdal
Hudiksvall
Hornslandet
Iggesund
Särna
Bollnäs
Söderhamn
Älvdalen
Mora
Rättvik
Gävle
Falun
Sandviken
Borlänge
Ludvika
Avesta
Fagersta
Sala
Uppsala
Norrtälje
Enköping
Västerås
Märsta
Täby
Arvika
Karlstad
Kristinehamn
Karlskoga
Arboga
Köping
Eskilstuna
Örebro
Kumla
Södertälje
Tumba
Västerhaninge
Nynäshamn
Säffle
Åmål
Katrineholm
Nyköping
Oxelösund
Mariestad
Finspång
Motala
Norrköping
Lidköping
Skövde
Linköping
Vänersborg
Uddevalla
Trollhättan
Lilla Edet
Skara
Falköping
Mjölby
Tranås
Kungälv
Alingsås
Göteborg
Lerum
Borås
Jönköping
Västervik
Mölnlycke
Kungsbacka
Nässjö
Eksjö
Kinna
Oskarshamn
Värnamo
Varberg
Växjö
Falkenberg
Ljungby
Nybro
Kalmar
Halmstad
Ängelholm
Hässleholm
Ronneby
Karlshamn
Karlskrona
Helsingborg
Landskrona
Kristianstad
Lund
Malmö
Ystad
Trelleborg
Visby
Mariehamn
Skagen
Grenen
Frederikshavn
Aalborg
Hobro
Randers
Grenaa
Århus
Skanderborg
Helsingør
Frederiksværk
Hillerød
Horsens
Kalundborg
Holbæk
Ringsted
Køge
Slagelse
Korsør
Nyborg
Svendborg
Næstved
Nakskov
Nykøbing
Middelfart
Rønne
Vaasa
Laihia
Lapua
Seinäjoki
Kurikka
Alavus
Närpes
Kauhajoki
Jyväskylä
Jämsänkoski
Kankaanpää
Näsijärvi
Längelmävesi
Ylöjärvi
Tampere
Pori
Vammala
Valkeakoski
Rauma
Hämeenlinna
Forssa
Riihimäki
Hyvinkää
Uusikaupunki
Raisio
Turku
Kaarina
Salo
Pargas
Espoo
Kirkkonummi
Kärdla
Haapsalu
Kuressaare
Pärnu
Kolkasrags
Ventspils
Talsi
Jūrmala
Kuldīga
Tukums
Akmenrags
Saldus
Dobele
Liepāja
Mažeikiai
Skuodas
Telšiai
Šiauliai
Kretinga
Plungė
Radviliškis
Klaipėda
Gargždai
Kelmė
Šilalė
Šilutė
Raseiniai
Tauragė
Nida
Jurbarkas
Sovetsk
Neman
Zelenogradsk
Svetlogorsk
Kaliningrad
Gur'yevsk
Chernyakhovsk
Gusev
Gvardeysk
Baltiysk
Mys Taran
Braniewo
Bartoszyce
Węgorzewo
Goldap
Suwałki
Ełk
Jezioro Łebsko
Ustka
Wejherowo
Lebork
Gdynia
Sopot
Słupsk
Gdańsk
Sławno
Tczew
Elbląg
Kołobrzeg
Koszalin
Bytów
Malbork
Białogard
Starogard Gdański
Olsztyn
Gryfice
Świdwin
Chojnice
Ostróda
Szczytno
Nowogard
Szczecinek
Iława
Grudziądz
Świecie
Chełmno
Brodnica
Działdowo
Nidzica
Łomża
Szczecin
Stargard Szczeciński
Wałcz
Mława
Choszczno
Piła
Bydgoszcz
Toruń
Ciechanów
Ostrów Mazowiecka
Pyrzyce
Gorzów
Inowrocław
Włocławek
Wyszków
Gryfino
Świnoujście
Wolgast
Greifswald
Stralsund
Bergen
Ribnitz-Damgarten
Rostock
Demmin
Güstrow
Teterow
Malchin
Wismar
Bad Schwartau
Lübeck
Bad Segeberg
Kiel
Norderstedt
Schwerin
Neubrandenburg
Pasewalk
Reinbek
Parchim
Waren
Müritz
Neustrelitz
Prenzlau
Ludwigslust
Perleberg
Wittstock
Wittenberge
Neuruppin
Kap Arkona
Żatoka Pomorska
0 100 200 km
0 50 100 miles

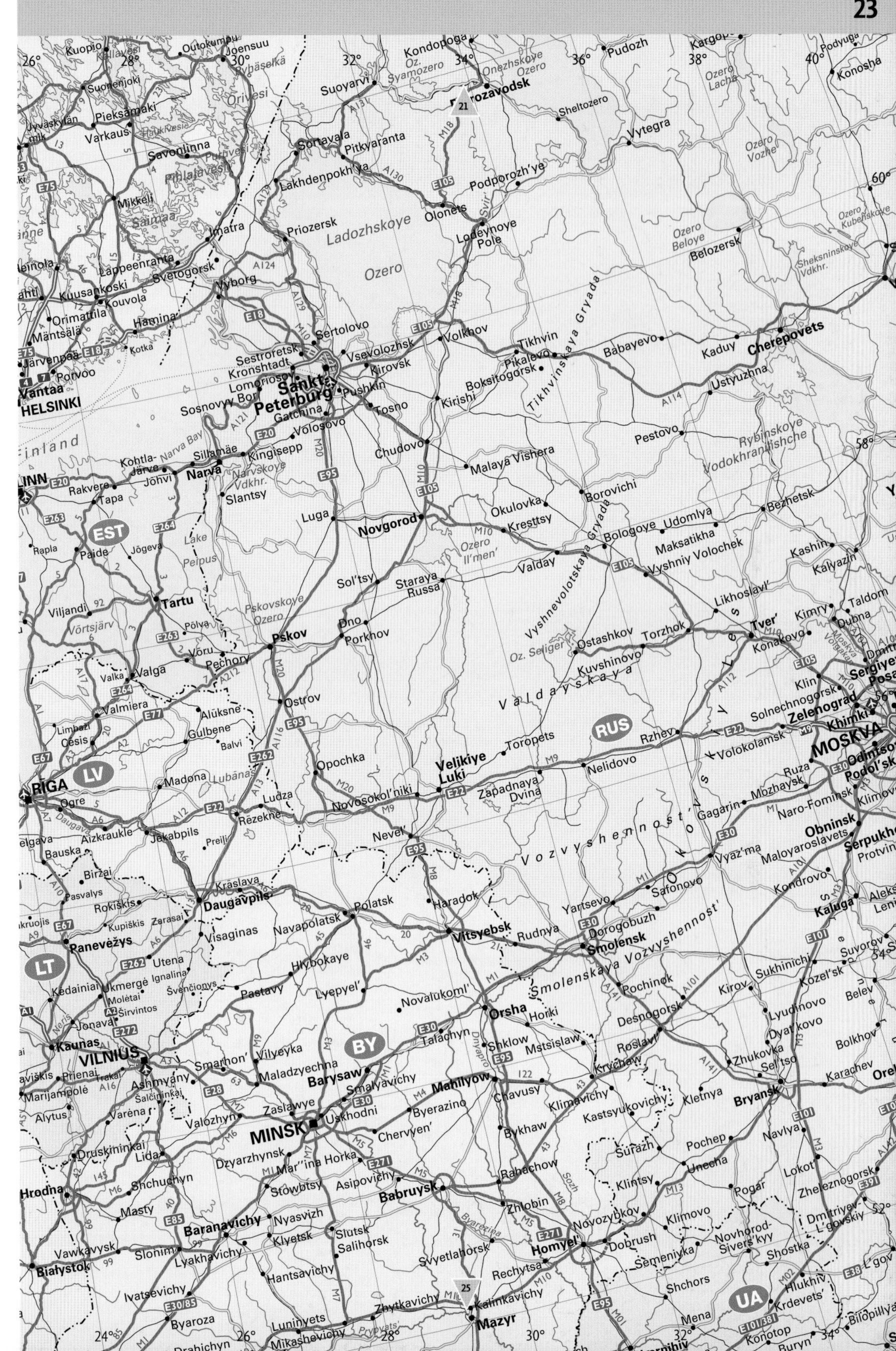

Kuopio
Outokumpu
Joensuu
Kondopoga
Pudozh
Kargopol'
Podyuga
Konosha
Suonenjoki
Orivesi
Suoyarvi
Syamozero
Onezhskoye Ozero
Petrozavodsk
Ozero Lacha
Jyväskylän mlk
Pieksämäki
Varkaus
Sheltozero
Vytegra
Savonlinna
Sortavala
Pitkyaranta
Ozero Vozhe'
Lakhdenpokh'ya
Podporozh'ye
Mikkeli
Saimaa
Olonets
Svir'
Imatra
Priozersk
Ladozhskoye Ozero
Lodeynoye Pole
Ozero Beloye
Belozersk
Ozero Kubenskoye
Sheksninskoye Vdkhr.
Lappeenranta
Svetogorsk
Kuusankoski
Kouvola
Vyborg
Orimattila
Mäntsälä
Hamina
Kotka
Järvenpää
Porvoo
Vantaa
HELSINKI
Sertolovo
Sestroretsk
Kronshtadt
Lomonosov
Sosnovyy Bor
Sankt-Peterburg
Vsevolozhsk
Kirovsk
Pushkin
Gatchina
Tosno
Volkhov
Tikhvin
Pikalevo
Boksitogorsk
Kirishi
Tikhvinskaya Gryada
Babayevo
Kaduy
Cherepovets
Ustyuzhna
Pestovo
Rybinskoye Vodokhranilishche
Volosovo
Kingisepp
Narva Bay
Kohtla-Järve
Sillamäe
Narva
Jõhvi
Narvskoye Vdkhr.
Slantsy
Chudovo
Malaya Vishera
Borovichi
Okulovka
Krestsy
Rakvere
Tapa
EST
Luga
Novgorod
Ozero Il'men'
Bologoye
Udomlya
Bezhetsk
Maksatikha
Vyshniy Volochek
Kashin
Kalyazin
Rapla
Paide
Jõgeva
Lake Peipus
Valday
Sol'tsy
Staraya Russa
Viljandi
Tartu
Pskovskoye Ozero
Võrtsjärv
Põlva
Dno
Porkhov
Pskov
Vyshnevolotskaya Gryada
Ostashkov
Torzhok
Likhoslavl'
Tver'
Kimry
Taldom
Dubna
Konakovo
Oz. Seliger
Kuvshinovo
Võru
Pechory
Valga
Valka
Valmiera
Alūksne
Ostrov
Valdayskaya Vozvyshennost'
Klin
Solnechnogorsk
Zelenograd
Khimki
Sergiyev Posad
Limbaži
Cēsis
Gulbene
Balvi
Toropets
RUS
Rzhev
Volokolamsk
MOSKVA
Odintsovo
Podol'sk
Opochka
Velikiye Luki
Nelidovo
Ruza
Mozhaysk
Naro-Fominsk
Klimovsk
RĪGA
LV
Madona
Lubānas
Ogre
Ludza
Novosokol'niki
Zapadnaya Dvina
Gagarin
Obninsk
Serpukhov
Daugava
Aizkraukle
Jēkabpils
Preiļi
Rēzekne
Nevel'
Vozvyshennost'
Vyaz'ma
Maloyaroslavets
Protvino
Jelgava
Bauska
Biržai
Pasvalys
Rokiškis
Krāslava
Daugavpils
Polatsk
Haradok
Yartsevo
Safonovo
Kondrovo
Kaluga
Kupiškis
Zarasai
Navapolatsk
Vitsyebsk
Rudnya
Dorogobuzh
Smolensk
Panevėžys
Visaginas
Smolenskaya Vozvyshennost'
Suvorov
Utena
Ignalina
Hlybokaye
LT
Kėdainiai
Ukmergė
Molėtai
Švenčionys
Pastavy
Lyepyel'
Pochinok
Sukhinichi
Kozel'sk
Belev
Širvintos
Jonava
Kaunas
Novalukoml'
Orsha
Horki
Desnogorsk
Kirov
Lyudinovo
VILNIUS
Prienai
Trakai
Vilyeyka
BY
Talachyn
Shklow
Mstsislaw
Roslavl'
Dyat'kovo
Zhukovka
Bolkhov
Ashmyany
Smarhon'
Maladzyechna
Barysaw
Mahilyow
Krychaw
Sel'tso
Karachev
Orel
Marijampolė
Šalčininkai
Smalyavichy
Chavusy
Klimavichy
Kletnya
Bryansk
Alytus
Varėna
Zaslawye
Byerazino
Kastsyukovichy
Valozhyn
MINSK
Uskhodni
Chervyen'
Druskininkai
Lida
Dzyarzhynsk
Mar"ina Horka
Bykhaw
Surazh
Pochep
Navlya
Unecha
Hrodna
Shchuchyn
Stowbtsy
Asipovichy
Rahachow
Klintsy
Lokot'
Zheleznogorsk
Babruysk
Pogar
Masty
Zhlobin
Novozybkov
Klimovo
Dmitriyev-L'govskiy
Baranavichy
Nyasvizh
Slutsk
Salihorsk
Dobrush
Novhorod-Sivers'kyy
Vawkavysk
Slonim
Lyakhavichy
Klyetsk
Svyetlahorsk
Homyel'
Semenivka
Shostka
L'gov
Białystok
Hantsavichy
Rechytsa
Shchors
Hlukhiv
Ivatsevichy
Kalinkavichy
Zhytkavichy
UA
Krolevets'
Byaroza
Luninyets
Mazyr
Mena
Bilopillya
Drahichyn
Mikashevichy
Chernihiv
Konotop
Buryn'

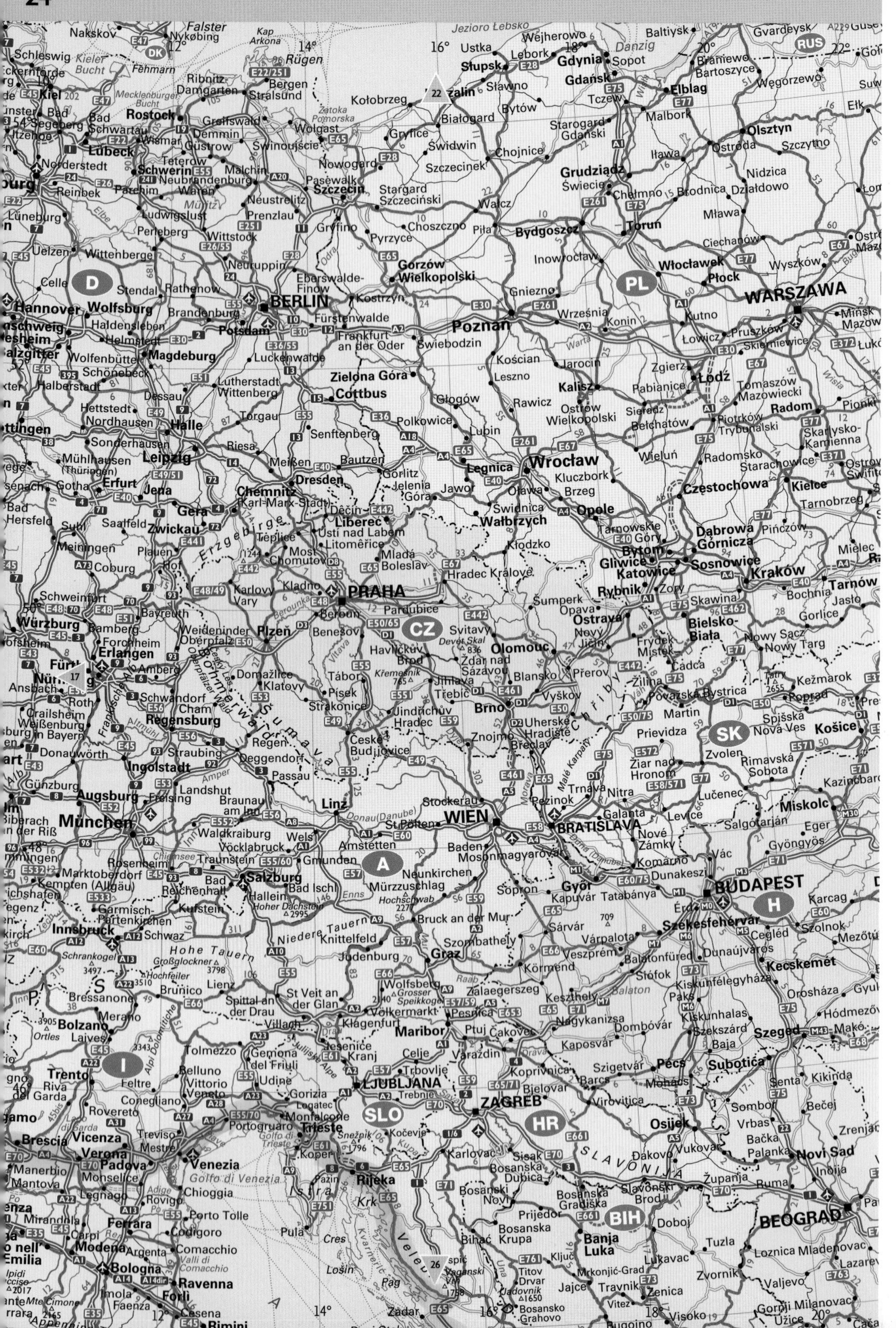

Falster
Nakskov
Nykøbing
DK
Kap Arkona
Rügen
Jezioro Łebsko
Ustka
Lebork
Wejherowo
Gdynia
Sopot
Danzig
Baltiysk
Gvardeysk
RUS
Braniewo
Bartoszyce
Węgorzewo
Schleswig
Kieler Bucht
Fehmarn
Ribnitz-Damgarten
Bergen
Stralsund
Słupsk
Sławno
Gdańsk
Tczew
Elbląg
Kiel
Mecklenburger Bucht
Kołobrzeg
Koszalin
Bytów
Malbork
Ełk
Segeberg
Bad Schwartau
Rostock
Greifswald
Zatoka Pomorska
Wolgast
Białogard
Starogard Gdański
Olsztyn
Itzehoe
Wismar
Demmin
Lübeck
Güstrow
Świnoujście
Gryfice
Świdwin
Chojnice
Iława
Ostróda
Szczytno
Norderstedt
Schwerin
Malchin
Nowogard
Szczecinek
Grudziądz
Nidzica
Neubrandenburg
Pasewalk
Świecie
Reinbek
Parchim
Waren
Müritz
Szczecin
Stargard Szczeciński
Chełmno
Brodnica
Działdowo
Lüneburg
Ludwigslust
Neustrelitz
Prenzlau
Wałcz
Mława
Elbe
Perleberg
Wittstock
Gryfino
Pyrzyce
Choszczno
Piła
Bydgoszcz
Toruń
Uelzen
Wittenberge
Ciechanów
Neuruppin
Eberswalde-Finow
Gorzów Wielkopolski
Inowrocław
Włocławek
Wyszków
Celle
D
Stendal
Rathenow
Płock
PL
Hannover
Wolfsburg
BERLIN
Kostrzyn
Gniezno
WARSZAWA
Haldensleben
Brandenburg
Fürstenwalde
Poznań
Września
Konin
Kutno
Mińsk Mazowiecki
Potsdam
Frankfurt an der Oder
Świebodzin
Łowicz
Pruszków
Salzgitter
Wolfenbüttel
Helmstedt
Magdeburg
Luckenwalde
Warta
Skierniewice
Kościan
Jarocin
Schönebeck
Zielona Góra
Leszno
Zgierz
Łódź
Halberstadt
Lutherstadt Wittenberg
Dessau
Cottbus
Kalisz
Pabianice
Tomaszów Mazowiecki
Głogów
Rawicz
Ostrów Wielkopolski
Sieradz
Radom
Hettstedt
Nordhausen
Halle
Torgau
Polkowice
Lubin
Bełchatów
Piotrków Trybunalski
Skarżysko-Kamienna
Sondershausen
Senftenberg
Riesa
Leipzig
Wrocław
Wieluń
Radomsko
Starachowice
Mühlhausen (Thüringen)
Meißen
Bautzen
Legnica
Görlitz
Kluczbork
Ostrowiec Świętokrzyski
Gotha
Erfurt
Jena
Dresden
Chemnitz (Karl-Marx-Stadt)
Jelenia Góra
Jawor
Oława
Brzeg
Częstochowa
Kielce
Bad Hersfeld
Suhl
Saalfeld
Gera
Zwickau
Děčín
Liberec
Świdnica
Wałbrzych
Opole
Tarnobrzeg
Meiningen
Plauen
Erzgebirge
Teplice
Ústí nad Labem
Litoměřice
Kłodzko
Tarnowskie Góry
Dąbrowa Górnicza
Pińczów
Coburg
Hof
Most
Chomutov
Mladá Boleslav
Hradec Králové
Bytom
Gliwice
Katowice
Sosnowiec
Mielec
Kraków
Karlovy Vary
Kladno
PRAHA
Rybnik
Żory
Tarnów
Schweinfurt
Bayreuth
Beroun
Pardubice
Šumperk
Opava
Skawina
Bochnia
Jasło
Würzburg
Bamberg
Weiden in der Oberpfalz
Plzeň
Benešov
Svitavy
Ostrava
Bielsko-Biała
Gorlice
Forchheim
CZ
Devět Skal
Olomouc
Nový Jičín
Frýdek-Místek
Nowy Sącz
Nowy Targ
Erlangen
Havlíčkův Brod
Žďár nad Sázavou
Fürth
Nürnberg
Amberg
Domažlice
Tábor
Křemešník
Jihlava
Blansko
Přerov
Čadca
Ansbach
Klatovy
Písek
Třebíč
Vyškov
Žilina
Tatry
Kežmarok
Roth
Schwandorf
Cham
Strakonice
Jindřichův Hradec
Brno
Považská Bystrica
Poprad
Crailsheim
Regensburg
Uherské Hradiště
Martin
Spišská Nová Ves
Weißenburg in Bayern
Regen
České Budějovice
Znojmo
Břeclav
Prievidza
SK
Košice
Donauwörth
Straubing
Deggendorf
Šumava
Zvolen
Rimavská Sobota
Ingolstadt
Passau
Žiar nad Hronom
Günzburg
Augsburg
Landshut
Freising
Braunau am Inn
Linz
Stockerau
Trnava
Nitra
Lučenec
Kazincbarcika
Biberach an der Riß
München
Donau (Danube)
St. Pölten
WIEN
Pezinok
Galanta
Levice
Miskolc
Waldkraiburg
Wels
Vöcklabruck
Amstetten
BRATISLAVA
Nové Zámky
Salgótarján
Eger
Memmingen
Rosenheim
Traunstein
Gmunden
A
Baden
Mosonmagyaróvár
Komárno
Gyöngyös
Vác
Marktoberdorf
Kempten (Allgäu)
Salzburg
Bad Ischl
Neunkirchen
Mürzzuschlag
Győr
Dunakeszi
Friedrichshafen
Bad Reichenhall
Hallein
Hoher Dachstein
Hochschwab
Sopron
Kapuvár
Tatabánya
BUDAPEST
Karcag
Garmisch-Partenkirchen
Kufstein
Bruck an der Mur
Sárvár
Érd
H
Innsbruck
Schwaz
Niedere Tauern
Knittelfeld
Szombathely
Várpalota
Székesfehérvár
Szolnok
Cegléd
Hohe Tauern
Judenburg
Graz
Veszprém
Balatonfüred
Dunaújváros
Schrankogel
Großglockner
Körmend
Kecskemét
Hochfeiler
Lienz
Brunico
Wolfsberg
Zalaegerszeg
Siófok
Kiskunfélegyháza
Bressanone
Spittal an der Drau
St Veit an der Glan
Großer Speikkogel
Keszthely
Balaton
Paks
Orosháza
Merano
Bolzano
Villach
Klagenfurt
Völkermarkt
Pesnica
Nagykanizsa
Kiskunhalas
Hódmezővásárhely
Ortles
Laives
Maribor
Ptuj
Čakovec
Dombóvár
Szekszárd
Szeged
Makó
Tolmezzo
Gemona del Friuli
Jesenice
Kranj
Celje
Varaždin
Kaposvár
Baja
Trento
I
Belluno
Feltre
Vittorio Veneto
Udine
Trbovlje
Koprivnica
Szigetvár
Pécs
Subotica
Riva del Garda
LJUBLJANA
Bjelovar
Barcs
Mohács
Senta
Kikinda
Conegliano
Gorizia
Logatec
Trebnje
ZAGREB
Virovitica
Sombor
Bečej
Rovereto
Monfalcone
SLO
HR
Osijek
Vrbas
Zrenjanin
Treviso
Portogruaro
Trieste
Kočevje
Snežnik
Bačka Palanka
Brescia
Vicenza
Mestre
Koper
Karlovac
Sisak
Đakovo
Vukovar
Novi Sad
Verona
Padova
Venezia
Golfo di Venezia
Bosanska Dubica
SLAVONIJA
Inđija
Manerbio
Mantova
Monselice
Chioggia
Rijeka
Bosanski Novi
Bosanska Gradiška
Slavonski Brod
Županja
Ruma
Legnago
Rovigo
Istra
Krk
Prijedor
BIH
Doboj
BEOGRAD
Mirandola
Ferrara
Porto Tolle
Pula
Cres
Bosanska Krupa
Banja Luka
Carpi
Codigoro
Bihać
Tuzla
Modena
Argenta
Comacchio
Lukavac
Loznica
Mladenovac
Lošinj
Ključ
Mrkonjić-Grad
Zvornik
Lazarevac
Bologna
Ravenna
Titov Drvar
Jajce
Travnik
Valjevo
Imola
Faenza
Forlì
Pag
Zenica
Vitez
Gornji Milanovac
Cesena
Rimini
Zadar
Bosansko Grahovo
Bugojno
Visoko
Užice
Čačak
Dugi Otok

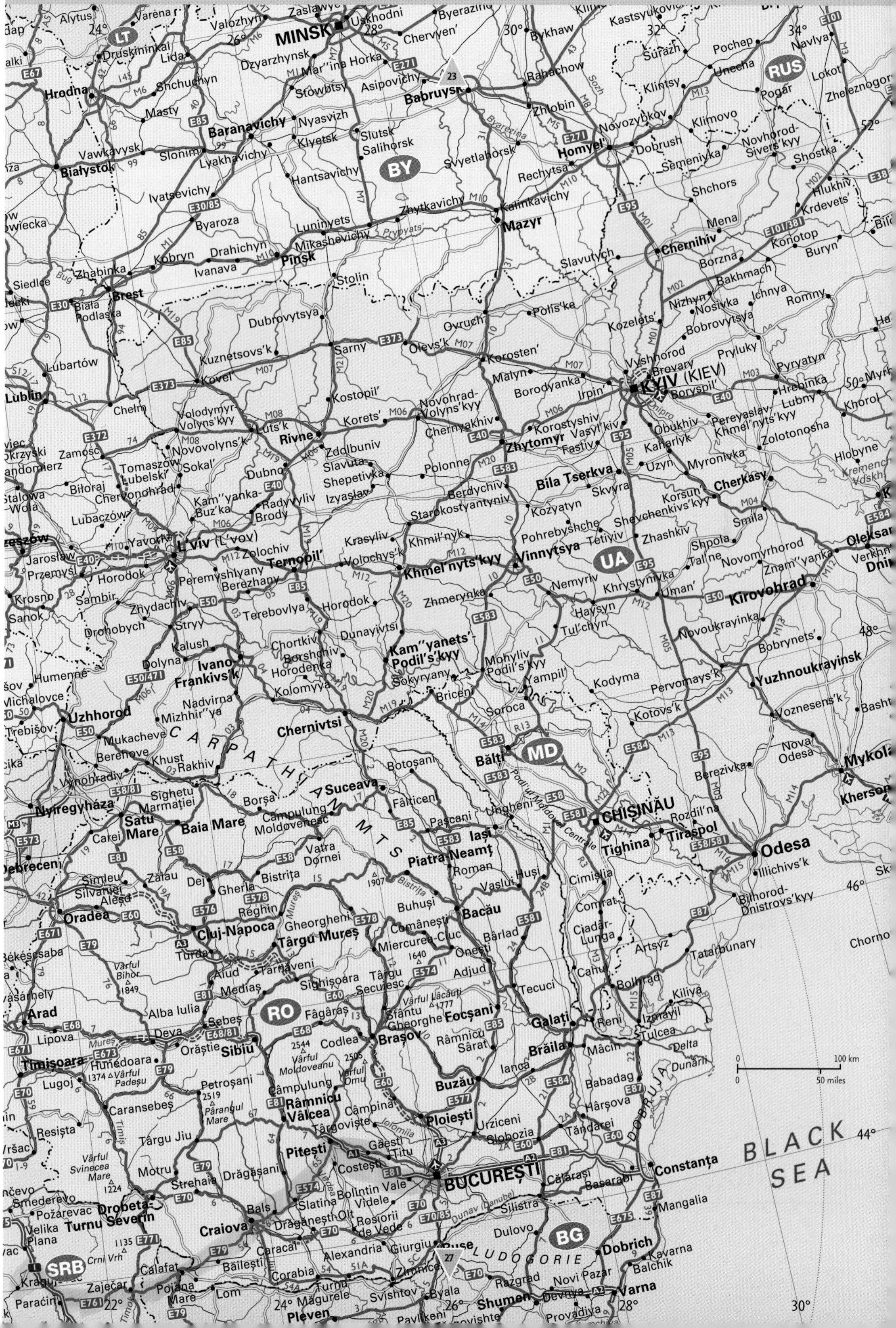

Alytus Varėna Valozhyn Zaslawye MINSK Uskhodni Byerazino Klimavichy Kastsyukovichy
24° LT 26° 28° Chervyen' 30° Bykhaw 32° 34°
Druskininkai Lida Dzyarzhynsk Mar''ina Horka Surazh Pochep Navlya
Hrodna Shchuchyn Stowbtsy Asipovichy Babruysk Rahachow Klintsy Unecha RUS Lokot' Pogar Zheleznogorsk
Masty Baranavichy Nyasvizh Slutsk Salihorsk Zhlobin Novozybkov Klimovo 52°
Vawkavysk Slonim Lyakhavichy Hantsavichy BY Svyetlahorsk Homyel' Dobrush Semenivka Novhorod-Sivers'kyy Shostka
Białystok Ivatsevichy Rechytsa Shchors Hlukhiv Krolevets'
Byaroza Luninyets Zhytkavichy Kalinkavichy Mazyr Mena
Kobryn Drahichyn Mikashevichy Pinsk Chernihiv Konotop Buryn'
Siedlce Zhabinka Ivanava Stolin Slavutych Borzna Bakhmach
Biała Podlaska Brest Dubrovytsya Ovruch Polis'ke Nizhyn Nosivka Ichnya Romny
Kuznetsovs'k Sarny Olevs'k Korosten' Kozelets' Bobrovytsya
Lubartów Kovel' Malyn Borodyanka Vyshhorod Brovary Pryluky Pyryatyn
Lublin Kostopil' Irpin' KYIV (KIEV) Boryspil' Hrebinka Lubny Khorol
Chełm Volodymyr-Volyns'kyy Luts'k Rivne Korets' Novohrad-Volyns'kyy Chernyakhiv Korostyshiv Vasyl'kiv Obukhiv Pereyaslav-Khmel'nyts'kyy Zolotonosha
Zamość Novovolyns'k Zdolbuniv Zhytomyr Fastiv Kaharlyk
Tomaszów Lubelski Sokal' Dubno Slavuta Shepetivka Polonne Uzyn Myronivka Hlobyne
Biłgoraj Chervonohrad Radyvyliv Izyaslav Berdychiv Bila Tserkva Skvyra Cherkasy
Kam''yanka-Buz'ka Brody Starokostyantyniv Kozyatyn Korsun'-Shevchenkivs'kyy Smila
Lubaczów Yavoriv Krasyliv Khmil'nyk Pohrebyshche Tetiyiv Zhashkiv Shpola Oleksandriya
Jarosław L'viv (L'vov) Zolochiv Ternopil' Volochys'k Khmel'nyts'kyy Vinnytsya UA Tal'ne Novomyrhorod Znam''yanka
Przemyśl Horodok Peremyshlyany Berezhany Nemyriv Khrystynivka Uman' Kirovohrad
Krosno Sambir Zhydachiv Terebovlya Horodok Zhmerynka Haysyn
Sanok Drohobych Stryy Chortkiv Dunayivtsi Tul'chyn Novoukrayinka Bobrynets' 48°
Kalush Borshchiv Kam''yanets'-Podil's'kyy Mohyliv Podil's'kyy Yampil'
Humenné Dolyna Ivano-Frankivs'k Horodenka Sokyryany Kodyma Pervomays'k Yuzhnoukrayinsk
Michalovce Nadvirna Kolomyya Briceni Soroca Voznesens'k Bashtanka
Uzhhorod Mizhhir''ya Kotovs'k
Trebišov Mukacheve CARPATHIAN MTS Chernivtsi MD
Berehove Khust Rakhiv Bălţi Nova Odesa Mykolayiv
Vynohradiv Botoşani Berezivka
Sighetu Marmaţiei Suceava Fălticeni Ungheni Podişul Moldovei Centrale Chişinău Rozdil'na Kherson
Nyíregyháza Satu Mare Baia Mare Borşa Câmpulung Moldovenesc Paşcani Tighina Tiraspol
Carei Iaşi Odesa
Debrecen Vatra Dornei Piatra Neamţ Roman Illichivs'k
Şimleu Silvaniei Zalău Dej Gherla Bistriţa 1907 Bistriţa Vaslui Huşi Cimişlia 46°
Aleşd Reghin Buhuşi Comrat Bilhorod-Dnistrovs'kyy
Oradea Cluj-Napoca Gheorgheni Comăneşti Bacău
Békéscsaba Turda Târgu Mureş Miercurea-Ciuc Bârlad Ciadâr-Lunga Artsyz Tatarbunary Chornomorsk
Vârful Bihor 1849 Aiud Târnăveni 1640 Oneşti Cahul
Sighişoara Târgu Secuiesc Adjud Bolhrad Kiliya
Arad Mediaş Vârful Lăcăuţi 1777
Alba Iulia Sebeş RO Făgăraş Sfântu Gheorghe Focşani Tecuci Galaţi Reni Izmayil
Lipova Deva Orăştie Sibiu Codlea Braşov Tulcea Delta Dunării
Timişoara Hunedoara 2544 Vârful Moldoveanu 2505 Vârful Omu Râmnicu Sărat Brăila Măcin
Lugoj 1374 Vârful Padeşu Petroşani Ianca Babadag
Caransebeş 2519 Parângul Mare Câmpulung Râmnicu Vâlcea Câmpina Buzău Hârşova DOBRUJA
Reşiţa Târgu Jiu Târgovişte Ploieşti Urziceni Slobozia Ţăndărei
Vršac Vârful Svinecea Mare 1224 Piteşti Găeşti Titu BLACK SEA 44°
Motru Drăgăşani Costeşti BUCUREŞTI Călăraşi Constanţa
Smederevo Strehaia Slatina Bolintin Vale Basarabi
Požarevac Drobeta-Turnu Severin Balş Videle Silistra Mangalia
Velika Plana Craiova Drăgăneşti-Olt Roşiorii de Vede Dunav (Danube) Dulovo BG
1135 Crni Vrh Caracal Alexandria Giurgiu Ruse LUDOGORIE Dobrich Kavarna
SRB Calafat Băileşti Corabia Zimnicea Razgrad Novi Pazar Balchik
Kragujevac Zaječar Poiana Mare Lom Turnu Măgurele Svishtov Byala Devnya Varna
Paraćin 22° 24° Pleven 26° Shumen Provadiya 28° 30°

0 100 km
0 50 miles

Sondrio
Lugano
Morbegno
Como
Lecco
Bergamo
Monza
Milano
Brescia
Trento
Riva del Garda
Rovereto
Vicenza
Verona
Padova
Treviso
Mestre
Venezia
Golfo di Venezia
Chioggia
Manerbio
Mantova
Cremona
Piacenza
Voghera
Legnago
Rovigo
Monselice
Feltre
Belluno
Vittorio Veneto
Conegliano
Tolmezzo
Gemona del Friuli
Udine
Gorizia
Monfalcone
Portogruaro
Trieste
Golfo di Trieste
Koper
Jesenice
Kranj
LJUBLJANA
Trbovlje
Celje
Logatec
Trebnje
Kočevje
Snežnik
1796
SLO
Varaždin
Koprivnica
ZAGREB
Bjelovar
Karlovac
Sisak
BIH
Virovitica
Szigetvár
Barcs
Pécs
Mohács
Subotica
Sombor
Osijek
Vrbas
Bačka Palanka
Vukovar
Đakovo
Županja
SLAVONIJA
Slavonski Brod
Bosanska Dubica
Bosanska Gradiška
Bosanski Novi
Prijedor
Bosanska Krupa
Bihać
Banja Luka
Doboj
Tuzla
Loznica
Zvornik
Lukavac
Zenica
Mrkonjić-Grad
Ključ
Jajce
Travnik
Vitez
Bugojno
Visoko
SARAJEVO
Goražde
Foča
Priboj
Pljevlja
HR
Gornji Vakuf
Livno
Jablanica
Konjic
Mostar
Nevesinje
Čapljina
Stolac
Trebinje
Nikšić
MNE
Cetinje
Bar
Dubrovnik
Korčula
Korčulanski Kanal
Lastovo
Hvar
Vis
Brač
Šolta
Split
Šibenik
DALMACIJA
Zadar
Dugi Otok
Pag
Velebit
Gospić
Titov Drvar
Bosansko Grahovo
Rijeka
Krk
Cres
Lošinj
Pula
Pazin
Istra
Kvarner
Ferrara
Porto Tolle
Codigoro
Comacchio
Valli di Comacchio
Mirandola
Carpi
Parma
Reggio nell' Emilia
Modena
Argenta
Bologna
Genova
Alpidi Succiso
2017
Imola
Faenza
Ravenna
Forlì
Cesena
Rimini
SAN MARINO
RSM
Sestri Levante
Mte Cimone
2165
La Spezia
Carrara
Massa
Pistoia
Prato
Viareggio
Lucca
Firenze
Pisa
Livorno
Empoli
Poggibonsi
Montevarchi
Rosignano Marittimo
Cecina
Siena
Arezzo
Poggio di Montieri
1051
Sinalunga
Cortona
Montepulciano
Follonica
Monte Amiata
1738
Portoferraio
Isola d'Elba
Monte Stello
1307
Bastia
Arcipelago Toscano
Grosseto
Lago di Bolsena
Orbetello
Monte Argentario
635
Tarquinia
Civitavecchia
Viterbo
Lago di Bracciano
Guidonia-Montecelio
ROMA
Tivoli
Frascati
Pomezia
Aprilia
Anzio
Latina
Sabaudia
Gaeta
Fondi
Formia
Sora
Frosinone
Cassino
Isernia
Avezzano
Piana del Fucino
Monte Greco
2283
Sulmona
Civita Castellana
Rieti
Narni
Terni
Orvieto
Todi
Spoleto
Foligno
Assisi
Perugia
Gubbio
Città di Castello
Sansepolcro
Urbino
Pesaro
Fano
Senigallia
Jesi
Ancona
Osimo
Fabriano
Macerata
Civitanova Marche
Fermo
Appennino Umbro-Marchigiano
Appennino Tosco-Emiliano
Ascoli Piceno
San Benedetto del Tronto
Giulianova
Roseto degli Abruzzi
Teramo
Monte Corno
2912
Montesilvano
Pescara
Penne
L'Aquila
Chieti
Ortona
Lanciano
Vasto
Guardiagrele
Atessa
Termoli
Appennino Abruzzese
ADRIATIC SEA
San Severo
Sannicandro Garganico
Vieste
Monte Sant'Angelo
Manfredonia
Golfo di Manfredonia
Campobasso
Lucera
Foggia
Barletta
Molfetta
Bari
Cerignola
Andria
Bitonto
Monopoli
Fasano
Ariano Irpino
Benevento
Caserta
Sessa Aurunca
Mondragone
Aversa
Golfo di Gaeta
Napoli
Vesuvio
1277
Torre del Greco
Castellammare di Stabia
Avellino
Salerno
Golfo di Salerno
Battipaglia
Eboli
Agropoli
Melfi
Minervino Murge
Le Murge
Gravina in Puglia
Altamura
Avigliano
Matera
Potenza
Ginosa
Taranto
Massafra
Brindisi
Mesagne
Francavilla Fontana
Lecce
Manduria
Copertino
Nardò
Galatina
Gallipoli
Casarano
Tricase
Capo Sta Maria di Leuca
Golfo di Taranto
Sala Consilina
Monte Cervati
1898
Monte del Papa
2005
Pisticci
Policoro
Lauria
2248
Monte Pollino
Castrovillari
Corigliano Calabro
Rossano
Cetraro
Acri
Montalto Uffugo
Cirò Marina
Paola
La Sila
San Giovanni in Fiore
Cosenza
Petilia Policastro
Crotone
Amantea
Nicastro
Isola di Capo Rizzuto
Golfo di Sta Eufemia
Catanzaro
Golfo di Squillace
Soverato
Vibo Valentia
Rosarno
Palmi
Taurianova
Villa San Giovanni
Reggio di Calabria
TYRRHENIAN SEA
Isola Stromboli
Isola di Ustica
Isole Lipari
Lipari
Capo Milazzo
Messina
Capo San Vito
Palermo
Trapani
Alcamo
Termini Imerese
Cefalù
1847
Monte Soro
Monte Etna
3323
Taormina
Giarre
Acireale
Marsala
Val di Mazara
Corleone
Castelvetrano
Adrano
Paternò
Mazara del Vallo
Casteltermini
Enna
Sciacca
Platani
Caltanissetta
Catania
Lentini
Canicattì
Agrigento
Caltagirone
Niscemi
Augusta
Licata
Gela
Serra di Burgio
883
Siracusa
Vittoria
Ragusa
Avola
Golfo di Noto
Pachino
SICILIA (SICILY)
Isola di Pantelleria
MEDITERRANEAN SEA
IONIAN SEA
Gozo
VALLETTA
Birkirkara
Malta
M
Isole Pelagie
Bizerte
Menzel Bourguiba
Golfe de Tunis
Cap Bon
TUNIS
L'Ariana
Ben Arous
Kelibia
Menzel Temime
Korba
Nabeul
Hammamet
Zaghouan
Golfe de Hammamet
TN
Kalaa Kebira
M'Saken
Sousse
Monastir
Moknine
Kairouan
Porto-Vecchio
La Maddalena
Olbia
Siniscola
Nuoro
Golfo di Orosei
Arbatax
I
F
Durrës
TIR
Lu
Vl
BEO
POD
Rtu Sant' Elena
46°
44°
42°
40°
38°
36°
10°
12°
14°
16°
18°
0
100
200 km
50
100 miles
24
19

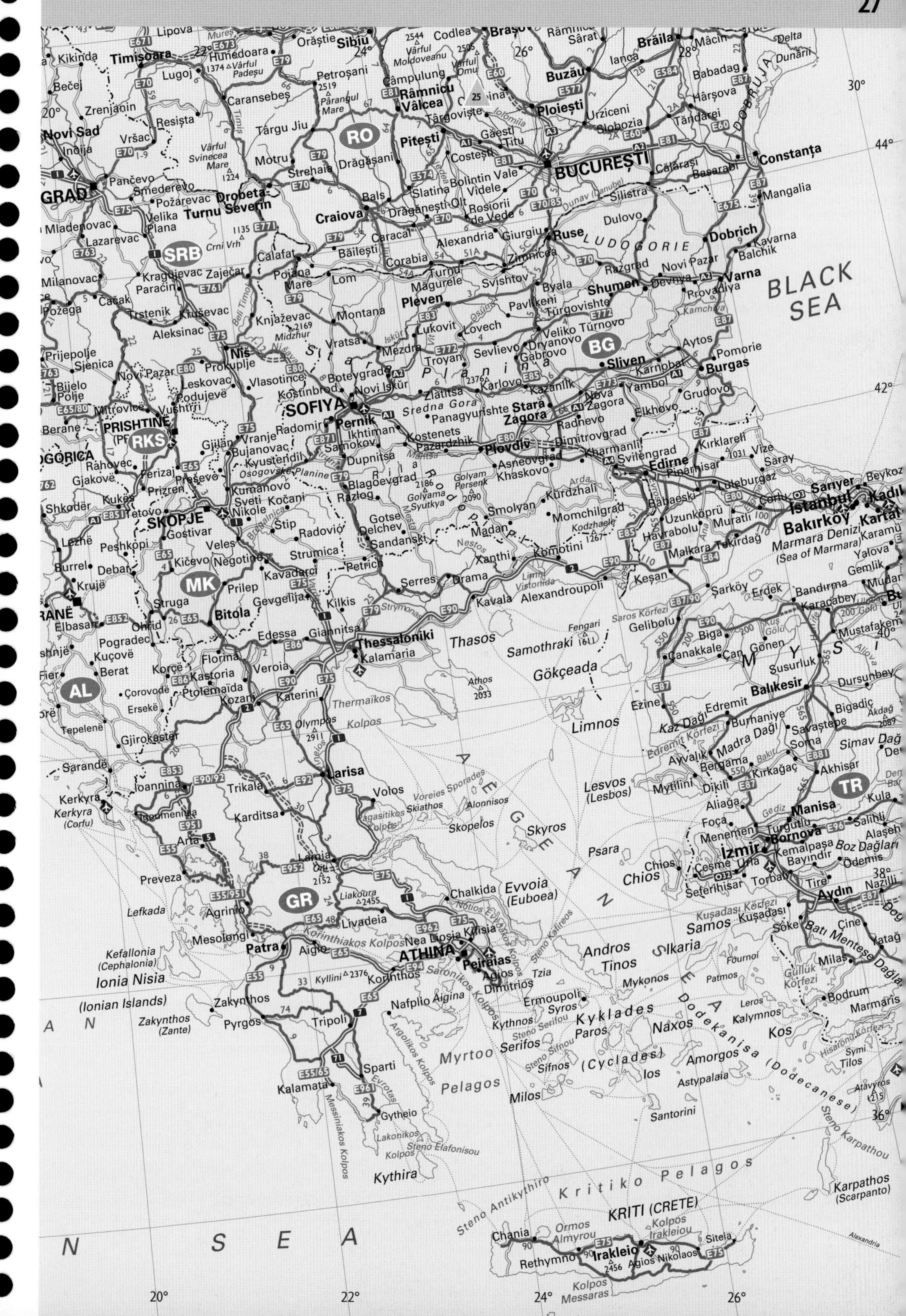
Lipova
Timişoara
Hunedoara
Orăştie
Sibiu
Codlea
Braşov
Râmnicu Sărat
Brăila
Măcin
Delta Dunării
Kikinda
Lugoj
Vârful Padeşu
Petroşani
Vârful Moldoveanu
Câmpulung
Vârful Omu
Buzău
Babadag
Bečej
Caransebeş
Vârful Păreangul Mare
Râmnicu Vâlcea
Târgovişte
Ploieşti
Urziceni
Hârşova
Zrenjanin
Reşiţa
Slobozia
Ţăndărei
Novi Sad
Vršac
Târgu Jiu
Piteşti
Găeşti
Titu
Inđija
Vârful Svinecea Mare
Motru
Drăgăşani
Costeşti
BUCUREŞTI
Călăraşi
Constanţa
Pančevo
Strehaia
Bolintin Vale
Slatina
Videle
Mangalia
Smederevo
Drobeta-Turnu Severin
Bals
Drăgăneşti-Olt
Roşiorii de Vede
Dunav (Danube)
Silistra
Požarevac
Craiova
Velika Plana
Caracal
Alexandria
Giurgiu
Ruse
Dulovo
Dobrich
Kavarna
Balchik
Mladenovac
Lazarevac
Crni Vrh
Băileşti
Calafat
LUDOGORIE
Corabia
Turnu Măgurele
Zimnicea
Razgrad
Novi Pazar
Varna
Milanovac
Kragujevac
Zaječar
Poiana Mare
Lom
Svishtov
Byala
Shumen
Devnya
Provadiya
BLACK SEA
Čačak
Paraćin
Pleven
Pavlikeni
Târgovishte
Požega
Trstenik
Kruševac
Knjaževac
Montana
Midzhur
Lukovit
Lovech
Veliko Târnovo
Kamchiya
Aleksinac
Vratsa
Mezdra
Dryanovo
Gabrovo
Aytos
Prijepolje
Sjenica
Niš
Troyan
Sevlievo
Sliven
Karnobat
Pomorie
Burgas
Novi Pazar
Prokuplje
Botevgrad
Stara Planina
Bijelo Polje
Leskovac
Vlasotince
Kostinbrod
Novi Iskŭr
Zlatitsa
Karlovo
Kazanlak
Yambol
Nova Zagora
Grudovo
Mitrovicë
Podujevë
Vushtrri
SOFIYA
Pernik
Sredna Gora
Panagyurishte
Stara Zagora
Elkhovo
Berane
PRISHTINË
Vranje
Radomir
Ikhtiman
Kostenets
Radnevo
Dimitrovgrad
Kırklareli
Vize
Gjilan
Bujanovac
Samokov
Pazardzhik
Plovdiv
Kharmanli
Svilengrad
Edirne
PODGORICA
Rahovec
Kyustendil
Dupnitsa
Rila
Asenovgrad
Haskovo
Pınarhisar
Saray
Ferizaj
Preševo
Osogovska Planine
Blagoevgrad
Golyam Persenk
Gjakovë
Prizren
Kumanovo
Razlog
Golyama Syutkya
Kurdzhali
Lüleburgaz
Sarıyer
Beykoz
Kukës
Sveti Nikole
Kočani
Babaeski
Çorlu
İstanbul
Kadıköy
Shkodër
Tetovo
SKOPJE
Gostivar
Bregalnica
Štip
Radoviš
Gotse Delchev
Smolyan
Momchilgrad
Uzunköprü
Bakırköy
Kartal
Rodopi
Mesta
Madan
Kodzhaele
Hayrabolu
Muratlı
Lezhë
Peshkopi
Veles
Strumica
Sandanski
Nestos
Komotini
Malkara
Tekirdağ
Marmara Denizi (Sea of Marmara)
Karamürsel
Yalova
Burrel
Debar
Kičevo
Negotino
Petrich
Xanthi
Gemlik
Mudanya
Krujë
Kavadarci
Serres
Drama
Limni Vistonida
Keşan
Bandırma
Prilep
Kilkis
Kavala
Alexandroupoli
Şarköy
Erdek
Karacabey
Struga
Gevgelija
Strymonas
TIRANË
Elbasan
Ohrid
Bitola
Edessa
Giannitsa
Saros Körfezi
Gelibolu
Mustafakemalpaşa
Pogradec
Thessaloniki
Thasos
Fengari
Samothraki
Biga
Kuş Gölü
Kalamaria
Çanakkale
Çan
Gönen
Kuçovë
Florina
Veroia
Gökçeada
Susurluk
Fier
Berat
Korçë
Kastoria
Ptolemaïda
Çorovodë
Ersekë
Kozani
Katerini
Athos
Balıkesir
Dursunbey
Thermaïkos Kolpos
Ezine
Edremit
Bigadiç
Akdağ
Tepelenë
Olympos
Limnos
Kaz Dağı
Burhaniye
Savaştepe
Gjirokastër
Edremit Körfezi
Madra Dağı
Soma
Simav Dağı
Sarandë
Ioannina
Larisa
Ayvalık
Bergama
Kırkağaç
Akhisar
Kerkyra
Kerkyra (Corfu)
Trikala
Volos
Voreies Sporades
Skiathos
Alonnisos
Lesvos (Lesbos)
Mytilini
Dikili
Kula
Igoumenitsa
Karditsa
Pagasitikos Kolpos
Skopelos
AEGEAN SEA
Aliağa
Gediz
Manisa
Salihli
Arta
Skyros
Foça
Turgutlu
Menemen
Bornova
Boz Dağları
Psara
Chios
İzmir
Kemalpaşa
Bayındır
Ödemiş
Preveza
Lamia
Oiti
Çeşme
Urla
Seferihisar
Torbalı
Tire
Chalkida
Evvoia (Euboea)
Aydın
Nazilli
Liakoura
Lefkada
Agrinio
Livadeia
Kuşadası Körfezi
Samos
Kuşadası
Söke
Çine
Mesolongi
Korinthiakos Kolpos
Nea Liosia
Kifisia
Steno Kafireos
Batı Menteşe Dağları
Yatağan
Kefallonia (Cephalonia)
Patra
Aigio
ATHINA
Peiraias
Andros
Tinos
Ikaria
Fournoi
Milas
Agios Dimitrios
Tzia
Güllük Körfezi
Ionia Nisia (Ionian Islands)
Kyllini
Korinthos
Saronikos Kolpos
Mykonos
Patmos
Bodrum
Zakynthos
Nafplio
Aigina
Ermoupoli
Syros
Leros
Marmaris
Zakynthos (Zante)
Pyrgos
Tripoli
Kythnos
Steno Serifou
Kyklades (Cyclades)
Naxos
Kalymnos
Dodekanisa (Dodecanese)
Argolikos Kolpos
Myrtoo Pelagos
Serifos
Paros
Kos
Hisarönü Körfezi
Sparti
Steno Sifnou
Sifnos
Amorgos
Symi
Tilos
Kalamata
Evrotas
Ios
Astypalaia
Messiniakos Kolpos
Milos
Atavyros
Gytheio
Santorini
Lakonikos Kolpos
Steno Elafonisou
Steno Karpathou
Kythira
Kritiko Pelagos
Steno Antikythiro
Karpathos (Scarpanto)
KRITI (CRETE)
Chania
Ormos Almyrou
Kolpos Irakleiou
Sitela
Rethymno
Irakleio
Agios Nikolaos
Kolpos Messaras
IONIAN SEA
RO
SRB
BG
RKS
MK
AL
GR
TR
20°
22°
24°
26°
28°
30°
44°
42°
38°
36°

	Road maps	Carte routière	Straßenkarten
E55	Euro route number	Route européenne	Europastraßennummer
A13	Motorway	Autoroute	Autobahn
	Motorway – toll	Autoroute à péage	Gebührenpflichtige Autobahn
37	Motorway junction – full access	Echangeur d'autoroute avec accès libre	Autobahnauffahrt mit vollem Zugang
12	Motorway junction – restricted access	Echangeur d'autoroute avec accès limité	Autobahnauffahrt mit beschränktem Zugang
	Motorway services	Aire de service sur autoroute	Autobahnraststätte
309	Main road – dual carriageway	Route principale à chaussées séparées	Hauptstraße - Zweispurig
	Main road – single carriageway	Route principale à une seule chaussée	Hauptstraße - Einspurig
516	Secondary road – dual carriageway	Route secondaire à chaussées séparées	Zweispurige Nebenstraße
	Secondary road – single carriageway	Route secondaire à une seule chaussée	Einspurige Nebenstraße
	Motorway tunnel	Tunnel (autoroute)	Tunnel (Autobahn)
	Main road tunnel	Tunnel (route principale)	Tunnel (Hauptstraße)
	Motorway/road under construction	Autoroute/route en construction	Autobahn/Straße im Bau
	Road toll	Route à péage	Gebührenpflichtige Straße
2587	Mountain pass (height in metres)	Col (altitude en mètres)	Pass (Höhe in Metern)
	International airport	Aéroport international	Internationaler Flughafen
	Railway	Chemin de fer	Eisenbahn
	Tunnel	Tunnel	Tunnel
Rotterdam	Car ferry	Bac pour autos	Autofähre
2587	Summit (height in metres)	Sommet (altitude en mètres)	Berg (Höhe in Metern)
	Volcano	Volcan	Vulkan
	Canal	Canal	Kanal
	International boundary	Frontière d'état	Landesgrenze
	Disputed International boundary	Frontière litigieuse	Umstrittene Staatsgrenze
D	Country abbreviation	Abréviation du pays	Nationalitätszeichen
	Urban area	Zone urbaine	Stadtgebiet
28	Adjoining page indicator	Indication de la page contiguë	Randhinweis auf Folgekarte
	National Park	Parc national	Nationalpark
	Scenic route	Parcours pittoresque	Landschaftlich schöne strecke

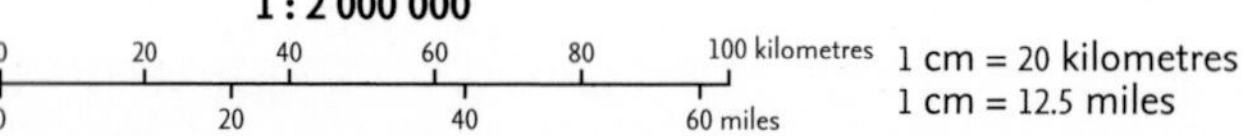

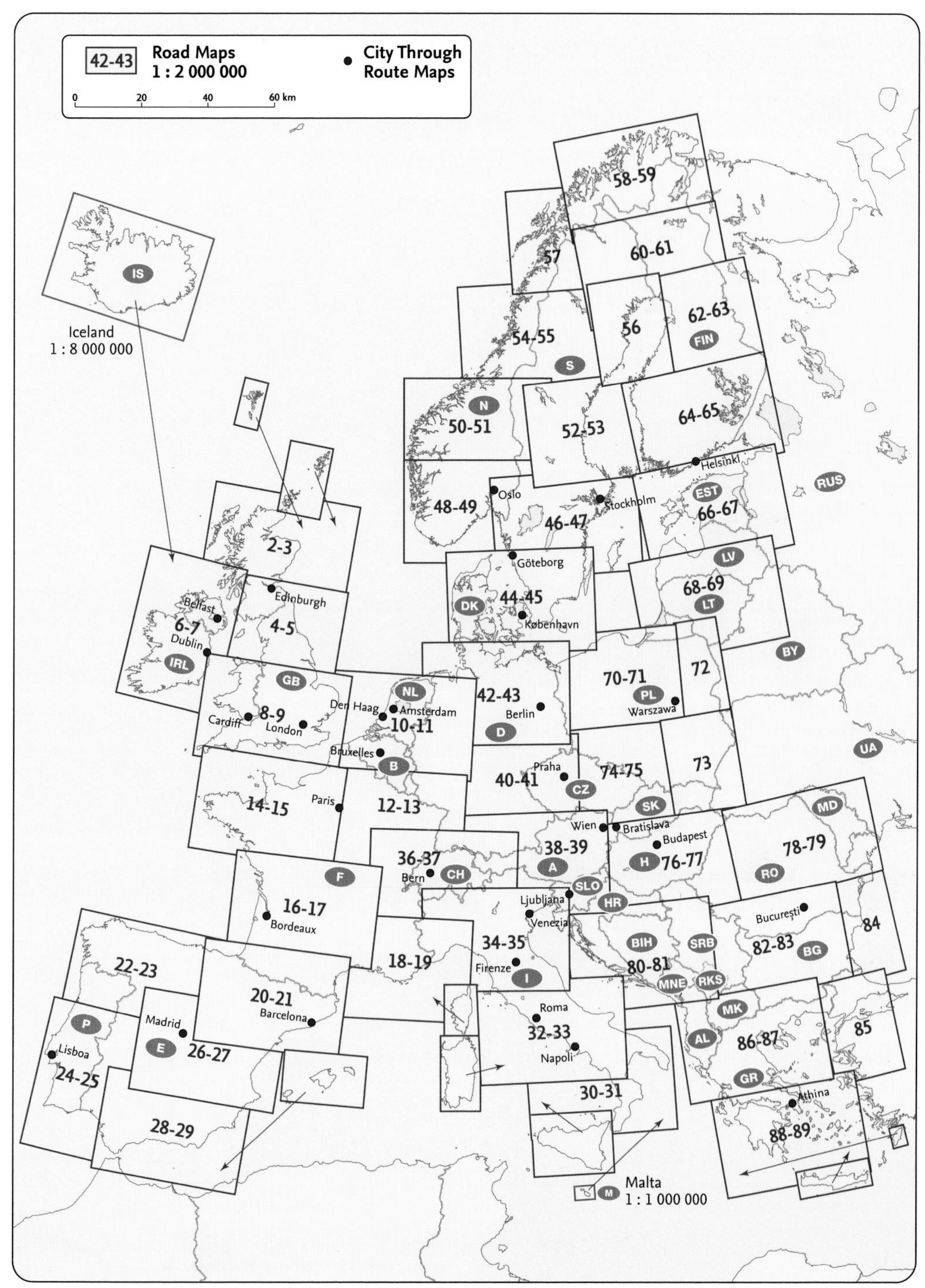
42-43 Road Maps 1 : 2 000 000
City Through Route Maps
0 20 40 60 km
Iceland 1 : 8 000 000
IS
58-59
57
60-61
54-55
56
62-63
FIN
S
N
50-51
52-53
64-65
Helsinki
48-49
Oslo
46-47
Stockholm
EST
66-67
RUS
2-3
Göteborg
DK
44-45
København
LV
68-69
LT
Edinburgh
Belfast
6-7
Dublin
IRL
4-5
BY
GB
8-9
Cardiff
London
Den Haag
NL
Amsterdam
10-11
Bruxelles
B
42-43
Berlin
D
70-71
PL
Warszawa
72
73
UA
14-15
Paris
12-13
40-41
Praha
CZ
74-75
SK
Wien
Bratislava
Budapest
38-39
A
H
76-77
MD
78-79
RO
36-37
Bern
CH
F
16-17
Bordeaux
SLO
Ljubljana
HR
Venezia
34-35
Firenze
I
BIH
SRB
80-81
MNE
RKS
București
82-83
BG
84
22-23
20-21
Barcelona
18-19
P
Madrid
E
26-27
Lisboa
24-25
Roma
32-33
Napoli
MK
AL
86-87
GR
85
28-29
30-31
Athina
88-89
Malta 1 : 1 000 000
M

1
2
3
4
5
6
B
C
D
E
F
G
H
Rona
Westray
Rousay
Brough Head
Birsay
Mainland
ORKNEY
ISLANDS
Stromness
Ward Hill
479
Hoy
Flotta
Pentland Firth
Island of Stroma
Dunnet Head
Strathy Point
Scrabster
Thurso
Wick
CAITHNESS
Cape Wrath
Butt of Lewis
Muirneag
248
Tolsta Head
Flannan Isles
Great Bernera
Tiumpan Head
Eye Peninsula
Stornoway
Mealisval
574
LEWIS
Scarp
Tirga Mor
679
Beinn Mhòr
572
Kebock Head
Tarbert
Scalpay
South Harris
Rodel
Pabbay
Berneray
Shiant Islands
THE MINCH
Handa Island
Cranstackie
802
Foinaven
915
Ben Hope
927
Ben Loyal
764
Beinn Stumanadh
527
Arkle
787
Ben Stack
721
Ben Hee
873
SUTHERLAND
Ben Klibreck
961
Quinag
808
Beinn Leoid
792
Canisp
846
Suilven
731
Ben More Assynt
998
Loch Shin
Rubha Coigeach
Summer Isles
Stac Pollaidh
613
Cul Mor
849
Greenstone Point
Meall Liath Choire
548
Ullapool
Ben Horn
521
Strath Halladale
Morven
706
Scaraben
626
Rubha Reidh
An Teallach
1062
Beinn Dearg
1084
Carn Chuinneag
898
Easter Ross
Dornoch Firth
Cnoc an t-Sabhail
379
Ben Wyvis
1046
Alness
Lossiemouth
Moray Firth
Rubha Hunish
North Uist
Lochmaddy
Sound of Harris
Sound of Monach
Monach Islands
Baleshare
Benbecula
Vaternish Point
Uig
Ben Geary
284
Trotternish
The Storr
719
Mullach Coire Mhic Fhearchair
1019
Slioch
980
Sgurr Mor
1110
Loch Maree
Beinn Alligin
985
Liathach
1054
Sgurr Ruadh
960
Sgurr a'Mhuilinn
879
Dingwall
Black Isle
Nairn
Forres
Elgin
Mill Buie
371
LITTLE MINCH
Portree
SKYE
Raasay
Inner Sound
Beinn Bhan
896
Sgurr a'Chaorachain
1053
Sgurr a'Choire Ghlais
1083
Inverness
GB
Carne na Loine
Ben Rinnes
840
Healabhal Bheag
488
South Uist
Beinn Mhor
620
Aonach Buidhe
899
Carn Eighe
1183
Glen Affric
Loch Ness
Carn Odhar
802
Grantown-on-Spey
Cook's Cairn
755
Carn Mor
804
Beinn Bhreac
445
Cuillin Hills
Sgurr Alasdair
993
Bla Bheinn
928
Scalpay
Kyle of Lochalsh
A'Chralaig
1120
NORTH WEST HIGHLANDS
Monadhliath Mountains
Strathspey
Aviemore
Geal Charn
821
Lochboisdale
Soay
Beinn Sgritheall
981
Carn a'Chuilinn
816
Carn Dearg
Cairn Gorm
1245
Ben Avon
1171
CAIRNGORMS
Ben Macdui
1309
Cairn Toul
1291
Eriskay
Sound of Barra
Barra
Vatersay
Castlebay
Canna
Cuillin Sound
Ardvasar
Sound of Sleat
Ladhar Bheinn
1020
Sea of the Hebrides
Rum
Askival
812
Mallaig
Sgurr na Ciche
1040
Loch Arkaig
Lochaber
Geal Charn
926
Creag Meagaidh
1130
Meall Chuaich
951
Braemar
Lochnagar
1155
Sandray
Pabbay
Mingulay
Berneray
Eigg
393
Loch Morar
Gulvain
987
Badenoch
An Sgarsoch
1006
Glas Maol
1068
Mayar
928
Sound of Arisaig
Muck
882
Fort William
Stob Choire Claurigh
1177
Ben Alder
1148
Beinn Dearg
1008
Carn nan Gabhar
1121
GRAMPIAN MOUNTAINS
Loch Shiel
Sgurr Dhomhnuill
888
Ben Nevis
1344
Binnein Mor
1128
Ardnamurchan
845
Beinn Resipol
Ben Hiant
528
Pitlochry
Coll
Fuar Bheinn
765
Glen Coe
Bidean nam Bian
1150
Rannoch Moor
Schiehallion
1083
Tobermory
Meall a'Bhuiridh
1108
Lyon
Blairgowrie
Tiree
Treshnish Isles
Lochaline
Loch Linnhe
Beinn Sgulaird
932
Stob Ghabhar
1087
Beinn Heasgarnich
1076
Breadalbane
Ben Lawers
1214
Loch Tay
Almond
Sidlaw Hills
Staffa
Ulva
Mull
Dùn da Ghaoithe
766
Ben More
966
Craignure
Lismore
Loch Etive
Ben Cruachan
1126
Ben Lui
1130
Ben More
1174
Ben Chonzie
931
Perth
Fionnphort
Iona
Loch Scridain
Ross of Mull
Ben Buie
717
Oban
Kerrera
Loch Awe
Beinn Bhuidhe
948
Ben Vorlich
943
Ben Vorlich
985
Crieff
Firth of Lorn
Seil
Beinn Chapull
515
Beinn Bhreac
526
Argyll
Beinn Ime
1011
Loch Lomond and the Trossachs
Ben Ledi
879
Callander
Luing
449
Scarba
Cruach Scarba
Ben Lomond
974
Dunblane
720
Glenrothes
Colonsay
Beinn Bhreac
467
Jura
Doune Hill
734
Loch Lomond
Stirling
Alloa
Cowdenbeath
Dunfermline
Oronsay
Sound of Jura
Lochgilphead
Beinn Mhor
742
Gargunnock Hills
570
Denny
Grangemouth
Tarbert
Beinn an Oir
Sgarbh Breac
364
Knapdale
Greenock
Helensburgh
Alexandria
Falkirk
Bo'ness
Edinburgh
Dumbarton
Cumbernauld
Port Askaig
785
Islay
Feolin Ferry
Beinn Bhreac
507
Dunoon
Tarbert
Bute
Rothesay
Clydebank
Glasgow
Bathgate
Broxburn
Livingston
Machir Bay
Bridgend
491
Beinn Bheigeir
Ardpatrick Point
Kintyre
Loch Fyne
Sound of Bute
Hill of Stake
522
Paisley
Barrhead
Largs
Hamilton
Coatbridge
Motherwell
Wishaw
East Kilbride
Portnahaven
Loch Indaal
Gigha
Beith
Ardrossan
Kilwinning
Strathaven
Lanark
Peebles
Penicuik
Mull Of Oa
The Oa
Port Ellen
Kilbrannan Sound
Goat Fell
874
Arran
Brodick
512
Saltcoats
Irvine
Kilmarnock
Galston
Tinto
707
Tweeddale
Beinn an Tuirc
454
Ard Bheinn
Troon
Crosshands
Culter Fell
Dun Rig
743

FØROYAR
FO
Villingadalsfjall 844
Slættaratindur 882
Svartbakstindur 803
Koppanni 790
Árnafjall 722
Krossafelli 546
Fuglafjørdur
Klaksvík
Eysturoy
Streymoy
Skælingsfjall 768
Miðvágur
Tórshavn
Tindur 479
Sandur
Knútur 392
Tvøroyri
Gluggarnir 610
Vágur
Seyðisfjörður
Esbjerg
Hanstholm
SHETLAND ISLANDS
Unst
Yell
Belmont
Fetlar
Yell Sound
Colgrave Sound
Ronas Hill 450
Hillswick
Ulsta
Toft
St Magnus Bay
Brae
Out Skerries
Muckle Roe
Papa Stour
Mainland
Whalsay
South Nesting Bay
Walls
Bressay
Lerwick
Isle of Noss
Foula
West Burra
Mousa
Sumburgh Head
Sumburgh
GB
Fair Isle
ORKNEY ISLANDS
Papa Westray
The North Sound
North Ronaldsay
Westray
North Ronaldsay Firth
Westray Firth
Sanday
Rousay
Eday
Sanday Sound
Brough Head
Birsay
Stronsay Firth
Stronsay
Mainland
Shapinsay
Stromness
Kirkwall
Ward Hill 479
Hoy
Scapa Flow
Flotta
Burray
St Margaret's Hope
South Ronaldsay
Pentland Firth
Island of Stroma
Pentland Skerries
Dunnet Head
Duncansby Head
Aberdeen
Kirkwall
Lerwick
Sanday
Sanday Sound
Eday
Stronsay Firth
Stronsay
Shapinsay
Burray
St Margaret's Hope
South Ronaldsay
Pentland Skerries
Duncansby Head
Buckie
Durn Hill
Knock Hill 430
Fraserburgh
Peterhead
Keith
Deveron
Strathbogie
Ythan
Hill of Dudwick
Tap o' Noth
Ellon
Inverurie
Don
Dyce
Mar
Morven 871
Westhill
Aberdeen
Banchory
Portlethen
Carnferg 525
Mount Keen 939
Stonehaven
Ben Tirran 896
Brechin
Kirriemuir
Montrose
Forfar
Arbroath
Monifieth
Carnoustie
Dundee
Firth of Tay
St Andrews
Cupar
Fife Ness
Leven
Isle of May
Buckhaven
Kirkcaldy
Firth of Forth
North Berwick
Dunbar
Haddington
Musselburgh
Dalkeith
Lammer Law 528
Gorebridge
Meikle Says Law 535
Berwick-upon-Tweed
Holy Island (Lindisfarne)
Windlestraw Law 659
Galashiels
Tweed
Cockenheugh 211
Minch Moor 567
Kelso
Selkirk
NORTH SEA
0 10 20 30 40 50 km
0 10 20 30 miles

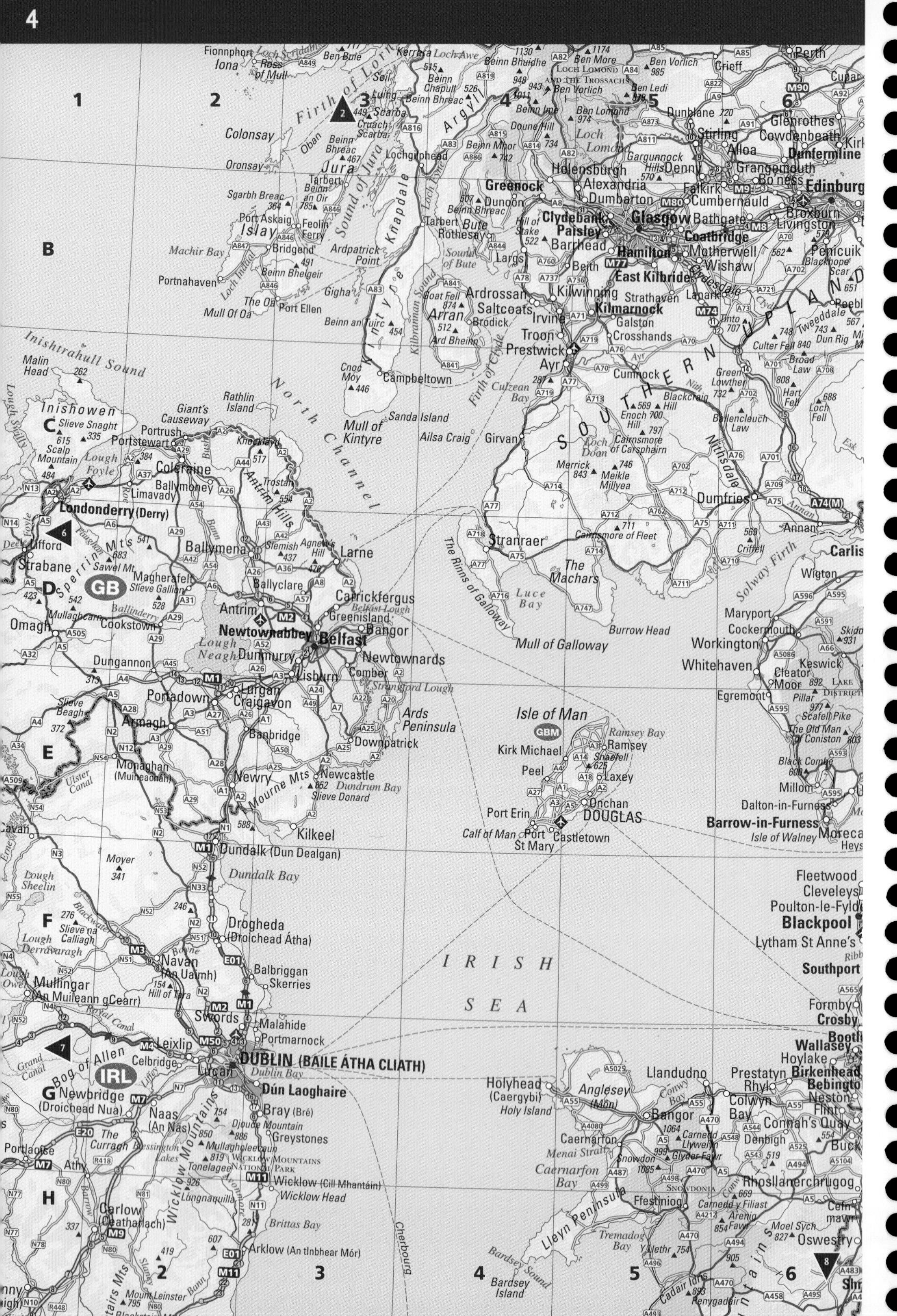

Fionnphort
Iona
Ross of Mull
Ben Buie
Kerrera
Loch Awe
Beinn Bhuidhe
Ben More
Loch Lomond and the Trossachs
Ben Vorlich
Crieff
Perth
Cupar
Firth of Lorn
Seil
Luing
Scarba
Cruach Scarba
Beinn Chapull
Beinn Bhreac
Argyll
Ben Ime
Ben Lomond
Ben Ledi
Dunblane
Stirling
Glenrothes
Cowdenbeath
Alloa
Dunfermline
Colonsay
Oban
Beinn Bhreac
Lochgilphead
Doune Hill
Beinn Mhor
Loch Lomond
Gargunnock Hills
Denny
Grangemouth
Bo'ness
Oronsay
Jura
Sound of Jura
Knapdale
Loch Fyne
Helensburgh
Alexandria
Falkirk
Edinburgh
Tarbert
Beinn an Oir
Greenock
Dunoon
Dumbarton
Cumbernauld
Broxburn
Sgarbh Breac
Beinn Bhreac
Hill of Stake
Clydebank
Glasgow
Bathgate
Livingston
Port Askaig
Feolin Ferry
Islay
Tarbert
Bute
Rothesay
Paisley
Coatbridge
Machir Bay
Bridgend
Ardpatrick Point
Sound of Bute
Barrhead
Hamilton
Motherwell
Penicuik
Wishaw
Blackhope Scar
Beinn Bheigeir
Largs
Beith
East Kilbride
Clydesdale
Portnahaven
Loch Indaal
Gigha
Kilbrannan Sound
Goat Fell
Ardrossan
Saltcoats
Kilwinning
Kilmarnock
Strathaven
Lanark
The Oa
Port Ellen
Mull Of Oa
Arran
Brodick
Irvine
Galston
Tinto
Tweeddale
Peebles
Beinn an Tuirc
Kintyre
Ard Bheinn
Troon
Crosshands
Prestwick
Ayr
Culter Fell
Dun Rig
Broad Law
Southern Uplands
Inishtrahull Sound
Malin Head
Cnoc Moy
Campbeltown
Firth of Clyde
Cumnock
Green Lowther
Hart Fell
Loch Fell
Culzean Bay
Lough Swilly
Inishowen
Rathlin Island
North Channel
Giant's Causeway
Slieve Snaght
Sanda Island
Mull of Kintyre
Ailsa Craig
Girvan
Enoch Hill
Blackcraig Hill
Ballencleuch Law
Portrush
Portstewart
Scalp Mountain
Lough Foyle
Coleraine
Knocklayd
Antrim Hills
Trostan
Loch Doon
Cairnsmore of Carsphairn
Merrick
Meikle Millyea
Nithsdale
Ballymoney
Limavady
Londonderry (Derry)
Dumfries
Annan
Strabane
Lifford
Sperrin Mts
Sawel Mt
Ballymena
Slemish
Agnew's Hill
Larne
Stranraer
Cairnsmore of Fleet
Criffell
Solway Firth
Carlisle
GB
Magherafelt
Slieve Gallion
Ballyclare
The Rinns of Galloway
The Machars
Wigton
Mullaghcarn
Ballinderry
Antrim
Carrickfergus
Greenisland
Belfast Lough
Luce Bay
Maryport
Cockermouth
Omagh
Cookstown
Newtownabbey
Belfast
Bangor
Burrow Head
Skiddaw
Lough Neagh
Dunmurry
Mull of Galloway
Workington
Dungannon
Newtownards
Whitehaven
Keswick
Lisburn
Comber
Strangford Lough
Cleator Moor
Lake District
Slieve Beagh
Portadown
Lurgan
Craigavon
Ards Peninsula
Isle of Man
Egremont
Pillar
Scafell Pike
Armagh
Banbridge
GBM
Ramsey Bay
Ramsey
The Old Man of Coniston
Downpatrick
Kirk Michael
Snaefell
Monaghan (Muineachán)
Ulster Canal
Newry
Newcastle
Dundrum Bay
Peel
Laxey
Black Combe
Mourne Mts
Slieve Donard
Millom
Onchan
Port Erin
DOUGLAS
Dalton-in-Furness
Barrow-in-Furness
Cavan
Kilkeel
Calf of Man
Port St Mary
Castletown
Isle of Walney
Morecambe
Heysham
Dundalk (Dun Dealgan)
Moyer
Dundalk Bay
Lough Sheelin
Fleetwood
Cleveleys
Poulton-le-Fylde
Blackpool
Lytham St Anne's
Blackwater
Slieve na Calliagh
Drogheda (Droichead Átha)
Lough Derravaragh
Navan (An Uaimh)
Boyne
IRISH SEA
Southport
Ribble
Balbriggan
Skerries
Lough Owel
Mullingar (An Muileann gCearr)
Hill of Tara
Formby
Crosby
Royal Canal
Swords
Malahide
Portmarnock
Bootle
Wallasey
Leixlip
Grand Canal
Bog of Allen
Celbridge
DUBLIN (BAILE ÁTHA CLIATH)
Dublin Bay
Lucan
Hoylake
Birkenhead
IRL
Liffey
Dún Laoghaire
Llandudno
Prestatyn
Bebington
Newbridge (Droichead Nua)
Holyhead (Caergybi)
Anglesey (Môn)
Conwy Bay
Rhyl
Colwyn Bay
Neston
Flint
Naas (An Nás)
Wicklow Mountains
Bray (Bré)
Holy Island
Bangor
Djouce Mountain
Greystones
Carnedd Llywelyn
Connah's Quay
The Curragh
Blessington Lakes
Mullaghcleevaun
Caernarfon
Menai Strait
Denbigh
Buckley
Portlaoise
Athy
Tonelagee
Wicklow Mountains National Park
Snowdon
Glyder Fawr
Caernarfon Bay
Wicklow (Cill Mhantáin)
Wicklow Head
Snowdonia
Rhosllanerchrugog
Lugnaquilla
Avonmore
Ffestiniog
Carnedd y Filiast
Barrow
Carlow (Ceatharlach)
Brittas Bay
Lleyn Peninsula
Arenig Fawr
Moel Sych
Cherbourg
Tremadog Bay
Oswestry
Arklow (An tInbhear Mór)
Bardsey Sound
Y Llethr
Berwyns
Slaney
Bardsey Island
Cadair Idris
Pennygadair
Shrewsbury
Mount Leinster
Blackstairs Mts
Blackstairs Mountain
1
2
3
4
5
6
B
C
D
E
F
G
H

St Andrews
Fife Ness
Isle of May
Firth of Forth
North Berwick
Dunbar
Berwick-upon-Tweed
Holy Island
(Lindisfarne)
Cheviot Hills
Alnwick
Amble
Ashington
Morpeth
Blyth
Bedlington
Cramlington
Ponteland
Whitley Bay
Newcastle upon Tyne
South Shields
Hexham
Prudhoe
Gateshead
Sunderland
Stanley
Washington
Consett
Durham
Seaham
Peterlee
Spennymoor
Hartlepool
Bishop Auckland
Billingham
Redcar
Newton Aycliffe
Stockton-on-Tees
Middlesbrough
Barnard Castle
Darlington
Guisborough
Whitby
Cleveland Hills
North York Moors
Richmond
Northallerton
Scalby
Scarborough
Eastfield
Thirsk
Pickering
Vale of Pickering
Filey
Flamborough Head
Ripon
Norton
Bridlington
Bridlington Bay
Knaresborough
Harrogate
York
Driffield
Pocklington
Hornsea
Beverley
Leeds
Bradford
Selby
Kingston upon Hull
Withernsea
Goole
Scunthorpe
Grimsby
Cleethorpes
Mouth of The Humber
Spurn Head
Doncaster
Rotherham
Sheffield
Manchester
Liverpool
Lincoln
Skegness
Louth
Boston
The Wash
Nottingham
Derby
Leicester
Peterborough
King's Lynn
Norwich
NORTH SEA
IJmuiden
Rotterdam, Zeebrugge
GB
8
9
10
11
12
B
C
D
E
F
G
H

1 2 3 4 5 6 7 8

B C D E F G

Ísafjörður
Straumnes
Horn
Grímsey
Rifstangi
Öxarfjörður
Fontur
Sauðárkrókur
Akureyri
Borgarfjörður
Seyðisfjörður
Egilsstaðir
Reiphólsfjöll 881
Húnaflói
Bjargtangar
Breiðafjörður
Ódáðahraun
Snæfell 1833
Tórshavn
Borgarnes
Faxaflói
1763
Bárðarbunga 2009
VATNAJÖKULL 1719
Sviahnúkar
Breiðdalsvík
IS
REYKJAVÍK
Keflavík
Reykjanestá
1491
2119
Hvannadalshnúkur
Vesturhorn
Vestmannaeyjar
Vestmannaeyjar
Surtsey
Vík
Kötlutangi
0 50 100 km
0 30 60 miles

Staffa
Ulva
Mull
Ben More 966
717
Ben Buie
Fionnphort
Iona
Ross of Mull
Loch Scridain
Kerrera
Oban
Ben Cruachan 1126
Ben Lui 1130
Beinn a' Chapuill
Beinn Bhuidhe 948
Beinn Bhreac 526
Ben Vorlich 943
1011
Beinn Ime
Seil
Luing
Scarba 449
Cruach Scarba
Firth of Lorn
Loch Awe
Loch Long
Loch Lomond
GB
Argyll
Colonsay
Oronsay
Jura 467
Beinn Bhreac
Tarbert
Beinn an Oir
Lochgilphead
Beinn Mhor 742
Helensburgh
Greenock
Dunoon
Sgarbh Breac
Port Askaig
364
785
Feolin Ferry
Sound of Jura
Knapdale
Loch Fyne
Rothesay
Largs
Islay
Bridgend
491
Ardpatrick Point
Tarbert
Sound of Bute
Bute
Machir Bay
Loch Indaal
Beinn Bheigeir
Gigha
Kintyre
Kilbrannan Sound
Goat Fell 874
Arran
Brodick
Ardrossan
Saltcoats
Irvine
Troon
Prestwick
Ayr
Portnahaven
The Oa
Port Ellen
Mull of Oa
Beinn an Tuirc 454
512
Ard Bheinn
Firth of Clyde
Troon
Cnoc Moy 446
Campbeltown
Sanda Island
Ailsa Craig
Girvan
Mull of Kintyre
North Channel
Rathlin Island
Inishtrahull Sound
Malin Head
262
Inishowen
Slieve Snaght 335
615
Lough Swilly
Scalp Mountain 484
Lough Foyle
Giant's Causeway
Portrush
Portstewart
384
Coleraine
Knocklayd 517
Antrim Hills
Trostan 554
Ballymoney
Limavady
Roe
Tory Sound
Horn Head
Muckish Mountain 670
Gweedore
The Rosses
Errigal 752
Derryveagh Mts
683
Slieve Snaght
Glenveagh National Park
Rosses Bay
Aran Island
Letterkenny
Londonderry (Derry)
Slievekirk 372
Lifford
Strabane
Sperrin Mts
Sawel Mt 683
541
Ballymena
Slemish 437
Agnew's Hill 474
Larne
Cark Mountain 367
Croaghgheen 383
Gweebarra Bay
598
Aghla Mountain
Blue Stack Mts
Blue Stack 676
525
Loughros More Bay
Slievetooey 444
353
504
494
Slieve League 601
Donegal
Lough Derg
448
423
542
Mullaghcarn
Omagh
Magherafelt
Slieve Gallion 528
Ballinderry
Cookstown
Ballyclare
Antrim
Carrickfergus
Belfast Lough
Greenisland
Newtownabbey
Belfast
Bangor
Newtownards
Lough Neagh
Dunmurry
Lisburn
Comber
Strangford Lough
Dungannon
313
Lurgan
Craigavon
Portadown
Ards Peninsula
Donegal Bay
Lower Lough Erne
Lough Melvin
Tullybrack 376
Darty Mts 522
Truskmore 643
Dough Mt 461
Benbulben 525
Sligo Bay
Sligo (Sligeach)
Enniskillen
Slieve Beagh 372
Armagh
Banbridge
Downpatrick
Broad Haven
Maumakeogh 380
Killala Bay
Ballina (Béal an Átha)
Knockalongy 542
Slieve Gamph (Ox Mountains)
Lough Gill
Shannon
Slievenakilla
Lough Allen
Lough Arrow
547
667
Cuilcagh
Iron Mts
387
Upper Lough Erne
Ulster Canal
Monaghan (Muineachán)
Newry
Mourne Mts
852
Slieve Donard
Newcastle
Dundrum Bay
Blacksod Bay
Slieve Car 772
Nephin Beg 629
700
Nephin 806
Lough Conn
Nephin Beg Range
Slieve More
Ballycroy National Park
Croaghaun 668
672
Achill Head
Achill Island
Corraun Peninsula
714
Slieve Anierin 586
Lough Key
IRL
Cavan
Lough Gara
125
Carrick-on-Shannon
Moyer 341
588
Kilkeel
Dundalk (Dun Dealgan)
Dundalk Bay
ATLANTIC OCEAN
0 10 20 30 40 50 km
0 10 20 30 miles
Stranraer
The Rinns of Galloway
Luce Bay
Mull of Galloway
Douglas, Heysham
Birkenhead
Port Erin
Port St Mary
2
4

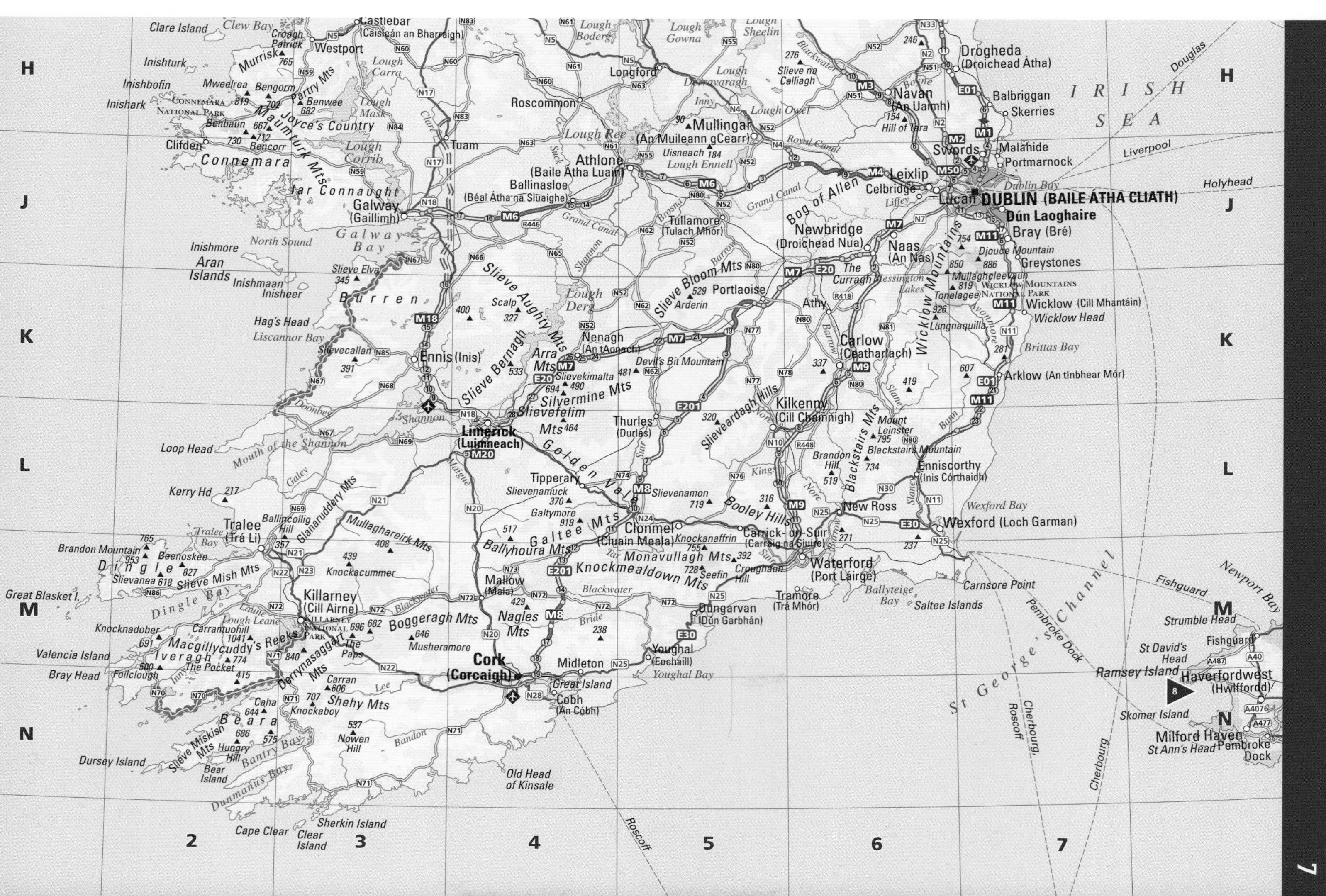
IRISH SEA
Douglas
Liverpool
Holyhead
DUBLIN (BAILE ÁTHA CLIATH)
Dún Laoghaire
Bray (Bré)
Greystones
Wicklow (Cill Mhantáin)
Wicklow Head
Arklow (An tInbhear Mór)
Brittas Bay
Drogheda (Droichead Átha)
Balbriggan
Skerries
Malahide
Portmarnock
Swords
Lucan
Leixlip
Celbridge
Dublin Bay
Liffey
Navan (An Uaimh)
Hill of Tara
Naas (An Nás)
Newbridge (Droichead Nua)
Bog of Allen
The Curragh
Wicklow Mountains
Wicklow Mountains National Park
Lugnaquilla
Mullaghcleevaun
Djouce Mountain
Tonelagee
Mount Leinster
Blackstairs Mts
Blackstairs Mountain
Brandon Hill
Carlow (Ceatharlach)
Athy
Kilkenny (Cill Chainnigh)
Slieveardagh Hills
Enniscorthy (Inis Córthaidh)
Wexford (Loch Garman)
Wexford Bay
New Ross
Waterford (Port Láirge)
Tramore (Trá Mhór)
Carrick-on-Suir (Carraig na Siúire)
Booley Hills
Carnsore Point
Saltee Islands
Ballyteige Bay
Dungarvan (Dún Garbhán)
Youghal (Eochaill)
Youghal Bay
Clonmel (Cluain Meala)
Knockanaffrin
Croughaun Hill
Seefin
Monavullagh Mts
Knockmealdown Mts
Galtee Mts
Galtymore
Slievenamuck
Golden Vale
Tipperary
Thurles (Durlas)
Slievenamon
Slieve Bloom Mts
Arderin
Portlaoise
Tullamore (Tullach Mhór)
Mullingar (An Muileann gCearr)
Lough Ennell
Uisneach
Lough Owel
Lough Sheelin
Lough Derravaragh
Lough Gowna
Lough Boderg
Longford
Athlone (Baile Átha Luain)
Lough Ree
Roscommon
Ballinasloe (Béal Átha na Sluaighe)
Grand Canal
Royal Canal
Shannon
Lough Derg
Nenagh (An tAonach)
Devil's Bit Mountain
Silvermine Mts
Slievekimalta
Slievefelim Mts
Arra Mts
Slieve Bernagh
Slieve Aughty Mts
Scalp
Limerick (Luimneach)
Ennis (Inis)
Burren
Slieve Elva
Slievecallan
Galway (Gaillimh)
Galway Bay
Iar Connaught
Tuam
Castlebar (Caisleán an Bharraigh)
Westport
Lough Mask
Lough Corrib
Lough Carra
Connemara
Connemara National Park
Joyce's Country
Maumturk Mts
Partry Mts
Clifden
Croagh Patrick
Murrisk
Mweelrea
Bengorm
Benwee
Benbaun
Bencorr
Clew Bay
Clare Island
Inishturk
Inishbofin
Inishark
Aran Islands
Inishmore
Inishmaan
Inisheer
North Sound
Hag's Head
Liscannor Bay
Doonbeg
Loop Head
Mouth of the Shannon
Kerry Hd
Tralee (Trá Lí)
Tralee Bay
Ballincollig Hill
Glanaruddery Mts
Mullaghareirk Mts
Slieve Mish Mts
Dingle
Dingle Bay
Brandon Mountain
Beenoskee
Slievanea
Great Blasket I.
Killarney (Cill Airne)
Killarney National Park
Lough Leane
Knockacummer
Macgillycuddy's Reeks
Carrantuohill
Knocknadober
Iveragh
The Pocket
Valencia Island
Bray Head
Foilclough
Derrynasaggart Mts
The Paps
Carran
Shehy Mts
Knockaboy
Boggeragh Mts
Musheramore
Nagles Mts
Mallow (Mala)
Ballyhoura Mts
Blackwater
Bride
Cork (Corcaigh)
Cobh (An Cóbh)
Great Island
Midleton
Old Head of Kinsale
Bandon
Nowen Hill
Bantry Bay
Dunmanus Bay
Beara
Caha
Hungry Hill
Slieve Miskish Mts
Dursey Island
Bear Island
Cape Clear
Clear Island
Sherkin Island
Roscoff
Cherbourg, Roscoff
Cherbourg
St George's Channel
Pembroke Dock
Fishguard
Newport Bay
Strumble Head
St David's Head
Ramsey Island
Skomer Island
St Ann's Head
Milford Haven
Haverfordwest (Hwlffordd)
Pembroke Dock
8
H
J
K
L
M
N
2
3
4
5
6
7

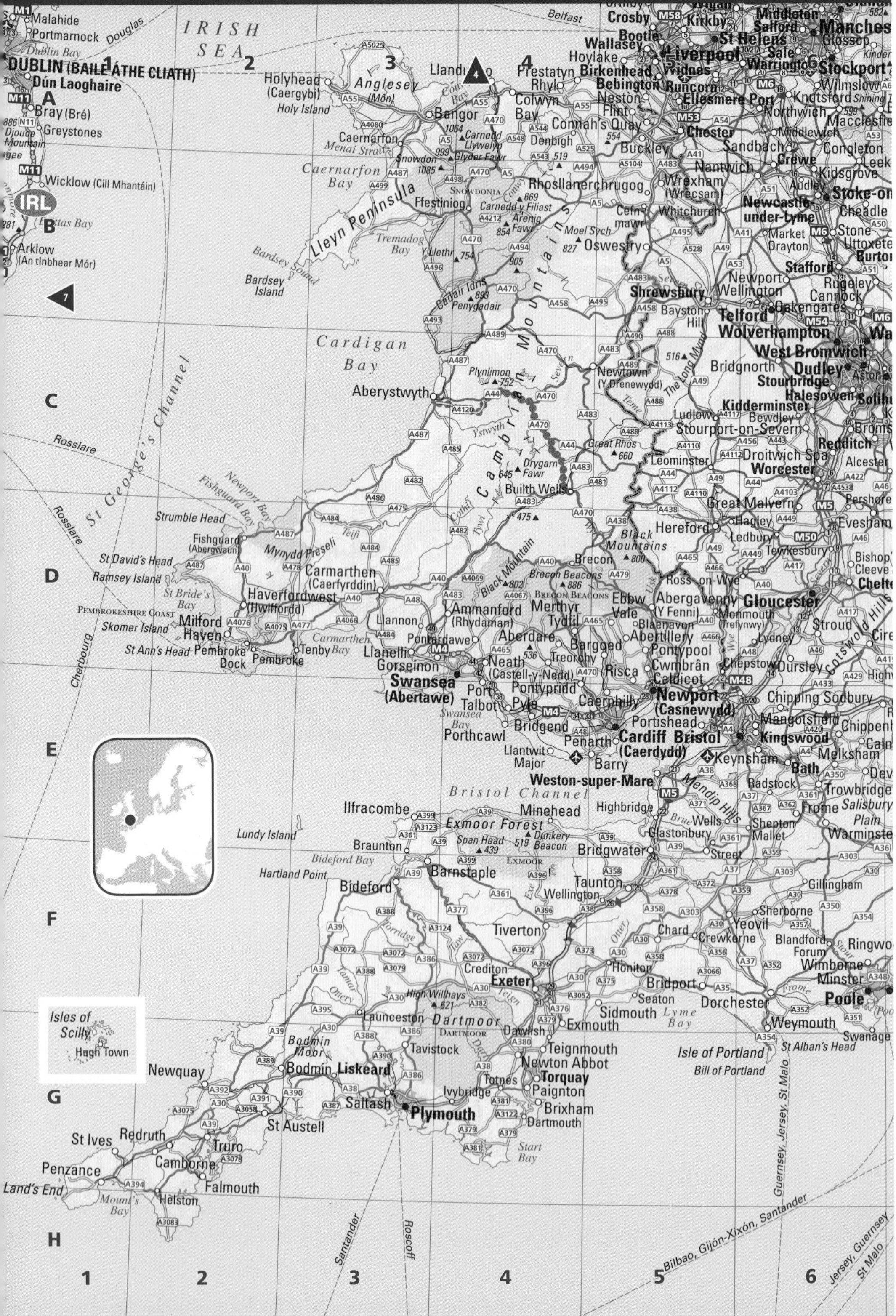

Malahide
Portmarnock
Dublin Bay
DUBLIN (BAILE ÁTHE CLIATH)
Dún Laoghaire
Bray (Bré)
Greystones
Djouce Mountain
Wicklow (Cill Mhantáin)
IRL
Brittas Bay
Arklow
(An tInbhear Mór)
Douglas
IRISH SEA
Belfast
Holyhead
(Caergybi)
Holy Island
Anglesey
(Môn)
Llandudno
Conwy Bay
Bangor
Caernarfon
Menai Strait
Caernarfon Bay
Carnedd Llywelyn
Snowdon
Glyder Fawr
Snowdonia
Lleyn Peninsula
Ffestiniog
Carnedd y Filiast
Arenig Fawr
Tremadog Bay
Y Llethr
Bardsey Sound
Bardsey Island
Cadair Idris
Penygadair
Cardigan Bay
Prestatyn
Rhyl
Colwyn Bay
Denbigh
Connah's Quay
Flint
Buckley
Rhosllanerchrugog
Moel Sych
Oswestry
Cambrian Mountains
Plynlimon
Aberystwyth
Ystwyth
Drygarn Fawr
Builth Wells
Great Rhos
Newtown
(Y Drenewydd)
Severn
Teme
Wye
The Long Mynd
Crosby
Bootle
Wallasey
Hoylake
Birkenhead
Bebington
Liverpool
Widnes
Runcorn
Kirkby
St Helens
Wigan
Salford
Manchester
Middleton
Sale
Warrington
Stockport
Glossop
Kinder
Ellesmere Port
Neston
Chester
Northwich
Knutsford
Wilmslow
Macclesfield
Middlewich
Sandbach
Congleton
Crewe
Nantwich
Leek
Kidsgrove
Audley
Wrexham
(Wrecsam)
Cefn-mawr
Whitchurch
Newcastle-under-Lyme
Stoke-on-Trent
Cheadle
Market Drayton
Stone
Uttoxeter
Burton
Stafford
Newport
Rugeley
Cannock
Shrewsbury
Bayston Hill
Wellington
Oakengates
Telford
Wolverhampton
Walsall
West Bromwich
Dudley
Aston
Stourbridge
Halesowen
Solihull
Bridgnorth
Kidderminster
Bewdley
Stourport-on-Severn
Bromsgrove
Redditch
Ludlow
Leominster
Droitwich Spa
Worcester
Alcester
Pershore
Great Malvern
Hagley
Evesham
Hereford
Ledbury
Tewkesbury
Bishop's Cleeve
Cheltenham
Black Mountains
Ross-on-Wye
Gloucester
Monmouth
(Trefynwy)
Stroud
Cirencester
Cotswold Hills
Lydney
Dursley
Chepstow
Chipping Sodbury
Mangotsfield
Kingswood
Chippenham
Calne
Melksham
Devizes
Keynsham
Bath
Radstock
Trowbridge
Frome
Salisbury Plain
Warminster
Shepton Mallet
Wells
Glastonbury
Street
Mendip Hills
Brue
Highbridge
Bridgwater
Weston-super-Mare
Bristol
Portishead
Cardiff
(Caerdydd)
Penarth
Barry
Llantwit Major
Newport
(Casnewydd)
Caldicot
Risca
Pontypool
Cwmbrân
Blaenavon
Abergavenny
(Y Fenni)
Ebbw Vale
Abertillery
Bargoed
Caerphilly
Pontypridd
Treorchy
Merthyr Tydfil
Aberdare
Brecon
Brecon Beacons
Usk
Black Mountain
Ammanford
(Rhydaman)
Llannon
Pontardawe
Neath
(Castell-y-Nedd)
Swansea
(Abertawe)
Port Talbot
Pyle
Bridgend
Porthcawl
Swansea Bay
Gorseinon
Llanelli
Carmarthen Bay
Carmarthen
(Caerfyrddin)
Cothi
Tywi
Teifi
Mynydd Preseli
Fishguard
(Abergwaun)
Fishguard Bay
Newport Bay
Strumble Head
St David's Head
Ramsey Island
St Bride's Bay
Pembrokeshire Coast
Haverfordwest
(Hwlffordd)
Milford Haven
Skomer Island
St Ann's Head
Pembroke Dock
Pembroke
Tenby
St George's Channel
Rosslare
Cherbourg
Bristol Channel
Ilfracombe
Exmoor Forest
Minehead
Dunkery Beacon
Span Head
Exmoor
Lundy Island
Braunton
Bideford Bay
Hartland Point
Barnstaple
Bideford
Taunton
Wellington
Torridge
Taw
Exe
Tiverton
Otter
Chard
Crewkerne
Yeovil
Sherborne
Gillingham
Blandford Forum
Stour
Ringwood
Wimborne Minster
Poole
Honiton
Bridport
Dorchester
Frome
Weymouth
Swanage
Isle of Portland
Bill of Portland
St Alban's Head
Crediton
Exeter
Teign
Sidmouth
Seaton
Lyme Bay
Exmouth
Dawlish
Teignmouth
Newton Abbot
Torquay
Paignton
Brixham
Dartmouth
Totnes
Start Bay
Dartmoor
High Willhays
Launceston
Tamar
Ottery
Tavistock
Bodmin Moor
Bodmin
Liskeard
Plymouth
Saltash
Ivybridge
Newquay
St Austell
St Ives
Redruth
Truro
Camborne
Falmouth
Penzance
Land's End
Mount's Bay
Helston
Isles of Scilly
Hugh Town
Santander
Roscoff
Bilbao, Gijón-Xixón, Santander
Guernsey, Jersey, St Malo
Jersey, Guernsey, St Malo

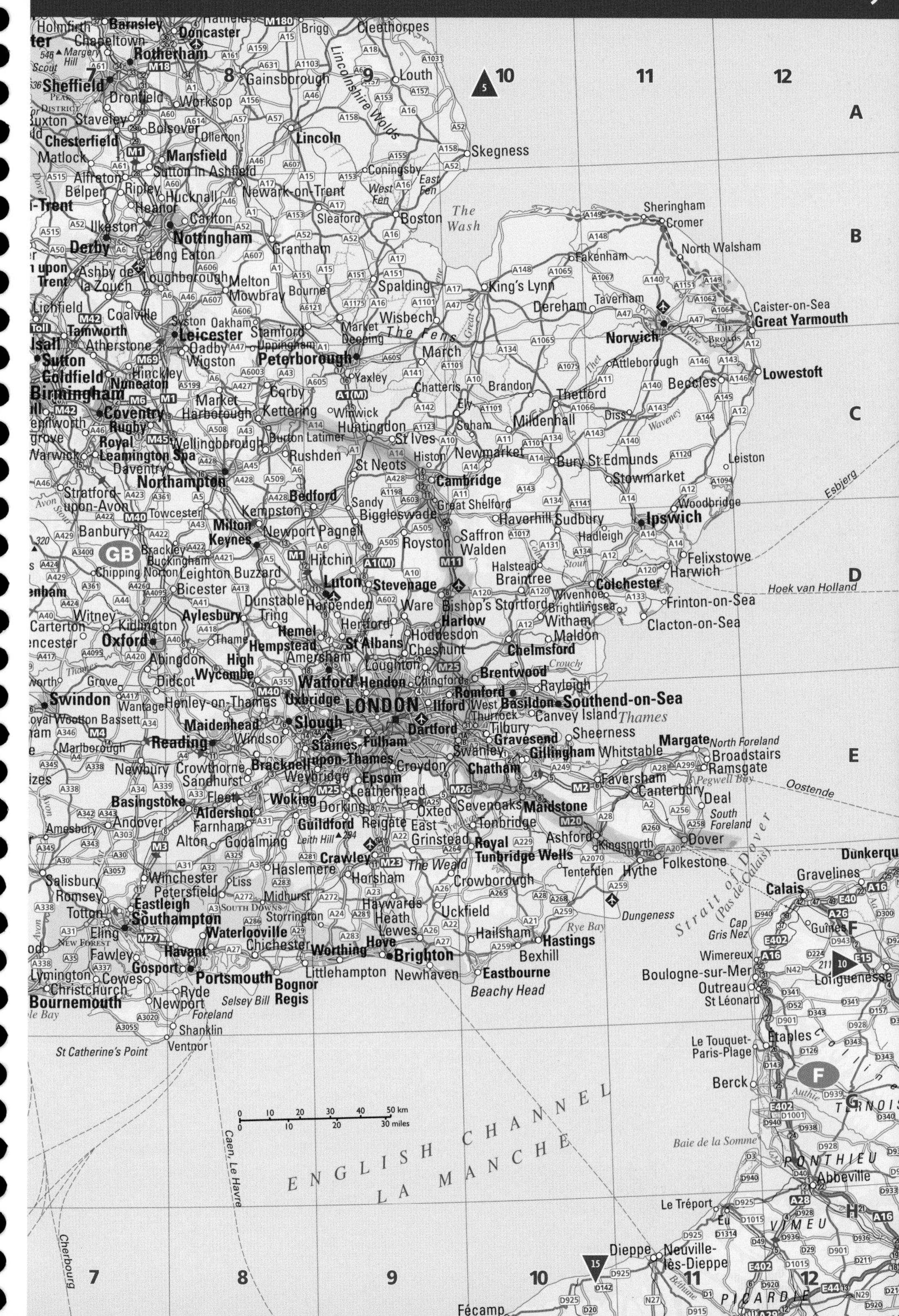

10
11
12
A
B
C
D
E
F
G
H
7
8
9
10
11
12
Barnsley
Doncaster
Brigg
Cleethorpes
Rotherham
Sheffield
Gainsborough
Louth
Lincolnshire Wolds
Dronfield
Worksop
Staveley
Bolsover
Chesterfield
Mansfield
Lincoln
Skegness
Matlock
Sutton in Ashfield
Coningsby
East Fen
West Fen
Alfreton
Belper
Ripley
Hucknall
Newark-on-Trent
Heanor
Carlton
Sleaford
Boston
The Wash
Sheringham
Cromer
Ilkeston
Nottingham
Derby
Long Eaton
Grantham
North Walsham
Fakenham
Ashby de la Zouch
Loughborough
Melton Mowbray
Bourne
Spalding
King's Lynn
Taverham
Caister-on-Sea
Great Yarmouth
Lichfield
Coalville
Syston
Oakham
Wisbech
Dereham
Norwich
Tamworth
Leicester
Stamford
Market Deeping
The Fens
The Broads
Atherstone
Oadby
Wigston
Uppingham
March
Sutton Coldfield
Peterborough
Attleborough
Beccles
Lowestoft
Nuneaton
Hinckley
Yaxley
Chatteris
Brandon
Thetford
Birmingham
Coventry
Market Harborough
Corby
Kettering
Winwick
Ely
Mildenhall
Diss
Waveney
Rugby
Huntingdon
Soham
Kenilworth
Royal Leamington Spa
Wellingborough
Burton Latimer
St Ives
Newmarket
Warwick
Daventry
Rushden
St Neots
Histon
Bury St Edmunds
Leiston
Northampton
Cambridge
Stowmarket
Stratford-upon-Avon
Bedford
Sandy
Biggleswade
Great Shelford
Woodbridge
Esbjerg
Towcester
Kempston
Haverhill
Sudbury
Ipswich
Banbury
Milton Keynes
Newport Pagnell
Royston
Saffron Walden
Hadleigh
Brackley
Buckingham
Hitchin
Halstead
Felixstowe
GB
Chipping Norton
Leighton Buzzard
Luton
Stevenage
Braintree
Colchester
Harwich
Hoek van Holland
Bicester
Dunstable
Harpenden
Ware
Bishop's Stortford
Wivenhoe
Brightlingsea
Frinton-on-Sea
Witney
Kidlington
Aylesbury
Tring
Hertford
Harlow
Witham
Clacton-on-Sea
Carterton
Hemel Hempstead
Hoddesdon
Maldon
Oxford
Thame
St Albans
Cheshunt
Chelmsford
Abingdon
High Wycombe
Amersham
Loughton
Crouch
Grove
Didcot
Watford
Hendon
Chingford
Brentwood
Rayleigh
Swindon
Wantage
Henley-on-Thames
Uxbridge
LONDON
Ilford
Romford
Basildon
Southend-on-Sea
West Thurrock
Canvey Island
Thames
Royal Wootton Bassett
Maidenhead
Slough
Dartford
Tilbury
Sheerness
Marlborough
Reading
Windsor
Staines
Fulham
Swanley
Gravesend
Gillingham
Whitstable
Margate
North Foreland
Broadstairs
Ramsgate
Newbury
Crowthorne
Sandhurst
Bracknell
Kingston upon Thames
Croydon
Chatham
Weybridge
Epsom
Faversham
Pegwell Bay
Oostende
Basingstoke
Fleet
Woking
Leatherhead
Canterbury
Deal
Aldershot
Dorking
Oxted
Sevenoaks
Maidstone
South Foreland
Amesbury
Andover
Farnham
Guildford
Reigate
East Grinstead
Tonbridge
Alton
Godalming
Leith Hill
Royal Tunbridge Wells
Ashford
Kingsnorth
Dover
Dunkerque
Crawley
The Weald
Tenterden
Hythe
Folkestone
Strait of Dover
(Pas de Calais)
Gravelines
Salisbury
Winchester
Haslemere
Horsham
Crowborough
Calais
Romsey
Petersfield
Liss
Midhurst
Haywards Heath
Uckfield
Dungeness
Guînes
Totton
Eastleigh
Southampton
South Downs
Storrington
Lewes
Hailsham
Rye Bay
Cap Gris Nez
Eling
Waterlooville
Hastings
New Forest
Havant
Chichester
Worthing
Hove
Brighton
Bexhill
Wimereux
Fawley
Gosport
Boulogne-sur-Mer
Longuenesse
Lymington
Cowes
Portsmouth
Bognor Regis
Littlehampton
Newhaven
Eastbourne
Outreau
Christchurch
Ryde
St Léonard
Bournemouth
Newport
Selsey Bill
Beachy Head
Foreland
Shanklin
Ventnor
St Catherine's Point
Le Touquet-Paris-Plage
Étaples
Berck
F
Authie
TERNOIS
0 10 20 30 40 50 km
0 10 20 30 miles
ENGLISH CHANNEL
LA MANCHE
Caen, Le Havre
Baie de la Somme
PONTHIEU
Abbeville
Cherbourg
Le Tréport
Eu
VIMEU
Dieppe
Neuville-lès-Dieppe
Béthune
PICARDIE
Fécamp
Neufchâtel-en-Bray

1 2 3 4 5 6

Newcastle upon Tyne
Kingston upon Hull
Esbjerg

0 10 20 30 40 50 km
0 10 20 30 miles

B
NORTH SEA
Sheringham
Cromer
North Walsham
Norwich
Caister-on-Sea
Great Yarmouth
The Broads
C
Attleborough
Beccles
Lowestoft
GB
Diss
Stowmarket
Leiston
Ipswich
D
Woodbridge
Felixstowe
Harwich
Frinton-on-Sea
Clacton-on-Sea
9
E
Margate
North Foreland
Broadstairs
Ramsgate
Canterbury
Pegwell Bay
Deal
South Foreland
Dover
Folkestone
F
Strait of Dover (Pas de Calais)
Calais
Cap Gris Nez
Wimereux
Boulogne-sur-Mer
Outreau
St Léonard
G
Étaples
Le Touquet-Paris-Plage
Berck
Baie de la Somme
H
Le Tréport
Eu
Abbeville
PONTHIEU
VIMEU
F
TERNOIS
Artois
Collines de l'Artois
Doullens
Amiens
Albert
12
Péronne
VERMANDOIS

Texel
Den Burg
Vlieland
Terschelling
Engelschmangat
Waddenzee
Den Helder
Anna Paulowna
Schagen
Medemblik
Langedijk
Bergen
Alkmaar
Hoorn
Heiloo
Castricum
Heemskerk
Beverwijk
Marker
Wormerveer
Zaandam
ZUID-KENNEMERLAND
Haarlem
Heemstede
Hoofddorp
AMSTERDAM
NORDSEE
Noordwijk-Binnen
Katwijk aan Zee
Wassenaar
Leiden
Hilversum
'S-GRAVENHAGE (DEN HAAG)
Zoetermeer
Utrecht
Monster
Delft
Gouda
's-Gravenzande
Europoort
Rotterdam
Vlaardingen
Spijkenisse
Dordrecht
De Biesbosch
Middelharnis
Made
Zierikzee
Zevenbergen
Breda
Oosterhout
Tilburg
Middelburg
Goes
Oosterschelde
Roosendaal
Vlissingen
Westerschelde
Essen
Eindhoven
Terneuzen
Zandvliet
Brecht
Turnhout
Knokke-Heist
Blankenberge
De Haan
Damme
Oostende (Ostend)
Brugge (Bruges)
Antwerpen (Anvers)
Kasterlee
Westende
Gistel
Beernem
Zelzate
Zwijndrecht
Borsbeek
Geel
Koksijde
Gent (Gand)
Lier
Dunkerque
Gravelines
Staden
St-Martens-Latem
Tielt
Deinze
Wichelen
Dendermonde
Zemst
Mechelen (Malines)
Beringen
Roeselare (Roulers)
Zulte
Aalst (Alost)
Hasselt
Guînes
Wormhout
Ieper
Gullegem
BRUXELLES (BRUSSEL)
Schaerbeek
Kortrijk
Anzegem
Wevelgem
Comines
Mont des Cats
Mouscron
Brakel
Dilbeek
St-Truiden
Longuenesse
Tourcoing
Bailleul
Halle
Braine-l'Alleud
Grez-Doiceau
Roubaix
Herne
Lille
Tubize
B
Hannut
Seclin
Tournai
Leuze-en-Hainaut
Soignies
Eghezée
Béthune
Divion
Avion
Mons
Namur
CONDROZ
Arras
Anzin
Charleroi
Maubeuge
Ciney
Aulnoye-Aymeries
Cambrai
Rochefort
L'Eau d'Heure
Caudry
Avesnes-sur-Helpe
Fagne
Couvin
Fourmies
Fumay
Revin
Plateau de
Meuse
Lesse
Oise

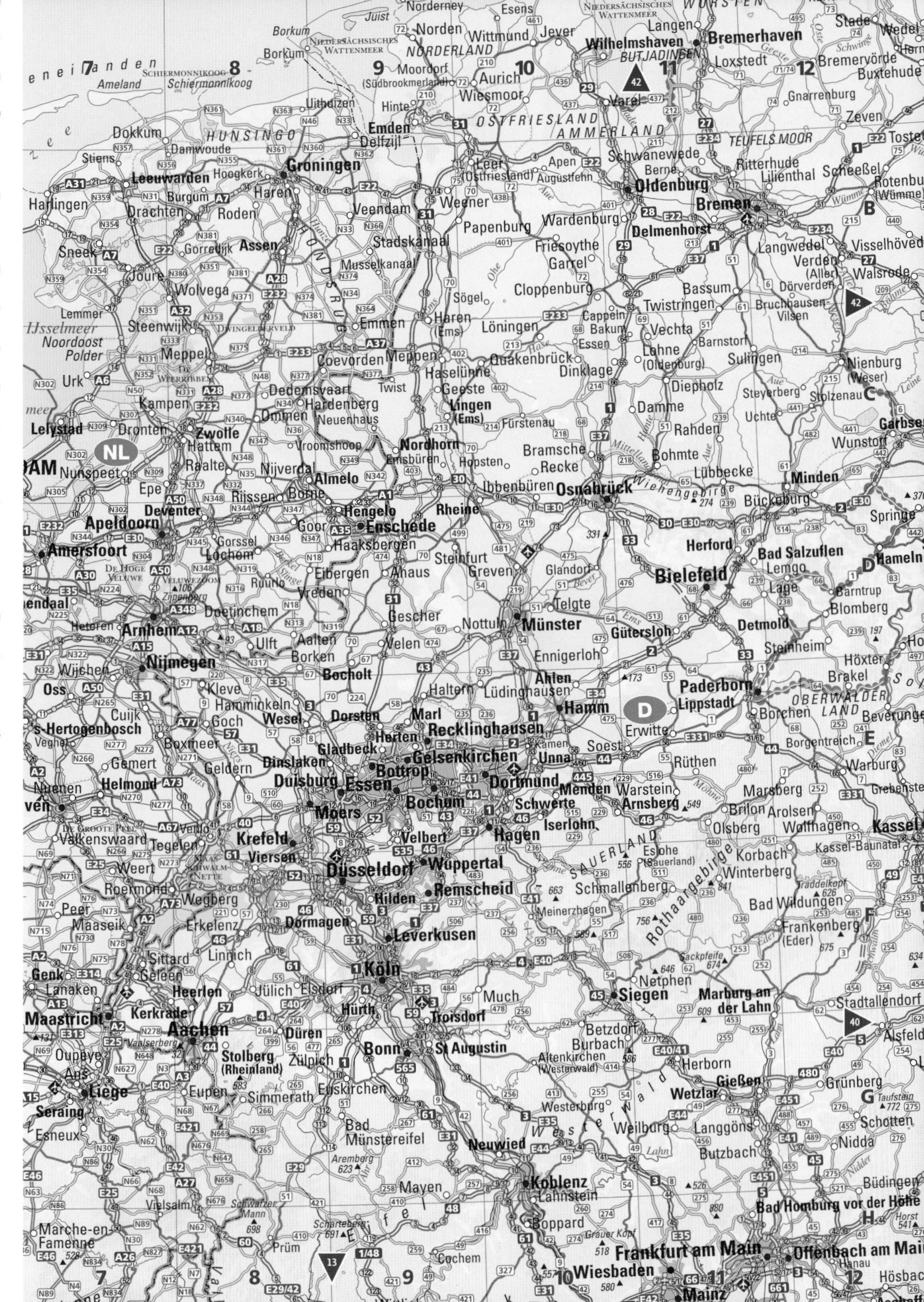

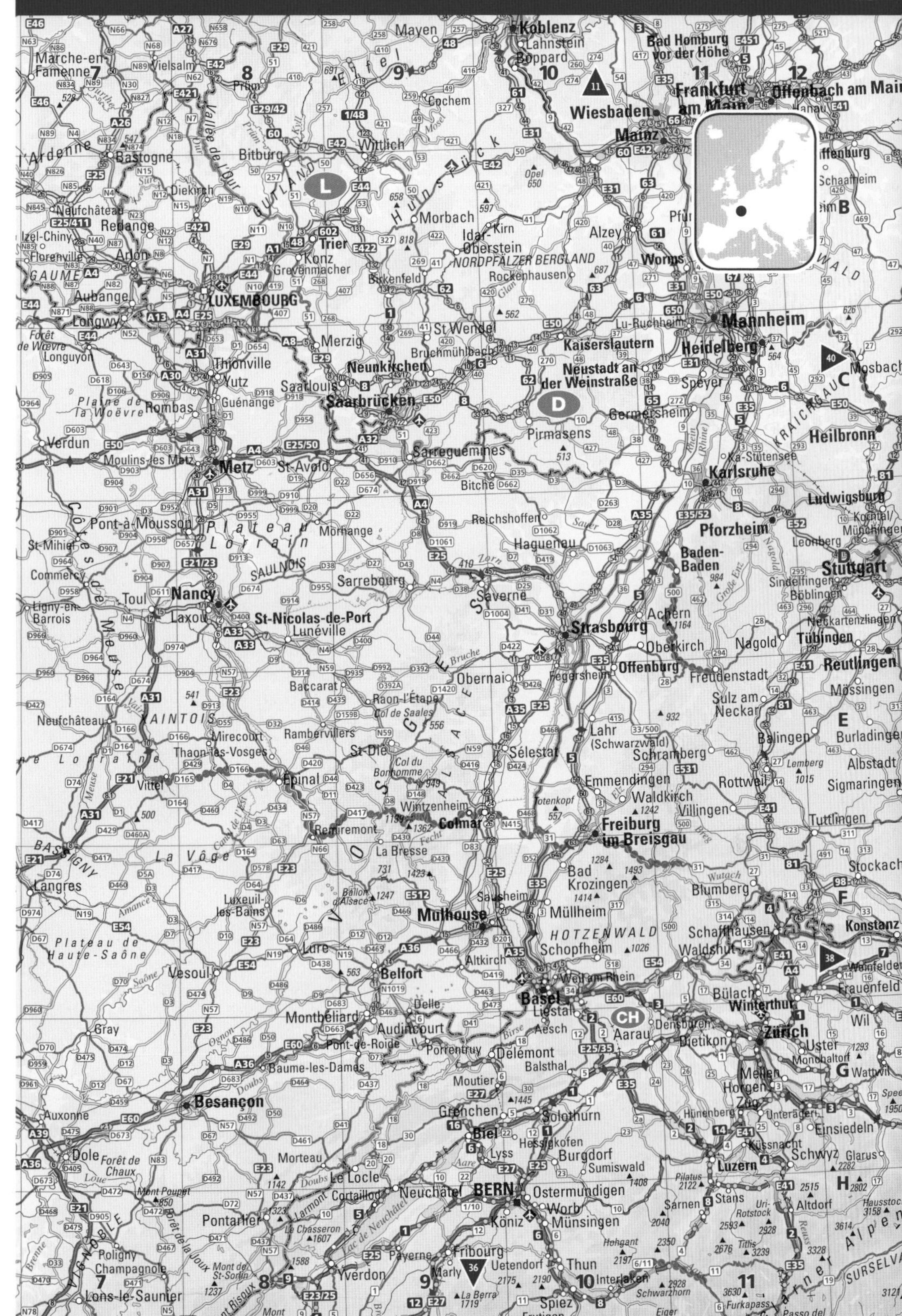
Koblenz
Mayen
Lahnstein
Boppard
Bad Homburg vor der Höhe
Marche-en-Famenne
Vielsalm
Prüm
Eifel
Cochem
Wiesbaden
Frankfurt am Main
Offenbach am Main
Mainz
Bastogne
Bitburg
Wittlich
Diekirch
GUTLAND
Hunsrück
Morbach
Idar-Oberstein
Alzey
Worms
Neufchâteau
Redange
Trier
Konz
Grevenmacher
NORDPFÄLZER BERGLAND
Rockenhausen
Arlon
Florenville
GAUME
Aubange
LUXEMBOURG
Birkenfeld
Longwy
Merzig
St Wendel
Mannheim
Heidelberg
Longuyon
Thionville
Yutz
Neunkirchen
Bruchmühlbach
Kaiserslautern
Neustadt an der Weinstraße
Speyer
Mosbach
Saarlouis
Saarbrücken
Guénange
Rombas
Plaine de la Woëvre
Germersheim
Pirmasens
Heilbronn
Verdun
Metz
Moulins-les-Metz
St-Avold
Sarreguemines
KRAICHGAU
Karlsruhe
Ka-Stutensee
Bitche
Ludwigsburg
Pont-à-Mousson
Plateau Lorrain
Morhange
Reichshoffen
Haguenau
Pforzheim
Kornwestheim
St-Mihiel
Côtes de Meuse
SAULNOIS
Commercy
Baden-Baden
Leonberg
Stuttgart
Sarrebourg
Sindelfingen
Böblingen
Toul
Nancy
Laxou
Ligny-en-Barrois
St-Nicolas-de-Port
Lunéville
Saverne
Strasbourg
Achern
Oberkirch
Offenburg
Nagold
Tübingen
Reutlingen
Neckartenzlingen
Baccarat
Raon-l'Étape
Obernai
Freudenstadt
Mössingen
Neufchâteau
XAINTOIS
Mirecourt
Thaon-les-Vosges
Rambervillers
St-Dié
Col de Saales
Lahr (Schwarzwald)
Sulz am Neckar
Balingen
Burladingen
Sélestat
Schramberg
Albstadt
Vittel
Épinal
Col du Bonhomme
Emmendingen
Waldkirch
Rottweil
Sigmaringen
Remiremont
Wintzenheim
Colmar
Villingen
Tuttlingen
Freiburg im Breisgau
La Bresse
La Vôge
BASSIGNY
Langres
Bad Krozingen
Stockach
Luxeuil-les-Bains
Ballon d'Alsace
Mulhouse
Sausheim
Müllheim
Blumberg
HOTZENWALD
Schaffhausen
Konstanz
Plateau de Haute-Saône
Lure
Belfort
Altkirch
Schopfheim
Waldshut
Vesoul
Weil am Rhein
Basel
Liestal
Bülach
Winterthur
Frauenfeld
Weinfelden
Montbéliard
Audincourt
Delle
Aesch
Aarau
Zürich
Wil
Gray
Pont-de-Roide
Porrentruy
Delémont
Dietikon
Uster
Baume-les-Dames
Balsthal
Meilen
Horgen
Wattwil
Besançon
Moutier
Zug
Auxonne
Grenchen
Solothurn
Einsiedeln
Biel
Hessigkofen
Dole
Forêt de Chaux
Morteau
Lyss
Burgdorf
Sumiswald
Küssnacht
Schwyz
Glarus
Le Locle
BERN
Ostermundigen
Luzern
Neuchâtel
Worb
Sarnen
Stans
Altdorf
Pontarlier
Köniz
Münsingen
Poligny
Champagnole
Fribourg
Payerne
Uetendorf
Thun
Yverdon
Marly
Interlaken
Lons-le-Saunier
Spiez
Frutigen
Bulle
Furkapass
Passo del San Gottardo
Wisconsin
SURSELVA
Glarner Alpen
VIGNOBLE

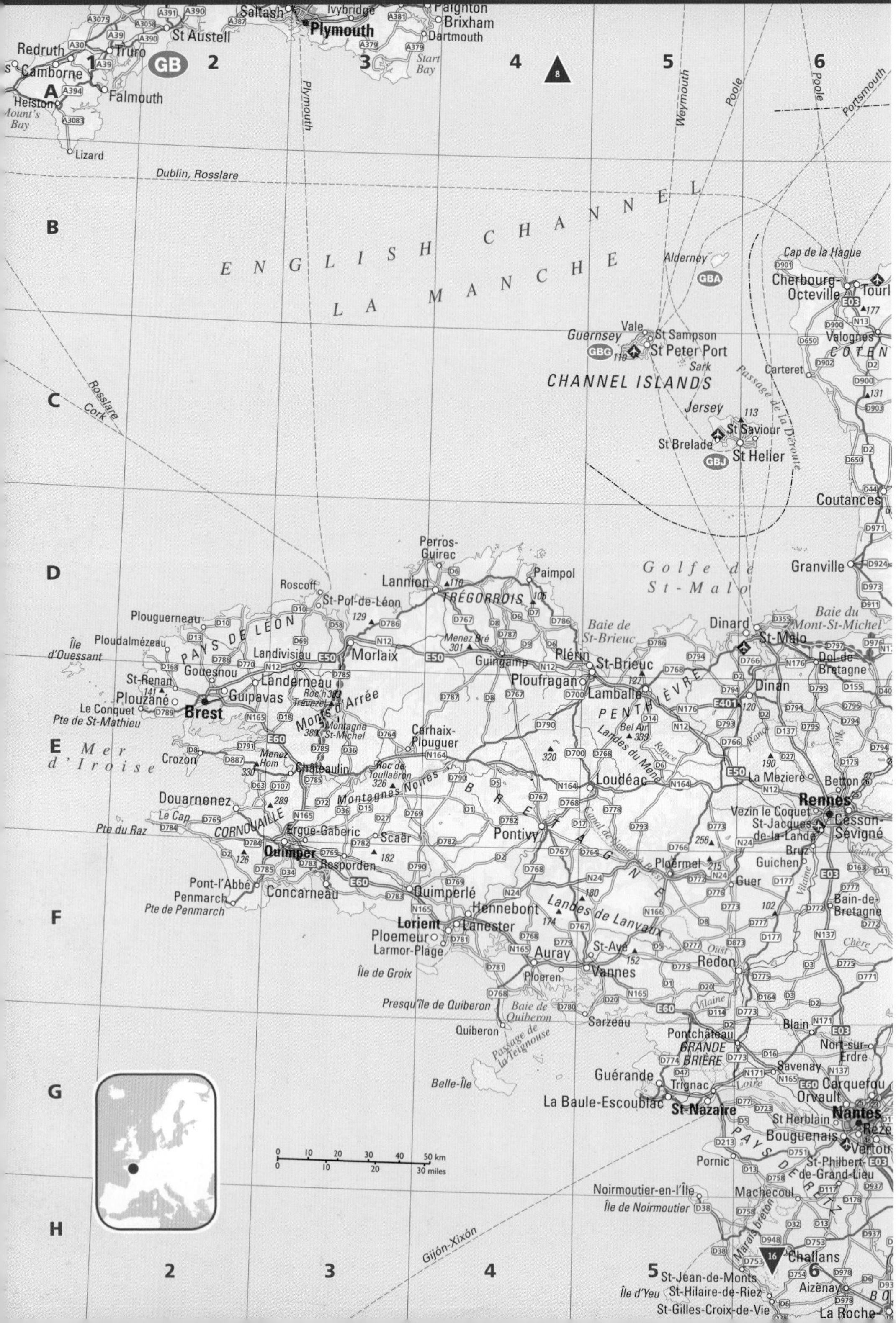

Saltash Ivybridge Paignton
Plymouth Brixham
Dartmouth
Start Bay
Redruth Truro St Austell
Camborne GB
Helston Falmouth
Mount's Bay
Lizard
Plymouth Weymouth Poole Poole Portsmouth
Dublin, Rosslare

ENGLISH CHANNEL
LA MANCHE

Alderney GBA
Cap de la Hague
Cherbourg-Octeville Tourl
Valognes
COTENTIN
Guernsey GBG Vale St Sampson St Peter Port
Sark
Carteret
CHANNEL ISLANDS
Passage de la Déroute
Jersey St Saviour
St Brelade St Helier GBJ
Rosslare Cork
Coutances
Granville
Golfe de St-Malo
Perros-Guirec Paimpol
Roscoff Lannion
St-Pol-de-Léon TRÉGORROIS
Plouguerneau
Île d'Ouessant Ploudalmézeau PAYS DE LÉON
Landivisiau Morlaix
Menez Bré Guingamp Plérin St-Brieuc
Baie de St-Brieuc
Dinard St-Malo
Baie du Mont-St-Michel
Dol-de-Bretagne
St-Renan Gouesnou Landerneau
Plouzané Guipavas Roc'h Trévezel
Le Conquet Brest Monts d'Arrée
Pte de St-Mathieu
Ploufragan Lamballe PENTHIÈVRE Dinan
Montagne St-Michel Carhaix-Plouguer
Bel Air Landes du Mené Rance
Mer d'Iroise Crozon Menez Hom Châteaulin
Roc de Toullaëron Montagnes Noires BRETAGNE
Loudéac La Mézière Betton
Rennes Cesson-Sévigné
Vezin le Coquet St-Jacques-de-la-Lande
Douarnenez CORNOUAILLE
Le Cap
Pte du Raz Ergué-Gaberic Scaër Pontivy Canal de Nantes à Brest
Quimper Rosporden
Ploërmel Bruz Guichen
Pont-l'Abbé Concarneau Guer
Penmarch Quimperlé
Pte de Penmarch Hennebont Landes de Lanvaux Bain-de-Bretagne
Lorient Lanester
Ploemeur
Larmor-Plage Auray St-Avé Oust Redon Chère
Île de Groix Ploeren Vannes Vilaine
Presqu'île de Quiberon Baie de Quiberon Sarzeau
Quiberon Passage de la Teignouse
Pontchâteau GRANDE BRIÈRE Blain
Nort-sur-Erdre
Belle-Île Guérande Savenay
Trignac Loire Carquefou
La Baule-Escoublac St-Nazaire Orvault
St Herblain Nantes
Bouguenais Rezé
PAYS DE RETZ Vertou
Pornic St-Philbert-de-Grand-Lieu
Noirmoutier-en-l'Île Machecoul
Île de Noirmoutier
Marais breton
Gijón-Xixón
Challans
St-Jean-de-Monts Aizenay
Île d'Yeu St-Hilaire-de-Riez
St-Gilles-Croix-de-Vie La Roche

0 10 20 30 40 50 km
0 10 20 30 miles

A B C D E F G H
1 2 3 4 5 6

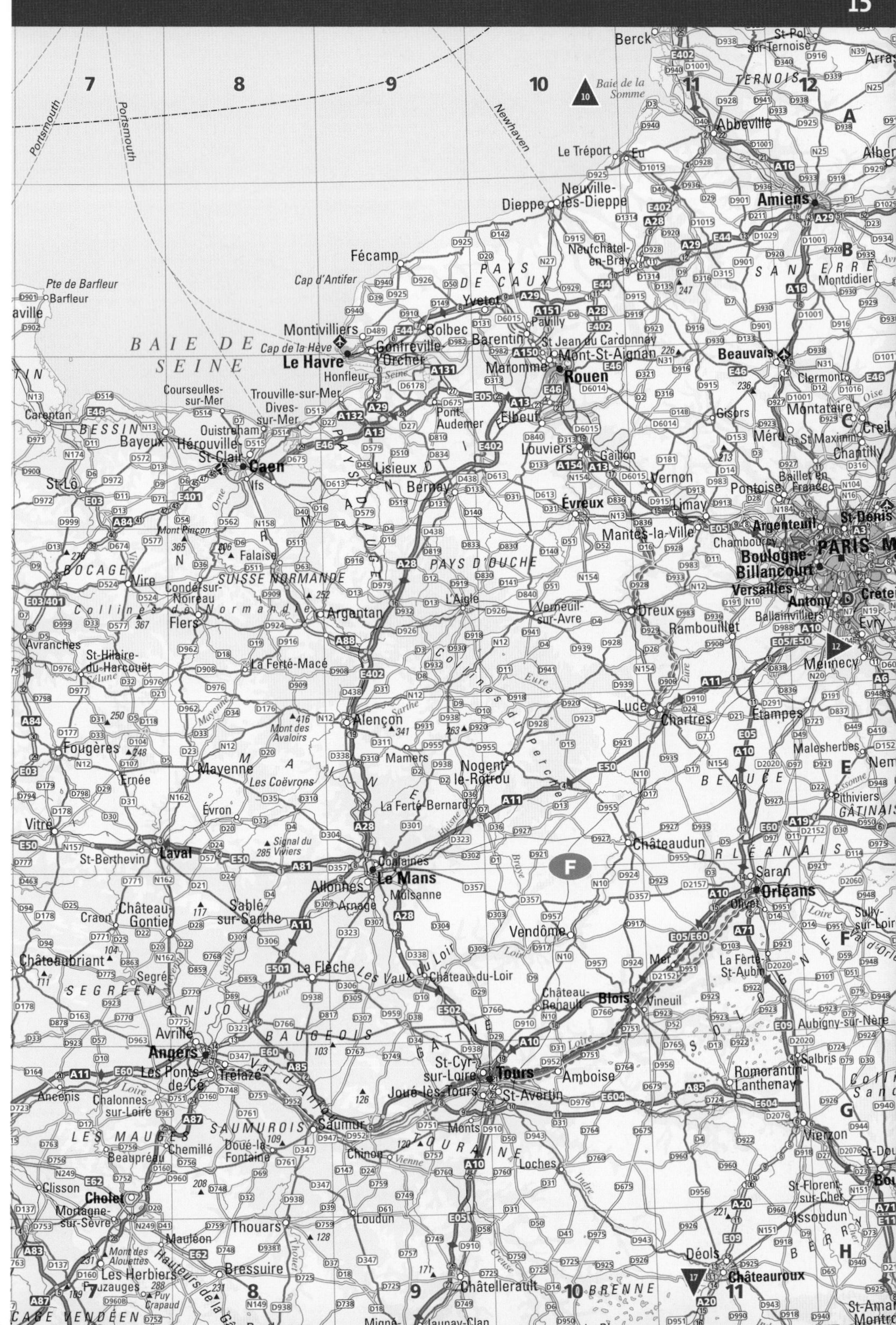

Berck
Baie de la Somme
Abbeville
Le Tréport
Eu
Dieppe
Neuville-lès-Dieppe
Amiens
Neufchâtel-en-Bray
Fécamp
Cap d'Antifer
PAYS DE CAUX
Yvetot
Bolbec
Montivilliers
Cap de la Hève
Le Havre
Gonfreville-l'Orcher
Barentin
Pavilly
St Jean du Cardonnay
Mont-St-Aignan
Maromme
Rouen
Beauvais
Clermont
Montdidier
SANTERRE
Pte de Barfleur
Barfleur
BAIE DE SEINE
Portsmouth
Newhaven
Honfleur
Trouville-sur-Mer
Dives-sur-Mer
Courseulles-sur-Mer
Ouistreham
Carentan
BESSIN
Bayeux
Hérouville-St-Clair
Caen
Ifs
Pont-Audemer
Elbeuf
Louviers
Gaillon
Gisors
Montataire
Creil
Méru
St Maximin
Chantilly
Lisieux
Bernay
PAYS D'AUGE
St-Lô
Évreux
Vernon
Pontoise
Bailleul en France
Limay
Mantes-la-Ville
Argenteuil
St-Denis
Chambourcy
PARIS
Boulogne-Billancourt
Versailles
Antony
Créteil
Ballainvilliers
Évry
Mennecy
Mont Pinçon
Falaise
BOCAGE
Vire
Condé-sur-Noireau
SUISSE NORMANDE
PAYS D'OUCHE
Collines de Normandie
Flers
Argentan
L'Aigle
Verneuil-sur-Avre
Dreux
Rambouillet
Avranches
St-Hilaire-du-Harcouët
La Ferté-Macé
Collines du Perche
Fougères
Alençon
Mont des Avaloirs
Lucé
Chartres
Étampes
Malesherbes
Mayenne
Ernée
Les Coëvrons
Mamers
Nogent-le-Rotrou
BEAUCE
Pithiviers
GÂTINAIS
Vitré
Évron
La Ferté-Bernard
Signal du Viviers
St-Berthevin
Laval
Coulaines
Le Mans
Allonnes
Mulsanne
Arnage
Châteaudun
ORLÉANAIS
Saran
Orléans
Olivet
Sully-sur-Loire
Craon
Château-Gontier
Sablé-sur-Sarthe
Vendôme
Châteaubriant
Segré
SEGRÉEN
La Flèche
Les Vaux du Loir
Château-du-Loir
Mer
La Ferté-St-Aubin
SOLOGNE
ANJOU
BAUGEOIS
Château-Renault
Blois
Vineuil
Aubigny-sur-Nère
Avrillé
Angers
GÂTINE
St-Cyr-sur-Loire
Tours
Amboise
Salbris
Romorantin-Lanthenay
Les Ponts-de-Cé
Trélazé
Val d'Anjou
Joué-lès-Tours
St-Avertin
Ancenis
Chalonnes-sur-Loire
Saumur
SAUMUROIS
Monts
Vierzon
LES MAUGES
Chemillé
Beaupréau
Doué-la-Fontaine
Chinon
TOURAINE
Loches
St-Florent-sur-Cher
Clisson
Cholet
Mortagne-sur-Sèvre
Thouars
Loudun
Issoudun
BERRY
Mauléon
Mont des Alouettes
Les Herbiers
Pouzauges
Puy Crapaud
Hauteurs de la Gâtine
Bressuire
Châtellerault
BRENNE
Déols
Châteauroux
BOCAGE VENDÉEN
Chantonnay
Parthenay
Mignê-Auxances
Jaunay-Clan
Buxerolles
Le Blanc
St-Amand-Montrond

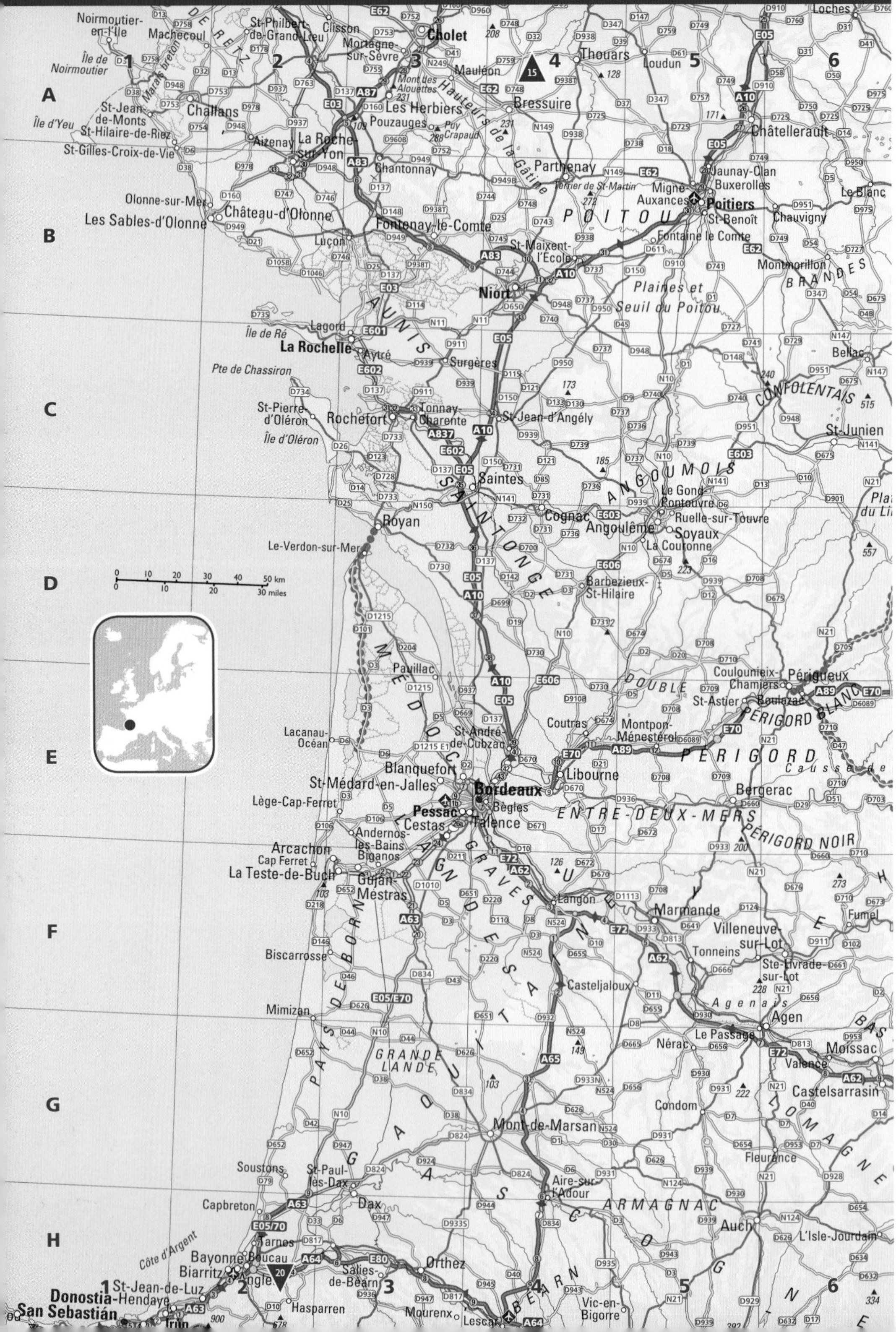

1 2 3 4 5 6

A B C D E F G H

0 10 20 30 40 50 km
0 10 20 30 miles

Noirmoutier-en-l'Île
Île de Noirmoutier
Machecoul
St-Philbert-de-Grand-Lieu
Clisson
Cholet
Mortagne-sur-Sèvre
Mauléon
Thouars
Loudun
Loches
St-Jean-de-Monts
Île d'Yeu
St-Hilaire-de-Riez
St-Gilles-Croix-de-Vie
Challans
Aizenay
La Roche-sur-Yon
Les Herbiers
Mont des Alouettes 231
Pouzauges
Puy Crapaud 288
Bressuire
Hauteurs de la Gâtine
Chantonnay
Parthenay
Terrier de St-Martin 272
Châtellerault
Jaunay-Clan
Buxerolles
Migné-Auxances
Poitiers
St-Benoît
Chauvigny
Le Blanc
Olonne-sur-Mer
Château-d'Olonne
Les Sables-d'Olonne
Fontenay-le-Comte
Luçon
POITOU
Fontaine le Comte
St-Maixent-l'École
Montmorillon
BRANDES
Niort
Plaines et Seuil du Poitou
AUNIS
Lagord
Île de Ré
La Rochelle
Aytré
Surgères
Pte de Chassiron
Bellac
CONFOLENTAIS
St-Pierre-d'Oléron
Île d'Oléron
Rochefort
Tonnay-Charente
St-Jean-d'Angély
St-Junien
Saintes
ANGOUMOIS
Le Gond-Pontouvre
Cognac
Angoulême
Ruelle-sur-Touvre
Soyaux
La Couronne
Royan
Le-Verdon-sur-Mer
SAINTONGE
Plateau du Limousin
Barbezieux-St-Hilaire
MÉDOC
Pauillac
DOUBLE
Coulounieix-Chamiers
Périgueux
St-Astier
Boulazac
PÉRIGORD BLANC
Lacanau-Océan
St-André-de-Cubzac
Coutras
Montpon-Ménestérol
PÉRIGORD
Causse de
Blanquefort
St-Médard-en-Jalles
Libourne
Bordeaux
Bergerac
Lège-Cap-Ferret
Pessac
Bègles
Cestas
Talence
ENTRE-DEUX-MERS
PÉRIGORD NOIR
Andernos-les-Bains
Arcachon
Cap Ferret
Biganos
La Teste-de-Buch
Gujan-Mestras
GRAVES
Langon
Marmande
Fumel
Villeneuve-sur-Lot
Tonneins
Ste-Livrade-sur-Lot
Biscarrosse
PAYS DE BORN
LANDES DE GASCOGNE
Casteljaloux
Agenais
Mimizan
Agen
Le Passage
Nérac
Moissac
Valence
BAS QUERCY
GRANDE LANDE
Castelsarrasin
Condom
LOMAGNE
Mont-de-Marsan
Fleurance
Soustons
St-Paul-lès-Dax
Dax
Aire-sur-l'Adour
ARMAGNAC
Capbreton
Auch
L'Isle-Jourdain
Tarnos
Côte d'Argent
Bayonne
Boucau
Biarritz
Anglet
Orthez
Salies-de-Béarn
St-Jean-de-Luz
Donostia-San Sebastián
Hendaye
Irún
Hasparren
Mourenx
Lescar
BÉARN
Vic-en-Bigorre
GASCOGNE

Bourges
St-Germain-du-Puy
St-Doulchard
St-Florent-sur-Cher
Issoudun
Varennes-Vauzelles
Nevers
Autun
Beaune
Chagny
Chalon-sur-Saône
Déols
Châteauroux
BERRY
BRENNE
BOISCHAUT
Argenton-sur-Creuse
St-Amand-Montrond
Forêt de Tronçais
Decize
Le Creusot
Montchanin
St-Rémy
Sevrey
Montceau-les-Mines
Bourbon-Lancy
Gueugnon
St-Vallier
Moulins
Yzeure
Plaines de la Loire et de l'Allier
Digoin
Paray-le-Monial
CHAROLLAIS
MÂCONNAIS
BOURBONNAIS
Domérat
Désertines
Montluçon
Commentry
St-Pourçain-sur-Sioule
Mâcon
Plateaux de la Marche
MARCHE
La Souterraine
BRIONNAIS
Guéret
St-Éloy-les-Mines
COMBRAILLE
Gannat
Cusset
Vichy
Roannais
Roanne
Riorges
Le Coteau
Monts du Beaujolais
Villefranche-sur-Saône
Tarare
Belleville
Trévoux
Aubusson
Riom
LIMAGNE
Puy de Montoncel
Monts de la Madeleine
Couzeix
Panazol
Limoges
St-Léonard-de-Noblat
Signal du Pic
Plateau de Gentioux
Chamalières
Cébazat
Gerzat
Thiers
Pont-du-Château
Lempdes
Clermont-Ferrand
Cournon-d'Auvergne
Monts du Forez
Lyon
Oullins
Vénissieux
Dardilly
Monts du Lyonnais
Monts du Limousin
Plateau de Millevaches
Mont de Bessou
Montbrison
Brignais
Rive-de-Gier
Givors
LIMOUSIN
Ussel
Monts Dore
Monts d'Auvergne
Issoire
Leiranoux
Ambert
Monts du Livradois
St-Just-St-Rambert
Veauche
St-Étienne
St-Chamond
Firminy
Suc-au-May
St-Yrieix-la-Perche
Égletons
Le Luguet
AUVERGNE
MASSIF
CENTRAL
Brioude
Monistrol-sur-Loire
Roussillon
Col de la République
Tulle
Annonay
Terrasson-Lavilledieu
Brive-la-Gaillarde
Massif du Cantal
Col de la Fageolle
Yssingeaux
VELAY
Le Puy-en-Velay
Tournon-sur-Rhône
St-Péray
PLANÈZE
St-Flour
Monts de la Margeride
Monts du Vivarais
Martel
Aurillac
SÉGALA DU QUERCY
CHÂTAIGNERAIE
La Voulte-sur-Rhône
Loriol-sur-Drôme
Sarlat-la-Canéda
Gourdon
St-Chély-d'Apcher
Privas
Col de l'Escrinet
QUERCY
Causse de Gramat
Signal de Randon
Sommet de Méjan
Figeac
Aubenas
Decazeville
Aubin
GÉVAUDAN
Marvejols
Le Teil
Mende
Mont Lozère
Cahors
Causse de Sauveterre
Causse de Limogne
Onet-le-Château
Causse Comtal
Rodez
Bourg-St-Andéol
Bollène
Villefranche-de-Rouergue
ROUERGUE
SÉGALA
Causse Méjean
CÉVENNES
La Grande-Combe
Pont-St-Esprit
Bagnols-sur-Cèze
Caussade
Forêt de la Grésigne
Causse Noir
Mont Aigoual
Alès
Orange
Millau
St-Christol-lès-Alès
Uzès
Villeneuve-lès-Avignon
Avignon
Montauban
Carmaux
Causse de St-Affrique
St-Affrique
Albi
Gaillac
ALBIGEOIS
Causse du Larzac
Montagne de la Séranne
GARRIGUES
Nîmes
Beaucaire
Grenade
Graulhet
Col de Sié
Lodève
Vauvert
Arles
Lavaur
L'Union
Colomiers
Toulouse
Tournefeuille
Cugnaux
Seysses
Muret
Monts de Lacaune
Castres
Monts de l'Espinouse
Clermont-l'Hérault
Montpellier
St Jean de Védas
Castelnau-le-Lez
Lunel
Mauguio
St-Gilles
CAMARGUE
Lattes
Le Grau-du-Roi
PETITE CAMARGUE
Stes-Maries-de-la-Mer
Ramonville-St-Agne
Labruguière
Sidobre
Col de la Feuille
Bédarieux
Pézenas
Frontignan
Mazamet
Revel
Montagne Noire
MINERVOIS
LANGUEDOC
Béziers
Sète
Agde
Auterive
LAURAGAIS

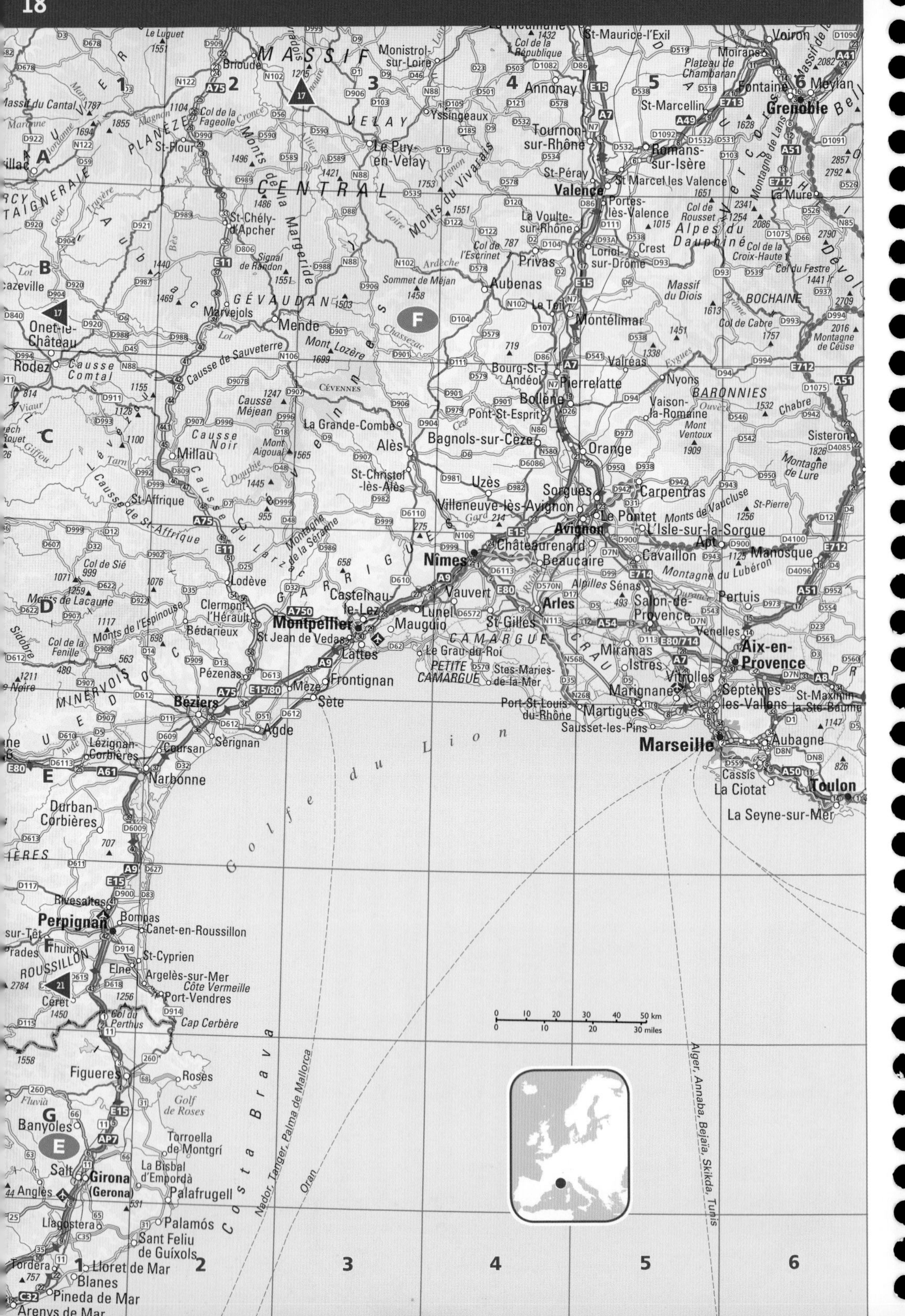
MASSIF CENTRAL
VELAY
GÉVAUDAN
Monts de la Margeride
Monts du Vivarais
Causse Comtal
Causse de Sauveterre
Causse Méjean
Causse Noir
Causse du Larzac
Cévennes
Mont Lozère
Mont Aigoual
Sommet de Mejan
Monts de Lacaune
Monts de l'Espinouse
MINERVOIS
Alpes du Dauphiné
Massif du Diois
BOCHAINE
BARONNIES
Mont Ventoux
Montagne de Lure
Monts de Vaucluse
Montagne du Lubéron
Alpilles
CAMARGUE
PETITE CAMARGUE
CRAU
ROUSSILLON
Côte Vermeille
Costa Brava
Golfe du Lion
Golf de Roses
Brioude
St-Flour
St-Chély-d'Apcher
Marvejols
Mende
Rodez
Onet-le-Château
Millau
St-Affrique
Lodève
Clermont-l'Hérault
Bédarieux
Pézenas
Béziers
Agde
Sérignan
Coursan
Lézignan-Corbières
Narbonne
Durban-Corbières
Rivesaltes
Perpignan
Bompas
Canet-en-Roussillon
St-Cyprien
Thuir
Elne
Argelès-sur-Mer
Port-Vendres
Cap Cerbère
Céret
Col du Perthus
Figueres
Roses
Banyoles
Girona (Gerona)
Salt
Anglès
Torroella de Montgrí
La Bisbal d'Empordà
Palafrugell
Palamós
Sant Feliu de Guíxols
Llagostera
Tordera
Lloret de Mar
Blanes
Pineda de Mar
Arenys de Mar
Monistrol-sur-Loire
Yssingeaux
Le Puy-en-Velay
Annonay
Tournon-sur-Rhône
St-Péray
Valence
La Voulte-sur-Rhône
Privas
Aubenas
Le Teil
Montélimar
Bourg-St-Andéol
Pierrelatte
Bollène
Pont-St-Esprit
Bagnols-sur-Cèze
La Grande-Combe
Alès
St-Christol-lès-Alès
Uzès
Orange
Sorgues
Carpentras
Villeneuve-lès-Avignon
Le Pontet
Avignon
L'Isle-sur-la-Sorgue
Châteaurenard
Beaucaire
Nîmes
Vauvert
Lunel
Montpellier
Castelnau-le-Lez
Mauguio
St Jean de Vedas
Lattes
Frontignan
Mèze
Sète
Le Grau-du-Roi
Stes-Maries-de-la-Mer
St-Gilles
Arles
Sénas
Salon-de-Provence
Miramas
Istres
Port-St-Louis-du-Rhône
Martigues
Marignane
Vitrolles
Sausset-les-Pins
Marseille
Septèmes-les-Vallons
Aix-en-Provence
Venelles
Pertuis
Cavaillon
Apt
Manosque
Sisteron
Aubagne
St-Maximin-la-Ste-Baume
Cassis
La Ciotat
Toulon
La Seyne-sur-Mer
Crest
Loriol-sur-Drôme
Portes-lès-Valence
St Marcel les Valence
Romans-sur-Isère
St-Marcellin
St-Maurice-l'Exil
Moirans
Voiron
Fontaine
Meylan
Grenoble
La Mure
Valréas
Nyons
Vaison-la-Romaine
Col de la Fageolle
Col de la République
Col de l'Escrinet
Col de Rousset
Col de la Croix-Haute
Col du Festre
Col de Cabre
Col de Sié
Col de la Fenille
Nador, Tanger, Palma de Mallorca
Oran
Alger, Annaba, Bejaia, Skikda, Tunis
0 10 20 30 40 50 km
0 10 20 30 miles
1 2 3 4 5 6
A B C D E F G

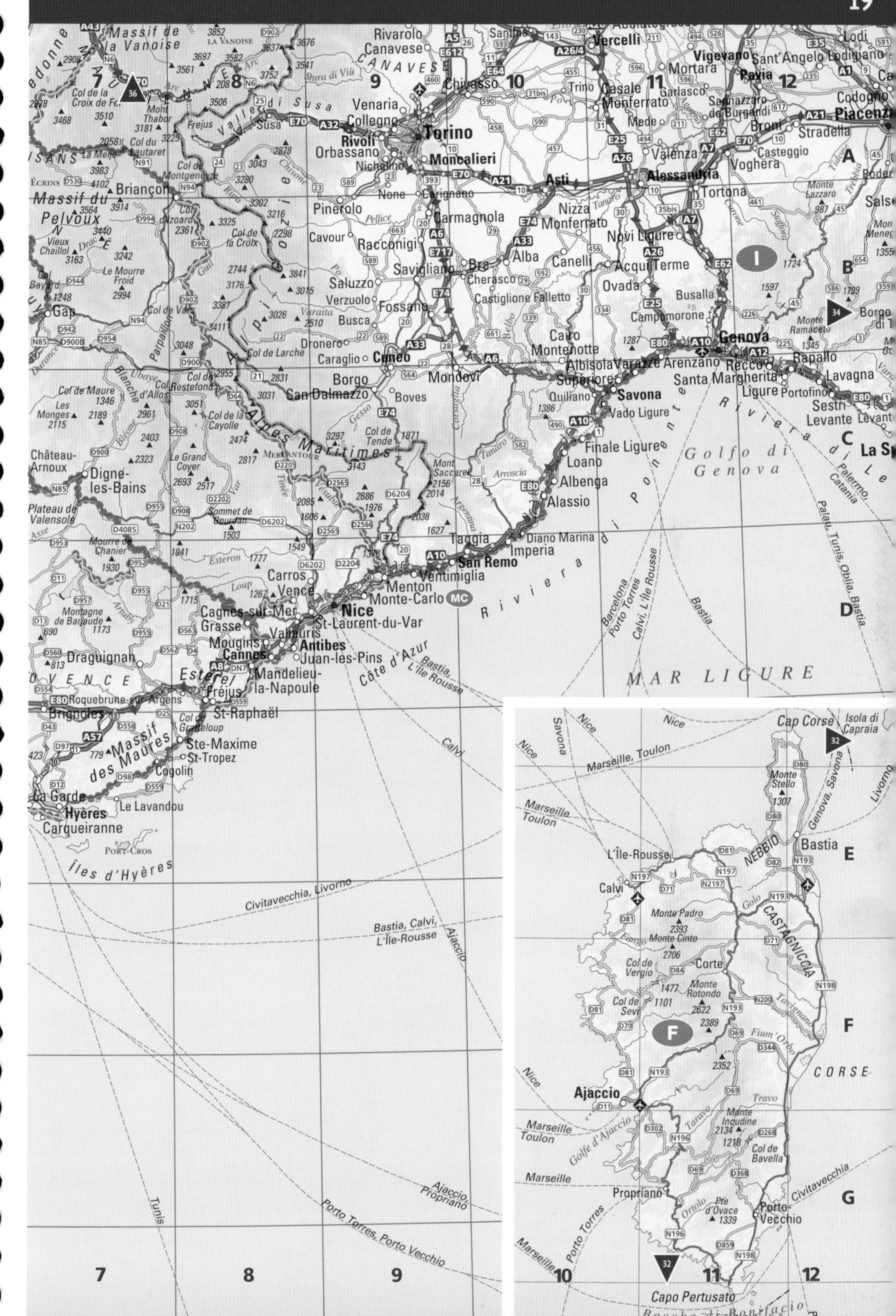
Massif de la Vanoise
Col de la Croix de Fer
Mont Thabor
Col du Lautaret
La Meije
Écrins
Massif du Pelvoux
Briançon
Col de Montgenèvre
Col d'Izoard
Col de la Croix
Vieux Chaillol
Le Mourre Froid
Gap
Col de Vars
Col de Larche
Col de Maure
Les Monges
Col de Restefond
Col d'Allos
Col de la Cayolle
Château-Arnoux
Digne-les-Bains
Le Grand Coyer
Plateau de Valensole
Sommet de Bourdan
Mourre de Chanier
Montagne de Barjaude
Draguignan
Roquebrune-sur-Argens
Brignoles
Col de Gratteloup
Massif des Maures
Ste-Maxime
St-Tropez
Cogolin
La Garde
Hyères
Carqueiranne
Le Lavandou
Port-Cros
Îles d'Hyères
Estérel
Fréjus
St-Raphaël
Mandelieu-la-Napoule
Cannes
Juan-les-Pins
Antibes
Mougins
Grasse
Vallauris
Cagnes-sur-Mer
St-Laurent-du-Var
Nice
Vence
Carros
Menton
Monte-Carlo
Ventimiglia
San Remo
Taggia
Imperia
Diano Marina
Alassio
Albenga
Loano
Finale Ligure
Vado Ligure
Savona
Quiliano
Albisola Superiore
Varazze
Arenzano
Genova
Recco
Santa Margherita Ligure
Portofino
Rapallo
Lavagna
Sestri Levante
Golfo di Genova
Riviera di Ponente
Riviera di Levante
Côte d'Azur
Mar Ligure
Alpes Maritimes
Mercantour
Col de Tende
Mont Saccarel
Alpi Cozie
Rivarolo Canavese
Canavese
Chivasso
Vercelli
Vigevano
Mortara
Pavia
Lodi
Sant'Angelo Lodigiano
Codogno
Piacenza
Stradella
Broni
Casteggio
Voghera
Tortona
Alessandria
Valenza
Casale Monferrato
Trino
Mede
Garlasco
Sannazzaro de' Burgondi
Asti
Nizza Monferrato
Novi Ligure
Acqui Terme
Ovada
Busalla
Campomorone
Canelli
Alba
Bra
Cherasco
Castiglione Falletto
Cairo Montenotte
Mondovì
Cuneo
Boves
Borgo San Dalmazzo
Caraglio
Dronero
Busca
Saluzzo
Verzuolo
Fossano
Savigliano
Racconigi
Carmagnola
Cavour
Pinerolo
None
Carignano
Moncalieri
Nichelino
Torino
Orbassano
Rivoli
Collegno
Venaria
Susa
Frejus
Valle di Susa
Cap Corse
Isola di Capraia
Monte Stello
Bastia
Nebbio
L'Île-Rousse
Calvi
Monte Padro
Monte Cinto
Castagniccia
Corte
Col de Vergio
Monte Rotondo
Col de Sevi
Corse
Ajaccio
Golfe d'Ajaccio
Monte Incudine
Col de Bavella
Propriano
Pte d'Ovace
Porto-Vecchio
Capo Pertusato
Bocche di Bonifacio
Civitavecchia, Livorno
Bastia, Calvi, L'Île-Rousse
Porto Torres, Porto Vecchio
Ajaccio, Propriano
Marseille, Toulon
Genova, Savona
Barcelona, Porto Torres
Palau, Tunis, Olbia, Bastia
Palermo, Catania
Tunis
A
B
C
D
E
F
G
7
8
9
10
11
12

1 2 3 4 5 6

A B C D E F G H

Portsmouth

Golfe de Gascogne

Golfo de Gascuña

Soustons
St-Paul-lès-Dax
Dax
Mont-de-Marsan
Adour
Aire-sur-l'Adour
Capbreton
Tarnos
Boucau
Bayonne
Biarritz
Anglet
Côte d'Argent
St-Jean-de-Luz
Hendaye
Irun
Errenteria
Hasparren
Salies-de-Béarn
Orthez
Mourenx
Lescar
Billère
Pau
Jurançon
Tarbes
Vic-en-Bigorre
Oloron-Ste-Marie
Lourdes
Col d'Ispéguy
Elizondo
Puerto de Velate
Puerto de Ibañeta
Col d'Aubisque
Des Pyrénées Occidentale
Col du Somport
Col du Pourtalet
Gabas

Santoña
Laredo
Castro-Urdiales
Algorta
Bermeo
Santurtzi
Portugalete
Barakaldo
Arizgoiti
Bilbao (Bilbo)
Basauri
Gernika-Lumo
Ondarroa
Zarautz
Donostia-San Sebastián
Balmaseda
Amorebieta
Durango
Ermua
Eibar
Billabona
Tolosa
Andoain
Anoeta
Llodio
Villasana de Mena
Arrasate
Zumarraga
Amurrio
Legazpi
Beasain
Urduña
Medina de Pomar
Sierra de Urquilla
Puerto Echegárate
Altsasu
Vitoria-Gasteiz
Puerto de Azáceta
Berriozar
Barañáin
Burlada
Pamplona (Iruñea)
Miranda de Ebro
Condado de Treviño
Estella
Ega
Arga
Tafalla
Haro
Briviesca
Bureba
Ebro
Logroño
Santo Domingo de la Calzada
Nájera
Ribera Navarra
Calahorra
Arnedo
Sierra de la Demanda
Ansó
Jaca
Torla
Ordesa - Monte Perdido
Sabiñánigo
Gállego
Sierra de Guara
Huesca
Somontano
Bárdenas Reales
Cinco Villas
Alfaro
Corella
Cintruénigo
Tudela
Ejea de los Caballeros
Puerto de Piqueras
Puerto de Oncala
Alhama
Tauste
Esteban
Tarazona
El Castellar
Zuera
Canal de Monegros
Flúmen
Los Monegros
San Caprasio
Alcanadre
Duero
Matute
Soria
Sierra de Cabrejas
Ardal
Ucero
Alto del Moncayo
Sierra del Moncayo
Huecha
Llano de Plasencia
Alagón
Canal Imperial de Aragón
Jalón
Zaragoza
Hinojedo
Abión
Campo de
Araviana
Isuela
El Burgo de Osma
Alto Cruz
Cabezo de Morés
La Almunia de Doña Godina
Huerva
Almazán
Nájima
Marquesado de Berlanga
Calatayud
Campo de Cariñena
Llanos de
Ebro
Gómara
Cuatro Mojones
Jalón
Aguasvivas
Caspe
Cabollera
Ocejón
Sorbe
Bornova
La Bodera
Sierra Ministra
Judes
Mesa
Piedra
Jiloca
Santa Cruz
Herrera
Cucutas
Desierto de Calanda
Alcañiz
Sigüenza
Dulce
Puerto de Maranchón
Aragoncillo
Sierra de Caldereros
Aguila
Retuerta
Martín
Escuriza
Andorra
Jarama
Henares
Badiel
Tajuña
Pinoso
Valdellosa
Pancrudo
Puerto de Minguez
San Just
Bergantes
Carrascal
Guadalajara
La Alcarria
Bernínches
Tajo
Serranía de Cuenca
San Ginés
Nevera
Juez
Bienvenida
Guadiela
Caimodorro
Puerto de Pozondón
Sierra Palomera
Alfambra
Guadalope
Puerto de Cabrillas
Ares
Alcalá de Henares
Torrejón de Ardoz
Morada del Campo
Arganda del Rey
Embalse de Buendía
Cuervo
San Felipe
Zaragozana
Peñarroya
El Maestrazgo
Montleó
de la Vega
Guadamajud
Mayor
Sierra de
Júcar
Losares
Collado Bajo
Javalón
Cabriel
Teruel
Puerto de Escandón
Mijares
Peñagolosa
Camarena

Mount labels: 592, 678, 900, 672, 1135, 1139, 822, 1418, 1057, 1472, 2050, 2613, 2692, 2334, 1180, 1475, 658, 2017, 2504, 1387, 1477, 2884, 2771, 3146, 2676, 1794, 1632, 2883, 3298, 3101, 3348, 1352, 981, 1770, 1929, 1154, 1517, 501, 1597, 2132, 2262, 2078, 1710, 1722, 2228, 1454, 742, 1429, 2313, 1215, 1375, 765, 1313, 1144, 890, 1408, 1310, 2048, 1290, 1423, 1346, 989, 1518, 1443, 1492, 1250, 1229, 1251, 1523, 1041, 1249, 1543, 1834, 1603, 1500, 1268, 1920, 1840, 1910, 1330, 1321, 2028, 1230, 1389, 1691, 1813

Road labels: A8, A63, A64, A65, E05/70, E80, E05/80, A1, A10, A12, A15, A21, AP1, AP15, AP68, AP2, E804, E07, E90, A23, A2, A22, N10, N134, R2

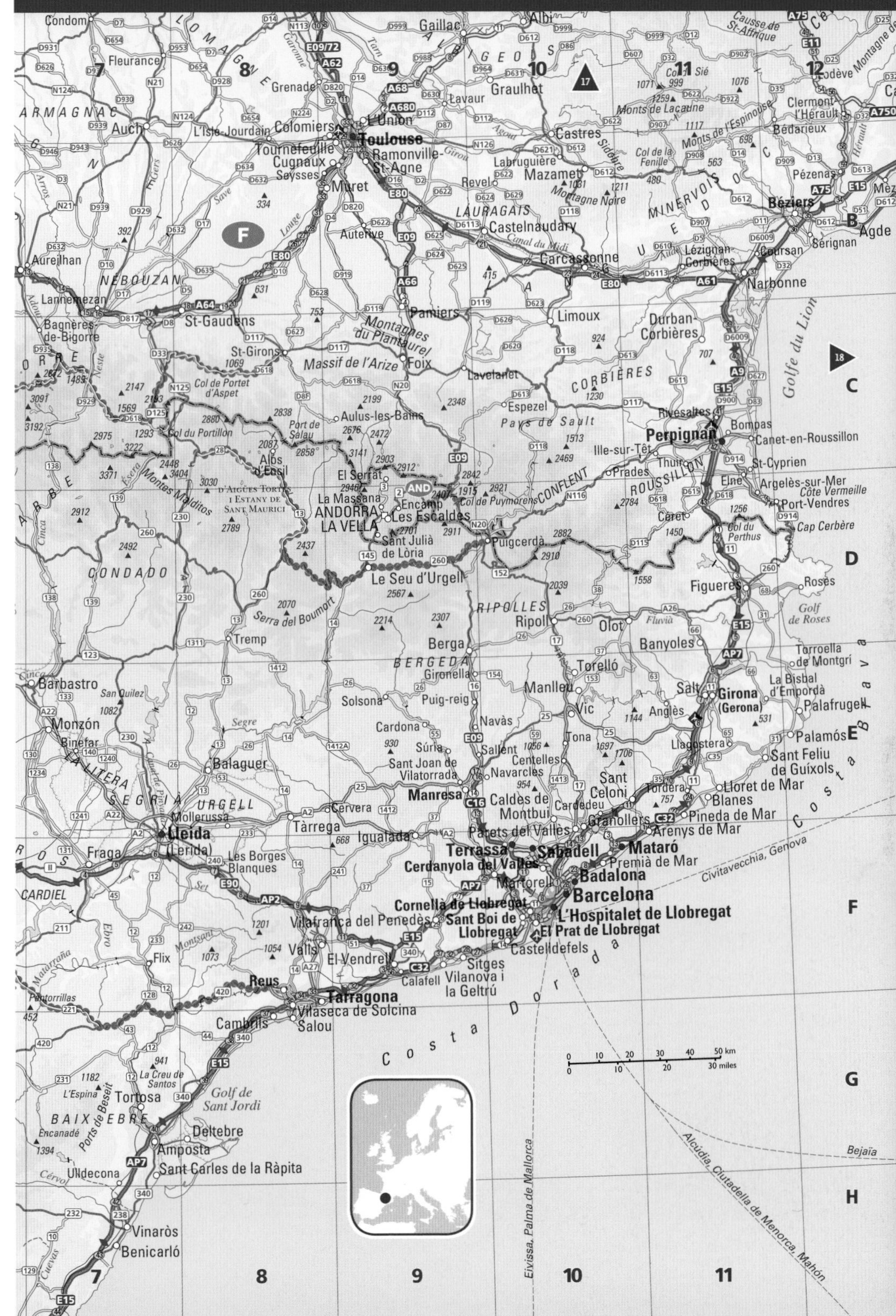
Condom
Gaillac
Albi
Fleurance
Grenade
Graulhet
Lavaur
ARMAGNAC
LOMAGNE
ALBIGEOIS
Auch
L'Isle-Jourdain
Colomiers
L'Union
Toulouse
Tournefeuille
Cugnaux
Ramonville-St-Agne
Seysses
Muret
Castres
Labruguière
Mazamet
Revel
Monts de Lacaune
Monts de l'Espinouse
Montagne Noire
LAURAGAIS
Castelnaudary
Canal du Midi
MINERVOIS
LANGUEDOC
Autérive
Carcassonne
Lézignan-Corbières
Coursan
Narbonne
Béziers
Agde
Sérignan
Pézenas
Bédarieux
Clermont-l'Hérault
Lodève
Causse de St-Affrique
Aureilhan
NEBOUZAN
Lannemezan
Bagnères-de-Bigorre
St-Gaudens
Pamiers
Limoux
Durban-Corbières
Montagnes du Plantaurel
Massif de l'Arize
St-Girons
Foix
Lavelanet
CORBIÈRES
Golfe du Lion
Col de Portet d'Aspet
Col du Portillon
Aulus-les-Bains
Port de Salau
Espezel
Pays de Sault
Rivesaltes
Perpignan
Bompas
Canet-en-Roussillon
Ille-sur-Têt
Thuir
Prades
CONFLENT
ROUSSILLON
St-Cyprien
Elne
Argelès-sur-Mer
Côte Vermeille
Port-Vendres
Cap Cerbère
Céret
Col du Perthus
Col de Puymorens
Alòs d'Isil
El Serrat
La Massana
Encamp
ANDORRA LA VELLA
Les Escaldes
Sant Julià de Lòria
Puigcerdà
D'AIGÜES TORTES I ESTANY DE SANT MAURICI
Montes Malditos
CONDADO
Le Seu d'Urgell
Serra del Boumort
RIPOLLES
Ripoll
Olot
Figueres
Roses
Golf de Roses
Tremp
Berga
BERGEDA
Banyoles
Torroella de Montgrí
Barbastro
San Quilez
Gironella
Torelló
Manlleu
Solsona
Puig-reig
Vic
Girona (Gerona)
La Bisbal d'Empordà
Palafrugell
Monzón
Binéfar
LA LITERA
Cardona
Súria
Navàs
Tona
Anglès
Palamós
Balaguer
Sant Joan de Vilatorrada
Sallent
Centelles
Navarcles
Llagostera
Sant Feliu de Guíxols
SEGRIÀ
URGELL
Mollerussa
Manresa
Caldes de Montbui
Sant Celoni
Tordera
Lloret de Mar
Blanes
Costa Brava
Lleida (Lérida)
Cervera
Tàrrega
Igualada
Cardedeu
Granollers
Pineda de Mar
Arenys de Mar
Fraga
Les Borges Blanques
Terrassa
Sabadell
Mataró
Parets del Vallès
Cerdanyola del Vallès
Premià de Mar
Badalona
Martorell
Barcelona
CARDIEL
Cornellà de Llobregat
Sant Boi de Llobregat
L'Hospitalet de Llobregat
El Prat de Llobregat
Vilafranca del Penedès
Castelldefels
Civitavecchia, Genova
Valls
El Vendrell
Calafell
Sitges
Vilanova i la Geltrú
Flix
Reus
Tarragona
Vilaseca de Solcina
Salou
Cambrils
Costa Dorada
La Creu de Santos
Tortosa
Golf de Sant Jordi
BAIX EBRE
Ports de Beseit
Deltebre
Amposta
Sant Carles de la Ràpita
Ulldecona
Vinaròs
Benicarló
Eivissa, Palma de Mallorca
Alcúdia, Ciutadella de Menorca, Mahón
Bejaïa
0 10 20 30 40 50 km
0 10 20 30 miles
A B C D E F G H
7 8 9 10 11 12

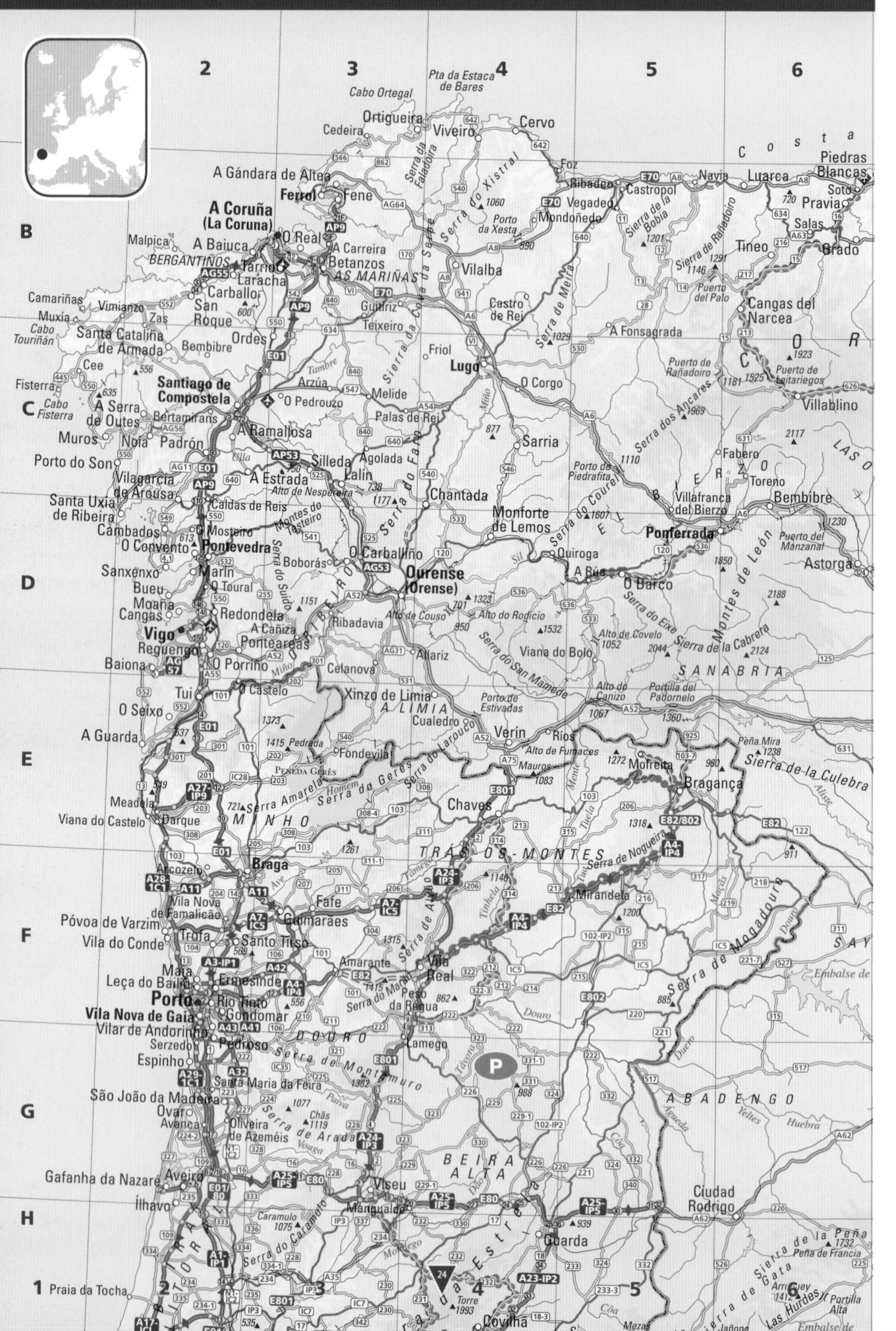
2
3
4
5
6
B
C
D
E
F
G
H
1
Pta da Estaca de Bares
Cabo Ortegal
Ortigueira
Cedeira
Viveiro
Cervo
Serra da Faladoira
Serra do Xistral
Foz
Ribadeo
Castropol
Navia
Luarca
Piedras Blancas
Soto
Pravia
Costa
A Gándara de Altea
Ferrol
Fene
A Coruña
(La Coruna)
O Real
A Carreira
Betanzos
Malpica
A Baiuca
BERGANTIÑOS
Tarrio
Laracha
AS MARIÑAS
Vegadeo
Mondoñedo
Porto da Xesta
Sierra de la Bobia
Sierra de Rañadoiro
Salas
Tineo
Grado
Puerto del Palo
Vilalba
Carballo
San Roque
Camariñas
Vimianzo
Muxía
Zas
Cabo Touriñán
Santa Catalina de Armada
Ordes
Guitiriz
Teixeiro
Castro de Rei
Serra de Meira
A Fonsagrada
Cangas del Narcea
Bembibre
Cee
Fisterra
Cabo Fisterra
Friol
Lugo
Sierra da Cova da Serpe
Puerto de Rañadoiro
Puerto de Leitariegos
Santiago de Compostela
A Serra de Outes
Arzúa
Melide
O Pedrouzo
Tambre
O Corgo
Serra dos Ancares
Villablino
Bertamirans
Palas de Rei
Muros
Noia
Padrón
A Ramallosa
Sarria
Porto do Son
Silleda
Agolada
Lalín
Serra do Faro
Vilagarcía de Arousa
A Estrada
Alto de Nespereira
Porto de Piedrafita
Fabero
Toreno
Santa Uxía de Ribeira
Caldas de Reis
Chantada
Villafranca del Bierzo
Bembibre
Montes do Testeiro
Monforte de Lemos
Serra do Courel
BIERZO
Cambados
O Mosteiro
O Convento
Pontevedra
Ponferrada
Puerto del Manzanal
Serra do Suido
O Carballiño
Quiroga
Astorga
Sanxenxo
Marín
Boborás
Bueu
O Toural
Ourense
(Orense)
A Rúa
O Barco
Montes de León
Moaña
Cangas
Redondela
Ribadavia
Alto de Couso
Alto do Rodicio
Serra do Eixe
Vigo
A Cañiza
Ponteareas
Viana do Bolo
Alto de Covelo
Sierra de la Cabrera
Reguengo
Allariz
Baiona
O Porriño
Celanova
Serra do San Mamede
SANABRIA
Tui
O Castelo
Xinzo de Limia
A LIMIA
Porto de Estivadas
Alto do Canizo
Portilla del Padornelo
O Seixo
Cualedro
A Guarda
Pedrada
Fondevila
Verín
Rios
Alto de Fumaces
Peña Mira
Serra do Larouco
Peneda Gerês
Mauros
Mofreita
Sierra de la Culebra
Serra do Gerês
Serra Amarela
Meadela
Viana do Castelo
Darque
MINHO
Chaves
Bragança
TRÁS-OS-MONTES
Serra de Nogueira
Braga
Arcozelo
Vila Nova de Famalicão
Fafe
Guimarães
Serra de Alvão
Mirandela
Serra de Mogadouro
Póvoa de Varzim
Vila do Conde
Trofa
Santo Tirso
Amarante
Vila Real
Maia
Leça do Bailio
Ermesinde
Serra do Marão
Peso da Régua
Porto
Rio Tinto
Gondomar
Vila Nova de Gaia
Vilar de Andorinho
Pedroso
DOURO
Douro
Lamego
Serzedo
Espinho
Serra de Montemuro
Santa Maria da Feira
São João da Madeira
Ovar
Avanca
Oliveira de Azeméis
Chãs
Serra de Arada
Vouga
ABADENGO
BEIRA ALTA
Gafanha da Nazaré
Aveiro
Viseu
Ílhavo
Mangualde
Ciudad Rodrigo
Caramulo
Serra do Caramulo
Serra da Estrela
Guarda
Sierra de la Peña
Peña de Francia
Praia da Tocha
Torre
Covilhã
Sierra de Gata
Las Hurdes
Portilla Alta
Embalse de Gabriel y Galán
Coimbra
Sierra de Malcata

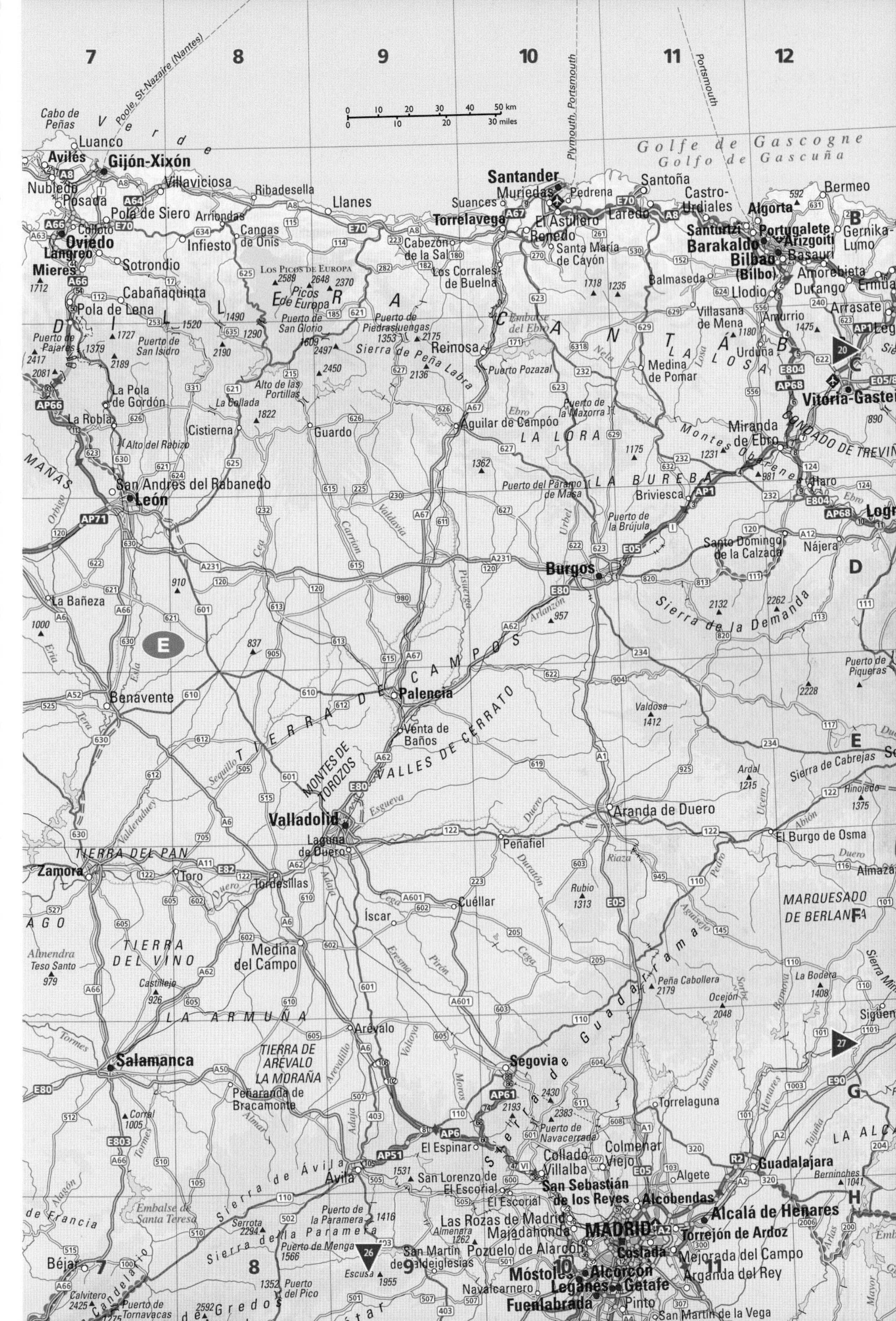
7
8
9
10
11
12
Poole, St-Nazaire (Nantes)
Plymouth, Portsmouth
Portsmouth
0 10 20 30 40 50 km
0 10 20 30 miles
Golfe de Gascogne
Golfo de Gascuña
Cabo de Peñas
Luanco
Avilés
Gijón-Xixón
Nubledo
Posada
Villaviciosa
Ribadesella
Llanes
Pola de Siero
Arriondas
Cangas de Onís
Oviedo
Langreo
Infiesto
Mieres
Sotrondio
Cabañaquinta
Pola de Lena
Los Picos de Europa
Picos de Europa
Puerto de San Glorio
Puerto de Pajares
Puerto de San Isidro
La Pola de Gordón
La Robla
Alto del Rabizo
Cistierna
La Collada
Alto de las Portillas
Guardo
Santander
Muriedas
Pedrena
Suances
Torrelavega
El Astillero
Renedo
Santa María de Cayón
Cabezón de la Sal
Los Corrales de Buelna
Puerto de Piedrasluengas
Sierra de Peña Labra
Reinosa
Embalse del Ebro
Puerto Pozazal
Aguilar de Campóo
Santoña
Laredo
Castro-Urdiales
Balmaseda
Villasana de Mena
Medina de Pomar
Puerto de la Mazorra
LA LORA
Bermeo
Algorta
Santurtzi
Portugalete
Arizgoiti
Gernika-Lumo
Barakaldo
Bilbao (Bilbo)
Basauri
Amorebieta
Durango
Ermua
Llodio
Amurrio
Arrasate
Urduña
Vitoria-Gasteiz
Miranda de Ebro
Montes Obarenes
CONDADO DE TREVIÑO
Haro
Briviesca
LA BUREBA
Puerto del Páramo de Masa
Puerto de la Brújula
Santo Domingo de la Calzada
Nájera
Logroño
Burgos
Sierra de la Demanda
Puerto de Piqueras
San Andrés del Rabanedo
León
La Bañeza
Benavente
E
Palencia
TIERRA DE CAMPOS
Venta de Baños
VALLES DE CERRATO
MONTES DE TOROZOS
Valladolid
Laguna de Duero
Valdosa
Aranda de Duero
Peñafiel
El Burgo de Osma
Sierra de Cabrejas
TIERRA DEL PAN
Zamora
Toro
Tordesillas
Cuéllar
Íscar
TIERRA DEL VINO
Medina del Campo
LA ARMUÑA
Arévalo
TIERRA DE ARÉVALO LA MORAÑA
Salamanca
Peñaranda de Bracamonte
Segovia
Sierra de Guadarrama
Peña Cabollera
Ocejón
MARQUESADO DE BERLANGA
La Bodera
Sigüenza
Torrelaguna
Puerto de Navacerrada
El Espinar
Collado Villalba
Colmenar Viejo
Ávila
Sierra de Ávila
San Lorenzo de El Escorial
El Escorial
San Sebastián de los Reyes
Alcobendas
Algete
Guadalajara
Alcalá de Henares
Torrejón de Ardoz
Las Rozas de Madrid
Majadahonda
MADRID
Coslada
Mejorada del Campo
Arganda del Rey
Pozuelo de Alarcón
San Martín de Valdeiglesias
Puerto de la Paramera
Puerto de Menga
Embalse de Santa Teresa
Móstoles
Alcorcón
Leganés
Getafe
Navalcarnero
Fuenlabrada
Pinto
San Martín de la Vega
Béjar
Puerto de Tornavacas
Puerto del Pico
Gredos
Sierra de Candelario
Almendra
Teso Santo
Castillejo
Corral
Serrota
Escusa
Calvitero
Riaza
Rubio
Ardal
Hinojedo
LA ALCARRIA
Berninches

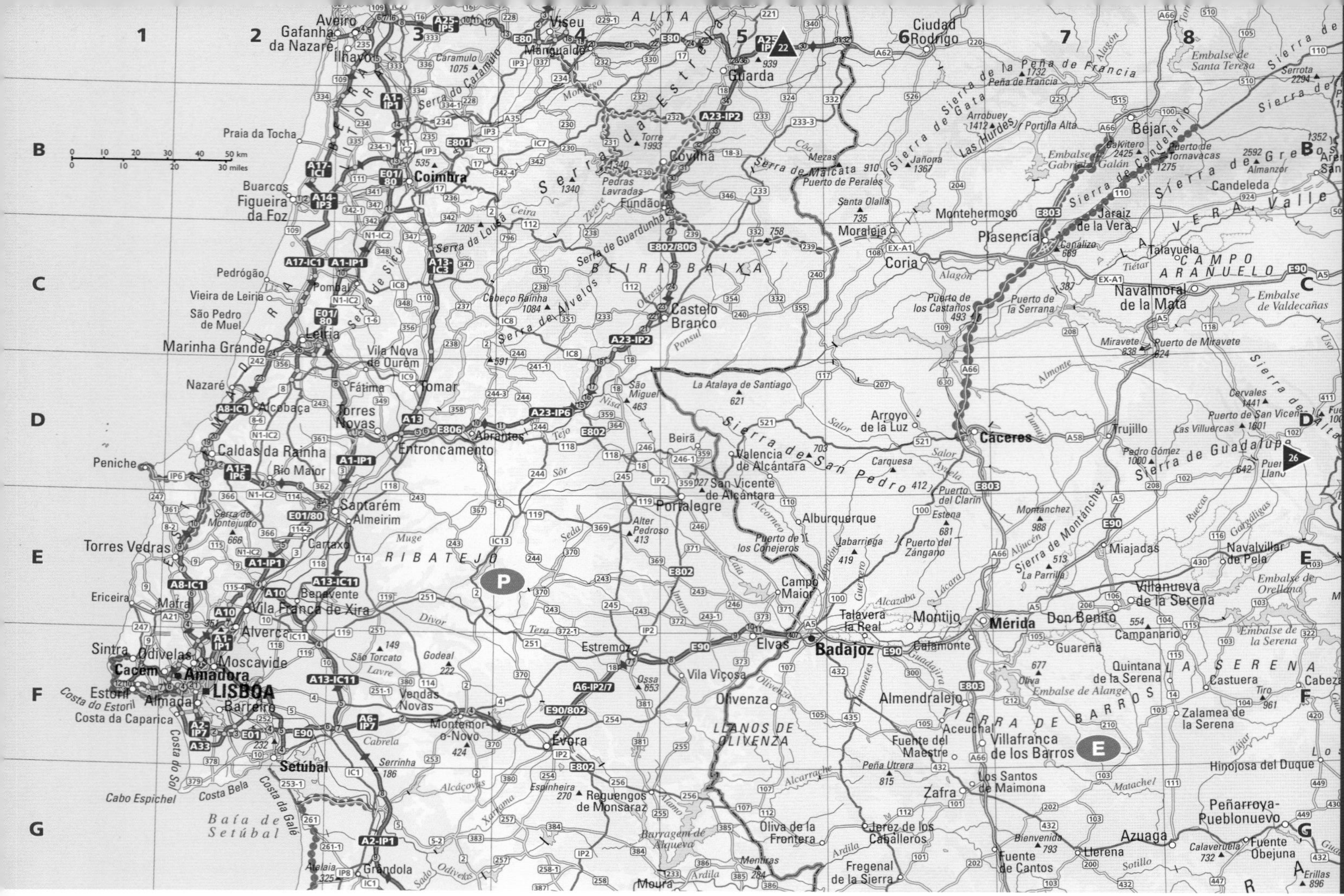

LISBOA
Setúbal
Évora
Badajoz
Mérida
Cáceres
Plasencia
Coimbra
Viseu
Guarda
Covilhã
Castelo Branco
Portalegre
Elvas
Santarém
Leiria
Aveiro
Figueira da Foz
Ciudad Rodrigo
Béjar
Navalmoral de la Mata
Trujillo
Don Benito
Villanueva de la Serena
Zafra
Llerena
Azuaga
Peñarroya-Pueblonuevo
Fuente Obejuna
Hinojosa del Duque
Almendralejo
Villafranca de los Barros
Montijo
Olivenza
Estremoz
Reguengos de Monsaraz
Montemor-o-Novo
Vendas Novas
Grândola
Torres Vedras
Peniche
Caldas da Rainha
Alcobaça
Nazaré
Marinha Grande
Tomar
Entroncamento
Abrantes
Torres Novas
Sintra
Cascais
Estoril
Almada
Barreiro
Amadora
Odivelas
Vila Franca de Xira
Coria
Moraleja
Arroyo de la Luz
Valencia de Alcántara
Alburquerque
Campo Maior
Vila Viçosa
Moura
Jerez de los Caballeros
Fregenal de la Sierra
Fuente de Cantos
Los Santos de Maimona
Miajadas
Guareña
Campanario
Castuera
Cabeza del Buey
Zalamea de la Serena
Quintana de la Serena

Santo André
Sines
Cercal
Zambujeira do Mar
Lagos
Portimão
Albufeira
Quarteira
Loulé
Faro
Olhão
Tavira
Beja
Aljustrel
Guadalupe
Ayamonte
Vila Real de Santo António
Isla Cristina
Lepe
Aljaraque
Gibraleón
Huelva
Punta Umbría
Trigueros
Moguer
Almonte
Bollullos Par del Condado
Valverde del Camino
Aracena
Cortegana
Nerva
Minas de Riotinto
Calañas
Alosno
Monesterio
Sierra de Aracena
Serra da Adiça
Serra de Monchique
EL ANDÉVALO
CONDADO DE NIEBLA
EL ALJARAFE
Aznalcóllar
Sevilla
Camas
Castilleja de la Cuesta
Coria del Río
Dos Hermanas
Alcalá de Guadaira
Utrera
La Rinconada
Brenes
Cantillana
Villaverde del Río
Guillena
Carmona
Marchena
La Puebla de Cazalla
Morón de la Frontera
Montellano
Lora del Río
Palma del Río
Posadas
Écija
Fuentes de Andalucía
Constantina
Cazalla de la Sierra
Los Palacios y Villafranca
Las Cabezas de San Juan
Lebrija
Trebujena
Sanlúcar de Barrameda
Chipiona
Rota
Jerez de la Frontera
El Puerto de Santa María
Cádiz
San Fernando
Puerto Real
Chiclana de la Frontera
Conil de la Frontera
Vejer de la Frontera
Barbate de Franco
Medina Sidonia
Arcos de la Frontera
Villamartín
Prado del Rey
Ubrique
Ronda
Olvera
Algodonales
Alcalá de los Gazules
Los Barrios
Algeciras
Tarifa
San Roque
La Línea
Gibraltar
Strait of Gibraltar
Ceuta
Tanger
Souk el Khemis
Souk Tleta Taghramet
Martil
Tétouan
Souk el Had
GOLFO DE CÁDIZ
Costa de la Luz
Las Marismas
Playa de Castilla
Tierra Llana de Huelva
ALENTEJO
ALGARVE
SIERRA
Islas Canarias
Madeira, Islas Canarias

H J K L M N
1 2 3 4 5 6 7 8

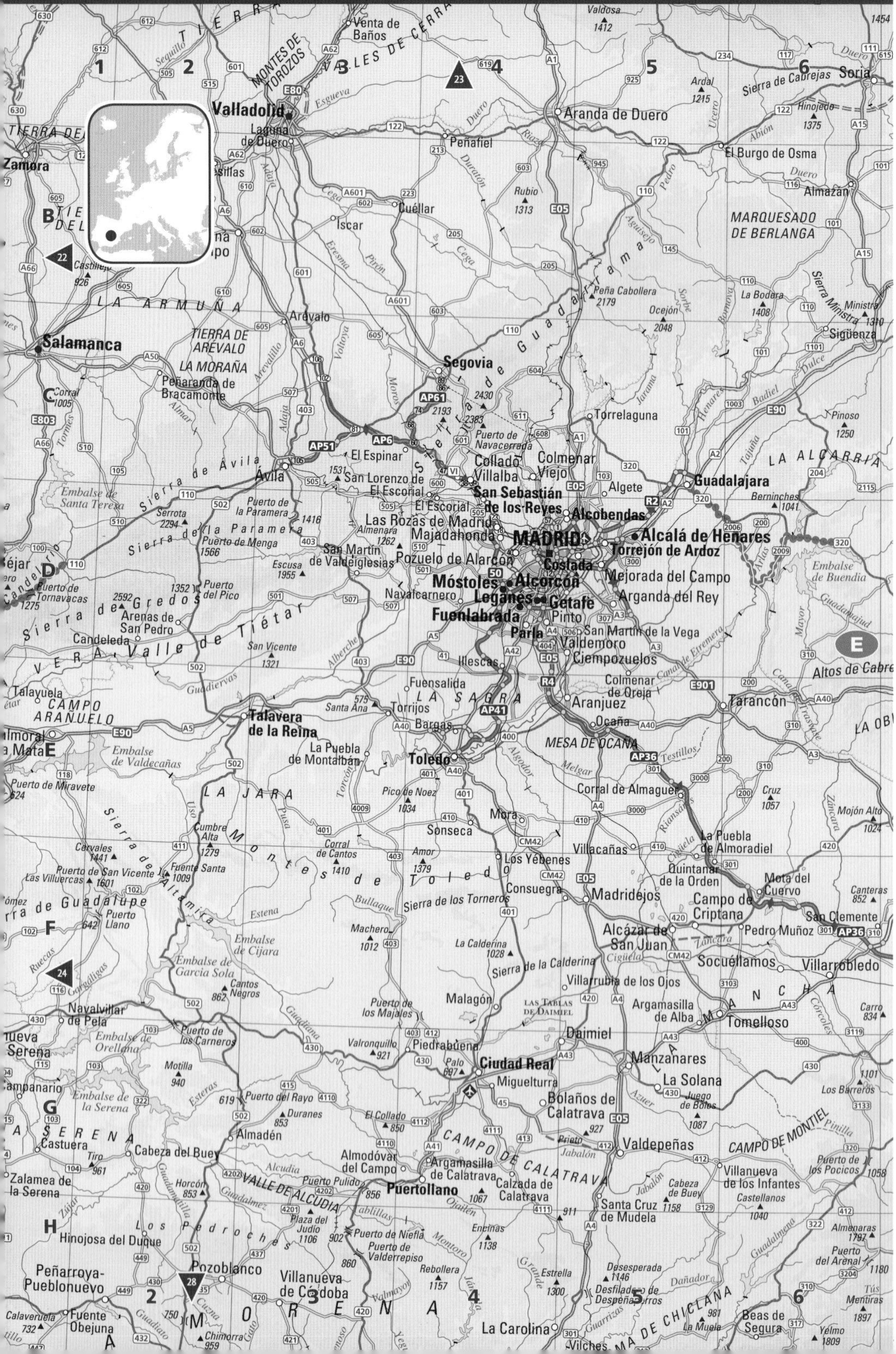

Tierra de Campos
Montes de Torozos
Valles de Cerrato
Venta de Baños
Valdosa 1412
Valladolid
Laguna de Duero
Aranda de Duero
Ardal 1215
Sierra de Cabrejas
Soria
Hinojedo 1375
Peñafiel
El Burgo de Osma
Almazán
Zamora
Tierra del Vino
Cuéllar
Iscar
Rubio 1313
Marquesado de Berlanga
Castillejo 926
La Armuña
Peña Cabollera 2179
Ocejón 2048
La Bodera 1408
Sierra Ministra
Ministra 1310
Sigüenza
Arévalo
Tierra de Arevalo
La Moraña
Salamanca
Peñaranda de Bracamonte
Segovia
Corral 1005
Torrelaguna
Pinoso 1250
Puerto de Navacerrada
2430
2193
2383
El Espinar
Collado Villalba
Colmenar Viejo
La Alcarria
Sierra de Guadarrama
Sierra de Ávila
Ávila
1531
San Lorenzo de El Escorial
El Escorial
San Sebastián de los Reyes
Alcobendas
Algete
Guadalajara
Berninches 1041
Embalse de Santa Teresa
Puerto de la Paramera
Serrota 2294
Sierra de la Paramera
1416
Las Rozas de Madrid
Almenara 1262
Majadahonda
MADRID
Alcalá de Henares
Torrejón de Ardoz
Puerto de Menga 1566
San Martín de Valdeiglesias
Pozuelo de Alarcón
Coslada
Escusa 1955
Móstoles
Alcorcón
Mejorada del Campo
Embalse de Buendía
Puerto de Tornavacas 1275
1352 Puerto del Pico
Sierra de Gredos
2592
Arenas de San Pedro
Navalcarnero
Leganés
Getafe
Arganda del Rey
Fuenlabrada
Pinto
Parla
San Martín de la Vega
Candeleda
La Vera
Valle de Tiétar
San Vicente 1321
Valdemoro
Ciempozuelos
Illescas
Altos de Cabrejas
Talayuela
Campo Arañuelo
Fuensalida
575
Santa Ana
Torrijos
La Sagra
Colmenar de Oreja
Aranjuez
Tarancón
Almoraz
Navalmoral de la Mata
Talavera de la Reina
Bargas
Ocaña
Mesa de Ocaña
La Obispalía
Embalse de Valdecañas
La Puebla de Montalbán
Toledo
Puerto de Miravete 624
La Jara
Pico de Noez 1034
Corral de Almaguer
Cruz 1057
Mojón Alto 1024
Cumbre Alta 1279
Mora
Sonseca
Cervales 1441
Corral de Cantos 1410
Amor 1379
Los Yébenes
Villacañas
La Puebla de Almoradiel
Montes de Toledo
Sierra de Altamira
Puerto de San Vicente
Fuente Santa 1009
Las Villuercas 1601
Quintanar de la Orden
Mota del Cuervo
Canteras 852
Consuegra
Madridejos
Campo de Criptana
Sierra de Guadalupe
Puerto Llano 642
Sierra de los Torneros
Pedro Muñoz
San Clemente
Machero 1012
La Calderina 1028
Alcázar de San Juan
Embalse de Cíjara
Embalse de García Sola
Sierra de la Calderina
Socuéllamos
Villarrobledo
Cantos Negros 862
Villarrubia de los Ojos
Malagón
Las Tablas de Daimiel
Argamasilla de Alba
La Mancha
Tomelloso
Carro 834
Navalvillar de Pela
Puerto de los Majales
Puerto de los Carneros
Embalse de Orellana
Daimiel
Vva. de la Serena
Valronquillo 921
Piedrabuena
Manzanares
Motilla 940
Palo 697
Ciudad Real
Miguelturra
La Solana
Los Barreros
Campanario
Embalse de la Serena
Puerto del Rayo 619
Bolaños de Calatrava
Juego de Bolos 1087
Duranes 853
El Collado 850
927
La Serena
Almadén
Campo de Calatrava
Campo de Montiel
Castuera
Cabeza del Buey
Tiro 961
Almodóvar del Campo
Argamasilla de Calatrava
Valdepeñas
Puerto de los Pocicos 1058
Zalamea de la Serena
Horcón 853
Valle de Alcudia
Puerto Pulido 856
Puertollano
1067
Calzada de Calatrava
Cabeza de Buey 1158
Villanueva de los Infantes
Castellanos 1040
Plaza del Judío 1106
902
Puerto de Niefla
Santa Cruz de Mudela
911
Hinojosa del Duque
Los Pedroches
Puerto de Valderrepiso
Encinas 1138
Almenaras 1797
Puerto del Arenal 1180
Peñarroya-Pueblonuevo
Pozoblanco
860
Rebollera 1157
Estrella 1300
Desesperada 1146
Desfiladero de Despeñaperros
Villanueva de Córdoba
Sierra Morena
Tús Mentiras 1897
Calaveruela 732
Fuente Obejuna
750
Chimorra 959
La Carolina
Vilches
Sierra de Chiclana
981 La Muela
Beas de Segura
Yelmo 1809

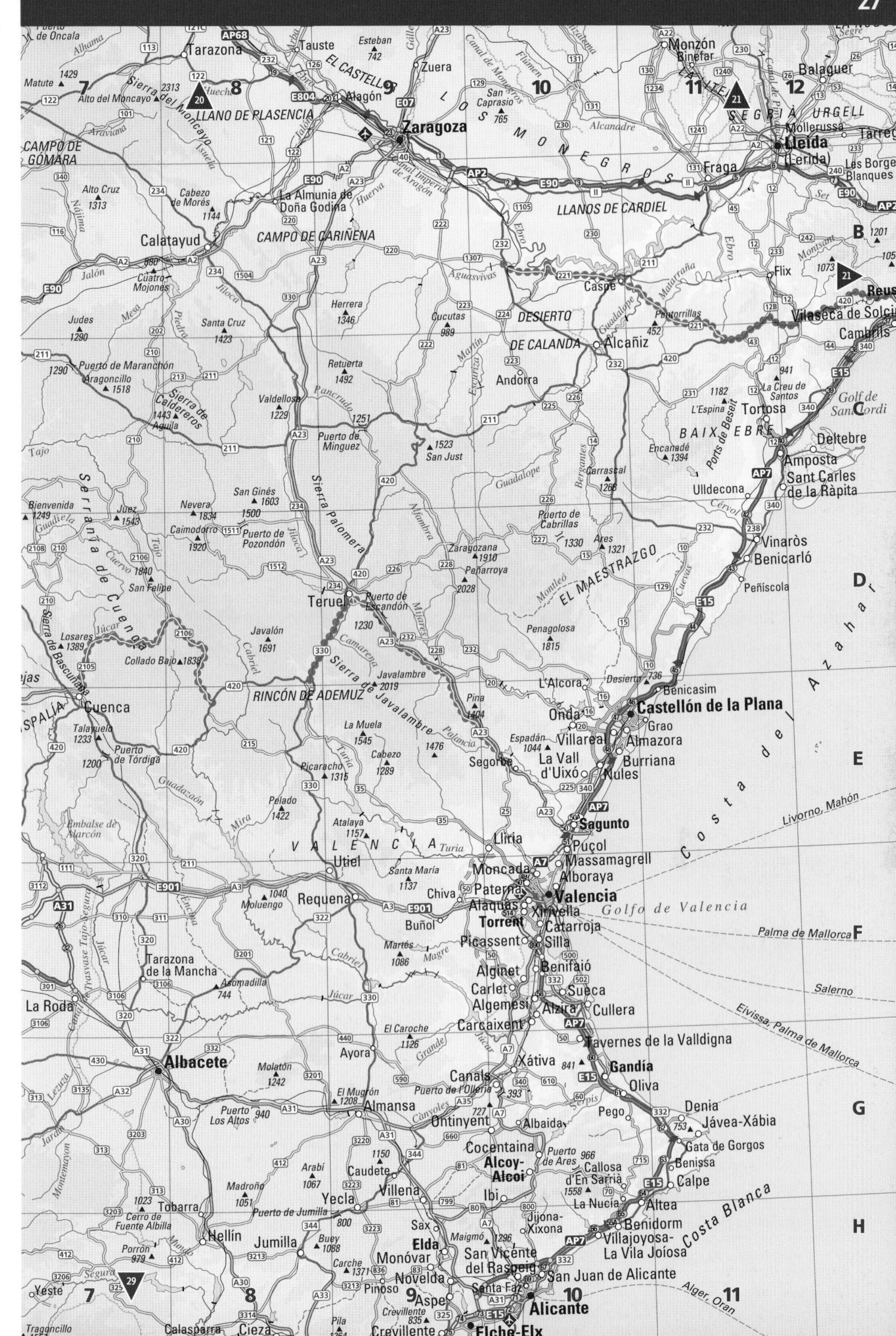

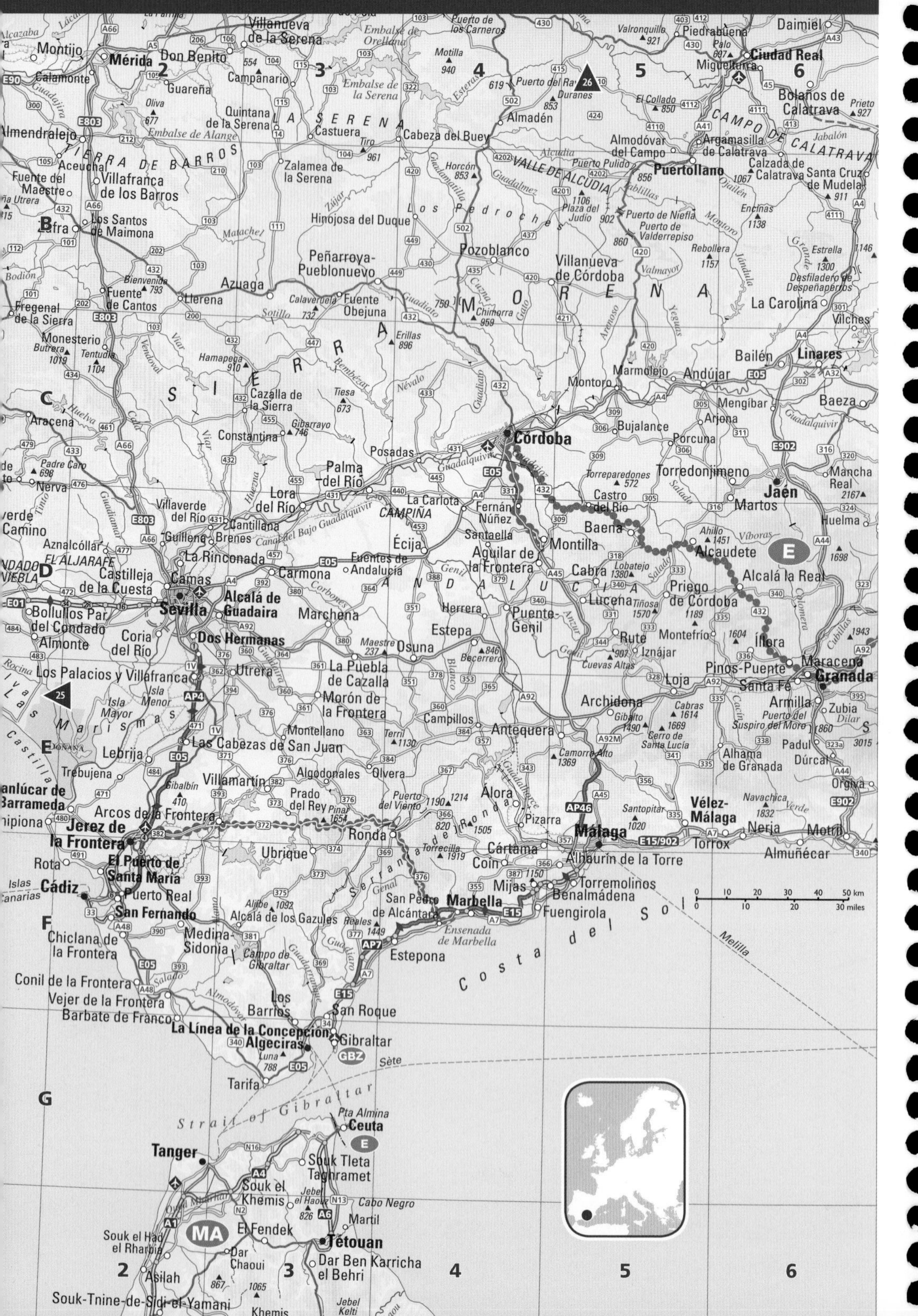
Villanueva de la Serena
Montijo
Mérida
Don Benito
Calamonte
Guareña
Campanario
Embalse de Orellana
Embalse de la Serena
Puerto de los Carneros
Motilla 940
Valronquillo 921
Piedrabuena
Palo 697
Daimiel
Miguelturra
Ciudad Real
Bolaños de Calatrava
Prieto 927
Puerto del Rayo
Duranes 853
El Collado 850
Almadén
Oliva 677
Quintana de la Serena
Embalse de Alange
L A S E R E N A
Castuera
Cabeza del Buey
Tiro 961
Almendralejo
TIERRA DE BARROS
Aceuchal
Villafranca de los Barros
Fuente del Maestre
Zalamea de la Serena
Horcón 853
VALLE DE ALCUDIA
Puerto Pulido 856
Almodóvar del Campo
Argamasilla de Calatrava
Puertollano
CAMPO DE CALATRAVA
Calzada de Calatrava
Santa Cruz de Mudela 911
Jabalón
1067
Plaza del Judío 902
1106
Puerto de Niefla
Puerto de Valderrepiso
860
Encinas 1138
Los Santos de Maimona
Zafra
Hinojosa del Duque
Los Pedroches
Pozoblanco
Villanueva de Córdoba
Rebollera 1157
Estrella 1300
Desfiladero de Despeñaperros
1146
Peñarroya-Pueblonuevo
Azuaga
Bienvenida 793
Fuente de Cantos
Llerena
Calaveruela 732
Fuente Obejuna
Chimorra 959
750
S I E R R A M O R E N A
La Carolina
Vilches
Fregenal de la Sierra
Monesterio
Butrera 1019
Tentudía 1104
Hamapega 910
Erillas 896
Linares
Bailén
Cazalla de la Sierra
Tiesa 673
Marmolejo
Andújar
Montoro
Baeza
Mengíbar
Arjona
Bujalance
Aracena
Constantina
Gibarrayo 746
Córdoba
Porcuna
Padre Caro 698
Nerva
Posadas
Palma del Río
Lora del Río
Torreparedones 572
Torredonjimeno
Jaén
Mancha Real
2167
Martos
Huelma
Villaverde del Río
Cantillana
La Carlota
Fernán Núñez
CAMPIÑA
Castro del Río
Baena
Santaella
Écija
Montilla
Alcaudete
Ahillo 1451
Víboras
1698
Aznalcóllar
EL ALJARAFE
Guillena
Brenes
La Rinconada
Castilleja de la Cuesta
Camas
Carmona
Fuentes de Andalucía
Aguilar de la Frontera
Cabra
Lobatejo 1380
Priego de Córdoba
Alcalá la Real
Sevilla
Alcalá de Guadaira
Marchena
A N D A L U C I A
Herrera
Lucena
Tiñosa 1570
1189
Bollullos Par del Condado
Almonte
Coria del Río
Dos Hermanas
Estepa
Puente-Genil
Rute
Montefrío
Íllora
1604
1943
Osuna
Maestre 237
Becerrero 846
Iznájar
907
Cuevas Altas
Pinos-Puente
Maracena
Granada
Los Palacios y Villafranca
Utrera
La Puebla de Cazalla
Loja
Santa Fé
Armilla
Zubia
Dilar
Isla Menor
Isla Mayor
Las Marismas
Morón de la Frontera
Archidona
Cabras 1614
Gibalto 1490
1669
Cerro de Santa Lucía
Puerto del Suspiro del Moro
1860
3015
Campillos
Antequera
Padul
Dúrcal
Doñana
Lebrija
Las Cabezas de San Juan
Montellano
Terril 1130
Camorro Alto 1369
Alhama de Granada
Trebujena
Algodonales
Olvera
Orgiva
Sanlúcar de Barrameda
Villamartín
Gibalbín 410
Prado del Rey
Pinar 1654
Puerto del Viento 1190
1214
Álora
Santopitar 1020
Vélez-Málaga
Navachica 1832
Chipiona
Jerez de la Frontera
Arcos de la Frontera
Ronda
820
1505
Pizarra
Málaga
Torrox
Nerja
Motril
Rota
El Puerto de Santa María
Ubrique
Torrecilla 1919
Cártama
Coín
Alhaurín de la Torre
Almuñécar
Islas Canarias
Cádiz
Puerto Real
San Fernando
Alijbe 1092
Alcalá de los Gazules
San Pedro de Alcántara
Marbella
Mijas
1150
Torremolinos
Benalmádena
Fuengirola
Costa del Sol
Chiclana de la Frontera
Medina-Sidonia
Reales 1449
Ensenada de Marbella
Estepona
Melilla
Campo de Gibraltar
Conil de la Frontera
Vejer de la Frontera
Barbate de Franco
Los Barrios
San Roque
La Línea de la Concepción
Algeciras
Gibraltar
Luna 788
Sète
Tarifa
Strait of Gibraltar
Pta Almina
Ceuta
Tanger
Souk Tleta Taghramet
Souk el Khemis
Jebel el Haouz 826
Cabo Negro
Martil
Souk el Had el Rharbia
El Fendek
Tétouan
Dar Chaoui
Dar Ben Karricha el Behri
Asilah
867
1065
Souk-Tnine-de-Sidi-el-Yamani
Khemis
Jebel Kelti
0 10 20 30 40 50 km
0 10 20 30 miles
1 2 3 4 5 6
B C D E F G

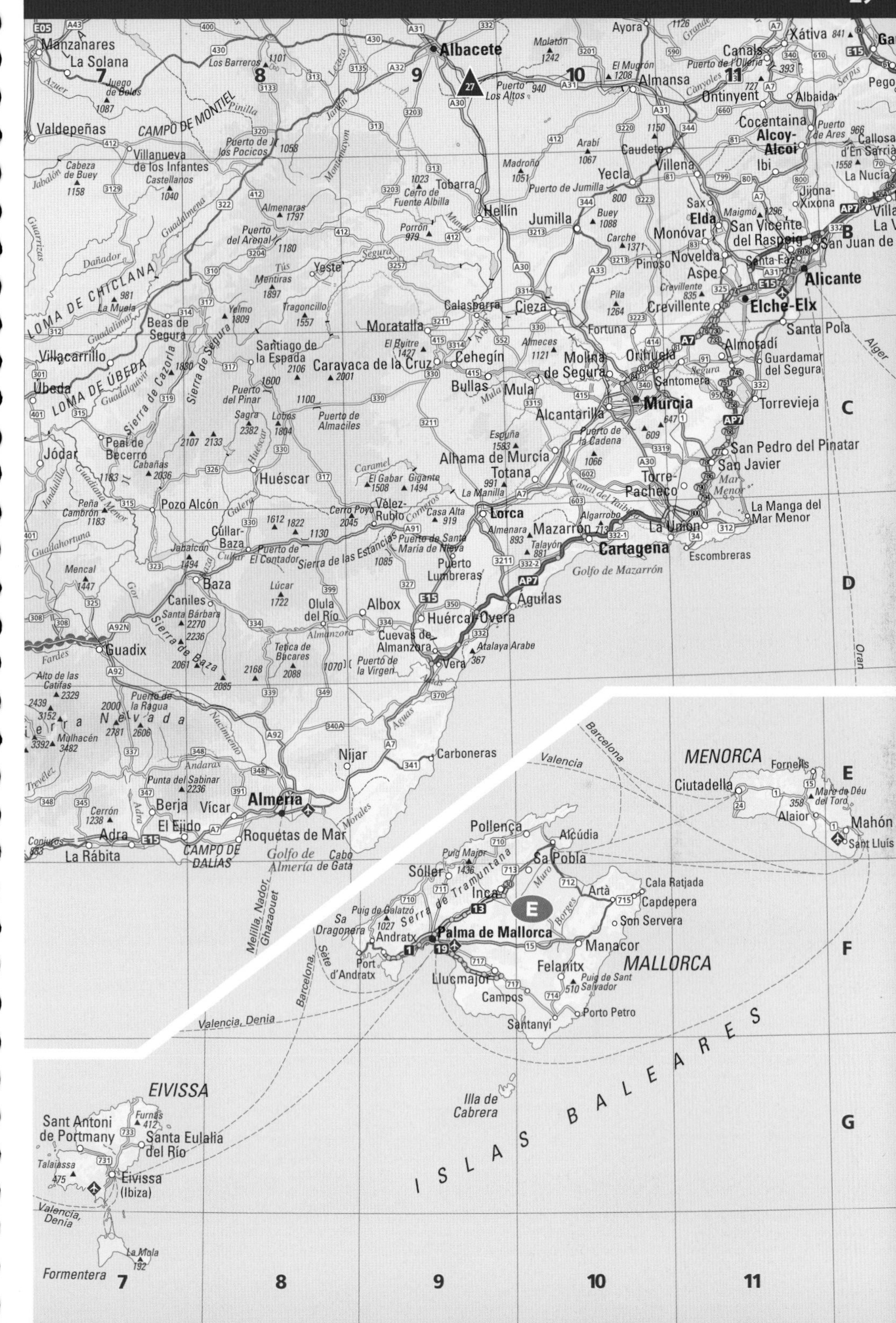
Manzanares
La Solana
Juego de Bolos
1087
Valdepeñas
CAMPO DE MONTIEL
Pinilla
Villanueva de los Infantes
Castellanos
1040
Cabeza de Buey
1158
Jabalón
Azuer
Puerto de los Pocicos
1058
Los Barreros
1101
Albacete
Puerto Los Altos
940
Molatón
1242
El Mugrón
1208
Almansa
Ayora
Xàtiva
841
Canals
Puerto de l'Olleria
393
Ontinyent
727
Albaida
Pego
Cocentaina
Puerto de Ares
966
Callosa d'En Sarrià
Alcoy-Alcoi
Ibi
1558
La Nucía
Jijona-Xixona
Vila
Maigmó
1296
San Vicente del Raspeig
San Juan de
Alicante
Elche-Elx
Santa Pola
Santa Faz
Arabí
1067
Caudete
Villena
1150
Madroño
1051
Yecla
Puerto de Jumilla
800
Buey
1088
Jumilla
Carche
1371
Sax
Elda
Monóvar
Novelda
Pinoso
Aspe
Crevillente
835
Pila
1264
Tobarra
1023
Cerro de Fuente Albilla
Hellín
Mundo
Almenaras
1797
Puerto del Arenal
1180
Porrón
979
Segura
Tús
Yeste
Mentiras
1897
Tragoncillo
1557
Guadalmena
Guarrizas
Dañador
LOMA DE CHICLANA
981
La Muela
Yelmo
1809
Beas de Segura
Guadalimar
Villacarrillo
Úbeda
LOMA DE ÚBEDA
Guadalquivir
Sierra de Cazorla
1880
Sierra de Segura
Santiago de la Espada
2106
1600
Caravaca de la Cruz
2001
Moratalla
El Buitre
1427
Calasparra
Cieza
Cehegín
Bullas
Mula
Almeces
1121
Fortuna
Molina de Segura
Orihuela
Santomera
Almoradí
Guardamar del Segura
Torrevieja
Murcia
647
609
Alcantarilla
Puerto del Pinar
1100
Sagra
2382
Lobos
1804
Puerto de Almaciles
2107
2133
Huéscar
Peal de Becerro
Jódar
Cabañas
2036
1183
Jandulilla
Guadiana Menor
Peña Cambrón
1183
Pozo Alcón
Caramel
El Gabar
1508
Gigante
1494
Vélez-Rubio
Cerro Poyo
2045
Corneros
Casa Alta
919
Lorca
Espuña
1583
Alhama de Murcia
Totana
991
La Manilla
Puerto de la Cadena
1066
San Pedro del Pinatar
San Javier
Mar Menor
Torre-Pacheco
La Manga del Mar Menor
La Unión
Cartagena
Escombreras
Algarrobo
Canal del Taibilla
Almenara
893
Mazarrón
713
Talayón
881
Golfo de Mazarrón
Galera
1612
1822
1130
Cúllar-Baza
Jabalcón
1494
Puerto de El Contador
Sierra de las Estancias
Puerto de Santa María de Nieva
1085
Puerto Lumbreras
Guadahortuna
Mencal
1447
Baza
Gor
Lúcar
1722
Olula del Río
Albox
Huércal-Overa
Águilas
Caniles
Santa Bárbara
2270
2236
Sierra de Baza
2061
2085
Almanzora
Cuevas de Almanzora
Tetica de Bacares
2088
2168
1070
Puerto de la Virgen
Vera
Atalaya Arabe
367
Guadix
Fardes
Alto de las Catifas
2329
2439
3152
Sierra Nevada
Mulhacén
3392
3482
2000
Puerto de la Ragua
2781
2606
Nacimiento
Andarax
Trevélez
Punta del Sabinar
2236
Cerrón
1238
Berja
Vícar
Adra
El Ejido
Almería
Roquetas de Mar
Níjar
Carboneras
Aguas
Morales
Conjuros
883
La Rábita
CAMPO DE DALÍAS
Golfo de Almería
Cabo de Gata
Melilla, Nador, Ghazaouet
Alger
Oran
Barcelona
Valencia
MENORCA
Fornells
Ciutadella
358
Mare de Déu del Toro
Alaior
Mahón
Sant Lluís
Pollença
Alcúdia
Puig Major
1436
Sóller
Sa Pobla
Serra de Tramuntana
Muro
Inca
Artà
Cala Ratjada
Capdepera
Son Servera
Borges
Puig de Galatzó
1027
Sa Dragonera
Andratx
Palma de Mallorca
Manacor
Port d'Andratx
Sete
Barcelona, Sete
Llucmajor
Felanitx
Puig de Sant Salvador
510
MALLORCA
Campos
Santanyí
Porto Petro
Valencia, Denia
ISLAS BALEARES
Illa de Cabrera
EIVISSA
Sant Antoni de Portmany
Furnás
412
Santa Eulalia del Río
Talaiassa
475
Eivissa (Ibiza)
Valencia, Denia
La Mola
192
Formentera
7
8
9
10
11
B
C
D
E
F
G

MARE TIRRENO

SICILIA

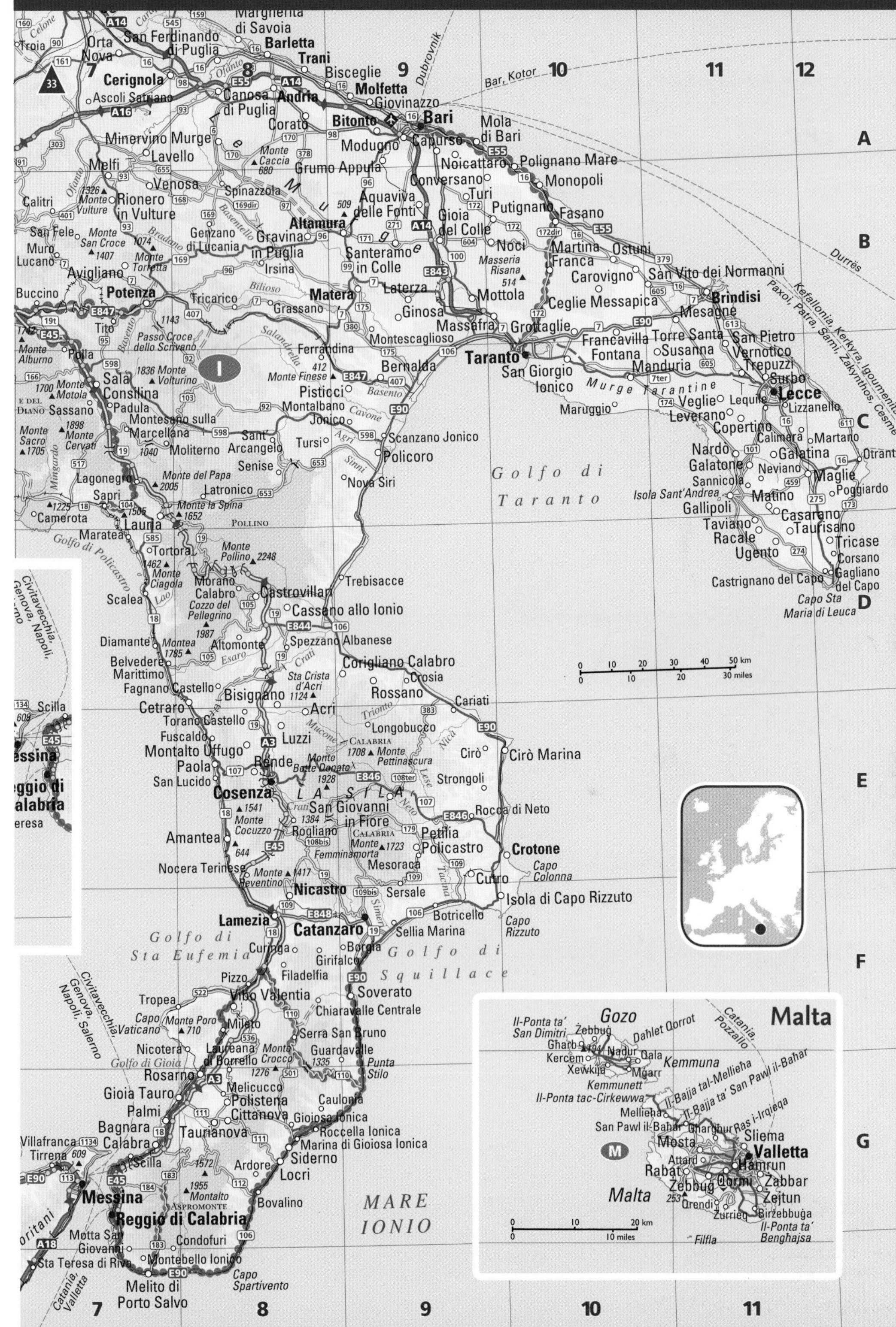

7
8
9
10
11
12
A
B
C
D
E
F
G
Margherita di Savoia
Barletta
Trani
Bisceglie
Molfetta
Giovinazzo
San Ferdinando di Puglia
Orta Nova
Troia
Cerignola
Ascoli Satriano
Canosa di Puglia
Andria
Corato
Bitonto
Bari
Mola di Bari
Modugno
Capurso
Minervino Murge
Lavello
Melfi
Venosa
Rionero in Vulture
Calitri
Spinazzola
Grumo Appula
Noicattaro
Polignano Mare
Monopoli
Conversano
Turi
Aquaviva delle Fonti
Altamura
Gioia del Colle
Putignano
Fasano
San Fele
Muro Lucano
Genzano di Lucania
Gravina in Puglia
Santeramo in Colle
Noci
Martina Franca
Ostuni
Avigliano
Irsina
Masseria Risana
Carovigno
San Vito dei Normanni
Brindisi
Buccino
Potenza
Tricarico
Grassano
Matera
Laterza
Mottola
Ceglie Messapica
Mesagne
Tito
Ginosa
Massafra
Grottaglie
Francavilla Fontana
Torre Santa Susanna
San Pietro Vernotico
Polla
Montescaglioso
Ferrandina
Taranto
San Giorgio Ionico
Manduria
Trepuzzi
Sala Consilina
Bernalda
Surbo
Padula
Sassano
Pisticci
Murge Tarantine
Lecce
Montesano sulla Marcellana
Montalbano Jonico
Maruggio
Veglie
Leverano
Lequile
Lizzanello
Moliterno
Sant' Arcangelo
Tursi
Scanzano Jonico
Copertino
Calimera
Martano
Policoro
Nardò
Galatina
Otranto
Senise
Galatone
Neviano
Maglie
Lagonegro
Nova Siri
Golfo di Taranto
Sannicola
Poggiardo
Latronico
Isola Sant'Andrea
Matino
Sapri
Gallipoli
Casarano
Camerota
Lauria
Taviano
Taurisano
Maratea
Racale
Tricase
Tortora
Ugento
Corsano
Golfo di Policastro
Monte Pollino
Gagliano del Capo
Castrignano del Capo
Trebisacce
Morano Calabro
Castrovillari
Scalea
Cassano allo Ionio
Capo Sta Maria di Leuca
Diamante
Spezzano Albanese
Altomonte
Belvedere Marittimo
Corigliano Calabro
Crosia
Fagnano Castello
Bisignano
Rossano
Cetraro
Acri
Cariati
Torano Castello
Longobucco
Fuscaldo
Luzzi
Montalto Uffugo
Cirò
Cirò Marina
Paola
Rende
San Lucido
Strongoli
Cosenza
La Sila
San Giovanni in Fiore
Rocca di Neto
Amantea
Rogliano
Petilia Policastro
Crotone
Mesoraca
Capo Colonna
Nocera Terinese
Cutro
Nicastro
Sersale
Isola di Capo Rizzuto
Lamezia
Catanzaro
Botricello
Sellia Marina
Capo Rizzuto
Golfo di Sta Eufemia
Curinga
Borgia
Golfo di Squillace
Girifalco
Filadelfia
Pizzo
Vibo Valentia
Soverato
Tropea
Chiaravalle Centrale
Capo Vaticano
Mileto
Serra San Bruno
Nicotera
Laureana di Borrello
Guardavalle
Punta Stilo
Golfo di Gioia
Rosarno
Melicucco
Gioia Tauro
Polistena
Caulonia
Palmi
Cittanova
Gioiosa Ionica
Bagnara Calabra
Taurianova
Roccella Ionica
Marina di Gioiosa Ionica
Villafranca Tirrena
Scilla
Siderno
Ardore
Locri
Messina
Aspromonte
Bovalino
Reggio di Calabria
Mare Ionio
Motta San Giovanni
Condofuri
Sta Teresa di Riva
Montebello Ionico
Capo Spartivento
Melito di Porto Salvo
Catania, Valletta
Civitavecchia, Genova, Napoli, Salerno
Dubrovnik
Bar, Kotor
Durrës
Kefallonia, Kerkyra, Igoumenitsa, Paxoi, Patra, Sami, Zakynthos, Cesme
Malta
Gozo
Il-Ponta ta' San Dimitri
Żebbuġ
Dahlet Qorrot
Gharb
Nadur
Qala
Kercem
Xewkija
Mġarr
Kemmuna
Kemmunett
Il-Ponta tac-Cirkewwa
Il-Bajja tal-Mellieħa
Il-Bajja ta' San Pawl il-Baħar
Mellieħa
Ras i-Irqieqa
San Pawl il-Baħar
Għargħur
Mosta
Sliema
Valletta
Attard
Ħamrun
Rabat
Żebbuġ
Qormi
Żabbar
Malta
Qrendi
Żejtun
Żurrieq
Birżebbuġa
Il-Ponta ta' Benghajsa
Filfla
Catania, Pozzallo
0 10 20 30 40 50 km
0 10 20 30 miles
0 10 20 km
0 10 miles

MARE TIRRENO
SARDEGNA
ROMA
Perugia
Grosseto
Viterbo
Terni
Latina
Sassari
Cagliari
Nuoro
Oristano
Civitavecchia
Olbia
Arcipelago Toscano
Bocche di Bonifacio
Isola di Capraia
Isole Ponziane
Isola di Ponza

MARE ADRIATICO
Sant'Elpidio a Mare
Montegranaro
Porto San Giorgio
Fermo
Grottammare
San Benedetto del Tronto
Ascoli Piceno
Spinetoli
Martinsicuro
Folignano
Civitella del Tronto
Alba Adriatica
Tortoreto
Giulianova
Campli
Teramo
Roseto degli Abruzzi
Gran Sasso e Monti della Laga
Monte Gorzano
Pineto
Silvi
Montorio al Vomano
Atri
Montesilvano
Penne
Spoltore
Pescara
Francavilla al Mare
Gran Sasso d'Italia
L'Aquila
Cepagatti
Ortona
Chieti
Manoppello
San Vito Chietino
Lanciano
Casalbordino
Vasto
Guardiagrele
Monte Velino
Monte Sirente
Pópoli
Maiella
Monte Amaro
Casoli
Atessa
San Salvo
Termoli
Campomarino
Celano
Avezzano
Sulmona
Monte Porrara
Monti dei Frentani
Colle della Sentinella
Monte d'Elio
Vico del Gargano
Vieste
Capistrello
Trasacco
Monte Viglio
Guglionesi
Lesina
Sannicandro Garganico
Promontorio del Gargano
Abruzzo
Monte Greco
Agnone
Monte Mauro
Serracapriola
Castèl di Sangro
Trivento
Larino
San Paolo di Civitate
Apricena
Monte Calvo
Mattinata
Monte Sant'Angelo
Alatri
Veroli
Sora
Torremaggiore
San Severo
San Giovanni Rotondo
Tavoliere
Isola del Liri
La Merta
Frosinone
Ripi
Isernia
Campobasso
Manfredonia
Golfo di Manfredonia
Arce
Monte Cairo
Sant Elia Fiumerapido
Lucera
Foggia
Ceccano
San Giovanni Incarico
Venafro
Monti del Matese
Monte Miletto
Bojano
Monti del Sannio
Riccia
San Bartolomeo in Galdo
Margherita di Savoia
Pontecorvo
Cassino
Monte Mutria
Morcone
Monte Cornacchia
Troia
San Ferdinando di Puglia
Barletta
Trani
Bisceglie
Fondi
Monti Aurunci
Monte Petrella
Vairano Patenora
Piedimonte Matese
Orta Nova
Cerignola
Formia
Teano
Guardia Sanframondi
Ascoli Satriano
Canosa di Puglia
Andria
Sessa Aurunca
Sparanise
Calazzo
Ariano Irpino
Golfo di Terracina
Gaeta
Corato
Bitonto
Mondragone
Capua
Benevento
Apice
Monte Taburno
Minervino Murge
Lavello
Golfo di Gaeta
Grazzanise
Caserta
Montesarchio
Mirabella Eclano
Grumo Appula
Marcianise
Maddaloni
Monte Caccia
Castèl Volturno
Aversa
Monti d'Avella
Altavilla Irpina
Melfi
Venosa
Spinazzola
Lusciano
Caivano
Afragola
Avellino
Monte Vulture
Rionero in Vulture
Giugliano in Campania
Baiano
Marigliano
Nusco
Calitri
Altamura
Napoli
Casoria
Vesuvio
Pozzuoli
San Giuseppe Vesuviano
Lioni
San Fele
Monte San Croce
Genzano di Lucania
Gravina in Puglia
Bacoli
Portici
Sarno
Monte Cervialto
Torre del Greco
Monti Picentini
Muro Lucano
Irsina
Forio
Torre Annunziata
Monte Mai
Baronissi
Avigliano
Matera
Monte Epomeo
Ischia
Isola d'Ischia
Golfo di Napoli
Gragnano
Cava de'Tirreni
Salerno
Buccino
Potenza
Tricarico
Grassano
Sorrento
Pontecagnano Faiano
Eboli
Battipaglia
Tito
Passo Croce dello Scrivano
Anacapri
Capri
Golfo di Salerno
Albanella
Polla
Ferrandina
Capaccio
Sala Consilina
Monte Volturino
Monte Finese
Pisticci
Agropoli
Cilento e del Vallo di Diano
Sassano
Padula
Montesano sulla Marcellana
Montalbano Jonico
Castellabate
Vallo della Lucania
Monte Cervati
Tursi
Monte della Stella
Moliterno
St Arcangelo
Policoro
Senise
Ascea
Lagonegro
Monte del Papa
Latronico
Nova Siri
Sapri
Monte la Spina
Camerota
Lauria
Pollino
Maratea
Golfo di Policastro
Tortora
Monte Ciagola
Monte Pollino
Trebisacce
Morano Calabro
Castrovillari
Cassano allo Ionio
Scalea
Cozzo del Pellegrino
Diamante
Montea
Altomonte
Spezzano Albanese
Belvedere Marittimo
Fagnano Castello
Bisignano
Sta Crista d'Acri
Acri
Cetraro
Torano Castello
Hvar
Viški Kanal
Vis
Split
Korčulanski Kanal
Vela Luka
HR
Lastovo
Ubli
Isole Tremiti
Palermo
Catania
Messina, Valletta
7
8
9
10
11
12
B
C
D
E
F
G
H
80
31

Bolzano
Appiano sulla Strada del Vino
Laives
Cles
Marmolada
Cima della Vezzana
Monte Civetta
Monte Duranno
Tolmezzo
Jesenice
Triglav
Bled
Radovljica
Kranj
Julijske Alpe
Gemona del Friuli
Tavagnacco
Škofja Loka
Tolmin
Cima Presanella
Gruppo di Brenta
Mezzolombardo
Lavis
Gardolo di Trento
Dolomiti Bellunesi
Ponte nelle Alpi
Maniago
Spilimbergo
Sedico
Belluno
Santa Giustina
Mel
Aviano
Udine
Cividale del Friuli
SLO
Idrija
Trento
Pergine Valsugana
Feltre
Vittorio Veneto
Cordenòns
Codroipo
Gorizia
Nova Gorica
Logatec
Vrhnika
Levico Terme
Sacile
Pordenone
Fiume Veneto
Ajdovščina
Riva del Garda
Arco
Asiago
Valdobbiadene
Conegliano
Cervignano del Friuli
Monfalcone
Rovereto
Mori
Ala
Bassano del Grappa
Montebelluna
Oderzo
Portogruaro
Latisana
Postojna
Sežana
Schio
Tezze sul Brenta
Treviso
Santo Stino di Livenza
Lignano Sabbiadoro
Grado
Trieste
Muggia
Valdagno
Dueville
Cittadella
San Donà di Piave
Izola
Piran
Koper
Ilirska Bistrica
I
Negrar
Arzignano
Creazzo
Vicenza
Piazzola sul Brenta
Eraclea
Caorle
Jesolo
Lucija
Bardolino
Bussolengo
Mestre
Spinea
Verona
Rubano
Vigonza
Mira
Venezia
HR
Opatija
Sommacampagna
Lonigo
Padova
Ponte San Nicolò
Golfo di Venezia
Istra (Istria)
Pazin
Poreč
Isola della Scala
Piove di Sacco
Goito
Cerea
Este
Monselice
Chioggia
Mantova
Solesino
Cavarzere
Labin
Roncoferraro
Badia Polesine
Villadose
Adria
Rosolina
Rovinj
Ostiglia
Lendinara
Rovigo
Porto Viro
Contarina
Suzzara
San Benedetto Po
Sermide
Porto Tolle
Ariano nel Polesine
Brijuni
Pula
Occhiobello
Mesola
Novellara
Mirandola
Bondeno
Copparo
Finale Emilia
Ferrara
Codigoro
Correggio
Carpi
Crevalcore
Cento
Portomaggiore
Modena
San Giovanni in Persiceto
Valli di Comacchio
Comacchio
Formigine
Castelfranco Emilia
Argenta
Mare Adriatico
Sassuolo
Bologna
Castenaso
Alfonsine
Vignola
Casalecchio di Reno
Medicina
Bagnacavallo
San Lazzaro di Savena
Lugo
Ravenna
Serramazzoni
Pavullo nel Frignano
Pianoro
Russi
Imola
Faenza
Cervia
Vergato
Cesenatico
Brisighella
Forlì
Forlimpopoli
Bellaria
Castrocaro Terme
Cesena
San Marcello Pistoiese
Vernio
Savignano sul Rubicone
Santarcangelo di Romagna
Rimini
Riccione
Borgo San Lorenzo
Serravalle
Cattolica
Pistoia
Pescia
Agliana
Vicchio
Mercato Saraceno
San Marino
RSM
Pesaro
Prato
Novafeltria
Sant'Angelo in Lizzola
Fano
Campi Bisenzio
Sesto Fiorentino
Monte Falterona, Campigna e delle Foreste Casentinesi
Montefeltro
Cartoceto
Firenze
Fucecchio
Scandicci
Empoli
Pontassieve
Poppi
Urbino
Mondolfo
Senigallia
Bagno a Ripoli
Fossombrone
Falconara Marittima
Impruneta
Reggello
Bibbiena
Fermignano
Corinaldo
Monte dei Frati
Urbania
Chiaravalle
Ancona
San Miniato
Castelfiorentino
Pergola
Monte Conero
Terranuova Bracciolini
Sansepolcro
San Giustino
Arcevia
Jesi
Camerano
Osimo
Certaldo
Peccioli
Greve in Chianti
Montevarchi
Cagli
Maiolati Spontini
Loreto
Poggibonsi
Sassoferrato
Castelfidardo
Porto Recanati
San Gimignano
Bucine
Arezzo
Città di Castello
Colle di Val d'Elsa
Cingoli
Recanati
Potenza Picena
Volterra
Castiglion Fiorentino
Gubbio
Fabriano
Macerata
Civitanova Marche
Monte San Savino
Porto Sant'Elpidio
Pomarance
Siena
Sovicille
Cortona
Umbertide
Matelica
Corridonia
Sinalunga
Gualdo Tadino
Tolentino
Montegranaro
Sant'Elpidio a Mare
Colline Metallifere
Monteroni d'Arbia
Torrita di Siena
Appennino Umbro-Marchigiano
Porto San Giorgio
Poggio di Montieri
Corciano
Perugia
Nocera Umbra
Camerino
Fermo
Montepulciano
Castiglione del Lago
Monte Fiegni
Montalcino
Chianciano Terme
Taverne di Corciano
Bastia
Assisi
Massa Marittima
Chiusi
Grottammare
Roccastrada
Spello
Monte Fema
San Benedetto del Tronto
Monte Leoni
Monte Amiata
Città della Pieve
Foligno
Monti Sibillini
Spinetoli
Martinsicuro
Abbadia San Salvatore
Marsciano
Ascoli Piceno
Alba Adriatica
Follonica
Montefalco
Trevi
Monte Vettore
Civitella del Tronto
Tortoreto
Monte Martano
Campli
Giulianova
Monte Faete
Monte Civitella
Todi
Spoleto
Sant'Anatolia di Narco
Castiglione della Pescaia
Grosseto
Acquapendente
Orvieto
Monte Coscerno
Gran Sasso e Monti della Laga
Teramo
Roseto
Pineto

Troyes
Bar-sur-Aube
Joinville
Neufchâteau
Chaumont
Mirecourt
Thaon-les-Vosges
Rambervillers
Baccarat
Raon-l'Étape
Obernai
Offenburg
Lahr
Sélestat
Épinal
Vittel
Plaine Lorraine
CHAMPAGNE HUMIDE
VALLAGE
BASSIGNY
La Vôge
Remiremont
La Bresse
Wintzenheim
Colmar
Emmendingen
Waldkirch
Freiburg im Breisgau
Bad Krozingen
Guebwiller
Ballon d'Alsace
Luxeuil-les-Bains
Plateau de Haute-Saône
Lure
Mulhouse
Müllheim
Schopfheim
Montbard
Vesoul
Belfort
Altkirch
SUNDGAU
Weil am Rhein
Basel
Semur-en-Auxois
Gray
Montbéliard
Audincourt
Delle
Aesch
Liestal
Talant
St-Apollinaire
Dijon
Chenôve
Porrentruy
Delémont
Aarau
Olten
Balsthal
Baume-les-Dames
Lomont
Auxonne
Massif de la Serre
Besançon
Moutier
Solothurn
Grenchen
Nuits-St-Georges
Dole
Chasseral
Biel
Beaune
Forêt de Chaux
Morteau
Le Locle
Neuchâtel
Lyss
Burgdorf
Autun
Chagny
Mont Poupet
Cortaillod
Hessigkofen
Sumiswald
BERN
Köniz
Worb
Münsingen
Le Creusot
Montchanin
Chalon-sur-Saône
Poligny
Pontarlier
Lac de Neuchâtel
Montceau-les-Mines
Champagnole
Forêt de la Joux
Mont Suchet
Payerne
Fribourg
Uetendorf
Thun
Spiez
Interlaken
St-Vallier
Sevrey
Lons-le-Saunier
Louhans
Yverdon
Marly
La Berra
Bulle
Tournus
Mont Risoux
Renens
Lausanne
Frutigen
Eiger
Morez
Morges
Vevey
Montreux
Saanen
BERNER ALPEN
St-Claude
Nyon
LAC LÉMAN
Évian-les-Bains
Balmhorn
Wildhorn
Gex
Thonon-les-Bains
Aigle
Ollon
Bex
Raron
Sierre
Mâcon
Bourg-en-Bresse
Oyonnax
Ferney-Voltaire
Versoix
Vernier
Genève
Le Lignon
Annemasse
Lancy
Monthey
Sion
Conthey
Chablais
Péronnas
Belleville
DOMBES
Bonneville
FAUCIGNY
Martigny
Weisshorn
Villefranche-sur-Saône
Ambérieu-en-Bugey
Cluses
Scionzier
Genevois
Rosablanche
Dent Blanche
Matterhorn
Monte Rosa
Trévoux
Meximieux
Tarare
Dardilly
Rillieux-la-Pape
Cran-Gevrier
Annecy
Sallanches
Chamonix-Mont-Blanc
Bornes
Grand Combin
Alpi Pennine
Dufourspitze
Rumilly
Seynod
Mont Joly
Mont Blanc
Lyon
Villeurbanne
Oullins
Vénissieux
Bron
Belley
Aix-les-Bains
Faverges
Ugine
Bauges
Albertville
Aosta
Valpelline
Corno Bianco
Brignais
Rive-de-Gier
Givors
Villefontaine
Bourgoin-Jallieu
Chambéry
La Ravoire
Cognin
Bourg-St-Maurice
Beaufortin
Becca du Lac
Monte Emilius
Biella
St-Chamond
St-Étienne
Vienne
St-Maurice-l'Exil
Mont Pourri
Gran Paradiso
Monte Giavino
Ivrea
Pontcharra
Le Cheval Noir
Pointe de la Grande Casse
Vanoise
Annonay
Rives
Voiron
Moirans
Voreppe
Massif de la Chartreuse
Belledonne
Massif de la Vanoise
Uia di Ciamarella
Cuorgnè
Rivarolo Canavese
CANAVESE
Plateau de Chambaran
St-Marcellin
Fontaine
Meylan
Grenoble
Aiguilles d'Arves
Punta Lunella
Caluso
Tournon-sur-Rhône
Romans-sur-Isère
Vercors
Montagne de Lans
Val di Susa
Susa
Fréjus
Venaria
Leini
Chivasso
Collegno
Rivoli
Torino
St-Péray
St-Marcel-lès-Valence
Grand Armet
La Meije
Écrins
Romanche
Orbassano
Moncalieri
Guilherand
Valence
La Mure
Punta Rognosa
Nichelino
La Voulte-sur-Rhône
Portes-lès-Valence
Massif du Pelvoux
Briançon
Grand Pic de Rochebrune
Pinerolo
None
Carignano
Privas
Loriol-sur-Drôme
Crest
Alpes du Dauphiné
Grande Tête de l'Obiou
Tête de Soulaure
Cavour
Carmagnola
Aubenas
Racconigi
Bra
Alba
Massif
Le Mourre Froid

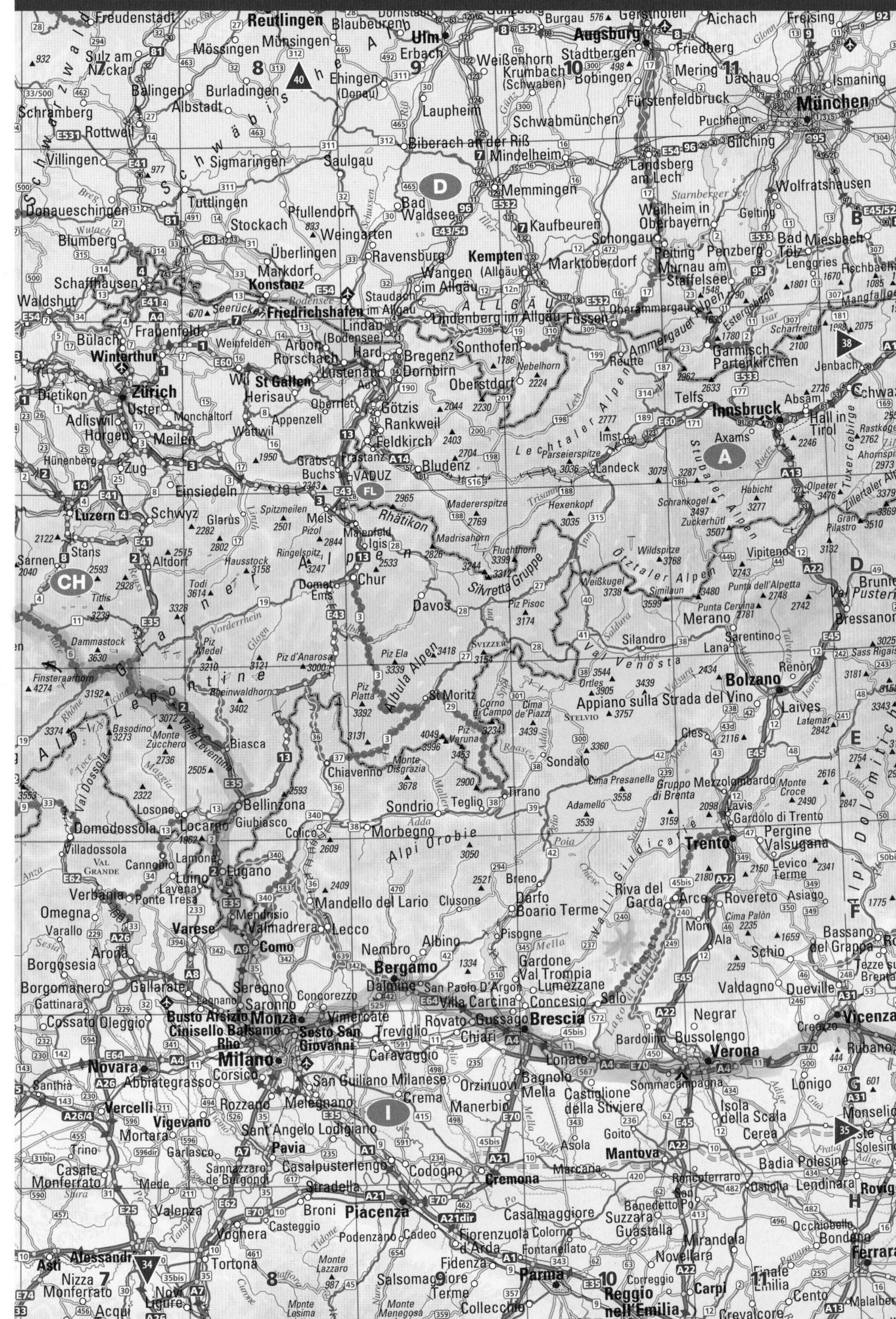

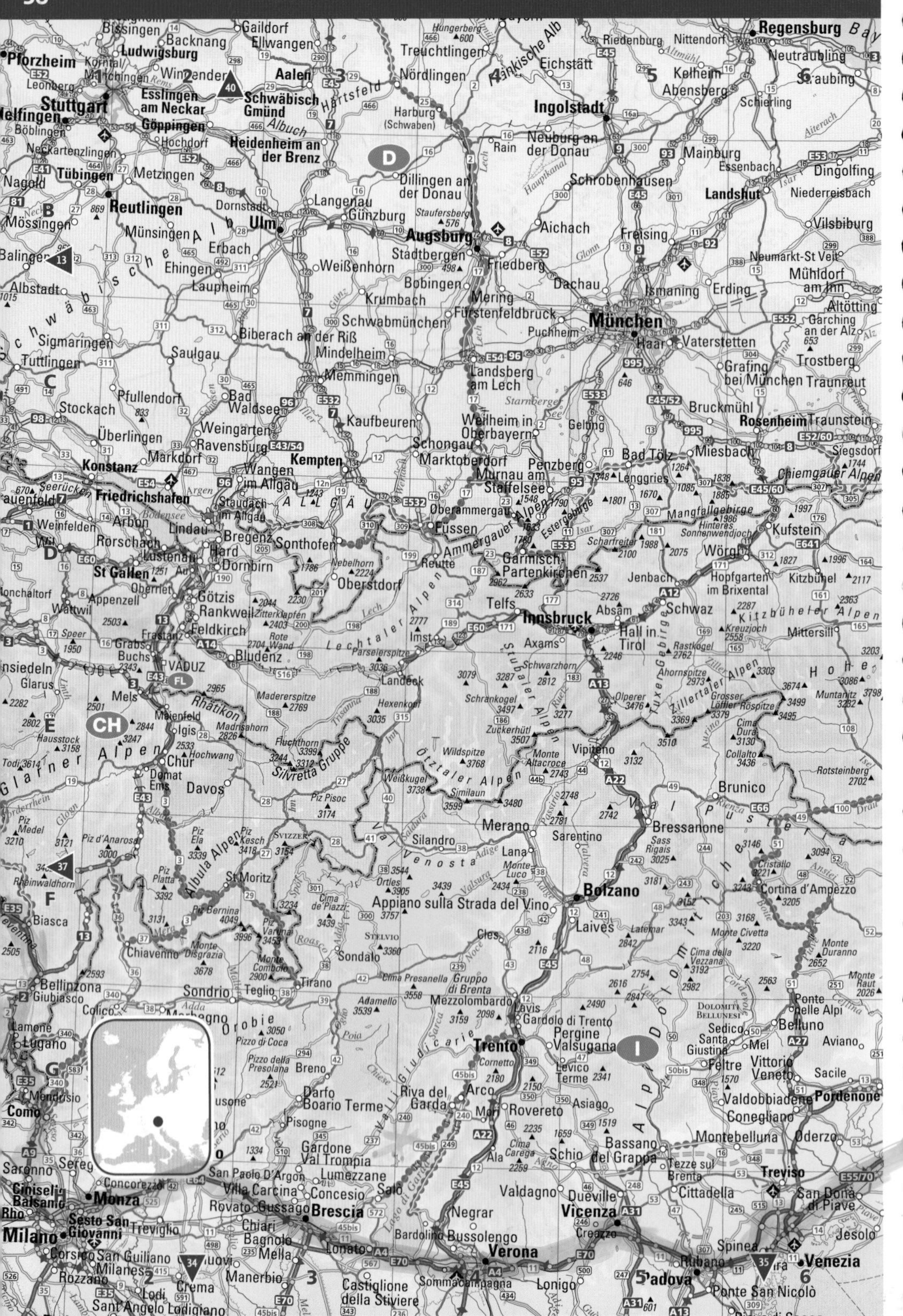

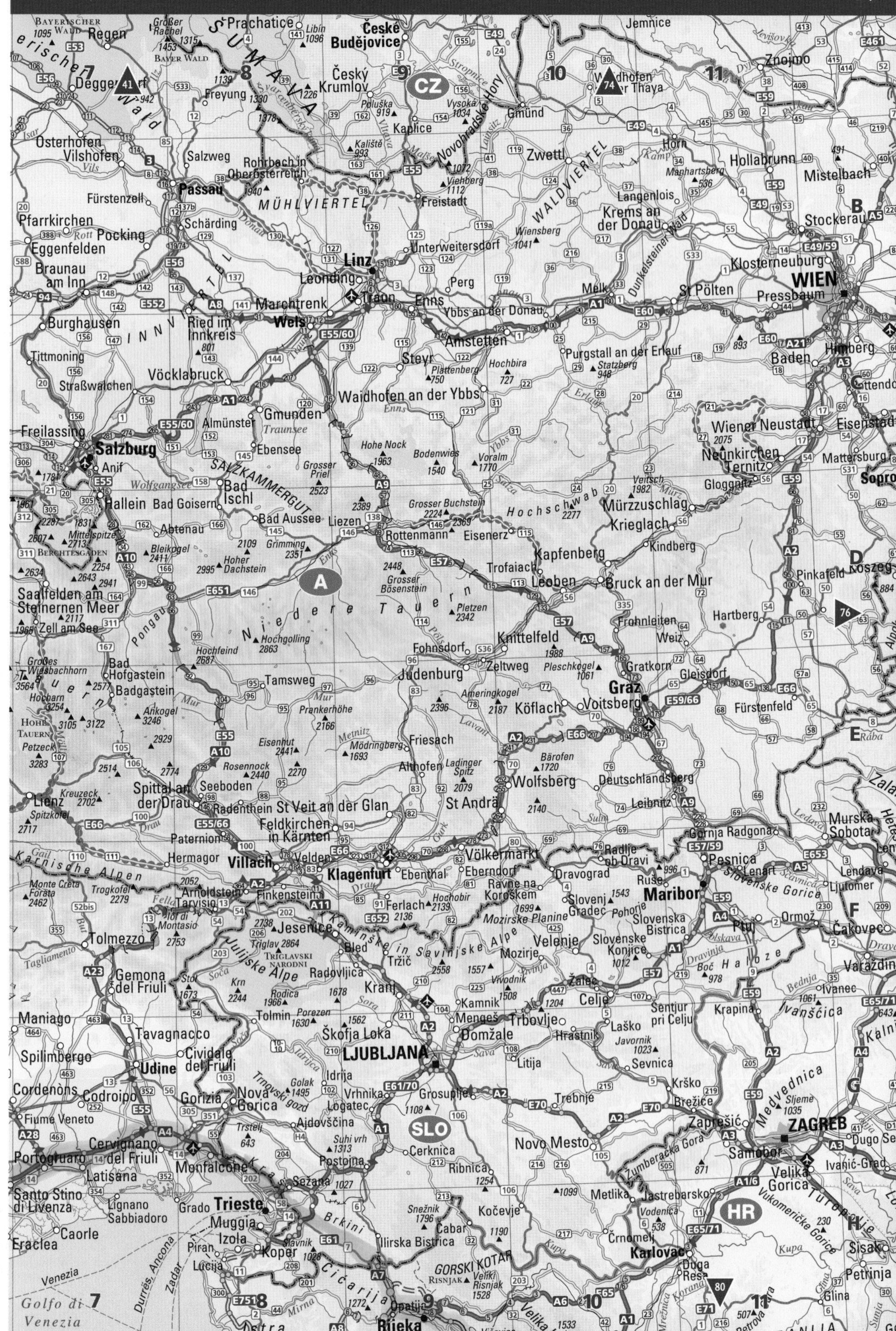
Regen
Prachatice
České Budějovice
Jemnice
Znojmo
Deggendorf
ŠUMAVA
Český Krumlov
CZ
Waidhofen an der Thaya
Freyung
Kaplice
Gmünd
Osterhofen
Vilshofen
Salzweg
Rohrbach in Oberösterreich
Zwettl
Horn
Hollabrunn
Mistelbach
Passau
MÜHLVIERTEL
Freistadt
WALDVIERTEL
Langenlois
Fürstenzell
Pfarrkirchen
Schärding
Pocking
Krems an der Donau
Stockerau
Eggenfelden
Unterweitersdorf
Braunau am Inn
Linz
Leonding
Perg
Klosterneuburg
WIEN
Marchtrenk
Traun
Enns
Melk
St Pölten
Pressbaum
Burghausen
Wels
Ried im Innkreis
Ybbs an der Donau
Amstetten
INNVIERTEL
Tittmoning
Steyr
Purgstall an der Erlauf
Baden
Himberg
Vöcklabruck
Straßwalchen
Waidhofen an der Ybbs
Gmunden
Wiener Neustadt
Eisenstadt
Freilassing
Almünster
Salzburg
Ebensee
Hohe Nock
Neunkirchen
Ternitz
Mattersburg
Sopron
Anif
SALZKAMMERGUT
Bad Ischl
Gloggnitz
Hallein
Bad Goisern
Bad Aussee
Liezen
Mürzzuschlag
Hochschwab
Abtenau
Rottenmann
Eisenerz
Krieglach
Kindberg
BERCHTESGADEN
Hoher Dachstein
Trofaiach
Kapfenberg
Kőszeg
A
Leoben
Bruck an der Mur
Pinkafeld
Saalfelden am Steinernen Meer
Niedere Tauern
Zell am See
Hartberg
Frohnleiten
Knittelfeld
Weiz
Fohnsdorf
Zeltweg
Gratkorn
Bad Hofgastein
Badgastein
Tamsweg
Judenburg
Graz
Gleisdorf
Fürstenfeld
Voitsberg
Köflach
Friesach
Rába
Spittal an der Drau
Seeboden
Althofen
Wolfsberg
Deutschlandsberg
Lienz
Radenthein
St Veit an der Glan
St Andrä
Leibnitz
Feldkirchen in Kärnten
Murska Sobota
Paternion
Gornja Radgona
Hermagor
Villach
Velden
Klagenfurt
Ebenthal
Völkermarkt
Eberndorf
Radlje ob Dravi
Pesnica
Lenart
Lendava
Karnische Alpen
Arnoldstein
Finkenstein
Tarvisio
Dravograd
Ravne na Koroškem
Ruše
Maribor
Ljutomer
Slovenske Gorice
Ferlach
Slovenj Gradec
Ptuj
Ormož
Čakovec
Jesenice
Bled
Mozirje
Velenje
Slovenska Bistrica
Slovenske Konjice
Tolmezzo
Julijske Alpe
Kamniške in Savinjske Alpe
Tržič
Radovljica
Varaždin
Gemona del Friuli
Kranj
Žalec
Celje
Ivanec
Kamnik
Šentjur pri Celju
Krapina
Ivanščica
Maniago
Tolmin
Mengeš
Trbovlje
Laško
Tavagnacco
Škofja Loka
Domžale
Hrastnik
Spilimbergo
Cividale del Friuli
Udine
LJUBLJANA
Litija
Sevnica
Idrija
Cordenòns
Codroipo
Gorizia
Nova Gorica
Vrhnika
Grosuplje
Trebnje
Krško
Medvednica
Logatec
Brežice
Fiume Veneto
Ajdovščina
SLO
Zaprešić
ZAGREB
Dugo Selo
Cervignano del Friuli
Novo Mesto
Portogruaro
Postojna
Cerknica
Samobor
Latisana
Monfalcone
Ribnica
Velika Gorica
Ivanić-Grad
Santo Stino di Livenza
Sežana
Metlika
Jastrebarsko
Lignano Sabbiadoro
Grado
Trieste
Kočevje
HR
Caorle
Muggia
Čabar
Črnomelj
Eraclea
Izola
Koper
Ilirska Bistrica
Karlovac
Sisak
Piran
Lucija
GORSKI KOTAR
Duga Resa
Petrinja
Golfo di Venezia
Opatija
Rijeka
Ogulin
Glina
Poreč
Pazin
Istra
Velika Kladuša
BANIJA
Zrinska Gora

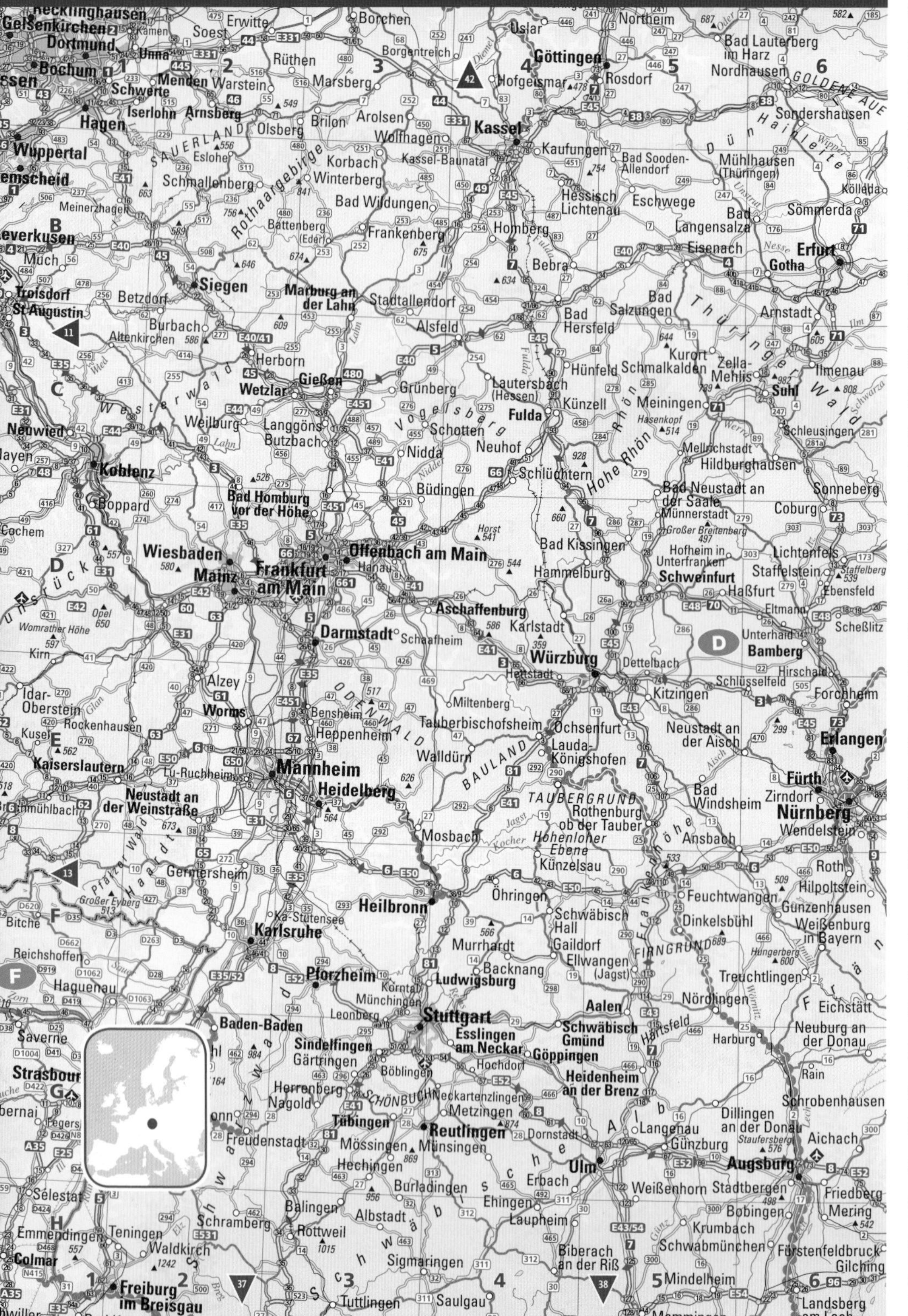
Recklinghausen
Gelsenkirchen
Dortmund
Unna
Bochum
Essen
Schwerte
Hagen
Wuppertal
Remscheid
Leverkusen
Troisdorf
St. Augustin
Neuwied
Koblenz
Mayen
Cochem
Boppard
Soest
Erwitte
Menden
Warstein
Iserlohn
Arnsberg
Olsberg
Brilon
Rüthen
Marsberg
Borchen
Borgentreich
Arolsen
Wolfhagen
Korbach
Winterberg
Schmallenberg
Eslohe
Meinerzhagen
Siegen
Betzdorf
Burbach
Altenkirchen
Herborn
Wetzlar
Gießen
Marburg an der Lahn
Stadtallendorf
Frankenberg (Eder)
Battenberg (Eder)
Bad Wildungen
Kassel
Kassel-Baunatal
Kaufungen
Hofgeismar
Uslar
Göttingen
Northeim
Rosdorf
Bad Lauterberg im Harz
Nordhausen
Sondershausen
Mühlhausen (Thüringen)
Bad Sooden-Allendorf
Hessisch Lichtenau
Eschwege
Bad Langensalza
Sömmerda
Kölleda
Erfurt
Gotha
Eisenach
Homberg
Bebra
Bad Hersfeld
Bad Salzungen
Arnstadt
Ilmenau
Zella-Mehlis
Suhl
Schmalkalden
Meiningen
Hünfeld
Alsfeld
Grünberg
Lautersbach (Hessen)
Fulda
Künzell
Schotten
Nidda
Neuhof
Schlüchtern
Büdingen
Butzbach
Langgöns
Weilburg
Bad Homburg vor der Höhe
Wiesbaden
Mainz
Frankfurt am Main
Offenbach am Main
Hanau
Aschaffenburg
Darmstadt
Schaafheim
Bad Kissingen
Hammelburg
Schweinfurt
Haßfurt
Bamberg
Coburg
Lichtenfels
Staffelstein
Sonneberg
Hildburghausen
Schleusingen
Bad Neustadt an der Saale
Münnerstadt
Karlstadt
Würzburg
Dettelbach
Kitzingen
Schlüsselfeld
Forchheim
Erlangen
Fürth
Nürnberg
Zirndorf
Wendelstein
Bad Windsheim
Neustadt an der Aisch
Ochsenfurt
Lauda-Königshofen
Tauberbischofsheim
Miltenberg
Walldürn
Rothenburg ob der Tauber
Ansbach
Alzey
Worms
Bensheim
Heppenheim
Mannheim
Heidelberg
Mosbach
Idar-Oberstein
Kirn
Rockenhausen
Kusel
Kaiserslautern
Lu-Ruchheim
Neustadt an der Weinstraße
Germersheim
Heilbronn
Öhringen
Künzelsau
Schwäbisch Hall
Gaildorf
Ellwangen (Jagst)
Feuchtwangen
Dinkelsbühl
Gunzenhausen
Weißenburg in Bayern
Roth
Hilpoltstein
Treuchtlingen
Eichstätt
Karlsruhe
Ka-Stutensee
Pforzheim
Murrhardt
Backnang
Ludwigsburg
Korntal-Münchingen
Leonberg
Stuttgart
Esslingen am Neckar
Sindelfingen
Böblingen
Gärtringen
Herrenberg
Nagold
Tübingen
Reutlingen
Metzingen
Göppingen
Schwäbisch Gmünd
Aalen
Nördlingen
Harburg
Heidenheim an der Brenz
Neuburg an der Donau
Rain
Schrobenhausen
Dillingen an der Donau
Langenau
Günzburg
Augsburg
Aichach
Friedberg
Stadtbergen
Bobingen
Mering
Ulm
Erbach
Ehingen
Weißenhorn
Laupheim
Biberach an der Riß
Krumbach
Schwabmünchen
Fürstenfeldbruck
Gilching
Mindelheim
Landsberg am Lech
Memmingen
Kaufbeuren
Baden-Baden
Freudenstadt
Mössingen
Münsingen
Hechingen
Burladingen
Balingen
Albstadt
Rottweil
Schramberg
Sigmaringen
Saulgau
Tuttlingen
Pfullendorf
Bad Waldsee
Stockach
Blumberg
Waldkirch
Teningen
Emmendingen
Freiburg im Breisgau
Bad Krozingen
Müllheim
Bitche
Reichshoffen
Haguenau
Saverne
Strasbourg
Sélestat
Colmar
Ensisheim
Westerwald
Sauerland
Rothaargebirge
Vogelsberg
Rhön
Hohe Rhön
Thüringer Wald
Hunsrück
Odenwald
Bauland
Taubergrund
Hohenloher Ebene
Frankenhöhe
Firngrund
Härtsfeld
Pfälzer Wald
Haardt
Schwarzwald
Schönbuch
Schwäbische Alb
Dün
Hainleite
Goldene Aue

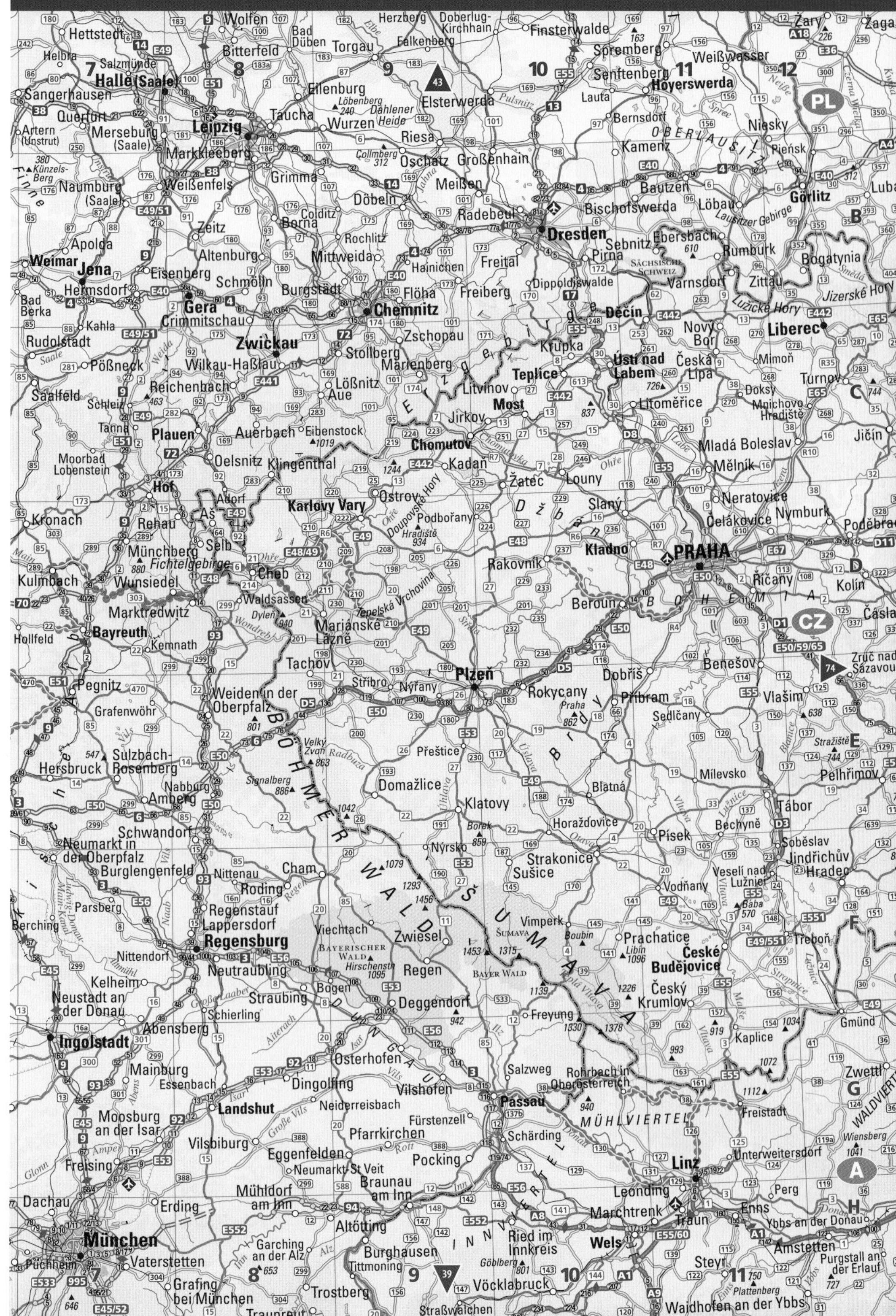
Hettstedt
Wolfen
Bad Düben
Torgau
Herzberg
Doberlug-Kirchhain
Finsterwalde
Żary
Żagań
Helbra
Salzmünde
Bitterfeld
Falkenberg
Spremberg
Weißwasser
Halle (Saale)
Eilenburg
Elsterwerda
Senftenberg
Hoyerswerda
Sangerhausen
Querfurt
Taucha
Löbenberg
Dahlener Heide
Lauta
Bernsdorf
PL
Artern (Unstrut)
Merseburg (Saale)
Leipzig
Wurzen
Riesa
Niesky
Markkleeberg
Collmberg
Oschatz
Großenhain
Kamenz
OBERLAUSITZ
Pieńsk
Naumburg (Saale)
Weißenfels
Grimma
Meißen
Bautzen
Görlitz
Luban
Colditz
Döbeln
Radebeul
Bischofswerda
Löbau
Lausitzer Gebirge
Zeitz
Borna
Rochlitz
Dresden
Sebnitz
Ebersbach
Rumburk
Apolda
Altenburg
Mittweida
Hainichen
Freital
Pirna
SÄCHSISCHE SCHWEIZ
Varnsdorf
Zittau
Bogatynia
Weimar
Jena
Eisenberg
Schmölln
Burgstädt
Dippoldiswalde
Hermsdorf
Gera
Flöha
Freiberg
Jizerské Hory
Bad Berka
Crimmitschau
Chemnitz
Děčín
Lužické Hory
Kahla
Zschopau
Nový Bor
Liberec
Rudolstadt
Zwickau
Stollberg
Krupka
Ústí nad Labem
Česká Lípa
Mimoň
Pößneck
Wilkau-Haßlau
Marienberg
Teplice
Turnov
Saalfeld
Reichenbach
Lößnitz
Aue
Litvínov
Most
Doksy
Mnichovo Hradiště
Schleiz
Jirkov
Litoměřice
Tanna
Plauen
Auerbach
Eibenstock
Chomutov
Jičín
Moorbad Lobenstein
Oelsnitz
Klingenthal
Kadaň
Mladá Boleslav
Žatec
Louny
Mělník
Hof
Adorf
Karlovy Vary
Ostrov
Slaný
Neratovice
Kronach
Rehau
Aš
Doupovské Hory
Podbořany
Hradiště
Čelákovice
Nymburk
Poděbrady
Selb
Münchberg
Fichtelgebirge
Kladno
PRAHA
Kulmbach
Wunsiedel
Cheb
Rakovník
Říčany
Kolín
Marktredwitz
Waldsassen
Tepelská Vrchovina
Beroun
BOHEMIA
Čáslav
Hollfeld
Bayreuth
Dyleň
Mariánské Lázně
CZ
Kemnath
Tachov
Zruč nad Sázavou
Benešov
Pegnitz
Weiden in der Oberpfalz
Stříbro
Nýřany
Plzeň
Rokycany
Dobříš
Příbram
Vlašim
Grafenwöhr
Praha
Brdy
Sedlčany
Sulzbach-Rosenberg
BÖHMER WALD
Velký Zvon
Radbuza
Přeštice
Stražiště
Hersbruck
Nabburg
Signalberg
Domažlice
Mílevsko
Pelhřimov
Amberg
Klatovy
Blatná
Tábor
Schwandorf
Borek
Horažďovice
Bechyně
Neumarkt in der Oberpfalz
Nýrsko
Písek
Soběslav
Burglengenfeld
Nittenau
Cham
Strakonice
Jindřichův Hradec
Sušice
Veselí nad Lužnicí
Roding
Vodňany
Parsberg
Regenstauf
ŠUMAVA
Bába
Lappersdorf
Viechtach
Vimperk
Berching
Regensburg
Zwiesel
Boubín
Prachatice
Třeboň
Nittendorf
BAYERISCHER WALD
Hirschenstein
Libín
České Budějovice
Neutraubling
Regen
BAYER WALD
Kelheim
Bogen
Český Krumlov
Neustadt an der Donau
Straubing
Deggendorf
Schierling
Freyung
Gmünd
Abensberg
Kaplice
Ingolstadt
Osterhofen
DUNGAU
Mainburg
Essenbach
Dingolfing
Vilshofen
Salzweg
Rohrbach in Oberösterreich
Zwettl
Landshut
Neiderreisbach
Passau
Freistadt
Moosburg an der Isar
Fürstenzell
MÜHLVIERTEL
WALDVIERTEL
Vilsbiburg
Pfarrkirchen
Schärding
Wiensberg
Eggenfelden
Pocking
Unterweitersdorf
Freising
Neumarkt-St Veit
A
Mühldorf am Inn
Braunau am Inn
Linz
Leonding
Perg
Dachau
Erding
Altötting
Marchtrenk
Enns
Traun
Ybbs an der Donau
München
Garching an der Alz
Ried im Innkreis
Wels
Amstetten
INNVIERTEL
Vaterstetten
Burghausen
Puchheim
Tittmoning
Göblberg
Steyr
Purgstall an der Erlauf
Grafing bei München
Trostberg
Vöcklabruck
Plattenberg
Waidhofen an der Ybbs
Gelting
Bruckmühl
Traunreut
Straßwalchen
Almünster
Gmunden
Traunstein

NORDSEE
Helgoländer Bucht
Nordfriesische Inseln
Halligen
Ostfriesische Inseln
Sylt
Föhr
Amrum
Pellworm
Nordstrand
Niebüll
Leck
Harrislee
Flensburg
Flensburg Fjord
Kappeln
Bagenkop
SCHWANSEN
Schleswig
Eckernförde
Kieler Förde
Kieler Bucht
Husum
Kropp
St Peter-Ording
SCHLESWIG-HOLSTEINISCHES WATTENMEER
Rendsburg
Kronshagen
Heikendorf
Kiel
Lütjenburg
Heide
Preetz
WAGRIEN
Malente
Eutin
Nortorf
Bordesholm
Plön
Büsum
Meldorf
Neumünster
HAMBURGISCHES WATTENMEER
Neuwerk
Marne
Brunsbüttel
Itzehoe
Bad Bramstedt
Ratekau
Lübeck
Cuxhaven
NIEDERSÄCHSISCHES WATTENMEER
Otterndorf
LAND HADELN
Glückstadt
Elmshorn
STORMARN
Bargteheide
Ratzeburg
Spiekeroog
Wangerooge
Langeoog
Norderney
Juist
Borkum
Nordholz
Mellum
LAND WURSTEN
Silberberg
LAND KEHDINGEN
Uetersen
Norderstedt
Mölln
Esens
Norden
Wittmund
Jever
Langen
Stade
Rellingen
Halstenbek
Trittau
Hamburg
Breitenfelde
NORDERLAND
HARLINGERLAND
Bremerhaven
BUTJADINGEN
Wedel (Holstein)
Schwarzenbek
Moordorf
Aurich
Hinte
Wilhelmshaven
Loxstedt
Bremervörde
Uithuizen
Wiesmoor
Zetel
Varel
Buxtehude
Geesthacht
Rosengarten
Seevetal
Boizenburg
Delfzijl
Emden
OSTFRIESLAND
Gnarrenburg
Groningen
AMMERLAND
Brake
Zeven
Tostedt
Lauenburg (Elbe)
Leer
Augustfehn
Apen
Rastede
TEUFELSMOOR
Winsen (Luhe)
Adendorf
Osterholz-Scharmbeck
Wilseder Berg
Lüneburg
Veendam
Weener
Oldenburg
Berne
Lemwerder
Scheeßel
Lilienthal
Rotenburg
Assen
Papenburg
Wardenburg
Bremen
Oyten
LÜNEBURGER HEIDE
Stadskanaal
Friesoythe
Bösel
Delmenhorst
Neuenkirchen
Musselkanaal
Achim
Soltau
Münster
NL
Garrel
Langwedel
Visselhövede
Uelzen
Sögel
Cloppenburg
Verden
D
Emmen
Haren
Bassum
Dörverden
Walsrode
Fallingbostel
Lüßberg
Twistringen
Bruchhausen-Vilsen
Bergen
Löningen
Bakum
Vechta
Coevorden
Meppen
Dinklage
Lohne
Barnstorf
Wittingen
Haselünne
Geeste
Quakenbrück
Sulingen
Winsen (Aller)
Twist
Celle
Diepholz
Steyerberg
Nienburg
Wietze
Neuenhaus
Lingen
Fürstenau
Damme
Stolzenau
Wathlingen
Vroomshoop
Uchte
Gifhorn
Nordhorn
Rahden
Garbsen
Uetze
Denekamp
Bramsche
Wunstorf
Wolfsburg
Almelo
Emsbüren
Recke
Bohmte
Hannover
Lehrte
Edemissen
Hopsten
Lübbecke
Ronnenberg
Hengelo
Osnabrück
Minden
Lehre
Enschede
Rheine
Wiehengebirge
Pattensen
Braunschweig
Neuenkirchen
Bissendorf
Bückeburg
Haaksbergen
Harsum
Salzgitter
Wolfenbüttel
Steinfurt
Springe
Ahaus
Greven
Herford
Weser
Glandorf
Hildesheim
Vreden
Bielefeld
Bad Salzuflen
Hameln
Thüster Berg
Schöppenstedt
Lemgo
Lage
Gescher
Nottuln
Münster
Teutoburger Wald
Barntrup
Bockenem
MÜNSTERLAND
Detmold
Alfeld (Leine)
Velen
Goslar
Bocholt
Ennigerloh
Gütersloh
Blomberg
Raesfeld
SENNE
Steinheim
Holzminden
Einbeck
Wernigerode
Lüdinghausen
Ahlen
Hamminkeln
Bad Lippspringe
Brocken
HOCHHARZ
Wesel
Haltern
Werne
Beckum
Paderborn
Höxter
Dassel
Marl
Hamm
Lippstadt
Solling
Northeim
HARZ
Dorsten
Herten
Recklinghausen
OBERWÄLDER LAND
Beverungen
Gladbeck
HOCHFLÄCHE
Uslar
Bottrop
Gelsenkirchen
Soest
Kamen
Unna
Eggegebirge
Bad Lauterberg im Harz
Ellrich
Essen
Dortmund
Rüthen
Diemel
Göttingen
Nordhausen
Bochum
Menden
Warstein
Marsberg
Hofgeismar
Schwerte
Arnsberg
Rosdorf
Iserlohn
Brilon
Arolsen
Hagen
Olsberg
Wolfhagen
Velbert
Wuppertal
Kassel
Kaufungen
Dün
Hainich
Düsseldorf
Korbach
Kassel-Baunatal
Bad Sooden-Allendorf
Unstrut
Mühlhausen (Thüringen)
SAUERLAND
Eslohe
Hilden
Remscheid
Winterberg
Sand
Eschwege
Rothaargebirge
Traddelkopf
Hessisch Lichtenau
Meinerzhagen
Leverkusen
Bad Wildungen

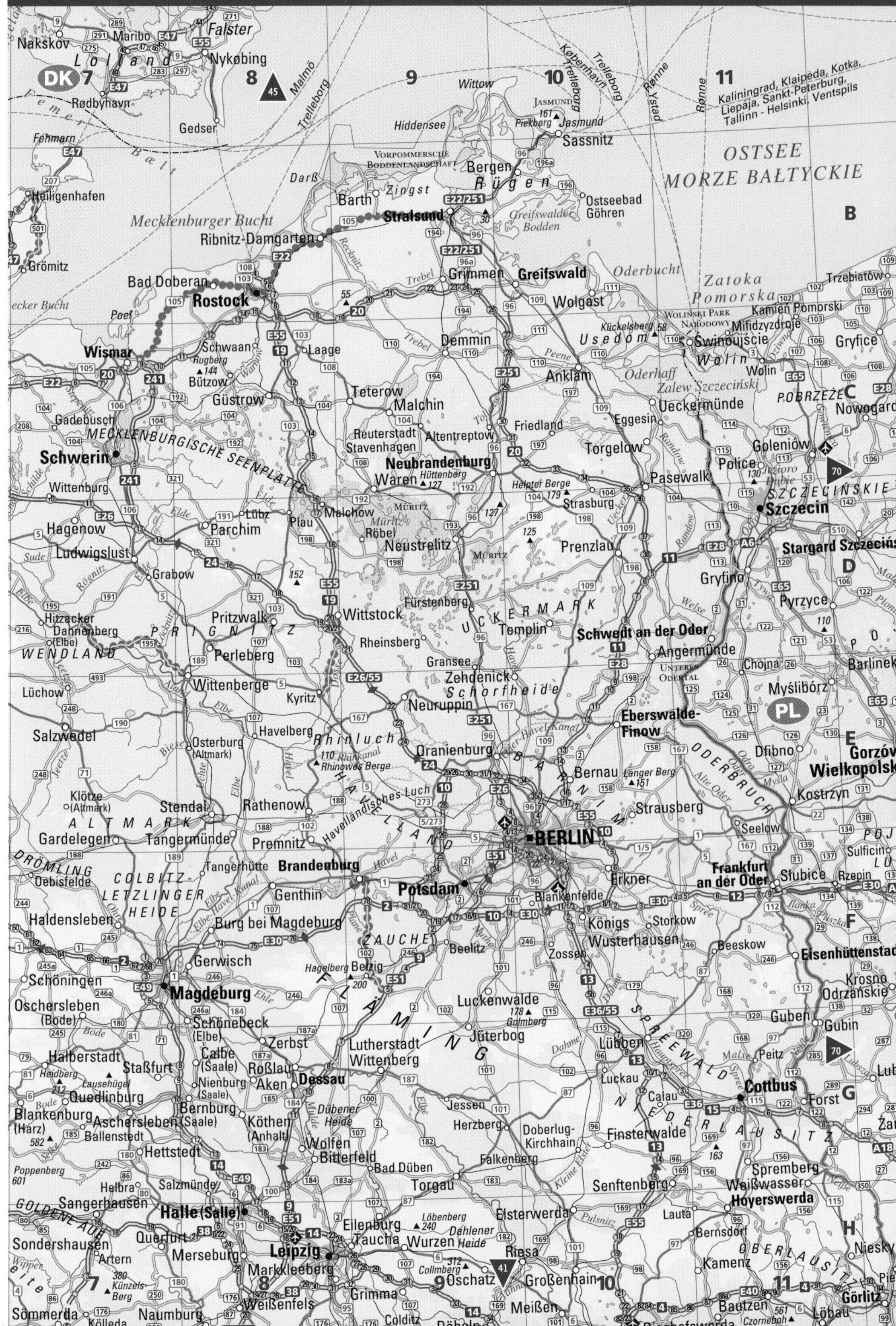
Nakskov
Maribo
Falster
Lolland
Nykøbing
Rødbyhavn
Gedser
Fehmarn
Heiligenhafen
Grömitz
Mecklenburger Bucht
Wittow
Hiddensee
Jasmund
Sassnitz
OSTSEE
MORZE BAŁTYCKIE
Vorpommersche Boddenlandschaft
Bergen
Rügen
Darß
Zingst
Barth
Stralsund
Ostseebad Göhren
Greifswalder Bodden
Ribnitz-Damgarten
Bad Doberan
Rostock
Poel
Wismar
Grimmen
Greifswald
Wolgast
Oderbucht
Zatoka Pomorska
Usedom
Świnoujście
Wolin
Międzyzdroje
Kamień Pomorski
Trzebiatów
Gryfice
Schwaan
Laage
Demmin
Anklam
Bützow
Güstrow
Teterow
Malchin
Oderhaff
Zalew Szczeciński
Ueckermünde
Nowogard
Gadebusch
Schwerin
Mecklenburgische Seenplatte
Reuterstadt Stavenhagen
Altentreptow
Friedland
Eggesin
Torgelow
Goleniów
Police
Neubrandenburg
Waren
Pasewalk
Szczecin
Wittenburg
Malchow
Müritz
Strasburg
Hagenow
Parchim
Plau
Röbel
Neustrelitz
Prenzlau
Stargard Szczeciński
Ludwigslust
Grabow
Gryfino
Pyrzyce
Wittstock
Fürstenberg
Uckermark
Templin
Schwedt an der Oder
Hitzacker
Dannenberg (Elbe)
Prignitz
Pritzwalk
Wendland
Perleberg
Rheinsberg
Angermünde
Barlinek
Wittenberge
Kyritz
Gransee
Zehdenick
Schorfheide
Chojna
Myślibórz
Lüchow
Salzwedel
Neuruppin
Eberswalde-Finow
Havelberg
Rhinluch
Oranienburg
Barnim
Oderbruch
Gorzów Wielkopolski
Osterburg (Altmark)
Bernau
Strausberg
Dębno
Klötze (Altmark)
Stendal
Rathenow
Havelland
Kostrzyn
Altmark
Gardelegen
Tangermünde
Premnitz
BERLIN
Seelow
Drömling
Oebisfelde
Colbitz-Letzlinger Heide
Tangerhütte
Brandenburg
Potsdam
Erkner
Frankfurt an der Oder
Słubice
Genthin
Blankenfelde
Haldensleben
Burg bei Magdeburg
Zauche
Königs Wusterhausen
Storkow
Beelitz
Zossen
Beeskow
Eisenhüttenstadt
Gerwisch
Schöningen
Magdeburg
Belzig
Fläming
Luckenwalde
Krosno Odrzańskie
Oschersleben (Bode)
Schönebeck (Elbe)
Guben
Gubin
Zerbst
Jüterbog
Halberstadt
Staßfurt
Calbe (Saale)
Roßlau
Lutherstadt Wittenberg
Lübben
Spreewald
Peitz
Quedlinburg
Nienburg (Saale)
Aken
Dessau
Luckau
Calau
Cottbus
Forst
Blankenburg (Harz)
Aschersleben
Bernburg (Saale)
Köthen (Anhalt)
Dübener Heide
Jessen
Herzberg
Doberlug-Kirchhain
Finsterwalde
Niederlausitz
Żary
Ballenstedt
Hettstedt
Wolfen
Bitterfeld
Falkenberg
Bad Düben
Torgau
Senftenberg
Spremberg
Weißwasser
Hoyerswerda
Helbra
Salzmünde
Sangerhausen
Halle (Saale)
Elsterwerda
Lauta
Bernsdorf
Goldene Aue
Sondershausen
Querfurt
Eilenburg
Taucha
Wurzen
Dahlener Heide
Riesa
Oberlausitz
Niesky
Artern
Merseburg
Leipzig
Markkleeberg
Oschatz
Großenhain
Kamenz
Grimma
Weißenfels
Meißen
Bautzen
Görlitz
Sömmerda
Kölleda
Naumburg
Colditz
Döbeln
Radebeul
Bischofswerda
Löbau
Dresden
Borna
DK
PL
Kaliningrad, Klaipėda, Kotka, Liepāja, Sankt-Peterburg, Tallinn - Helsinki, Ventspils

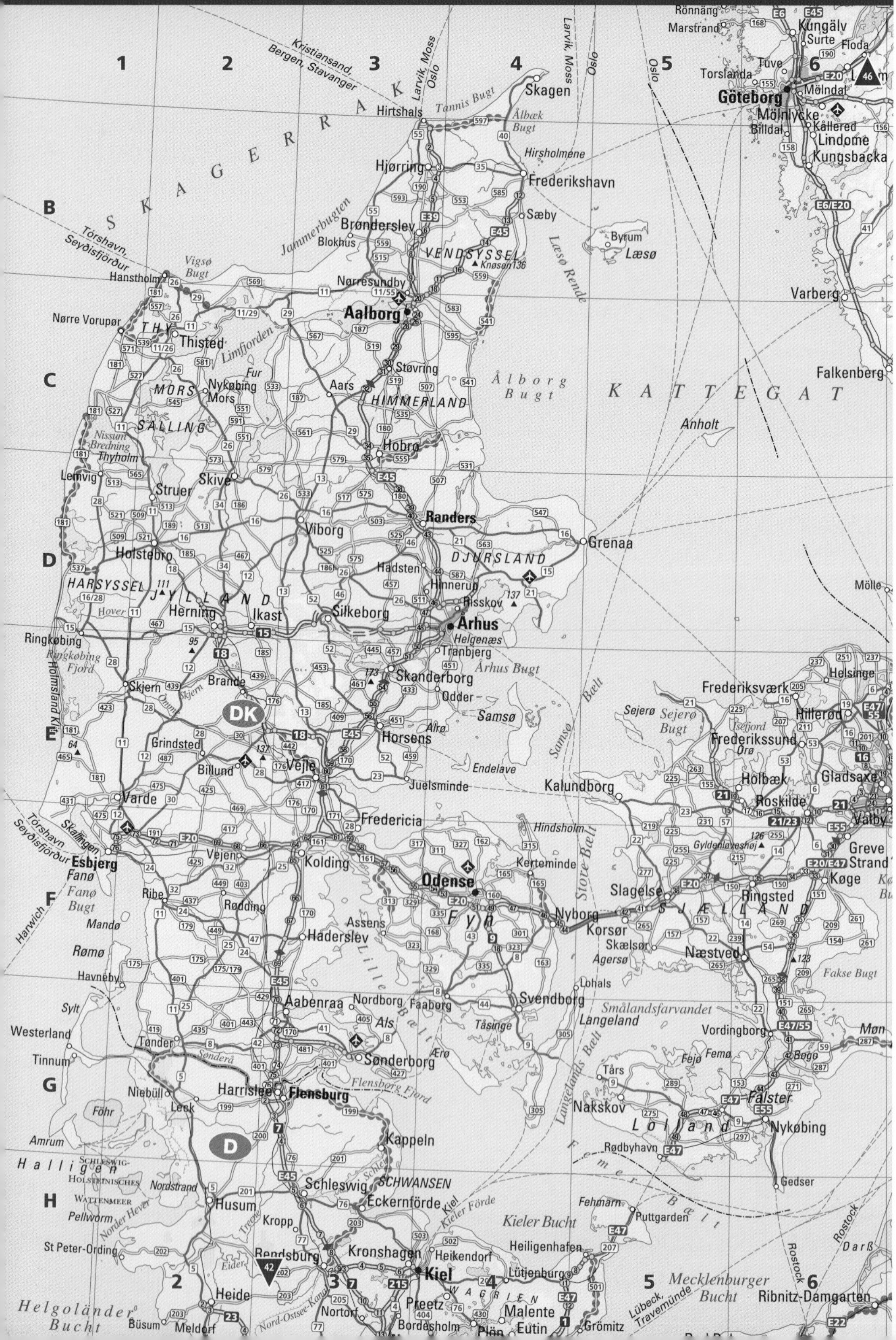

1 2 3 4 5 6

Rönnäng
Marstrand
Kungälv
Surte
Floda
Kristiansand, Bergen, Stavanger
Larvik, Moss Oslo
Larvik, Moss
Oslo
Oslo
Torslanda
Tuve
Skagen
Göteborg
Mölndal
S K A G E R R A K
Hirtshals
Tannis Bugt
Ålbæk Bugt
Mölnlycke
Billdal
Kållered
Lindome
Kungsbacka
Hirsholmene
Hjørring
Frederikshavn
B
Jammerbugten
Sæby
Brønderslev
Blokhus
Byrum
Læsø
Læsø Rende
Tórshavn, Seyðisfjörður
Vigsø Bugt
VENDSYSSEL
Knøsen 136
Hanstholm
Nørresundby
Varberg
Aalborg
Nørre Vorupør
THY
Thisted
Limfjorden
C
Fur
MORS
Nykøbing Mors
Aars
Støvring
Ålborg Bugt
K A T T E G A T
Falkenberg
HIMMERLAND
SALLING
Nissum Bredning
Anholt
Thyholm
Hobro
Lemvig
Struer
Skive
Randers
Viborg
Grenaa
D
Holstebro
DJURSLAND
Hadsten
HARSYSSEL
111
JYLLAND
Hinnerup
Risskov
137
Mölle
Herning
Ikast
Hover
Silkeborg
Århus
Ringkøbing
95
Helgenæs
Ringkøbing Fjord
Tranbjerg
Århus Bugt
Holmsland Klit
173
Skanderborg
Helsinge
Skjern
Brande
Odder
Frederiksværk
Skjern Å
DK
Samsø
Sejerø
Sejerø Bugt
Samsø Bælt
Hillerød
E
Grindsted
137
Horsens
Alrø
Isefjord
Frederikssund
64
Orø
Vejle
Billund
Endelave
Holbæk
Gladsaxe
Juelsminde
Kalundborg
Roskilde
Varde
Valby
Fredericia
Tórshavn Seyðisfjörður
Skallingen
Hindsholm
126
Gyldenløveshøj
Greve Strand
Esbjerg
Vejen
Kolding
Kerteminde
Fanø
Odense
Køge
Køge Bugt
F
Fanø Bugt
Ribe
Store Bælt
Slagelse
Ringsted
Rødding
Nyborg
SJÆLLAND
Harwich
Fyn
Korsør
Mandø
Assens
Haderslev
Skælskør
Agersø
Næstved
Rømø
Lille Bælt
123
Fakse Bugt
Havneby
Lohals
Sylt
Aabenraa
Nordborg
Faaborg
Svendborg
Smålandsfarvandet
Langeland
Westerland
Tåsinge
Vordingborg
Møn
Als
Tønder
Ærø
Tinnum
Sønderå
Sønderborg
Fejø
Femø
Bogø
G
Flensborg Fjord
Tårs
Langelands Bælt
Niebüll
Harrislee
Flensburg
Falster
Leck
Nakskov
Föhr
Lolland
Nykøbing
Kappeln
Amrum
D
Rødbyhavn
Femer Bælt
Halligen
Schleswig-Holsteinisches Wattenmeer
Nordstrand
Schleswig
SCHWANSEN
Gedser
H
Husum
Eckernförde
Kiel
Kieler Förde
Fehmarn
Puttgarden
Pellworm
Norder Hever
Kropp
Kieler Bucht
Treene
Rostock
St Peter-Ording
Kronshagen
Heikendorf
Heiligenhafen
Rendsburg
Darß
Eider
42
Kiel
Lütjenburg
2
3
4
5
Mecklenburger Bucht
6
Heide
WAGRIEN
Lübeck, Travemünde
Ribnitz-Damgarten
Preetz
Nord-Ostsee-Kanal
Helgoländer Bucht
Nortorf
Malente
Büsum
Meldorf
Bordesholm
Plön
Eutin
Grömitz

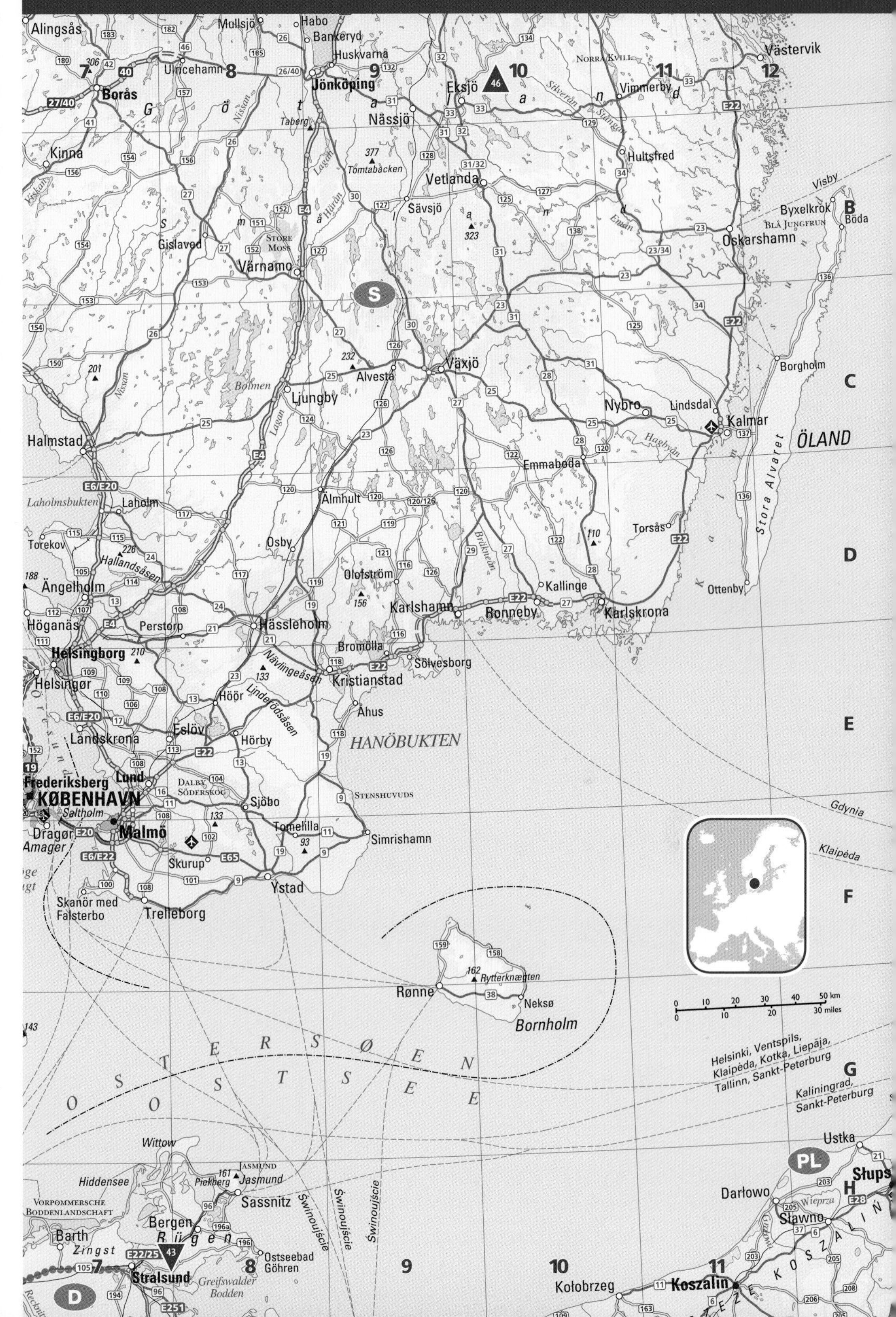

Alingsås
Borås
Ulricehamn
Jönköping
Huskvarna
Bankeryd
Habo
Mullsjö
Eksjö
Nässjö
Vimmerby
Västervik
Hultsfred
Vetlanda
Sävsjö
Tomtabacken
Taberg
Kinna
Gislaved
Värnamo
Store Mosse
Oskarshamn
Byxelkrok
Böda
Blå Jungfrun
Visby
Växjö
Alvesta
Ljungby
Bolmen
Halmstad
Laholmsbukten
Laholm
Torekov
Hallandsåsen
Ängelholm
Höganäs
Helsingborg
Helsingør
Perstorp
Hässleholm
Älmhult
Osby
Olofström
Karlshamn
Ronneby
Kallinge
Karlskrona
Nybro
Lindsdal
Kalmar
Emmaboda
Torsås
Ottenby
Borgholm
Öland
Stora Alvaret
Bromölla
Sölvesborg
Kristianstad
Nävlingeåsen
Linderödsåsen
Åhus
Hanöbukten
Höör
Hörby
Eslöv
Landskrona
Lund
Frederiksberg
København
Saltholm
Dragør
Amager
Malmö
Dalby Söderskog
Sjöbo
Stenshuvuds
Tomelilla
Simrishamn
Skurup
Ystad
Trelleborg
Skanör med Falsterbo
Rønne
Rytterknægten
Nekső
Bornholm
Østersøen
Ostsee
Gdynia
Klaipėda
Helsinki, Ventspils, Klaipėda, Kotka, Liepāja, Tallinn, Sankt-Peterburg
Kaliningrad, Sankt-Peterburg
Ustka
Słupsk
Darłowo
Sławno
Wieprza
Koszalin
Kołobrzeg
Wittow
Hiddensee
Jasmund
Piekberg
Sassnitz
Vorpommersche Boddenlandschaft
Bergen
Rügen
Barth
Zingst
Stralsund
Greifswalder Bodden
Ostseebad Göhren
Świnoujście
S
DK
D
PL
0 10 20 30 40 50 km
0 10 20 30 miles

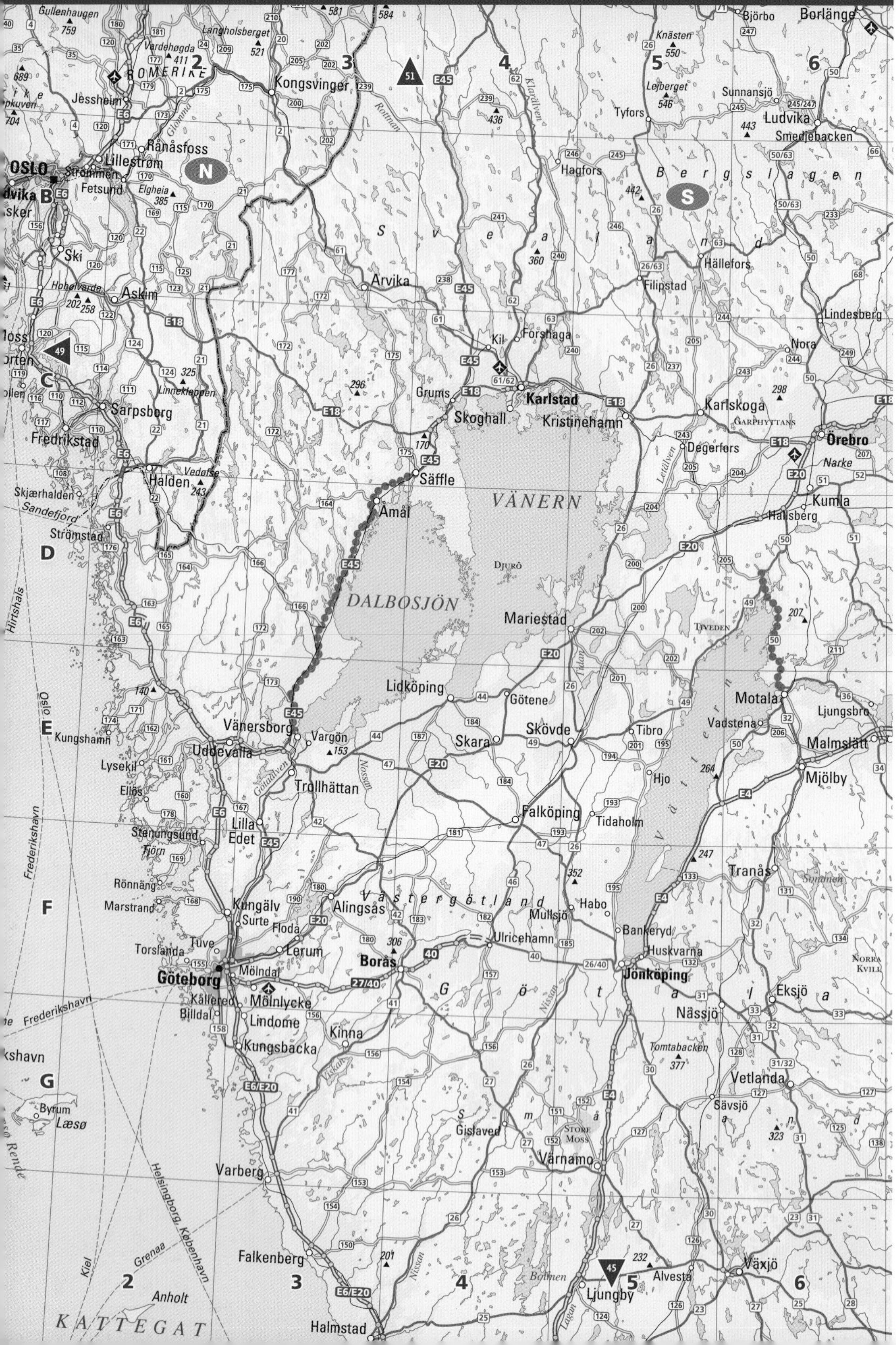

Gullenhaugen 759
Langholsberget 521
Vardehøgda 411
ROMERIKE
Kongsvinger
Klarälven
Knästen 550
Björbo
Borlänge
Jessheim
Glomma
Rottnan
Lejberget 546
Tyfors
Sunnansjö
Ludvika
Smedjebacken
Rånåsfoss
Lillestrøm
OSLO
Strømmen
Fetsund
Elgheia 385
N
Hagfors
Bergslagen
S
Ski
Svealand
Hällefors
Hobølvarde 202 258
Askim
Arvika
Filipstad
Lindesberg
Kil
Forshaga
Nora
Linnekleppen 325
Karlstad
Grums
Skoghall
Kristinehamn
Karlskoga
Garphyttans
Sarpsborg
Fredrikstad
Degerfors
Letälven
Örebro
Narke
Halden
Vedafjell 243
Säffle
Skjærhalden
Sandefjord
Strömstad
Åmål
VÄNERN
Kumla
Hallsberg
D
Djurö
DALBOSJÖN
Hirtshals
Mariestad
Tiveden
Lidköping
Götene
Motala
Ljungsbro
Oslo
E
Kungshamn
Vänersborg
Vargön
Skara
Skövde
Tibro
Vadstena
Malmslätt
Uddevalla
Lysekil
Ellös
Trollhättan
Götaälven
Nossan
Hjo
Mjölby
Vättern
Frederikshavn
Stenungsund
Tjörn
Lilla Edet
Falköping
Tidaholm
Rönnäng
Marstrand
F
Kungälv
Surte
Alingsås
Västergötland
Mullsjö
Habo
Tranås
Sommen
Bankeryd
Torslanda
Tuve
Floda
Lerum
Borås
Ulricehamn
Huskvarna
Göteborg
Mölndal
Jönköping
Norra Kvill
Kållered
Mölnlycke
Billdal
Lindome
Frederikshavn
Götaland
Eksjö
Nässjö
Kinna
Kungsbacka
Tomtabacken 377
G
Byrum
Læsø
Vetlanda
Sävsjö
Småland
Gislaved
Store Moss
Värnamo
Varberg
Helsingborg, København
Kiel
Grenaa
Falkenberg
Nissan
Bolmen
Alvesta
Växjö
Ljungby
Lagan
2
3
4
5
6
Anholt
KATTEGAT
Halmstad

STOCKHOLM
Uppsala
Västerås
Eskilstuna
Södertälje
Norrköping
Linköping
Nyköping
Oxelösund
Norrtälje
Kapellskär
Furusund
Nynäshamn
Visby
GOTLAND
ÖLAND
Åland
Mariehamn
Södra Kvarken
Ålands Hav
Östersjön
Gotska Sandön
Helsinki, Tallinn
Paldiski
Riga
Ventspils
Gdansk
Naantali, Turku
Oskarshamn
Västervik
Fårösund
Ljugarn
Burgsvik
Borgholm
Lindsdal
Köping
Arboga
Fagersta
Avesta
Hedemora
Sala
Enköping
Strängnäs
Katrineholm
Finspång
Söderköping
Åtvidaberg
Vimmerby
Hultsfred
Tierp
Forsmark
Grisslehamn
Märsta
Täby
Lidingö
Åkersberga
Vallentuna
Tumba
Västerhaninge
Saltsjöbaden
Trosa
Flen
Arkösund
Gryt
Loftahammar
Gamleby
Byxelkrok
Böda
Lärbro
Ala
0 10 20 30 40 50 km
0 10 20 30 miles

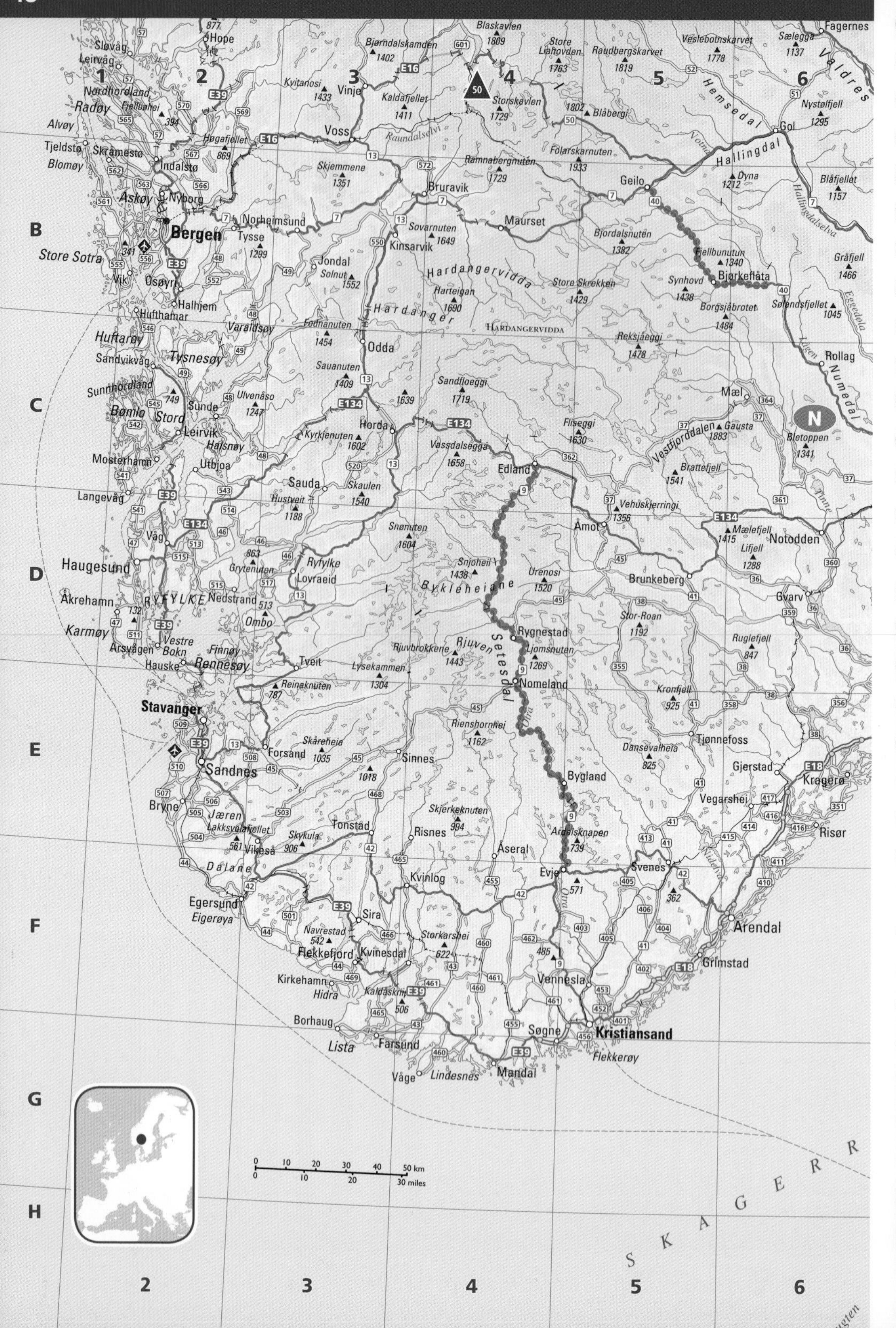
Fagernes
Valdres
Hemsedal
Hallingdal
Gol
Geilo
Voss
Vinje
Hope
Sløvåg
Leirvåg
Nordhordland
Radøy
Alvøy
Tjeldstø
Skråmestø
Blomøy
Indalstø
Askøy
Nyborg
Bergen
Store Sotra
Norheimsund
Tysse
Bruravik
Maurset
Kinsarvik
Jondal
Hardangervidda
Hardanger
Osøyri
Halhjem
Hufthamar
Huftarøy
Varaldsøy
Odda
Sandvikvåg
Tysnesøy
Sunnhordland
Bømlo
Stord
Sunde
Leirvik
Halsnøy
Mosterhamn
Utbjoa
Langevåg
Horda
Sauda
Våg
Haugesund
Ryfylke
Lovraeid
Nedstrand
Ombo
Åkrehamn
Karmøy
Vestre Bokn
Finnøy
Arsvågen
Hauske
Rennesøy
Tveit
Stavanger
Forsand
Sandnes
Sinnes
Bryne
Jæren
Vikeså
Dalane
Tonstad
Egersund
Eigerøya
Sira
Flekkefjord
Kvinesdal
Kirkehamn
Hidra
Borhaug
Lista
Farsund
Våge
Lindesnes
Mandal
Søgne
Kristiansand
Flekkerøy
Vennesla
Evje
Åseral
Kvinlog
Risnes
Bygland
Nomeland
Rygnestad
Setesdal
Bykleheiane
Edland
Åmot
Brunkeberg
Notodden
Gvarv
Tjønnefoss
Gjerstad
Kragerø
Vegarshei
Risør
Svenes
Arendal
Grimstad
Rollag
Numedal
Mæl
Vestfjorddalen
Gausta 1883
Bjørkeflåta
Hardangervidda
Skagerrak
50 km
30 miles

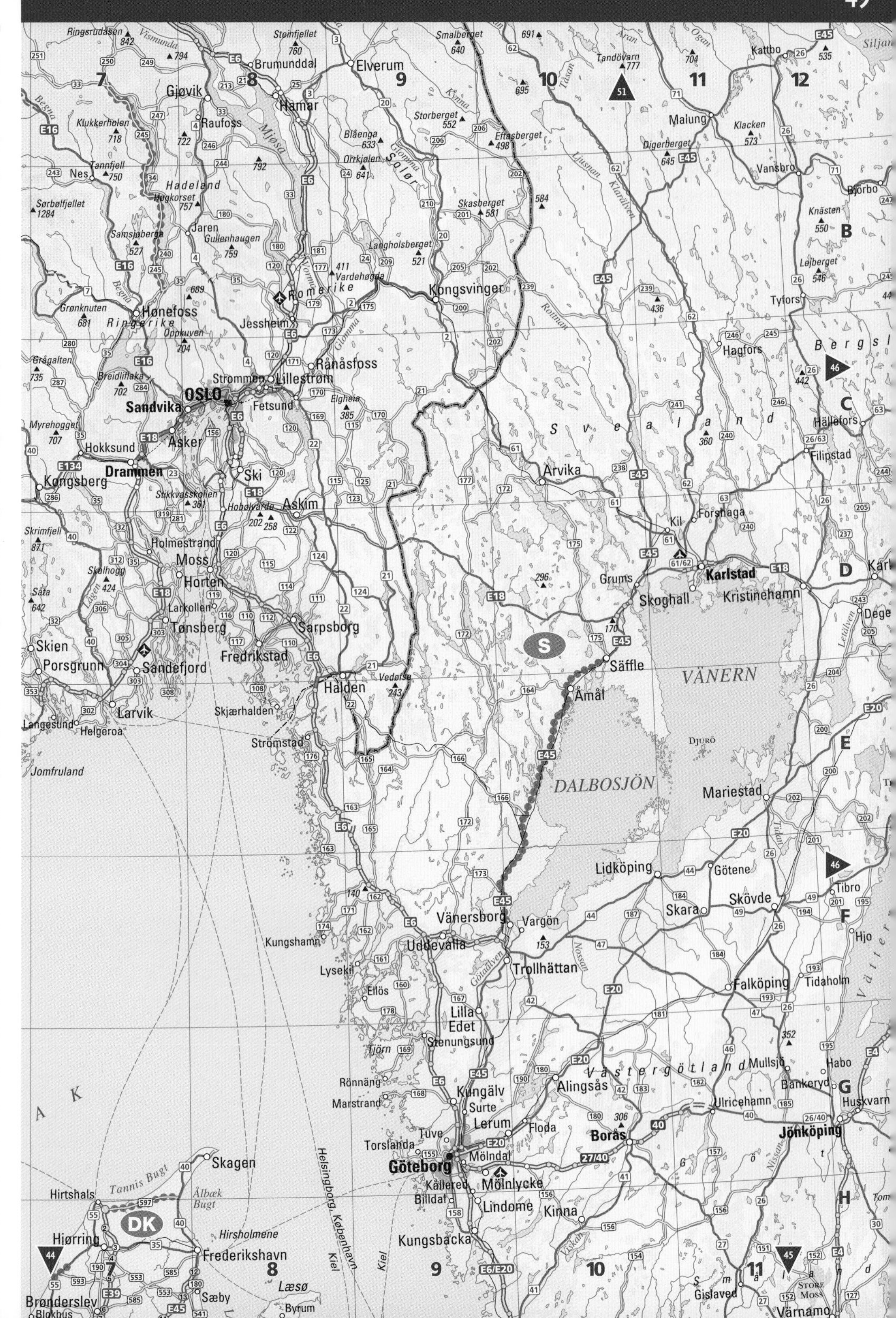
Ringsrudåsen
842
Vismunda
Steinfjellet
760
Smalberget
640
691
Tandövarn
777
704
Kattbo
535
Siljan
7
8
9
10
11
12
Gjøvik
Brumunddal
Elverum
Hamar
Raufoss
Mjøsa
Klukkerholen
718
722
792
Blåenga
633
Orrkjølen
641
Glomma
Solør
Storberget
552
Eftasberget
498
Malung
Klacken
573
Digerberget
645
Tannfjell
750
Nes
Hadeland
Høgkorset
757
Sørbølfjellet
1284
Skasberget
581
584
Vansbro
Björbo
Knästen
550
B
Jaren
Gullenhaugen
759
Samsjøberga
527
Langholsberget
521
411
Vardehøgda
Romerike
Kongsvinger
Lejberget
546
Tyfors
Grønknuten
681
Hønefoss
Ringerike
Oppkuven
704
Jessheim
436
Hagfors
Bergsl
Rånåsfoss
Lillestrøm
Strømmen
Grågalten
735
Breidliflaka
702
OSLO
Sandvika
Fetsund
Elgheia
385
442
C
Hällefors
Myrehogget
707
Asker
Hokksund
Drammen
Ski
Svealand
360
Filipstad
Kongsberg
Stikkvasskollen
361
Askim
Hobølvarda
202
258
Arvika
Skrimfjell
871
Holmestrand
Moss
Horten
Kil
Forshaga
Skalhogg
424
Såta
642
Larkollen
296
Grums
Karlstad
Skoghall
Kristinehamn
D
Karl
Dege
Tønsberg
Sarpsborg
Skien
Porsgrunn
Sandefjord
Fredrikstad
170
Säffle
Halden
Vedøise
243
Åmål
VÄNERN
Larvik
Langesund
Helgeroa
Skjærhalden
Strömstad
Djurö
E
Jomfruland
DALBOSJÖN
Mariestad
Lidköping
Götene
Tibro
140
Skara
Skövde
F
Vänersborg
Vargön
153
Hjo
Kungshamn
Uddevalla
Trollhättan
Lysekil
Falköping
Tidaholm
Ellös
Lilla Edet
352
Tjörn
Stenungsund
Västergötland
Mullsjö
Habo
Rönnäng
Kungälv
Alingsås
Bankeryd
G
Marstrand
Surte
Lerum
Floda
306
Ulricehamn
Huskvarn
Tuve
Torslanda
Borås
Jönköping
Skagen
Göteborg
Mölndal
Tannis Bugt
Hirtshals
Ålbæk Bugt
Kållered
Mölnlycke
Billdal
Lindome
Kinna
H
DK
Hirsholmene
Hjørring
Frederikshavn
Kungsbacka
Helsingborg, København
Kiel
8
9
10
11
Læsø
Brønderslev
Blokhus
Sæby
Byrum
Gislaved
Värnamo
Store Mosse
Småland
Vättern

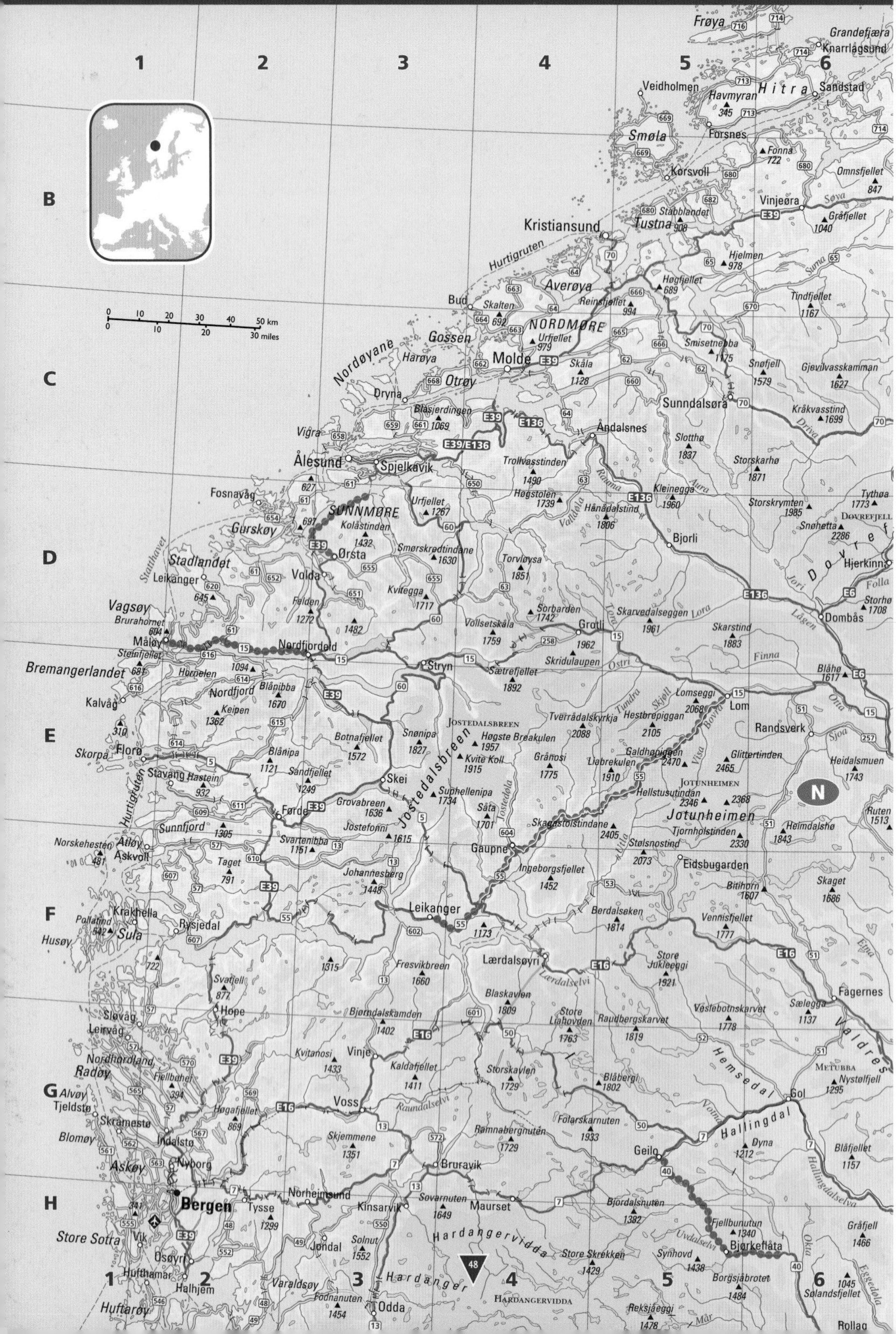

1 2 3 4 5 6

B C D E F G H

0 10 20 30 40 50 km
0 10 20 30 miles

Frøya
Grandefjæra
Knarrlagsund
Veidholmen
Havmyran 345
Hitra
Sandstad
Smøla
Forsnes
Fonna 722
Korsvoll
Omnsfjellet 847
Kristiansund
Stabblandet
Tustna 908
Vinjeøra
Søya
Gråfjellet 1040
Hurtigruten
Hjelmen 978
Averøya
Høgfjellet 689
Bud
Skalten 692
Reinsfjellet 994
Tindfjellet 1167
NORDMØRE
Urfjellet 979
Smisetnebba 1175
Nordøyane
Gossen
Harøya
Molde
Skåla 1128
Snøfjell 1579
Gjevilvasskamman 1627
Otrøy
Dryna
Sunndalsøra
Kråkvasstind 1699
Blåsjerdingen 1069
Driva
Vigra
Åndalsnes
Slotthø 1837
Ålesund
Spjelkavik
Trollvasstinden 1490
Storskarhø 1871
627
Høgstolen 1739
Rauma
Aura
Fosnavåg
Urfjellet 1267
Kleinegga 1960
Tythøa 1773
SUNNMØRE
Hånådalstind 1806
Storskrymten 1985
Gurskøy
697
Kolåstinden 1432
Valldøla
Snøhetta 2286
DOVREFJELL
Statthavet
Ørsta
Bjorli
Stadlandet
Smørskredtindane 1630
Dovre
Hjerkinn
Leikanger
Volda
Torvløysa 1851
Jori
Folla
645
Kvitegga 1717
Vagsøy
Felden 1272
Sorbarden 1742
Skarvedalseggen 1961
Lora
Storhø 1708
Brurahornet 604
1482
Vollsetskåla 1759
Grotli
Skarstind 1883
Dombås
Lågen
Måløy
Nordfjordeid
1962
Steinfjellet 681
Hornelen 1094
Stryn
Skridulaupen
Ostri
Finna
Bremangerlandet
Sætrefjellet 1892
Blåhø 1617
Nordfjord
Blånibba 1670
Tundra
Skjøll
Lomseggi 2068
Lom
Otta
Kalvåg
Keipen 1362
JOSTEDALSBREEN
Tverrådalskyrkja 2088
Hestbrepiggan 2105
Randsverk
Sjoa
310
Botnafjellet 1572
Snønipa 1827
Høgste Breakulen 1957
Galdhøpiggen 2470
Glittertinden 2465
Skorpa
Florø
Blånipa 1121
Jostedalsbreen
Kvite Koll 1915
Grånosi 1775
Ljabrekulen 1910
Visa
Bøvra
Heidalsmuen 1743
Stavang
Hastein 932
Sandfjellet 1249
Skei
Suphellenipa 1734
JOTUNHEIMEN
Hellstusutindan 2346
2368
N
Hurtigruten
Grovabreen 1636
Førde
Såta 1701
Jostedøla
Jotunheimen
Ruten 1513
Sunnfjord 1305
Jostefonni 1615
Skagastølstindane 2405
Tjornholstinden 2330
Heimdalshø 1843
Norskehesten 481
Atløy
Askvoll
Svartenibba 1151
Gaupne
Stølsnostind 2073
Utla
Taget 791
Johannesberg 1448
Ingeborgsfjellet 1452
Eidsbugarden
Bitihorn 1607
Skaget 1686
Krakhella
Pallatind 542
Sula
Rysjedal
Leikanger
Berdalseken 1814
Vennisfjellet 1777
Husøy
1173
Lærdalsøyri
Etna
722
1315
Fresvikbreen 1660
Store Jukleeggi 1921
Lærdalselvi
Svatjell 877
Blaskavlen 1809
Fagernes
Hope
Sløvåg
Bjørndalskamden 1402
Store Liahovden 1763
Raudbergskarvet 1819
Veslebotnskarvet 1778
Sælegga 1137
Leirvåg
Valdres
Nordhordland
Radøy
Kvitanosi 1433
Vinje
Hemsedal
Fjellbuher 394
Kaldafjellet 1411
Storskavlen 1729
Blåbergi 1802
METUBBA
Nystølfjell 1295
Alvøy
Tjeldstø
Høgafjellet 869
Voss
Raundalselvi
Gol
Skråmestø
Folarskarnuten 1933
Hallingdal
Blomøy
Indalstø
Skjemmene 1351
Ramnabergnuten 1729
Geilo
Øyna 1212
Blåfjellet 1157
Askøy
Nyborg
Bruravik
Hallingdalselva
Bergen
Tysse 1299
Norheimsund
Kinsarvik
Sovarnuten 1649
Maurset
Bjordalsnuten 1382
Fjellbunutun 1340
Store Sotra
Vik
Jondal
Solnut 1552
Hardangervidda
Store Skrekken 1429
Uvdalselvi
Synhovd 1438
Bjørkeflåta
Gråfjell 1466
Osøyri
48
Hufthamar
Halhjem
Varaldsøy
Hardanger
Borgsjåbrotet 1484
1045 Sølandsfjellet
Okta
Eggedøla
Fodnanuten 1454
Odda
HARDANGERVIDDA
Huftarøy
Reksjåeggi 1478
Mår
Rollag

1 2 3 4 5 6

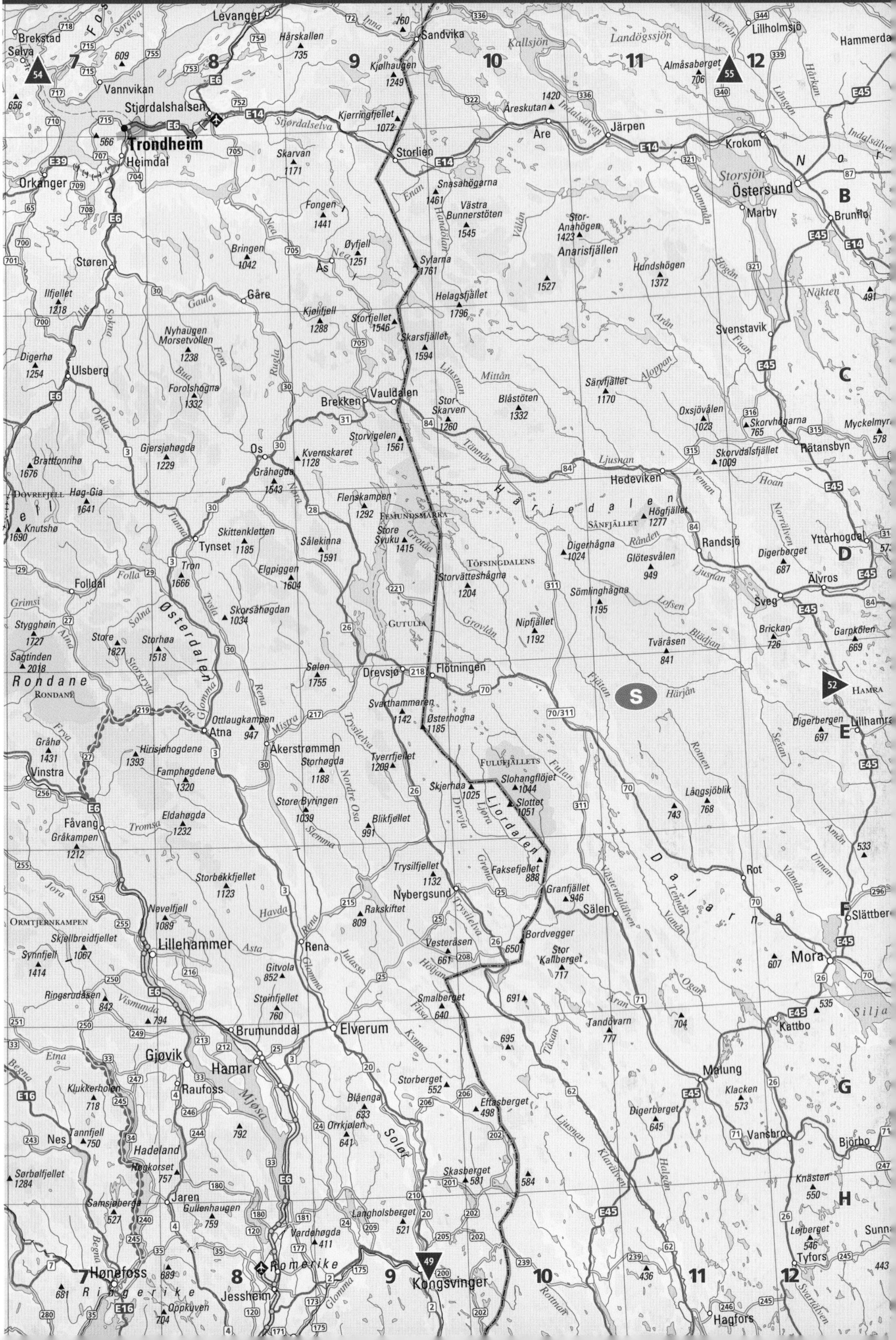

Brekstad
Selva
54
7
Fos
Sørelva
609
Levanger
8
Hårskallen 735
9
Inna
760
Sandvika
10
Kallsjön
Landögssjön
11
Almåsaberget 706
55
12
Lillholmsjö
Hammerdal
Åkerån
Kjølhaugen 1249
Vannvikan
656
Stjørdalshalsen
Kjerringfjellet 1072
Stjørdalselva
1420
Åreskutan
Indalsälven
Järpen
Åre
Krokom
Indalsälven
Trondheim
566
Heimdal
Orkanger
Skarvan 1171
Storlien
Storsjön
Östersund
N o r
B
Enan
Snasahögarna 1461
Västra Bunnerstöten 1545
Fongen 1441
Marby
Brunflo
Handölan
Vålån
Stor-Anahögen 1423
Anarisfjällen
Dammån
Bringen 1042
Nea
Øyfjell 1251
Ås
Støren
Sylarna 1761
Hundshögen 1372
Höggån
1527
Nälden
491
Gåre
Gaula
Helagsfjället 1796
Ilfjellet 1218
Kjølifjell 1288
Storfjellet 1546
Skarsfjället 1594
Svenstavik
Arån
Fuan
Nyhaugen Morsetvollen 1238
Sokna
Fora
Rugla
Digerhø 1254
Ulsberg
Bua
Forolshogna 1332
Ljusnan
Mittån
Aloppan
Särvfjället 1170
C
Brekken
Vauldalen
Stor-Skarven 1260
Blåstöten 1332
Oxsjövålen 1023
Skorvhögarna 765
Myckelmyr 578
Orkla
Storvigelen 1561
Tännån
Gjersjøhøgda 1229
Os
Kvernskaret 1128
Brattfonnhø 1676
Gråhøgda 1543
Ljusnan
Hedeviken
Skorvdalsfjället 1009
Rätansbyn
Hoan
Dovrefjell
Høg-Gia 1641
Flenskampen 1292
Femundsmarka
H ä r j e d a l e n
Sånfjället
Högfjället 1277
Veman
Norrälven
Knutshø 1690
Tunna
Tynset
Skittenkletten 1185
Sålekinna 1591
Store Svuku 1415
Digerhågna 1024
Rånden
Randsjö
Glötesvålen 949
Digerberget 687
Ytterhogdal
D
Tron 1666
Elgpiggen 1604
Grøtia
Töfsingdalens
Storvätteshågna 1204
Ljusnan
Folldal
Folla
Tysla
Älvros
Sveg
Grimsi
Sömlinghågna 1195
Lofsen
Østerdalen
Skorsåhøgdan 1034
Gutulia
Grovlån
Nipfjället 1192
Stygghøin 1727
Store 1827
Storhøa 1518
Brickan 726
Garpkölen 669
Blådjan
Tväråsen 841
Atna
Glomma
Sagtinden 2018
Rondane
Rena
Sølen 1755
Drevsjø
Flötningen
Fjätan
S
Härjån
52
Hamra
Storerya
Svarthammaren 1142
Østerhogna 1185
Ottlaugkampen 947
Atna
Mistra
Trysilelva
Digerbergen 697
E
Lillhamra
Gråhø 1431
Hirisjøhogdene 1393
Åkerstrømmen
Storhøgda 1188
Tverrfjellet 1209
Fulufjällets
Slohangflöjet 1044
Fulan
Romnen
Sexan
Vinstra
Famphøgdene 1320
Nordre Osa
Skjerhøa 1025
Ljordalen
Slottet 1051
Långsjöblik 768
743
Fåvang
Eldahøgda 1232
Store Byringen 1039
Blikfjellet 991
Drevja
Ljøra
Tromsa
Gråkampen 1212
Slemma
Trysilfjellet 1132
Faksefjellet 888
D a l a r n a
Unnan
Åmån
533
Rot
Vämån
Jora
Storbekkfjellet 1123
Nybergsund
Grøna
Granfjället 946
Sälen
Västerdalälven
Tennån
Ormtjernkampen
Nevelfjell 1089
Havda
Rakkskiftet 809
Trysilelva
Vanån
F
Slättberg
Skjellbreidfjellet
Lillehammer
Asta
Rena
Vesteråsen 661
Bordvegger 650
Stor Kallberget 717
607
Mora
Synnfjell 1414
1067
Gitvola 852
Juloassa
Höljan
Ogan
Ringsrudåsen 842
Vismunda
794
Steinfjellet 760
Smalberget 640
691
Åran
Tandövarn 777
704
Kattbo
535
Silja
Brumunddal
Elverum
Flisa
Kynna
695
Gjøvik
Etna
Hamar
Tåsan
Malung
Begna
Klukkerholen 718
Raufoss
Mjøsa
Blåenga 633
Storberget 552
Eftasberget 498
Ljusnan
Klacken 573
G
Orrkjølen 641
Digerberget 645
Vansbro
Björbo
Nes
Tannfjell 750
792
Solør
Hadeland
Klarälven
Sørbølfjellet 1284
Høgkorset 757
Skasberget 581
584
Halgån
Knästen 550
H
Samsjøberga 527
Jaren
Gullenhaugen 759
Langholsberget 521
Vardehøgda 411
Lejberget 546
Sunne
Tyfors
443
7
Hønefoss
689
Romerike
49
Kongsvinger
436
10
11
12
681
R i n g e r i k e
8
Jessheim
9
Glomma
Rottnan
Svartälven
Oppkuven 704
Hagfors

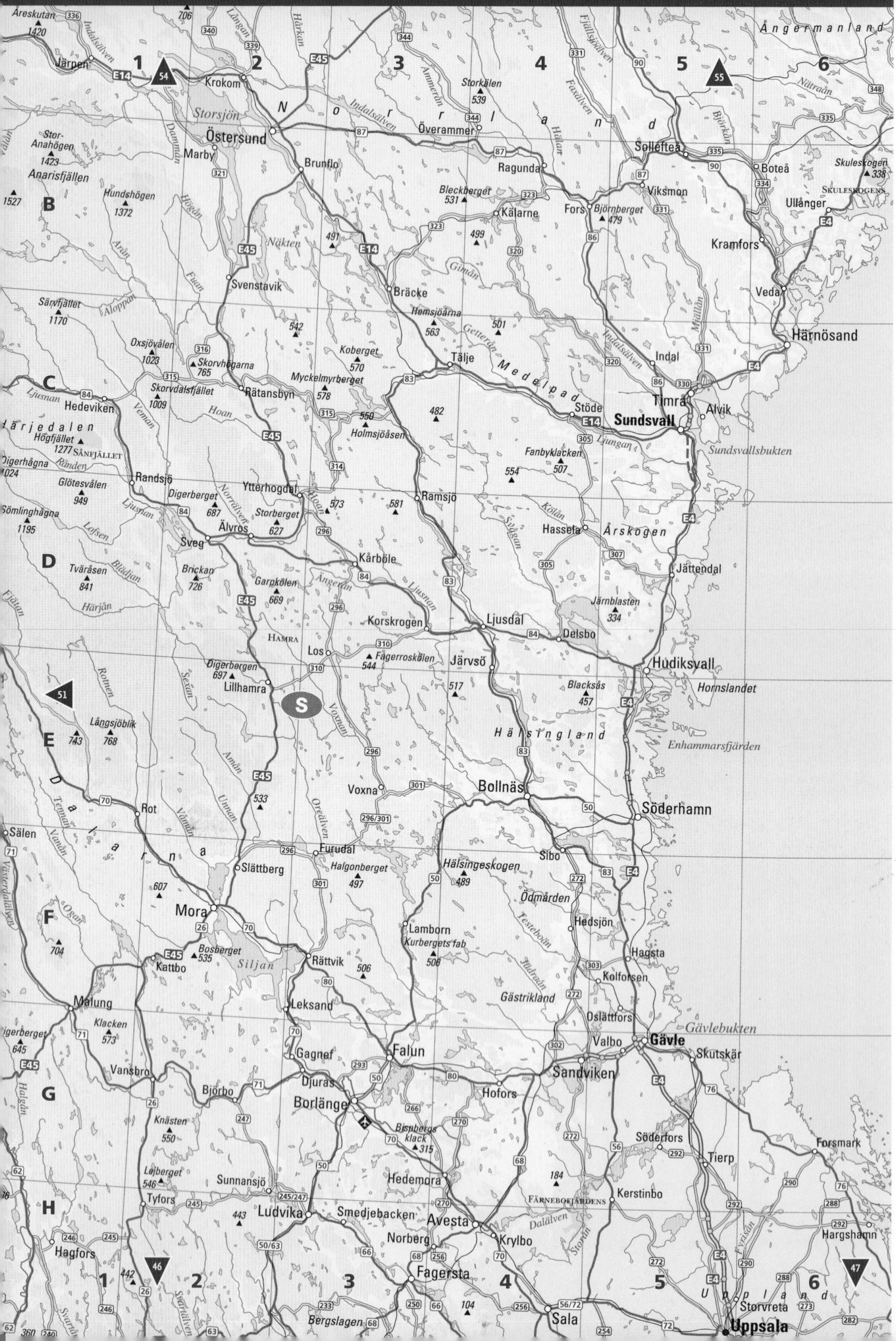

Åreskutan 1420
Järpen
Krokom
Storsjön
Östersund
Marby
Brunflo
Stor-Anahögen 1423
Anarisfjällen
Hundshögen 1372
Norrland
Indalsälven
Överammer
Storkälen 539
Ragunda
Sollefteå
Ångermanland
Nätraån
Boteå
Skuleskogen 338
Skuleskogens
Viksmon
Fors
Björnberget 479
Bleckberget 531
Kälarne
Ullånger
Kramfors
Veda
Härnösand
Nökten
Svenstavik
Bräcke
Hemsjöarna 563
Särvfjället 1170
Oxsjövålen 1023
Skorvhögarna 765
Koberget 570
Tälje
Indal
Medelpad
Timrå
Alvik
Skorvdalsfjället 1009
Hedeviken
Rätansbyn
Myckelmyrberget 578
Holmsjöåsen
Stöde
Sundsvall
Sundsvallsbukten
Härjedalen
Högfjället 1277
Sånfjället
Digerhågna
Glötesvålen 949
Randsjö
Digerberget 687
Ytterhogdal
Storberget 627
Ramsjö
Fanbyklacken 507
Hassela
Årskogen
Sömlinghågna 1195
Sveg
Älvros
Kårböle
Jättendal
Tväråsen 841
Brickan 726
Garpkölen 669
Järnblasten 334
Korskrogen
Ljusdal
Delsbo
Hamra
Los
Fagerroskölen 544
Järvsö
Hudiksvall
Hornslandet
Digerbergen 697
Lillhamra
Blacksås 457
Långsjöblik 768
Hälsingland
Enhammarsfjärden
Voxna
Bollnäs
Söderhamn
Rot
Sälen
Dalarna
Furudal
Slättberg
Halgonberget 497
Hälsingeskogen 489
Sibo
Ödmården
Mora
Bosberget 535
Siljan
Kattbo
Rättvik
Lamborn
Kurbergets fäb 506
Hedsjön
Hagsta
Kolforsen
Gästrikland
Malung
Klacken 573
Leksand
Oslättfors
Gävlebukten
Gagnef
Falun
Valbo
Gävle
Skutskär
Vansbro
Djurås
Sandviken
Björbo
Borlänge
Hofors
Knästen 550
Bisbergs klack 315
Söderfors
Forsmark
Tierp
Lejberget 546
Sunnansjö
Hedemora
Tyfors
Ludvika
Smedjebacken
Avesta
Krylbo
Färnebofjärdens
Kerstinbo
Dalälven
Hargshamn
Hagfors
Norberg
Fagersta
Uppland
Storvreta
Bergslagen
Sala
Uppsala

Örnsköldsvik
Norra Kvarken
Umeå
Norra Gloppet
Östra Gloppet
Södra Gloppet
Björköby
Vaasa (Vasa)
Laihia
Molpe
Nyby
Pörtom
Närpes
Kauhava
Lapua
Kauhajoki
Kurikka
Seinäjoki
Nurmo
Karvala
Alajärvi
Ruona
Alavus
Jalasjärvi
Virrat
Parkano
Kuru
Kauhanevan Pohjankankaan
Lauhavuori 230
Pohjankangas
Hämeenkangas
Kankaanpää
S A T A K U
FIN
Ylöjärvi
Tampere
Nokia
Pirkkala
Lempäälä
Toijala
Vammala
Reposaari
Mäntyluoto
Pihlava
Pori
Friitala
Harjavalta
Kokemäki
Huittinen
Puurijärven ja Isonsuon
Eura
Rauma
Laitila
Uusikaupunki
Varsinais-Suomi
Loimaa
Forssa
Somero
Torronsuon
Kustavi
Hakkenpää
Raisio
Naantali
Turku (Åbo)
Littoinen
Kaarina
Paimio
Salo
Pargas (Parainen)
Dalsbruk (Taalintehdas)
Bromarv
Ekenäs (Tammisaari)
Hanko (Hangö)
Ekenäskärgårds
Skärgårdshavets
Åland
Geta
Södra Kvarken
Storby
Vårdö
Delet
Teili
Kihti Skiftet
Lumparland
Mariehamn
Grisslehamn
Stockholm
Kökar
Kökarsfjärden
Ålands Hav
B O T T E N H A V E T
S E L K Ä M E R I
Kyrönjoki
Lapuanjoki
Nurmonjoki
Seinäjoki
Isojoki
Karvianjoki
Loimijoki
Aurajoki
Mynäjoki
Gideälven
Husån
0 10 20 30 40 50 km
0 10 20 30 miles
7 8 9 10 11 12
B C D E F G H
56 64 66

1 2 3 4 5 6

B C D E F G H

0 10 20 30 40 50 km
0 10 20 30 miles

Meløya
Glomsteet 1288
Ågskaret
1454
Blokktinden 1032
Snøtinden 1594
Nesøya
Jektvik
Hestmona
Saltfjellet Svartisen
Hestmona 568
Trænfjorden
Kilboghamn
Lurøya
Strandtindan 1173
1268
Høgtuva
Langvatnet
Snøfjellet 1196
619
Lovunden
Sjona
Sjonbotn
Nesna
Hemnesberget
Hemnesøy
Glein
Levang
Lihodet 842
Toven 991
Korgen
Dønna
Dønmannen 838
Engan
Sandnessjøen
Vefsnfjord
Røssvassbukta
Mosjøen
Røssvatnet
Tjøtta
1559
Geittind
Vefsna
Vågsodden
Vega
Trolltinden 797
Elsfjord
Horn
Anddalsvågen
Trofors
Vefsna
Ivarrud
Bjørgefjellet
Vennesund
Holm
Børgefjell
Gutuvikfjellet 594
Leka
422
Abjøra
Terråk
593
Skatollet 981
Drottendalsfjellet 927
Søre Steinfjellet 1008
Nursfjellet 1182
Vikna
Vikna
606
Kjøringvassfjellet 806
Mealhkoe 1160
Røyrvik
Jåavma 1170
Geisnes
Namdalen
Namsen
Mariafjellet 793
Abelvær
1056
Salfjella 759
Hurtigruten
Skorva 665
757
Skorovatn
Tommervikfjellet 446
Heimdalshaugen 1150
Nesåpiggen 988
Portfjellet 838
648
Lauvsnes
Skogmo
Sanddøla
Namsos
685
540
Eidet
Vestre Brandsfjellet 1072
Geitfjellet 872
Formofoss
Reinsjøfjellet 726
Lura
Osen
Langnesfjellet 775
Gressåmoen
Stordselva
Finnhuva 995
Holdeelva
Snåsavatnet
Imsa
Kjerringheia 540
Finnvollheia 675
Forra
Sprova
Imsdalsfjellet 941
Blåfjellshatten 1332
Harsvik
Brannheiklumpen 818
Steinkjer
Innherad
Frohavet
Åfjord
Storfjellet 664
Måhkene 1266
Løvsmundhatten 1090
Lorrön
Skjækra
Tarva
Fosna
1248
Mjölksvattsfjället
Ansätten 1091
Sandfjället 1230
Frøya
Verdalsøra
Brekstad
Grandefjæra
Levanger
Skäckerfjällen
Åkersjön
Knarrlagsund
Sørelva
Selva
609
Hårskallen 735
1035
Inna
760
Sandvika
Kallsjön
Landögssjön
Sandstad
Hitra
Kristiansund, Ålesund, Bergen
656
Vannvikan
Kjølhaugen 1249
Almåsaberget 706
Orsnes
Stjørdalshalsen
Kjerringfjellet 1072
Åreskutan 1420
Indalsälven
Fonna 722
566
Trondheim
Heimdal
Järpen
Omnsfjellet 847
Skarvan 1171
Storlien
Åre
Orkanger
Søya
Vinjeøra
Gråfjellet 1040
Fongen 1441
Nea
Enan
Snasahögarna 1461

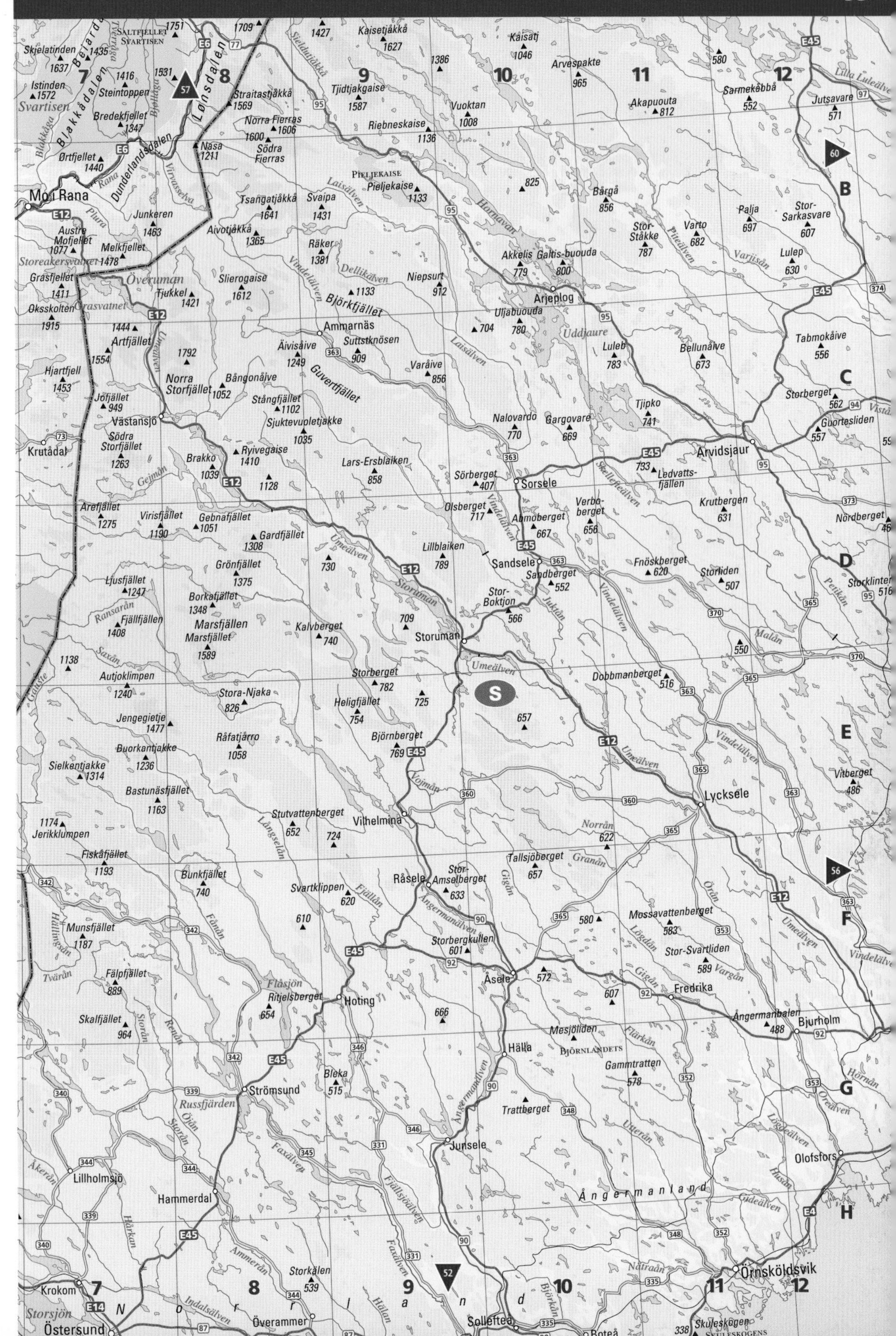
Mo i Rana
Skjelatinden 1637
1435
Istinden 1572
Svartisen
Saltfjellet Svartisen
1751
Blakkådalen
Beiarda
Bredekfjellet 1347
Steintoppen 1416
1531
Lønsdalen
Ørtfjellet 1440
Dunderlandsdalen
Nasa 1211
Straitastjåkkå 1569
1709
1427
Kaisetjåkkå 1627
Tjidtjakgaise 1587
Norra Fierras 1606
Södra Fierras 1600
Riebneskaise 1136
Vuoktan 1008
1386
Kaisatj 1046
Arvespakte 965
Akapuouta 812
580
Sarmekåbbå 552
Jutsavare 571
Lilla Luleälven
Pieljekaise 1133
Tsangatjåkkå 1641
Svaipa 1431
Junkeren 1463
Aivotjåkkå 1365
Räker 1381
Austre Mofjellet 1077
Melkfjellet 1478
Storeakersvatnet
825
Bårgå 856
Stor-Ståkke 787
Varto 682
Palja 697
Stor-Sarkasvare 607
Lulep 630
Akkelis 779
Galtis-buouda 800
Arjeplog
Uljabuouda 780
Uddjaure
Grasfjellet 1411
Överuman
Tjukkel 1421
Sliergaise 1612
1133
Niepsurt 912
Björkfjället
Oksskolten 1915
Grasvatnet
Ammarnäs
Äivisåive 1249
Suttstknösen 909
704
Luleb 783
Bellunåive 673
Tabmokåive 556
Artfjället 1554
1444
1792
Norra Storfjället
Bångonåive 1052
Guvertfjället
Varåive 856
Hjartfjell 1453
Jofjället 949
Stångfjället 1102
Sjuktevuoletjakke 1035
Västansjö
Nalovardo 770
Gargovare 669
Tjipko 741
Storberget 562
Guorteslideen 557
Arvidsjaur
Krutådal
Södra Storfjället 1263
Brakko 1039
Ryivegaise 1410
Lars-Ersblaiken 858
733
Ledvatts-fjällen
Sörberget 407
Sorsele
1128
Olsberget 717
Verbo-berget 656
Krutbergen 631
Nördberget
Arefjället 1275
Virisfjället 1190
Gebnafjället 1051
Gardfjället 1308
Abmoberget 667
Lillblaiken 789
Sandsele
Sandberget 552
Fnöskberget 620
Storliden 507
Grönfjället 1375
730
Ljusfjället 1247
Borkafjället 1348
Fjällfjällen 1408
Marsfjällen
Marsfjället 1589
Kalvberget 740
709
Storuman
Stor-Boktjon 566
550
Umeälven
1138
Autjoklimpen 1240
Storberget 782
725
Dobbmanberget 516
Stora-Njaka 826
Heligfjället 754
657
Jengegietje 1477
Råfatjärro 1058
Björnberget 769
Buorkantjakke 1236
Sielkentjakke 1314
Bastunäsfjället 1163
Lycksele
Vitberget 486
1174
Jerikklumpen
Stutvattenberget 652
724
Vilhelmina
622
Fiskåfjället 1193
Tallsjöberget 657
Bunkfjället 740
Råsele
Stor-Amselberget 633
Svartklippen 620
Munsfjället 1187
610
580
Mossavattenberget 583
Storbergkullen 601
Stor-Svartliden 589
Fälpfjället 889
Flåsjön
Åsele
572
607
Fredrika
Ritjelsberget 654
Hoting
666
Ångermanbalen 488
Bjurholm
Skalfjället 964
Mesjöliden
Hälla
Björnlandets
Gammtratten 578
Bleka 515
Strömsund
Russfjärden
Trattberget
Junsele
Olofsfors
Lillholmsjö
Hammerdal
Ångermanland
Storkälen 539
Örnsköldsvik
Krokom
Norrland
Storsjön
Östersund
Överammer
Sollefteå
Boteå
Skuleskogen
Skuleskogens
338
7
8
9
10
11
12
B
C
D
E
F
G
H
S
52
56
57
60
E4
E6
E12
E14
E45

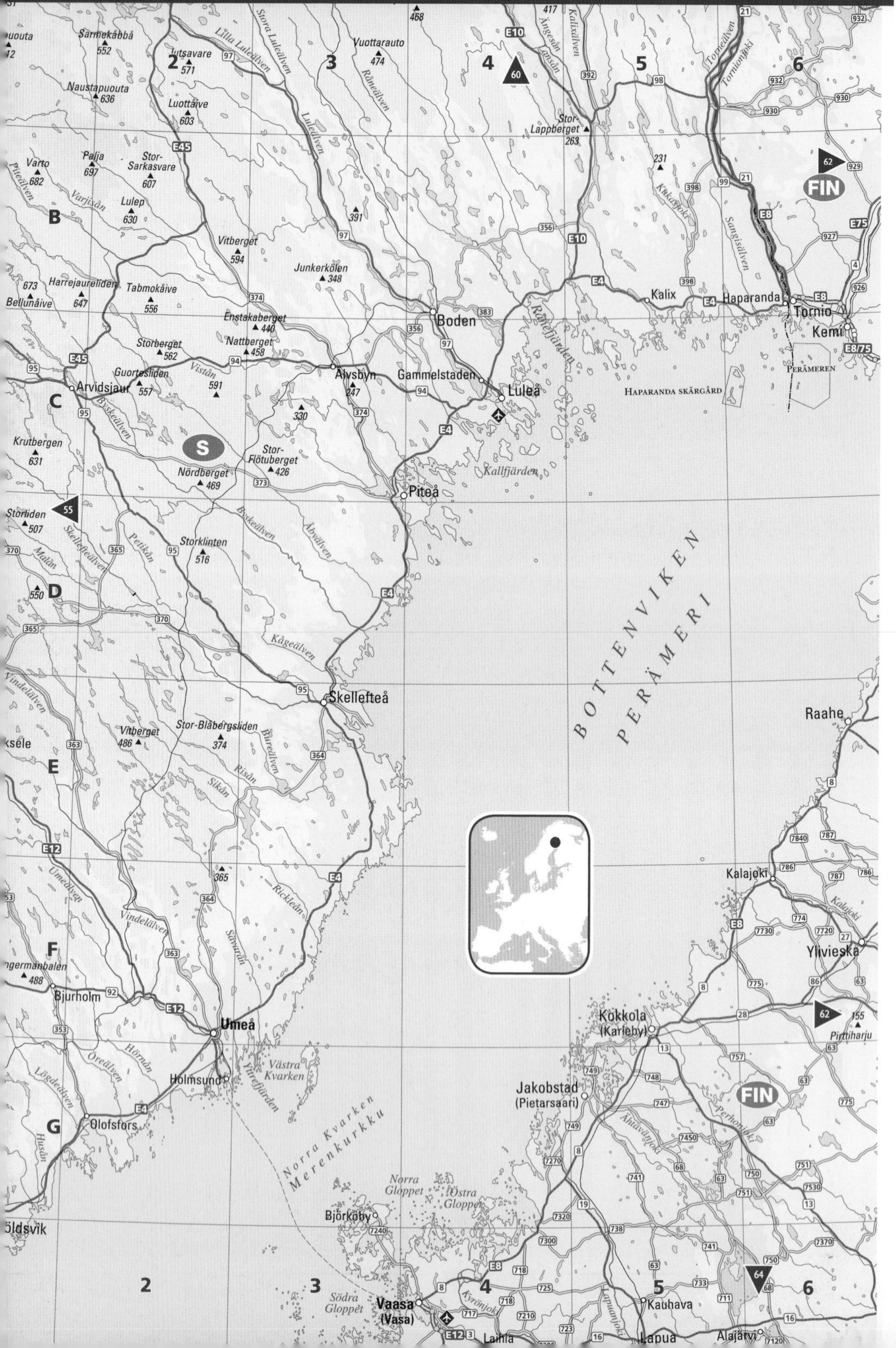

Sarmekåbbå 552
Jutsavare 571
Naustapuouta 636
Luottåive 603
Vuottarauto 474
468
417
Stor-Lappberget 263
231
391
Varto 682
Palja 697
Stor-Sarkasvare 607
Lulep 630
Vitberget 594
Junkerkölen 348
673
Harrejaureliden 647
Bellunåive
Tabmokåive 556
Enstakaberget 440
Nattberget 458
Storberget 562
Guortesliden 557
591
247
330
Krutbergen 631
Stor-Flötuberget 426
Nördberget 469
Storliden 507
Storklinten 516
550
Vitberget 486
Stor-Blåbergsliden 374
365
488
155
Pirttiharju

Lilla Luleälven
Stora Luleälven
Luleälven
Råneälven
Ängesån
Lansån
Kalixälven
Torneälven
Tornionjoki
Kukasjoki
Sangisälven
Piteälven
Varjisån
Vistån
Byskeälven
Råneälven
Skellefteälven
Malån
Petikån
Åbyälven
Kågeälven
Vindelälven
Bureälven
Risån
Sikån
Rickleån
Umeälven
Sävarån
Öreälven
Hörnån
Lögdeälven
Husån
Kyrönjoki
Lapuanjoki
Ähtävänjoki
Perhonjoki
Kalajoki

Boden
Gammelstaden
Luleå
Älvsbyn
Arvidsjaur
Piteå
Kalix
Haparanda
Tornio
Kemi
Skellefteå
Umeå
Bjurholm
Holmsund
Olofsfors
Björköby
Vaasa (Vasa)
Laihia
Kauhava
Lapua
Alajärvi
Kokkola (Karleby)
Jakobstad (Pietarsaari)
Raahe
Kalajoki
Ylivieska

Råneфjärden
Kallfjärden
Haparanda skärgård
Perämeren
BOTTENVIKEN
PERÄMERI
Västra Kvarken
Ytterfjärden
Norra Kvarken
Merenkurkku
Norra Gloppet
Östra Gloppet
Södra Gloppet

S
FIN
FIN

E10 E45 E4 E8 E75 E8/75 E12
97 392 98 21 932 930 929 99 398 356 927 4 926 383 356 374 95 94 373 365 370 363 364 353 92 8 7840 787 786 774 7720 7730 27 775 86 63 28 13 757 749 748 747 7450 7270 741 68 751 750 7530 7370 7320 7300 738 19 733 711 718 725 7210 717 723 16 7120 3 7240

ıuouta
ksele
ngermanbalen
Öldsvik

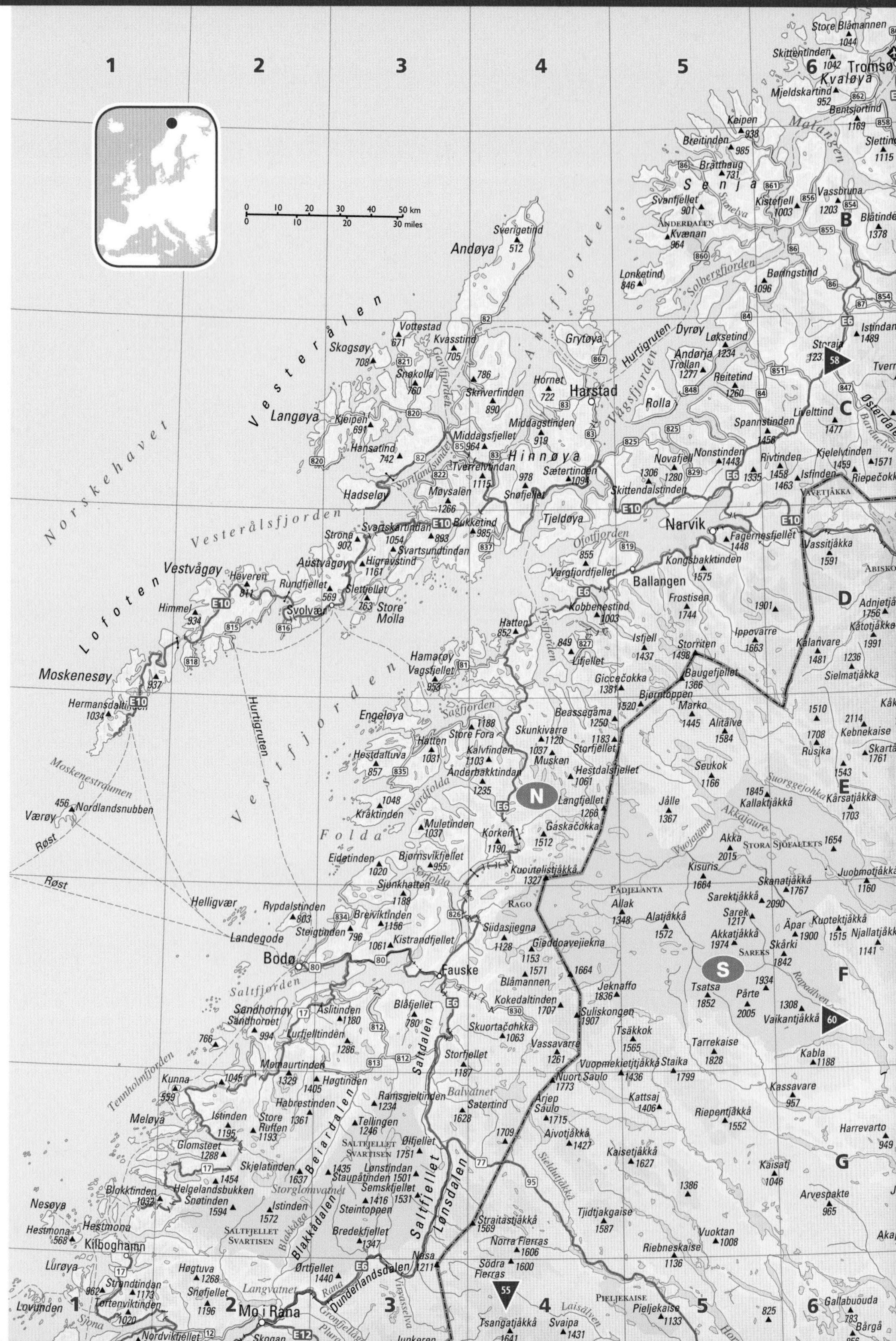
1
2
3
4
5
6
A
B
C
D
E
F
G
0 10 20 30 40 50 km
0 10 20 30 miles
Tromsø
Kvaløya
Store Blåmannen 1044
Skittentinden 1042
Mjeldskartind 952
Bentsjordtind 1169
Sletting 1115
Keipen 938
Breitinden 985
Malangen
Bråtthaug 731
Senja
Svanfjellet 901
Kistefjell 1003
Vassbruna 1203
Blåtinden 1378
Anderdalen
Kvænan 964
Lonketind 846
Solbergfjorden
Børingstind 1096
Istindan 1489
Storaja 1231
Andøya
Sverigetind 512
Andfjorden
Vesterålen
Vottestad 671
Kvasstind 705
Skogsøy 708
Snøkolla 760
Gavlfjorden
Grytøya
Dyrøy
Løksetind 1234
Andørja
Trollan 1277
Hurtigruten
Reitetind 1260
Østerdalen
Bardueiva
Langøya
Kjeipen 691
786
Skriverfinden 890
Hornet 722
Harstad
Vågsfjorden
Rolla
Livelttind 1477
Spannstinden 1456
Norskehavet
Hansatind 742
Middagsfjellet 964
Middagstinden 919
Hinnøya
Nonstinden 1443
Novafjell 1280
1306
Rivtinden 1458 1463
Kjelelvtinden 1459
1571
Riepečokka
Isfinden
Vaivetjåkka
Hadseløy
Sortlandsundet
Tverrelvtinden 1115
978
Sætertinden 1094
Snøfjellet
Skittendalstinden
Møysalen 1266
Vesterålsfjorden
Svartskartindan 1054
Bukketind 985
893
Tjeldøya
Narvik
Fagernesfjellet 1448
Vassitjåkka 1591
Abisko
Strona 907
Svartsundtinden
Ofotfjorden
855
Vargfjordfjellet
Kongsbakktinden 1575
Ballangen
Lofoten
Vestvågøy
Austvågøy
Higravstind 1161
Haveren 811
Rundfjellet
Slettfjellet 569
763
Store Molla
Svolvær
Himmel 934
Kobbenestind 1003
Frostisen 1744
1901
Adnjetjåkka 1756
Kåtotjåkka 1991
Hatten 852
849
Lifjellet
Isfjell 1437
Storriten 1498
Ippovarre 1663
Kalanvare 1481
1236
Sielmatjåkka
Moskenesøy
937
Hamarøy
Vagsfjellet 953
Tysfjorden
Gicceċokka 1381
Baugefjellet 1366
Hermansdaltinden 1034
Vestfjorden
Hurtigruten
Bjørntoppen 1520
Beassagáma 1250
Marko 1445
Alitaive 1584
1510
2114
Kebnekaise
Kåk
Engeløya
Sagfjorden
Store Fora 1188
Skunkivarre 1120
1037
1183
Storfjellet
1708
Rusjka
Skarta 1761
Hatten 1031
Hestdaltuva 857
Kalvfinden 1103
Musken
Anderbakktindan 1235
Hestdalsfjellet 1061
Seukok 1166
1543
Moskenestraumen
Suorggejohka
1845
Kallaktjåkkå
Kårsatjåkka 1703
Nordfolda
N
Langfjellet 1266
Jålle 1367
Akkajaure
Værøy
456 Nordlandsnubben
1048
Kråktinden
Muletinden 1037
Gaskačokka 1512
Vuojatätno
Akka 2015
Stora Sjöfallets
1654
Røst
Folda
Korken 1190
Eidøtinden 1020
Bjørnsvikfjellet 955
Kuoutelistjåkkå 1327
Kisuris 1664
Skanatjåkkå 1767
Juobmotjåkka 1160
Sjunkhatten 1188
Padjelanta
Sarektjåkkå 2090
Helligvær
Rypdalstinden 803
Breiviktinden 1156
Rago
Allak 1348
Alatjåkkå 1572
Sarek 1217
Äpar 1900
Kuotektjåkkå 1515
Njallatjåkka 1141
Steigtinden 796
Siidasjiegna 1128
Akkatjåkkå 1974
Landegode
Kistrandfjellet 1061
Gieddoavejiekna
Skårki 1842
Sareks
Bodø
Fauske
1153
1571
Blåmannen
1664
S
Saltfjorden
Jeknaffo 1836
Tsatsa 1852
1934
Pårte 2005
Rapadälven
Sandhornøy
Sandhornet 994
Aslitinden 1180
Blåfjellet 780
Kokedaltinden 1707
Suliskongen 1907
1308
Vaikantjåkkå
60
Lurfjelltinden 1286
766
Skuortačohkka 1063
Tsäkkok 1565
Tarrekaise 1828
Kabla 1188
Saltdalen
Storfjellet 1187
Vassavarre 1261
Tennholmfjorden
Kunna 559
1046
Mømaurtinden 1329
1405
Høgtinden
Vuopmekietjtjåkkå 1436
Nuort Saulo 1773
Staika 1799
Kassavare 957
Habrestinden 1361
Ramsgjeltinden 1234
Balvatnet
Sætertind 1628
Kattsaj 1406
Meløya
Istinden 1195
Store Ruffen 1193
Tellingen 1246
Arjep Saulo 1715
Riepentjåkkå 1552
Beiardalen
Aivotjåkkå 1427
Harrevarto 949
Glomsteet 1288
Saltfjellet Svartisen
Ølfjellet 1751
1709
Kaisetjåkkå 1627
Kaisatj 1046
Skjelatinden 1637
1454
Lønstindan
1435
Staupåtinden 1501
Semskfjellet 1531
Storglomvatnet
Helgelandsbukken
Snøtinden 1594
Blokktinden 1032
Istinden 1572
1416
Steintoppen
Saltfjellet
Lønsdalen
Sieldutjåkka
1386
Arvespakte 965
Nesøya
Hestmona
Hestmona 568
Blakkådalen
Bredekfjellet 1347
Straitastjåkkå 1569
Tjidtjakgaise 1587
Aka
Kilboghamn
Norra Fierras 1606
Vuoktan 1008
Lurøya
Høgtuva 1268
Snøfjellet 1196
Ørtfjellet 1440
Dunderlandsdalen
Nasa 1211
Södra Fierras 1600
Riebneskaise 1136
Strandtindan 1173
962
Tortenviktinden 1020
Langvatnet
Rana
55
Pieljekaise
Pieljekaise 1133
Lovunden
Sjona
Mo i Rana
Vindelälven
Laisälven
825
Gallabuouda 783
Bårgå 856
Nordviktfjellet 842
Skogan 799
Austre
Gronfjelldal
Plura
Junkeren 1463
Tsangatjåkkå 1641
Svaipa 1431
Aivotjåkkå
Hornavan

1 2 3 4 5 6

B

0 10 20 30 40 50 km
0 10 20 30 miles

NORDISHAVET
Hurtigruten
Rolvsøysundet
580
Hammerfest
Kvaløya
Svartfjellet
630
Sørøya
Vatnafjellet
656
882
C
Lopphavet
Hasvik
Sørøysundet
94
Seiland
1079
985
Skinnfjellet
710
Nord-Kvaløy
Fugløya
Fugløykallen
753
628
Eliassen
939
949
Stjernøya
698
Alangen
737
Vanna
Arnøya
1168
Middagsfjellet
1071
1066
Øksfjord
1304
Stjernsundet
Altafjorden
E6
Rebbenesøy
Vanntinden
1033
Kvænangen
Nevernesfjellet
1181
Fjelltindnasen
1041
882
Liv'luvarri
958
883
Navgastat
713
Svartevasstind
876
Hansnes
Hurtigruten
Skjervøy
Kågen
1098
E6
Lassefjellet
1166
Ringvassøy
Reinøy
Reinskartind
884
Uløya
866
Reisafjorden
Alta
740
D
Istind
953
863
Tverrbakktind
1390
Blåtind
1142
Stuora
Hal'di
1149
Gierdoidvarri
810
Grøtsundet
Ullsfjorden
Lyngen
E6
Store Blåmannen
1044
Ullstind
1094
Vaggastinden
1398
Mattiselva
93
Skittentinden
1042
Stortind
1512
Bæssetinden
1312
Rieppesgai'sa
1337
Altaelva
Cæv'dni
672
Tromsø
Tromsdalen
Kvaløya
E6
Nubivarri
841
Mjeldskartind
952
862
Tromsdalstind
1238
E8
91
Nordmannviktind
1336
91
Badajokka
N
Jiesjávri
Vir'dnečák'ka
590
Bentsjordtind
1169
Malangen
Lavangsdalen
Sennedalfjellet
1385
Fornesfjellet
1478
868
E6
865
1301
Breitinden
985
Slettind
1115
Jiehkkevarri
1833
Manndalen
Isfjellet
1375
Bæccæhal'di
1326
Čuonjaoai'vi
1089
858
Lakselvtinden
1617
E
Balsfjorden
Henriktind
1219
Skibotndalen
Čiččenvárri
1312
Reisaelva
Mállejus
975
861
856
Senja
Kistefjell
1003
E8
Piggtind
1505
E6/8
Skibotnelva
Rássanibba
1252
1365
Čáravárri
887
86
854
Halti
1328
93
ANDERDALEN
860
855
Blåtinden
1378
858
86
Lille
Russetind
1527
87
Mannfjellet
1533
Goahteråssa
1371
E8
REISA
Solbergfjorden
E6
Børingstind
1096
84
86
Stormauken
1249
857
Báras
1419
Kåhperusvaarat
1144
Poroeno
Vuoskuvárri
527
Vrøy
854
87
942
Saana
1029
Jollanoaivi
1029
84
87
Moskkugáisi
1523
Målselva
Divielva
Rostadalen
Rostaelva
Rommaeno
Storaia
1237
E6
Istindan
1489
Dividalen
Langfjelltind
1504
Bas'tevarri
658
Reitetind
1260
F
851
84
21
Peeravaara
933
93
1271
Siebejokka
847
Østerdalen
Kjerkestinden
1677
Könkämäälven
Torniseno
Spannstinden
1456
Liveltind
1477
Barduelva
Njumis
1713
491
Vonstinden
1443
Jerta
1428
E8
Ropi
945
Urtivaara
633
Rivtinden
1458
Kjelelvtinden
1571
ØVRE DIVIDAL
Paltaive
915
Rostonsölkä
Tarju
735
E6
Altevatnet
Kistefjell
1633
Råstäeno
Ruutusoive
842
21
Lätäseno
Jietajoki
Tarvantovaara
591
Jierstivaara
647
57
VAVETJÅKKA
Råkkunbårri
1659
Tarvantojoki
Poroejoki
E6
E10
Tsåktso
1119
Lainioälven
93
Näkkäläjoki
Vassitjåkka
1591
Tuoptejåkkah
1604
Máissávarri
1022
Roopi
799
G
ABISKO
Torneträsk
E45
99
956
21
Palojoki
93
Pyhäkero
711
1901
E10
S
Rakisvare
985
Puollanåive
796
Ippovarre
1663
Kåtotjåkka
1991
Lulep-Patsajåkel
782
Outtakka
723
957
E8
Kalahvare
1481
Rassepautastjåkka
1750
PALLAS JA OUNASTUNTURIN
KANSALLISPUISTO
H
Råppe
1014
Vittangivaara
836
60
Leavasjohka
Visttasjohka
Nunasvaara
580
Taivaskero
807
21
1510
612
Merasjoki
Kebnekaise
2114
Rusjka
1708
2
1017
3
4
Lainioälven
Saankijoki
5
Halju
551
99
6
Keimiötunturi
610
Skartåive
1761
Vittangiälven
E45
79
1543
Piedjastjåkka
Kiruna
Rautusakara

7
8
9
10
11
12
B
C
D
E
F
G
H
Nordkapp
Trollvikfjellet 392
Geitingsfjellet 373
Gråkollfjellet 417
Breisundet
Havøysund
Magerøya
E69
Molvikfjell 518
Fiskatind 491
889
Porsangerhalvøya
Vilgesrassa 563
Revsbotn
Gar'devarri 634
Erdalsfjellet 681
656
396
E6
Porsangen
Gukkesguravarri 525
Børselva
Sværholthalvøya
Sauhaugen 578
Golpusfjellet 525
169
Laksefjorden
Nordkinn 237
Søre Bjørnsviktuva 370
888
894
Nordkynhalvøya
Kifjord
Sandfjellet 487
Dalhaugen 442
Trolltind 555
Perletind 639
Langfjordelva
Blåfjell 487
Bædnatgai'sa 620
Flattind 673
Tanafjorden
Berlevåg
Hurtigruten
Storelva
Raggučærro 480
890
Midtfjellet 475
Straumen
Båtsfjordfjellet 481
891
Stangenestind 724
Oar'dujåkka
Tanafjellet 570
Julelva
Sandfjordelva
Langryggen 405
Vardø
Svartnes
Skipskjølen 633
Varangerhalvøya
98
Njuk'čagai'sa 478
Brattfjellet 446
Urdfjellet 460
Falkefjellet 545
Komagelva
Bergebyelva
Guk'kčærro 250
Holmfjellet 286
Čal'bmeraigvarri 650
Stuorrajåkskai'di 715
Ul'ugai'sa 602
Lak'sjåkka
E75
Vadsø
Stabbursdalen
Mad'de Ndæidan 631
Spal'čavarri 766
Duolbaš 694
895
E6/75
Varangerfjorden
Særbačåk'ka 404
Čuokkaraš'ša 950
Rastegai'sa 1067
Tenojoki
Hal'kavarri 1045
Suonjergai'sa 1007
970
Korgåsen 419
Bieg'gavatgai'sa 1117
Orušoaivi 502
4
Vetsijoki
Pulmankijoki
504
Khrebet Pasari-Tunturi 503
Kirkenes
887
886
Viksjøfjellet 391
Villavaara 344
893
Näätämöjoki
Guorboaivi 443
9703
Utsjoki
Guivi 641
E105
Zapolyarnyy
Nikel'
10
Stuorra Guorbmit 434
Kevojoki
971
Vaijoki
885
Ailigas 620
92
Jiešjokka
Gora Kuorpukas 631
Pechenga
Iškuras 643
Gora Shuort 322
Keätkepåssi 520
Inarijoki
Karasjokka
Peäldoaivi 567
Øvre Pasvik
Gora Kuchintundra 578
Koarvikodds 590
Galmat 539
Gosjokka
Paatsjoki
Inarijärvi
Vaskojoki
9553
Otsamo 418
Bavtajokka
Anarjokka
Øvre Anárjohka
Kietsimäjoki
Landjoivi 593
Lemmenjoki
955
969
Sarmitunturi 411
RUS
Verkhnetu
Morgam-Viibus 599
Suukisjoki
Lemmenjoen kansallispuisto
Hammastunturi 531
91
Suorsapää 471
Lotta
FIN
Repojoki
Repokaira
Ivalojoki
Tolosjoki
Lutto
Gora Nyurmtundra 653
Kakkalöjoki
Kivipää 466
Korsatunturi 462
Ivalojoki
Kiilopää 546
Suomujoki
Kuikkapää 678
Gora Ionn-N'yugoayv 713
Gora Chiltal'd 90
Lupukkapää 620
Saariselkä
Sokosti 718
Puljutunturi 471
Uurrekarkia 390
633
Talkkunapää
Yavr
Suku-Nattanen 544
Urho Kekkosen kansallispuisto
Nota
Pokka
Kitinen
Kapsajoki
Nattaset
Jaurujoki
Korvatunturi 483
Oanasjoki
61
Naltiotunturi 430
Nuorttijoki
Pomokaira
Isolaki 421
Koitelaisenkaira
Kitinen
Sorvortantunturi 423
Nuorttitunturi 482
Gora Vaynatundr 600
79

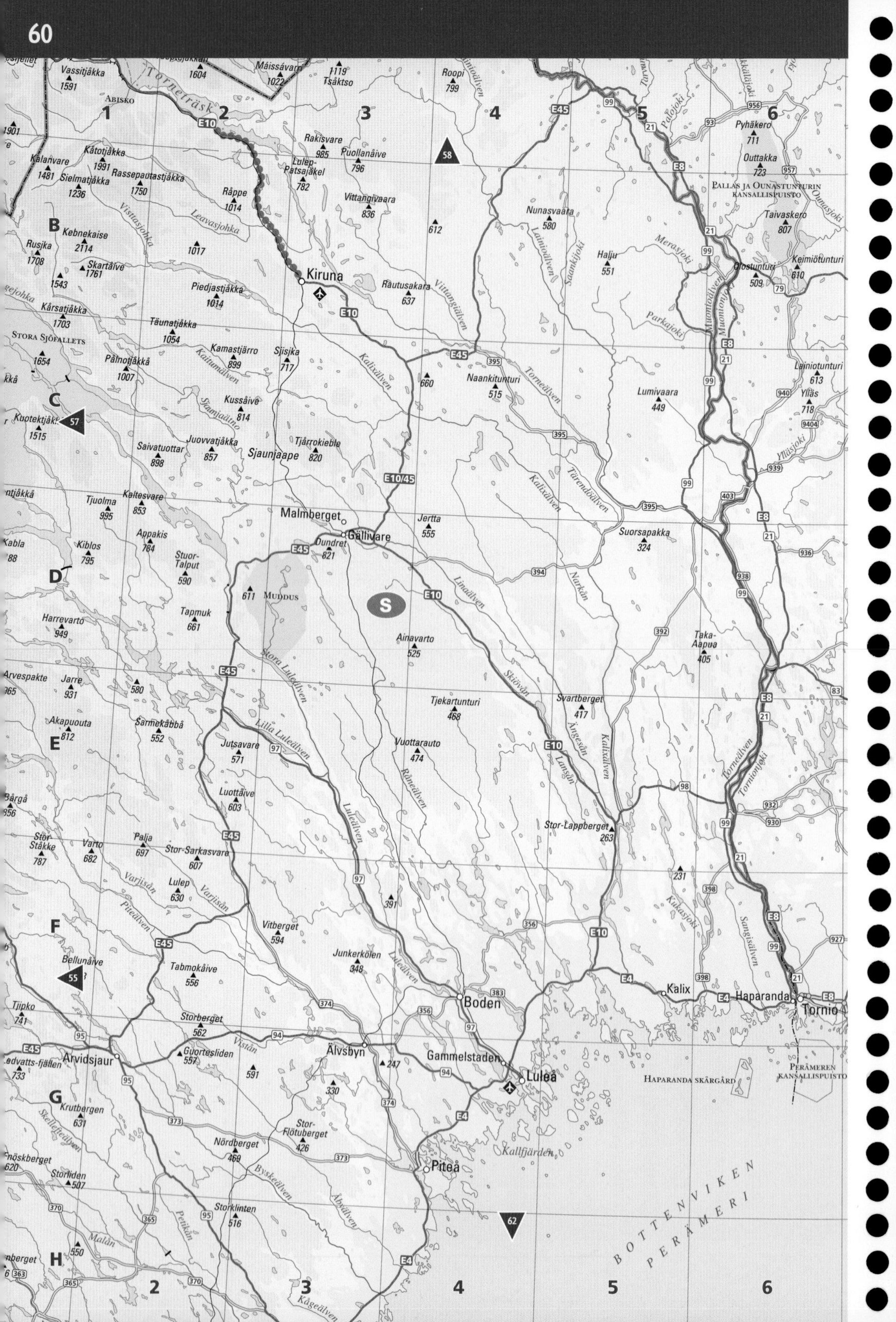
Kiruna
Gällivare
Malmberget
Boden
Luleå
Piteå
Älvsbyn
Arvidsjaur
Kalix
Haparanda
Tornio
Gammelstaden
Sjaunjaape
Abisko
Torneträsk
Kebnekaise
2114
Stora Sjöfallets
Muddus
Pallas ja Ounastunturin kansallispuisto
Haparanda skärgård
Perämeren kansallispuisto
Bottenviken
Perämeri
Kallfjärden
Kalixälven
Torneälven
Luleälven
Lilla Luleälven
Stora Luleälven
Råneälven
Piteälven
Skellefteälven
Byskeälven
Åbyälven
Muonioälven
Tornionjoki
Lainioälven
Linaälven
Kaitumälven
Vittangiälven
Tärendöälven
E10
E45
E4
E8
E10/45
S
58
57
55
62

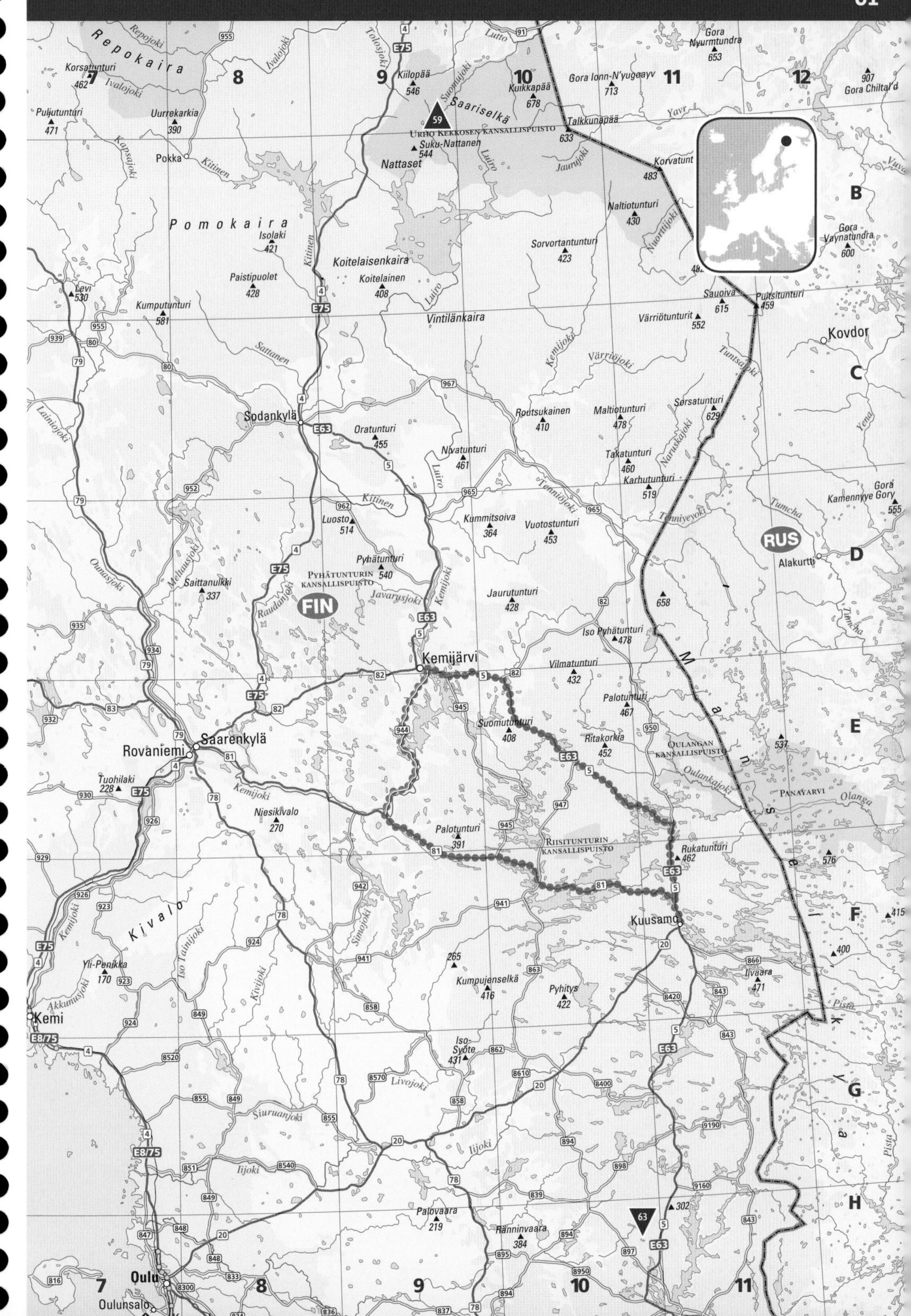

1 2 3 4 5 6

Luottåive 603
Stor-Sarkasvare 607
Rånealven
Luleälven
Lansån
Stor-Lappberget 263
Torniojoki
Saarenkylä
Rovaniemi
Tuohilaki 228
231
391
Varjisån
Vitberget 594
Piteälven
Kukasjoki
Sangisälven
Kivalo
Iso Tainijoki
Kemijoki
Junkerkölen 348
Luleälven
B
Kåive 556
Enstakaberget 440
Nattberget 458
Storberget 562
Vistån
Boden
Kalix
Haparanda
Tornio
Kemi
Akkunusjoki
Yli-Penikka 170
Simojoki
S
Älvsbyn
247
Gammelstaden
Luleå
Råneälven
591
330
Haparanda skärgård
Perämeren
Stor-Flötuberget 426
Nördberget 469
C
Piteå
Kallfjärden
0 10 20 30 40 50 km
0 10 20 30 miles
56
Storklinten 516
Byskeälven
Åbyälven
Kågeälven
D
Oulu
Oulunsalo
Kempele
Skellefteå
Bureälven
Stor-Blåbergsliden 374
Sikån
Risån
Bottenviken
Perämeri
Raahe
Siikajoki
E
365
Rickleån
Liminkaoja
Piipsanjoki
Kalajoki
Oulainen
Pyhäjoki
186
Sävarån
Kalajoki
Ylivieska
F
Umeå
Holmsund
Västra Kvarken
Ytterfjärden
Kokkola (Karleby)
Nivala
Pirttiharju 155
Kalajoki
Pyhäjoki
Jakobstad (Pietarsaari)
Lestijoki
Perhonjoki
Ähtävänjoki
Norra Kvarken
Merenkurkku
G
Norra Gloppet
Östra Gloppet
Björköby
Kolima
Salamajärven Kansallispuisto
Södra Gloppet
Vaasa (Vasa)
Kyrönjoki
Lapuanjoki
Kauhava
64
60
Laihia
Lapua 132
Alajärvi
2 3 4 5 6
Pyhä-Häkin

Kuusamo
Kajaani
Kuhmo
Kiuruvesi
Iisalmi
Nurmes
Lieksa
Siilinjärvi
Kuopio
Kalevala
Kostomuksha
Reboly
FIN
RUS
Oulangan Kansallispuisto
Riisitunturin Kansallispuisto
Rokuan Kansallispuisto
Hiidenportin Kansallispuisto
Tiilikkajärven Kansallispuisto
Kolin Kansallispuisto
Patvinsuon Kansallispuisto
Oulujärvi
Pielinen
Panayarvi
Ritakorkia 452
Palotunturi 391
Rukatunturi 462
Njesikivalo 270
Kumpujenselkä 416
Pyhitys 422
Iivaara 471
Iso-Syöte 431
Palovaara 219
Ränninvaara 384
Paljakka 384
Rokuanvaara 194
Saukkovaara 325
Naulavaara 368
Kinahmi 314
Pisa 271
Koli 347
Korpivaara 283
Kemijoki
Iijoki
Oulujoki
Siikajoki
Kiiminginjoki
Livojoki
Siuruanjoki
Kärsämäenjoki
Lieksanjoki
Koitere
Keitele
Savo
Oz. Topozero
Ozero Pyaozero
Ozero Nyuk
Oz. Lekshozero
Olanga
Pista
Livo
Kuma
Poncha
Kepa

Södra Gloppet
Vaasa (Vasa)
Laihia
Kauhava
Karvala
Lapua
Alajärvi
Salamajärven kansallispuisto
Seinäjoki
Nurmo
Ruona
Pyhä-Häkin kansallispuisto
Saarijärvi
Kurikka
Alavus
Äänekoski
Suolahti
Närpes
Kauhajoki
Keuruu
Jyväskylä
Pirttimäki 243
Lauhanvuoren kansallispuisto
Lauhavuori 230
Kauhanevan-Pohjankankaan kansallispuisto
Pohjankangas
Helvetinjärven kansallispuisto
Parkano
Mänttä
Jämsänkoski
Seitsemisen kansallispuisto
Kankaanpää
Hämeenkangas
S A T A K U N T A
Jämsä
Reposaari
Mäntyluoto
Pihlava
Orivesi
Isojärven kansallispuisto
FIN
Ylöjärvi
Pori
Tampere
Nokia
Friitala
Pirkkala
Kangasala
Päijänne
Päijänteen kansallispuisto
Vammala
Harjavalta
Lempäälä
Kokemäki
Puurijärven ja Isosuon kansallispuisto
Valkeakoski
Rauma
Huittinen
Eura
Toijala
H Ä M E
Loimijoki
Hämeenlinna
Lahti
Hollola
Laitila
Turenki
Uusikaupunki
Varsinais-Suomi
Loimaa
Forssa
Orimattila
Mynäjoki
Torronsuon kansallispuisto
Riihimäki
Liesjärven kansallispuisto
Kustavi
Somero
Hyvinkää
Mäntsälä
Hakkenpää
Raisio
U U S I
Naantali
Littoinen
Paimio
Karkkila
Järvenpää
Porvoo (Borgå)
Turku (Åbo)
Kaarina
Salo
Tuusula
Kerava
Klaukkala
Korso
Pargas (Parainen)
Nummela
Vantaa (Vanda)
Tikkurila
Lohja
Nuuksion kansallispuisto
Kauniainen
Virkkala
Espoo (Esbo)
HELSINKI (HELSINGFORS)
Mariehamn, Stockholm
Kirkkonummi (Kyrkslätt)
Kökar
Dalsbruk (Taalintehdas)
Bromarv
Karis
Ekenäs (Tammisaari)
Skärgårdshavets
Kökarsfjärde
Hanko (Hangö)
Ekenässkärgårds
Mariehamn, Stockholm
Lübeck, Travemünde
Tallinn, Rostock
Tallinn, Rostock
Kaliningrad, Sassnitz, Lübeck
SUO (Fi
Prangli
Kolima

2 3 4 5 6
B C D E F G

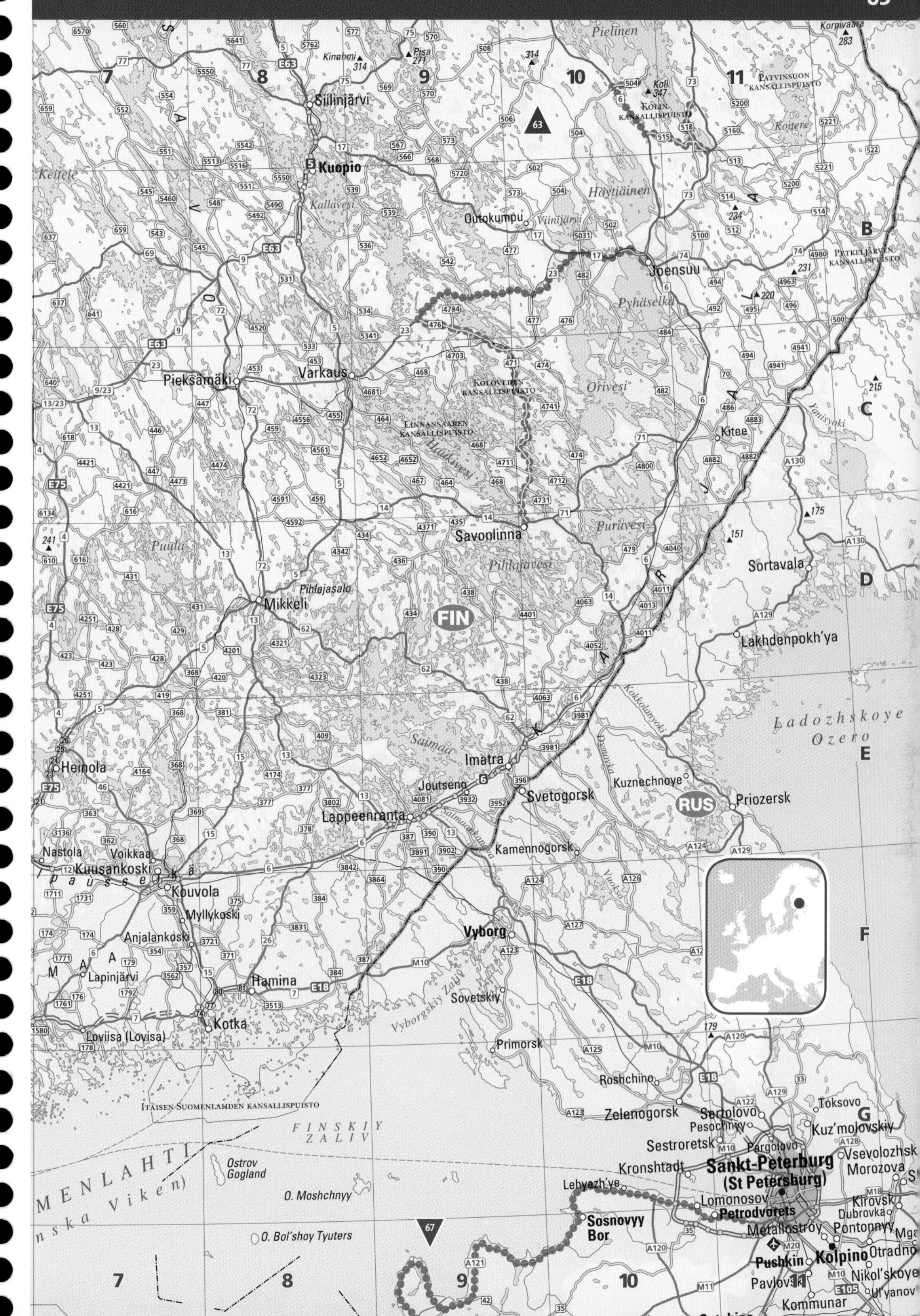
Siilinjärvi
Kuopio
Kallavesi
Outokumpu
Joensuu
Pyhäselkä
Höytiäinen
Pielinen
Koli
Kolin Kansallispuisto
Patvinsuon Kansallispuisto
Petkeljärven Kansallispuisto
Pieksämäki
Varkaus
Koloveden Kansallispuisto
Linnansaaren Kansallispuisto
Haukivesi
Orivesi
Kitee
Puruvesi
Savonlinna
Pihlajavesi
Puula
Mikkeli
Pihlajasalo
FIN
Sortavala
Lakhdenpokh'ya
Ladozhskoye Ozero
Saimaa
Imatra
Joutseno
Svetogorsk
Lappeenranta
Kuznechnoye
RUS
Priozersk
Kamennogorsk
Heinola
Nastola
Voikkaa
Kuusankoski
Kouvola
Myllykoski
Anjalankoski
Lapinjärvi
Hamina
Kotka
Loviisa (Lovisa)
Vyborg
Vyborgskiy Zaliv
Sovetskiy
Primorsk
Itäisen Suomenlahden Kansallispuisto
Finskiy Zaliv
Ostrov Gogland
O. Moshchnyy
O. Bol'shoy Tyuters
Roshchino
Zelenogorsk
Sertolovo
Pesochnyy
Toksovo
Kuz'molovskiy
Sestroretsk
Pargolovo
Vsevolozhsk
Kronshtadt
Sankt-Peterburg
(St Petersburg)
Morozova
Lebyazh'ye
Lomonosov
Petrodvorets
Kirovsk
Dubrovka
Sosnovyy Bor
Metallostroy
Pontonnyy
Pushkin
Kolpino
Otradnoye
Nikol'skoye
Pavlovsk
Kommunar
Gatchina
Ul'yanovka

Virkkala
Lohja
Espoo (Esbo)
Kauniainen
Kirkkonummi (Kyrkslätt)
HELSINKI (HELSINGFORS)
Karis
Ekenäs (Tammisaari)
Hanko (Hangö)
FIN
Kökar
Kökarsfjärden
SKÄRGÅRDSHAVETS
EKENÄSKÄRGÅRDS
POHJANLAHTI
SUOMENLAHTI
SOOME
FINSKA VIKEN
Prangli
Naissaar
Mariehamn, Stockholm
Kapellskär
0 10 20 30 40 50 km
0 10 20 30 miles
TALLINN
Maardu
Paldiski
Keila
Väänna
Pirita
Vihterpalu
Vormsi
Voosi kurk
Hari kurk
Paralepa
Haapsalu
Rapla
Hiiumaa
Kuivastu
Kassari
Kassaare laht
MATSALU RAHVUSPARK
Kasari
Vigala
Türi
EST
LÄÄNEMERI
Lübeck, Travemünde, Rostock
Muhu
Virtsu
Tagamõisa poolsaar
Vilsandi
Loonalaid
VILSANDI RAHVUSPARK
Navesti
Pärnu
SOOMAA RAHVUSPARK
Raudna
Halliste
Reiu
Sauga
Kuressaare
Saaremaa
Abruka
Kihnu
Kaliningrad, Sassnitz, Lübeck
Stockholm
Mõntu
LIIVI LAHT
Kura kurk
Ruhnu
Nynäshamn
Irbes šaurums
Salaca
Rūja
Burtnieku ezers
Lübeck
Irbe
Ziemeļkursas Augstiene
Zilais kalns 127
Valmiera
Limbaži
Ventspils
Rinda
Rīgas Jūras Līcis
Āģe
Cēsis
GAUJAS
LV
Talsi
Kamparkalns 174
Venta
Abava
Gauja
Sigulda
BALTIJAS JŪRA
Kuldīga
Tukums
Jūrmala
RĪGA
KEMERU NACIONĀLAIS PARKS
Vidzemes Centrālā Augstiene
Salaspils
Maza Jugla
Ogre
Aizpute
Austrumkursas Augstiene
Olaine
Ķekava
Lielupe
Daugava
Lielvārde
Skrunda
Saldus
Jelgava
Dobele
Liepāja
Krievukalns 182
Liepājas ezers
Iecava
Aizkraukle
A 1 2 3 4 5 6
B C D E F G H
E20 E263 E67 E22 E77 A1 A2 A3 A4 A5 A6 A7 A8 A9 A10

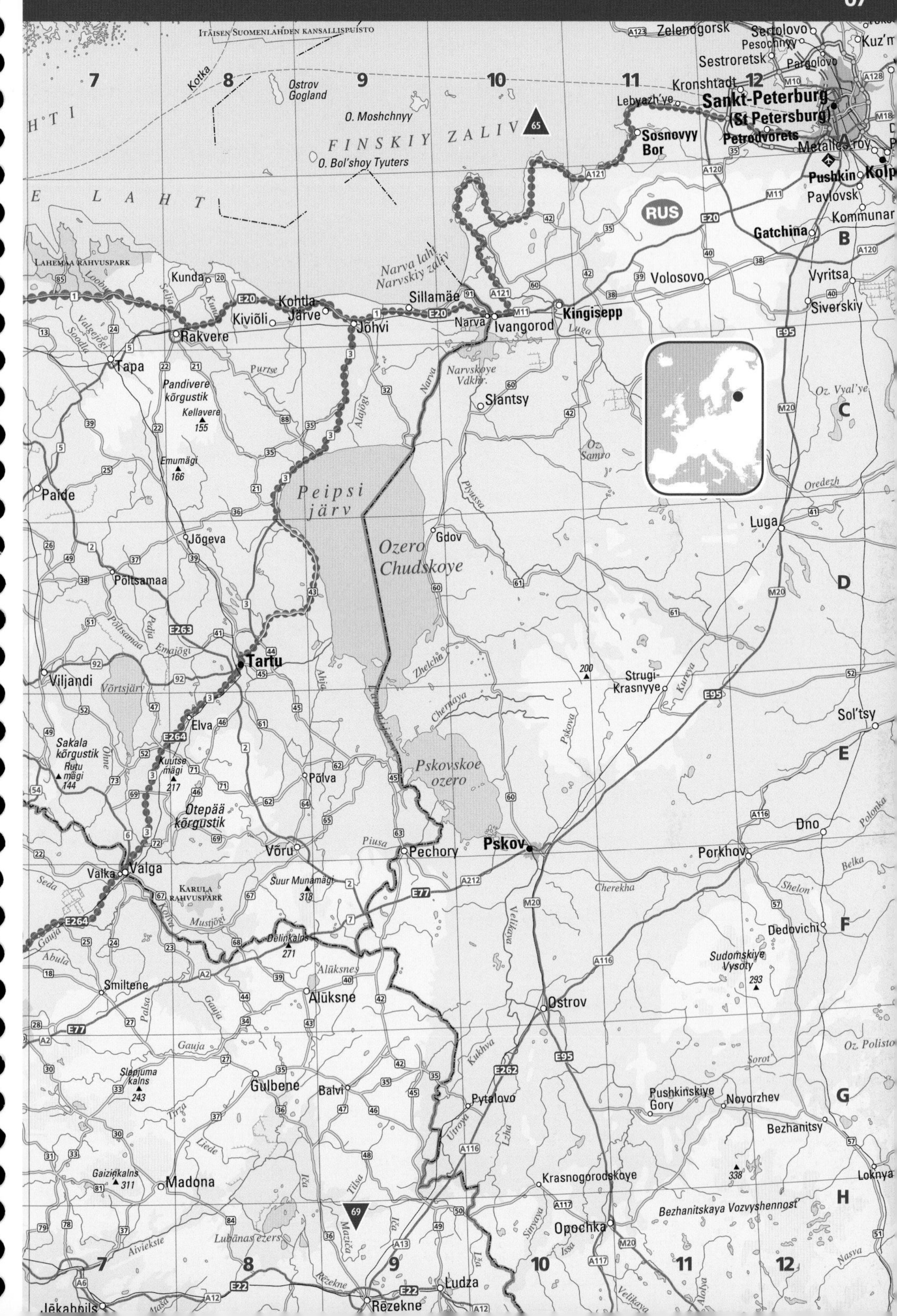

Zelenogorsk
Sertolovo
Pesochnyy
Kuz'm
Sestroretsk
Pargolovo
Kronshtadt
Lebyazh'ye
Sankt-Peterburg
(St Petersburg)
Sosnovyy Bor
Petrodvorets
Pushkin
Pavlovsk
Kommunar
Gatchina
Volosovo
Vyritsa
Siverskiy
Kingisepp
Ivangorod
Narva
Sillamäe
Kohtla-Järve
Kiviõli
Jõhvi
Kunda
Rakvere
Tapa
Paide
Jõgeva
Põltsamaa
Viljandi
Tartu
Elva
Põlva
Võru
Valga
Valka
Pechory
Pskov
Slantsy
Gdov
Luga
Strugi-Krasnyye
Sol'tsy
Dno
Porkhov
Dedovichi
Ostrov
Pytalovo
Pushkinskiye Gory
Novorzhev
Bezhanitsy
Loknya
Krasnogorodskoye
Opochka
Smiltene
Alūksne
Gulbene
Balvi
Madona
Ludza
Rēzekne
Jēkabpils
Ostrov Gogland
O. Moshchnyy
O. Bol'shoy Tyuters
FINSKIY ZALIV
Narva laht
Narvskiy zaliv
Peipsi järv
Ozero Chudskoye
Pskovskoe ozero
Võrtsjärv
Narvskoye Vdkhr.
Lahemaa rahvuspark
Karula rahvuspark
Itäisen Suomenlahden kansallispuisto
Pandivere kõrgustik
Kellavere 155
Emumägi 166
Sakala kõrgustik
Rutu mägi 144
Kuutse mägi 217
Otepää kõrgustik
Suur Munamägi 318
Delinkalns 271
Sleņjuma kalns 243
Gaiziņkalns 311
Sudomskiye Vysoty 293
Bezhanitskaya Vozvyshennost'
RUS

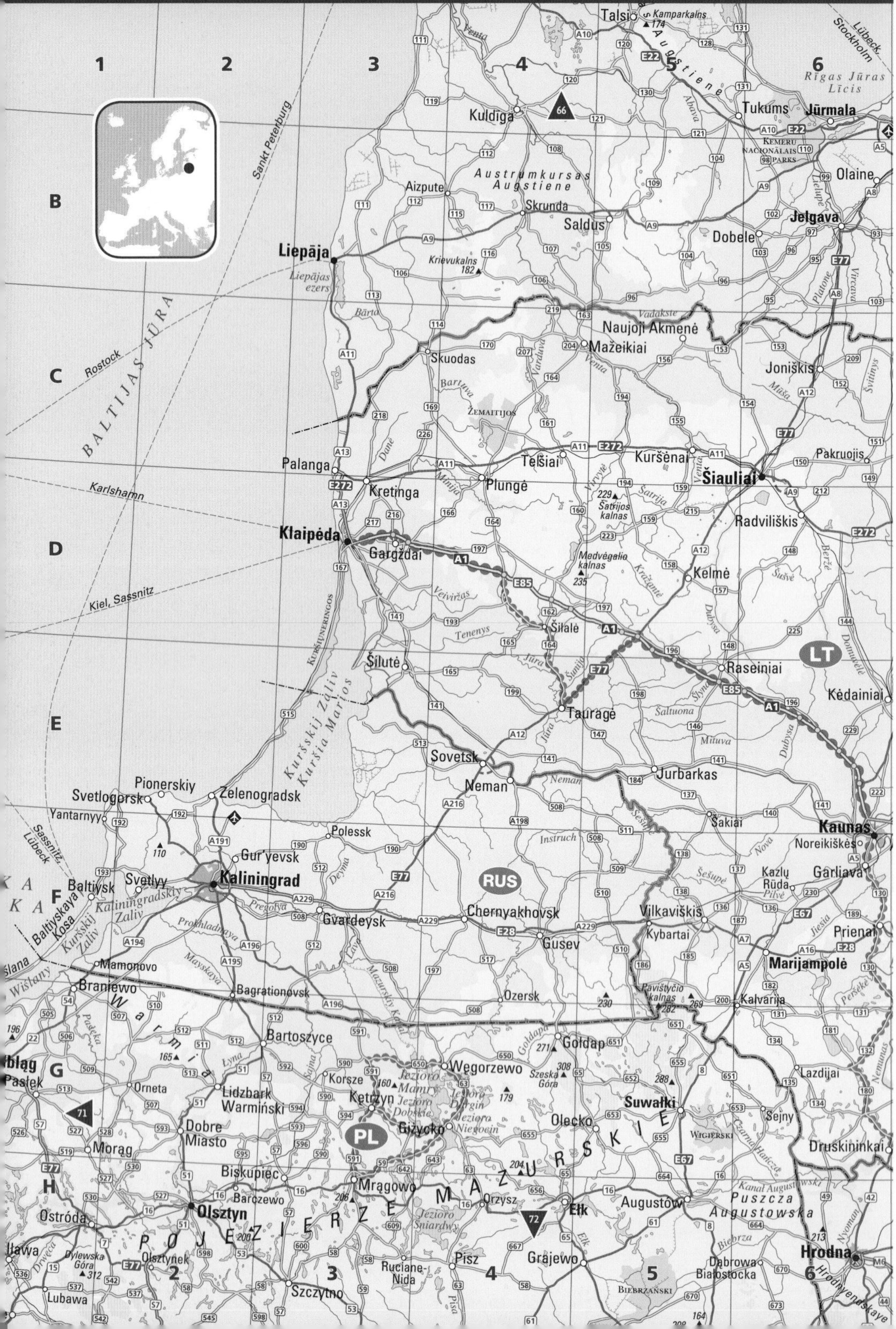

1 2 3 4 5 6

B C D E F G H

Talsi
Kamparkalns 174
Tukums
Jūrmala
Rīgas Jūras Līcis
Lübeck, Stockholm
Kuldīga
Austrumkursas Augstiene
Kemeru Nacionālais Parks
Olaine
Aizpute
Skrunda
Saldus
Dobele
Jelgava
Liepāja
Liepājas ezers
Krievukalns 182
Sankt Peterburg
Baltijas Jūra
Rostock
Karlshamn
Kiel, Sassnitz
Sassnitz, Lübeck
Naujoji Akmenė
Mažeikiai
Skuodas
Joniškis
Žemaitijos
Palanga
Kretinga
Plungė
Telšiai
Kuršėnai
Šiauliai
Pakruojis
Šatrijos kalnas 229
Radviliškis
Klaipėda
Gargždai
Medvėgalio kalnas 235
Kelmė
Kuršių Nerijos
Šilalė
Šilutė
Raseiniai
Kuršskij Zaliv
Kuršių Marios
Tauragė
Kėdainiai
LT
Sovetsk
Neman
Jurbarkas
Pionerskiy
Svetlogorsk
Zelenogradsk
Yantarnyy
Polessk
Šakiai
Kaunas
Noreikiškės
Gur'yevsk
Kaliningrad
Svetlyy
Baltiysk
Baltiyskaya Kosa
Kaliningradskiy Zaliv
RUS
Kazlų Rūda
Garliava
Gvardeysk
Chernyakhovsk
Vilkaviškis
Kybartai
Prienai
Gusev
Marijampolė
Mamonovo
Braniewo
Bagrationovsk
Ozersk
Pavištyčio kalnas 282
Kalvarija
Warmia
Bartoszyce
Gołdap
Lazdijai
Elbląg
Pasłek
Orneta
Lidzbark Warmiński
Korsze
Węgorzewo
Jezioro Mamry
Kętrzyn
Suwałki
Sejny
Morąg
Dobre Miasto
Giżycko
PL
Olecko
Wigierski
Druskininkai
Biskupiec
Mrągowo
Orzysz
Ełk
Augustów
Puszcza Augustowska
Ostróda
Olsztyn
Barczewo
Jezioro Śniardwy
Pojezierze Mazurskie
Iława
Olsztynek
Ruciane-Nida
Pisz
Grajewo
Biebrzański
Dąbrowa Białostocka
Hrodna
Lubawa
Szczytno
Nemunas
Neris

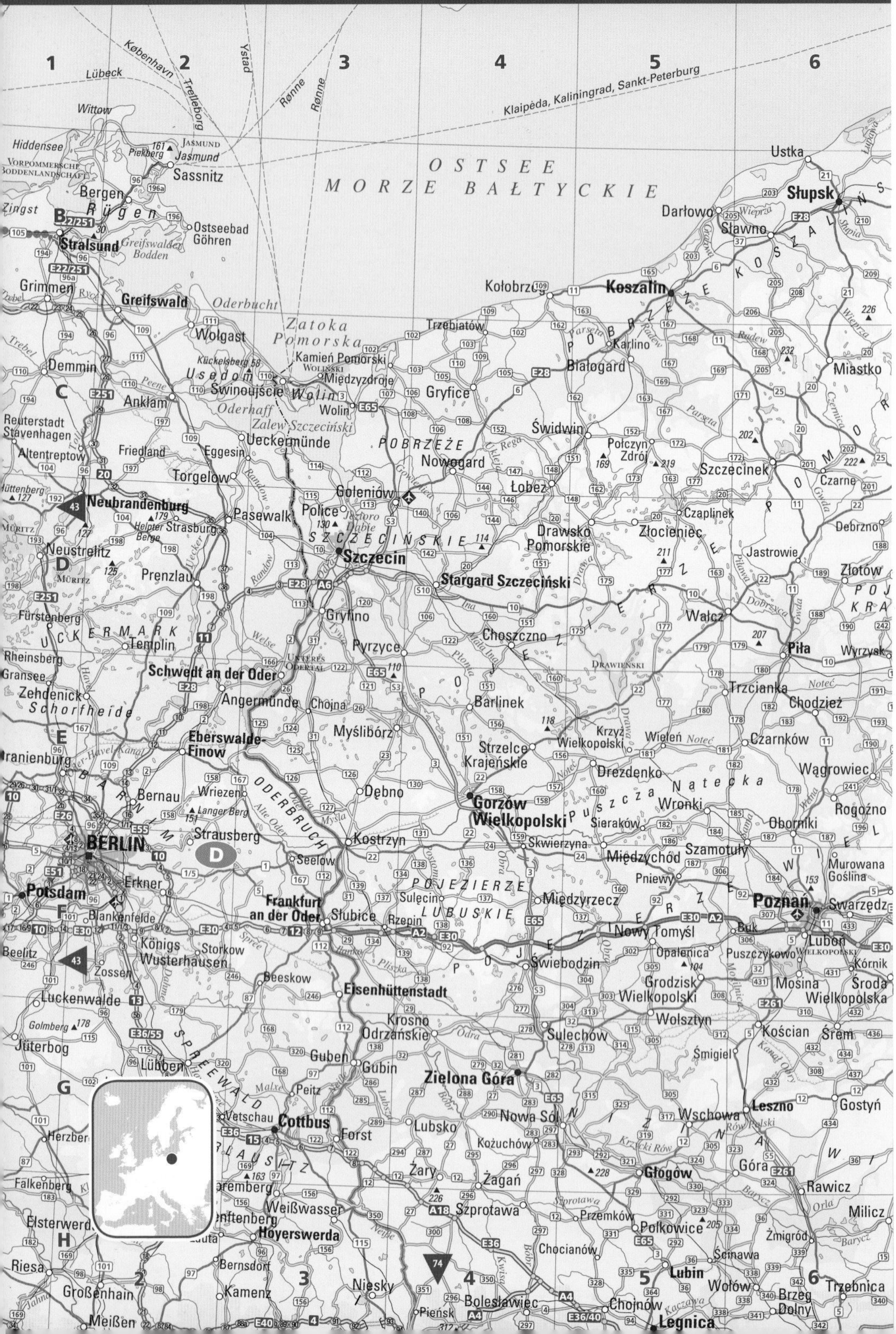

1 2 3 4 5 6

København
Ystad
Lübeck
Trelleborg
Rønne
Rønne
Klaipėda, Kaliningrad, Sankt-Peterburg
Wittow
Hiddensee
Jasmund
Piekberg 161
Jasmund
Vorpommersche Boddenlandschaft
Sassnitz
OSTSEE
MORZE BAŁTYCKIE
Bergen
Rügen
Zingst
Stralsund
Ostseebad Göhren
Greifswalder Bodden
Grimmen
Greifswald
Oderbucht
Zatoka Pomorska
Wolgast
Kückelsberg 58
Usedom
Świnoujście
Wolin
Kamień Pomorski
Woliński
Międzyzdroje
Wolin
Demmin
Anklam
Oderhaff
Zalew Szczeciński
Reuterstadt Stavenhagen
Altentreptow
Friedland
Eggesin
Ueckermünde
Torgelow
Neubrandenburg
Helpter Berge 179
Strasburg
Pasewalk
Police
Jezioro Dąbie
Goleniów
Szczecin
Szczecińskie
Neustrelitz
Müritz
Prenzlau
Fürstenberg
Uckermark
Templin
Rheinsberg
Gransee
Zehdenick
Schorfheide
Schwedt an der Oder
Unteres Odertal
Angermünde
Chojna
Gryfino
Pyrzyce
Myślibórz
Eberswalde-Finow
Oranienburg
Barnim
Bernau
Wriezen
Oderbruch
Langer Berg 151
Dębno
Kostrzyn
Strausberg
BERLIN
Seelow
Potsdam
Erkner
Frankfurt an der Oder
Słubice
Rzepin
Sulęcin
Pojezierze Lubuskie
Königs Wusterhausen
Storkow
Beelitz
Zossen
Beeskow
Eisenhüttenstadt
Luckenwalde
Golmberg 178
Jüterbog
Lübben
Spreewald
Krosno Odrzańskie
Guben
Gubin
Peitz
Vetschau
Cottbus
Forst
Lusatia
Lausitz
Herzberg
Falkenberg
Spremberg
Weißwasser
Senftenberg
Hoyerswerda
Lauta
Elsterwerda
Riesa
Großenhain
Meißen
Kamenz
Bernsdorf
Niesky
Pieńsk
Bolesławiec
Kołobrzeg
Trzebiatów
Koszalin
Darłowo
Sławno
Słupsk
Ustka
Białogard
Karlino
Pobrzeże Koszalińskie
Gryfice
Nowogard
Pobrzeże Szczecińskie
Świdwin
Połczyn Zdrój
Łobez
Drawsko Pomorskie
Złocieniec
Czaplinek
Szczecinek
Czarne
Miastko
Jastrowie
Debrzno
Złotów
Stargard Szczeciński
Wałcz
Choszczno
Piła
Wyrzysk
Drawieński
Trzcianka
Chodzież
Barlinek
Pojezierze Pomorskie
Strzelce Krajeńskie
Krzyż Wielkopolski
Wieleń
Czarnków
Drezdenko
Wągrowiec
Gorzów Wielkopolski
Puszcza Notecka
Wronki
Rogoźno
Skwierzyna
Sieraków
Oborniki
Międzychód
Szamotuły
Murowana Goślina
Pniewy
Międzyrzecz
Poznań
Swarzędz
Nowy Tomyśl
Buk
Luboń
Świebodzin
Opalenica
Puszczykowo
Kórnik
Grodzisk Wielkopolski
Mosina
Środa Wielkopolska
Wolsztyn
Sulechów
Kościan
Śrem
Śmigiel
Zielona Góra
Nowa Sól
Wschowa
Leszno
Gostyń
Lubsko
Kożuchów
Żary
Żagań
Szprotawa
Głogów
Góra
Rawicz
Przemków
Polkowice
Milicz
Chocianów
Żmigród
Ścinawa
Lubin
Wołów
Trzebnica
Brzeg Dolny
Chojnów
Legnica
Wielkopolski
Pojezierze Wielkopolskie
Kaczawa
Barycz
Odra

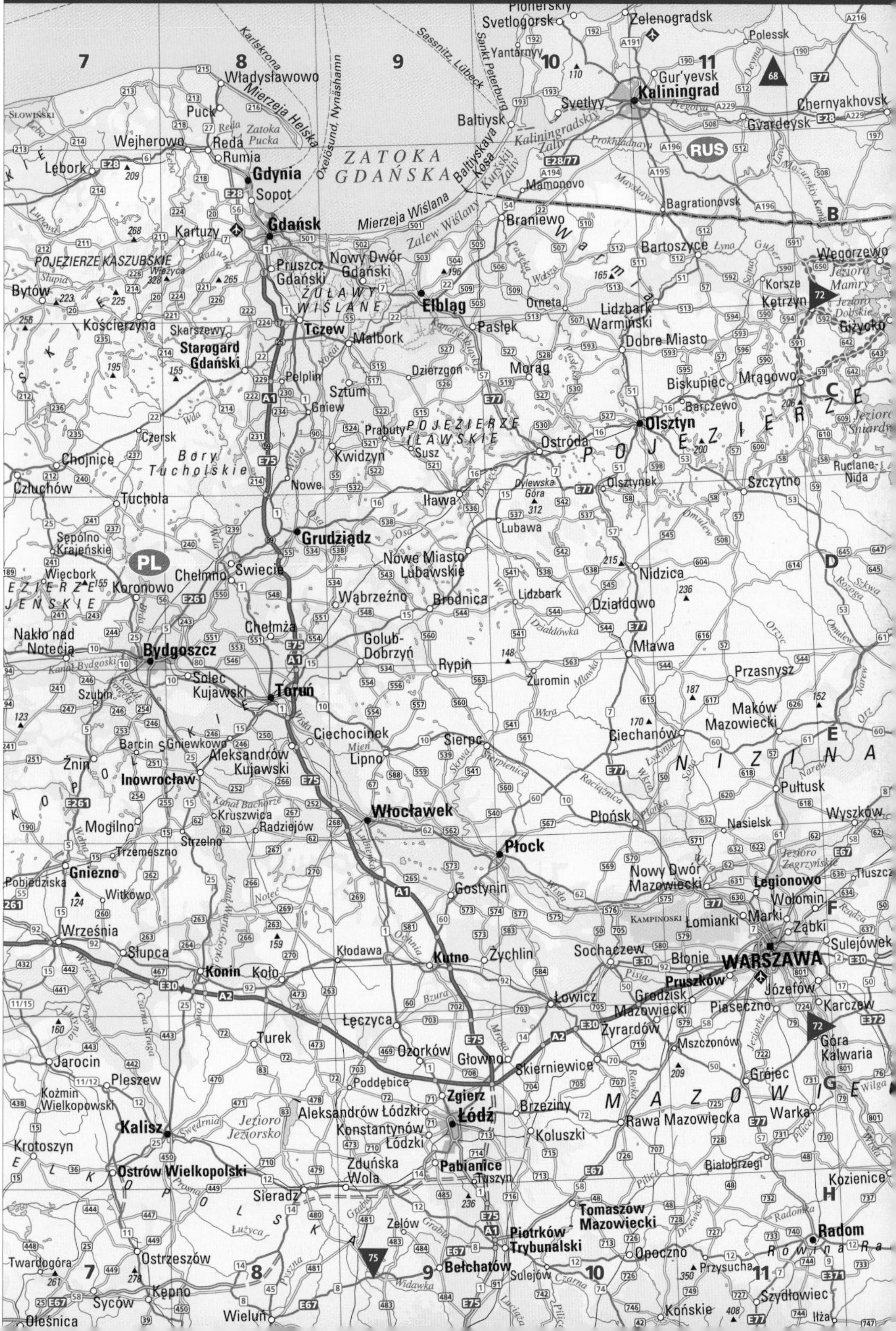

7 8 9 10 11

Svetlogorsk
Zelenogradsk
Polessk
Yantarnyy
Władysławowo
Mierzeja Helska
Gur'yevsk
Kaliningrad
Puck
Zatoka Pucka
Svetlyy
Baltiysk
Chernyakhovsk
Gvardeysk
Słowiński
Wejherowo
Reda
Rumia
Kaliningradskiy Zaliv
RUS
Lębork
Gdynia
ZATOKA GDAŃSKA
Baltiyskaya Kosa
Kurskij Zaliv
Mamonovo
Sopot
Bagrationovsk
Gdańsk
Mierzeja Wiślana
Zalew Wiślany
Braniewo
Kartuzy
Warmia
Bartoszyce
Węgorzewo
POJEZIERZE KASZUBSKIE
Pruszcz Gdański
Nowy Dwór Gdański
Jezioro Mamry
Bytów
ŻUŁAWY WIŚLANE
Elbląg
Orneta
Lidzbark Warmiński
Korsze
Kętrzyn
Jezioro Dobskie
Giżycko
Kościerzyna
Skarszewy
Tczew
Malbork
Pasłęk
Dobre Miasto
Starogard Gdański
Pelplin
Dzierzgoń
Morąg
Biskupiec
Mrągowo
Sztum
Gniew
Barczewo
POJEZIERZE IŁAWSKIE
Prabuty
Olsztyn
Czersk
Susz
Ostróda
Chojnice
Bory Tucholskie
Kwidzyn
Człuchów
Nowe
Olsztynek
Szczytno
Ruciane-Nida
Tuchola
Iława
Dylewska Góra
Lubawa
Sępólno Krajeńskie
Grudziądz
PL
Nowe Miasto Lubawskie
Więcbork
Chełmno
Świecie
Nidzica
Koronowo
Wąbrzeźno
Brodnica
Lidzbark
Działdowo
Nakło nad Notecią
Chełmża
Golub-Dobrzyń
Mława
Bydgoszcz
Kanał Bydgoski
Rypin
Przasnysz
Solec Kujawski
Szubin
Toruń
Żuromin
Barcin
Gniewkowo
Ciechocinek
Maków Mazowiecki
Żnin
Aleksandrów Kujawski
Lipno
Sierpc
Ciechanów
Inowrocław
NIZINA
Pułtusk
Mogilno
Kruszwica
Radziejów
Włocławek
Płońsk
Wyszków
Strzelno
Trzemeszno
Nasielsk
Płock
Gniezno
Nowy Dwór Mazowiecki
Legionowo
Witkowo
Gostynin
Wołomin
Kampinoski
Łomianki
Marki
Ząbki
Września
Słupca
Kłodawa
Kutno
Żychlin
Sochaczew
Błonie
WARSZAWA
Sulejówek
Konin
Koło
Pruszków
Grodzisk Mazowiecki
Józefów
Łowicz
Piaseczno
Karczew
Łęczyca
Żyrardów
Turek
Ozorków
Głowno
Skierniewice
Mszczonów
Góra Kalwaria
Jarocin
Pleszew
Poddębice
Grójec
Koźmin Wielkopolski
Zgierz
MAZOWIECKIE
Aleksandrów Łódzki
Łódź
Brzeziny
Warka
Kalisz
Jezioro Jeziorsko
Konstantynów Łódzki
Rawa Mazowiecka
Koluszki
Krotoszyn
Zduńska Wola
Pabianice
Tuszyn
Białobrzegi
Ostrów Wielkopolski
Kozienice
Sieradz
Tomaszów Mazowiecki
Zelów
Piotrków Trybunalski
Radom
Twardogóra
Ostrzeszów
Opoczno
Bełchatów
Sulejów
Przysucha
Syców
Kępno
Szydłowiec
Oleśnica
Wieluń
Końskie
Iłża

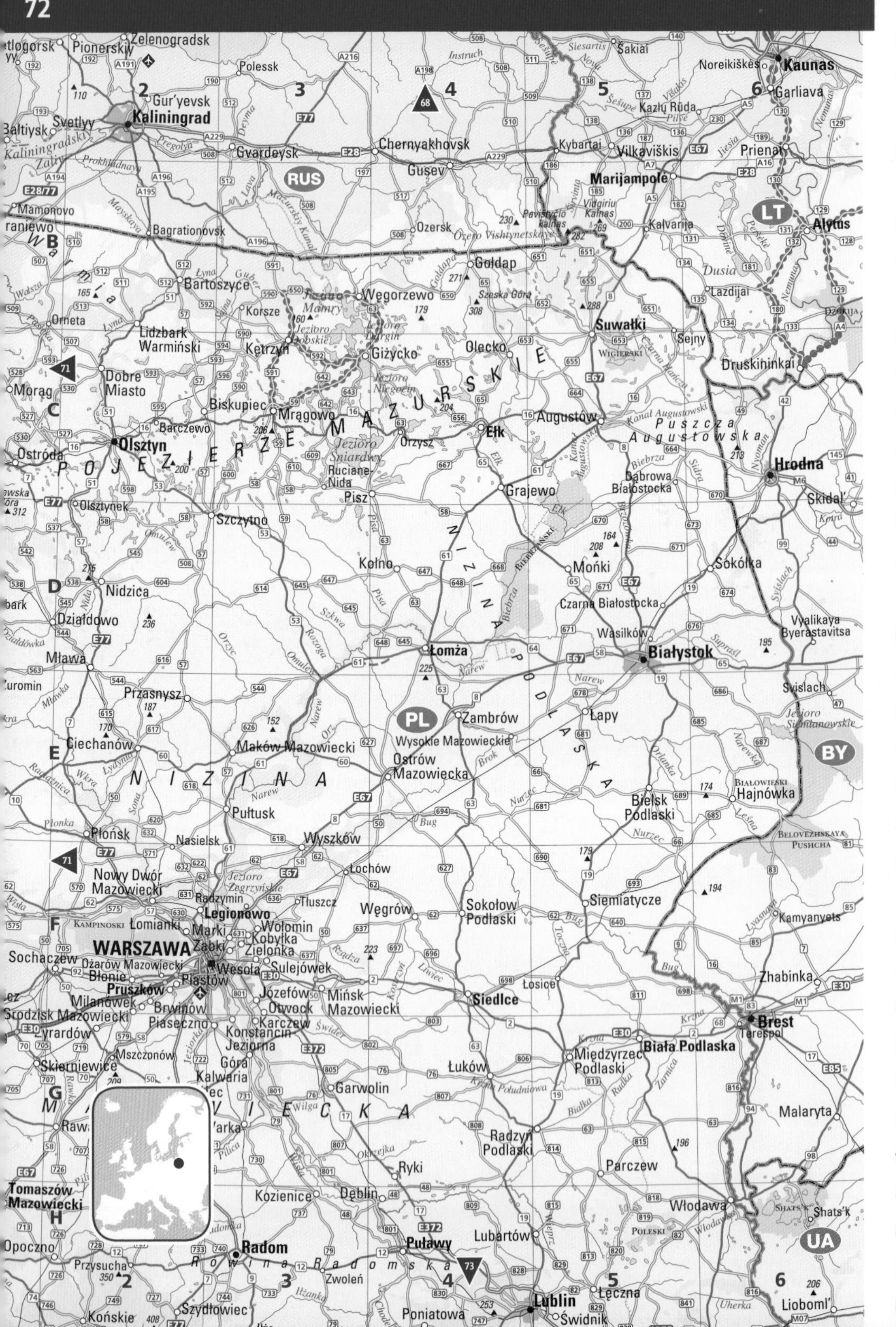
Zelenogradsk
Pionerskiy
Polessk
Kaliningrad
Gur'yevsk
Svetlyy
Baltiysk
Kaliningradskiy Zaliv
Gvardeysk
Chernyakhovsk
Gusev
RUS
Mamonovo
Bagrationovsk
Ozersk
Sakiai
Kaunas
Noreikiškės
Garliava
Kazlų Rūda
Kybartai
Vilkaviškis
Prienai
Marijampolė
Kalvarija
Alytus
LT
Lazdijai
Druskininkai
Goldap
Węgorzewo
Bartoszyce
Korsze
Orneta
Lidzbark Warmiński
Kętrzyn
Giżycko
Olecko
Suwałki
Sejny
Dobre Miasto
Morąg
Biskupiec
Mrągowo
Augustów
Ełk
Olsztyn
Barczewo
Ostróda
POJEZIERZE MAZURSKIE
Ruciane-Nida
Pisz
Grajewo
Hrodna
Dąbrowa Białostocka
Skidal'
Olsztynek
Szczytno
Kolno
Mońki
Sokółka
Nidzica
Działdowo
Czarna Białostocka
Wasilków
Białystok
Vyalikaya Byerastavitsa
Łomża
Mława
Przasnysz
Zambrów
Łapy
Svislach
PL
BY
Ciechanów
Maków Mazowiecki
Wysokie Mazowieckie
Ostrów Mazowiecka
NIZINA PODLASKA
Bielsk Podlaski
Hajnówka
Pułtusk
Płońsk
Nasielsk
Wyszków
Nowy Dwór Mazowiecki
Łochów
Radzymin
Legionowo
Tłuszcz
Węgrów
Sokołów Podlaski
Siemiatycze
Kamyanyets
Łomianki
Marki
Wołomin
Kobyłka
WARSZAWA
Ząbki
Zielonka
Sochaczew
Ożarów Mazowiecki
Błonie
Wesoła
Sulejówek
Pruszków
Piastów
Józefów
Mińsk Mazowiecki
Milanówek
Brwinów
Otwock
Siedlce
Łosice
Zhabinka
Grodzisk Mazowiecki
Piaseczno
Karczew
Brest
Terespol
Żyrardów
Konstancin-Jeziorna
Biała Podlaska
Skierniewice
Mszczonów
Góra Kalwaria
Łuków
Międzyrzec Podlaski
Garwolin
Malaryta
Rawa
Radzyń Podlaski
Ryki
Parczew
Tomaszów Mazowiecki
Kozienice
Dęblin
Włodawa
Shats'k
UA
Lubartów
Puławy
Radom
Opoczno
Przysucha
Zwoleń
Łęczna
Końskie
Szydłowiec
Poniatowa
Lublin
Świdnik
Liuboml'
NIZINA MAZOWIECKA
Rowina Radomska

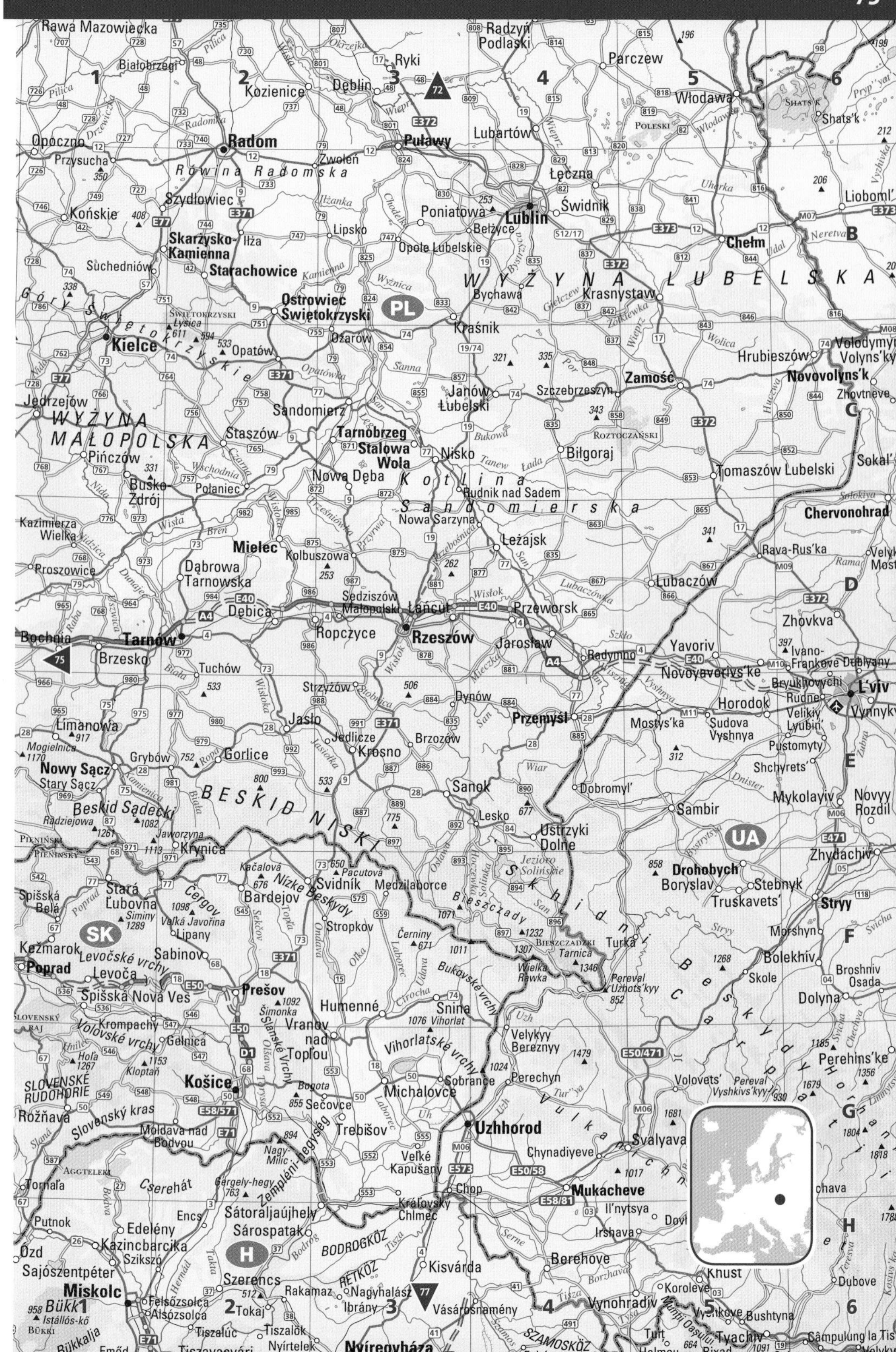
Rawa Mazowiecka
Radzyń Podlaski
Parczew
Białobrzegi
Kozienice
Dęblin
Ryki
Włodawa
Shats'k
Opoczno
Radom
Puławy
Lubartów
Przysucha
Równina Radomska
Zwoleń
Łęczna
Szydłowiec
Poniatowa
Lublin
Świdnik
Liuboml'
Końskie
Lipsko
Bełżyce
Skarżysko-Kamienna
Iłża
Opole Lubelskie
Chełm
Suchedniów
Starachowice
Wyżyna Lubelska
Bychawa
Krasnystaw
Góry Świętokrzyskie
Ostrowiec Świętokrzyski
PL
Kraśnik
Kielce
Opatów
Ożarów
Hrubieszów
Volodymyr-Volyns'kyy
Novovolyns'k
Jędrzejów
Sandomierz
Janów Lubelski
Szczebrzeszyn
Zamość
Zhovtneve
Wyżyna Małopolska
Staszów
Tarnobrzeg
Stalowa Wola
Nisko
Biłgoraj
Pińczów
Busko-Zdrój
Połaniec
Nowa Dęba
Kotlina Sandomierska
Rudnik nad Sanem
Tomaszów Lubelski
Sokal'
Chervonohrad
Kazimierza Wielka
Nowa Sarzyna
Mielec
Kolbuszowa
Leżajsk
Rava-Rus'ka
Velyki Mosty
Proszowice
Dąbrowa Tarnowska
Lubaczów
Dębica
Sędziszów Małopolski
Łańcut
Przeworsk
Zhovkva
Bochnia
Tarnów
Ropczyce
Rzeszów
Jarosław
Brzesko
Tuchów
Radymno
Yavoriv
Novoyavorivs'ke
Ivano-Frankove
Dublyany
L'viv
Strzyżów
Dynów
Horodok
Rudne
Vynnyky
Limanowa
Jasło
Jedlicze
Krosno
Brzozów
Przemyśl
Mostys'ka
Sudova Vyshnya
Velikiy Lyubin'
Pustomyty
Gorlice
Grybów
Nowy Sącz
Stary Sącz
Shchyrets'
Beskid Niski
Sanok
Dobromyl'
Mykolayiv
Novyy Rozdil
Beskid Sądecki
Lesko
Sambir
Ustrzyki Dolne
UA
Krynica
Zhydachiv
Bardejov
Svidník
Medzilaborce
Drohobych
Boryslav
Stebnyk
Truskavets'
Stryy
Stará Ľubovňa
Nízke Beskydy
Stropkov
Bieszczady
SK
Lipany
Morshyn
Kežmarok
Sabinov
Turka
Bolekhiv
Poprad
Levoča
Prešov
Skole
Spišská Nová Ves
Humenné
Snina
Dolyna
Krompachy
Vranov nad Topľou
Gelnica
Vihorlat
Velykyy Bereznyy
Perehins'ke
Košice
Michalovce
Sobrance
Perechyn
Volovets'
Rožňava
Slovenský kras
Sečovce
Trebišov
Uzhhorod
Svalyava
Moldava nad Bodvou
Veľké Kapušany
Chynadiyeve
Tornaľa
Chop
Mukacheve
Sátoraljaújhely
Sárospatak
Kráľovský Chlmec
Il'nytsya
Putnok
Edelény
Irshava
Ózd
Kazincbarcika
Kisvárda
Berehove
Sajószentpéter
Szerencs
Khust
Miskolc
Tokaj
Rakamaz
Nagyhalász
Vásárosnamény
Vynohradiv
Dubove
Bükk
Tiszalúc
Tiszalök
Nyírtelek
Nyíregyháza
Bushtyna
Tyachiv
Câmpulung la Tisa
H

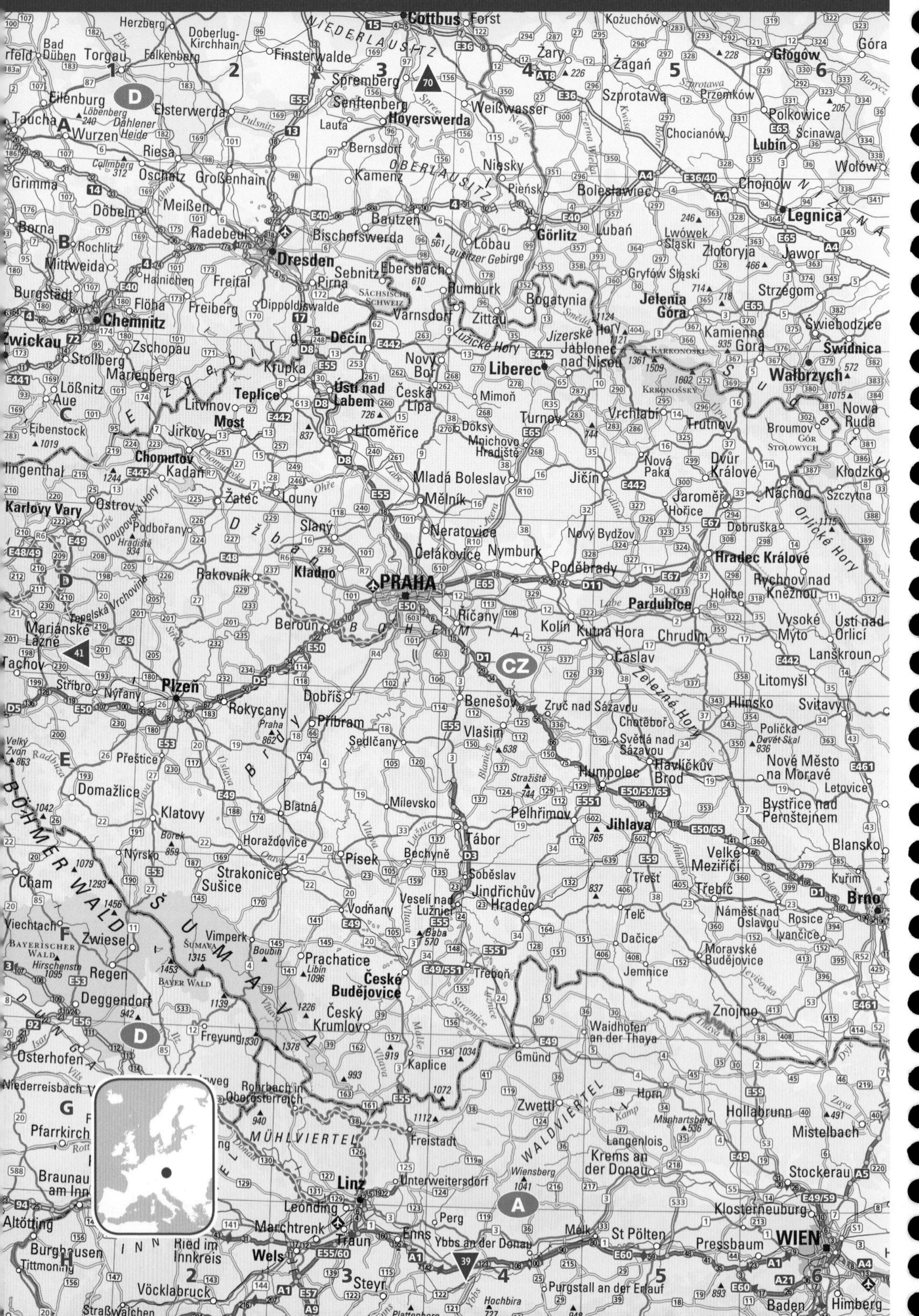
Cottbus
Dresden
Chemnitz
Děčín
Ústí nad Labem
Teplice
Most
Liberec
Jelenia Góra
Wałbrzych
Legnica
Głogów
Hradec Králové
Pardubice
PRAHA
Kladno
Plzeň
Karlovy Vary
Tábor
Jihlava
České Budějovice
Linz
Wels
St Pölten
WIEN
Brno
Görlitz
Bautzen
Hoyerswerda
Lubin
Świdnica
Krems an der Donau

NIZINA WIELKOPOLSKA
Kalisz
Krotoszyn
Rawicz
Ostrów Wielkopolski
Sieradz
Zduńska Wola
Pabianice
Koluszki
Tuszyn
Białobrzegi
Tomaszów Mazowiecki
Piotrków Trybunalski
Bełchatów
Zelów
Milicz
Żmigród
Ostrzeszów
Trzebnica
Twardogóra
Kępno
Syców
Oleśnica
Brzeg Dolny
Wrocław
Bierutów
Namysłów
Jelcz-Laskowice
Wieluń
Pajęczno
Praszka
Wołczyn
Kluczbork
Oława
Brzeg
Olesno
Kłobuck
Częstochowa
Blachownia
WYŻYNA KRAKOWSKO-CZĘSTOCHOWSKA
Radomsko
Sulejów
Opoczno
Przysucha
Końskie
Szydłowiec
Skarżysko-Kamienna
Suchedniów
Góry Świętokrzyskie
Kielce
Włoszczowa
Koniecpol
PL
Strzelin
Lewin Brzeski
Grodków
Niemodlin
Opole
Ozimek
Lubliniec
Ząbkowice Śląskie
Ziębice
Zawadzkie
Strzelce Opolskie
Kalety
Myszków
Zawiercie
Jędrzejów
WYŻYNA MAŁOPOLSKA
Pińczów
Busko-Zdrój
Otmuchów
Nysa
Krapkowice
Tarnowskie Góry
Paczków
Pyskowice
Zdzieszowice
Bytom
Będzin
Dąbrowa Górnicza
Wolbrom
Miechów
Głuchołazy
Prudnik
Kędzierzyn-Koźle
Gliwice
Zabrze
Sosnowiec
Olkusz
Kazimierza Wielka
Jeseník
Głubczyce
Czerwionka-Leszczyny
Katowice
Jaworzno
Proszowice
Vrbno pod Pradědem
Racibórz
Rybnik
Tychy
Chrzanów
Bieruń
Kraków
Krnov
Rydułtowy
Żory
Oświęcim
Skawina
Wieliczka
Bochnia
Brzesko
Hrubý Jeseník
Bruntál
Jastrzębie-Zdrój
Brzeszcze
Opava
Bohumín
Kęty
Wadowice
Dobczyce
Šumperk
Rýmařov
Bielsko-Biała
Zábřeh
Ostrava
Karviná
Andrychów
Myślenice
Mohelnice
Uničov
Bílovec
Havířov
Cieszyn
Maków Podhalański
Limanowa
Moravská Třebová
Šternberk
Studénka
Třinec
Żywiec
Mszana Dolna
Nowy Sącz
Litovel
Odry
Frýdek-Místek
Wisła
KARPATY
Rabka
Olomouc
Hranice
Nový Jičín
Jablunkov
Nowy Targ
Boskovice
Valašské Meziříčí
Čadca
Prostějov
Přerov
Krásno nad Kysucou
Trstená
Zakopane
Stará Ľubovňa
Vyškov
Holešov
Vsetín
Kysucké Nové Mesto
Oravská Magura
TATRY
Kroměříž
Zlín
Javorníky
Bytča
Žilina
Dolný Kubín
Spišská Belá
MORAVA
Chřiby
Valašské Klobouky
Púchov
Liptovský Mikuláš
Kežmarok
Bučovice
Uherské Hradiště
Slavičín
Považská Bystrica
Martin
Ružomberok
Poprad
Levoča
Kyjov
Uherský Brod
Veľká Fatra
Spišská Nová Ves
Hustopeče
Veselí nad Moravou
Nová Dubnica
NÍZKE TATRY
Strážnice
Turčianske Teplice
Brezno
Skalica
Trenčín
Bojnice
Prievidza
Břeclav
Holíč
Banská Bystrica
Čierny Balog
Revúca
Rožňava
Senica
Nové Mesto nad Váhom
Bánovce nad Bebravou
SK
Poľana
Partizánske
Žiar nad Hronom
Piešťany
Zvolen
Detva
Hriňová
Hnúšťa
Vrbové
Topoľčany
Malacky
Malé Karpaty
TRIBEČ
Zlaté Moravce
Banská Štiavnica
Javorie
Poltár
Tornaľa
Hlohovec
Nová Baňa
Trnava
Krupina
Lučenec
Rimavská Sobota
Putnok
Gänserndorf
Pezinok
Modra
Sereď
Strasshof an der Nordbahn
Stupava
Nitra
Vráble
Tlmače
Krupinská Planina
Fiľakovo
Senec
Galanta
Levice
Veľký Krtíš
Ózd
Hainburg an der Donau
BRATISLAVA
Šaľa
Šurany
Šahy
H
Salgótarján
Szécsény
Balassagyarmat
Želiezovce
Šamorín
Dunajská Streda
Nové Zámky
Bátonyterenye
Cserhát

Stockerau
Klosterneuburg
St.Pölten
WIEN
Malacky
Gänserndorf
Pezinok
Modra
Stupava
Trnava
Hlohovec
Sereď
Senec
Nitra
Zlaté Moravce
Nová Baňa
Banská Štiavnica
Krupina
Vráble
Tlmače
Levice
Galanta
Šaľa
Šurany
BRATISLAVA
Hainburg an der Donau
Pressbaum
Baden
Himberg
Dunajská Streda
Šamorín
Nové Zámky
Želiezovce
Šahy
Balassagyarmat
Szécsény
Cserhát
Wiener Neustadt
Eisenstadt
Neusiedler See
Mosonmagyaróvár
Kolárovo
Veľký Meder
Hurbanovo
Štúrovo
Esztergom
Vác
Neunkirchen
Ternitz
Gloggnitz
Mattersburg
Jánossomorja
Komárno
Komárom
Nyergesújfalu
Lábatlan
Tát
Tokod
Dorog
Szentendre
Göd
Mürzzuschlag
Sopron
Hanság
Győr
Ács
Tata
Pilisvörösvár
Dunakeszi
Aszód
Kapuvár
Csorna
Tatabánya
Pilisszentiván
Fót
Gödöllő
Kerepestarcsa
Pécel
BUDAPEST
Kisbér
Oroszlány
Bicske
Budaörs
Törökbálint
Pinkafeld
Kőszeg
Pápa
Mór
Érd
Dunaharaszti
Vecsés
Monor
Hartberg
Oberwart
Sárvár
Celldömölk
Bakony
Zirc
Szigetszentmiklós
Gyál
Százhalombatta
Ócsa
Szombathely
Székesfehérvár
Várpalota
Ercsi
Dunavarsány
Bugyi
Dabas
Gárdony
Kiskunlacháza
Ráckeve
Pusztaszabolcs
Fürstenfeld
Vasvár
Devecser
Ajka
Veszprém
Berhida
Polgárdi
Dömsöd
Körmend
Balatonalmádi
Kunszentmiklós
Lajosmizse
Sümeg
Zalaszentgrót
Balatonfüred
Dunaújváros
Tapolca
Enying
Zalaegerszeg
Siófok
Sárbogárd
Szabadszállás
Keszthely
Balatonboglár
Solt
Izsák
Fonyód
Dunaföldvár
Murska Sobota
Tab
Külső-Somogy
Lenti
Tamási
Paks
Kiskőrös
Lendava
Marcali
Soltvadkert
Ljutomer
Nagykanizsa
Kecel
Kalocsa
Ptuj
Ormož
Čakovec
Dombóvár
Tolna
Szekszárd
Kiskunhalas
Varaždin
Kaposvár
Bonyhád
Jánoshalma
Ivanec
Csurgó
Nagyatád
Komló
Bátaszék
Baja
Koprivnica
Mecsek
Križevci
Szigetvár
Pécs
Mélykút
Bácsalmás
Đurđevac
Barcs
Szentőrinc
Mohács
Tavankut
Bjelovar
Pitomača
Bajmok
Virovitica
Siklós
Stanišić
ZAGREB
Dugo Selo
Ivanić-Grad
Ormánság
Bezdan
Stara Moravica
Velika Gorica
Donji Miholjac
Beli Manastir
Sombor
Kljajićevo
Sivac
Slatina
Belišće
Valpovo
Apatin
Crvenka
Kula
Daruvar
Darda
Sonta
Ruski Krstur
Kutina
Osijek
Čepin
Petrinja
Sisak
Pakrac
Našice
Tenja
Dalj
Karavukovo
Odžaci
Glina
Novska
Požega
Borovo Selo
Bač
Bački Petrovac
Nova Gradiška
Đakovo
Ivankovo
Vukovar
Bačka Palanka
Vinkovci
Dubica
Bosanska Gradiška
Slavonski Brod
Bosanski Brod
Otok
Ilok
Šid
Županja
Bosanski Šamac
Bosanska Krupa
Derventa
Modriča
Sremska
Bihać
Prnjavor
Gradačac
Brčko
Gunja
Sanski Most
Banja Luka
Doboj
Bijeljina
SK
A
H
SLO
HR
BIH

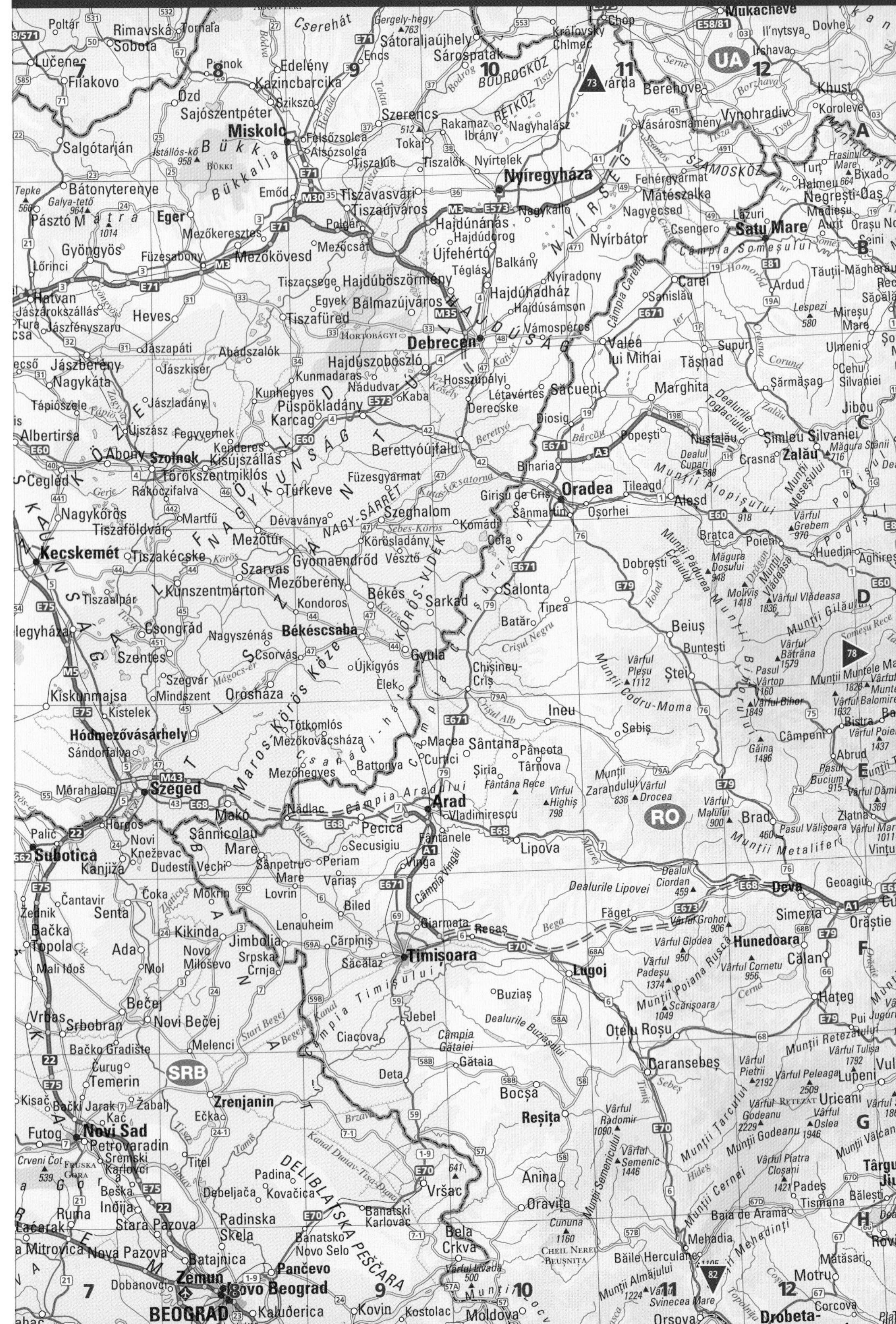
Poltár
Rimavská Sobota
Tornaľa
Cserehát
Gergely-hegy
763
Sátoraljaújhely
Mukacheve
Chop
Kráľovský Chlmec
Il'nytsya
Dovhe
Lučenec
7
Fiľakovo
8
Edelény
9
Encs
Sárospatak
10
BODROGKÖZ
11
Várda
Irshava
UA
12
Berehove
Khust
Kazincbarcika
Ózd
Sajószentpéter
Szikszó
Szerencs
RÉTKÖZ
Rakamaz
Nagyhalász
Ibrány
Vásárosnamény
Vynohradiv
Koroleve
Miskolc
Felsőzsolca
Alsózsolca
Tokaj
Salgótarján
Istállós-kő
958
B ü k k
Bükki
Tiszalúc
Tiszalök
Nyírtelek
A
Nyíregyháza
SZAMOSKÖZ
Fehérgyarmat
Turț
Bixad
Halmeu
Negrești-Oaș
Bátonyterenye
Bükkalja
Emőd
Tiszavasvári
Mátészalka
Galya-tető
964
Pásztó
M á t r a
1014
Eger
Tiszaújváros
Nagykálló
Nagyecsed
Lazuri
Madiesu
Aurit
Orașu Nou
Polgár
Hajdúnánás
Hajdúdorog
N Y Í R S É G
Csengeri
Satu Mare
Mezőkeresztes
Mezőcsát
Nyírbátor
Câmpia Someșului
Gyöngyös
Füzesabony
Mezőkövesd
Újfehértó
Balkány
B
Lőrinci
Téglás
Nyíradony
Carei
Tăuții-Măgherăuș
Hatvan
Jászárokszállás
Tiszacsege
Hajdúböszörmény
Hajdúhadház
Ardud
Egyek
Balmazújváros
Hajdúsámson
Sanislău
Jászfényszaru
Heves
Tiszafüred
Câmpia Careiului
Lespezi
580
Mireșu Mare
Hortobágyi
Debrecen
H A J D Ú S Á G
Vámospércs
Valea lui Mihai
Supur
Ulmeni
Jászapáti
Abádszalók
Hajdúszoboszló
Tășnad
Jászberény
Jászkisér
Kunmadaras
Hosszúpályi
Cehu Silvaniei
Nagykáta
Kunhegyes
Nádudvar
Kaba
Létavértes
Săcueni
Marghita
Șărmășag
Tápiószele
Jászladány
Püspökladány
Derecske
Dealurile Toglaciului
Jibou
Albertirsa
Újszász
Fegyvernek
Karcag
Diosig
Popești
Nusfalău
Șimleu Silvaniei
C
Kenderes
Berettyóújfalu
Dealul Cupari
588
Crasna
Zalău
Măgura Stânii
716
Abony
Szolnok
Kisújszállás
Biharia
Munții Plopișului
Munții Meseșului
Cegléd
Törökszentmiklós
Füzesgyarmat
Oradea
Tileagd
Aleșd
Rákóczifalva
Túrkeve
Girișu de Criș
Nagykőrös
Martfű
Szeghalom
Sânmartin
Oșorhei
918
Vârful Grebem
970
Tiszaföldvár
Dévaványa
NAGY-SÁRRÉT
Komádi
Mezőtúr
Körösladány
Cefa
Bratca
Poieni
Kecskemét
Tiszakécske
Gyomaendrőd
Vésztő
Huedin
Aghireșu
Szarvas
Dobrești
Munții Pădurea Craiului
Măgura Dosului
948
Munții Vlădeasa
Mezőberény
Salonta
Kunszentmárton
Békés
Sarkad
Moliviș
1418
Vârful Vlădeasa
1836
D
Tiszaalpár
Kondoros
Tinca
Munții Gilăului
Csongrád
Nagyszénás
Békéscsaba
Batăr
Beiuș
KÖRÖS-VIDÉK
Crișul Negru
Buntești
Szentes
Csorvás
Gyula
Chișineu-Criș
Vârful Pleșu
1112
Ștei
Vârful Bătrâna
1579
Pasul Vârtop
1160
78
Munții Muntele Mare
Szegvár
Újkígyós
Elek
Munții Codru-Moma
Kiskunmajsa
Mindszent
Orosháza
Ineu
Vârful Bihor
1849
Vârful Balomireasa
1632
Kistelek
Crișul Alb
Sebiș
Câmpeni
Hódmezővásárhely
Tótkomlós
Mezőkovácsháza
Macea
Sântana
Pâncota
Gâina
1486
Vârful Poienița
1437
Sándorfalva
Csanádi-hát
Battonya
Curtici
Șiria
Târnova
Abrud
Mezőhegyes
Fântâna Rece
Munții Zarandului
Vârful Highiș
798
Vârful Drocea
836
Pasul Bucium
915
E
Mórahalom
Szeged
Maros-Körös Köze
Câmpia Aradului
Arad
Vârful Dâmbău
1369
Makó
Nădlac
Vladimirescu
RO
Vârful Măgului
900
Brad
Zlatna
Palić
Horgoš
Sânnicolau Mare
Pecica
Fântânele
Lipova
Pasul Vălișoara
460
Vârful Mare
1011
Subotica
Novi Kneževac
Secusigiu
Munții Metaliferi
Vințu de
Kanjiža
Dudestii Vechi
Sânpetru Mare
Periam
Vinga
Čantavir
Čoka
Mokrin
Variaș
Lovrin
Dealurile Lipovei
Dealul Ciordan
459
Deva
Geoagiu
Senta
Biled
Câmpia Vingăi
Orăștie
Žednik
Bačka Topola
Kikinda
Lenauheim
Giarmata
Recaș
Făget
Vârful Grohot
906
Simeria
Ada
Novo Miloševo
Jimbolia
Cărpiniș
Timișoara
Vârful Glodea
950
Hunedoara
F
Mali Iđoš
Mol
Srpska Crnja
Săcălaz
Lugoj
Vârful Padeșu
1374
Vârful Cornetu
956
Călan
Câmpia Timișului
Buziaș
Munții Poiana Ruscă
Hațeg
Bečej
Jebel
Scărișoara
1049
Vrbas
Srbobran
Novi Bečej
Dealurile Buziașului
Oțelu Roșu
Pui
Ciacova
Câmpia Gătaiei
Munții Retezatului
Bačko Gradište
Melenci
Gătaia
Vârful Tulișa
1792
Čurug
Temerin
SRB
Deta
Caransebeș
Vârful Pietrii
2192
Vârful Peleaga
2509
Lupeni
Vulcan
Kisač
Bački Jarak
Žabalj
Zrenjanin
Bocșa
Reșița
Vârful Radomir
1090
Retezat
Uricani
Kać
Ečka
Vârful Godeanu
2229
Vârful Oslea
1946
G
Futog
Novi Sad
Petrovaradin
Munții Țarcului
Munții Godeanu
Munții Vâlcanului
Crveni Čot
539
Fruška Gora
Sremski Karlovci
Titel
DELIBLATSKA PEŠČARA
Padina
Vârful Semenic
1446
Vârful Platra Closani
Târgu Jiu
Beška
Debeljača
Kovačica
641
Anina
Munții Semenicului
Munții Cernei
1421
Padeș
Bălești
Inđija
Vršac
Oravița
Tismana
Ruma
Stara Pazova
Padinska Skela
Banatski Karlovac
Cununa
1160
Baia de Aramă
H
Lăcarak
Mitrovica
Nova Pazova
Banatsko Novo Selo
Bela Crkva
Cheil Nerei-Beușnița
Mehadia
Munții Mehedinți
Batajnica
Pančevo
Vârful Lilvada
500
Băile Herculane
Mătăsari
Dobanovci
Zemun
Novo Beograd
7
9
10
11
12
Munții Almăjului
Vârful Svinecea Mare
1224
Motru
Kovin
Kostolac
Moldova Nouă
82
BEOGRAD
Kaluđerica
Orșova
Corcova
Drobeta-Turnu Severin
Sremčica

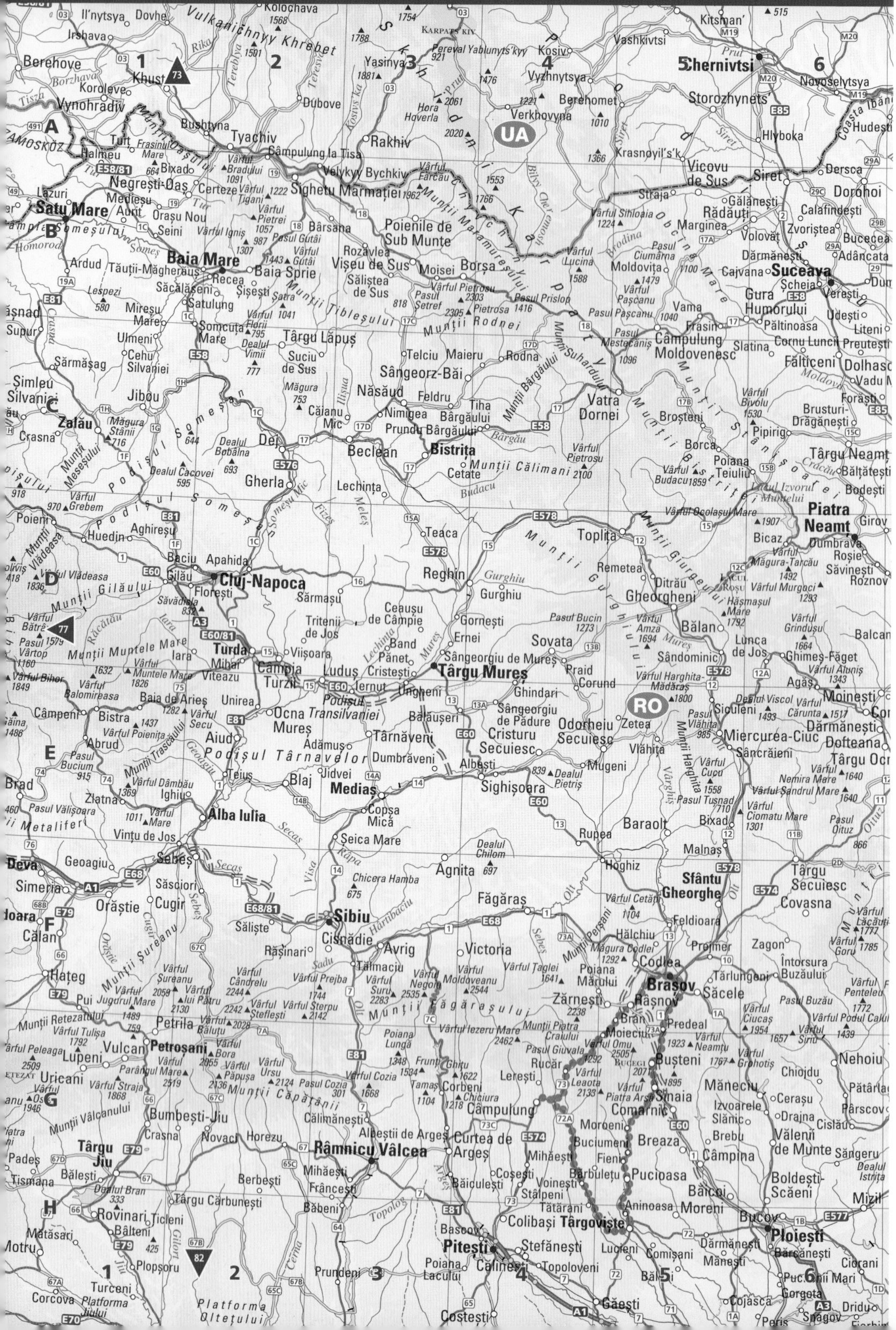

1 2 3 4 5 6

A B C D E F G H

Il'nytsya Dovhe Vulkanichnyy Khrebet Kolochava 1568 1754 Kitsman' 515
Irshava Riko Tereblya 1501 Teresva 1788 Karpats'kiy Vashkivtsi M19 M20
Berehove Khust 73 Yasinya 1881 Pereval Yablunyts'kyy 921 Kosiv Prut Chernivtsi
Borzhava Koroleve Dubove Kosivs'ka Prut 2061 Hora Hoverla 1476 Vyzhnytsya Berehomet Storozhynets' Novoselytsya Coasta Ibănești
Tisza Vynohradiv Bushtyna Tyachiv Rakhiv 2020 1221 Verkhovyna UA 1010 E85 Hlyboka Hudești
Tamosköz Tur Frasinului Mare Halmeu Munții Oașului Câmpulung la Tisa Velykyy Bychkiv Vârful Farcău 1553 1366 Krasnoyil's'k Siret Vicovu de Sus Dersca
E58/81 664 Bixad Vârful Bradului 1091 Negrești-Oaș Certeze Vârful Țiganu 1222 Sighetu Marmației 1962 Munții Maramureșului 1766 Bilyy Cheremosh Straja Gălănești Dorohoi
Lazuri Satu Mare Medieșu Aurit Orașu Nou Vârful Pietrei 1057 Bârsana Poienile de Sub Munte Vârful Sihloaia 1224 Rădăuți Calafindești
Câmpia Someșului Seini Vârful Igniș 987 Pasul Gutâi 1307 1443 Vârful Gutâi Marginea Volovăț Zvoriștea Bucecea
Homorod Someș Baia Mare Baia Sprie Rozavlea Vișeu de Sus Moisei Borșa Vârful Lucina 1588 Brodina Pasul Ciumârna Obcina Mare Dărmănești Adâncata
Ardud Tăuții-Măgherăuș Recea Șișești Săliștea de Sus Moldovița 1100 Cajvana Suceava
19A Săcălășeni Lespezi 580 Satulung Șatra 1041 Munții Țibleșului Vârful Pietrosu 2303 Pasul Prislop 1416 Vârful Pașcanu 1479 Șcheia Verești Dumbrava
Asnad Crasna Mireșu Mare Vârful Florii 795 818 Pasul Șetref 2305 Pietrosa Pasul Pașcanu 1040 Vama Gura Humorului E58 Udești
Supur Ulmeni Șomcuta Mare Dealul Vimii 777 Târgu Lăpuș Munții Rodnei Munții Suhardului Pasul Mestecăniș Câmpulung Moldovenesc Frasin Păltinoasa Liteni
Sărmășag Cehu Silvaniei E58 Suciu de Sus Telciu Maieru Rodna 1096 Slatina Cornu Luncii Preutești
Șimleu Silvaniei Jibou Măgura 753 Sângeorz-Băi Munții Bârgăului Vatra Dornei Munții Bistriței Fălticeni Dolhasca
Zalău Măgura Stânii 716 Someșan Ilișua Căianu Mic Năsăud Feldru Tiha Bârgăului Broșteni Vârful Bivolu 1530 Moldova Vadu Moldovei
Crasna Munții Meseșului 644 Dealul Bobâlna 693 Dej Nimigea Prundu Bârgăului Bârgău E58 17B Brusturi-Drăgănești Forăști E85
Podișul Someșan Dealul Cacovei 595 Gherla E576 Beclean Bistrița Cetate Munții Călimani Vârful Pietrosu 2100 Borca Pipirig Târgu Neamț
918 Vârful Grebem 970 Someșu Mic Fizeș Lechința Meleș Budacu Vârful Budacu 1859 Poiana Teiului Crăcău Bălțătești
Poieni Munții Vlădeasa Huedin Aghireșu E81 15A Teaca Vârful Ocolașul Mare Lacul Izvorul Muntelui Bodești
Apahida Baciu E578 Toplița 1907 Piatra Neamț Girov
Olivis 418 Vârful Vlădeasa 1836 E60 Gilău Cluj-Napoca Reghin Munții Gurghiului Remetea Bicaz Dumbrava Roșie
Munții Gilăului Florești Sărmașu Gurghiu Ditrău Vârful Măgura-Tarcău 1492 Săvinești Roznov
Vârful Bătrâna 77 Săvădisla 832 Ceaușu de Câmpie Gornești Gheorgheni Lacul Roșu Vârful Murgoci 1293
Pasul Vârtop 1160 Rădăuțiu Iara A3 E60/81 Tritenii de Jos Band Pasul Bucin 1273 Vârful Amza 1694 Mureș Bălan Hășmașul Mare 1792 Vârful Grinduș Balcani
Vârful Bihor 1849 Munții Muntele Mare Vârful Muntele Mare 1826 1632 Turda Mihai Viteazu Iara Viișoara Pănet Cristești Ernei Sângeorgiu de Mureș Sovata Sândominic Lunca de Jos 1664 Ghimeș-Făget
Vârful Balomireasa Câmpia Turzii Luduș Iernut Târgu Mureș Ungheni Praid Corund Vârful Harghita-Mădăraș 1800 Vârful Aluniș 1343 Agăș
Câmpeni Baia de Arieș 1282 Unirea Podișul Transilvaniei Ghindari Sângeorgiu de Pădure RO Dealul Viscol 1493 Vârful Cărunta 1517 Moinești
Găina 1486 Bistra 1437 Vârful Secu E81 Ocna Mureș Bălăușeri Cristuru Secuiesc Odorheiu Secuiesc Zetea Pasul Vlăhița 985 Siculeni Dărmănești
Abrud Vârful Poienița Munții Trascăului Aiud Adămuș Târnăveni E60 Vlăhița Munții Harghita Miercurea-Ciuc Sâncrăieni Dofteana
Pasul Bucium 915 Vârful Dâmbău 1369 Geoagiu Podișul Târnavelor Dumbrăveni Albești Mugeni Vârful Cucu 1558 Târgu Ocna
Brad Zlatna Ighiu Teiuș Blaj Jidvei Mediaș Sighișoara Dealul Pietriș 839 Vârghiș Vârful Șandru Mare 1640 Nemira Mare 1640
460 Pasul Vălișoara Munții Metaliferi 1011 Vârful Mare Alba Iulia Secaș Copșa Mică E60 Baraolt Pasul Tușnad 710 Bixad Vârful Ciomatu Mare 1301 Pasul Oituz
Vințu de Jos Seica Mare Rupea Malnaș 866
Deva Geoagiu Sebeș Secaș Vârful Chilom 697 Agnita Hoghiz Sfântu Gheorghe Târgu Secuiesc
Simeria A1 E68 Săsciori Chicera Hamba 675 E578 E574 Covasna
Hunedoara Orăștie Cugir E68/81 Sebeș Făgăraș Vârful Cetății 1104 Vârful Lăcăuți 1777
Călan Săliște Sibiu Hârtibaciu Cisnădie Avrig Victoria Munții Perșani Hălchiu Feldioara Prejmer Zagon 1785 Vârful Goru
Hațeg Munții Șureanu Rășinari Sadu Tălmaciu Vârful Negoiu Vârful Moldoveanu 2544 Vârful Țaglei 1641 Măgura Codlei 1292 Poiana Mărului Codlea Tărlungeni Întorsura Buzăului
Vârful Șureanu 2059 Vârful Căndrelu 2244 Vârful Prejba 1744 Vârful Suru 2283 2535 Zărnești 2238 Brașov Săcele Vârful Penteleu 1772
Pui Vârful Jugurul Mare 1489 Vârful lui Pătru 2130 2242 Vârful Ștefleşti Vârful Sterpu 2142 Munții Făgărașului Râșnov Pasul Buzău Vârful Podul Calului
Munții Retezatului Vârful Tulișa 1792 759 Petrila Vârful Băluțu 2028 Vârful Iezeru Mare 2462 Munții Piatra Craiului Bran Moieciu Predeal Vârful Ciucaș 1954 1657 Vârful Siriu 1439
Vârful Peleaga 2509 Lupeni Vulcan Petroșani Vârful Bora 2055 Poiana Lungă 1348 Frunți Ghițu 1622 Pasul Giuvala Vârful Omu 2505 1923 Vârful Neamțu 1767 Vârful Grohotiș Nehoiu
Uricani Vârful Parângul Mare 2519 Vârful Păpușa 2136 Vârful Ursu 2124 Pasul Cozia 301 Vârful Cozia 1668 Tamaș 1534 Rucăr Bucegi 2071 Bușteni 1895 Chiojdu
Vârful Oslea 1946 Vârful Straja 1868 Munții Căpățânii Corbeni 1104 Vârful Chiciura 1218 Lerești Vârful Leaota 2133 Vârful Piatra Arsă Sinaia Măneciu Cerașu Pătârlagele
Munții Vâlcanului Bumbești-Jiu Călimănești Câmpulung Comarnic Izvoarele Drajna Pârscov
Crasna Novaci Horezu Albeștii de Argeș Curtea de Argeș E574 Moroeni Slănic Cislău
Târgu Jiu E79 Râmnicu Vâlcea Mihăești Buciumeni Breaza Brebu Vălenii de Munte Săngeru
Padeș Bălești Berbești Mihăești Coșești Fieni Câmpina
Tismana Dealul Bran 333 Frâncești Băiculești Voinești Bărbulețu Pucioasa Boldești-Scăeni Dealul Istriței
Rovinari Ticleni Târgu Cărbunești Băbeni Topolog Stâlpeni Tătărani Aninoasa Moreni Băicoi Mizil
Bâlteni 425 Argeș Colibași Târgoviște Bucov E577
Motru Plopșoru Gilort 82 Cerna Bascov Pitești Ștefănești Lucieni Dărmănești Ploiești
Turceni Prundeni Poiana Lacului Călinești Topoloveni Comișani Mănești Bărcănești Ciorani
Corcova Platforma Jiului Platforma Olteţului Costești Găești Băleni Cojasca Puchenii Mari Gorgota Dridu
A1 A3 Snagov Periș

Roads: 03 19 18 1C 1H 1G 1F 1 E81 E60 E58 E576 E578 17 17C 17D 15A 15 16 12 12C 13B 12A 13A 14 14A 14B 13 2D 11B 1A 73 73A 73C 72A 7C 7 67 67C 67B 65C 66 68B E79 E68 E70 E81 E574 E60 71 72 1B 65 E85 29A 29B 29C 2 17A 17B 15B 15C 11 75 74 76

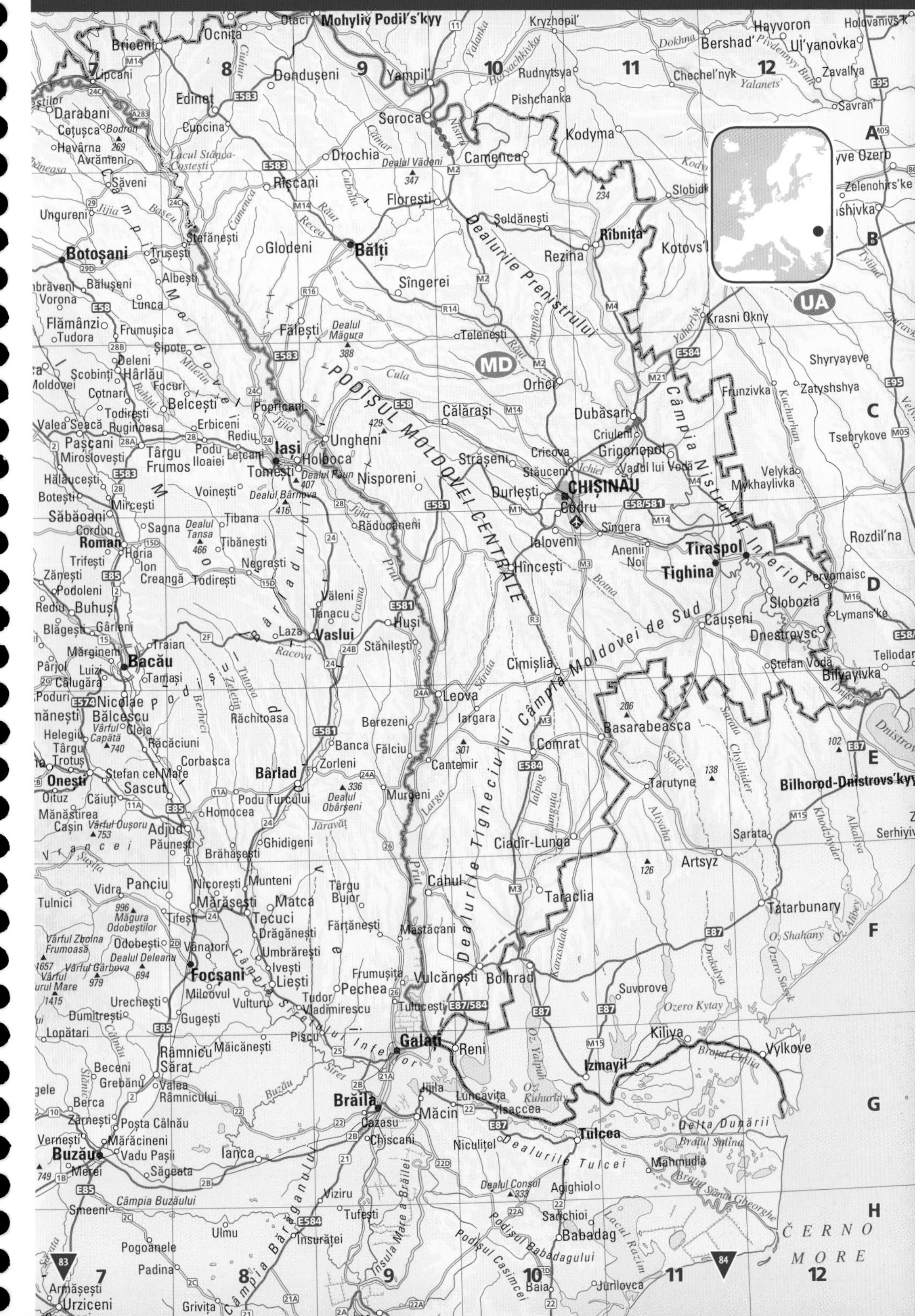
Mohyliv Podil's'kyy
Otaci
Ocnița
Briceni
Lipcani
Edineț
Dondușeni
Yampil'
Kryzhopil'
Hayvoron
Bershad'
Ul'yanovka
Rudnytsya
Chechel'nyk
Zavallya
Pishchanka
Savran'
Darabani
Soroca
Kodyma
Cupcina
Drochia
Camenca
Rîșcani
Florești
Slobidka
Săveni
Șoldănești
Rîbnița
Ungureni
Ștefănești
Botoșani
Glodeni
Bălți
Rezina
Kotovs'k
Sîngerei
Dealurile Prenistrului
Fălești
Telenești
Krasni Okny
MD
UA
PODIȘUL MOLDOVEI CENTRALE
Orhei
Hîrlău
Belcești
Cotnari
Podu Iloaiei
Iași
Holboca
Ungheni
Călărași
Dubăsari
Câmpia Nistrului Inferior
Pașcani
Târgu Frumos
Strășeni
Cricova
Grigoriopol
Nisporeni
Durlești
CHIȘINĂU
Codru
Sîngera
Ialoveni
Hîncești
Anenii Noi
Tiraspol
Tighina
Roman
Rozdil'na
Pervomaisc
Slobozia
Căușeni
Dnestrovsc
Buhuși
Vaslui
Huși
Bacău
Cimișlia
Câmpia Moldovei de Sud
Ștefan Vodă
Bilyayivka
Tellodar
Leova
Basarabeasca
Comrat
Onești
Bârlad
Cantemir
Tarutyne
Bilhorod-Dnistrovs'kyy
Adjud
Ciadîr-Lunga
Sarata
Artsyz
Panciu
Mărășești
Tecuci
Cahul
Taraclia
Tatarbunary
Focșani
Vulcănești
Bolhrad
Suvorove
Pechea
Galați
Reni
Kiliya
Vylkove
Izmayil
Râmnicu Sărat
Brăila
Măcin
Isaccea
Tulcea
Delta Dunării
Buzău
Mahmudia
Dealurile Tulcei
Babadag
ČERNO MORE
Urziceni
Hârșova
Jurilovca
Podișul Babadagului
Câmpia Bărăganului
A
B
C
D
E
F
G
H
7
8
9
10
11
12
83
84

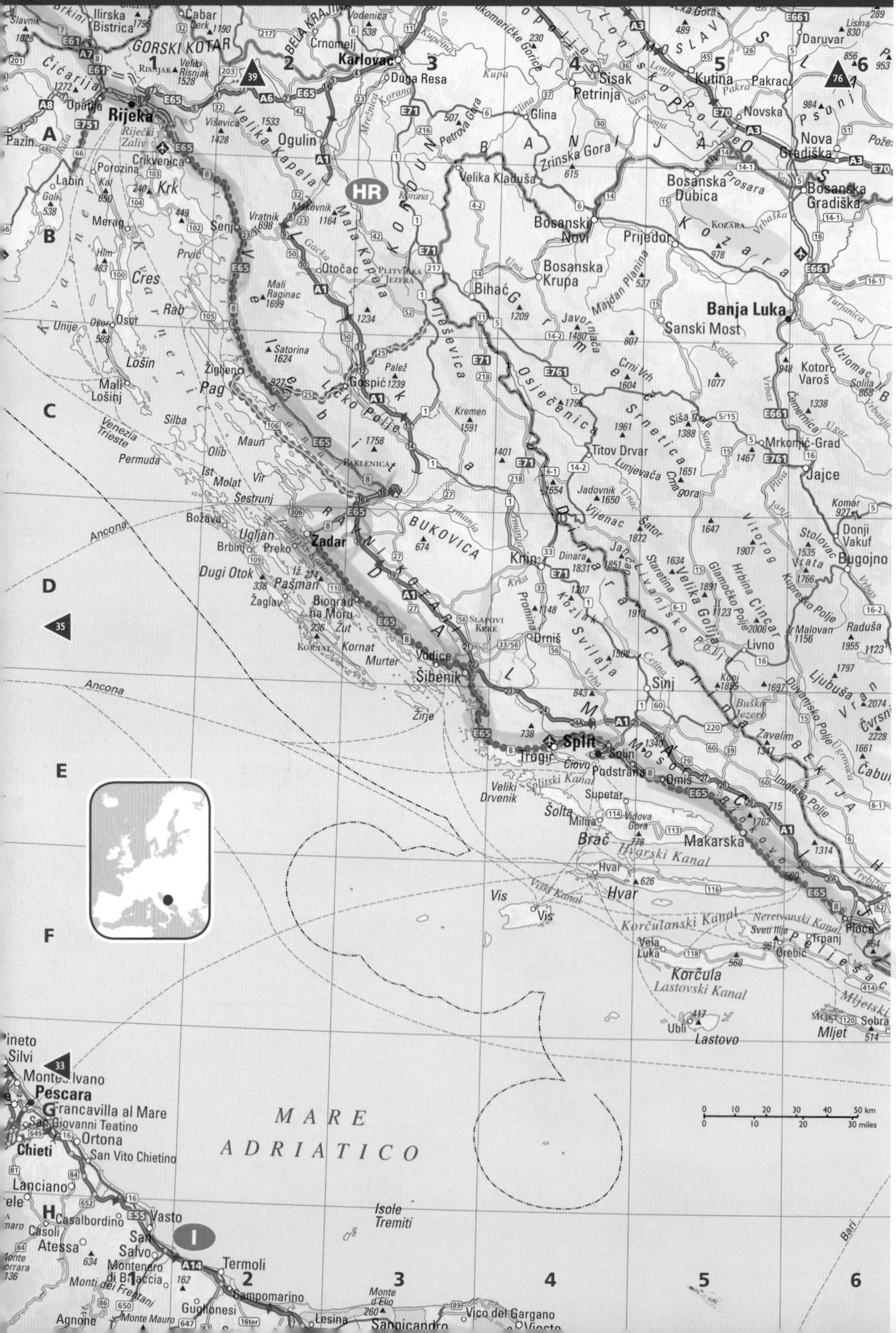

Ilirska Bistrica
Čabar
GORSKI KOTAR
Risnjak
Čićarija
Opatija
Rijeka
Riječki Zaliv
Pazin
Labin
Crikvenica
Porozina
Krk
Senj
Merag
Cres
Prvić
Rab
Unije
Osor
Lošinj
Mali Lošinj
Pag
Žigljen
Silba
Venezia Trieste
Permuda
Olib
Maun
Ist
Molat
Vir
Sestrunj
Božava
Ugljan
Brbinj
Preko
Zadar
Dugi Otok
Iž
Pašman
Žaglav
Biograd na Moru
Žut
Kornat
Murter
Vodice
Šibenik
Žirje
Trogir
Split
Čiovo
Solin
Podstrana
Omiš
Veliki Drvenik
Šolta
Milna
Supetar
Brač
Makarska
Hvar
Vis
Korčula
Vela Luka
Lastovo
Ubli
Mljet
Sobra
Pelješac
Orebić
Trpanj
Sveti Ilija
Ploče
Karlovac
Duga Resa
Crnomelj
BELA KRAJINA
Ogulin
Velika Kapela
Mala Kapela
Otočac
Plitvička Jezera
Gospić
Ličko Polje
Velebit
Paklenica
Ravni Kotari
BUKOVICA
Zrmanja
Knin
Drniš
Kozjak
Svilaja
Sinj
Dinara
Sisak
Petrinja
Glina
Kutina
Novska
Pakrac
Daruvar
Nova Gradiška
Bosanska Gradiška
Bosanska Dubica
Bosanski Novi
Prijedor
Bosanska Krupa
Bihać
Velika Kladuša
Sanski Most
Banja Luka
Kotor Varoš
Mrkonjić-Grad
Jajce
Donji Vakuf
Bugojno
Titov Drvar
Glamočko Polje
Livno
Kupresko Polje
Duvanjsko Polje
Imotsko Polje
Buško Jezero
Zavelim
Biokovo
Mosor
Ljubuša
MARE ADRIATICO
Isole Tremiti
Pineto
Silvi
Montesilvano
Pescara
Francavilla al Mare
San Giovanni Teatino
Chieti
Ortona
San Vito Chietino
Lanciano
Casalbordino
Vasto
San Salvo
Atessa
Montenero di Bisaccia
Termoli
Campomarino
Guglionesi
Lesina
Vico del Gargano
Monte d'Elio
Agnone
Ancona
Bari
HR
I
0 10 20 30 40 50 km
0 10 20 30 miles

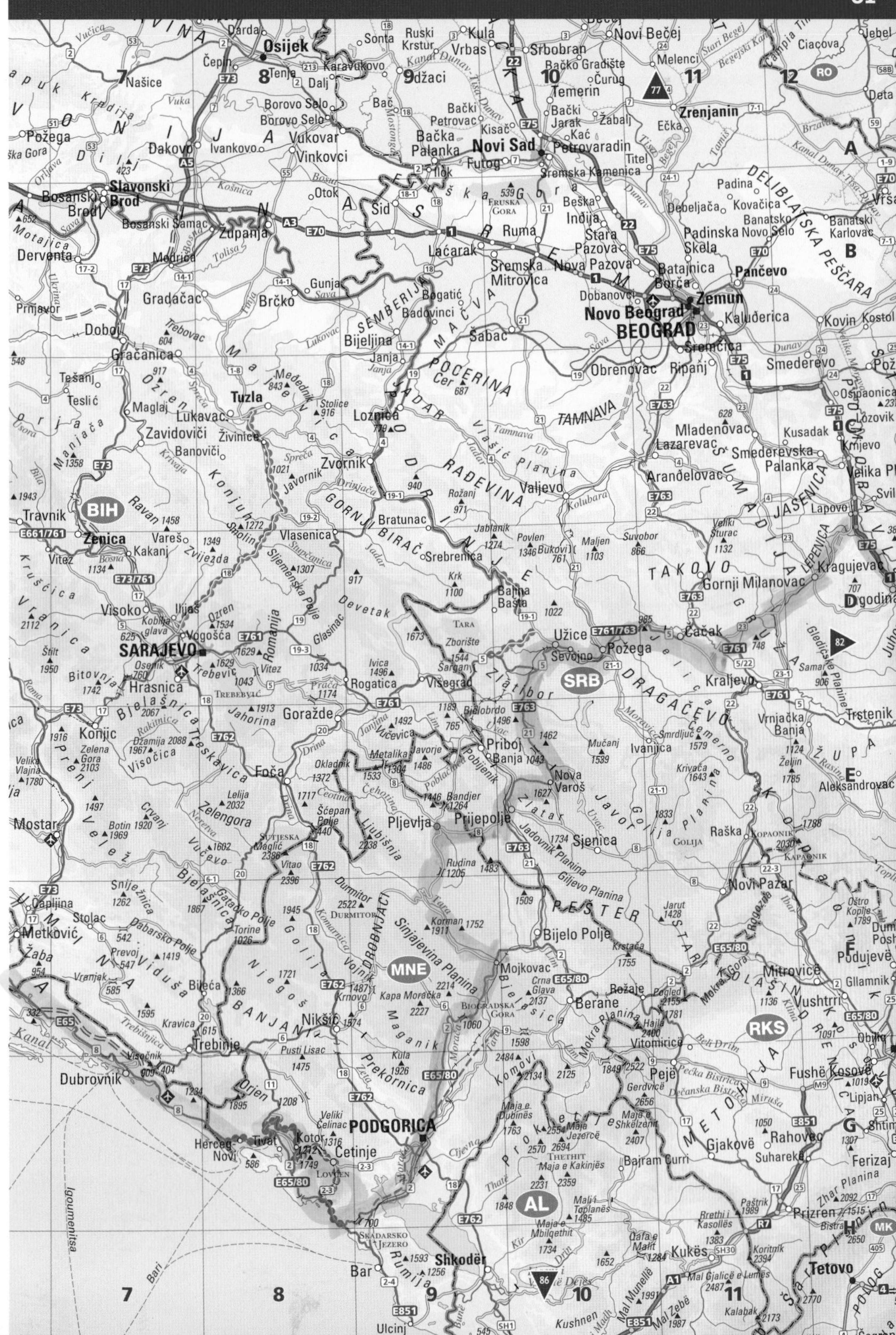

Padina
Kovačica
Banatsko Novo Selo
Padinska Skela
Pančevo
Zemun
BEOGRAD
Kaluđerica
Vršac
Banatski Karlovac
DELIBLATSKA PEŠČARA
Anina
Oravița
Bela Crkva
Kovin
Kostolac
Smederevo
Požarevac
Moldova Nouă
Munții Locvei
Munții Almăjului
Munții Cernei
Munții Mehedinți
Munții Godeanu
Băile Herculane
Mehadia
Orșova
Drobeta-Turnu Severin
Kladovo
Șimian
Baia de Aramă
Tismana
Padeș
Bumbești-Jiu
Crasna
Novaci
Horezu
Târgu Jiu
Bălești
Berbești
Târgu Cărbunești
Rovinari
Țicleni
Bâlteni
Mătăsari
Motru
Plopșoru
Corcova
Turceni
Strehaia
Platforma Olteţului
Podișul Getic
Țânțăreni
Filiași
Bălcești
Argetoaia
Craiova
Balș
Podari
Malu Mare
Coșoveni
Leu
Osipaonica
Lozovik
Kusadak
Krnjevo
Smederevska Palanka
Velika Plana
Kučevo
Petrovac
Majdanpek
HOMOLJE
Homoljske Planine
Vânju Mare
Gogoșu
Câmpia Blahniței
Negotin
Gârla Mare
Plenița
Svilajnac
Lapovo
RESAVA
Beljanica
Kragujevac
Jagodina
Ćuprija
Paraćin
Bor
Zaječar
Kučajske Planine
Deli Jovan
Cetate
Moțăței
Galicea Mare
Bratovoești
Segarcea
Câmpia Băileștilor
Vidin
Calafat
Maglavit
Băilești
Poiana Mare
Ciupercenii Noi
Piscu Vechi
Valea Stanciului
Goicea
Sadova
Daneți
Celaru
Mârșani
Kula
Vrŭshka Chuka
Lom
Kozloduy
Ostroveni
Oryakhovo
Dăbuleni
Vŭlchedrŭm
Zlatiyata
Miziya
Kraljevo
Ćićevac
Sokobanja
Knjaževac
Trstenik
Vrnjačka Banja
Kruševac
Aleksinac
ŽUPA
Aleksandrovac
Veliki Jastrebac
Belogradchik
Shiroka Planina
Midzhur
Montana
Knezha
Byala Slatina
Svrljig
Svrljiške Planine
Niš
SRB
TOPLICA
Prokuplje
Kuršumlija
Novi Pazar
Suva Planina
Bela Palanka
Pirot
Berkovitsa
Vŭrshets
Vratsa
Cherven Bryag
Mezdra
Koznitsa
Petrokhanski Prokhod
Leskovac
Vlasotince
Lebane
Dimitrovgrad
Godech
Svoge
Golema Planina
Botevgrad
Etropole
Mitrovicë
Podujevë
Vushtrri
Gllamnik
Vladičin Han
Surdulica
Slivnitsa
Kostinbrod
Novi Iskŭr
PRISHTINË (PRIŠTINA)
Obiliq
Fushë Kosovë
Janjevë
Lipjan
RKS
Kosovska Kamenicë
Vranje
Breznik
Bankya
SOFIYA
Elin Pelin
Pernik
Radomir
Vitosha
Ikhtiman
Bresalc
Gjilan
Shtime
Suharekë
Ferizaj
Bujanovac
Bosilegrad
Kyustendil
Konyavska Planina
Bobovdol
PALAKARIYATA
Kostenets
Samokov
Preševo
Kaçanik
Prizren
Dupnitsa
Belovo
Septemvri
SLAVIŠTE
Kriva Palanka
Osogovske Planine
Kumanovo
Kratovo
Aračinovo
Probištip
MK
Kočani
Blagoevgrad
Yakoruda
Velingrad
Rila
Rakitovo
Delčevo
Vinica
Trabotivište
Simitli
Razlog
Bansko
Gostivar
Vrapčište
Sveti Nikole
Ovče Pole
Štip
Veles
Radoviš
Berovo
MALEŠEVO
Pirin
Vikhren
Kičevo
Brod
Sandanski
Gotse Delchev
Negotino

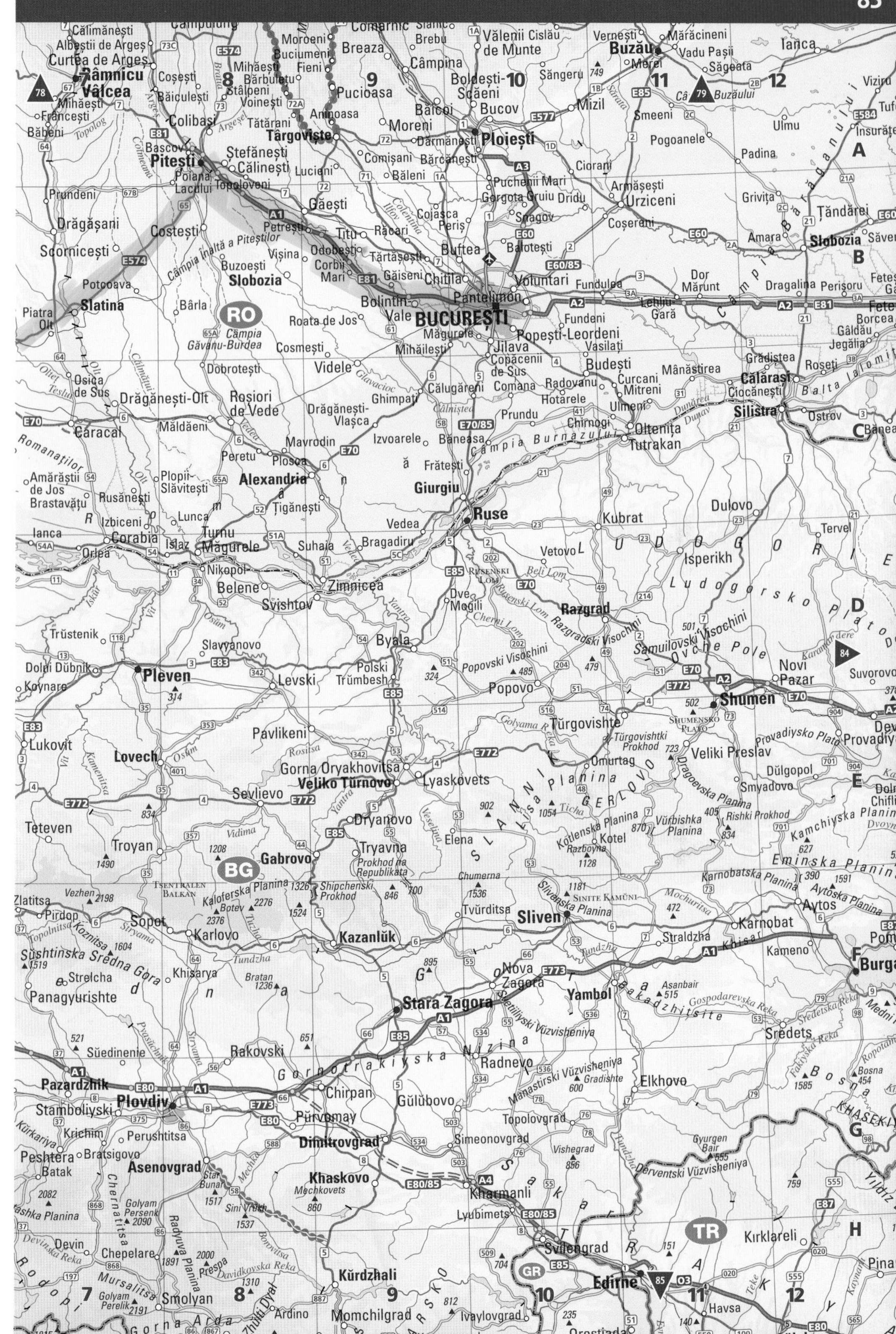
Călimănești
Albeștii de Argeș
Curtea de Argeș
Râmnicu Vâlcea
Mihăești
Frâncești
Băbeni
Coșești
Băiculești
Colibași
Bascov
Pitești
Poiana Lacului
Ștefănești
Călinești
Topoloveni
Moroeni
Buciumeni
Fieni
Mihăești
Bărbulețu
Stâlpeni
Voinești
Tătărani
Aninoasa
Târgoviște
Comarnic
Breaza
Brebu
Câmpina
Pucioasa
Moreni
Vălenii de Munte
Cislău
Boldești-Scăeni
Băicoi
Bucov
Ploiești
Dărmănești
Bărcănești
Comișani
Băleni
Lucieni
Găești
Titu
Răcari
Petrești
Cojasca
Periș
Mizil
Sângeru
Buzău
Verneşti
Mărăcineni
Vadu Pașii
Săgeata
Merei
Smeeni
Pogoanele
Ianca
Viziru
Ulmu
Tufești
Însurăței
Padina
Grivița
Țăndărei
Slobozia
Săveni
Amara
Cioranii
Puchenii Mari
Gorgota
Gruiu
Dridu
Armășești
Urziceni
Coșereni
Snagov
Balotești
Buftea
Chitila
Voluntari
Pantelimon
București
Bolintin-Vale
Roata de Jos
Cosmești
Măgurele
Mihăilești
Jilava
Popești-Leordeni
Fundeni
Vasilați
Fundulea
Lehliu-Gară
Dor Mărunt
Dragalina
Perișoru
Fetești
Borcea
Gâldău
Jegălia
Grădiștea
Roseți
Călărași
Ciocănești
Silistra
Ostrov
Băneasa
Mânăstirea
Budești
Curcani
Mitreni
Radovanu
Hotarele
Ulmeni
Chirnogi
Oltenița
Tutrakan
Copăcenii de Sus
Comana
Călugăreni
Prundu
Ghimpați
Drăgănești-Vlașca
Videle
Vișina
Odobești
Tărtășești
Găiseni
Corbii Mari
Buzoești
Slobozia
Costești
Drăgășani
Prundeni
Scornicești
Potcoava
Slatina
Piatra Olt
Bârla
Câmpia Găvanu-Burdea
Câmpia Înaltă a Piteștilor
Dobrotești
Osica de Sus
Drăgănești-Olt
Roșiori de Vede
Caracal
Măldăeni
Mavrodin
Peretu
Plosca
Alexandria
Izvoarele
Băneasa
Frătești
Giurgiu
Câmpia Burnazului
Amărăștii de Jos
Brastavățu
Rusănești
Plopii-Slăvitești
Lunca
Izbiceni
Țigănești
Ianca
Corabia
Orlea
Islaz
Turnu Măgurele
Suhaia
Bragadiru
Vedea
Ruse
Kubrat
Dulovo
Tervel
Vetovo
Isperikh
Nikopol
Belene
Svishtov
Zimnicea
Dve Mogili
Rusenski Lom
Razgrad
Ludogorsko Plato
Samuilovski Visochini
Razgradski Visochini
Ovche Pole
Novi Pazar
Suvorovo
Shumen
Trŭstenik
Slavyanovo
Byala
Dolni Dŭbnik
Koynare
Pleven
Levski
Polski Trŭmbesh
Popovski Visochini
Popovo
Lukovit
Pavlikeni
Tŭrgovishte
Tŭrgovishtki Prokhod
Omurtag
Veliki Preslav
Provadiysko Plato
Provadiya
Dŭlgopol
Smyadovo
Lovech
Gorna Oryakhovitsa
Veliko Tŭrnovo
Lyaskovets
Sevlievo
Teteven
Dryanovo
Elena
Kotel
Kotlenska Planina
Vŭrbishka Planina
Rishki Prokhod
Kamchiyska Planina
Troyan
Tryavna
Gabrovo
Prokhod na Republikata
Shipchenski Prokhod
Tsentralen Balkan
Kaloferska Planina
Botev
Zlatitsa
Pirdop
Sopot
Karlovo
Kazanlŭk
Tvŭrditsa
Chumerna
Sliven
Sinite Kamŭni
Slivenska Planina
Karnobat
Aytos
Eminska Planina
Karnobatska Planina
Aytoska Planina
Straldzha
Kameno
Burgas
Sŭshtinska Sredna Gora
Strelcha
Panagyurishte
Khisarya
Nova Zagora
Yambol
Stara Zagora
Sredets
Bakadzhitsite
Sŭedinenie
Rakovski
Radnevo
Gornotrakiyska Nizina
Elkhovo
Manastirski Vŭzvisheniya
Pazardzhik
Plovdiv
Stamboliyski
Chirpan
Gŭlŭbovo
Pŭrvomay
Krichim
Perushtitsa
Bratsigovo
Peshtera
Batak
Asenovgrad
Dimitrovgrad
Simeonovgrad
Topolovgrad
Khaskovo
Kharmanli
Lyubimets
Svilengrad
Derventski Vŭzvisheniya
Devin
Chepelare
Smolyan
Kŭrdzhali
Ardino
Momchilgrad
Krumovgrad
Ivaylovgrad
Madan
Dzhebel
Edirne
Kırklareli
Havsa
Lüleburgaz
Orestiada
RO
BG
TR
GR
A
B
C
D
E
F
G
H
7
8
9
10
11
12
78
79
84
85

Tulcea
Delta Dunării
Buzău
Slobozia
Călărași
Constanța
Mangalia
Dobrich
Varna
Shumen
Burgas
Edirne
Kırklareli
RO
BG
TR
DOBRUJA
LUDOGORIE
Ludogorsko Plato
ČERNO MORE

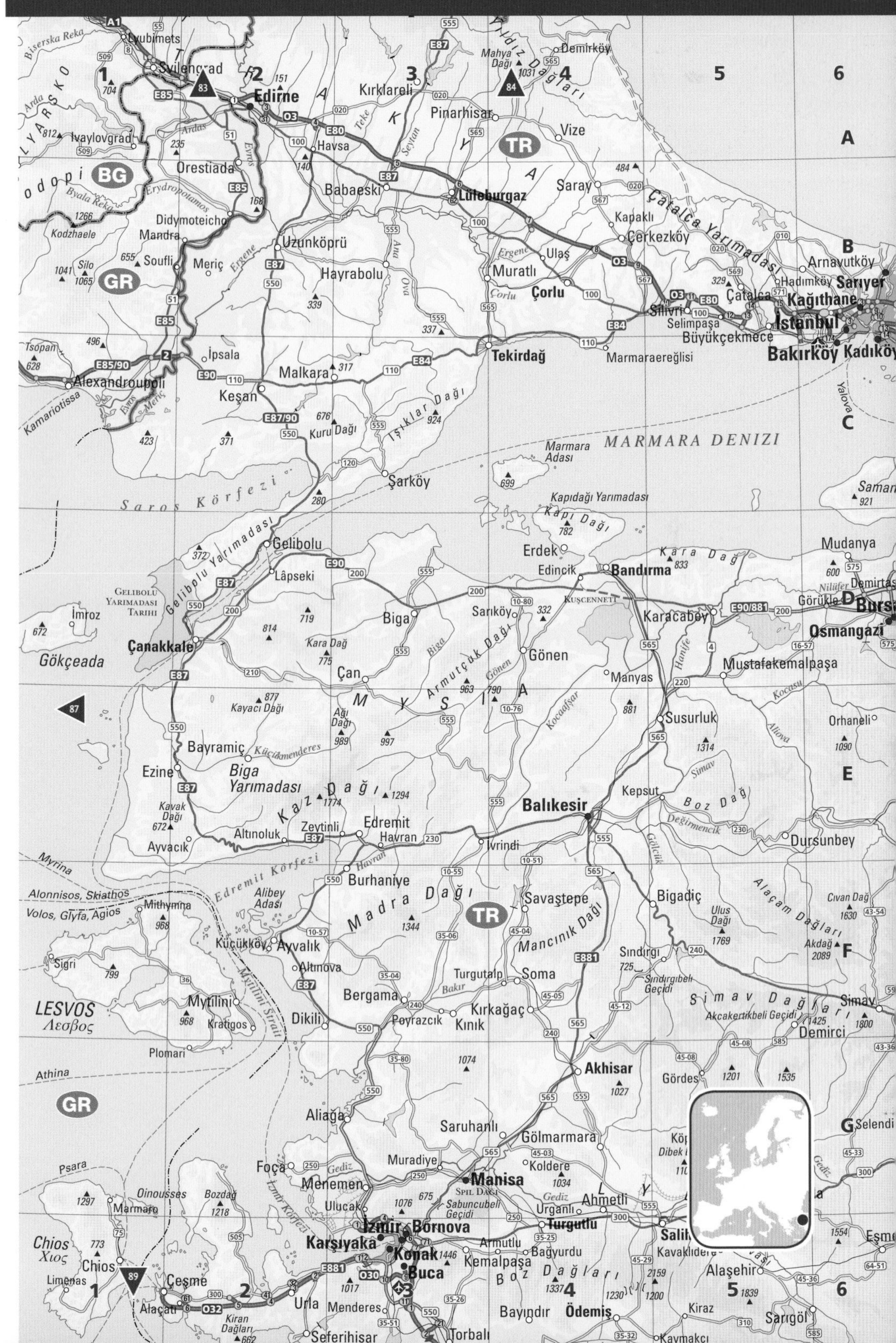

Lyubimets
Svilengrad
Edirne
Kırklareli
Mahya Dağı
Demirköy
Yıldız Dağları
Pinarhisar
Vize
Ivaylovgrad
Havsa
Orestiada
BG
TR
Babaeski
Lüleburgaz
Saray
Rodopi
Didymoteicho
Mandra
Kapaklı
Çatalca Yarımadası
Çerkezköy
Uzunköprü
Soufli
Meriç
GR
Hayrabolu
Muratlı
Ulaş
Çorlu
Silivri
Çatalca
Hadımköy
Arnavutköy
Sarıyer
Kağıthane
İstanbul
Selimpaşa
Büyükçekmece
Bakırköy
Kadıköy
Tekirdağ
Marmaraereğlisi
İpsala
Alexandroupoli
Malkara
Keşan
Kuru Dağı
Işıklar Dağı
Yalova
MARMARA DENIZI
Marmara Adası
Şarköy
Saros Körfezi
Kapıdağı Yarımadası
Kapı Dağı
Gelibolu
Gelibolu Yarımadası
Erdek
Mudanya
Lâpseki
Edincik
Bandırma
Kara Dağ
GELIBOLU YARIMADASI TARIHI
İmroz
Biga
Sarıköy
KUŞCENNETI
Karacabey
Görükle
Bursa
Osmangazi
Çanakkale
Gökçeada
Kara Dağ
Armutçuk Dağı
Gönen
Çan
Manyas
Mustafakemalpaşa
MYSIA
Kayacı Dağı
Ağı Dağı
Susurluk
Orhaneli
Bayramiç
Küçükmenderes
Ezine
Biga Yarımadası
Kaz Dağı
Kavak Dağı
Kepsut
Balıkesir
Boz Dağ
Zeytinli
Edremit
Altınoluk
Havran
İvrindi
Dursunbey
Ayvacık
Edremit Körfezi
Burhaniye
Myrina
Alonnisos, Skiathos
Volos, Glyfa, Agios
Mithymna
Alibey Adası
Madra Dağı
Savaştepe
Bigadiç
Alaçam Dağları
Civan Dağ
Ulus Dağı
Küçükköy
Ayvalık
Mancınık Dağı
Akdağ
Sındırgı
Sındırgıbeli Geçidi
Sigri
Altınova
Turgutalp
Soma
Simav Dağları
Simav
LESVOS
Λεσβος
Mytilini
Kratigos
Mytilini Straiti
Dikili
Bergama
Poyrazcık
Kınık
Kırkağaç
Akcakertikbeli Geçidi
Demirci
Plomari
Athina
Akhisar
Gördes
GR
Aliağa
Saruhanlı
Gölmarmara
Selendi
Psara
Foça
Muradiye
Koldere
Menemen
Manisa
Spil Dağı
Sabuncubeli Geçidi
Oinoussas
Bozdağ
Marmaro
Ulucak
Urganlı
Ahmetli
İzmir Körfezi
İzmir
Bornova
Turgutlu
Salihli
Chios
Χιος
Karşıyaka
Konak
Armutlu
Bağyurdu
Kavaklıdere
Alaşehir
Eşme
Limenas
Çeşme
Buca
Kemalpaşa
Boz Dağları
Alaçatı
Urla
Menderes
Bayındır
Ödemiş
Kiraz
Sarıgöl
Kiran Dağları
Seferihisar
Torbalı
Kaymakçı

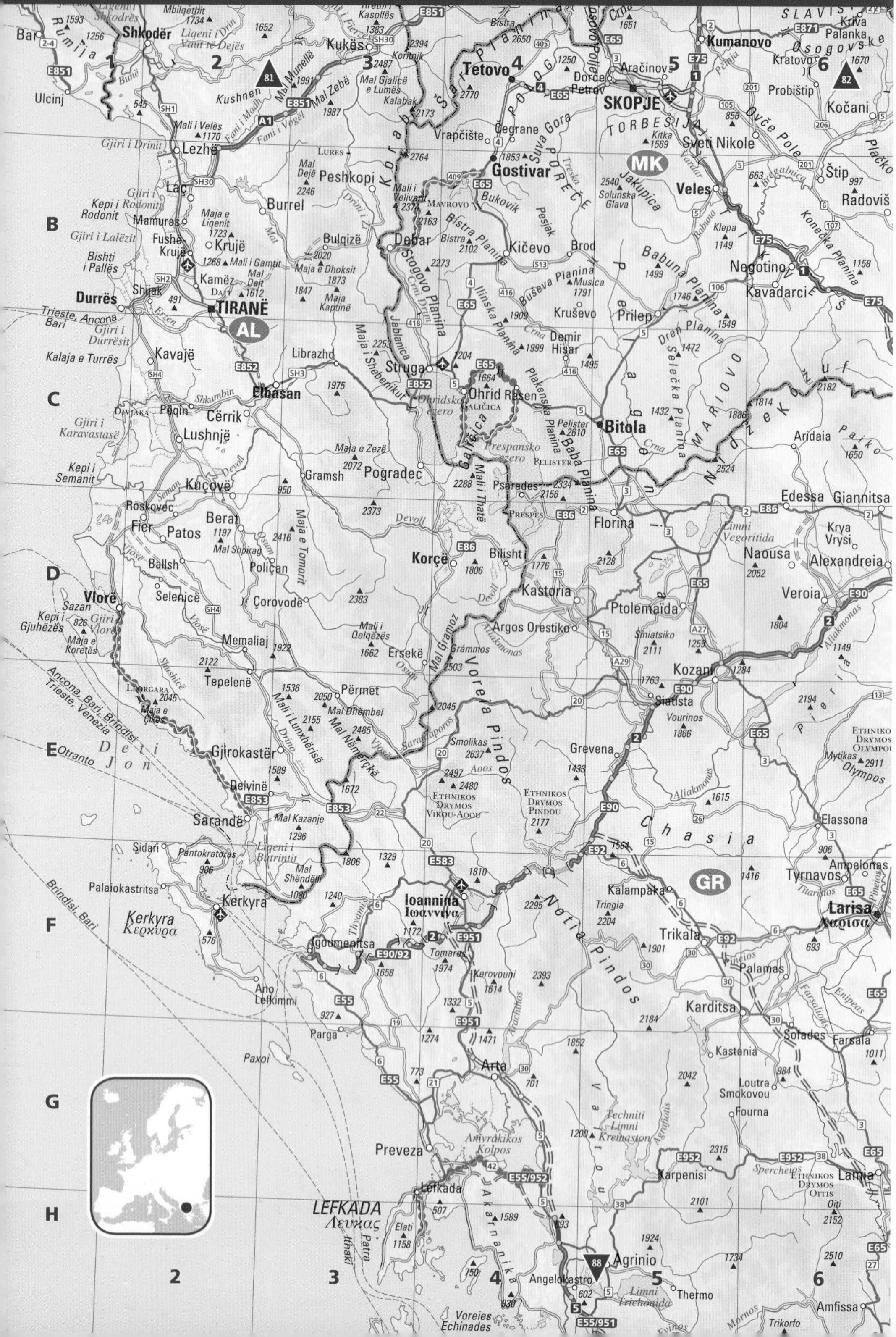

Bar
Rumija
Shkodër
Liqeni i Shkodrës
Ulcinj
Mbilqethit
Liqeni i Drin
Vaut të Dejës
Kukës
Kushnen
Mal Munellë
Mal Zebë
Mal Gjalicë e Lumës
Kalabak
Koritnik
Mali i Velës
Fani i Madh
Fani i Vogël
Gjiri i Drinit
Lezhë
Laç
Gjiri i Rodonit
Kepi i Rodonit
Mamuras
Maja e Liqenit
Burrel
Mal Dejë
Peshkopi
Drini i Zi
Mali i Velivarit
Gjiri i Lalëzit
Fushë Krujë
Krujë
Mali i Gamtit
Bishti i Pallës
Kamëz
Mal Dajt
Durrës
TIRANË
AL
Trieste, Ancona, Bari
Gjiri i Durrësit
Kalaja e Turrës
Kavajë
Librazhd
Shkumbin
Elbasan
Divjaka
Peqin
Cërrik
Gjiri i Karavastasë
Lushnjë
Kepi i Semanit
Seman
Devoll
Kuçovë
Gramsh
Roskovec
Fier
Patos
Berat
Mal Shpirag
Osum
Ballsh
Poliçan
Maja e Tomorit
Vlorë
Sazan
Kepi i Gjuhëzës
Gjiri i Vlorës
Selenicë
Çorovodë
Maja e Koretës
Memaliaj
Tepelenë
Llogara
Maja e Çikës
Ancona, Bari, Brindisi, Trieste, Venezia
Deti Jon
Otranto
Gjirokastër
Mali i Lunxhërisë
Mal Dhëmbel
Mal Nëmërçkë
Përmet
Delvinë
Sarandë
Mal Kazanje
Sidari
Pantokratoras
Liqeni i Butrintit
Mal Shëndëlli
Palaiokastritsa
Kerkyra
Κερκυρα
Brindisi, Bari
Igoumenitsa
Ano Lefkimmi
Parga
Paxoi
Preveza
Lefkada
LEFKADA
Λευκας
Ithaki
Elati
Voreies Echinades
Tetovo
Šar Planina
Korab
Bistra
Polog
Vrapčište
Čegrane
Gostivar
Mavrovo
Bukovik
Bistra Planina
Debar
Stogovo Planina
Crni Drim
Jablanica
Maja i Shebenikut
Struga
Ohrid
Ohridsko ezero
Galičica
Resen
Prespansko ezero
Pelister
Mali i Thatë
Pogradec
Maja e Zezë
Psarades
Prespes
Kičevo
Brod
Ilinska Planina
Buševa Planina
Musica
Kruševo
Demir Hisar
Plakenska Planina
Pesjak
Suva Gora
Poreče
Treska
Skopje
Đorče Petrov
Aračinovo
Kumanovo
Torbešija
Kitka
Sveti Nikole
MK
Jakupica
Solunska Glava
Veles
Babuna
Babuna Planina
Prilep
Pelagonija
Bitola
Baba Planina
Dren Planina
Selečka Planina
Mariovo
Nidže
Kožuf
Crna
Negotino
Kavadarci
Štip
Radoviš
Konečka Planina
Ovče Pole
Kočani
Probištip
Kratovo
Kriva Palanka
Osogovske
Slavište
Pčinja
Tikveš
Vardar
Bregalnica
Korçë
Bilisht
Devoll
Maja i Qelqëzës
Ersekë
Mal Gramoz
Grammos
Florina
Kastoria
Argos Orestiko
Aliakmonas
Ptolemaida
Vegoritida
Limni Vegoritida
Edessa
Giannitsa
Aridaia
Paiko
Krya Vrysi
Naousa
Alexandreia
Veroia
Sniatsiko
Kozani
Siatista
Vourinos
Grevena
Smolikas
Voreia Pindos
Sarantaporos
Aoos
Ethnikos Drymos Vikou-Aoou
Ethnikos Drymos Pindou
Ethnikos Drymos Olympou
Mytikas
Olympos
Pieria
Elassona
Chasia
Ampelonas
Tyrnavos
Titarisios
Pineios
Larisa
Λαρισα
GR
Kalampaka
Tringia
Trikala
Palamas
Karditsa
Enipeas
Farsaliotis
Sofades
Farsala
Kastania
Loutra Smokovou
Fourna
Notia Pindos
Ioannina
Ιωαννινα
Thyamis
Tomaros
Kerovouni
Arachthos
Arta
Amvrakikos Kolpos
Akarnanika
Agrafiotis
Techniti Limni Kremaston
Valtou
Karpenisi
Spercheios
Ethnikos Drymos Oitis
Oiti
Lamia
Agrinio
Angelokastro
Limni Trichonida
Thermo
Evinos
Mornos
Trikorfo
Amfissa
A B C D E F G H
1 2 3 4 5 6
E65 E75 E90 E92 E86 E851 E852 E853 E583 E951 E952 E55 E55/951 E55/952 E90/92 E871
A1 SH1 SH2 SH4 SH30

Plovdiv
Pazardzhik
Blagoevgrad
Asenovgrad
Khaskovo
Dimitrovgrad
Kŭrdzhali
Smolyan
Velingrad
Bansko
Sandanski
Gotse Delchev
Petrich
Strumica
Gevgelija
Kilkis
Serres
Drama
Xanthi
Komotini
Kavala
Καβαλα
Alexandroupoli
Thasos
Θασος
Thessaloniki
Θεσσαλονικη
Kalamaria
Polygyros
Ouranoupoli
Athos
Katerini
Thermaïkos Kolpos
Kolpos Kassandras
Kolpos Agiou Orous
Sithonia
Kassandra
Thrakiko Pelagos
Samothraki
Gökçeada
Limnos
Λημνος
Myrina
Agios Efstratios
Egeon Pelagos
Voreies Sporades
Βορειοι Σποραδες
Skiathos
Skopelos
Alonnisos
Skyros
Volos
Nea Ionia
Almyros
Pagasitikos Kolpos
Voreios Evvoikos Kolpos
Chalkida
Psachna
Kymi
Atalanti
Orchomenos
RHODOPE MOUNTAINS
Rila
Pirin
BG
Mytilini
Sigri
Psara

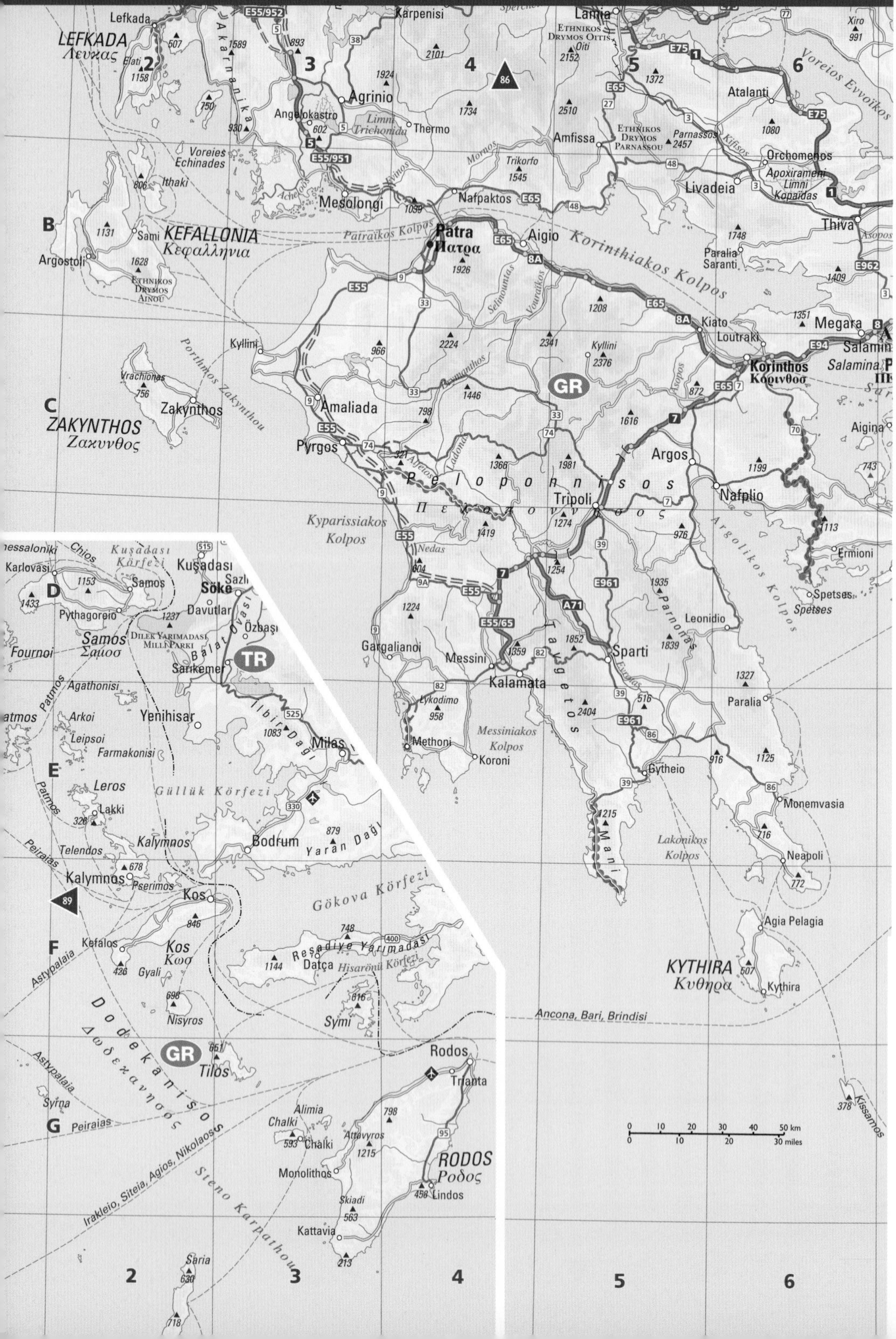

LEFKADA
Λευκας
Lefkada
Akarnanika
Karpenisi
Lamia
Ethnikos Drymos Oitis
Oiti
Xiro
Agrinio
Angelokastro
Limni Trichonida
Thermo
Voreios Evvoikos
Atalanti
Amfissa
Ethnikos Drymos Parnassou
Parnassos
Orchomenos
Apoxirameni Limni Kopaidas
Livadeia
Thiva
Voreies Echinades
Ithaki
Mesolongi
Nafpaktos
Trikorfo
Mornos
KEFALLONIA
Κεφαλληνια
Sami
Argostoli
Ethnikos Drymos Ainou
Patraikos Kolpos
Patra
Πατρα
Aigio
Korinthiakos Kolpos
Paralia Saranti
Kiato
Megara
Loutraki
Korinthos
Κορινθος
Salamina
Kyllini
Porthmos Zakynthou
Vrachionas
Zakynthos
ZAKYNTHOS
Ζακυνθος
Amaliada
Pyrgos
GR
Aigina
Argos
Tripoli
Nafplio
Peloponnisos
Πελοποννησος
Kyparissiakos Kolpos
Argolikos Kolpos
Ermioni
Spetses
Nedas
Leonidio
Parnonas
Taygetos
Sparti
Gargaliano
Messini
Kalamata
Lykodimo
Methoni
Koroni
Messiniakos Kolpos
Paralia
Gytheio
Monemvasia
Mani
Lakonikos Kolpos
Neapoli
Agia Pelagia
KYTHIRA
Κυθηρα
Kythira
Ancona, Bari, Brindisi
Kissamos
Thessaloniki
Chios
Kuşadası Körfezi
Kuşadası
Karlovasi
Samos
Söke
Davutlar
Pythagoreio
Özbaşı
Dilek Yarimadasi Milli Parki
Samos
Σαμος
Fournoi
Balat Ovası
TR
Sarıkemer
Agathonisi
Patmos
Arkoi
Yenihisar
Leipsoi
Farmakonisi
İlbir Dağı
Milas
Leros
Lakki
Güllük Körfezi
Kalymnos
Bodrum
Yaran Dağı
Telendos
Kalymnos
Pserimos
Kos
Gökova Körfezi
Kefalos
Kos
Κως
Gyali
Reşadiye Yarımadası
Datça
Hisarönü Körfezi
Nisyros
Symi
Dodekanisos
Δωδεκανησος
Tilos
Rodos
Trianta
Astypalaia
Syrna
Peiraias
Alimia
Chalki
Attavyros
RODOS
Ροδος
Monolithos
Lindos
Skiadi
Kattavia
Iraklelo, Siteia, Agios Nikolaos
Steno Karpathou
Saria
0 10 20 30 40 50 km
0 10 20 30 miles

Skyros
Linaria
Kochylas
Limnos, Kavala
Lesvos
Psara
Antipsara
Marmaro
Oinousses
Bozdağ
Foça
Chios
Χιος
Çeşme
Alaçatı
Limenas
Kiran Dağlari
TR
Pyxaria
Kymi
Psachna
Nea Artaki
Chalkida
Notios Evvoïkos Kolpos
EVVOIA
Ευβοια
Avlonas
Parnithas
Agia Marina
Nea Styra
Nea Liosia
Kifisia
Nea Makri
ATHINA
ΑΘΗΝΑΙ
Chalandri
Zografou
Marmari
Karystos
Spata
Petalioi
Kolpos Petalion
Peiraias
ΠΕΙΡΑΙΑΣ
Kallithea
Glyfada
Voula
Keratea
Agios Dimitrios
Ethnikos Drymos Souniou
Makronisos
Lavrio
Aigina
Saronikos Kolpos
Egeon Pelagos
Samos, Kos, Rodos
Andros
Ανδρος
Gavrio
Tinos
Τηνος
Ikaria
Ικαρια
Evdilos
Fournoi
Samos
Korisia
Tzia
Κεα
Gyaros
Syros
Συρος
Ermoupoli
Mykonos
Μυκονος
Rineia
Kythnos
Κυθνος
Merichas
Patmos
Skala
Ydra
Kyklades
Κυκλαδες
Serifos
Donoussa
Paros
Παρος
Paroikia
Naxos
Ναξος
Antiparos
Sifnos
Σιφνος
Kamares
Koufonisi
Kinaros
Levitha
Kalymnos, Rodos
Schoinoussa
Irakleia
Keros
Katapola
Amorgos
MYRTOO PELAGOS
Antimilos
Kimolos
Polyaigos
Adamas
Milos
Μηλος
Sikinos
Ios
Ιος
Folegandros
Astypalaia
Oia
Santorini
Θηρα
Anafi
Rethymno
Chania
Irakleio
Agios Nikolaos
Syrna
Kythira
Peiraias
Paros
Thira
Milos, Peiraias
Karpathos, Rodos, Lemesos
Kolpos Chanion
Chania
Kissamos
Platanos
KRITI
Κρητη
Ormos Almyrou
Dia
Elos
Lefka Ori
Rethymno
Irakleio
Kolpos Irakleiou
Nea Alikarnassos
Palaiochora
Ethnikos Drymos Samarias
Chora Sfakion
Geropotamos
Psiloreitis
GR
Selena
Agios Nikolaos
Kolpos Mirampellou
Siteia
Palaikastro
Karpathos, Rodos
Dikti
Zakros
Kolpos Messaras
Matala
Kofinas
Ierapetra
Gavdos

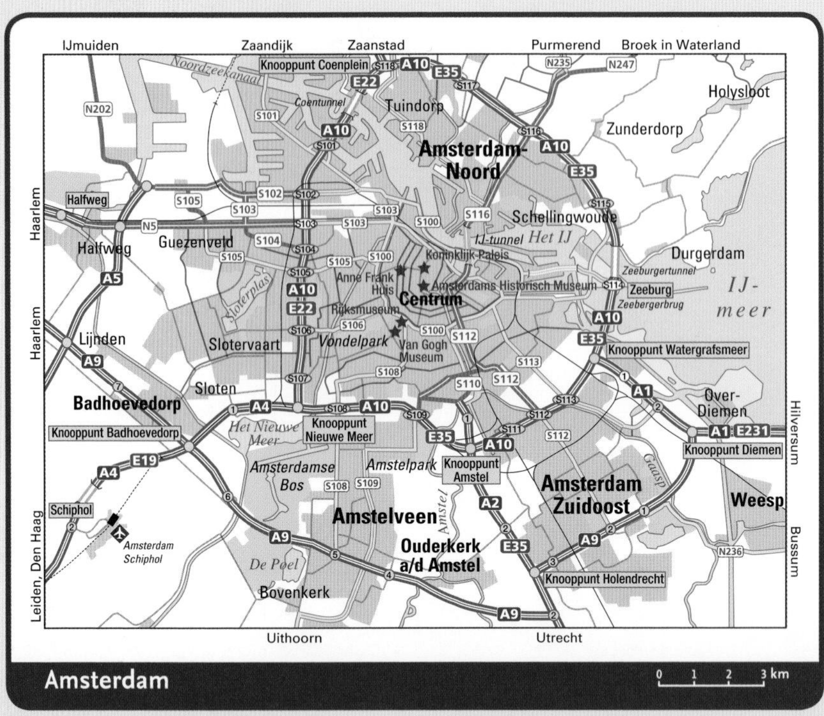

Amsterdam

0 1 2 3 km

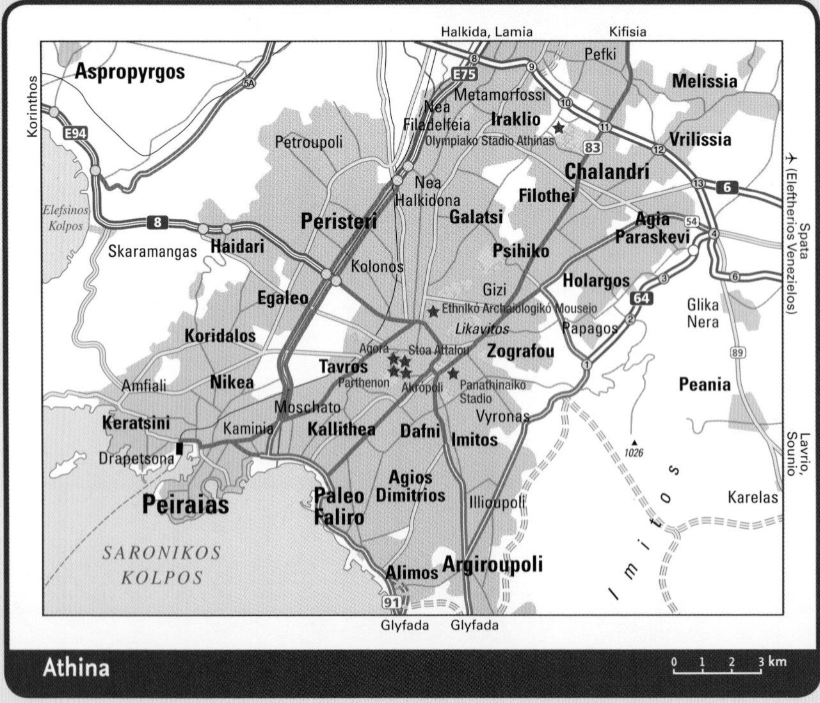

Athina

0 1 2 3 km

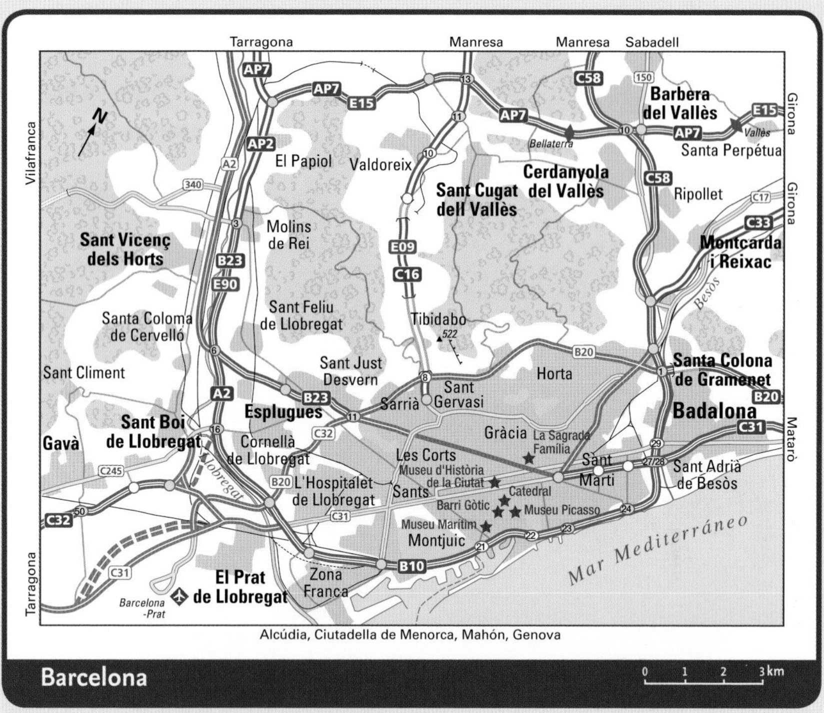
Tarragona
Manresa
Manresa
Sabadell
Vilafranca
Girona
Girona
Mataró
Tarragona
Alcúdia, Ciutadella de Menorca, Mahón, Genova
Barbera del Vallès
Santa Perpétua
Cerdanyola del Vallès
Sant Cugat dell Vallès
El Papiol
Valdoreix
Ripollet
Molins de Rei
Sant Vicenç dels Horts
Montcarda i Reixac
Santa Coloma de Cervelló
Sant Feliu de Llobregat
Tibidabo
Sant Climent
Sant Just Desvern
Horta
Santa Colona de Gramenet
Sant Gervasi
Sarrià
Badalona
Esplugues
Sant Boi de Llobregat
Gavà
Cornellà de Llobregat
Gràcia
La Sagrada Família
Les Corts
Museu d'Història de la Ciutat
Sant Martí
Sant Adrià de Besòs
L'Hospitalet de Llobregat
Sants
Catedral
Barri Gòtic
Museu Picasso
Museu Marítim
Montjuic
Mar Mediterráneo
El Prat de Llobregat
Zona Franca
Barcelona -Prat
Barcelona
0 1 2 3 km

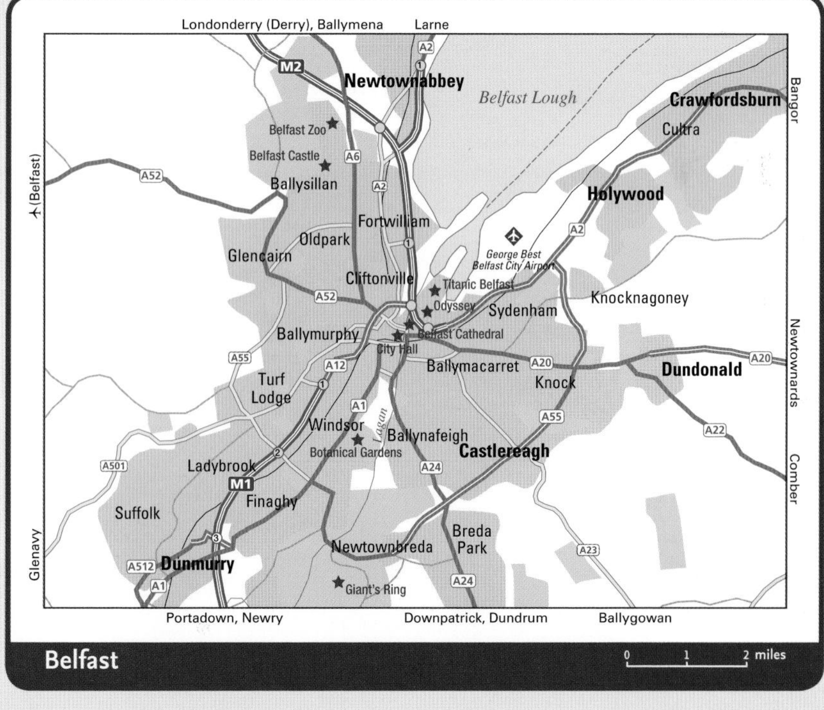
Londonderry (Derry), Ballymena
Larne
Bangor
Newtownards
Comber
(Belfast)
Glenavy
Portadown, Newry
Downpatrick, Dundrum
Ballygowan
Newtownabbey
Belfast Lough
Crawfordsburn
Cultra
Belfast Zoo
Belfast Castle
Ballysillan
Holywood
Fortwilliam
Oldpark
Glencairn
George Best Belfast City Airport
Cliftonville
Titanic Belfast
Knocknagoney
Odyssey
Sydenham
Ballymurphy
Belfast Cathedral
City Hall
Ballymacarret
Knock
Dundonald
Turf Lodge
Windsor
Ballynafeigh
Botanical Gardens
Castlereagh
Ladybrook
Finaghy
Suffolk
Breda Park
Newtownbreda
Dunmurry
Giant's Ring
Belfast
0 1 2 miles

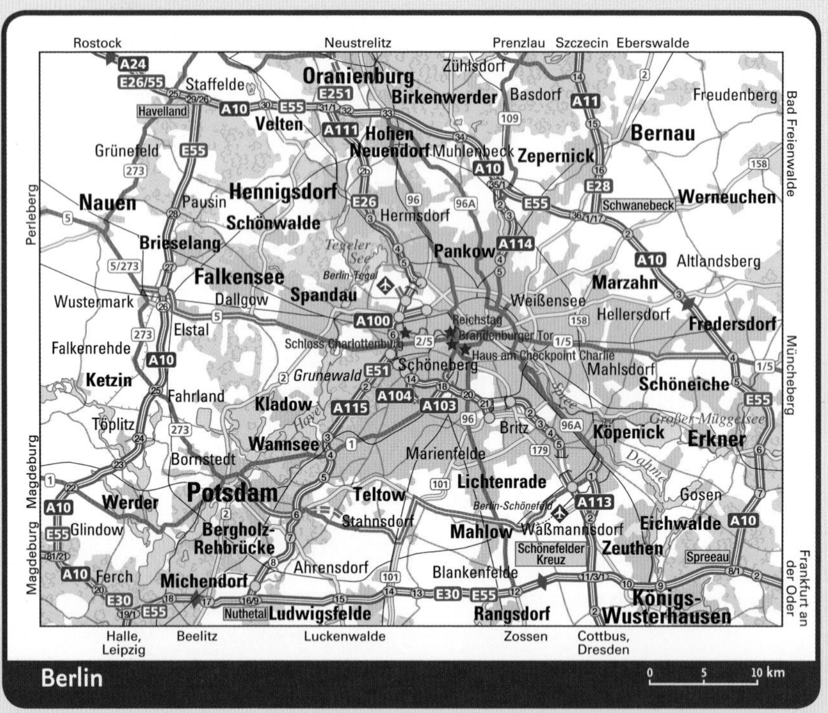
Rostock
Neustrelitz
Prenzlau
Szczecin
Eberswalde
Oranienburg
Zühlsdorf
Staffelde
Birkenwerder
Basdorf
Freudenberg
Havelland
Velten
Hohen Neuendorf
Mühlenbeck
Zepernick
Bernau
Grünefeld
Nauen
Pausin
Hennigsdorf
Hermsdorf
Schwanebeck
Werneuchen
Schönwalde
Brieselang
Tegeler See
Pankow
Altlandsberg
Falkensee
Berlin-Tegel
Marzahn
Wustermark
Dallgow
Spandau
Weißensee
Hellersdorf
Elstal
Reichstag
Brandenburger Tor
Fredersdorf
Falkenrehde
Schloss Charlottenburg
Haus am Checkpoint Charlie
Mahlsdorf
Ketzin
Grunewald
Schöneberg
Schöneiche
Fahrland
Kladow
Spree
Großer Müggelsee
Töplitz
Havel
Britz
Köpenick
Erkner
Wannsee
Marienfelde
Bornstedt
Dahme
Lichtenrade
Werder
Potsdam
Teltow
Gosen
Berlin-Schönefeld
Stahnsdorf
Glindow
Bergholz-Rehbrücke
Mahlow
Waßmannsdorf
Eichwalde
Schönefelder Kreuz
Zeuthen
Spreeau
Ahrensdorf
Ferch
Blankenfelde
Michendorf
Königs-Wusterhausen
Nuthetal
Ludwigsfelde
Rangsdorf
Perleberg
Magdeburg
Bad Freienwalde
Müncheberg
Frankfurt an der Oder
Halle, Leipzig
Beelitz
Luckenwalde
Zossen
Cottbus, Dresden
0 5 10 km

Berlin

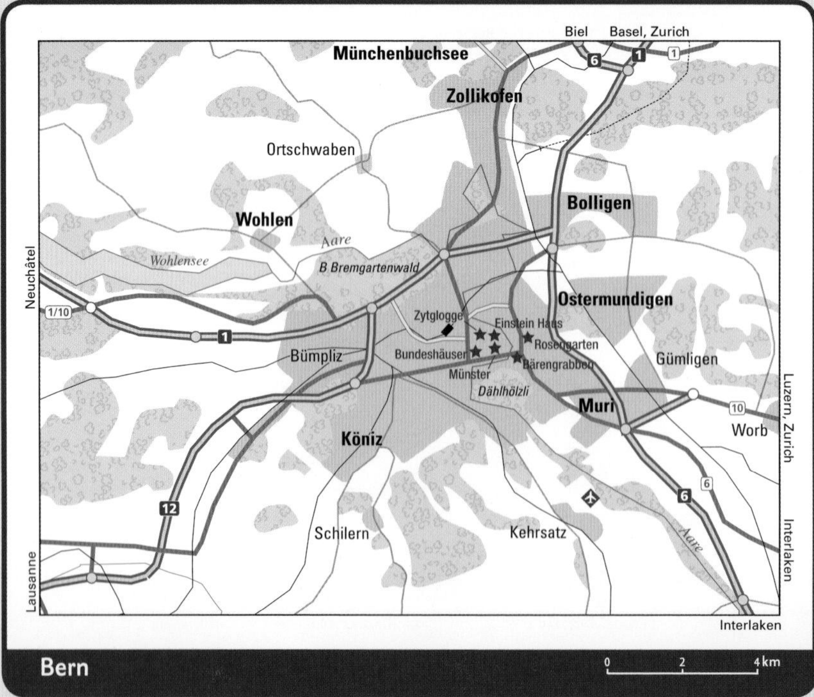
Biel
Basel, Zurich
Münchenbuchsee
Zollikofen
Ortschwaben
Bolligen
Wohlen
Aare
Wohlensee
B Bremgartenwald
Ostermundigen
Zytglogge
Einstein Haus
Rosengarten
Bundeshäuser
Bärengraben
Münster
Gümligen
Bümpliz
Dählhölzli
Muri
Worb
Köniz
Schilern
Kehrsatz
Neuchâtel
Lausanne
Luzern, Zurich
Interlaken
0 2 4 km

Bern

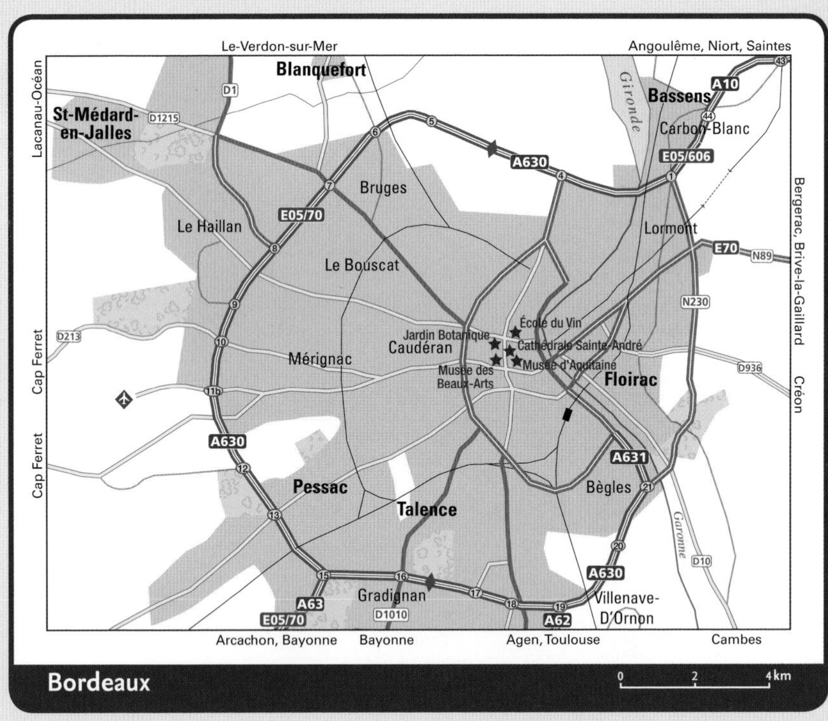

Bordeaux

0 2 4 km

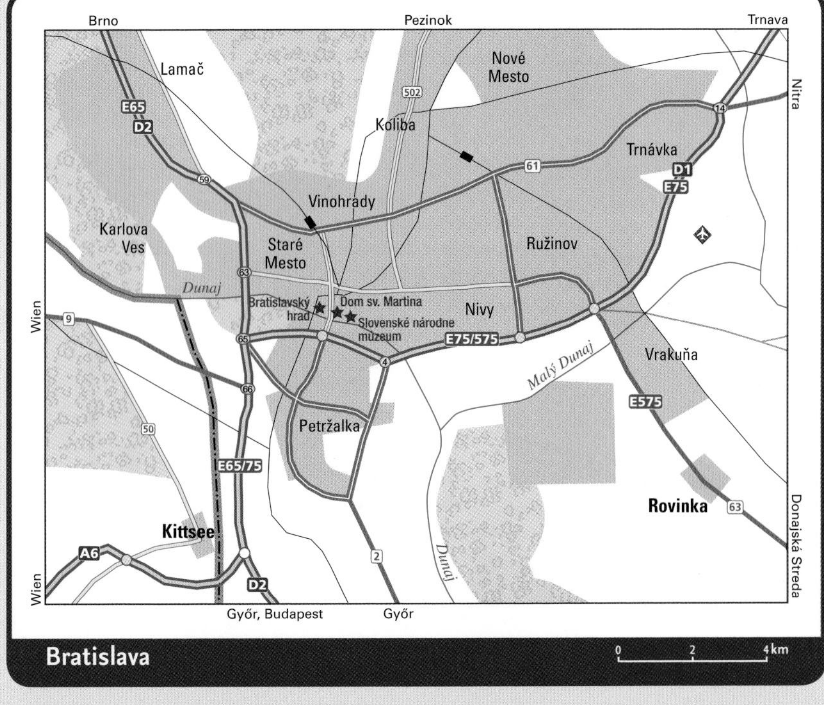

Bratislava

0 2 4 km

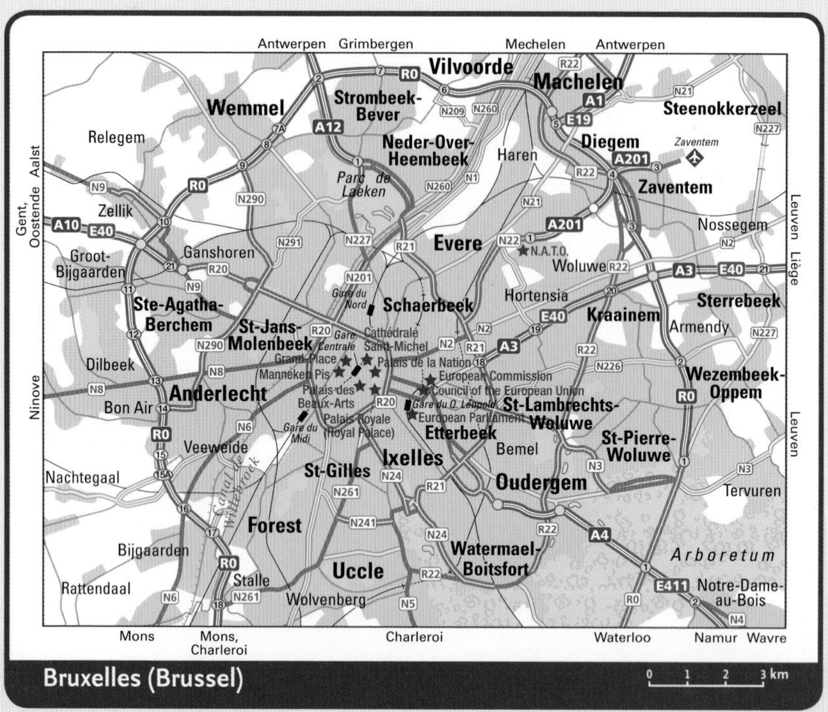

Bruxelles (Brussel)

0 1 2 3 km

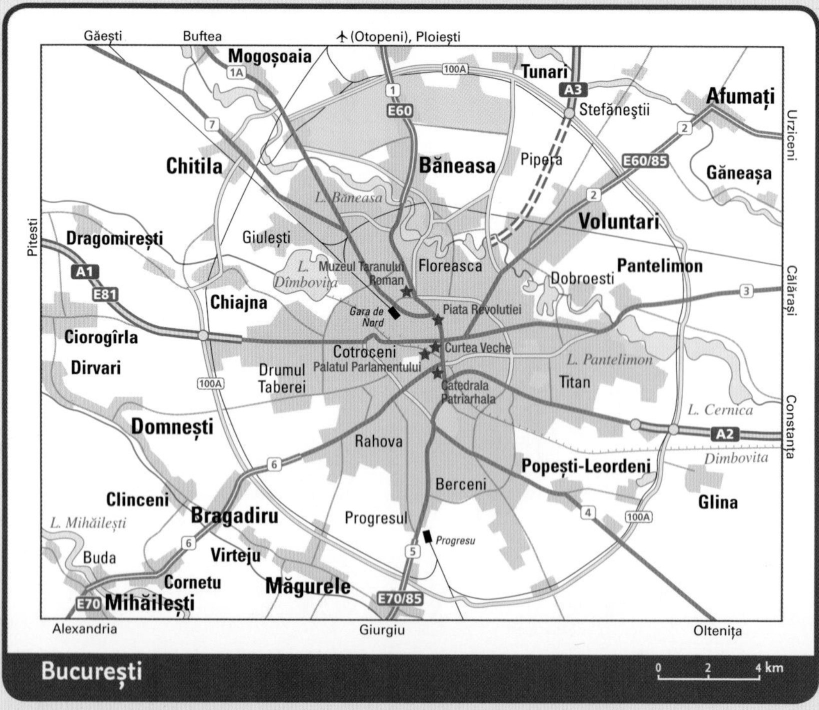

București

0 2 4 km

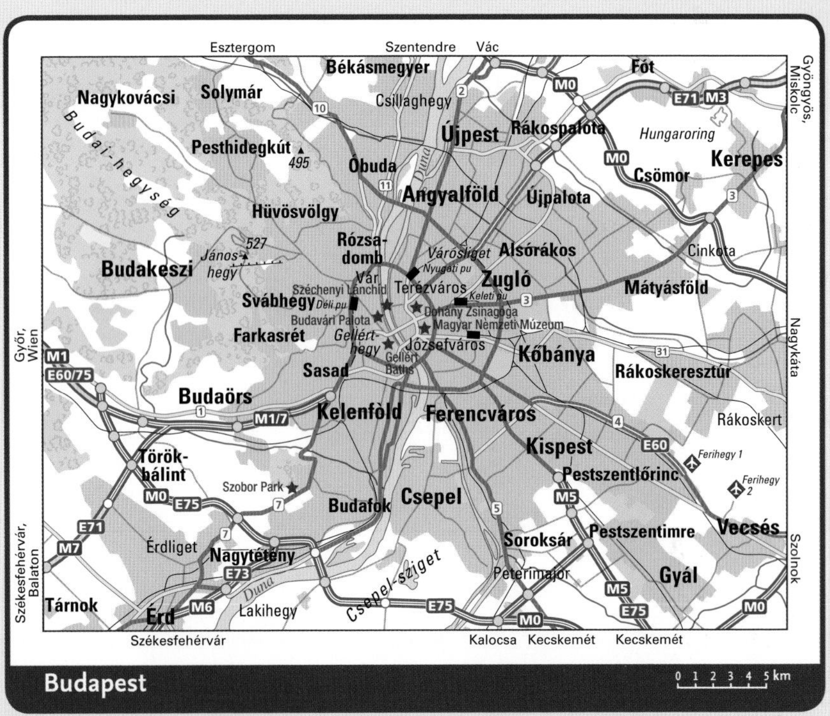

Budapest

0 1 2 3 4 5 km

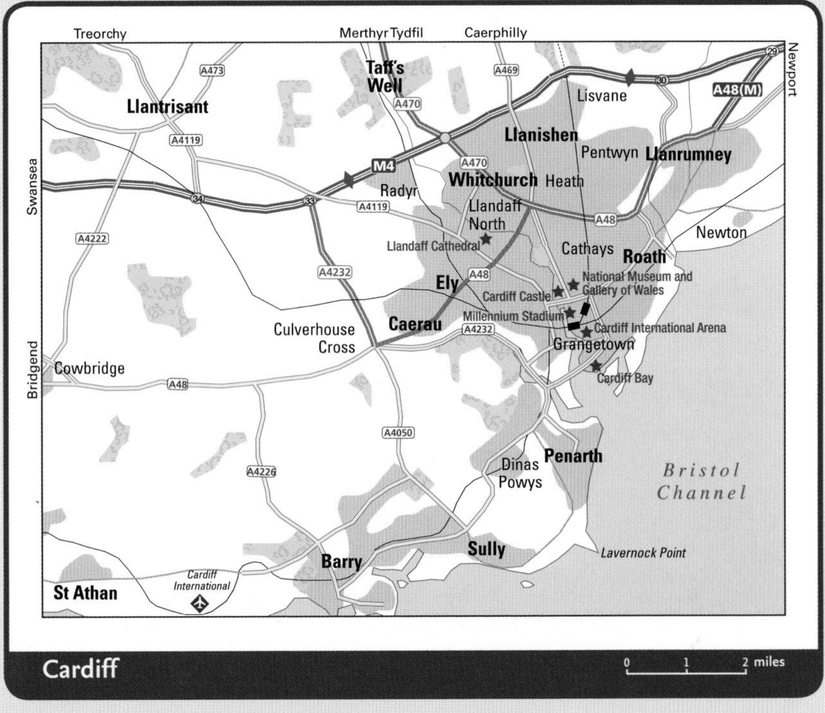

Cardiff

0 1 2 miles

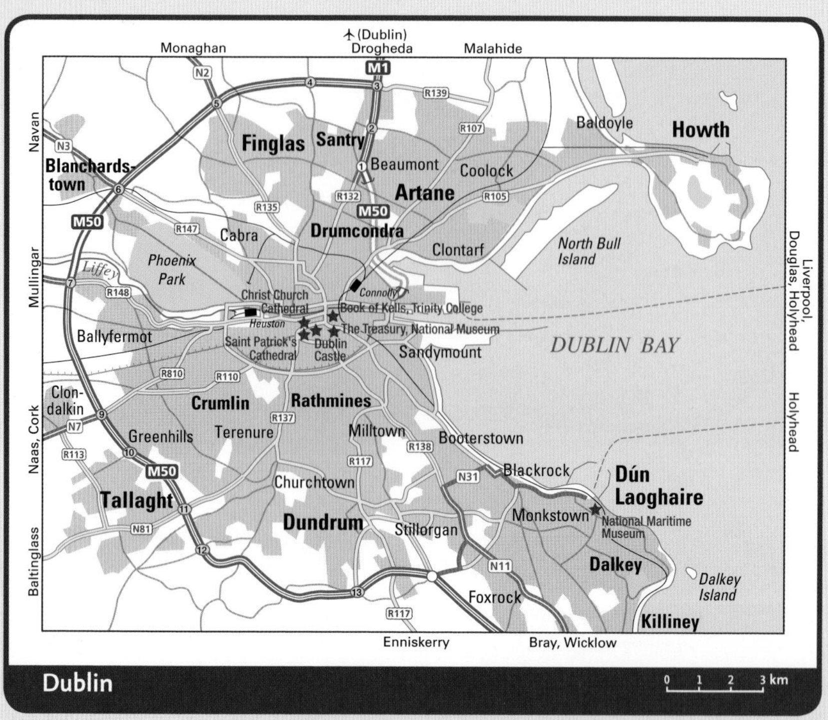

Dublin

0 1 2 3 km

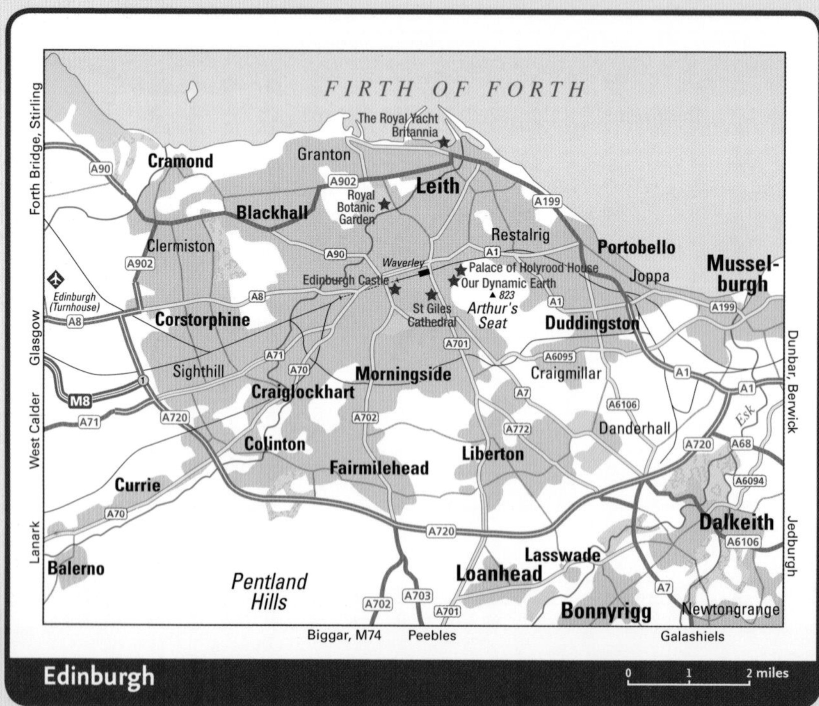

Edinburgh

0 1 2 miles

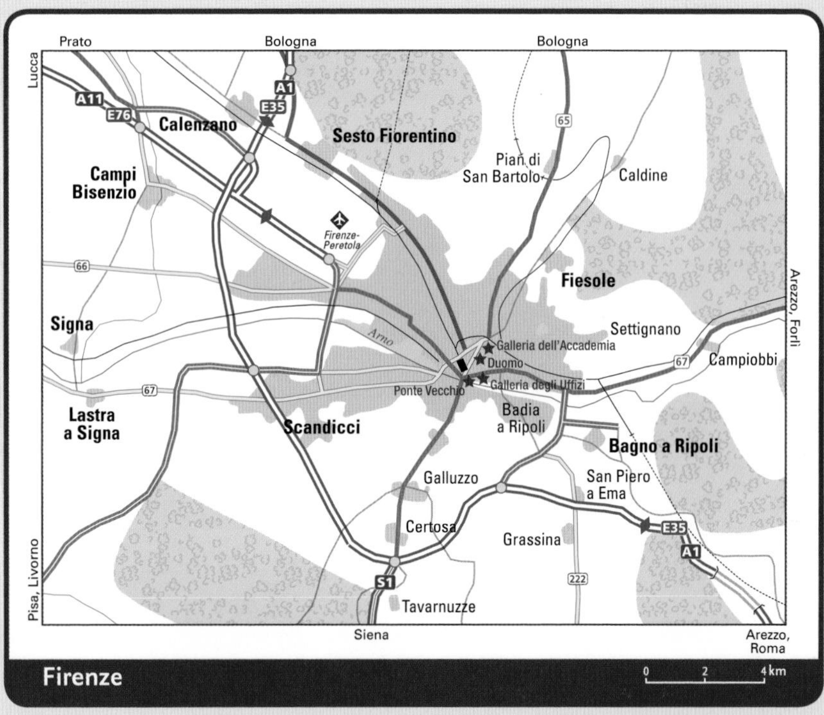
Prato
Bologna
Bologna
Lucca
Calenzano
Sesto Fiorentino
Pian di San Bartolo
Caldine
Campi Bisenzio
Firenze-Peretola
Fiesole
Signa
Arno
Settignano
Galleria dell'Accademia
Duomo
Campiobbi
Ponte Vecchio
Galleria degli Uffizi
Badia a Ripoli
Lastra a Signa
Scandicci
Bagno a Ripoli
Galluzzo
San Piero a Ema
Certosa
Grassina
Tavarnuzze
Pisa, Livorno
Arezzo, Forlì
Siena
Arezzo, Roma
Firenze
0 2 4 km

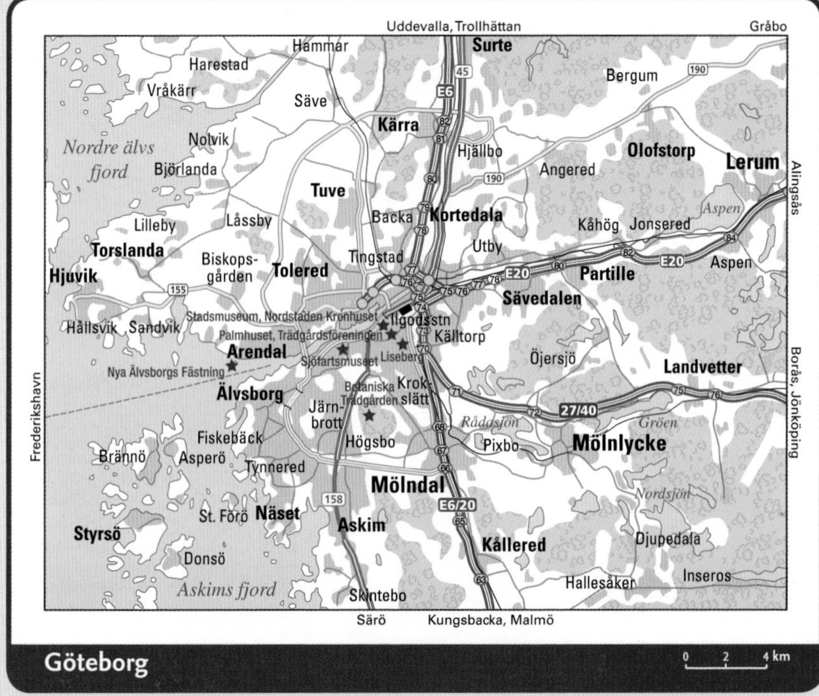
Uddevalla, Trollhättan
Gråbo
Hammar
Surte
Harestad
Bergum
Vråkärr
Säve
Kärra
Nordre älvs fjord
Nolvik
Hjällbo
Björlanda
Angered
Olofstorp
Lerum
Tuve
Backa
Kortedala
Aspen
Lilleby
Låssby
Kåhög
Jonsered
Torslanda
Utby
Hjuvik
Biskopsgården
Tolered
Tingstad
Partille
Aspen
Sävedalen
Hällsvik
Sandvik
Stadsmuseum, Nordstaden Kronhuset
Ilgodsstn
Palmhuset, Trädgårdsföreningen
Källtorp
Arendal
Nya Älvsborgs Fästning
Sjöfartsmuseet
Liseberg
Öjersjö
Landvetter
Älvsborg
Botaniska Trädgården
Krokslätt
Järnbrott
Rådasjön
Gröen
Fiskebäck
Högsbo
Pixbo
Mölnlycke
Brännö
Asperö
Tynnered
Mölndal
Nordsjön
St. Förö
Näset
Askim
Styrsö
Kållered
Djupedala
Donsö
Askims fjord
Hallesåker
Inseros
Skintebo
Fredrikshavn
Alingsås
Borås, Jönköping
Särö
Kungsbacka, Malmö
Göteborg
0 2 4 km

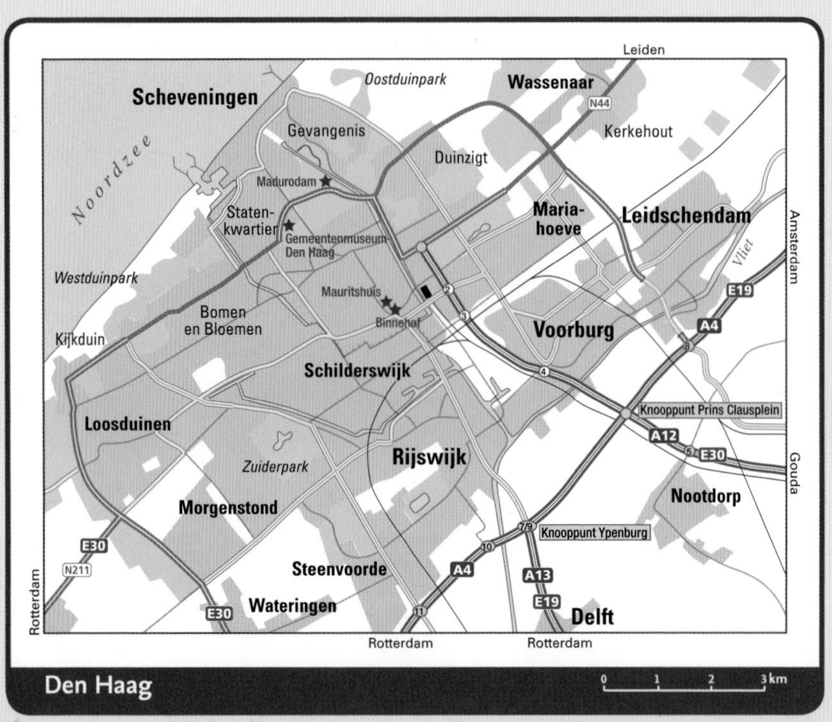

Den Haag

0 1 2 3 km

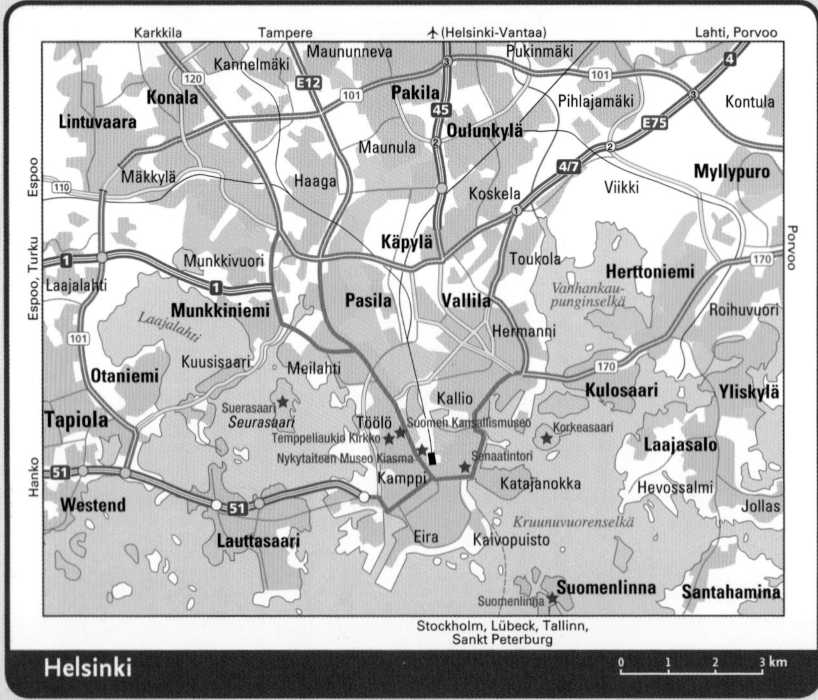

Helsinki

0 1 2 3 km

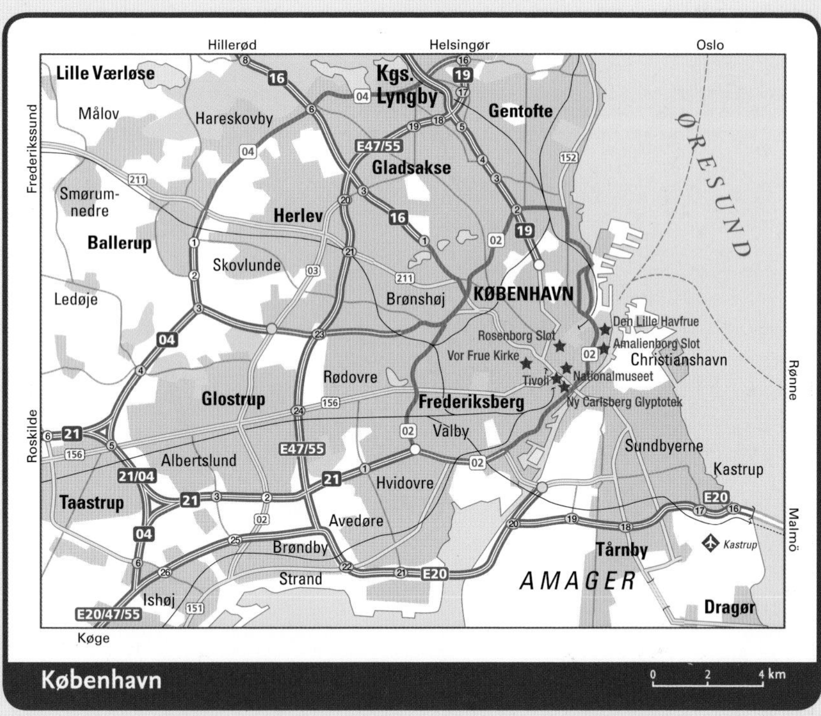
Hillerød
Helsingør
Oslo
Lille Værløse
Kgs. Lyngby
Gentofte
Målov
Hareskovby
ØRESUND
Frederikssund
Gladsakse
Smørum-
nedre
Herlev
Ballerup
Skovlunde
Ledøje
Brønshøj
KØBENHAVN
Den Lille Havfrue
Rosenborg Slot
Amalienborg Slot
Vor Frue Kirke
Christianshavn
Tivoli
Nationalmuseet
Rødovre
Rønne
Glostrup
Frederiksberg
Ny Carlsberg Glyptotek
Roskilde
Valby
Sundbyerne
Albertslund
Kastrup
Hvidovre
Taastrup
Avedøre
Malmö
Brøndby
Kastrup
Tårnby
Strand
AMAGER
Ishøj
Dragør
Køge
E20/47/55
E47/55
E20
21/04
København
0 2 4 km

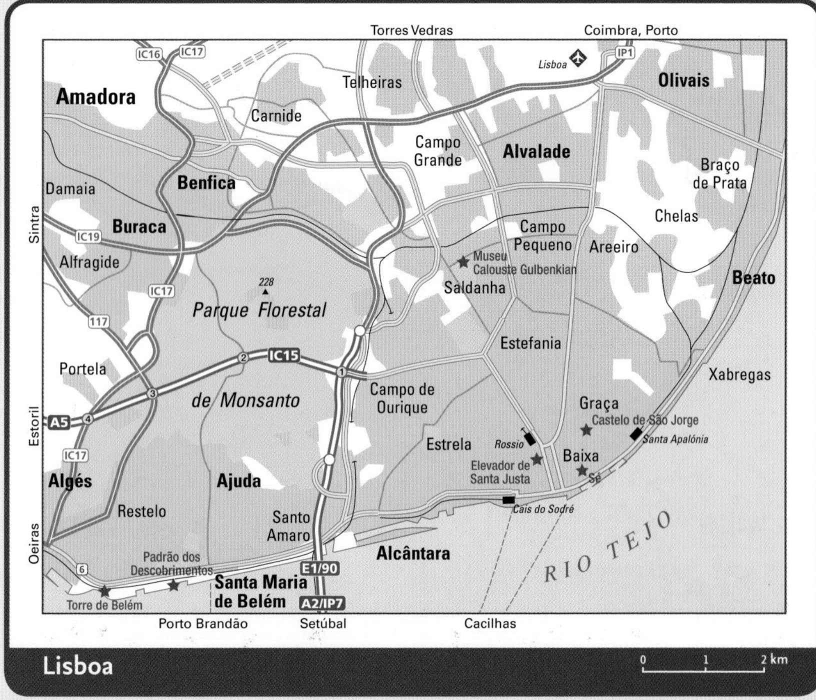
Torres Vedras
Coimbra, Porto
Lisboa
Telheiras
Olivais
Amadora
Carnide
Campo
Grande
Alvalade
Braço
de Prata
Damaia
Benfica
Chelas
Sintra
Buraca
Campo
Pequeno
Areeiro
Alfragide
Museu
Calouste Gulbenkian
Beato
Saldanha
228
Parque Florestal
Estefania
Portela
Xabregas
Campo de
Ourique
de Monsanto
Graça
Castelo de São Jorge
Estoril
Estrela
Rossio
Santa Apolónia
Baixa
Elevador de
Santa Justa
Sé
Algés
Ajuda
Restelo
Cais do Sodré
Santo
Amaro
RIO TEJO
Oeiras
Alcântara
Padrão dos
Descobrimentos
Santa Maria
de Belém
Torre de Belém
Porto Brandão
Setúbal
Cacilhas
Lisboa
0 1 2 km

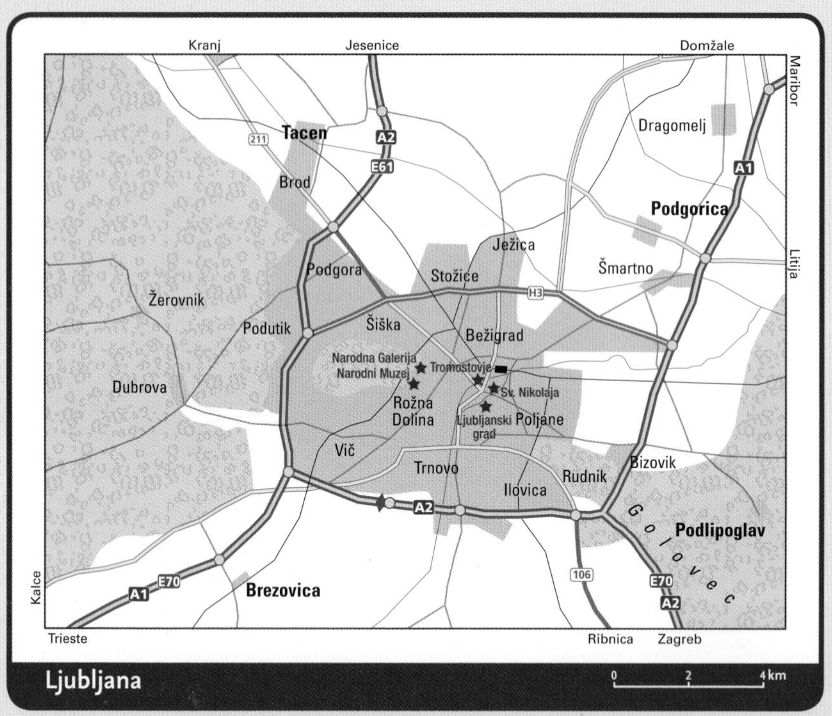

Ljubljana

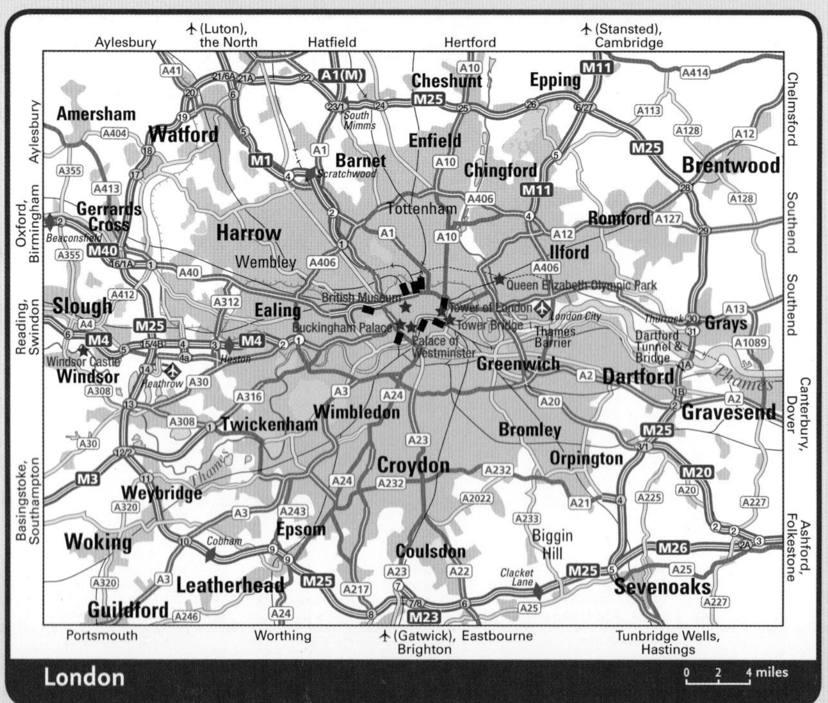

London

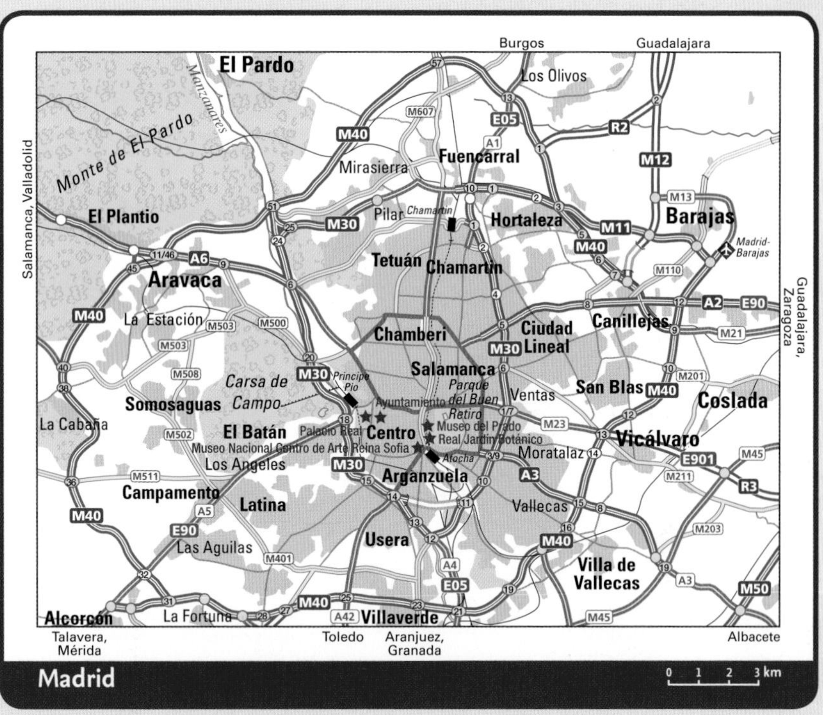
Madrid
Burgos
Guadalajara
El Pardo
Los Olivos
Monte de El Pardo
Manzanares
Mirasierra
Fuencarral
El Plantio
Pilar
Chamartín
Hortaleza
Barajas
Madrid-Barajas
Aravaca
Tetuán
Chamartín
La Estación
Chamberí
Ciudad Lineal
Canillejas
Salamanca
Príncipe Pío
Carsa de Campo
Somosaguas
Parque del Buen Retiro
Ayuntamiento
Ventas
San Blas
Coslada
La Cabaña
El Batán
Palacio Real
Centro
Museo del Prado
Real Jardín Botánico
Museo Nacional Centro de Arte Reina Sofia
Vicálvaro
Los Angeles
Atocha
Moratalaz
Arganzuela
Campamento
Latina
Vallecas
Las Aguilas
Usera
Villa de Vallecas
Alcorcón
La Fortuna
Villaverde
Salamanca, Valladolid
Guadalajara, Zaragoza
Talavera, Mérida
Toledo
Aranjuez, Granada
Albacete
0 1 2 3 km

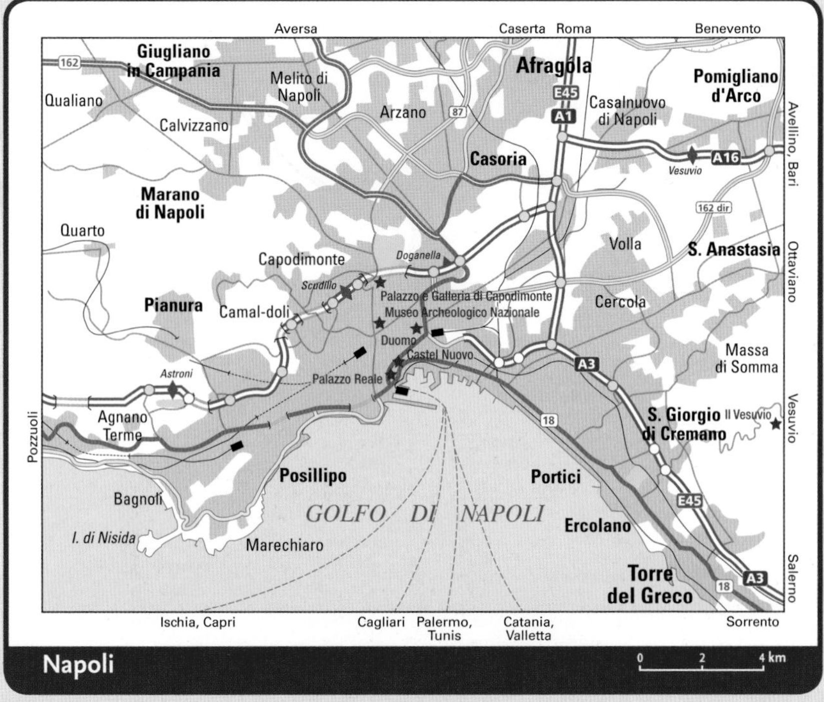
Napoli
Aversa
Caserta
Roma
Benevento
Giugliano in Campania
Melito di Napoli
Afragóla
Pomigliano d'Arco
Qualiano
Casalnuovo di Napoli
Arzano
Calvizzano
Casoria
Vesuvio
Avellino, Bari
Marano di Napoli
Quarto
Volla
S. Anastasia
Capodimonte
Doganella
Scudillo
Palazzo e Galleria di Capodimonte
Pianura
Camal-doli
Museo Archeologico Nazionale
Cercola
Duomo
Castel Nuovo
Ottaviano
Massa di Somma
Astroni
Palazzo Reale
Agnano Terme
S. Giorgio di Cremano
Il Vesuvio
Vesuvio
Pozzuoli
Posillipo
Portici
Bagnoli
GOLFO DI NAPOLI
Ercolano
I. di Nisida
Marechiaro
Torre del Greco
Salerno
Ischia, Capri
Cagliari
Palermo, Tunis
Catania, Valletta
Sorrento
0 2 4 km

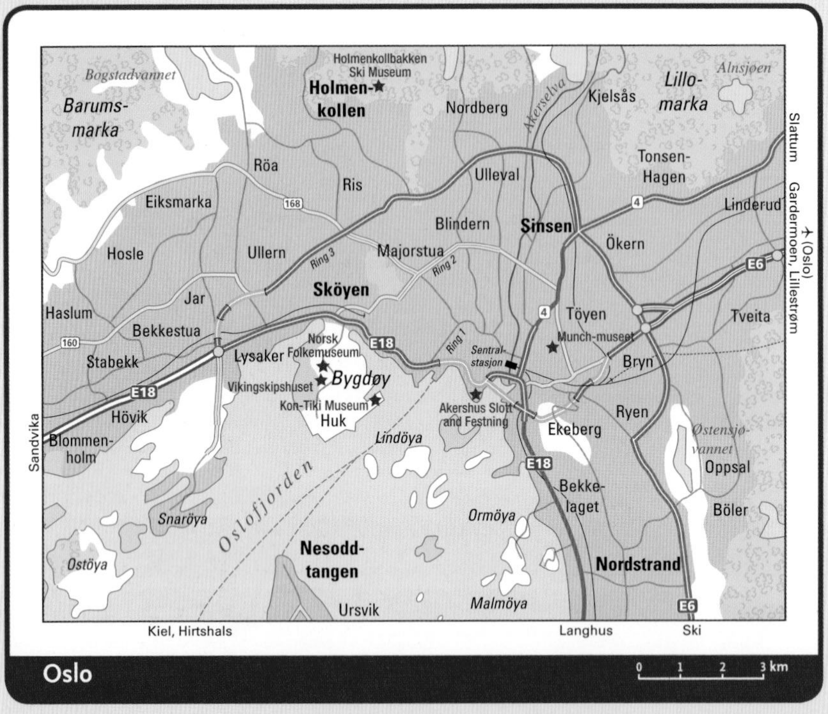

Oslo

0 1 2 3 km

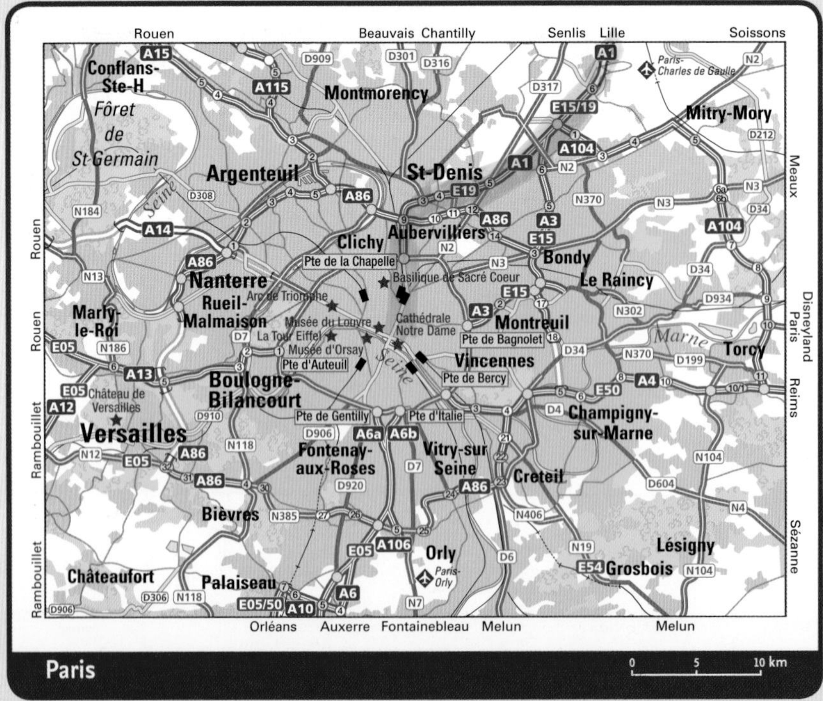

Paris

0 5 10 km

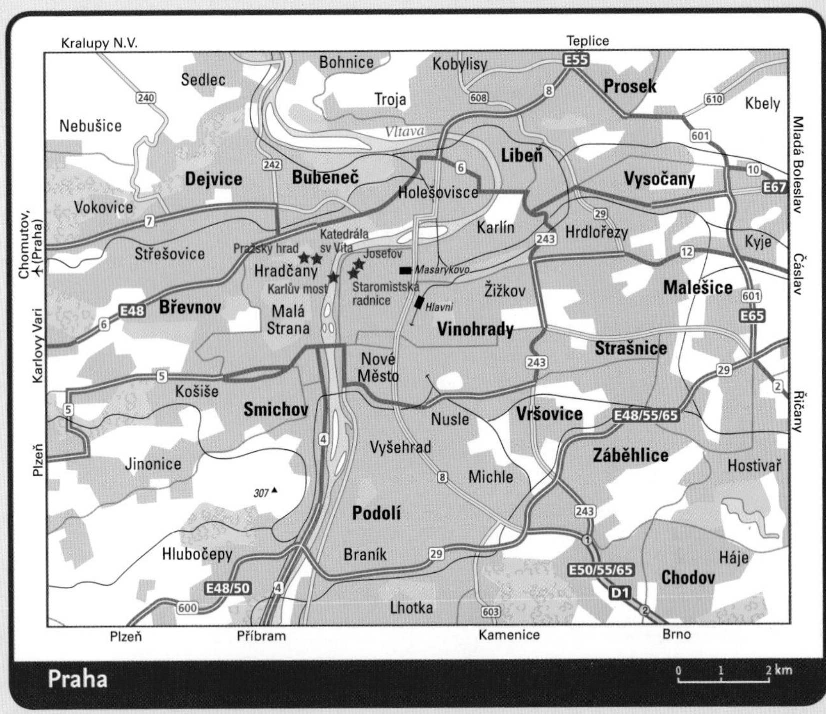
Kralupy N.V.
Teplice
Sedlec
Bohnice
Kobylisy
Prosek
Kbely
Nebušice
Troja
Vltava
Mladá Boleslav
Dejvice
Bubeneč
Libeň
Vysočany
Holešovisce
Vokovice
Karlín
Hrdlořezy
Kyje
Chomutov, (Praha)
Střešovice
Pražský hrad
Katedrála sv Víta
Josefov
Masarykovo
Hradčany
Karlův most
Staroměstská radnice
Hlavní
Žižkov
Malešice
Čáslav
Břevnov
Malá Strana
Vinohrady
Strašnice
Karlovy Vari
Nové Město
Košiše
Smichov
Nusle
Vršovice
Říčany
Vyšehrad
Záběhlice
Hostivař
Plzeň
Jinonice
Michle
Podolí
Hlubočepy
Braník
Háje
Chodov
Lhotka
Plzeň
Příbram
Kamenice
Brno
0 1 2 km

Praha

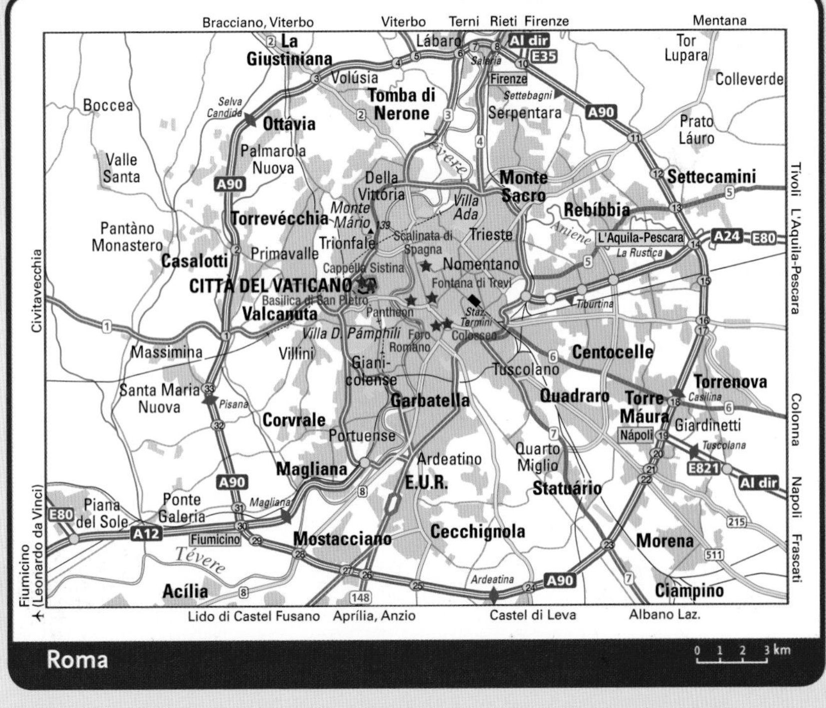
Bracciano, Viterbo
Viterbo
Terni
Rieti
Firenze
Mentana
La Giustiniana
Lábaro
Tor Lupara
Volúsia
Salaria
Colleverde
Boccea
Selva Candida
Tomba di Nerone
Settebagni
Serpentara
Ottávia
Prato Láuro
Valle Santa
Palmarola Nuova
Tevere
Della Vittória
Monte Sacro
Settecamini
Tivoli
Rebíbbia
Pantàno Monastero
Torrevécchia
Monte Mário
Villa Ada
Trieste
Aniene
L'Aquila-Pescara
Trionfale
Scalinata di Spagna
La Rustica
Casalotti
Primavalle
Cappella Sistina
Nomentano
Civitavecchia
CITTÀ DEL VATICANO
Fontana di Trevi
Basilica di San Pietro
Tiburtina
Valcanuta
Pantheon
Staz. Termini
Villa D. Pámphili
Foro Romano
Colosseo
Massimina
Villini
Gianicolense
Centocelle
Tuscolano
Santa Maria Nuova
Pisana
Garbatella
Quadraro
Torre Máura
Torrenova
Casilina
Corvrale
Giardinetti
Colonna
Portuense
Nápoli
Tuscolana
Ardeatino
Quarto Miglio
Magliana
E.U.R.
Statuário
Napoli
Piana del Sole
Ponte Galeria
Magliana
Fiumicino
Mostacciano
Cecchignola
Morena
Frascati
Fiumicino (Leonardo da Vinci)
Tévere
Ardeatina
Acília
Ciampino
Lido di Castel Fusano
Aprília, Anzio
Castel di Leva
Albano Laz.
0 1 2 3 km

Roma

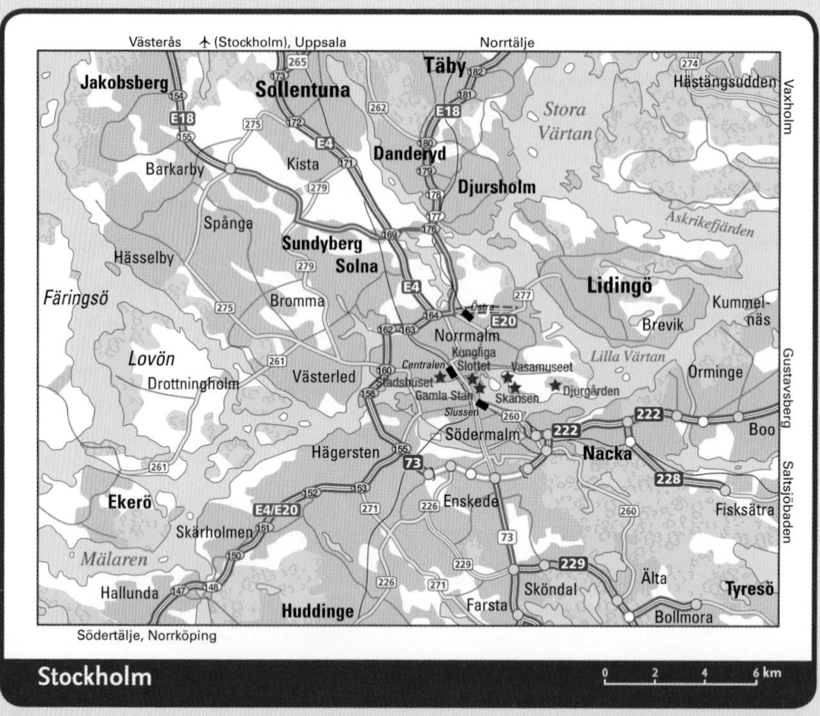

Stockholm

0 2 4 6 km

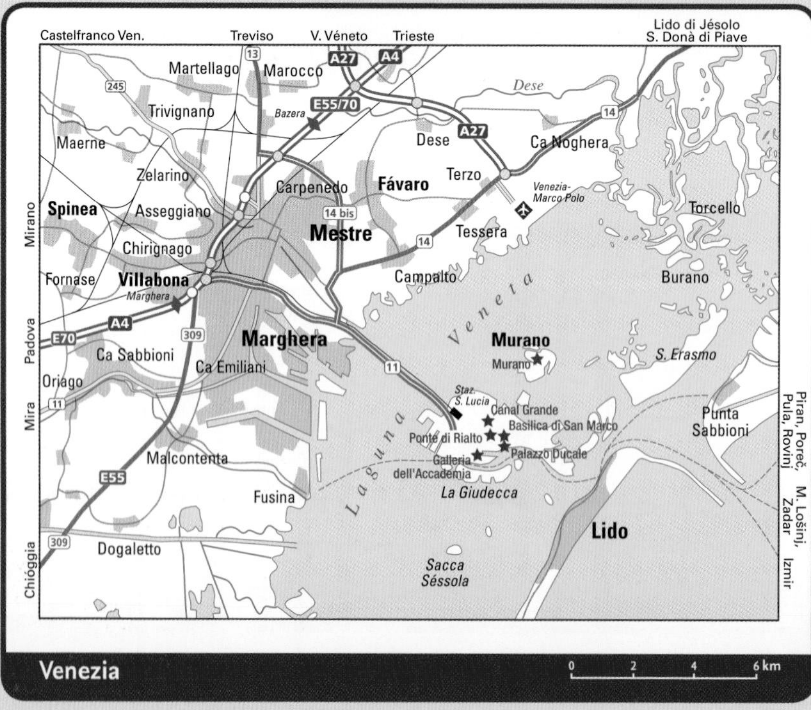

Venezia

0 2 4 6 km

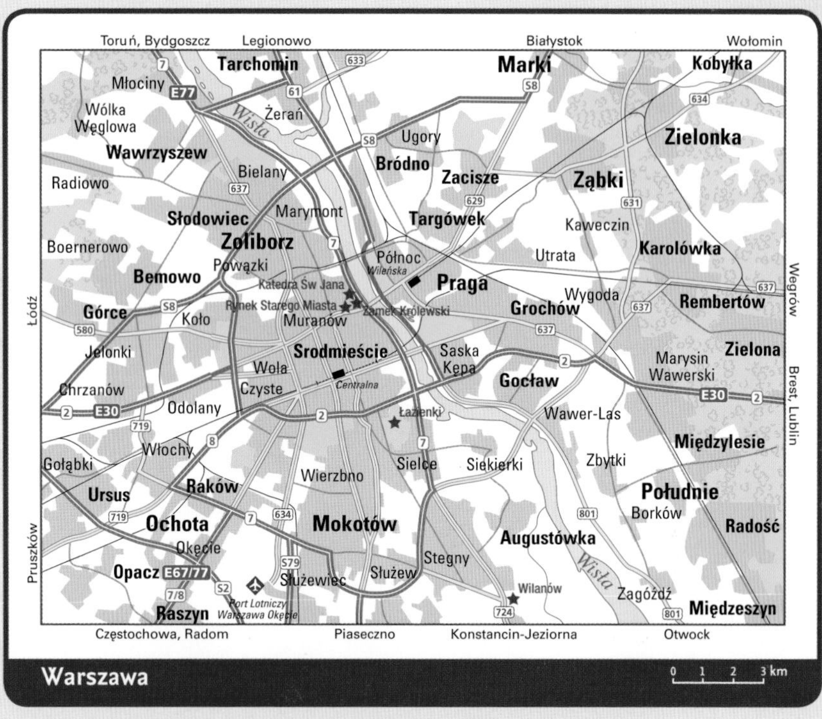

Warszawa

0 1 2 3 km

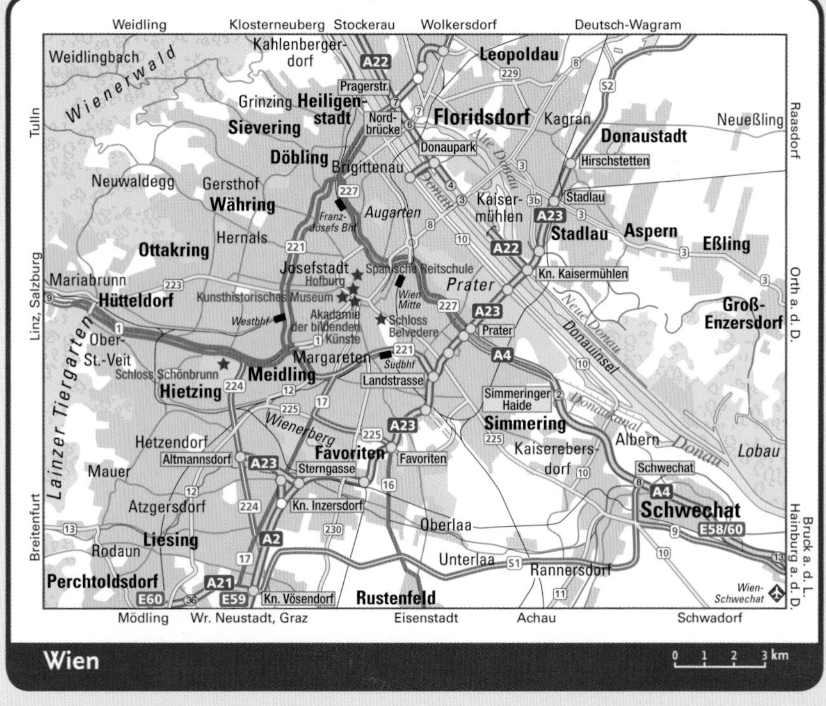

Wien

0 1 2 3 km

Index

The index contains a selection of the major towns and cities found on the reference map section of the atlas.
All indexed entries have a page and grid reference.

Entries which have a ❐ symbol instead of a grid reference are located on small insets within the appropriate page.

A	Austria
AL	Albania
AND	Andorra
B	Belgium
BG	Bulgaria
BIH	Bosnia and Herzogovina
BY	Belarus
CH	Switzerland
CZ	Czech Republic
D	Germany
DK	Denmark
E	Spain
EST	Estonia
F	France
FIN	Finland
FL	Liechtenstein
FO	Faroe Islands
GB	United Kingdom
GBG	Guernsey
GBJ	Jersey
GBM	Isle of Man
GBZ	Gibraltar
GR	Greece
H	Hungary
HR	Croatia
I	Italy
IRL	Ireland
IS	Iceland
L	Luxembourg
LT	Lithuania
LV	Latvia
M	Malta
MA	Morocco
MC	Monaco
MD	Moldova
MK	Macedonia (F.Y.R.O.M.)
MNE	Montenegro
N	Norway
NL	Netherlands
P	Portugal
PL	Poland
RKS	Kosovo
RO	Romania
RSM	San Marino
RUS	Russia
S	Sweden
SK	Slovakia
SLO	Slovenia
SRB	Serbia
TR	Turkey
UA	Ukraine

A

Place	Country	Page	Grid
Aabenraa	DK	44	G3
Aachen	D	11	G8
Aalborg	DK	44	C4
Aalen	D	38	A3
Aalst	B	10	F5
Aalten	NL	11	D8
Äänekoski	FIN	64	B6
Aarau	CH	13	G10
Aars	DK	44	C3
Abádszalók	H	77	C8
A Baiuca	E	22	B2
Abarán	E	29	B10
Abbadia San Salvatore	I	32	B4
Abbeville	F	9	G12
Abelvær	N	54	E4
Abensberg	D	38	A5
Aberdare	GB	8	D4
Aberdeen	GB	3	E8
Abergavenny	GB	8	D5
Abergwaun	GB	8	D2
Abertawe	GB	8	D4
Abertillery	GB	8	D5
Aberystwyth	GB	8	C3
Abingdon	GB	9	D7
Åbo	FIN	53	G11
Abony	H	77	C7
Abrantes	P	24	D3
Abrud	RO	77	E12
Absam	A	37	C11
Abtenau	A	39	D7
Åby	S	47	D7
A Cañiza	E	22	D3
A Carreira	E	22	B3
Acate	I	30	G5
Accrington	GB	5	F7
Acerra	I	30	B5
Aceuchal	E	24	F6
Acharnes	GR	89	B7
Achern	D	13	D10
Aci Castello	I	30	F6
Aci Catena	I	30	F6
Acireale	I	30	F6
Aci Sant'Antonio	I	30	F6
A Coruña	E	22	B3
Acquapendente	I	32	B4
Acquedolci	I	30	E5
Acqui Terme	I	19	B11
Acri	I	31	E8
Ács	H	76	B4
Ada	SRB	77	F7
Adamas	GR	89	E8
Adămuș	RO	78	E3
Adâncata	RO	78	B6
Adendorf	D	42	D6
Adjud	RO	79	E8
Adorf	D	41	C8
Adra	E	29	E7
Adrano	I	30	F5
Adunații-Copăceni	RO	83	C10
Aesch	CH	13	G10
A Estrada	E	22	C2
Åfjord	N	54	G3
A Fonsagrada	E	22	B5
Afragola	I	30	B5
Afumați	RO	83	B10
A Gándara de Altea	E	22	B3
Agăș	RO	78	D6
Agde	F	18	E2
Agen	F	16	F6
Aghireșu	RO	77	D12
Agia Marina	GR	89	B8
Agia Pelagia	GR	88	F6
Agighiol	RO	79	G10
Agios Charalampos	GR	87	C12
Agios Dimitrios	GR	89	C7
Agios Efstratios	GR	87	F11
Agios Nikolaos	GR	89	G11
Agira	I	30	F5
Agliana	I	35	F7
Agnita	RO	78	F3
Agnone	I	33	D8
Agolada	E	22	C3
Agrigento	I	30	F3
Agrinio	GR	86	H5
Agropoli	I	30	C6
Ågskaret	N	57	G2
A Guarda	E	22	E2
Aguilar de Campóo	E	23	C9
Aguilar de la Frontera	E	28	D4
Águilas	E	29	D10
Ahaus	D	11	D9
Ahlen	D	11	E10
Ahmetli	TR	85	G4
Ahrensburg	D	42	C6
Åhus	S	45	E9
Aichach	D	38	B4
Aidone	I	30	F5
Aigina	GR	88	C7
Aigio	GR	88	B4
Aigle	CH	36	E5
Aigues-Mortes	F	17	H11
Ailly-sur-Somme	F	12	B2
Aire-sur-l'Adour	F	16	G4
Aiud	RO	78	E2
Aix-en-Provence	F	18	D6
Aix-les-Bains	F	36	F3
Aizenay	F	16	A2
Aizkraukle	LV	69	B8
Aizpute	LV	66	H2
Ajaccio	F	19	F10
Ajdovščina	SLO	35	B12
Ajka	H	76	C3
Åkarp	S	45	E8
Aken	D	43	G8
Åkersberga	S	47	C10
Åkerstrømmen	N	51	E8
Akhisar	TR	85	G4
Åkrehamn	N	48	D2
Ala	S	47	G10
Alaçatı	TR	89	B11
Alagón	E	20	E5
Alaior	E	29	E11
Alajärvi	FIN	53	B12
Alakurtti	RUS	61	D12
Alaquàs	E	27	F10
Alașehir	TR	85	H5
Alassio	I	19	C10
Alatri	I	33	D7
Alavus	FIN	53	C12
Alba	I	19	B10
Alba Adriatica	I	33	B8
Albacete	E	27	G7
Albaida	E	27	G10
Alba Iulia	RO	78	E2
Albanella	I	30	C6
Albano Laziale	I	32	D5
Albaville	I	34	B4
Albenga	I	19	C10
Albert	F	12	B3
Albertirsa	H	77	C7
Albertville	F	36	F4
Albești	RO	78	E4
Albești	RO	79	B7
Albeștii de Argeș	RO	78	G3
Albi	F	17	G8
Albino	I	34	B5
Albisola Superiore	I	19	C11
Alboraya	E	27	F10
Albox	E	29	D9
Albstadt	D	13	E12
Albufeira	P	25	K3
Alburquerque	E	24	E5
Alcalá de Guadaira	E	25	J7
Alcalá de Henares	E	23	H11
Alcalá de los Gazules	E	25	M7
Alcalá la Real	E	28	D6
Alcamo	I	30	E2
Alcañiz	E	20	G6
Alcantarilla	E	29	C10
Alcaudete	E	28	D5
Alcázar de San Juan	E	26	F5
Alcester	GB	8	C7
Alcobaça	P	24	D2
Alcobendas	E	23	H10
Alcorcón	E	23	H10
Alcoy-Alcoi	E	27	G10
Alcúdia	E	29	E10
Aldershot	GB	9	E8
Aleksandrovac	SRB	81	E12
Aleksandrów Kujawski	PL	71	E8
Aleksandrów Łódzki	PL	71	G9
Aleksinac	SRB	82	D2
Alençon	F	15	E9
Alès	F	17	G11
Aleșd	RO	77	C11
Alessandria	I	19	A11
Alessandria della Rocca	I	30	F3
Alessano	I	31	D12
Ålesund	N	50	C3
Alexandreia	GR	86	D6
Alexandria	RO	83	C9
Alexandria	GB	2	G5
Alexandroupoli	GR	85	C1
Alezio	I	31	C11
Alfaro	E	20	D3
Alfeld (Leine)	D	42	G5
Alfreton	GB	5	G9
Algeciras	E	25	M8
Algemesí	E	27	F10
Algete	E	23	G11
Alghero	I	32	E1
Alginet	E	27	F10
Algodonales	E	25	L8
Algorta	E	20	B1
Alhama de Granada	E	28	E6
Alhama de Murcia	E	29	C10
Alhaurín de la Torre	E	28	F5
Aliağa	TR	85	G3
Alicante	E	27	H10
Alingsås	S	46	F3
Aljaraque	E	25	K5
Aljustrel	P	25	H3
Alkmaar	NL	10	C6
Allariz	E	22	D4
Allevard	F	36	G4
Alliste	I	31	D11

Name	Country	Page	Grid
Alloa	GB	2	G6
Allonnes	F	15	F9
Almada	P	24	F2
Almadén	E	26	G2
Almansa	E	27	G9
Almazán	E	20	F2
Almazora	E	27	E10
Almeirim	P	24	E3
Almelo	NL	11	C8
Almendralejo	E	24	F6
Almería	E	29	E8
Älmhult	S	45	D9
Almodóvar del Campo	E	26	G4
Almonte	E	25	K6
Almoradí	E	29	C11
Almuñécar	E	28	E6
Almünster	A	39	C8
Almyros	GR	87	G7
Alness	GB	2	D5
Alnwick	GB	5	C8
Álora	E	28	E4
Alós d'Ensil	E	21	C8
Alosno	E	25	J5
Alost	B	10	F5
Alsfeld	D	11	G12
Alsózsolca	H	77	A9
Alta	N	58	D6
Älta	S	47	C9
Altamura	I	31	B9
Altavilla Irpina	I	30	B6
Altavilla Silentina	I	30	B6
Altdorf	CH	13	H11
Altea	E	27	G10
Altenburg	D	41	B8
Altenkirchen (Westerwald)	D	11	G10
Altentreptow	D	43	C9
Althofen	A	39	E9
Altınoluk	TR	85	E2
Altınova	TR	85	F2
Altkirch	F	13	F9
Altofonte	I	30	E3
Altomonte	I	31	D8
Alton	GB	9	E8
Altopascio	I	35	F6
Altötting	D	38	B6
Alüksne	LV	67	F8
Alverca	P	24	E2
Alvesta	S	45	C9
Alvik	S	52	C5
Älvros	S	51	D12
Älvsbyn	S	56	C3
Alytus	LT	69	G7
Alzey	D	13	B11
Alzira	E	27	F10
Amadora	P	24	F2
Åmål	S	46	D3
Amalfi	I	30	B5
Amaliada	GR	88	C3
Amantea	I	31	E8
Amara	RO	83	B12
Amarante	P	22	F3
Amărăştii de Jos	RO	83	C7
Amberg	D	41	E7
Ambérieu-en-Bugey	F	36	F3
Ambert	F	17	D11
Amble	GB	5	C8
Amboise	F	15	G10
Amelia	I	32	B5
Amersfoort	NL	11	D7
Amersham	GB	9	D8
Amesbury	GB	9	E7
Amfissa	GR	88	A5
Amiens	F	12	B2
Amilly	F	12	F3
Ammanford	GB	8	D4
Ammarnäs	S	55	C9
Amorebieta	E	20	B2
Åmot	N	48	D5
Ampelokipoi	GR	87	D7
Ampelonas	GR	86	F6
Amposta	E	21	G7
Amsterdam	NL	10	C6
Amurrio	E	20	C1
Anacapri	I	30	B5
Anafi	GR	89	F10
Anagni	I	32	D6
Anan'yiv	UA	79	B12
Ancenis	F	15	G7
An Cóbh	IRL	7	N4
Ancona	I	35	G11
Åndalsnes	N	50	C4
Anddalsvågen	N	54	C5
Andernos-les-Bains	F	16	E3
Andoain	E	20	B3
Andorra	E	20	G6
Andorra la Vella	AND	21	D9
Andover	GB	9	E7
Andrano	I	31	D12
Andratx	E	29	F9
Andria	I	31	A8
Andrychów	PL	75	D10
Andújar	E	28	C5
Anenii Noi	MD	79	D11
Ängelholm	S	45	D7
Angelokastro	GR	88	A3
Angermünde	D	43	D10
Angers	F	15	G8
Anglès	E	18	G1
Anglet	F	16	H2
Angoulême	F	16	D5
Angri	I	30	B5
Anguillara Sabazia	I	32	C5
Anif	A	39	C7
Anina	RO	77	G10
Aninoasa	RO	78	H5
Anjalankoski	FIN	65	F7
Anklam	D	43	C10
Anlaby	GB	5	F10
An Muileann gCearr	IRL	4	F1
Annan	GB	4	D6
Anna Paulowna	NL	10	B6
An Nás	IRL	4	G2
Annecy	F	36	F4
Annemasse	F	36	E4
Annonay	F	17	D12
Ano Lefkimmi	GR	86	F2
Anould	F	13	E9
Ans	B	11	G7
Ansbach	D	40	E5
Ansó	E	20	C5
An tAonach	IRL	7	K4
Antequera	E	28	E5
Antibes	F	19	D8
An tInbhear Mór	IRL	4	H3
Antony	F	12	D2
Antrim	GB	4	D2
Antwerpen	B	10	F5
An Uaimh	IRL	4	F2
Anvers	B	10	F5
Anykščiai	LT	69	D8
Anzegem	B	10	F4
Anzin	F	10	G4
Anzio	I	32	D5
Aosta	I	34	B1
Apahida	RO	78	D2
Apatin	SRB	76	F5
Apeldoorn	NL	11	D7
Apen	D	11	B10
Apice	I	30	A6
Apolda	D	41	B7
Appenzell	CH	37	C8
Appiano sulla Strada del Vino	I	37	E11
Apricena	I	33	D10
Aprilia	I	32	D5
Apt	F	18	D5
Aquaviva delle Fonti	I	31	B9
Aracena	E	25	H6
Aračinovo	MK	82	G2
Arad	RO	77	E9
Aradeo	I	31	C11
Aragona	I	30	F3
A Ramallosa	E	22	C2
Aranda de Duero	E	23	E10
Aranđelovac	SRB	81	C11
Aranjuez	E	26	E5
Arbatax	I	32	F4
Arboga	S	47	C7
Arbon	CH	37	C8
Arbroath	GB	3	F7
Arbus	I	32	G2
Arcachon	F	16	F3
Arce	I	33	D7
Arcevia	I	35	G10
Archidona	E	28	E5
Arco	I	35	B7
Arcos de la Frontera	E	25	L7
Arcozelo	P	22	F2
Ardea	I	32	D5
Ardino	BG	87	B11
Ardore	I	31	G8
Ardres	F	9	F12
Ardrossan	GB	4	B4
Ardud	RO	77	B12
Ardvasar	GB	2	E3
Åre	S	51	A10
Arenas de San Pedro	E	26	D2
Arendal	N	48	F6
Arenys de Mar	E	21	F11
Arenzano	I	19	B11
Arès	F	16	E3
Arévalo	E	23	G9
Arezzo	I	35	G8
Argamasilla de Alba	E	26	F5
Argamasilla de Calatrava	E	26	G4
Arganda del Rey	E	26	D5
Argelès-sur-Mer	F	18	F2
Argenta	I	35	E8
Argentan	F	15	D8
Argenteuil	F	12	D2
Argenton-sur-Creuse	F	17	B7
Argetoaia	RO	82	B5
Argos	GR	88	C5
Argos Orestiko	GR	86	D4
Argostoli	GR	88	B2
Århus	DK	44	D4
Ariano Irpino	I	30	A6
Ariano nel Polesine	I	35	D9
Ariccia	I	32	D5
Arizgoiti	E	20	B2
Arjeplog	S	55	B10

Place	Country	Page	Grid
Arjona	*E*	**28**	C5
Arklow	*IRL*	**4**	H3
Arkösund	*S*	**47**	E8
Arles	*F*	**17**	H12
Arlon	*B*	**13**	B7
Armagh	*GB*	**4**	E2
Armăşeşti	*RO*	**83**	B11
Armilla	*E*	**28**	E6
Armutlu	*TR*	**85**	H4
Arnage	*F*	**15**	F9
Arnavutköy	*TR*	**85**	B6
Arnedo	*E*	**20**	D3
Arnhem	*NL*	**11**	D7
Arnoldstein	*A*	**39**	F8
Arnsberg	*D*	**11**	E10
Arnstadt	*D*	**40**	B6
Arolsen	*D*	**11**	E12
Arona	*I*	**34**	B3
Arpino	*I*	**33**	D7
Arras	*F*	**10**	H3
Arrasate	*E*	**20**	C2
Arriondas	*E*	**23**	B8
Arroyo de la Luz	*E*	**24**	D6
Arsta	*S*	**47**	C9
Arsvågen	*N*	**48**	D2
Arta	*GR*	**86**	G4
Artà	*E*	**29**	F10
Artena	*I*	**32**	D6
Artern (Unstrut)	*D*	**41**	A6
Artsyz	*UA*	**79**	F11
A Rúa	*E*	**22**	D5
Arvidsjaur	*S*	**55**	C12
Arvika	*S*	**46**	B3
Arzachena	*I*	**32**	D3
Arzúa	*E*	**22**	C3
Aš	*CZ*	**41**	D8
Ås	*N*	**51**	B9
Ascea	*I*	**30**	C6
Aschaffenburg	*D*	**13**	B12
Aschersleben	*D*	**43**	G7
Ascoli Piceno	*I*	**33**	B7
Ascoli Satriano	*I*	**31**	A7
Åsele	*S*	**55**	F10
Asenovgrad	*BG*	**83**	G8
Åseral	*N*	**48**	E4
A Serra de Outes	*E*	**22**	C2
Ashby de la Zouch	*GB*	**5**	H8
Ashford	*GB*	**9**	E10
Ashington	*GB*	**5**	C8
Ashmyany	*BY*	**69**	F9
Asiago	*I*	**35**	B8
Asilah	*MA*	**28**	H2
Asker	*N*	**49**	C7
Askim	*N*	**46**	C2
Askvoll	*N*	**50**	F1
Aspe	*E*	**27**	H9
Aspropyrgos	*GR*	**89**	B7
Assemini	*I*	**32**	G2
Assen	*NL*	**11**	B8
Assens	*DK*	**44**	F4
Assisi	*I*	**32**	A5
Assoro	*I*	**30**	F5
Asti	*I*	**19**	A10
Astillero	*E*	**23**	B10
Aston	*GB*	**8**	C6
Astorga	*E*	**22**	D6
Åstorp	*S*	**45**	D7
Astravyets	*BY*	**69**	F9
Aszód	*H*	**76**	B6
Atalanti	*GR*	**87**	H7
Atessa	*I*	**33**	C8
Athens	*GR*	**89**	C7
Atherstone	*GB*	**9**	C7
Athina	*GR*	**89**	C7
Athlone	*IRL*	**7**	J5
Athy	*IRL*	**4**	H2
Atna	*N*	**51**	E8
Atri	*I*	**33**	B8
Atripalda	*I*	**30**	B6
Attleborough	*GB*	**9**	C11
Åtvidaberg	*S*	**47**	E7
Au	*CH*	**37**	C9
Aubagne	*F*	**18**	E6
Aubange	*B*	**13**	B7
Aubenas	*F*	**17**	F12
Aubigny-sur-Nère	*F*	**12**	G2
Auch	*F*	**16**	H5
Audierne	*F*	**14**	E2
Audincourt	*F*	**13**	G9
Aue	*D*	**41**	C9
Auerbach	*D*	**41**	C8
Augsburg	*D*	**38**	B4
Augusta	*I*	**30**	F6
Augustfehn	*D*	**11**	B10
Augustów	*PL*	**68**	H5
Aulla	*I*	**34**	E5
Aulnoye-Aymeries	*F*	**10**	H4
Aulus-les-Bains	*F*	**21**	C9
Auray	*F*	**14**	F4
Aurec-sur-Loire	*F*	**17**	D11
Aureilhan	*F*	**21**	B7
Aurich	*D*	**11**	A10
Aurillac	*F*	**17**	E9
Auriol	*F*	**18**	E6
Auterive	*F*	**21**	B9
Autun	*F*	**12**	H5
Auxerre	*F*	**12**	F4
Auxonne	*F*	**13**	G7
Avallon	*F*	**12**	F5
Avanca	*P*	**22**	G2
Aveiro	*P*	**22**	G2
Avella	*I*	**30**	B5
Avellino	*I*	**30**	B6
Aversa	*I*	**30**	B5
Avesnes-sur-Helpe	*F*	**10**	H5
Avesta	*S*	**47**	A7
Avetrano	*I*	**31**	C11
Avezzano	*I*	**33**	C7
Aviano	*I*	**35**	B10
Avigliano	*I*	**31**	B7
Avignon	*F*	**18**	C5
Ávila	*E*	**23**	G9
Avilés	*E*	**23**	B7
Avlonas	*GR*	**89**	B7
Avola	*I*	**30**	G6
Avonmouth	*GB*	**8**	E5
Avrămeni	*RO*	**79**	A7
Avranches	*F*	**15**	D7
Avrig	*RO*	**78**	F3
Avrillé	*F*	**15**	F8
Axams	*A*	**37**	C11
Ayamonte	*E*	**25**	K5
Aylesbury	*GB*	**9**	D8
Aylsham	*GB*	**9**	B11
Ayora	*E*	**27**	G9
Ayr	*GB*	**4**	C4
Aytos	*BG*	**83**	F12
Aytré	*F*	**16**	C3
Ayvacık	*TR*	**85**	E2
Ayvalık	*TR*	**85**	F2
Azanja	*SRB*	**81**	C12
Azkoitia	*E*	**20**	B2
Aznalcóllar	*E*	**25**	J7
Azuaga	*E*	**24**	G8

B

Place	Country	Page	Grid
Babadag	*RO*	**79**	H10
Babaeski	*TR*	**85**	B3
Băbeni	*RO*	**78**	H3
Bač	*SRB*	**76**	G6
Bacău	*RO*	**79**	D7
Baccarat	*F*	**13**	E9
Baciu	*RO*	**78**	D2
Bačka Palanka	*SRB*	**76**	G6
Bačka Topola	*SRB*	**77**	F7
Bački Jarak	*SRB*	**77**	G7
Bački Petrovac	*SRB*	**77**	G7
Bačko Gradište	*SRB*	**77**	F7
Bacoli	*I*	**30**	B4
Bácsalmás	*H*	**76**	E6
Badajoz	*E*	**24**	F5
Badalona	*E*	**21**	F10
Bad Aussee	*A*	**39**	D8
Bad Berka	*D*	**41**	B6
Bad Bramstedt	*D*	**42**	C5
Bad Doberan	*D*	**43**	B8
Bad Düben	*D*	**43**	G9
Baden	*A*	**39**	C12
Baden-Baden	*D*	**13**	D11
Badgastein	*A*	**39**	E7
Bad Goisern	*A*	**39**	D8
Bad Hersfeld	*D*	**40**	B4
Bad Hofgastein	*A*	**39**	E7
Badia Polesine	*I*	**35**	D8
Bad Ischl	*A*	**39**	C8
Bad Kissingen	*D*	**40**	D5
Bad Krozingen	*D*	**13**	F10
Bad Lauterberg im Harz	*D*	**42**	G6
Bad Münstereifel	*D*	**11**	G9
Bad Neustadt an der Saale	*D*	**40**	C5
Badovinci	*SRB*	**81**	B9
Bad Salzuflen	*D*	**11**	D11
Bad Salzungen	*D*	**40**	B5
Bad Sooden-Allendorf	*D*	**40**	B5
Bad Waldsee	*D*	**37**	B9
Bad Wildungen	*D*	**11**	F12
Bad Windsheim	*D*	**40**	E5
Baena	*E*	**28**	D5
Baeza	*E*	**28**	C6
Bagheria	*I*	**30**	E3
Bagnacavallo	*I*	**35**	E9
Bagnara Calabra	*I*	**31**	G7
Bagnères-de-Bigorre	*F*	**21**	C7
Bagno a Ripoli	*I*	**35**	F8
Bagno di Romagna	*I*	**35**	F9
Bagnolo Mella	*I*	**34**	C6
Bagnols-sur-Cèze	*F*	**17**	G12
Bagrationovsk	*RUS*	**68**	G2
Bagshot	*GB*	**9**	E8
Bağyurdu	*TR*	**85**	H4
Baia	*RO*	**84**	B5
Baia de Aramă	*RO*	**77**	H12
Baia de Arieş	*RO*	**78**	E1
Baia Mare	*RO*	**78**	B2
Baiano	*I*	**30**	B5
Baia Sprie	*RO*	**78**	B2
Băicoi	*RO*	**78**	G5
Băiculeşti	*RO*	**78**	G3

B

Place	Country	Page	Grid
Baile Átha Cliath	*IRL*	**4**	G2
Baile Átha Luain	*IRL*	**7**	J5
Băile Herculane	*RO*	**77**	H11
Bailén	*E*	**28**	C6
Băilești	*RO*	**82**	C5
Baillargues	*F*	**17**	H11
Bailleul	*F*	**10**	G3
Bain-de-Bretagne	*F*	**14**	F6
Baiona	*E*	**22**	D2
Baja	*H*	**76**	E5
Bajina Bašta	*SRB*	**81**	D10
Bajmok	*SRB*	**76**	F6
Bajram Curri	*AL*	**81**	G10
Bakırköy	*TR*	**85**	C6
Bakum	*D*	**11**	C11
Balaguer	*E*	**21**	E8
Bălan	*RO*	**78**	D5
Balassagyarmat	*H*	**76**	A6
Balatonalmádi	*H*	**76**	C4
Balatonboglár	*H*	**76**	D3
Balatonfüred	*H*	**76**	D4
Bălăușeri	*RO*	**78**	E3
Balbriggan	*IRL*	**4**	F3
Balcani	*RO*	**79**	D7
Bălcești	*RO*	**82**	B6
Balchik	*BG*	**84**	D4
Băleni	*RO*	**78**	H5
Bălești	*RO*	**78**	G1
Balestrate	*I*	**30**	E2
Balıkesir	*TR*	**85**	E4
Balingen	*D*	**13**	E12
Balkány	*H*	**77**	B10
Ballainvilliers	*F*	**12**	D2
Ballangen	*N*	**57**	D5
Ballenstedt	*D*	**43**	G7
Ballerup	*DK*	**44**	E7
Ballina	*IRL*	**6**	G3
Ballinasloe	*IRL*	**7**	J4
Ballsh	*AL*	**86**	D2
Ballycastle	*GB*	**4**	C2
Ballyclare	*GB*	**4**	D3
Ballymena	*GB*	**4**	D2
Ballymoney	*GB*	**4**	C2
Ballynahinch	*GB*	**4**	E3
Balmaseda	*E*	**20**	B1
Balmazújváros	*H*	**77**	B9
Balotești	*RO*	**83**	B10
Balș	*RO*	**82**	B6
Bålsta	*S*	**47**	C9
Balsthal	*CH*	**13**	G10
Balta	*UA*	**79**	B12
Bălțătești	*RO*	**78**	C6
Bâlteni	*RO*	**78**	H1
Bălți	*MD*	**79**	B9
Baltiysk	*RUS*	**68**	F1
Bălușeni	*RO*	**79**	B7
Balvi	*LV*	**67**	G9
Bamberg	*D*	**40**	D6
Banatski Karlovac	*SRB*	**77**	G9
Banatsko Novo Selo	*SRB*	**77**	H8
Banbridge	*GB*	**4**	E2
Banbury	*GB*	**9**	D7
Banca	*RO*	**79**	E9
Banchory	*GB*	**3**	E7
Band	*RO*	**78**	D3
Bandırma	*TR*	**85**	D4
Băneasa	*RO*	**83**	C10
Băneasa	*RO*	**84**	C3
Bangor	*GB*	**4**	D3
Bangor	*GB*	**4**	G5
Banja	*SRB*	**81**	E9
Banja Luka	*BIH*	**80**	B5
Bankeryd	*S*	**46**	F5
Bankya	*BG*	**82**	F5
Bánovce nad Bebravou	*SK*	**75**	G9
Banovići	*BIH*	**81**	C8
Banská Bystrica	*SK*	**75**	G10
Banská Štiavnica	*SK*	**75**	G10
Bansko	*BG*	**82**	G5
Banyoles	*E*	**18**	G1
Bar	*MNE*	**81**	H9
Barakaldo	*E*	**20**	B1
Barañain	*E*	**20**	C4
Baraolt	*RO*	**78**	E5
Barbastro	*E*	**21**	E7
Barbate de Franco	*E*	**25**	M7
Barberá del Vallès	*E*	**21**	F10
Barberino di Mugello	*I*	**35**	F7
Bărbulețu	*RO*	**78**	G4
Bărcănești	*RO*	**78**	H6
Barcellona Pozzo di Gotto	*I*	**30**	E6
Barcelona	*E*	**21**	F10
Barcin	*PL*	**71**	E7
Barcs	*H*	**76**	F3
Barczewo	*PL*	**68**	H2
Bardejov	*SK*	**73**	F2
Barentin	*F*	**15**	B10
Barfleur	*F*	**15**	B7
Barga	*I*	**34**	F6
Bargas	*E*	**26**	E4
Bargoed	*GB*	**8**	D5
Bargteheide	*D*	**42**	C6
Bari	*I*	**31**	A9
Bârla	*RO*	**83**	B8
Bârlad	*RO*	**79**	E8
Bar-le-Duc	*F*	**12**	D6
Barletta	*I*	**33**	E11
Barlinek	*PL*	**70**	E4
Barnard Castle	*GB*	**5**	D8
Barnoldswick	*GB*	**5**	F8
Barnsley	*GB*	**5**	F8
Barnstaple	*GB*	**8**	F3
Barnstorf	*D*	**11**	C11
Barntrup	*D*	**11**	D12
Baronissi	*I*	**30**	B6
Barr	*F*	**13**	E10
Barrafranca	*I*	**30**	F4
Barreiro	*P*	**24**	F2
Barrhead	*GB*	**2**	H5
Barrow-in-Furness	*GB*	**4**	E6
Barry	*GB*	**8**	E5
Bârsana	*RO*	**78**	B2
Bar-sur-Aube	*F*	**12**	E6
Barth	*D*	**43**	B9
Barton-upon-Humber	*GB*	**5**	F10
Bartoszyce	*PL*	**68**	G3
Basarabeasca	*MD*	**79**	E11
Basarabi	*RO*	**84**	C4
Basauri	*E*	**23**	B12
Bascov	*RO*	**78**	H4
Basel	*CH*	**13**	F10
Basildon	*GB*	**9**	E10
Basingstoke	*GB*	**9**	E8
Bassano del Grappa	*I*	**35**	B8
Basse-Goulaine	*F*	**14**	G6
Bassens	*F*	**16**	E4
Bassum	*D*	**11**	B11
Bastia	*F*	**19**	E12
Bastia	*I*	**32**	A5
Batajnica	*SRB*	**77**	H8
Batak	*BG*	**83**	G7
Batăr	*RO*	**77**	D10
Bátaszék	*H*	**76**	E5
Bath	*GB*	**8**	E6
Bathgate	*GB*	**2**	G6
Bátonyterenye	*H*	**77**	B7
Battenberg (Eder)	*D*	**40**	B3
Battipaglia	*I*	**30**	B6
Battle	*GB*	**9**	F10
Battonya	*H*	**77**	E9
Baume-les-Dames	*F*	**13**	G8
Baunatal	*D*	**11**	F12
Bauska	*LV*	**69**	B7
Bavay	*F*	**10**	H4
Bayeux	*F*	**15**	C7
Bayonne	*F*	**16**	H2
Bayramiç	*TR*	**85**	E2
Bayreuth	*D*	**41**	D7
Bayston Hill	*GB*	**8**	B5
Baza	*E*	**29**	D8
Béal an Átha	*IRL*	**6**	G3
Béal Átha na Sluaighe	*IRL*	**7**	J4
Beasain	*E*	**20**	C3
Beas de Segura	*E*	**29**	B7
Beaucaire	*F*	**17**	G12
Beaumont-lès-Valence	*F*	**18**	B5
Beaune	*F*	**12**	G6
Beaupréau	*F*	**15**	G7
Beauvais	*F*	**12**	C2
Bebington	*GB*	**5**	G6
Bebra	*D*	**40**	B4
Beccles	*GB*	**9**	C11
Bečej	*SRB*	**77**	F7
Beceni	*RO*	**79**	G7
Bechyně	*CZ*	**41**	F11
Beclean	*RO*	**78**	C3
Bédarieux	*F*	**17**	H10
Bédarrides	*F*	**18**	C5
Bedford	*GB*	**9**	C9
Bedlington	*GB*	**5**	C8
Będzin	*PL*	**75**	C10
Beelitz	*D*	**43**	F9
Beernem	*B*	**10**	F4
Beeskow	*D*	**43**	F11
Begles	*F*	**16**	E4
Beith	*GB*	**2**	H5
Beiuș	*RO*	**77**	D11
Beja	*P*	**25**	H4
Béjar	*E*	**23**	H7
Békés	*H*	**77**	D9
Békéscsaba	*H*	**77**	D9
Bela Crkva	*SRB*	**77**	H10
Bela Palanka	*SRB*	**82**	E3
Belcești	*RO*	**79**	C7
Bełchatów	*PL*	**71**	H9
Belene	*BG*	**83**	D8
Belfast	*GB*	**4**	D3
Belfort	*F*	**13**	F9
Belgrade	*SRB*	**81**	B11
Beli Manastir	*HR*	**76**	F5
Belišće	*HR*	**76**	F5
Bellac	*F*	**16**	C6
Bellaria	*I*	**35**	F9
Belleville	*F*	**17**	C12
Belley	*F*	**36**	F3
Bellinzona	*CH*	**34**	A4
Bellizzi	*I*	**30**	B6
Belluno	*I*	**35**	B9
Belmont	*GB*	**3**	B12
Belogradchik	*BG*	**82**	D4

Place	Country	Page	Grid
Belovo	*BG*	**82**	G6
Belpasso	*I*	**30**	F6
Belper	*GB*	**5**	G8
Belvedere Marittimo	*I*	**31**	D7
Belzig	*D*	**43**	F9
Bełżyce	*PL*	**73**	B3
Bembibre	*E*	**22**	C2
Bembibre	*E*	**22**	C6
Benalmádena	*E*	**28**	F5
Benavente	*P*	**24**	E2
Benavente	*E*	**23**	E7
Benešov	*CZ*	**41**	E11
Benevento	*I*	**30**	A6
Benfeld	*F*	**13**	E10
Benicarló	*E*	**21**	H7
Benicasim	*E*	**27**	E11
Benidorm	*E*	**27**	H10
Benifaió	*E*	**27**	F10
Benissa	*E*	**27**	G11
Benson	*GB*	**9**	D8
Beograd	*SRB*	**81**	B11
Berane	*MNE*	**81**	F10
Berat	*AL*	**86**	D2
Berbeşti	*RO*	**78**	G2
Berca	*RO*	**79**	G7
Berceni	*RO*	**78**	H6
Berching	*D*	**41**	F7
Berck	*F*	**9**	G11
Berehomet	*UA*	**78**	A5
Berehove	*UA*	**73**	H4
Berettyóújfalu	*H*	**77**	C10
Berezeni	*RO*	**79**	E9
Berga	*E*	**21**	D9
Bergama	*TR*	**85**	F3
Bergamo	*I*	**34**	C5
Bergara	*E*	**20**	B2
Bergen	*D*	**42**	E5
Bergen	*D*	**43**	B10
Bergen	*NL*	**10**	C6
Bergen	*N*	**48**	B2
Bergerac	*F*	**16**	E5
Bergues	*F*	**10**	F2
Berhida	*H*	**76**	C4
Beringen	*B*	**10**	F6
Berja	*E*	**29**	E7
Berkovitsa	*BG*	**82**	E5
Berlevåg	*N*	**59**	B10
Berlin	*D*	**43**	E10
Bermeo	*E*	**20**	B2
Bern	*CH*	**13**	H10
Bernalda	*I*	**31**	C9
Bernau	*D*	**43**	E10
Bernay	*F*	**15**	C9
Bernburg (Saale)	*D*	**43**	G8
Berne	*D*	**11**	B11
Bernsdorf	*D*	**41**	A10
Beroun	*CZ*	**41**	D10
Berovo	*MK*	**82**	H4
Berre-l'Étang	*F*	**18**	D5
Berriozar	*E*	**20**	C4
Bertamirans	*E*	**22**	C2
Bertinoro	*I*	**35**	F9
Berwick-upon-Tweed	*GB*	**3**	H8
Besançon	*F*	**13**	G8
Beška	*SRB*	**77**	G7
Betanzos	*E*	**22**	B3
Béthune	*F*	**10**	G3
Bettembourg	*L*	**13**	B8
Betton	*F*	**14**	E6
Betzdorf	*D*	**11**	G10

Place	Country	Page	Grid
Beverley	*GB*	**5**	F10
Beverwijk	*NL*	**10**	C6
Bewdley	*GB*	**8**	C6
Bex	*CH*	**36**	E5
Bexhill	*GB*	**9**	F10
Bezdan	*SRB*	**76**	F5
Bezhanitsy	*RUS*	**67**	G12
Béziers	*F*	**18**	E2
Biała Podlaska	*PL*	**72**	G5
Białobrzegi	*PL*	**71**	G11
Białogard	*PL*	**70**	C5
Białystok	*PL*	**72**	D5
Biancavilla	*I*	**30**	F5
Biarritz	*F*	**16**	H2
Biasca	*CH*	**37**	E8
Bibbiena	*I*	**35**	G8
Biberach an der Riß	*D*	**37**	B9
Bicaz	*RO*	**78**	D6
Bicester	*GB*	**9**	D8
Bicske	*H*	**76**	B5
Bideford	*GB*	**8**	F3
Biel	*CH*	**13**	G9
Bielefeld	*D*	**11**	D11
Biella	*I*	**34**	C2
Bielsko-Biała	*PL*	**75**	D10
Bielsk Podlaski	*PL*	**72**	E5
Bieruń	*PL*	**75**	D10
Bierutów	*PL*	**75**	B8
Biga	*TR*	**85**	D3
Bigadiç	*TR*	**85**	F5
Biganos	*F*	**16**	F3
Biggleswade	*GB*	**9**	D9
Biguglia	*F*	**19**	E12
Bihać	*BIH*	**80**	B3
Biharia	*RO*	**77**	C10
Bijeljina	*BIH*	**81**	B9
Bijelo Polje	*MNE*	**81**	F10
Bilbao	*E*	**20**	B1
Bilbo	*E*	**20**	B1
Bileća	*BIH*	**81**	F8
Biled	*RO*	**77**	F9
Biłgoraj	*PL*	**73**	C4
Bilisht	*AL*	**86**	D4
Billabona	*E*	**20**	B3
Billdal	*S*	**44**	B6
Billère	*F*	**20**	B6
Billingham	*GB*	**5**	D9
Billingshurst	*GB*	**9**	F9
Billund	*DK*	**44**	E3
Bílovec	*CZ*	**75**	E8
Bilyayivka	*UA*	**79**	E12
Binefar	*E*	**21**	E7
Bingen	*D*	**37**	A8
Binic	*F*	**14**	D4
Biograd na Moru	*HR*	**80**	D3
Birchington	*GB*	**9**	E11
Birkenfeld	*D*	**13**	B9
Birkenhead	*GB*	**5**	G6
Birkerød	*DK*	**44**	E7
Birmingham	*GB*	**8**	C7
Birsay	*GB*	**3**	E9
Biržai	*LT*	**69**	C7
Bisacquino	*I*	**30**	E3
Biscarrosse	*F*	**16**	F3
Bisceglie	*I*	**31**	A9
Bischofswerda	*D*	**41**	B11
Bishop Auckland	*GB*	**5**	D8
Bishop's Cleeve	*GB*	**8**	D6
Bishop's Stortford	*GB*	**9**	D9
Bishop's Waltham	*GB*	**9**	F7

Place	Country	Page	Grid
Bisignano	*I*	**31**	D8
Biskupiec	*PL*	**68**	H3
Bistra	*RO*	**77**	E12
Bistrița	*RO*	**78**	C3
Bitburg	*D*	**13**	B8
Bitche	*F*	**13**	C10
Bitetto	*I*	**31**	A9
Bitola	*MK*	**86**	C5
Bitonto	*I*	**31**	A9
Bitterfeld	*D*	**43**	G8
Bivona	*I*	**30**	F3
Bixad	*RO*	**78**	B1
Bixad	*RO*	**78**	E5
Bjärred	*S*	**45**	E7
Bjelovar	*HR*	**76**	F2
Bjerringbro	*DK*	**44**	D3
Björbo	*S*	**52**	G2
Bjørkeflåta	*N*	**48**	B5
Björköby	*FIN*	**53**	A10
Bjorli	*N*	**50**	D5
Bjurholm	*S*	**55**	G12
Bjuv	*S*	**45**	E7
Blachownia	*PL*	**75**	C10
Blackburn	*GB*	**5**	F7
Blackpool	*GB*	**4**	F6
Blaenavon	*GB*	**8**	D5
Blăgeşti	*RO*	**79**	D7
Blagoevgrad	*BG*	**82**	G5
Blain	*F*	**14**	G6
Blairgowrie	*GB*	**2**	F6
Blaj	*RO*	**78**	E2
Blandford Forum	*GB*	**8**	F6
Blanes	*E*	**21**	E11
Blankenberge	*B*	**10**	E3
Blankenburg (Harz)	*D*	**43**	G7
Blankenfelde	*D*	**43**	F10
Blanquefort	*F*	**16**	E3
Blansko	*CZ*	**74**	E6
Blatná	*CZ*	**41**	E10
Bled	*SLO*	**39**	F9
Blejoi	*RO*	**78**	H6
Bléré	*F*	**15**	G10
Blois	*F*	**15**	F10
Blokhus	*DK*	**44**	B3
Blomberg	*D*	**11**	D12
Błonie	*PL*	**71**	F11
Bludenz	*A*	**37**	C9
Blumberg	*D*	**13**	F11
Blyth	*GB*	**5**	C8
Bobingen	*D*	**37**	A10
Boborás	*E*	**22**	D3
Bobovdol	*BG*	**82**	F5
Bochnia	*PL*	**73**	D1
Bocholt	*D*	**11**	D8
Bochum	*D*	**11**	E9
Bockenem	*D*	**42**	F6
Bocşa	*RO*	**77**	G10
Böda	*S*	**45**	B12
Boden	*S*	**56**	B4
Bodeşti	*RO*	**78**	C6
Bodmin	*GB*	**8**	G2
Bodø	*N*	**57**	F2
Bodrum	*TR*	**88**	E3
Boën	*F*	**17**	C11
Bogatić	*SRB*	**76**	H6
Bogatynia	*PL*	**41**	B12
Bogdanci	*MK*	**87**	C7
Bognor Regis	*GB*	**9**	F8
Bohmte	*D*	**11**	C11
Bohumín	*CZ*	**75**	D9

Place	Country	Page	Grid
Bois-Guillaume	F	**15**	C10
Boizenburg	D	**42**	D6
Bojano	I	**33**	D8
Bojnice	SK	**75**	G9
Bolaños de Calatrava	E	**26**	G4
Bolbec	F	**15**	B9
Boldești-Scăeni	RO	**78**	G6
Bolekhiv	UA	**73**	F6
Bolesławiec	PL	**74**	B5
Bolhrad	UA	**79**	F10
Bolintin-Deal	RO	**83**	B9
Bolintin-Vale	RO	**83**	B9
Bollène	F	**18**	C4
Bollnäs	S	**52**	E4
Bollullos Par del Condado	E	**25**	J6
Bologna	I	**35**	E8
Bolsover	GB	**5**	G9
Bolton	GB	**5**	F7
Bolzano	I	**37**	E11
Bompas	F	**18**	F1
Bondeno	I	**35**	D8
Bo'ness	GB	**2**	G6
Bonn	D	**11**	G9
Bonneville	F	**36**	F4
Bonyhád	H	**76**	E5
Boo	S	**47**	C9
Bootle	GB	**5**	G7
Boppard	D	**11**	H10
Bor	SRB	**82**	C3
Borås	S	**45**	A7
Borca	RO	**78**	C5
Borcea	RO	**84**	B3
Bordeaux	F	**16**	E4
Bordesholm	D	**42**	B5
Bordighera	I	**19**	D9
Bordușani	RO	**84**	B3
Borgholm	S	**45**	C12
Borgia	I	**31**	F9
Borgo	F	**19**	E12
Borgomanero	I	**34**	C3
Borgo San Dalmazzo	I	**19**	C9
Borgo San Lorenzo	I	**35**	F8
Borgosesia	I	**34**	B2
Borgo Val di Taro	I	**34**	E5
Borhaug	N	**48**	F3
Borken	D	**11**	D9
Borkum	D	**42**	C1
Borlänge	S	**52**	G3
Borna	D	**41**	B8
Bornova	TR	**85**	H3
Borovo Selo	HR	**76**	G5
Borșa	RO	**78**	B3
Borsbeek	B	**10**	F5
Boryslav	UA	**73**	F5
Bosa	I	**32**	E2
Bosanska Dubica	BIH	**76**	G2
Bosanska Gradiška	BIH	**76**	G3
Bosanska Krupa	BIH	**80**	B4
Bosanski Brod	BIH	**76**	G4
Bosanski Novi	BIH	**76**	G1
Bosanski Šamac	BIH	**76**	G5
Boscotrecase	I	**30**	B5
Bosilegrad	SRB	**82**	F4
Boskovice	CZ	**74**	E6
Boston	GB	**5**	H10
Boteå	S	**52**	B6
Botești	RO	**79**	C7
Botevgrad	BG	**82**	E6
Botoroaga	RO	**83**	C9
Botoșani	RO	**79**	B7
Botricello	I	**31**	F9
Boucau	F	**16**	H2
Bouc-Bel-Air	F	**18**	D6
Bouchemaine	F	**15**	G8
Bouguenais	F	**14**	G6
Bouillargues	F	**17**	G12
Boulazac	F	**16**	E6
Boulogne-Billancourt	F	**12**	D2
Boulogne-sur-Mer	F	**9**	F12
Bourbon-Lancy	F	**17**	B11
Bourg-en-Bresse	F	**36**	E2
Bourges	F	**12**	G2
Bourgoin-Jallieu	F	**36**	G2
Bourg-St-Andéol	F	**17**	F12
Bourg-St-Maurice	F	**36**	F5
Bourgueil	F	**15**	G9
Bourne	GB	**5**	H10
Bournemouth	GB	**8**	F7
Bourron-Marlotte	F	**12**	E3
Bovalino	I	**31**	G8
Boves	I	**19**	C9
Boville Ernica	I	**33**	D7
Boxmeer	NL	**11**	E7
Božava	HR	**80**	D2
Bra	I	**19**	B10
Bracciano	I	**32**	C5
Bräcke	S	**52**	B3
Brackley	GB	**9**	D8
Bracknell	GB	**9**	E8
Brad	RO	**77**	E12
Bradford	GB	**5**	F8
Brae	GB	**3**	B12
Braga	P	**22**	F2
Bragadiru	RO	**83**	B10
Bragadiru	RO	**83**	D9
Bragança	P	**22**	E5
Brăhășești	RO	**79**	E8
Brăila	RO	**79**	G9
Braine-l'Alleud	B	**10**	G5
Braintree	GB	**9**	D10
Brakel	B	**10**	F4
Bramming	DK	**44**	F2
Bramsche	D	**11**	C10
Bran	RO	**78**	F5
Brande	DK	**44**	E3
Brandenburg	D	**43**	F9
Brandon	GB	**9**	C10
Brănești	RO	**83**	B10
Braniewo	PL	**68**	G1
Braslaw	BY	**69**	D10
Brașov	RO	**78**	F5
Brastavățu	RO	**83**	C7
Bratca	RO	**77**	D12
Bratislava	SK	**75**	H7
Bratovoești	RO	**82**	C6
Bratsigovo	BG	**83**	G7
Bratunac	BIH	**81**	D9
Braunau am Inn	A	**39**	B7
Braunschweig	D	**42**	F6
Braunton	GB	**8**	E3
Bray	IRL	**4**	G3
Brbinj	HR	**80**	D2
Brčko	BIH	**76**	H5
Bré	IRL	**4**	G3
Breaza	RO	**78**	G5
Brebu	RO	**78**	G5
Brechin	GB	**3**	F7
Brecht	B	**10**	E6
Břeclav	CZ	**75**	G7
Brecon	GB	**8**	D4
Breda	NL	**10**	E6
Bregenz	A	**37**	C9
Breitenfelde	D	**42**	C6
Brekken	N	**51**	C9
Brekstad	N	**54**	G2
Bremen	D	**11**	B12
Bremerhaven	D	**42**	C4
Bremervörde	D	**11**	A12
Brenes	E	**25**	J7
Brentwood	GB	**9**	D10
Bresalc	RKS	**82**	F2
Brescia	I	**34**	C6
Bressanone	I	**37**	D12
Bressuire	F	**15**	H8
Brest	BY	**72**	G6
Brest	F	**14**	E2
Brevik	S	**47**	C9
Brežice	SLO	**39**	G11
Breznik	BG	**82**	F5
Brezno	SK	**75**	F11
Briançon	F	**19**	A8
Briare	F	**12**	F3
Bridgend	GB	**2**	H3
Bridgend	GB	**8**	E4
Bridgnorth	GB	**8**	C6
Bridgwater	GB	**8**	E5
Bridlington	GB	**5**	E10
Bridport	GB	**8**	F5
Brig	CH	**34**	A2
Brigg	GB	**5**	F10
Brightlingsea	GB	**9**	D11
Brighton	GB	**9**	F9
Brignais	F	**36**	F2
Brignoles	F	**19**	D7
Brilon	D	**11**	E11
Brindisi	I	**31**	B11
Brioude	F	**17**	D10
Brisighella	I	**35**	E8
Bristol	GB	**8**	E6
Brive-la-Gaillarde	F	**17**	E7
Briviesca	E	**20**	D1
Brixham	GB	**8**	G4
Brixworth	GB	**9**	C8
Brno	CZ	**74**	F6
Bro	S	**47**	C9
Broadstairs	GB	**9**	E11
Brod	MK	**86**	B4
Brodick	GB	**4**	B4
Brodnica	PL	**71**	D9
Bromarv	FIN	**53**	H11
Bromma	S	**47**	C9
Bromölla	S	**45**	E9
Bromsgrove	GB	**8**	C6
Bron	F	**36**	F2
Brønderslev	DK	**44**	B4
Bronte	I	**30**	E5
Broșteni	RO	**78**	C5
Brou	F	**15**	E10
Broumov	CZ	**74**	C6
Broxburn	GB	**2**	G6
Bruchhausen-Vilsen	D	**11**	B12
Bruchmühlbach	D	**13**	C10
Bruck an der Mur	A	**39**	D10
Bruges	B	**10**	F4
Brugge	B	**10**	F4
Brumunddal	N	**51**	G8
Brunflo	S	**51**	B12
Brunico	I	**38**	E5
Brunkeberg	N	**48**	D5

Place	Country	Page	Grid
Brunsbüttel	*D*	**42**	C4
Bruntál	*CZ*	**75**	D8
Bruravik	*N*	**48**	B3
Brussel	*B*	**10**	F5
Brusturi-Drăgănești	*RO*	**78**	C6
Bruxelles	*B*	**10**	F5
Bruz	*F*	**14**	E6
Brymbo	*GB*	**4**	G6
Bryne	*N*	**48**	E2
Bryukhovychi	*UA*	**73**	E6
Brzeg	*PL*	**75**	B8
Brzeg Dolny	*PL*	**75**	B7
Brzesko	*PL*	**73**	D1
Brzeszcze	*PL*	**75**	D10
Brzeziny	*PL*	**71**	G10
Brzozów	*PL*	**73**	E3
Buarcos	*P*	**24**	B2
Buca	*TR*	**85**	H3
Buccino	*I*	**31**	B7
Bucecea	*RO*	**78**	B6
Bucharest	*RO*	**83**	B10
Buchs	*CH*	**37**	C8
Bucine	*I*	**35**	G8
Buciumeni	*RO*	**78**	G5
Bückeburg	*D*	**11**	D12
Buckhaven	*GB*	**3**	G7
Buckie	*GB*	**3**	D7
Buckingham	*GB*	**9**	D8
Buckley	*GB*	**4**	G6
Bucov	*RO*	**78**	H6
Bučovice	*CZ*	**75**	F7
București	*RO*	**83**	B10
Bud	*N*	**50**	B4
Budaörs	*H*	**76**	C5
Budapest	*H*	**76**	C6
Buddusò	*I*	**32**	E3
Budești	*RO*	**83**	C10
Bueu	*E*	**22**	D2
Buftea	*RO*	**83**	B10
Bugojno	*BIH*	**80**	D6
Bugyi	*H*	**76**	C6
Buhuși	*RO*	**79**	D7
Builth Wells	*GB*	**8**	C4
Bujalance	*E*	**28**	C5
Bujanovac	*SRB*	**82**	F3
Buk	*PL*	**70**	F6
Bullas	*E*	**29**	C9
Bulle	*CH*	**36**	D5
Bulqizë	*AL*	**86**	B3
Bumbești-Jiu	*RO*	**78**	G1
Buñol	*E*	**27**	F9
Buntești	*RO*	**77**	D11
Burbach	*D*	**11**	G10
Burgas	*BG*	**83**	F12
Burg bei Magdeburg	*D*	**43**	F8
Burgdorf	*CH*	**13**	G10
Burghausen	*D*	**39**	C7
Burglengenfeld	*D*	**41**	F8
Burgos	*E*	**23**	D10
Burgstädt	*D*	**41**	B9
Burgsvik	*S*	**47**	H9
Burgum	*NL*	**11**	B8
Burhaniye	*TR*	**85**	F3
Burlada	*E*	**20**	C4
Burnley	*GB*	**5**	F7
Burntisland	*GB*	**2**	G6
Burrel	*AL*	**86**	B2
Burriana	*E*	**27**	E10
Burton Latimer	*GB*	**9**	C8
Burton upon Trent	*GB*	**5**	H8
Burwell	*GB*	**9**	C10
Bury	*GB*	**5**	F7
Bury St Edmunds	*GB*	**9**	C10
Busalla	*I*	**19**	B11
Busca	*I*	**19**	B9
Bushtyna	*UA*	**78**	A1
Busko-Zdrój	*PL*	**73**	C1
Bussolengo	*I*	**35**	C7
Bușteni	*RO*	**78**	G5
Busto Arsizio	*I*	**34**	C3
Büsum	*D*	**42**	B4
Butera	*I*	**30**	G4
Butzbach	*D*	**11**	G11
Bützow	*D*	**43**	C8
Buxerolles	*F*	**16**	B5
Buxtehude	*D*	**42**	D5
Buxton	*GB*	**5**	G8
Büyükçekmece	*TR*	**85**	B5
Buzău	*RO*	**79**	G7
Buziaș	*RO*	**77**	F10
Buzoești	*RO*	**83**	B8
Byahoml'	*BY*	**69**	F12
Byala	*BG*	**83**	D9
Byala Slatina	*BG*	**82**	D6
Byarozawka	*BY*	**69**	H8
Bychawa	*PL*	**73**	B4
Bydgoszcz	*PL*	**71**	D7
Bygland	*N*	**48**	E5
Byrum	*DK*	**44**	B5
Bystřice nad Pernštejnem	*CZ*	**74**	E6
Bytča	*SK*	**75**	F9
Bytom	*PL*	**75**	C10
Bytów	*PL*	**71**	B7
Byxelkrok	*S*	**45**	B12

C

Place	Country	Page	Grid
Cabañaquinta	*E*	**23**	B7
Čabar	*HR*	**39**	H9
Cabeza del Buey	*E*	**26**	G2
Cabezón de la Sal	*E*	**23**	B9
Cabra	*E*	**28**	D5
Cabras	*I*	**32**	F2
Čačak	*SRB*	**81**	D11
Caccamo	*I*	**30**	E3
Cacém	*P*	**24**	F2
Cáceres	*E*	**24**	D6
Čadca	*SK*	**75**	E9
Cadeo	*I*	**34**	D5
Cádiz	*E*	**25**	L7
Caen	*F*	**15**	C8
Caerdydd	*GB*	**8**	E5
Caerfyrddin	*GB*	**8**	D3
Caergybi	*GB*	**4**	G4
Caernarfon	*GB*	**4**	G5
Caerphilly	*GB*	**8**	E5
Cagli	*I*	**35**	G10
Cagliari	*I*	**32**	G3
Cagnano Varano	*I*	**33**	D11
Cagnes-sur-Mer	*F*	**19**	D8
Cahors	*F*	**17**	F7
Cahul	*MD*	**79**	F9
Căianu Mic	*RO*	**78**	C3
Caiazzo	*I*	**30**	A5
Cairo Montenotte	*I*	**19**	B10
Caisleán an Bharraigh	*IRL*	**7**	H3
Caister-on-Sea	*GB*	**9**	B12
Căiuți	*RO*	**79**	E7
Caivano	*I*	**30**	B5
Cajvana	*RO*	**78**	B6
Čakovec	*HR*	**76**	E1
Calafat	*RO*	**82**	C5
Calafell	*E*	**21**	F9
Calafindești	*RO*	**78**	B6
Calahorra	*E*	**20**	D3
Calais	*F*	**9**	F12
Calamonte	*E*	**24**	F6
Călan	*RO*	**77**	F12
Calañas	*E*	**25**	J6
Călărași	*MD*	**79**	C10
Călărași	*RO*	**82**	D6
Călărași	*RO*	**83**	C12
Calascibetta	*I*	**30**	F4
Calasetta	*I*	**32**	H1
Calasparra	*E*	**29**	B9
Calatafimi	*I*	**30**	E2
Calatayud	*E*	**20**	F4
Calbe (Saale)	*D*	**43**	G8
Caldas da Rainha	*P*	**24**	D2
Caldas de Reis	*E*	**22**	C2
Caldes de Montbui	*E*	**21**	E10
Caldicot	*GB*	**8**	E5
Calenzano	*I*	**35**	F7
Călimănești	*RO*	**78**	G3
Calimera	*I*	**31**	C11
Călinești	*RO*	**78**	H4
Calitri	*I*	**31**	B7
Callosa d'En Sarrià	*E*	**27**	G10
Calne	*GB*	**8**	E6
Calpe	*E*	**27**	G11
Caltabellotta	*I*	**30**	F3
Caltagirone	*I*	**30**	F5
Caltanissetta	*I*	**30**	F4
Caltavuturo	*I*	**30**	E4
Călugăreni	*RO*	**83**	C10
Calvi	*F*	**19**	E10
Calzada de Calatrava	*E*	**26**	G4
Camariñas	*E*	**22**	B1
Camas	*E*	**25**	J7
Cambados	*E*	**22**	D2
Camborne	*GB*	**8**	G2
Cambrai	*F*	**10**	H4
Cambridge	*GB*	**9**	C9
Cambrils	*E*	**21**	G8
Camenca	*MD*	**79**	A10
Camerano	*I*	**35**	G11
Camerino	*I*	**35**	H10
Camerota	*I*	**31**	C7
Cammarata	*I*	**30**	F3
Campagnano di Roma	*I*	**32**	C5
Campanario	*E*	**24**	F8
Campbeltown	*GB*	**4**	C3
Câmpeni	*RO*	**77**	E12
Câmpia Turzii	*RO*	**78**	D2
Campi Bisenzio	*I*	**35**	F7
Campiglia Marittima	*I*	**32**	A2
Campillos	*E*	**28**	E4
Câmpina	*RO*	**78**	G5
Campi Salentina	*I*	**31**	C11
Campli	*I*	**33**	B7
Campobasso	*I*	**33**	D9
Campobello di Licata	*I*	**30**	F4
Campobello di Mazara	*I*	**30**	F2
Campo de Criptana	*E*	**26**	F5
Campofelice di Roccella	*I*	**30**	E4
Campo Maior	*P*	**24**	E5
Campomarino	*I*	**33**	C9
Campomorone	*I*	**19**	B11

C

Place	Country	Page	Grid
Campos	*E*	**29**	F10
Câmpulung	*RO*	**78**	G4
Câmpulung la Tisa	*RO*	**78**	B2
Câmpulung Moldovenesc	*RO*	**78**	B5
Çan	*TR*	**85**	D3
Çanakkale	*TR*	**85**	D2
Canals	*E*	**27**	G10
Cancale	*F*	**14**	D6
Candeleda	*E*	**24**	B8
Canelli	*I*	**19**	B10
Canet-en-Roussillon	*F*	**18**	F2
Cangas	*E*	**22**	D2
Cangas del Narcea	*E*	**22**	B6
Cangas de Onís	*E*	**23**	B8
Canicattì	*I*	**30**	F4
Canicattini Bagni	*I*	**30**	G6
Caniles	*E*	**29**	D8
Canino	*I*	**32**	B4
Cannes	*F*	**19**	D8
Cannobio	*I*	**34**	B3
Cannock	*GB*	**8**	B6
Canosa di Puglia	*I*	**31**	A8
Čantavir	*SRB*	**77**	F7
Cantemir	*MD*	**79**	E9
Canterbury	*GB*	**9**	E11
Cantillana	*E*	**25**	J7
Canvey Island	*GB*	**9**	E10
Caorle	*I*	**35**	C10
Capaccio	*I*	**30**	C6
Capaci	*I*	**30**	E3
Capannori	*I*	**34**	F6
Capbreton	*F*	**16**	H2
Capdenac-Gare	*F*	**17**	F8
Capdepera	*E*	**29**	F10
Cap Ferret	*F*	**16**	F2
Capistrello	*I*	**33**	C7
Čapljina	*BIH*	**80**	F6
Capo d'Orlando	*I*	**30**	E5
Capoterra	*I*	**32**	G2
Capri	*I*	**30**	B5
Capua	*I*	**30**	A5
Capurso	*I*	**31**	A9
Caracal	*RO*	**83**	C7
Caraglio	*I*	**19**	B9
Caransebeş	*RO*	**77**	G11
Caravaca de la Cruz	*E*	**29**	C9
Carballo	*E*	**22**	B2
Carboneras	*E*	**29**	E9
Carbonia	*I*	**32**	G2
Carcaixent	*E*	**27**	F10
Carcare	*I*	**19**	C10
Carcassonne	*F*	**21**	B10
Cardedeu	*E*	**21**	E10
Cardiff	*GB*	**8**	E5
Cardona	*E*	**21**	E9
Carei	*RO*	**77**	B11
Carentan	*F*	**15**	C7
Carhaix-Plouguer	*F*	**14**	E3
Cariati	*I*	**31**	E9
Carignano	*I*	**19**	A9
Carini	*I*	**30**	E3
Carlentini	*I*	**30**	F6
Carlet	*E*	**27**	F10
Carlisle	*GB*	**5**	D7
Carloforte	*I*	**32**	G1
Carlow	*IRL*	**4**	H2
Carlton	*GB*	**5**	H9
Carmagnola	*I*	**19**	B9
Carmarthen	*GB*	**8**	D3
Carmaux	*F*	**17**	G8
Carmiano	*I*	**31**	C11
Carmona	*E*	**25**	J8
Carnac	*F*	**14**	F4
Carnforth	*GB*	**5**	E7
Carnoustie	*GB*	**3**	F7
Carnoux-en-Provence	*F*	**18**	E6
Carosino	*I*	**31**	C10
Carovigno	*I*	**31**	B10
Carpentras	*F*	**18**	C5
Carpi	*I*	**35**	D7
Carpineto Romano	*I*	**32**	D6
Cărpiniş	*RO*	**77**	F9
Carpino	*I*	**33**	D11
Carquefou	*F*	**14**	G6
Carqueiranne	*F*	**18**	E7
Carraig na Siuire	*IRL*	**7**	L5
Carrara	*I*	**34**	F5
Carrickfergus	*GB*	**4**	D3
Carrick-on-Shannon	*IRL*	**6**	G4
Carrick-on-Suir	*IRL*	**7**	L5
Carros	*F*	**19**	D8
Carryduff	*GB*	**4**	D3
Carry-le-Rouet	*F*	**18**	E5
Cartagena	*E*	**29**	D11
Cártama	*E*	**28**	E4
Cartaxo	*P*	**24**	E2
Carteret	*F*	**14**	C6
Carterton	*GB*	**9**	D7
Cartoceto	*I*	**35**	F10
Casagiove	*I*	**30**	A5
Casalbordino	*I*	**33**	C9
Casalecchio di Reno	*I*	**35**	E7
Casale Monferrato	*I*	**19**	A11
Casalmaggiore	*I*	**34**	D6
Casalpusterlengo	*I*	**34**	D5
Casamassima	*I*	**31**	B9
Casarano	*I*	**31**	C11
Cascina	*I*	**34**	G6
Caserta	*I*	**30**	A5
Čáslav	*CZ*	**74**	D5
Casnewydd	*GB*	**8**	E5
Casoli	*I*	**33**	C8
Casoria	*I*	**30**	B5
Caspe	*E*	**20**	F6
Cassano allo Ionio	*I*	**31**	D8
Cassino	*I*	**33**	D7
Cassis	*F*	**18**	E6
Castagneto Carducci	*I*	**34**	H6
Casteggio	*I*	**19**	A12
Castèl Bolognese	*I*	**35**	E8
Castelbuono	*I*	**30**	E4
Castèl di Iudica	*I*	**30**	F5
Castèl di Sangro	*I*	**33**	D8
Castelfidardo	*I*	**35**	G11
Castelfiorentino	*I*	**35**	G7
Castellabate	*I*	**30**	C6
Castellammare del Golfo	*I*	**30**	E2
Castellammare di Stabia	*I*	**30**	B5
Castellaneta	*I*	**31**	B9
Castelldefels	*E*	**21**	F10
Castellón de la Plana	*E*	**27**	E10
Castell-y-Nedd	*GB*	**8**	D4
Castelnaudary	*F*	**21**	B10
Castelnau-le-Lez	*F*	**17**	H11
Castelnovo ne'Monti	*I*	**34**	E6
Castelnuovo di Garfagnana	*I*	**34**	F6
Castelnuovo di Porto	*I*	**32**	C5
Castelo Branco	*P*	**24**	C5
Castèl San Pietro Terme	*I*	**35**	E8
Castelsardo	*I*	**32**	D2
Castelsarrasin	*F*	**16**	G6
Casteltermini	*I*	**30**	F3
Castelu	*RO*	**84**	C4
Castelvetrano	*I*	**30**	F2
Castèl Volturno	*I*	**30**	A4
Castiglione dei Pepoli	*I*	**35**	F7
Castiglione del Lago	*I*	**35**	H9
Castiglione della Pescaia	*I*	**32**	B2
Castiglione Falletto	*I*	**19**	B10
Castiglion Fiorentino	*I*	**35**	G9
Castilleja de la Cuesta	*E*	**25**	J7
Castillon-la-Bataille	*F*	**16**	E4
Castlebar	*IRL*	**7**	H3
Castlebay	*GB*	**2**	E1
Castres	*F*	**17**	H8
Castricum	*NL*	**10**	C6
Castries	*F*	**17**	H11
Castrignano del Capo	*I*	**31**	D12
Castrocaro Terme	*I*	**35**	F9
Castro del Río	*E*	**28**	D5
Castro de Rei	*E*	**22**	B4
Castropol	*E*	**22**	B5
Castro-Urdiales	*E*	**20**	B1
Castrovillari	*I*	**31**	D8
Castuera	*E*	**24**	F8
Çatalca	*TR*	**85**	B5
Catania	*I*	**30**	F6
Catanzaro	*I*	**31**	F9
Catarroja	*E*	**27**	F10
Cattolica	*I*	**35**	F10
Cattolica Eraclea	*I*	**30**	F3
Caudete	*E*	**27**	G9
Caudry	*F*	**10**	H4
Caulonia	*I*	**31**	G8
Căuşeni	*MD*	**79**	D11
Caussade	*F*	**17**	G7
Cava de'Tirreni	*I*	**30**	B6
Cavaillon	*F*	**18**	D5
Cavalaire-sur-Mer	*F*	**19**	E7
Cavan	*IRL*	**4**	F1
Cavour	*I*	**19**	B9
Cavriglia	*I*	**35**	G8
Cazalla de la Sierra	*E*	**25**	H7
Cazasu	*RO*	**79**	G9
Ceatharlach	*IRL*	**4**	H2
Ceauşu de Câmpie	*RO*	**78**	D3
Cébazat	*F*	**17**	C10
Ceccano	*I*	**33**	D7
Cecina	*I*	**34**	G6
Cedeira	*E*	**22**	A3
Cee	*E*	**22**	C1
Cefa	*RO*	**77**	D10
Cefalù	*I*	**30**	E4
Cefn-mawr	*GB*	**4**	H6
Cegléd	*H*	**77**	C7
Ceglie Messapica	*I*	**31**	B10
Čegrane	*MK*	**82**	G1
Cehegín	*E*	**29**	C9
Cehu Silvaniei	*RO*	**77**	C12
Čelákovice	*CZ*	**41**	D11
Celano	*I*	**33**	C7
Celanova	*E*	**22**	D3
Celaru	*RO*	**83**	C7
Celbridge	*IRL*	**4**	G2
Celje	*SLO*	**39**	F10
Celldömölk	*H*	**76**	C2
Celle	*D*	**42**	E5
Centelles	*E*	**21**	E10
Cento	*I*	**35**	D7
Centuripe	*I*	**30**	F5

Place	Country	Page	Grid
Cepagatti	I	33	C8
Čepin	HR	76	F5
Ceprano	I	33	D7
Cerașu	RO	78	G6
Cerda	I	30	E4
Cerdanyola del Vallès	E	21	F10
Cerea	I	35	D7
Céret	F	18	F1
Cerignola	I	31	A8
Çerkezköy	TR	85	B4
Cerknica	SLO	39	G9
Cernavodă	RO	84	B4
Cernica	RO	83	B10
Cërrik	AL	86	C2
Certaldo	I	35	G7
Cervera	E	21	E8
Cerveteri	I	32	C5
Cervia	I	35	E9
Cervignano del Friuli	I	35	B11
Cervo	E	22	A4
Cesena	I	35	F9
Cesenatico	I	35	E9
Cēsis	LV	66	F6
Česká Lípa	CZ	41	C11
České Budějovice	CZ	41	F11
Český Krumlov	CZ	39	A9
Çeşme	TR	89	B11
Cesson-Sévigné	F	14	E6
Cestas	F	16	E3
Cetate	RO	78	C3
Cetate	RO	82	C5
Cetinje	MNE	81	G8
Cetraro	I	31	D8
Ceuta		28	G3
Ceva	I	19	C10
Chabeuil	F	18	A5
Chagny	F	12	H6
Chalandri	GR	89	B7
Chalastra	GR	87	D7
Chalford	GB	8	D6
Chalki	GR	88	G3
Chalkida	GR	89	B7
Challans	F	14	H6
Chalonnes-sur-Loire	F	15	G7
Châlons-en-Champagne	F	12	D5
Chalon-sur-Saône	F	12	H6
Cham	D	41	F8
Chamalières	F	17	C10
Chambéry	F	36	G3
Chambourcy	F	15	D11
Chamonix-Mont-Blanc	F	36	F5
Champagnole	F	13	H7
Champ-sur-Drac	F	18	A6
Changé	F	15	F9
Chania	GR	89	F8
Chantada	E	22	C4
Chantilly	F	12	C2
Chantonnay	F	16	B3
Chapeltown	GB	5	G8
Chard	GB	8	F5
Charleroi	B	10	G5
Charleville-Mézières	F	12	B6
Charlieu	F	17	C11
Charly	F	12	D4
Charmes	F	13	E8
Chartres	F	12	E1
Château-Arnoux	F	18	C6
Châteaubriant	F	15	F7
Château-d'Olonne	F	16	B2
Château-du-Loir	F	15	F9
Châteaudun	F	15	E10
Châteaugiron	F	14	E6
Château-Gontier	F	15	F7
Châteaulin	F	14	E3
Châteaurenard	F	18	D5
Château-Renault	F	15	F10
Châteauroux	F	15	H11
Château-Thierry	F	12	C4
Châtelguyon	F	17	C10
Châtellerault	F	15	H9
Chatham	GB	9	E10
Châtillon-sur-Seine	F	12	F5
Chatteris	GB	9	C9
Chaumont	F	12	E6
Chauny	F	12	B4
Chauvigny	F	16	B6
Chaves	P	22	E4
Cheadle	GB	5	H8
Cheb	CZ	41	D8
Chechel'nyk	UA	79	A11
Chełm	PL	73	B5
Chełmno	PL	71	D8
Chelmsford	GB	9	D10
Chełmża	PL	71	D8
Cheltenham	GB	8	D6
Chemillé	F	15	G7
Chemnitz	D	41	B9
Chenôve	F	12	G6
Chepelare	BG	83	H7
Chepstow	GB	8	D5
Cherasco	I	19	B10
Cherbourg-Octeville	F	14	B6
Chernyakhovsk	RUS	68	F4
Cherven Bryag	BG	82	E6
Cheshunt	GB	9	D9
Chester	GB	5	G7
Chesterfield	GB	5	G8
Chiajna	RO	83	B10
Chianciano Terme	I	32	A4
Chiaramonte Gulfi	I	30	G5
Chiaravalle	I	35	G11
Chiaravalle Centrale	I	31	F8
Chiari	I	34	C5
Chiavenno	I	34	A4
Chichester	GB	9	F8
Chiclana de la Frontera	E	25	M7
Chieti	I	33	C8
Chingford	GB	9	D9
Chinon	F	15	G9
Chioggia	I	35	C9
Chiojdu	RO	78	G6
Chios	GR	85	H1
Chipiona	E	25	L6
Chippenham	GB	8	E6
Chipping Norton	GB	9	D7
Chipping Sodbury	GB	8	E6
Chirnogi	RO	83	C11
Chirpan	BG	83	G9
Chiscani	RO	79	G9
Chișinău	MD	79	C10
Chișineu-Criș	RO	77	D10
Chitila	RO	83	B10
Chiusi	I	32	A4
Chiva	E	27	F9
Chivasso	I	19	A10
Chocianów	PL	70	H5
Chodzież	PL	70	E6
Chojna	PL	43	E11
Chojnice	PL	71	C7
Chojnów	PL	74	B5
Cholet	F	15	G7
Chomutov	CZ	41	C9
Chop	UA	73	G3
Chora	GR	87	G9
Chora Sfakion	GR	89	G8
Chorley	GB	5	F7
Choszczno	PL	70	D4
Chotěboř	CZ	74	E5
Christchurch	GB	9	F7
Chrudim	CZ	74	D5
Chrysoupoli	GR	87	C10
Chrzanów	PL	75	D10
Chur	CH	37	D9
Chynadiyeve	UA	73	G4
Ciacova	RO	77	F9
Ciadîr-Lunga	MD	79	E10
Ciampino	I	32	D5
Cianciana	I	30	F3
Cicciano	I	30	B5
Ćićevac	SRB	82	D2
Ciechanów	PL	71	E11
Ciechocinek	PL	71	E8
Ciempozuelos	E	26	D4
Čierny Balog	SK	75	G11
Cieszyn	PL	75	E9
Cieza	E	29	B10
Cill Airne	IRL	7	M3
Cill Chainnigh	IRL	7	L5
Cill Mhantáin	IRL	4	H3
Cimișlia	MD	79	D10
Ciney	B	10	H6
Cingoli	I	35	G11
Cinisello Balsamo	I	34	C4
Cinquefrondi	I	31	G8
Cintruénigo	E	20	E3
Ciocănești	RO	83	B9
Ciocănești	RO	83	C11
Ciorani	RO	78	H6
Cirencester	GB	8	D6
Cirò	I	31	E9
Cirò Marina	I	31	E10
Cislău	RO	78	G6
Cisnădie	RO	78	F3
Cisterna di Latina	I	32	D6
Cisternino	I	31	B10
Cistierna	E	23	C8
Città della Pieve	I	32	A4
Città di Castello	I	35	G9
Cittanova	I	31	G8
Città Sant'Angelo	I	33	B8
Ciudad Real	E	26	G4
Ciudad Rodrigo	E	22	G6
Ciupercenii Noi	RO	82	C5
Ciutadella	E	29	E11
Cividale del Friuli	I	35	B11
Civita Castellana	I	32	C5
Civitanova Marche	I	35	G12
Civitavecchia	I	32	C4
Civitella del Tronto	I	33	B7
Civitella in Val di Chiana	I	35	G8
Clacton-on-Sea	GB	9	D11
Clamecy	F	12	G4
Cleator Moor	GB	4	D6
Cleethorpes	GB	5	F10
Cleja	RO	79	E7
Cléon	F	15	C10
Clermont	F	12	C2
Clermont-Ferrand	F	17	C10
Clermont-l'Hérault	F	17	H10
Cles	I	37	E11

Name	Country	Page	Grid
Cleveleys	*GB*	**4**	F6
Clisson	*F*	**15**	G7
Clitheroe	*GB*	**5**	F7
Clonmel	*IRL*	**7**	L5
Cloppenburg	*D*	**11**	B10
Cluain Meala	*IRL*	**7**	L5
Cluj-Napoca	*RO*	**78**	D2
Cluses	*F*	**36**	F4
Clydebank	*GB*	**2**	G5
Coalville	*GB*	**9**	B7
Coatbridge	*GB*	**2**	H5
Cobadin	*RO*	**84**	C4
Cobh	*IRL*	**7**	N4
Coburg	*D*	**40**	D6
Cocentaina	*E*	**27**	G10
Cochem	*D*	**11**	H9
Cockenzie and Port Seton	*GB*	**3**	G7
Cockermouth	*GB*	**4**	D6
Codigoro	*I*	**35**	D9
Codlea	*RO*	**78**	F5
Codroipo	*I*	**35**	B10
Codru	*MD*	**79**	D10
Coevorden	*NL*	**11**	C9
Cogealac	*RO*	**84**	B4
Cognac	*F*	**16**	D4
Cognin	*F*	**36**	G3
Cogolin	*F*	**19**	E7
Coimbra	*P*	**24**	B3
Coín	*E*	**28**	F4
Cojasca	*RO*	**83**	B9
Čoka	*SRB*	**77**	F7
Colchester	*GB*	**9**	D10
Colditz	*D*	**41**	B9
Coleraine	*GB*	**4**	C2
Colibași	*RO*	**78**	H4
Colico	*I*	**34**	B4
Collado Villalba	*E*	**23**	G10
Collecchio	*I*	**34**	D6
Colle di Val d'Elsa	*I*	**35**	G7
Colleferro	*I*	**32**	D6
Collegno	*I*	**19**	A9
Collepasso	*I*	**31**	C11
Collesalvetti	*I*	**34**	G6
Colloto	*E*	**23**	B7
Colmar	*F*	**13**	E9
Colmenar de Oreja	*E*	**26**	D5
Colmenar Viejo	*E*	**23**	G10
Colne	*GB*	**5**	F8
Colombelles	*F*	**15**	C8
Colomiers	*F*	**17**	H7
Colorno	*I*	**34**	D6
Colwyn Bay	*GB*	**4**	G6
Comacchio	*I*	**35**	E9
Comana	*RO*	**83**	C10
Comănești	*RO*	**78**	E6
Comarnic	*RO*	**78**	G5
Comber	*GB*	**4**	D3
Comines	*B*	**10**	G3
Comișani	*RO*	**78**	H5
Comiso	*I*	**30**	G5
Commentry	*F*	**17**	B9
Commercy	*F*	**13**	D7
Como	*I*	**34**	B4
Compiègne	*F*	**12**	C3
Comrat	*MD*	**79**	E10
Concarneau	*F*	**14**	F3
Concesio	*I*	**34**	C6
Conches-en-Ouche	*F*	**15**	D10
Concorezzo	*I*	**34**	B4
Condé-sur-Noireau	*F*	**15**	D8
Condofuri	*I*	**31**	G7
Condom	*F*	**16**	G5
Conegliano	*I*	**35**	B9
Congleton	*GB*	**5**	G7
Conil de la Frontera	*E*	**25**	M7
Connah's Quay	*GB*	**4**	G6
Consett	*GB*	**5**	D8
Constanța	*RO*	**84**	C5
Constantina	*E*	**25**	H8
Consuegra	*E*	**26**	F5
Contarina	*I*	**35**	D9
Contes	*F*	**19**	D9
Conthey	*CH*	**36**	E5
Conversano	*I*	**31**	B10
Cookstown	*GB*	**4**	D2
Copăcenii de Sus	*RO*	**83**	C10
Copenhagen	*DK*	**45**	E7
Copertino	*I*	**31**	C11
Copparo	*I*	**35**	D8
Copșa Mică	*RO*	**78**	E3
Corabia	*RO*	**83**	D7
Corato	*I*	**31**	A8
Corbasca	*RO*	**79**	E8
Corbeni	*RO*	**78**	G3
Corbii Mari	*RO*	**83**	B9
Corby	*GB*	**9**	C8
Corcaigh	*IRL*	**7**	N4
Corciano	*I*	**35**	H9
Corcova	*RO*	**82**	B5
Cordenòns	*I*	**35**	B10
Córdoba	*E*	**28**	C4
Cordun	*RO*	**79**	D7
Corella	*E*	**20**	D3
Cori	*I*	**32**	D6
Coria	*E*	**24**	C6
Coria del Río	*E*	**25**	K7
Coriano	*I*	**35**	F10
Corigliano Calabro	*I*	**31**	D9
Corinaldo	*I*	**35**	G10
Cork	*IRL*	**7**	N4
Corleone	*I*	**30**	E3
Çorlu	*TR*	**85**	B4
Cormontreuil	*F*	**12**	C5
Cornellà de Llobregat	*E*	**21**	F10
Cornu Luncii	*RO*	**78**	C6
Çorovodë	*AL*	**86**	D3
Corral de Almaguer	*E*	**26**	E5
Correggio	*I*	**35**	D7
Corridonia	*I*	**35**	G11
Corsano	*I*	**31**	D12
Corsico	*I*	**34**	C4
Cortaillod	*CH*	**13**	H9
Corte	*F*	**19**	F11
Cortegana	*E*	**25**	H6
Cortona	*I*	**35**	G9
Coruña	*E*	**22**	B3
Corund	*RO*	**78**	E4
Cosenza	*I*	**31**	E8
Coșereni	*RO*	**83**	B11
Coșești	*RO*	**78**	G4
Coslada	*E*	**23**	H11
Cosmești	*RO*	**83**	B9
Cosne-Cours-sur-Loire	*F*	**12**	G3
Coșoveni	*RO*	**82**	C6
Cossato	*I*	**34**	C2
Costa da Caparica	*P*	**24**	F2
Costești	*RO*	**83**	B8
Cotignola	*I*	**35**	E9
Cotnari	*RO*	**79**	C7
Cotronei	*I*	**31**	E9
Cottbus	*D*	**43**	G11
Cottenham	*GB*	**9**	C9
Coțușca	*RO*	**79**	A7
Couëron	*F*	**14**	G6
Coulaines	*F*	**15**	E9
Coulommiers	*F*	**12**	D3
Coulounieix-Chamiers	*F*	**16**	E6
Cournon-d'Auvergne	*F*	**17**	C10
Coursan	*F*	**18**	E2
Courseulles-sur-Mer	*F*	**15**	C8
Courtrai	*B*	**10**	F4
Coutances	*F*	**14**	C6
Coutras	*F*	**16**	E4
Couvin	*B*	**12**	A5
Couzeix	*F*	**17**	C7
Covasna	*RO*	**78**	F6
Cove Bay	*GB*	**3**	E8
Coventry	*GB*	**9**	C7
Covilhã	*P*	**24**	B5
Cowdenbeath	*GB*	**2**	G6
Cowes	*GB*	**9**	F7
Craigavon	*GB*	**4**	E2
Craignure	*GB*	**2**	F3
Craiova	*RO*	**82**	B6
Cramlington	*GB*	**5**	C8
Cran-Gevrier	*F*	**36**	F4
Crasna	*RO*	**77**	C12
Crasna	*RO*	**78**	G2
Crawley	*GB*	**9**	E9
Creazzo	*I*	**35**	C8
Crêches-sur-Saône	*F*	**17**	B12
Crécy-la-Chapelle	*F*	**12**	D3
Crediton	*GB*	**8**	F4
Creil	*F*	**12**	C2
Crema	*I*	**34**	C5
Cremlingen	*D*	**42**	F6
Cremona	*I*	**34**	D5
Crest	*F*	**18**	B5
Créteil	*F*	**12**	D2
Crevalcore	*I*	**35**	D7
Crevedia	*RO*	**83**	B10
Crevedia Mare	*RO*	**83**	B9
Crevillente	*E*	**29**	B11
Crewe	*GB*	**5**	G7
Crewkerne	*GB*	**8**	F5
Cricova	*MD*	**79**	C10
Crieff	*GB*	**2**	G6
Crikvenica	*HR*	**80**	B1
Crimmitschau	*D*	**41**	B8
Crispiano	*I*	**31**	B10
Cristești	*RO*	**78**	D3
Cristuru Secuiesc	*RO*	**78**	E4
Criuleni	*MD*	**79**	C11
Črnomelj	*SLO*	**39**	H10
Cromer	*GB*	**9**	B11
Crosby	*GB*	**4**	G6
Crosia	*I*	**31**	D9
Crosshands	*GB*	**4**	B5
Crotone	*I*	**31**	E10
Crowborough	*GB*	**9**	F9
Crowthorne	*GB*	**9**	E8
Crozon	*F*	**14**	E2
Crvenka	*SRB*	**76**	F6
Csenger	*H*	**77**	B12
Csongrád	*H*	**77**	D7
Csorna	*H*	**76**	B3
Csorvás	*H*	**77**	D9
Csurgó	*H*	**76**	E2
Cualedro	*E*	**22**	E4
Cuéllar	*E*	**23**	F9

Place	Country	Page	Grid
Cuenca	*E*	**27**	E7
Cuers	*F*	**19**	E7
Cuevas de Almanzora	*E*	**29**	D9
Cugir	*RO*	**78**	F1
Cugnaux	*F*	**17**	H7
Cuijk	*NL*	**11**	E7
Cúllar-Baza	*E*	**29**	D8
Cullera	*E*	**27**	F10
Cullompton	*GB*	**8**	F4
Cumbernauld	*GB*	**2**	G5
Cumnock	*GB*	**4**	C5
Cumpăna	*RO*	**84**	C4
Cuneo	*I*	**19**	C9
Cuorgnè	*I*	**34**	C1
Cupar	*GB*	**3**	G7
Cupcina	*MD*	**79**	A8
Ćuprija	*SRB*	**82**	C2
Curcani	*RO*	**83**	C11
Curinga	*I*	**31**	F8
Curtea de Argeş	*RO*	**78**	G3
Curtici	*RO*	**77**	E9
Čurug	*SRB*	**77**	G7
Cusset	*F*	**17**	C10
Cutro	*I*	**31**	E9
Cutrofiano	*I*	**31**	C11
Cuxhaven	*D*	**42**	C4
Cwmbrân	*GB*	**8**	D5
Czaplinek	*PL*	**70**	D5
Czarna Białostocka	*PL*	**72**	D5
Czarne	*PL*	**70**	C6
Czarnków	*PL*	**70**	E6
Czersk	*PL*	**71**	C7
Czerwionka-Leszczyny	*PL*	**75**	D9
Częstochowa	*PL*	**75**	B10
Człuchów	*PL*	**71**	C7
D			
Dabas	*H*	**76**	C6
Dąbrowa Białostocka	*PL*	**68**	H6
Dąbrowa Górnicza	*PL*	**75**	C10
Dąbrowa Tarnowska	*PL*	**73**	D2
Dăbuleni	*RO*	**82**	D6
Dachau	*D*	**37**	A11
Dačice	*CZ*	**74**	F5
Dafni	*GR*	**89**	B7
Daimiel	*E*	**26**	G5
Đakovo	*HR*	**76**	G5
Dalarö	*S*	**47**	C10
Dalby	*S*	**45**	E8
Dalj	*HR*	**76**	G5
Dalkeith	*GB*	**3**	H7
Dalmine	*I*	**34**	C5
Dalsbruk	*FIN*	**53**	H11
Dalton-in-Furness	*GB*	**4**	E6
Damme	*B*	**10**	F4
Damme	*D*	**11**	C11
Damwoude	*NL*	**11**	B8
Daneţi	*RO*	**82**	C6
Dannenberg (Elbe)	*D*	**43**	D7
Darabani	*RO*	**79**	A7
Dărăşti Ilfov	*RO*	**83**	C10
Dar Ben Karricha el Behri	*MA*	**28**	H3
Dar Chaoui	*MA*	**28**	H3
Darda	*HR*	**76**	F5
Dardilly	*F*	**36**	F2
Darfo Boario Terme	*I*	**34**	B6
Darlington	*GB*	**5**	D8
Darłowo	*PL*	**45**	H12
Dărmăneşti	*RO*	**78**	B6
Dărmăneşti	*RO*	**78**	E6
Dărmăneşti	*RO*	**78**	H5
Darmstadt	*D*	**13**	B11
Darque	*P*	**22**	E2
Dartford	*GB*	**9**	E10
Dartmouth	*GB*	**8**	G4
Daruvar	*HR*	**76**	F3
Dassel	*D*	**42**	G5
Datça	*TR*	**88**	F3
Daugavpils	*LV*	**69**	D10
Daventry	*GB*	**9**	C8
Davoli	*I*	**31**	F8
Davos	*CH*	**37**	D9
Davutlar	*TR*	**88**	D2
Dawlish	*GB*	**8**	G4
Dax	*F*	**16**	G3
Deal	*GB*	**9**	E11
Debar	*MK*	**86**	B3
Debeljača	*SRB*	**77**	G8
Dębica	*PL*	**73**	D2
Dęblin	*PL*	**72**	H4
Dębno	*PL*	**43**	E11
Debrecen	*H*	**77**	B10
Debrzno	*PL*	**70**	D6
Decazeville	*F*	**17**	F8
Děčín	*CZ*	**41**	C11
Decize	*F*	**12**	H4
Dedemsvaart	*NL*	**11**	C8
Dedovichi	*RUS*	**67**	F12
Degerfors	*S*	**46**	C5
Deggendorf	*D*	**39**	A7
De Haan	*B*	**10**	F3
Deinze	*B*	**10**	F4
Dej	*RO*	**78**	C2
Delčevo	*MK*	**82**	G4
Delémont	*CH*	**13**	G9
Deleni	*RO*	**79**	C7
Delft	*NL*	**10**	D5
Delfzijl	*NL*	**11**	A9
Delia	*I*	**30**	F4
Delle	*F*	**13**	F9
Delmenhorst	*D*	**11**	B11
Delsbo	*S*	**52**	D4
Deltebre	*E*	**21**	G8
Delvinë	*AL*	**86**	E3
Demirci	*TR*	**85**	F5
Demir Hisar	*MK*	**86**	C4
Demirköy	*TR*	**84**	G3
Demmin	*D*	**43**	C9
Denbigh	*GB*	**4**	G6
Den Burg	*NL*	**10**	B6
Dendermonde	*B*	**10**	F5
Den Haag	*NL*	**10**	D5
Den Helder	*NL*	**10**	B6
Denia	*E*	**27**	G11
Denny	*GB*	**2**	G5
Densburen	*CH*	**13**	G10
Déols	*F*	**15**	H11
Derby	*GB*	**5**	H8
Derecske	*H*	**77**	C10
Dereham	*GB*	**9**	B11
Derry	*GB*	**4**	D1
Dersca	*RO*	**78**	B6
Derventa	*BIH*	**76**	H4
Descartes	*F*	**15**	H10
Dessau	*D*	**43**	G8
Deta	*RO*	**77**	G9
Detmold	*D*	**11**	D12
Dettelbach	*D*	**40**	D5
Detva	*SK*	**75**	G10
Deutschlandsberg	*A*	**39**	E10
Deva	*RO*	**77**	F12
Dévaványa	*H*	**77**	C9
Devecser	*H*	**76**	C3
Deventer	*NL*	**11**	D8
Devin	*BG*	**83**	H7
Devizes	*GB*	**8**	E6
Devnya	*BG*	**83**	E12
Dewsbury	*GB*	**5**	F8
Diamante	*I*	**31**	D7
Diano Marina	*I*	**19**	C10
Didcot	*GB*	**9**	D7
Didymoteicho	*GR*	**85**	B2
Diekirch	*L*	**13**	B8
Diepholz	*D*	**11**	C11
Dieppe	*F*	**9**	H11
Dietikon	*CH*	**13**	G11
Digne-les-Bains	*F*	**19**	C7
Digoin	*F*	**17**	B11
Dijon	*F*	**12**	G6
Dikili	*TR*	**85**	F2
Dilbeek	*B*	**10**	F5
Dimitrovgrad	*BG*	**83**	G9
Dimitrovgrad	*SRB*	**82**	E4
Dinan	*F*	**14**	E6
Dinard	*F*	**14**	D6
Dingolfing	*D*	**38**	B6
Dingwall	*GB*	**2**	D5
Dinkelsbühl	*D*	**40**	F5
Dinklage	*D*	**11**	C11
Diosig	*RO*	**77**	C11
Dippoldiswalde	*D*	**41**	B10
Diss	*GB*	**9**	C11
Dităru	*RO*	**78**	D5
Dives-sur-Mer	*F*	**15**	C8
Djurås	*S*	**52**	G3
Dnestrovsc	*MD*	**79**	D12
Dno	*RUS*	**67**	E12
Dobanovci	*SRB*	**81**	B11
Dobczyce	*PL*	**75**	D11
Dobele	*LV*	**66**	H4
Döbeln	*D*	**41**	B9
Doberlug-Kirchhain	*D*	**43**	G10
Doboj	*BIH*	**81**	B7
Dobre Miasto	*PL*	**68**	G2
Dobreşti	*RO*	**77**	D11
Dobrich	*BG*	**84**	D3
Dobříš	*CZ*	**41**	E11
Dobroteşti	*RO*	**83**	C8
Dobruška	*CZ*	**74**	D6
Doetinchem	*NL*	**11**	D8
Dofteana	*RO*	**78**	E7
Dokkum	*NL*	**11**	A7
Dokshytsy	*BY*	**69**	F11
Doksy	*CZ*	**41**	C11
Dole	*F*	**13**	G7
Dolhasca	*RO*	**79**	C7
Dolianova	*I*	**32**	G3
Dolni Chiflik	*BG*	**84**	E3
Dolni Dŭbnik	*BG*	**83**	D7
Dolný Kubín	*SK*	**75**	F10
Dolyna	*UA*	**73**	F6
Domat Ems	*CH*	**37**	D8
Domažlice	*CZ*	**41**	E9
Dombås	*N*	**50**	D6
Dombóvár	*H*	**76**	E4
Domérat	*F*	**17**	B9
Domneşti	*RO*	**83**	B10
Domodossola	*I*	**34**	B3

D

Dömsöd	*H*	**76**	C6
Domusnovas	*I*	**32**	G2
Domžale	*SLO*	**39**	G9
Donaghadee	*GB*	**4**	D3
Don Benito	*E*	**24**	E7
Doncaster	*GB*	**5**	F9
Donduşeni	*MD*	**79**	A8
Donji Miholjac	*HR*	**76**	F4
Donji Vakuf	*BIH*	**80**	D6
Donostia-San Sebastián	*E*	**20**	B3
Đorče Petrov	*MK*	**82**	G2
Dorchester	*GB*	**8**	F6
Dordrecht	*NL*	**10**	E6
Dorgali	*I*	**32**	E3
Dorking	*GB*	**9**	E9
Dormagen	*D*	**11**	F9
Dor Mărunt	*RO*	**83**	B11
Dornbirn	*A*	**37**	C9
Dorog	*H*	**76**	B5
Dorohoi	*RO*	**78**	B6
Dorsten	*D*	**11**	E9
Dortmund	*D*	**11**	E10
Dörverden	*D*	**11**	B12
Dos Hermanas	*E*	**25**	K7
Douarnenez	*F*	**14**	E2
Doué-la-Fontaine	*F*	**15**	G8
Douglas	*GBM*	**4**	E5
Douvaine	*F*	**36**	E4
Dover	*GB*	**9**	E11
Dovhe	*UA*	**73**	H5
Downham Market	*GB*	**9**	B10
Downpatrick	*GB*	**4**	E3
Drachten	*NL*	**11**	B8
Dragalina	*RO*	**83**	B12
Drăgăneşti	*RO*	**78**	H6
Drăgăneşti	*RO*	**79**	F8
Drăgăneşti-Olt	*RO*	**83**	C7
Drăgăneşti-Vlaşca	*RO*	**83**	C9
Drăgăşani	*RO*	**83**	B7
Dragør	*DK*	**45**	F7
Draguignan	*F*	**19**	D7
Drajna	*RO*	**78**	G6
Drama	*GR*	**87**	C9
Drammen	*N*	**49**	C7
Dravograd	*SLO*	**39**	F10
Drawsko Pomorskie	*PL*	**70**	D5
Dresden	*D*	**41**	B10
Dreux	*F*	**12**	D1
Drevsjø	*N*	**51**	E9
Drezdenko	*PL*	**70**	E5
Dridu	*RO*	**83**	B10
Driffield	*GB*	**5**	E10
Drniš	*HR*	**80**	D4
Drobeta-Turnu Severin	*RO*	**82**	B4
Drochia	*MD*	**79**	A9
Drogheda	*IRL*	**4**	F2
Drohobych	*UA*	**73**	F5
Droichead Átha	*IRL*	**4**	F2
Droichead Nua	*IRL*	**4**	G2
Droitwich Spa	*GB*	**8**	C6
Dronero	*I*	**19**	B9
Dronfield	*GB*	**5**	G8
Dronten	*NL*	**11**	C7
Druskininkai	*LT*	**69**	G7
Dryanovo	*BG*	**83**	E9
Dryna	*N*	**50**	C3
Dubăsari	*MD*	**79**	C11
Dublin	*IRL*	**4**	G2
Dublyany	*UA*	**73**	E6
Dubove	*UA*	**78**	A2
Dubrovnik	*HR*	**81**	G7
Dudestii Vechi	*RO*	**77**	E8
Dudley	*GB*	**8**	C6
Dueville	*I*	**35**	C8
Duga Resa	*HR*	**39**	H11
Dugo Selo	*HR*	**39**	G12
Dŭlgopol	*BG*	**83**	E12
Dulovo	*BG*	**83**	C12
Dumbarton	*GB*	**2**	G5
Dumbrava Roşie	*RO*	**78**	D6
Dumbrăveni	*RO*	**78**	B6
Dumbrăveni	*RO*	**78**	E3
Dumfries	*GB*	**4**	C6
Dumitreşti	*RO*	**79**	F7
Dumnicë e Poshtme	*RKS*	**82**	E2
Dunaföldvár	*H*	**76**	D5
Dunaharaszti	*H*	**76**	C6
Dunajská Streda	*SK*	**76**	B3
Dunakeszi	*H*	**76**	B6
Dunaújváros	*H*	**76**	D5
Dunavarsány	*H*	**76**	C6
Dunbar	*GB*	**3**	G7
Dunblane	*GB*	**2**	G5
Dundalk	*IRL*	**4**	E2
Dun Dealgan	*IRL*	**4**	E2
Dundee	*GB*	**3**	F7
Dunfermline	*GB*	**2**	G6
Dungannon	*GB*	**4**	D2
Dún Garbhán	*IRL*	**7**	M5
Dungarvan	*IRL*	**7**	M5
Dunkerque	*F*	**10**	F2
Dún Laoghaire	*IRL*	**4**	G3
Dunmurry	*GB*	**4**	D3
Dunoon	*GB*	**2**	G4
Dunstable	*GB*	**9**	D8
Dupnitsa	*BG*	**82**	G5
Durango	*E*	**20**	B2
Durban-Corbières	*F*	**18**	E1
Dúrcal	*E*	**28**	E6
Đurđevac	*HR*	**76**	E2
Düren	*D*	**11**	G8
Durham	*GB*	**5**	D8
Durlas	*IRL*	**7**	L5
Durleşti	*MD*	**79**	C10
Durrës	*AL*	**86**	B1
Dursley	*GB*	**8**	D6
Dursunbey	*TR*	**85**	E5
Düsseldorf	*D*	**11**	F9
Dve Mogili	*BG*	**83**	D9
Dvůr Králové	*CZ*	**74**	C5
Dyce	*GB*	**3**	E8
Dynów	*PL*	**73**	E3
Dzhebel	*BG*	**87**	B11
Działdowo	*PL*	**71**	D10
Dzierzgoń	*PL*	**71**	C9
Dzyarzhynsk	*BY*	**69**	H10

E

Eastbourne	*GB*	**9**	F10
Eastfield	*GB*	**5**	E10
East Grinstead	*GB*	**9**	E9
East Kilbride	*GB*	**2**	H5
Eastleigh	*GB*	**9**	F7
East Wittering	*GB*	**9**	F8
Ebbw Vale	*GB*	**8**	D5
Ebensee	*A*	**39**	C8
Ebensfeld	*D*	**40**	D6
Ebenthal	*A*	**39**	F9
Eberndorf	*A*	**39**	F9
Ebersbach	*D*	**41**	B11
Eberswalde-Finow	*D*	**43**	E10
Eboli	*I*	**30**	B6
Écija	*E*	**28**	D4
Ečka	*SRB*	**77**	G8
Eckernförde	*D*	**42**	B5
Eckington	*GB*	**5**	G9
Edelény	*H*	**73**	H1
Edemissen	*D*	**42**	F6
Edessa	*GR*	**86**	C6
Edinburgh	*GB*	**2**	G6
Edincik	*TR*	**85**	D4
Edineţ	*MD*	**79**	A8
Edirne	*TR*	**83**	H11
Edland	*N*	**48**	C4
Edremit	*TR*	**85**	E3
Eforie	*RO*	**84**	C5
Eger	*H*	**77**	B8
Egersund	*N*	**48**	F3
Eggesin	*D*	**43**	C10
Eghezée	*B*	**10**	G6
Egremont	*GB*	**4**	E6
Éguilles	*F*	**18**	D5
Egyek	*H*	**77**	B9
Ehingen (Donau)	*D*	**37**	A9
Eibar	*E*	**20**	B2
Eibenstock	*D*	**41**	C8
Eibergen	*NL*	**11**	D8
Eichstätt	*D*	**38**	A4
Eidet	*N*	**54**	F6
Eidsbugarden	*N*	**50**	F5
Eilenburg	*D*	**41**	A8
Einbeck	*D*	**42**	G5
Eindhoven	*NL*	**11**	E7
Einsiedeln	*CH*	**13**	G11
Eisenach	*D*	**40**	B5
Eisenberg	*D*	**41**	B7
Eisenerz	*A*	**39**	D10
Eisenhüttenstadt	*D*	**43**	F11
Eisenstadt	*A*	**76**	B1
Eivissa	*E*	**29**	G7
Ejea de los Caballeros	*E*	**20**	D4
Ekenäs	*FIN*	**64**	G4
Ekerö	*S*	**47**	C9
Eksjö	*S*	**45**	A10
Elassona	*GR*	**86**	E6
El Astillero	*E*	**23**	B10
Elbasan	*AL*	**86**	C2
Elbeuf	*F*	**15**	C10
Elbląg	*PL*	**71**	B9
El Burgo de Osma	*E*	**20**	F1
Elche-Elx	*E*	**29**	B11
Elda	*E*	**27**	H9
Elefsina	*GR*	**89**	B7
El Ejido	*E*	**29**	E7
Elek	*H*	**77**	D9
Elektrėnai	*LT*	**69**	F7
Elena	*BG*	**83**	E9
El Escorial	*E*	**23**	H10
El Espinar	*E*	**23**	G9
El Fendek	*MA*	**28**	H3
Elgin	*GB*	**2**	D6
Elin Pelin	*BG*	**82**	F6
Elizondo	*E*	**20**	B4
Ełk	*PL*	**68**	H4
Elkhovo	*BG*	**83**	G11
Elland	*GB*	**5**	F8
Ellesmere Port	*GB*	**5**	G7
Ellon	*GB*	**3**	E8

Ellös	S	**46**	E2
Ellwangen (Jagst)	D	**40**	F5
Elmshorn	D	**42**	C5
Elne	F	**18**	F1
Elos	GR	**89**	G7
El Prat de Llobregat	E	**21**	F10
El Puerto de Santa María	E	**25**	L7
Elsdorf	D	**11**	F8
El Serrat	AND	**21**	C9
Elsterwerda	D	**41**	A10
Eltmann	D	**40**	D6
Elva	EST	**67**	E8
Elvas	P	**24**	F5
El Vendrell	E	**21**	F9
Elverum	N	**51**	G9
Ely	GB	**9**	C10
Embrun	F	**19**	B7
Emden	D	**11**	A9
Emmaboda	S	**45**	C11
Emmen	NL	**11**	C9
Emőd	H	**77**	B9
Empoli	I	**35**	F7
Emsbüren	D	**11**	C9
Encamp	AND	**21**	D9
Encs	H	**73**	H2
Engan	N	**54**	B5
Enköping	S	**47**	B8
Enna	I	**30**	F4
Ennigerloh	D	**11**	D10
Ennis	IRL	**7**	K3
Enniscorthy	IRL	**7**	L6
Enniskillen	GB	**6**	F5
Enns	A	**39**	B9
Enschede	NL	**11**	D9
Entroncamento	P	**24**	D3
Enying	H	**76**	D4
Eochaill	IRL	**7**	M5
Epe	NL	**11**	C7
Épernay	F	**12**	C5
Épinal	F	**13**	E8
Epsom	GB	**9**	E9
Eraclea	I	**35**	C10
Erbach	D	**38**	B2
Erbach	D	**38**	B3
Erbiceni	RO	**79**	C8
Erchie	I	**31**	C11
Ercsi	H	**76**	C5
Érd	H	**76**	C5
Erdek	TR	**85**	D4
Erfurt	D	**40**	B6
Ergué-Gabéric	F	**14**	F3
Erice	I	**30**	E2
Erkelenz	D	**11**	F8
Erkner	D	**43**	F10
Erlangen	D	**40**	E6
Ermesinde	P	**22**	F2
Ermioni	GR	**88**	D6
Ermoupoli	GR	**89**	D9
Ermua	E	**20**	B2
Ernée	F	**15**	E7
Ernei	RO	**78**	D3
Errenteria	E	**20**	B3
Erritsø	DK	**44**	F3
Ersekë	AL	**86**	D3
Esbjerg	DK	**44**	F2
Esbo	FIN	**64**	G5
Eschwege	D	**40**	B5
Escombreras	E	**29**	D11
Esens	D	**42**	C2
Eskilstuna	S	**47**	C8

Eslohe (Sauerland)	D	**11**	F11
Eslöv	S	**45**	E8
Esneux	B	**11**	G7
Espalion	F	**17**	F9
Esparreguera	E	**21**	F9
Espergærde	DK	**45**	E7
Espezel	F	**21**	C10
Espinho	P	**22**	G2
Espoo	FIN	**64**	G5
Essen	B	**10**	E5
Essen	D	**11**	E9
Essenbach	D	**38**	B6
Esslingen am Neckar	D	**38**	A2
Este	I	**35**	C8
Estella	E	**20**	C3
Estepa	E	**28**	D4
Estepona	E	**28**	F4
Estoril	P	**24**	F1
Estremoz	P	**24**	F4
Esztergom	H	**76**	B5
Étampes	F	**12**	E2
Étaples	F	**9**	G12
Etropole	BG	**82**	E6
Eu	F	**9**	H11
Eupen	B	**11**	G8
Eura	FIN	**53**	F10
Euskirchen	D	**11**	G9
Eutin	D	**42**	B6
Evdilos	GR	**89**	C11
Evesham	GB	**8**	D6
Évian-les-Bains	F	**36**	E4
Evje	N	**48**	F5
Évora	P	**24**	F4
Evosmos	GR	**87**	D7
Évreux	F	**15**	C10
Évron	F	**15**	E8
Évry	F	**12**	D2
Exeter	GB	**8**	F4
Exmouth	GB	**8**	F4
Exochi	GR	**87**	B9
Eyguières	F	**18**	D5
Ezine	TR	**85**	E2
Ézy-sur-Eure	F	**12**	D1

F

Faaborg	DK	**44**	G4
Fabero	E	**22**	C5
Fabrègues	F	**17**	H11
Fabriano	I	**35**	G10
Fabrica di Roma	I	**32**	C5
Făcăeni	RO	**84**	B3
Faenza	I	**35**	E8
Fafe	P	**22**	F3
Făgăraș	RO	**78**	F4
Fagernes	N	**50**	F6
Fagersta	S	**47**	B7
Făget	RO	**77**	F11
Fagnano Castello	I	**31**	D8
Fagnières	F	**12**	D5
Fakenham	GB	**9**	B10
Falaise	F	**15**	D8
Fălciu	RO	**79**	E9
Falconara Marittima	I	**35**	F11
Fălești	MD	**79**	B9
Falkenberg	D	**43**	G9
Falkenberg	S	**44**	C7
Falkirk	GB	**2**	G6
Falköping	S	**46**	E4

Fallingbostel	D	**42**	E5
Falmouth	GB	**8**	G2
Fălticeni	RO	**78**	C6
Falun	S	**52**	G3
Fano	I	**35**	F10
Fântânele	RO	**78**	E4
Fara in Sabina	I	**32**	C6
Faringdon	GB	**9**	D7
Farnham	GB	**9**	E8
Faro	P	**25**	K4
Fårösund	S	**47**	F10
Farsala	GR	**86**	F6
Farsund	N	**48**	G3
Fărțănești	RO	**79**	F9
Fasano	I	**31**	B10
Fátima	P	**24**	D3
Fauske	N	**57**	F3
Fåvang	N	**51**	E7
Favara	I	**30**	F3
Faverges	F	**36**	F4
Faversham	GB	**9**	E10
Fawley	GB	**9**	F7
Fayence	F	**19**	D8
Fazeley	GB	**9**	B7
Fécamp	F	**15**	B9
Fegersheim	F	**13**	E10
Fegyvernek	H	**77**	C8
Fehérgyarmat	H	**77**	B11
Felanitx	E	**29**	F10
Feldioara	RO	**78**	F5
Feldkirch	A	**37**	C9
Feldkirchen in Kärnten	A	**39**	E8
Feldru	RO	**78**	C3
Felixstowe	GB	**9**	D11
Felsőzsolca	H	**73**	H1
Feltre	I	**35**	B9
Fene	E	**22**	B3
Feolin Ferry	GB	**2**	H3
Ferentino	I	**32**	D6
Ferizaj	RKS	**81**	G12
Ferlach	A	**39**	F9
Fermignano	I	**35**	G10
Fermo	I	**35**	H12
Fernán Núñez	E	**28**	D4
Ferney-Voltaire	F	**36**	E4
Ferrandina	I	**31**	C8
Ferrara	I	**35**	D8
Ferrol	E	**22**	B3
Ferryhill	GB	**5**	D8
Fetești	RO	**84**	B3
Fetești-Gară	RO	**84**	B3
Fetsund	N	**46**	B2
Feuchtwangen	D	**40**	F5
Feytiat	F	**17**	C7
Ffestiniog	GB	**4**	H5
Fiano Romano	I	**32**	C5
Ficarazzi	I	**30**	E3
Fidenza	I	**34**	D5
Fieni	RO	**78**	G5
Fier	AL	**86**	D2
Fiesole	I	**35**	F7
Figeac	F	**17**	F8
Figline Valdarno	I	**35**	G8
Figueira da Foz	P	**24**	B2
Figueres	E	**18**	G1
Filadelfia	I	**31**	F8
Fiľakovo	SK	**75**	H11
Filey	GB	**5**	E10
Filiași	RO	**82**	B6
Filipeștii de Pădure	RO	**78**	H5

F

F

Name	Country	Page	Grid
Filipstad	*S*	**46**	B5
Filottrano	*I*	**35**	G11
Finale Emilia	*I*	**35**	D8
Finale Ligure	*I*	**19**	C10
Finkenstein	*A*	**39**	F8
Finspång	*S*	**47**	D7
Finsterwalde	*D*	**43**	G10
Fionnphort	*GB*	**2**	G2
Fiorenzuola d'Arda	*I*	**34**	D5
Firenze	*I*	**35**	F7
Fishguard	*GB*	**8**	D2
Fisksätra	*S*	**47**	C9
Fismes	*F*	**12**	C4
Fisterra	*E*	**22**	C1
Fiuggi	*I*	**32**	D6
Fiumefreddo di Sicilia	*I*	**30**	E6
Fivizzano	*I*	**34**	E6
Flămânzi	*RO*	**79**	B7
Fleet	*GB*	**9**	E8
Fleetwood	*GB*	**4**	F6
Flekkefjord	*N*	**48**	F3
Flen	*S*	**47**	D8
Flensburg	*D*	**44**	G3
Flers	*F*	**15**	D8
Fleurance	*F*	**16**	G6
Flint	*GB*	**4**	G6
Flix	*E*	**21**	F7
Floda	*S*	**44**	A7
Flöha	*D*	**41**	B9
Floirac	*F*	**16**	E4
Florence	*I*	**35**	F7
Florenville	*B*	**13**	B7
Florești	*MD*	**79**	B10
Florești	*RO*	**78**	D2
Florești-Stoenești	*RO*	**83**	B9
Floridia	*I*	**30**	G6
Florina	*GR*	**86**	D5
Florø	*N*	**50**	E1
Flötningen	*S*	**51**	E9
Foča	*BIH*	**81**	E8
Foça	*TR*	**85**	G2
Focșani	*RO*	**79**	F8
Focuri	*RO*	**79**	C8
Foggia	*I*	**33**	D10
Fohnsdorf	*A*	**39**	D9
Foix	*F*	**21**	C9
Folignano	*I*	**33**	B7
Foligno	*I*	**32**	A6
Folkestone	*GB*	**9**	F11
Folldal	*N*	**51**	D7
Follonica	*I*	**32**	A2
Fondevila	*E*	**22**	E3
Fondi	*I*	**33**	E7
Fonsorbes	*F*	**17**	H7
Fontaine	*F*	**18**	A6
Fontainebleau	*F*	**12**	E3
Fontaine le Comte	*F*	**16**	B5
Fontanellato	*I*	**34**	D6
Fontenay-le-Comte	*F*	**16**	B3
Fonyód	*H*	**76**	D3
Forăști	*RO*	**78**	C6
Forcalquier	*F*	**18**	C6
Forchheim	*D*	**40**	E6
Førde	*N*	**50**	E2
Fordingbridge	*GB*	**9**	F7
Forfar	*GB*	**3**	F7
Forio	*I*	**30**	B4
Forlì	*I*	**35**	E9
Forlimpopoli	*I*	**35**	F9
Formby	*GB*	**4**	F6
Formello	*I*	**32**	C5
Formia	*I*	**30**	A4
Formofoss	*N*	**54**	F5
Forres	*GB*	**2**	D6
Fors	*S*	**52**	B4
Forsand	*N*	**48**	E3
Forshaga	*S*	**46**	C4
Forsmark	*S*	**52**	G6
Forsnes	*N*	**50**	A5
Forssa	*FIN*	**53**	F12
Forst	*D*	**43**	G11
Fortuna	*E*	**29**	C10
Fort William	*GB*	**2**	F4
Fosnavåg	*N*	**50**	D2
Fossano	*I*	**19**	B9
Fossombrone	*I*	**35**	G10
Fót	*H*	**76**	B6
Fougères	*F*	**15**	E7
Fourmies	*F*	**12**	A5
Fourna	*GR*	**86**	G5
Fournoi	*GR*	**89**	C12
Foz	*E*	**22**	B4
Fraga	*E*	**21**	F7
Fragagnano	*I*	**31**	C10
Francavilla al Mare	*I*	**33**	B8
Francavilla di Sicilia	*I*	**30**	E6
Francavilla Fontana	*I*	**31**	B10
Francești	*RO*	**78**	G3
Francofonte	*I*	**30**	F5
Frankenberg (Eder)	*D*	**11**	F11
Frankfurt am Main	*D*	**11**	H11
Frankfurt an der Oder	*D*	**43**	F11
Frascati	*I*	**32**	D5
Fraserburgh	*GB*	**3**	D8
Frasin	*RO*	**78**	B5
Frastanz	*A*	**37**	C9
Frătești	*RO*	**83**	C10
Frauenfeld	*CH*	**13**	F12
Fredensborg	*DK*	**44**	E7
Fredericia	*DK*	**44**	F3
Frederiksberg	*DK*	**44**	E7
Frederikshavn	*DK*	**44**	B4
Frederikssund	*DK*	**44**	E6
Frederiksværk	*DK*	**44**	E6
Fredrika	*S*	**55**	F11
Fredrikstad	*N*	**46**	C1
Fregenal de la Sierra	*E*	**24**	G6
Freiberg	*D*	**41**	B9
Freiburg im Breisgau	*D*	**13**	E10
Freilassing	*D*	**39**	C7
Freising	*D*	**38**	B5
Freistadt	*A*	**39**	B9
Freital	*D*	**41**	B10
Fréjus	*F*	**19**	D8
Freudenstadt	*D*	**13**	E11
Freyung	*D*	**39**	A8
Fribourg	*CH*	**13**	H9
Friedberg	*D*	**38**	B4
Friedland	*D*	**43**	C10
Friesach	*A*	**39**	E9
Friesoythe	*D*	**11**	B10
Friitala	*FIN*	**53**	E10
Frinton-on-Sea	*GB*	**9**	D11
Friol	*E*	**22**	C4
Friville-Escarbotin	*F*	**9**	H11
Frohnleiten	*A*	**39**	D10
Frome	*GB*	**8**	E6
Frontignan	*F*	**18**	D3
Frosinone	*I*	**33**	D7
Frumușica	*RO*	**79**	B7
Frumușița	*RO*	**79**	F9
Frunzivka	*UA*	**79**	C12
Frutigen	*CH*	**36**	E6
Frýdek-Místek	*CZ*	**75**	E9
Fucecchio	*I*	**35**	F7
Fuengirola	*E*	**28**	F4
Fuenlabrada	*E*	**26**	D4
Fuensalida	*E*	**26**	E3
Fuente de Cantos	*E*	**24**	G6
Fuente del Maestre	*E*	**24**	F6
Fuente Obejuna	*E*	**24**	G8
Fuentes de Andalucía	*E*	**25**	J8
Fuglafjørður	*FO*	**3**	B9
Fulda	*D*	**40**	C4
Fumay	*F*	**12**	B6
Fumel	*F*	**16**	F6
Fundão	*P*	**24**	B5
Fundeni	*RO*	**83**	B10
Fundulea	*RO*	**83**	B11
Fürstenau	*D*	**11**	C10
Fürstenberg	*D*	**43**	D9
Fürstenfeld	*A*	**39**	E11
Fürstenfeldbruck	*D*	**37**	A11
Fürstenzell	*D*	**39**	B7
Fürth	*D*	**40**	E6
Furudal	*S*	**52**	F3
Furusund	*S*	**47**	B10
Fuscaldo	*I*	**31**	E8
Fushë Kosovë	*RKS*	**81**	G12
Fushë-Krujë	*AL*	**86**	B2
Füssen	*D*	**37**	C10
Futog	*SRB*	**77**	G7
Füzesabony	*H*	**77**	B8
Füzesgyarmat	*H*	**77**	C9

G

Name	Country	Page	Grid
Gabicce Mare	*I*	**35**	F10
Gabrovo	*BG*	**83**	E9
Gadebusch	*D*	**43**	C7
Găești	*RO*	**83**	B9
Gaeta	*I*	**30**	A4
Gafanha da Nazaré	*P*	**22**	G2
Gagliano del Capo	*I*	**31**	D12
Gagnef	*S*	**52**	G3
Gaildorf	*D*	**40**	F4
Gaillac	*F*	**17**	G8
Gaillimh	*IRL*	**7**	J3
Gaillon	*F*	**15**	C10
Gainsborough	*GB*	**5**	G9
Găiseni	*RO*	**83**	B9
Gălănești	*RO*	**78**	B5
Galanta	*SK*	**75**	H8
Galashiels	*GB*	**5**	B7
Galata	*BG*	**84**	E3
Galați	*RO*	**79**	G9
Galatina	*I*	**31**	C11
Galatone	*I*	**31**	C11
Gâldău	*RO*	**83**	B12
Galicea Mare	*RO*	**82**	C5
Gallardon	*F*	**12**	D1
Gallipoli	*I*	**31**	C11
Gällivare	*S*	**60**	D3
Galston	*GB*	**4**	B5
Galway	*IRL*	**7**	J3
Gamleby	*S*	**47**	F7
Gammelstaden	*S*	**56**	C4
Gand	*B*	**10**	F4
Gandía	*E*	**27**	G10

Name	Country	Page	Grid
Ganges	*F*	**17**	G11
Gangi	*I*	**30**	E4
Gannat	*F*	**17**	C10
Gap	*F*	**19**	B7
Garbsen	*D*	**42**	F5
Garching an der Alz	*D*	**38**	C6
Gardanne	*F*	**18**	D6
Gardelegen	*D*	**43**	E7
Gardone Val Trompia	*I*	**34**	C6
Gárdony	*H*	**76**	C5
Gåre	*N*	**51**	B8
Garforth	*GB*	**5**	F9
Gargalianoi	*GR*	**88**	D4
Gargždai	*LT*	**68**	D3
Gârla Mare	*RO*	**82**	C4
Gârleni	*RO*	**79**	D7
Garliava	*LT*	**68**	F6
Garmisch-Partenkirchen	*D*	**37**	C11
Garrel	*D*	**11**	B10
Garstang	*GB*	**5**	F7
Garwolin	*PL*	**72**	G3
Gata de Gorgos	*E*	**27**	G11
Gătaia	*RO*	**77**	G10
Gatchina	*RUS*	**67**	B12
Gateshead	*GB*	**5**	D8
Gattinara	*I*	**34**	C3
Gauchy	*F*	**12**	B4
Gaupne	*N*	**50**	E4
Gävle	*S*	**52**	G5
Gavrio	*GR*	**89**	C9
Gdańsk	*PL*	**71**	B8
Gdov	*RUS*	**67**	D9
Gdynia	*PL*	**71**	B8
Gedser	*DK*	**43**	A8
Geel	*B*	**10**	F6
Geeste	*D*	**11**	C9
Geesthacht	*D*	**42**	D6
Geilo	*N*	**48**	B5
Geisnes	*N*	**54**	E4
Gela	*I*	**30**	G4
Geldern	*D*	**11**	E8
Geleen	*NL*	**11**	F7
Gelibolu	*TR*	**85**	D2
Gelnica	*SK*	**73**	G2
Gelting	*D*	**37**	B11
Gémenos	*F*	**18**	E6
Gemert	*NL*	**11**	E7
Gemona del Friuli	*I*	**35**	A11
General Toshevo	*BG*	**84**	D4
Genève	*CH*	**36**	E4
Genk	*B*	**11**	F7
Genova	*I*	**19**	B11
Gent	*B*	**10**	F4
Genthin	*D*	**43**	F8
Genzano di Lucania	*I*	**31**	B8
Genzano di Roma	*I*	**32**	D5
Geoagiu	*RO*	**77**	F12
Gera	*D*	**41**	B8
Germersheim	*D*	**13**	C11
Gernika-Lumo	*E*	**20**	B2
Gerona	*E*	**18**	G1
Gerwisch	*D*	**43**	F8
Gerzat	*F*	**17**	C10
Gescher	*D*	**11**	D9
Geta	*FIN*	**53**	G8
Getafe	*E*	**26**	D4
Gevgelija	*MK*	**87**	C6
Gex	*F*	**36**	E4
Gheorgheni	*RO*	**78**	D5
Gherla	*RO*	**78**	C2
Ghidigeni	*RO*	**79**	E8
Ghimeș-Făget	*RO*	**78**	D6
Ghimpați	*RO*	**83**	C9
Ghindari	*RO*	**78**	E4
Giannitsa	*GR*	**86**	D6
Giardini-Naxos	*I*	**30**	E6
Giarmata	*RO*	**77**	F9
Giarre	*I*	**30**	E6
Gibellina Nuova	*I*	**30**	E2
Gibraleón	*E*	**25**	J5
Gibraltar	*GBZ*	**28**	G3
Gien	*F*	**12**	F3
Gießen	*D*	**11**	G11
Gifhorn	*D*	**42**	F6
Gijón-Xixón	*E*	**23**	B7
Gilău	*RO*	**78**	D1
Gillingham	*GB*	**8**	F6
Gillingham	*GB*	**9**	E10
Ginosa	*I*	**31**	B9
Gioia del Colle	*I*	**31**	B9
Gioia Tauro	*I*	**31**	G8
Gioiosa Ionica	*I*	**31**	G8
Gioiosa Marea	*I*	**30**	E5
Giovinazzo	*I*	**31**	A9
Girifalco	*I*	**31**	F8
Girișu de Criș	*RO*	**77**	C10
Giromagny	*F*	**13**	F9
Girona	*E*	**18**	G1
Gironella	*E*	**21**	E9
Girov	*RO*	**78**	D7
Girvan	*GB*	**4**	C4
Gislaved	*S*	**45**	B8
Gisors	*F*	**12**	C1
Gistel	*B*	**10**	F3
Giubiasco	*CH*	**34**	B4
Giugliano in Campania	*I*	**30**	B5
Giulianova	*I*	**33**	B8
Giurgiu	*RO*	**83**	C10
Givors	*F*	**17**	D12
Giżycko	*PL*	**68**	G4
Gjakovë	*RKS*	**81**	G11
Gjerstad	*N*	**48**	E6
Gjilan	*RKS*	**82**	F2
Gjirokastër	*AL*	**86**	E3
Gjøvik	*N*	**49**	A8
Gladsaxe	*DK*	**44**	E7
Glandorf	*D*	**11**	D10
Glarus	*CH*	**37**	D8
Glasgow	*GB*	**2**	H5
Glastonbury	*GB*	**8**	E5
Glein	*N*	**54**	B5
Gleisdorf	*A*	**39**	E11
Glenrothes	*GB*	**2**	G6
Glina	*HR*	**76**	G1
Glina	*RO*	**83**	B10
Gliwice	*PL*	**75**	D9
Gllamnik	*RKS*	**81**	F12
Glodeni	*MD*	**79**	B8
Gloggnitz	*A*	**39**	D11
Głogów	*PL*	**70**	G5
Glossa	*GR*	**87**	G8
Glossop	*GB*	**5**	G8
Gloucester	*GB*	**8**	D6
Głowno	*PL*	**71**	G10
Głubczyce	*PL*	**75**	D8
Głuchołazy	*PL*	**75**	C7
Glückstadt	*D*	**42**	C5
Glyfada	*GR*	**89**	C7
Gmünd	*A*	**39**	A10
Gnarrenburg	*D*	**11**	A12
Gniew	*PL*	**71**	C8
Gniewkowo	*PL*	**71**	E8
Gniezno	*PL*	**71**	F7
Goch	*D*	**11**	E8
Göd	*H*	**76**	B6
Godalming	*GB*	**9**	E8
Godech	*BG*	**82**	E5
Godmanchester	*GB*	**9**	C9
Gödöllő	*H*	**76**	B6
Goes	*NL*	**10**	E4
Gogoșu	*RO*	**82**	B4
Göhren, Ostseebad	*D*	**43**	B10
Goicea	*RO*	**82**	C6
Gökçeören	*TR*	**85**	G5
Gol	*N*	**48**	A6
Gołdap	*PL*	**68**	G4
Goleniów	*PL*	**43**	C11
Golfo Aranci	*I*	**32**	D3
Gölmarmara	*TR*	**85**	G4
Golub-Dobrzyń	*PL*	**71**	D9
Gondomar	*P*	**22**	F2
Gönen	*TR*	**85**	D4
Gonfreville-l'Orcher	*F*	**15**	B9
Gonnesa	*I*	**32**	G1
Goole	*GB*	**5**	F9
Goor	*NL*	**11**	D8
Göppingen	*D*	**38**	A2
Góra	*PL*	**70**	G6
Góra Kalwaria	*PL*	**71**	G11
Goražde	*BIH*	**81**	E8
Gördes	*TR*	**85**	G5
Gorebridge	*GB*	**3**	H7
Gorgota	*RO*	**83**	B10
Gorizia	*I*	**35**	B11
Gorlice	*PL*	**73**	E2
Görlitz	*D*	**41**	B12
Gorna Oryakhovitsa	*BG*	**83**	E9
Gornești	*RO*	**78**	D3
Gornja Radgona	*SLO*	**39**	F11
Gornji Milanovac	*SRB*	**81**	D11
Gorredijk	*NL*	**11**	B8
Gorseinon	*GB*	**8**	D3
Gorssel	*NL*	**11**	D8
Görükle	*TR*	**85**	D6
Gorzów Wielkopolski	*PL*	**70**	E4
Gosforth	*GB*	**5**	C8
Goslar	*D*	**42**	G6
Gospić	*HR*	**80**	C2
Gosport	*GB*	**9**	F8
Gostivar	*MK*	**82**	H1
Gostyń	*PL*	**70**	G6
Gostynin	*PL*	**71**	F9
Göteborg	*S*	**44**	A6
Götene	*S*	**46**	E4
Gotha	*D*	**40**	B6
Gothenburg	*S*	**44**	A6
Gotse Delchev	*BG*	**87**	B8
Göttingen	*D*	**40**	A5
Götzis	*A*	**37**	C9
Gouda	*NL*	**10**	D6
Gouesnou	*F*	**14**	E2
Grabow	*D*	**43**	D7
Grabs	*CH*	**37**	C8
Gračanica	*BIH*	**81**	B7
Gradačac	*BIH*	**76**	H5
Grădiștea	*RO*	**83**	C12
Grado	*I*	**35**	C11
Grado	*E*	**22**	B6
Grafenwöhr	*D*	**41**	E7
Gragnano	*I*	**30**	B5

Place	Country	Page	Grid
Grajewo	*PL*	**68**	H5
Grammichele	*I*	**30**	F5
Gramsh	*AL*	**86**	C3
Granada	*E*	**28**	E6
Grândola	*P*	**24**	G3
Grangemouth	*GB*	**2**	G6
Granollers	*E*	**21**	E10
Gransee	*D*	**43**	D9
Grantham	*GB*	**5**	H9
Granville	*F*	**14**	D6
Grao	*E*	**27**	E11
Grassano	*I*	**31**	B8
Grasse	*F*	**19**	D8
Gratkorn	*A*	**39**	E10
Graulhet	*F*	**17**	G8
Gravelines	*F*	**9**	F12
Gravesend	*GB*	**9**	E10
Gravina di Catania	*I*	**30**	F6
Gravina in Puglia	*I*	**31**	B8
Gray	*F*	**13**	G7
Graz	*A*	**39**	E10
Grazzanise	*I*	**30**	A5
Great Dunmow	*GB*	**9**	D10
Great Gonerby	*GB*	**5**	H9
Great Malvern	*GB*	**8**	C6
Great Shelford	*GB*	**9**	C9
Great Torrington	*GB*	**8**	F3
Great Yarmouth	*GB*	**9**	C12
Grebănu	*RO*	**79**	G7
Greenisland	*GB*	**4**	D3
Greenock	*GB*	**2**	G4
Greifswald	*D*	**43**	B10
Grenaa	*DK*	**44**	D5
Grenade	*F*	**17**	G7
Grenchen	*CH*	**13**	G10
Grenoble	*F*	**18**	A6
Greve in Chianti	*I*	**35**	G8
Greven	*D*	**11**	D10
Grevena	*GR*	**86**	E5
Grevenmacher	*L*	**13**	B8
Greystones	*IRL*	**4**	G3
Grez-Doiceau	*B*	**10**	G6
Grigiškės	*LT*	**69**	F8
Grigoriopol	*MD*	**79**	C11
Grimma	*D*	**41**	B9
Grimmen	*D*	**43**	B9
Grimsby	*GB*	**5**	F10
Grimstad	*N*	**48**	F5
Grindsted	*DK*	**44**	E2
Grisslehamn	*S*	**47**	A10
Grivița	*RO*	**83**	B12
Grocka	*SRB*	**81**	C11
Grodków	*PL*	**75**	C7
Grodzisk Mazowiecki	*PL*	**71**	F11
Grodzisk Wielkopolski	*PL*	**70**	F5
Grójec	*PL*	**71**	G11
Grömitz	*D*	**43**	B7
Groningen	*NL*	**11**	B8
Großenhain	*D*	**41**	B10
Grosseto	*I*	**32**	B3
Grosuplje	*SLO*	**39**	G9
Grotli	*N*	**50**	D4
Grottaferrata	*I*	**32**	D5
Grottaglie	*I*	**31**	B10
Grottammare	*I*	**33**	A7
Grotte	*I*	**30**	F4
Grove	*GB*	**9**	D7
Grudziądz	*PL*	**71**	D8
Grumo Appula	*I*	**31**	A9
Grums	*S*	**46**	C4
Grünberg	*D*	**11**	G12
Grybów	*PL*	**73**	E2
Gryfice	*PL*	**43**	C12
Gryfino	*PL*	**43**	D11
Gryt	*S*	**47**	E8
Guadalajara	*E*	**20**	G1
Guadix	*E*	**29**	D7
Gualdo Cattaneo	*I*	**32**	B5
Gualdo Tadino	*I*	**35**	G10
Guarda	*P*	**22**	H4
Guardamar del Segura	*E*	**29**	C11
Guardavalle	*I*	**31**	F8
Guardiagrele	*I*	**33**	C8
Guardia Sanframondi	*I*	**30**	A5
Guardo	*E*	**23**	C8
Guareña	*E*	**24**	F7
Guastalla	*I*	**34**	D6
Gubbio	*I*	**35**	G10
Guben	*D*	**43**	G11
Gubin	*PL*	**43**	G11
Guénange	*F*	**13**	C8
Guer	*F*	**14**	F5
Guérande	*F*	**14**	G5
Guéret	*F*	**17**	C8
Gueugnon	*F*	**17**	B11
Gugești	*RO*	**79**	F8
Guglionesi	*I*	**33**	C9
Guichen	*F*	**14**	F6
Guidel	*F*	**14**	F4
Guidonia-Montecelio	*I*	**32**	C6
Guildford	*GB*	**9**	E8
Guillena	*E*	**25**	J7
Guimarães	*P*	**22**	F3
Guînes	*F*	**9**	F12
Guingamp	*F*	**14**	D4
Guipavas	*F*	**14**	E2
Guisborough	*GB*	**5**	D9
Guitiriz	*E*	**22**	B3
Gujan-Mestras	*F*	**16**	F3
Gulbene	*LV*	**67**	G8
Gullegem	*B*	**10**	F4
Gülŭbovo	*BG*	**83**	G9
Gunja	*HR*	**76**	H5
Günzburg	*D*	**38**	B3
Gunzenhausen	*D*	**40**	F6
Gura Humorului	*RO*	**78**	B5
Gurghiu	*RO*	**78**	D4
Gur'yevsk	*RUS*	**68**	F2
Gusev	*RUS*	**68**	F4
Guspini	*I*	**32**	G2
Gussago	*I*	**34**	C6
Gustavsberg	*S*	**47**	C10
Güstrow	*D*	**43**	C8
Gütersloh	*D*	**11**	D11
Gvardeysk	*RUS*	**68**	F3
Gvarv	*N*	**48**	D6
Gyál	*H*	**76**	C6
Gyomaendrőd	*H*	**77**	D8
Gyöngyös	*H*	**77**	B7
Győr	*H*	**76**	B3
Gytheio	*GR*	**88**	E5
Gyula	*H*	**77**	D9

H

Place	Country	Page	Grid
Haaksbergen	*NL*	**11**	D9
Haapsalu	*EST*	**66**	C4
Haarlem	*NL*	**10**	C6
Habo	*S*	**46**	F5
Haddington	*GB*	**3**	G7
Haderslev	*DK*	**44**	F3
Hadımköy	*TR*	**85**	B5
Hadleigh	*GB*	**9**	D11
Hadsten	*DK*	**44**	D4
Hagen	*D*	**11**	E10
Hagenow	*D*	**43**	D7
Hagfors	*S*	**46**	B4
Hagsta	*S*	**52**	F5
Haguenau	*F*	**13**	D10
Hailsham	*GB*	**9**	F10
Hainburg an der Donau	*A*	**75**	H7
Hainichen	*D*	**41**	B9
Hajdúböszörmény	*H*	**77**	B10
Hajdúdorog	*H*	**77**	B10
Hajdúhadház	*H*	**77**	B10
Hajdúnánás	*H*	**77**	B10
Hajdúsámson	*H*	**77**	B10
Hajdúszoboszló	*H*	**77**	C9
Hajnówka	*PL*	**72**	E6
Hakkenpää	*FIN*	**53**	G10
Hăläucești	*RO*	**79**	C7
Halberstadt	*D*	**43**	G7
Hălchiu	*RO*	**78**	F5
Halden	*N*	**46**	C2
Haldensleben	*D*	**43**	F7
Halesowen	*GB*	**8**	C6
Halesworth	*GB*	**9**	C11
Halhjem	*N*	**48**	B2
Halifax	*GB*	**5**	F8
Hälla	*S*	**55**	G10
Halle	*B*	**10**	G5
Halle (Saale)	*D*	**41**	A7
Hällefors	*S*	**46**	B5
Hallein	*A*	**39**	D7
Hall in Tirol	*A*	**37**	C11
Hallsberg	*S*	**46**	D6
Hallstahammar	*S*	**47**	B7
Halmeu	*RO*	**77**	B12
Halmstad	*S*	**45**	C7
Halstead	*GB*	**9**	D10
Halstenbek	*D*	**42**	C5
Haltingen	*D*	**13**	F10
Ham	*F*	**12**	B3
Hamar	*N*	**49**	A8
Hamburg	*D*	**42**	C5
Hämeenlinna	*FIN*	**64**	E5
Hameln	*D*	**11**	D12
Hamilton	*GB*	**2**	H5
Hamina	*FIN*	**65**	F8
Hamm	*D*	**11**	E10
Hammel	*DK*	**44**	D3
Hammelburg	*D*	**40**	D4
Hammerdal	*S*	**55**	G8
Hammerfest	*N*	**58**	B6
Hamminkeln	*D*	**11**	E8
Hanau	*D*	**13**	A12
Hanko	*FIN*	**64**	H4
Hannover	*D*	**42**	F5
Hannut	*B*	**10**	G6
Hansnes	*N*	**58**	D3
Haparanda	*S*	**56**	B6
Harburg (Schwaben)	*D*	**38**	A4
Hard	*A*	**37**	C9
Hardenberg	*NL*	**11**	C8
Haren (Ems)	*D*	**11**	C9
Hargshamn	*S*	**47**	A10
Harjavalta	*FIN*	**53**	E10
Hârlău	*RO*	**79**	C7
Harlingen	*NL*	**11**	B7

Harlow	*GB*	**9**	D9
Härnösand	*S*	**52**	C6
Haro	*E*	**20**	D2
Harpenden	*GB*	**9**	D9
Harrislee	*D*	**44**	G3
Harrogate	*GB*	**5**	F8
Hârşova	*RO*	**84**	B3
Harstad	*N*	**57**	C4
Harsum	*D*	**42**	F5
Harsvik	*N*	**54**	F2
Hartberg	*A*	**39**	D11
Hartlepool	*GB*	**5**	D9
Harwich	*GB*	**9**	D11
Haselünne	*D*	**11**	C10
Haslemere	*GB*	**9**	F8
Haslev	*DK*	**44**	F6
Hasparren	*F*	**20**	B4
Haspe	*D*	**11**	E10
Hassela	*S*	**52**	D4
Hasselt	*B*	**11**	F7
Haßfurt	*D*	**40**	D5
Hässleholm	*S*	**45**	D8
Hastings	*GB*	**9**	F10
Hasvik	*N*	**58**	C5
Haţeg	*RO*	**77**	F12
Hatfield	*GB*	**5**	F9
Hattem	*NL*	**11**	C8
Hatvan	*H*	**77**	B7
Haugesund	*N*	**48**	D2
Hauske	*N*	**48**	D2
Havant	*GB*	**9**	F8
Havârna	*RO*	**79**	A7
Havelberg	*D*	**43**	E8
Haverfordwest	*GB*	**8**	D2
Haverhill	*GB*	**9**	D10
Havířov	*CZ*	**75**	E9
Havlíčkův Brod	*CZ*	**74**	E5
Havneby	*DK*	**44**	G2
Havøysund	*N*	**59**	B7
Havran	*TR*	**85**	E3
Havsa	*TR*	**84**	H2
Hawick	*GB*	**5**	C7
Haxby	*GB*	**5**	E9
Hayrabolu	*TR*	**85**	B3
Haywards Heath	*GB*	**9**	F9
Heanor	*GB*	**5**	G9
Hedemora	*S*	**47**	A7
Hedeviken	*S*	**51**	C11
Heemskerk	*NL*	**10**	C6
Heemstede	*NL*	**10**	C6
Heeren	*D*	**11**	E10
Heerlen	*NL*	**11**	F7
Heide	*D*	**42**	B4
Heidelberg	*D*	**13**	C11
Heidenheim an der Brenz	*D*	**38**	B3
Heikendorf	*D*	**42**	B6
Heilbronn	*D*	**40**	F4
Heiligenhafen	*D*	**43**	B7
Heiloo	*NL*	**10**	C6
Heimdal	*N*	**51**	B7
Heinola	*FIN*	**65**	E7
Helbra	*D*	**43**	G7
Helegiu	*RO*	**79**	E7
Helensburgh	*GB*	**2**	G4
Helgeroa	*N*	**49**	E7
Hellín	*E*	**27**	H8
Helmond	*NL*	**11**	E7
Helsingborg	*S*	**45**	E7
Helsinge	*DK*	**44**	E6
Helsingfors	*FIN*	**64**	G6
Helsingør	*DK*	**45**	E7
Helsinki	*FIN*	**64**	G6
Helston	*GB*	**8**	G2
Hemel Hempstead	*GB*	**9**	D9
Hemnesberget	*N*	**54**	B6
Hemsby	*GB*	**9**	B12
Hendaye	*F*	**20**	B3
Hengelo	*NL*	**11**	D9
Henley-on-Thames	*GB*	**9**	E8
Hennebont	*F*	**14**	F4
Herborn	*D*	**11**	G11
Herceg-Novi	*MNE*	**81**	G8
Hereford	*GB*	**8**	D5
Herford	*D*	**11**	D11
Herlev	*DK*	**44**	E7
Hermagor	*A*	**39**	F7
Hermsdorf	*D*	**41**	B7
Herne	*B*	**10**	G5
Herning	*DK*	**44**	D2
Hérouville-St-Clair	*F*	**15**	C8
Herrera	*E*	**28**	D4
Hersbruck	*D*	**41**	E7
Hertford	*GB*	**9**	D9
Herzberg	*D*	**43**	G9
Hesdin	*F*	**9**	G12
Hessigkofen	*CH*	**13**	G10
Hessisch Lichtenau	*D*	**40**	B4
Hettstadt	*D*	**40**	E4
Hettstedt	*D*	**43**	G7
Heves	*H*	**77**	B8
Hexham	*GB*	**5**	D8
Heysham	*GB*	**5**	E7
Highbridge	*GB*	**8**	E5
Highworth	*GB*	**9**	D7
High Wycombe	*GB*	**9**	D8
Hildburghausen	*D*	**40**	C6
Hildesheim	*D*	**42**	F5
Hillerød	*DK*	**44**	E6
Hillswick	*GB*	**3**	B11
Hilpoltstein	*D*	**40**	F6
Hilversum	*NL*	**10**	D6
Hînceşti	*MD*	**79**	D10
Hinckley	*GB*	**9**	C7
Hinnerup	*DK*	**44**	D4
Hinojosa del Duque	*E*	**26**	H2
Hinte	*D*	**11**	A9
Hirschaid	*D*	**40**	D6
Hirson	*F*	**12**	B5
Hirtshals	*DK*	**44**	B4
Histon	*GB*	**9**	C9
Hitchin	*GB*	**9**	D9
Hitzacker	*D*	**43**	D7
Hjerkinn	*N*	**50**	D6
Hjo	*S*	**46**	E5
Hjørring	*DK*	**44**	B4
Hlinsko	*CZ*	**74**	E5
Hlohovec	*SK*	**75**	G8
Hlyboka	*UA*	**78**	A6
Hlybokaye	*BY*	**69**	E11
Hnúšťa	*SK*	**75**	G11
Hobro	*DK*	**44**	C3
Hochdorf	*D*	**40**	G4
Hoddesdon	*GB*	**9**	D9
Hódmezővásárhely	*H*	**77**	E8
Hof	*D*	**41**	C7
Hofheim in Unterfranken	*D*	**40**	D5
Hofors	*S*	**52**	G4
Höganäs	*S*	**45**	D7
Hoghiz	*RO*	**78**	F5
Hokksund	*N*	**49**	C7
Holbæk	*DK*	**44**	E6
Holbeach	*GB*	**5**	H10
Holboca	*RO*	**79**	C8
Holešov	*CZ*	**75**	E8
Holíč	*SK*	**75**	F7
Holice	*CZ*	**74**	D5
Hollabrunn	*A*	**39**	B11
Hollfeld	*D*	**41**	D7
Hollola	*FIN*	**64**	E6
Holmestrand	*N*	**49**	D7
Holmfirth	*GB*	**5**	F8
Holmsund	*S*	**56**	G2
Holstebro	*DK*	**44**	D2
Holyhead	*GB*	**4**	G4
Holywood	*GB*	**4**	D3
Holzminden	*D*	**11**	D12
Homocea	*RO*	**79**	E8
Hønefoss	*N*	**49**	B7
Honfleur	*F*	**15**	C9
Honiton	*GB*	**8**	F5
Honley	*GB*	**5**	F8
Hoofddorp	*NL*	**10**	C6
Hook	*GB*	**9**	E8
Höör	*S*	**45**	E8
Hoorn	*NL*	**10**	C6
Hope	*N*	**50**	F2
Hopsten	*D*	**11**	C10
Horažďovice	*CZ*	**41**	E10
Hörby	*S*	**45**	E8
Horda	*N*	**48**	C3
Horezu	*RO*	**78**	G2
Horgoš	*SRB*	**77**	E7
Horia	*RO*	**79**	D7
Hořice	*CZ*	**74**	C5
Horn	*A*	**39**	B11
Horn	*N*	**54**	C5
Horncastle	*GB*	**5**	G10
Hørning	*DK*	**44**	E4
Hornsea	*GB*	**5**	F10
Horodok	*UA*	**73**	E5
Horsens	*DK*	**44**	E3
Horsham	*GB*	**9**	F9
Hørsholm	*DK*	**44**	E7
Horten	*N*	**49**	D7
Horwich	*GB*	**5**	F7
Hosszúpályi	*H*	**77**	C10
Hotarele	*RO*	**83**	C10
Hoting	*S*	**55**	F9
Hove	*GB*	**9**	F9
Höxter	*D*	**11**	E12
Hoyerswerda	*D*	**41**	A11
Hoylake	*GB*	**4**	G6
Hradec Králové	*CZ*	**74**	D5
Hranice	*CZ*	**75**	E8
Hrasnica	*BIH*	**81**	D7
Hrastnik	*SLO*	**39**	G10
Hriňová	*SK*	**75**	G11
Hrodna	*BY*	**68**	H6
Hrubieszów	*PL*	**73**	C6
Hucknall	*GB*	**5**	G9
Huddersfield	*GB*	**5**	F8
Hudeşti	*RO*	**78**	A7
Hudiksvall	*S*	**52**	D5
Huedin	*RO*	**77**	D12
Huelma	*E*	**28**	D6
Huelva	*E*	**25**	K5
Huenenberg	*CH*	**37**	C7
Huércal-Overa	*E*	**29**	D9
Huesca	*E*	**20**	D6
Huéscar	*E*	**29**	C8

Hufthamar	*N*	**48**	B2
Hugh Town	*GB*	**8**	G1
Huittinen	*FIN*	**53**	F11
Hull	*GB*	**5**	F10
Hultsfred	*S*	**45**	B11
Humenné	*SK*	**73**	F3
Humlebæk	*DK*	**45**	E7
Hundested	*DK*	**44**	E6
Hunedoara	*RO*	**77**	F12
Hünfeld	*D*	**40**	C4
Huntingdon	*GB*	**9**	C9
Hurbanovo	*SK*	**76**	B4
Hürth	*D*	**11**	F9
Huşi	*RO*	**79**	D9
Huskvarna	*S*	**45**	A9
Hustopeče	*CZ*	**75**	F7
Husum	*D*	**42**	B4
Hvar	*HR*	**80**	F4
Hvidovre	*DK*	**44**	E7
Hwlffordd	*GB*	**8**	D2
Hyères	*F*	**19**	E7
Hythe	*GB*	**9**	F11
Hyvinkää	*FIN*	**64**	F5

I

Ialoveni	*MD*	**79**	D10
Ianca	*RO*	**79**	G8
Ianca	*RO*	**83**	D7
Iara	*RO*	**78**	D2
Iargara	*MD*	**79**	E10
Iaşi	*RO*	**79**	C8
Ibi	*E*	**27**	G10
Ibrány	*H*	**73**	H3
Idar-Oberstein	*D*	**13**	B9
Idrija	*SLO*	**35**	B12
Idron-Ousse-Sendets	*F*	**20**	B6
Iecava	*LV*	**69**	B7
Ieper	*B*	**10**	F3
Ierapetra	*GR*	**89**	G11
Iernut	*RO*	**78**	E3
Ifs	*F*	**15**	C8
Ighiu	*RO*	**78**	E2
Igis	*CH*	**37**	D9
Iglesias	*I*	**32**	G2
Ignalina	*LT*	**69**	E9
Igoumenitsa	*GR*	**86**	F3
Igualada	*E*	**21**	F9
Iisalmi	*FIN*	**63**	G8
Ikast	*DK*	**44**	D3
Ikhtiman	*BG*	**82**	F6
Iława	*PL*	**71**	D9
Ilford	*GB*	**9**	E9
Ilfracombe	*GB*	**8**	E3
Ílhavo	*P*	**22**	G2
Ilijaš	*BIH*	**81**	D7
Ilirska Bistrica	*SLO*	**35**	C12
Ilkeston	*GB*	**5**	H9
Ilkley	*GB*	**5**	F8
Illescas	*E*	**26**	D4
Ille-sur-Têt	*F*	**18**	F1
Íllora	*E*	**28**	D6
Ilmenau	*D*	**40**	C6
Il'nytsya	*UA*	**73**	H5
Ilok	*HR*	**76**	G6
Iłża	*PL*	**73**	B2
Imatra	*FIN*	**65**	E9
Immingham	*GB*	**5**	F10
Imola	*I*	**35**	E8
Imotski	*HR*	**80**	E6
Imperia	*I*	**19**	D10
Imphy	*F*	**12**	H4
Impruneta	*I*	**35**	G7
İmroz	*TR*	**85**	D1
Imst	*A*	**37**	C10
Inca	*E*	**29**	F9
Incisa in Val d'Arno	*I*	**35**	G8
Indal	*S*	**52**	C5
Indalstø	*N*	**48**	B2
Inđija	*SRB*	**77**	G7
Ineu	*RO*	**77**	E10
Infiesto	*E*	**23**	B8
Ingolstadt	*D*	**38**	A5
Inis	*IRL*	**7**	K3
Inis Córthaidh	*IRL*	**7**	L6
Innsbruck	*A*	**37**	C11
Inowrocław	*PL*	**71**	E8
Însurăţei	*RO*	**79**	H8
Interlaken	*CH*	**36**	D6
Întorsura Buzăului	*RO*	**78**	F6
Inverkeithing	*GB*	**2**	G6
Inverness	*GB*	**2**	D5
Inverurie	*GB*	**3**	E7
Ioannina	*GR*	**86**	F4
Ion Creangă	*RO*	**79**	D7
İpsala	*TR*	**85**	C2
Ipswich	*GB*	**9**	D11
Irakleio	*GR*	**89**	G10
Iraklion	*GR*	**89**	G10
Irshava	*UA*	**73**	H5
Irsina	*I*	**31**	B8
Irun	*E*	**20**	B3
Irunea	*E*	**20**	C4
Irvine	*GB*	**4**	B4
Isaccea	*RO*	**79**	G10
Íscar	*E*	**23**	F9
Ischia	*I*	**30**	B4
Iserlohn	*D*	**11**	E10
Isernia	*I*	**33**	D8
Isla Cristina	*E*	**25**	K5
Islaz	*RO*	**83**	D8
Isola del Gran Sasso d'Italia	*I*	**33**	B7
Isola del Liri	*I*	**33**	D7
Isola di Capo Rizzuto	*I*	**31**	F10
Isperikh	*BG*	**83**	D11
Ispica	*I*	**30**	G6
Issoire	*F*	**17**	D10
Issoudun	*F*	**12**	H2
Is-sur-Tille	*F*	**12**	F6
İstanbul	*TR*	**85**	B6
Istres	*F*	**18**	D5
Ittiri	*I*	**32**	E2
Itzehoe	*D*	**42**	C5
Ivančice	*CZ*	**74**	F6
Ivanec	*HR*	**39**	F11
Ivangorod	*RUS*	**67**	B10
Ivanić-Grad	*HR*	**76**	F1
Ivanjica	*SRB*	**81**	E11
Ivankovo	*HR*	**76**	G5
Ivano-Frankove	*UA*	**73**	D6
Ivarrud	*N*	**54**	D6
Ivaylovgrad	*BG*	**85**	A1
Iveşti	*RO*	**79**	F8
Ivrea	*I*	**34**	C2
İvrindi	*TR*	**85**	E3
Ivry Sur Seine	*F*	**12**	D2
Ivybridge	*GB*	**8**	G4
Iwye	*BY*	**69**	G9
Izbiceni	*RO*	**83**	C7
Izel-Chiny	*B*	**13**	B7
Izmayil	*UA*	**79**	G10
İzmir	*TR*	**85**	H3
Iznájar	*E*	**28**	D5
Izola	*SLO*	**35**	C11
Izsák	*H*	**76**	D6
Izvoarele	*RO*	**78**	G6
Izvoarele	*RO*	**83**	C9

J

Jablunkov	*CZ*	**75**	E9
Jaca	*E*	**20**	D5
Jaén	*E*	**28**	C6
Jagodina	*SRB*	**81**	D12
Jajce	*BIH*	**80**	C6
Jakobstad	*FIN*	**56**	G5
Jalasjärvi	*FIN*	**53**	C11
Jämsä	*FIN*	**64**	D6
Jämsänkoski	*FIN*	**64**	C6
Janja	*BIH*	**81**	C9
Janjevë	*RKS*	**82**	F2
Jánoshalma	*H*	**76**	E6
Jánossomorja	*H*	**76**	B2
Janów Lubelski	*PL*	**73**	C4
Janzé	*F*	**14**	F6
Jaraiz de la Vera	*E*	**24**	C7
Jaren	*N*	**49**	B8
Jargeau	*F*	**12**	F2
Järna	*S*	**47**	D9
Jarocin	*PL*	**71**	G7
Jaroměř	*CZ*	**74**	C5
Jarosław	*PL*	**73**	D4
Järpen	*S*	**51**	B11
Järvenpää	*FIN*	**64**	F6
Järvsö	*S*	**52**	D4
Jasło	*PL*	**73**	E2
Jassans-Riottier	*F*	**17**	C12
Jastrebarsko	*HR*	**39**	H11
Jastrowie	*PL*	**70**	D6
Jastrzębie-Zdrój	*PL*	**75**	D9
Jászapáti	*H*	**77**	B7
Jászárokszállás	*H*	**77**	B7
Jászberény	*H*	**77**	C7
Jászfényszaru	*H*	**77**	B7
Jászkisér	*H*	**77**	C8
Jászladány	*H*	**77**	C7
Jättendal	*S*	**52**	D5
Jaunay-Clan	*F*	**16**	B5
Jávea-Xábia	*E*	**27**	G11
Jawor	*PL*	**74**	B6
Jaworzno	*PL*	**75**	D10
Jebel	*RO*	**77**	F9
Jedlicze	*PL*	**73**	E3
Jędrzejów	*PL*	**73**	C1
Jegălia	*RO*	**83**	B12
Jēkabpils	*LV*	**69**	B9
Jektvik	*N*	**54**	A6
Jelcz-Laskowice	*PL*	**75**	B7
Jelenia Góra	*PL*	**74**	B5
Jelgava	*LV*	**66**	H4
Jemnice	*CZ*	**74**	F5
Jena	*D*	**41**	B7
Jenbach	*A*	**37**	C12
Jerez de la Frontera	*E*	**25**	L7
Jerez de los Caballeros	*E*	**24**	G6
Jesenice	*SLO*	**39**	F8
Jeseník	*CZ*	**75**	D7
Jesi	*I*	**35**	G11

H

Place	Country	Page	Grid
Jesolo	*I*	**35**	C10
Jessen	*D*	**43**	G9
Jessheim	*N*	**46**	A2
Jever	*D*	**42**	C3
Jiana	*RO*	**82**	B4
Jibou	*RO*	**77**	C12
Jičín	*CZ*	**74**	C5
Jidvei	*RO*	**78**	E2
Jihlava	*CZ*	**74**	E5
Jijila	*RO*	**79**	G9
Jijona-Xixona	*E*	**27**	H10
Jilava	*RO*	**83**	B10
Jimbolia	*RO*	**77**	F8
Jindřichův Hradec	*CZ*	**41**	F12
Jirkov	*CZ*	**41**	C10
Jódar	*E*	**29**	C7
Joensuu	*FIN*	**65**	B10
Jõgeva	*EST*	**67**	D8
Jõhvi	*EST*	**67**	B9
Joigny	*F*	**12**	F4
Joinville	*F*	**12**	E6
Joița	*RO*	**83**	B9
Jonava	*LT*	**69**	E7
Jondal	*N*	**48**	B3
Joniškis	*LT*	**68**	C6
Jönköping	*S*	**45**	A9
Jonzac	*F*	**16**	D4
Jordbro	*S*	**47**	C9
Joué-lès-Tours	*F*	**15**	G9
Joure	*NL*	**11**	B7
Joutseno	*FIN*	**65**	E9
Józefów	*PL*	**71**	F11
Juan-les-Pins	*F*	**19**	D8
Judenburg	*A*	**39**	E9
Jülich	*D*	**11**	F8
Jumilla	*E*	**27**	H8
Junsele	*S*	**55**	G9
Jurançon	*F*	**20**	B6
Jurbarkas	*LT*	**68**	E5
Jurilovca	*RO*	**84**	B5
Jūrmala	*LV*	**66**	G4
Jüterbog	*D*	**43**	G9
Jyllinge	*DK*	**44**	E6
Jyväskylä	*FIN*	**64**	C6

K

Place	Country	Page	Grid
Kaarina	*FIN*	**53**	G11
Kaba	*H*	**77**	C9
Kać	*SRB*	**77**	G7
Kaçanik	*RKS*	**82**	G2
Kadaň	*CZ*	**41**	C9
Kağıthane	*TR*	**85**	B6
Kahla	*D*	**41**	C7
Kaiserslautern	*D*	**13**	C10
Kajaani	*FIN*	**63**	E8
Kakanj	*BIH*	**81**	D7
Kalajoki	*FIN*	**56**	F6
Kalamaki	*GR*	**89**	C7
Kalamaria	*GR*	**87**	D7
Kalamata	*GR*	**88**	D4
Kalampaka	*GR*	**86**	F5
Kälarne	*S*	**52**	B4
Kalety	*PL*	**75**	C10
Kalevala	*RUS*	**63**	C12
Kaliningrad	*RUS*	**68**	F2
Kalisz	*PL*	**71**	G7
Kalix	*S*	**56**	B5
Kållered	*S*	**44**	A6
Kallinge	*S*	**45**	D10
Kallithea	*GR*	**89**	C7
Kalmar	*S*	**45**	C12
Kalocsa	*H*	**76**	D5
Kaluđerica	*SRB*	**81**	B11
Kalundborg	*DK*	**44**	E5
Kalvåg	*N*	**50**	E1
Kalvarija	*LT*	**68**	F6
Kalymnos	*GR*	**88**	F2
Kamares	*GR*	**89**	E9
Kamariotissa	*GR*	**87**	D11
Kamennogorsk	*RUS*	**65**	E10
Kameno	*BG*	**83**	F12
Kamenz	*D*	**41**	B11
Kamëz	*AL*	**86**	B2
Kamienna Gora	*PL*	**74**	C6
Kamień Pomorski	*PL*	**43**	C11
Kamnik	*SLO*	**39**	F9
Kampen	*NL*	**11**	C7
Kamyanyets	*BY*	**72**	F6
Kangasala	*FIN*	**64**	D5
Kanjiža	*SRB*	**77**	E7
Kankaanpää	*FIN*	**53**	D11
Kapaklı	*TR*	**85**	B4
Kapellskär	*S*	**47**	B10
Kapfenberg	*A*	**39**	D10
Kaplice	*CZ*	**39**	A9
Kaposvár	*H*	**76**	E3
Kappeln	*D*	**42**	A5
Kapuvár	*H*	**76**	B2
Karacabey	*TR*	**85**	D5
Karavukovo	*SRB*	**76**	G6
Kårböle	*S*	**52**	D3
Karcag	*H*	**77**	C9
Karczew	*PL*	**71**	G11
Karditsa	*GR*	**86**	F6
Kärdla	*EST*	**66**	C3
Karis	*FIN*	**64**	G4
Karkkila	*FIN*	**64**	F5
Karleby	*FIN*	**56**	F5
Karlino	*PL*	**70**	C5
Karlovac	*HR*	**39**	H11
Karlovasi	*GR*	**88**	D2
Karlovo	*BG*	**83**	F8
Karlovy Vary	*CZ*	**41**	D9
Karlshamn	*S*	**45**	D10
Karlskoga	*S*	**46**	C5
Karlskrona	*S*	**45**	D11
Karlsruhe	*D*	**13**	C11
Karlstad	*S*	**46**	C4
Karlstadt	*D*	**40**	D4
Karnobat	*BG*	**83**	F11
Karpenisi	*GR*	**86**	G5
Karşıyaka	*TR*	**85**	H3
Kartal	*H*	**76**	B6
Kartuzy	*PL*	**71**	B8
Karvala	*FIN*	**53**	B12
Karviná	*CZ*	**75**	D9
Karystos	*GR*	**89**	B8
Kassel	*D*	**40**	A4
Kastania	*GR*	**86**	G5
Kaštel Stari	*HR*	**80**	E4
Kaštel Sućurac	*HR*	**80**	E4
Kasterlee	*B*	**10**	F6
Kastoria	*GR*	**86**	D4
Ka-Stutensee	*D*	**13**	C11
Katapola	*GR*	**89**	E11
Katerini	*GR*	**87**	E7
Katowice	*PL*	**75**	D10
Katrineholm	*S*	**47**	D7
Kattavia	*GR*	**88**	H3
Kattbo	*S*	**51**	G12
Katwijk aan Zee	*NL*	**10**	D5
Kaufbeuren	*D*	**37**	B10
Kaufungen	*D*	**40**	B4
Kauhajoki	*FIN*	**53**	C10
Kauhava	*FIN*	**53**	B11
Kaunas	*LT*	**68**	F6
Kauniainen	*FIN*	**64**	G5
Kavadarci	*MK*	**86**	B6
Kavajë	*AL*	**86**	C2
Kavaklıdere	*TR*	**85**	H5
Kavala	*GR*	**87**	C10
Kavarna	*BG*	**84**	D4
Kävlinge	*S*	**45**	E8
Kaysersberg	*F*	**13**	E9
Kazanlŭk	*BG*	**83**	F9
Kazimierza Wielka	*PL*	**73**	D1
Kazlų Rūda	*LT*	**68**	F6
Kecel	*H*	**76**	D6
Kecskemét	*H*	**77**	D7
Kėdainiai	*LT*	**68**	E6
Kędzierzyn-Koźle	*PL*	**75**	C9
Kefalos	*GR*	**88**	F2
Keighley	*GB*	**5**	F8
Keila	*EST*	**66**	B5
Ķekava	*LV*	**66**	G5
Kelheim	*D*	**41**	F7
Kelmė	*LT*	**68**	D5
Kelso	*GB*	**5**	B7
Kemalpaşa	*TR*	**85**	H3
Kemi	*FIN*	**56**	C6
Kemijärvi	*FIN*	**61**	D9
Kemnath	*D*	**41**	D7
Kempele	*FIN*	**62**	D6
Kempston	*GB*	**9**	C9
Kempten (Allgäu)	*D*	**37**	B10
Kendal	*GB*	**5**	E7
Kenderes	*H*	**77**	C8
Kenilworth	*GB*	**9**	C7
Kępno	*PL*	**75**	B8
Kepsut	*TR*	**85**	E5
Keramoti	*GR*	**87**	C10
Keratea	*GR*	**89**	C7
Kerava	*FIN*	**64**	G6
Kerepestarcsa	*H*	**76**	B6
Kerkrade	*NL*	**11**	F8
Kerkyra	*GR*	**86**	F2
Kerstinbo	*S*	**47**	A8
Kerteminde	*DK*	**44**	F4
Keşan	*TR*	**85**	C2
Keszthely	*H*	**76**	D3
Kętrzyn	*PL*	**68**	G3
Kettering	*GB*	**9**	C8
Kęty	*PL*	**75**	D10
Keuruu	*FIN*	**64**	C5
Keynsham	*GB*	**8**	E6
Kežmarok	*SK*	**73**	F1
Kharmanli	*BG*	**83**	G9
Khaskovo	*BG*	**83**	G9
Khisarya	*BG*	**83**	F8
Khust	*UA*	**73**	H5
Kiato	*GR*	**88**	B5
Kičevo	*MK*	**86**	B4
Kidderminster	*GB*	**8**	C6
Kidlington	*GB*	**9**	D7
Kidsgrove	*GB*	**5**	G7
Kiel	*D*	**42**	B6
Kielce	*PL*	**73**	C1
Kietrz	*PL*	**75**	D8

Kifisia GR 89 B7
Kifjord N 59 B9
Kikinda SRB 77 F8
Kil S 46 C4
Kilboghamn N 54 B6
Kiliya UA 79 G11
Kilkeel GB 4 E3
Kilkenny IRL 7 L5
Kilkis GR 87 C7
Killarney IRL 7 M3
Kilmarnock GB 4 B5
Kilwinning GB 4 B4
Kindberg A 39 D10
Kingisepp RUS 67 B10
Kingsbridge GB 8 G4
King's Lynn GB 5 H11
Kingsnorth GB 9 E10
Kingston upon Hull GB 5 F10
Kingswood GB 8 E6
Kınık TR 85 F3
Kinna S 45 B7
Kinsarvik N 48 B3
Kırkağaç TR 85 F4
Kirkby GB 5 G7
Kirkcaldy GB 2 G6
Kirkehamn N 48 F3
Kirkenes N 59 D11
Kirkkonummi FIN 64 G5
Kırklareli TR 83 H12
Kirkwall GB 3 E10
Kirn D 13 B10
Kirriemuir GB 3 F7
Kiruna S 60 B3
Kisač SRB 77 G7
Kisbér H 76 B4
Kiskőrös H 76 D6
Kiskunfélegyháza H 77 D7
Kiskunhalas H 76 E6
Kiskunlacháza H 76 C6
Kiskunmajsa H 77 E7
Kissamos GR 89 F7
Kistelek H 77 E7
Kisújszállás H 77 C8
Kisvárda H 73 H3
Kitee FIN 65 C11
Kitzbühel A 38 D6
Kitzingen D 40 E5
Kiuruvesi FIN 63 F7
Kiviõli EST 67 B8
Kladno CZ 41 D11
Kladovo SRB 82 B4
Klagenfurt A 39 F9
Klaipėda LT 68 D3
Klaksvík FO 3 B9
Klatovy CZ 41 E9
Klaukkala FIN 64 G5
Kleinmachnow D 43 E10
Kleve D 11 E8
Klingenthal D 41 C8
Klippan S 45 D8
Kljajićevo SRB 76 F6
Kłobuck PL 75 B10
Kłodawa PL 71 F9
Kłodzko PL 74 C6
Klosterneuburg A 39 B12
Klötze (Altmark) D 43 E7
Kluczbork PL 75 B9
Knaresborough GB 5 E8
Knarrlagsund N 54 G1
Knezha BG 82 D6
Knin HR 80 D4
Knittelfeld A 39 D10
Knivsta S 47 B9
Knjaževac SRB 82 D3
Knokke-Heist B 10 E4
Knottingley GB 5 F9
Knutsford GB 5 G7
København DK 45 E7
Koblenz D 11 G10
Kočani MK 82 G4
Kočevje SLO 39 H10
Kodyma UA 79 A11
Köflach A 39 E10
Køge DK 44 F6
Kohtla-Järve EST 67 B9
Kokemäki FIN 53 E11
Kokkola FIN 56 F5
Koksijde B 10 F3
Kolárovo SK 76 B4
Kolbuszowa PL 73 D3
Koldere TR 85 G4
Kolding DK 44 F3
Kolín CZ 41 D12
Kölleda D 40 B6
Köln D 11 F9
Kolno PL 72 D4
Koło PL 71 F8
Kołobrzeg PL 70 B4
Kolochava UA 73 G6
Koluszki PL 71 G10
Komádi H 77 C10
Komárno SK 76 B4
Komárom H 76 B4
Komló H 76 E4
Komotini GR 87 C11
Konak TR 85 H3
Kondoros H 77 D9
Kongens Lyngby DK 44 E7
Kongsberg N 49 C7
Kongsvinger N 46 A3
Koniecpol PL 75 C11
Königs Wusterhausen D 43 F10
Konin PL 71 F8
Köniz CH 13 H10
Konjic BIH 81 E7
Końskie PL 73 B1
Konstanz D 37 B8
Konz D 13 B8
Koper SLO 35 C12
Köping S 47 C7
Koprivnica HR 76 E2
Köprübaşı TR 85 G5
Korbach D 11 F12
Korçë AL 86 D4
Korgen N 54 B6
Korinthos GR 88 C6
Korisia GR 89 C8
Körmend H 76 C2
Kórnik PL 70 F6
Korntal D 13 D12
Koroleve UA 73 H5
Koroni GR 88 E4
Koronowo PL 71 D7
Koropi GR 89 C7
Körösladány H 77 D9
Korskrogen S 52 D3
Korso FIN 64 G6
Korsør DK 44 F5
Korsvoll N 50 B5
Korsze PL 68 G3
Kortrijk B 10 F4
Kos GR 88 F2
Kościan PL 70 G6
Kościerzyna PL 71 B7
Košice SK 73 G2
Kosovska Kamenicë RKS 82 F2
Kostenets BG 82 F6
Kostinbrod BG 82 E5
Kostolac SRB 81 B12
Kostomuksha RUS 63 E11
Kostrzyn PL 43 E11
Koszalin PL 70 B5
Kőszeg H 76 C1
Kotel BG 83 E10
Köthen (Anhalt) D 43 G8
Kotka FIN 65 F8
Kotor MNE 81 G8
Kotor Varoš BIH 80 C6
Kotovs'k UA 79 B12
Koufalia GR 87 C7
Kouvola FIN 65 F7
Kovačica SRB 77 G8
Kovdor RUS 61 C12
Kovin SRB 81 B12
Koynare BG 83 D7
Kozani GR 86 D5
Kozienice PL 72 H3
Kozloduy BG 82 D6
Koźmin Wielkopowski PL 71 G7
Kożuchów PL 70 G4
Kragerø N 48 E6
Kragujevac SRB 81 D12
Krakhella N 50 F1
Kraków PL 75 D11
Kraljevo SRB 81 D11
Kráľovský Chlmec SK 73 G3
Kramfors S 52 B6
Kranj SLO 39 F9
Krapina HR 39 G11
Krapkowice PL 75 C8
Krāslava LV 69 D10
Kraśnik PL 73 B3
Krasni Okny UA 79 B11
Krasnogorodskoye RUS 67 G10
Krásno nad Kysucou SK 75 E10
Krasnoyil's'k UA 78 A5
Krasnystaw PL 73 B5
Kratovo MK 82 G3
Krefeld D 11 E8
Krems an der Donau A 39 B11
Kretinga LT 68 D3
Krichim BG 83 G7
Krieglach A 39 D11
Kristiansand N 48 F5
Kristianstad S 45 E9
Kristiansund N 50 B4
Kristinehamn S 46 C5
Kriva Palanka MK 82 G4
Križevci HR 76 E1
Krnjevo SRB 81 C12
Krnov CZ 75 D8
Krokom S 51 B12
Krokstadelva N 49 C7
Kroměříž CZ 75 F7
Krompachy SK 73 F1
Kronach D 41 D7
Kronshagen D 42 B5
Kronshtadt RUS 65 G10
Kropp D 42 B5
Krosno PL 73 E3

Place	Country	Page	Grid
Krosno Odrzańskie	*PL*	**70**	G4
Krotoszyn	*PL*	**71**	G7
Krško	*SLO*	**39**	G10
Krujë	*AL*	**86**	B2
Krumbach (Schwaben)	*D*	**37**	A10
Krumovgrad	*BG*	**87**	B12
Krupina	*SK*	**75**	G10
Krupka	*CZ*	**41**	C10
Kruševac	*SRB*	**82**	D2
Kruševo	*MK*	**86**	B4
Kruszwica	*PL*	**71**	E8
Krutådal	*N*	**55**	C7
Krya Vrysi	*GR*	**86**	D6
Krylbo	*S*	**47**	A7
Krynica	*PL*	**73**	E2
Krzyż Wielkopolski	*PL*	**70**	E5
Kubrat	*BG*	**83**	D10
Kučevo	*SRB*	**82**	B2
Kuçovë	*AL*	**86**	D2
Küçükçekmece	*TR*	**85**	B6
Küçükköy	*TR*	**85**	F2
Kufstein	*A*	**38**	D6
Kuhmo	*FIN*	**63**	E10
Kukës	*AL*	**81**	H11
Kula	*BG*	**82**	C4
Kula	*SRB*	**76**	F6
Kula	*TR*	**85**	G5
Kuldīga	*LV*	**66**	G2
Kulmbach	*D*	**41**	D7
Kulykiv	*UA*	**73**	D6
Kumanovo	*MK*	**82**	G3
Kumla	*S*	**46**	C6
Kunda	*EST*	**67**	B8
Kungälv	*S*	**46**	F2
Kungsängen	*S*	**47**	C9
Kungsbacka	*S*	**44**	B6
Kungshamn	*S*	**46**	E2
Kungsör	*S*	**47**	C7
Kunhegyes	*H*	**77**	C8
Kunmadaras	*H*	**77**	C8
Kunszentmárton	*H*	**77**	D8
Kunszentmiklós	*H*	**76**	C6
Künzell	*D*	**40**	C4
Künzelsau	*D*	**40**	F4
Kuopio	*FIN*	**65**	B8
Kupiškis	*LT*	**69**	D8
Kŭrdzhali	*BG*	**83**	H9
Kuressaare	*EST*	**66**	E3
Kurikka	*FIN*	**53**	C11
Kuřim	*CZ*	**74**	F6
Kurort Schmalkalden	*D*	**40**	C5
Kuršėnai	*LT*	**68**	C5
Kuršumlija	*SRB*	**82**	E2
Kurtzea	*E*	**20**	B2
Kuru	*FIN*	**53**	D12
Kusadak	*SRB*	**81**	C12
Kuşadası	*TR*	**88**	D2
Küssnacht	*CH*	**13**	G11
Kustavi	*FIN*	**53**	G10
Kutina	*HR*	**76**	G2
Kutno	*PL*	**71**	F9
Kuusamo	*FIN*	**61**	F11
Kuusankoski	*FIN*	**65**	E7
Kuz'molovskiy	*RUS*	**65**	G11
Kuznechnoye	*RUS*	**65**	E10
Kvinesdal	*N*	**48**	F4
Kvinlog	*N*	**48**	F4
Kwidzyn	*PL*	**71**	C9
Kybartai	*LT*	**68**	F5
Kyjov	*CZ*	**75**	F7
Kyllini	*GR*	**88**	C3
Kymi	*GR*	**87**	H9
Kyritz	*D*	**43**	E8
Kysucké Nové Mesto	*SK*	**75**	E9
Kythira	*GR*	**88**	F6
Kyustendil	*BG*	**82**	G4

L

Place	Country	Page	Grid
Laage	*D*	**43**	C8
La Almunia de Doña Godina	*E*	**20**	F4
La Bañeza	*E*	**23**	D7
Lábatlan	*H*	**76**	B5
La Baule-Escoublac	*F*	**14**	G5
Labin	*HR*	**35**	D12
La Bisbal d'Empordà	*E*	**18**	G2
La Bresse	*F*	**13**	E9
La Broque	*F*	**13**	E9
Labruguière	*F*	**17**	H8
Laç	*AL*	**86**	B2
Lacanau-Océan	*F*	**16**	E3
Laćarak	*SRB*	**76**	G6
La Carlota	*E*	**28**	D4
La Carolina	*E*	**28**	B6
La Charité-sur-Loire	*F*	**12**	G3
La Châtre	*F*	**17**	B8
La Ciotat	*F*	**18**	E6
La Coruna	*E*	**22**	B3
La Côte-St-André	*F*	**36**	G2
La Couronne	*F*	**16**	D5
La Crau	*F*	**19**	E7
Ladispoli	*I*	**32**	C4
Lærdalsøyri	*N*	**50**	F4
La Fare-les-Oliviers	*F*	**18**	D5
La Ferté-Alais	*F*	**12**	E2
La Ferté-Bernard	*F*	**15**	E9
La Ferté-Gaucher	*F*	**12**	D4
La Ferté-Macé	*F*	**15**	D8
La Ferté-sous-Jouarre	*F*	**12**	D3
La Ferté-St-Aubin	*F*	**12**	F2
La Flèche	*F*	**15**	F8
La Garde	*F*	**19**	E7
Lage	*D*	**11**	D11
Lagkadas	*GR*	**87**	D7
Lagnieu	*F*	**36**	F3
Lagonegro	*I*	**31**	C7
Lagord-la-Rochelle	*F*	**16**	C3
Lagos	*P*	**25**	K3
La Grande-Combe	*F*	**17**	F11
Laguna de Duero	*E*	**23**	F9
Laholm	*S*	**45**	D7
Lahoysk	*BY*	**69**	G11
Lahr (Schwarzwald)	*D*	**13**	E10
Lahti	*FIN*	**64**	E6
L'Aigle	*F*	**15**	D9
Laihia	*FIN*	**53**	B10
Laitila	*FIN*	**53**	F10
Laives	*I*	**37**	E11
Lajosmizse	*H*	**76**	C6
Lakhdenpokh'ya	*RUS*	**65**	D11
Lakki	*GR*	**88**	E2
L'Alcora	*E*	**27**	E10
Lalín	*E*	**22**	C3
La Línea de la Concepción	*E*	**28**	G3
La Londe-les-Maures	*F*	**19**	E7
La Maddalena	*I*	**32**	C3
La Manga del Mar Menor	*E*	**29**	D11
La Massana	*AND*	**21**	D9
Lamballe	*F*	**14**	E5
Lambesc	*F*	**18**	D5
Lamborn	*S*	**52**	F3
Lamego	*P*	**22**	G4
Lamezia	*I*	**31**	F8
Lamia	*GR*	**86**	G6
La Mure	*F*	**18**	A6
Lana	*I*	**37**	D11
Lanaken	*B*	**11**	F7
Lanark	*GB*	**2**	H6
Lancaster	*GB*	**5**	E7
Lanciano	*I*	**33**	C8
Łańcut	*PL*	**73**	D3
Lancy	*CH*	**36**	E4
Landeck	*A*	**37**	C10
Landerneau	*F*	**14**	E2
Landivisiau	*F*	**14**	D3
Landsberg am Lech	*D*	**37**	B10
Landshut	*D*	**38**	B6
Landskrona	*S*	**45**	E7
Lanester	*F*	**14**	F4
Langedijk	*NL*	**10**	C6
Langen	*D*	**42**	C4
Langenlois	*A*	**39**	B11
Langesund	*N*	**49**	E7
Langevåg	*N*	**48**	C2
Langgöns	*D*	**11**	G11
Langoiran	*F*	**16**	E4
Langon	*F*	**16**	F4
Langreo	*E*	**23**	B7
Langres	*F*	**13**	F7
Langwedel	*D*	**11**	B12
Lannemezan	*F*	**21**	B7
Lannilis	*F*	**14**	D2
Lannion	*F*	**14**	D4
Lanškroun	*CZ*	**74**	D6
La Nucía	*E*	**27**	G10
Lanusei	*I*	**32**	F3
Laon	*F*	**12**	B4
Lapinjärvi	*FIN*	**65**	F7
La Pola de Gordón	*E*	**23**	C7
La Pommeraye	*F*	**15**	G7
Lapovo	*SRB*	**81**	D12
Lappeenranta	*FIN*	**65**	E9
Lappersdorf	*D*	**41**	F8
Lâpseki	*TR*	**85**	D2
Lapua	*FIN*	**53**	B11
La Puebla de Almoradiel	*E*	**26**	F5
La Puebla de Cazalla	*E*	**25**	K8
La Puebla de Montalbán	*E*	**26**	E3
Łapy	*PL*	**72**	E5
L'Aquila	*I*	**33**	C7
Laracha	*E*	**22**	B2
La Ravoire	*F*	**36**	G3
Larbert	*GB*	**2**	G6
Lärbro	*S*	**47**	F10
Laredo	*E*	**20**	B1
La Réole	*F*	**16**	F4
Largs	*GB*	**2**	H4
Lari	*I*	**34**	G6
La Riche	*F*	**15**	G9
La Rinconada	*E*	**25**	J7
Larino	*I*	**33**	D9
Larisa	*GR*	**86**	F6
Larkollen	*N*	**49**	D8
Larmor-Plage	*F*	**14**	F4
Larne	*GB*	**4**	D3
La Robla	*E*	**23**	C7
La Rochelle	*F*	**16**	C3
La Roche-sur-Yon	*F*	**16**	B2
La Roda	*E*	**27**	F7

Place	Country	Page	Grid
Larvik	N	**49**	E7
Las Cabezas de San Juan	E	**25**	K7
La Seyne-sur-Mer	F	**18**	E6
Laško	SLO	**39**	G10
La Solana	E	**26**	G5
La Souterraine	F	**17**	B7
La Spezia	I	**34**	F5
Las Rozas de Madrid	E	**23**	H10
Lastra a Signa	I	**35**	F7
La Suze-sur-Sarthe	F	**15**	F9
Laterza	I	**31**	B9
La Teste-de-Buch	F	**16**	F3
Latiano	I	**31**	B11
Latina	I	**32**	D6
Latisana	I	**35**	B10
La Tremblade	F	**16**	C3
La Trinité	F	**19**	D9
Latronico	I	**31**	C8
Lattes	F	**17**	H11
La Turballe	F	**14**	G5
Lauda-Königshofen	D	**40**	E4
Laudun	F	**17**	G12
Lauenburg (Elbe)	D	**42**	D6
Launceston	GB	**8**	F3
La Unión	E	**29**	D11
Laupheim	D	**37**	A9
Laureana di Borrello	I	**31**	G8
Lauria	I	**31**	C7
Lausanne	CH	**36**	E4
Lauta	D	**41**	A11
Lautersbach (Hessen)	D	**40**	C4
Lauvsnes	N	**54**	F3
Lavagna	I	**19**	C12
Lavagna	I	**34**	E4
Laval	F	**15**	E7
La Vall d'Uixó	E	**27**	E10
Lavaur	F	**17**	H8
Lavelanet	F	**21**	C9
Lavello	I	**31**	A7
Lavena Ponte Tresa	I	**34**	B3
Lavìs	I	**35**	B7
La Voulte-sur-Rhône	F	**18**	B4
Lavrio	GR	**89**	C8
Laxou	F	**13**	D8
Laza	RO	**79**	D8
Lazarevac	SRB	**81**	C11
Lazdijai	LT	**68**	G6
Lazuri	RO	**77**	B12
Leamington Spa, Royal	GB	**9**	C7
Leatherhead	GB	**9**	E9
Lebane	SRB	**82**	E3
Le Blanc	F	**16**	B6
Lębork	PL	**71**	B7
Lebrija	E	**25**	K7
Lebyazh'ye	RUS	**65**	G10
Leça do Bailio	P	**22**	F2
Le Cannet	F	**19**	D8
Lecce	I	**31**	C11
Lecco	I	**34**	B4
Lechința	RO	**78**	C3
Leck	D	**44**	G2
Le Conquet	F	**14**	E2
Le Coteau	F	**17**	C11
Le Creusot	F	**12**	H5
Łęczna	PL	**73**	B4
Łęczyca	PL	**71**	G9
Ledbury	GB	**8**	D6
Leeds	GB	**5**	F8
Leek	GB	**5**	G8
Leer (Ostfriesland)	D	**11**	B10
Leeuwarden	NL	**11**	B7
Lefkada	GR	**86**	G4
Leganés	E	**26**	D4
Legazpi	E	**20**	C2
Lège-Cap-Ferret	F	**16**	E3
Legionowo	PL	**71**	F11
Legnano	I	**34**	C4
Legnica	PL	**74**	B6
Le Gond-Pontouvre	F	**16**	D5
Le Grand-Lemps	F	**36**	G3
Le Grand-Quevilly	F	**15**	C10
Le Grau-du-Roi	F	**17**	H11
Le Havre	F	**15**	B9
Lehliu-Gară	RO	**83**	B11
Lehre	D	**42**	F6
Lehrte	D	**42**	F5
Leibnitz	A	**39**	E11
Leicester	GB	**9**	B8
Leiden	NL	**10**	D5
Leighton Buzzard	GB	**9**	D8
Leikanger	N	**50**	D2
Leikanger	N	**50**	F3
Leioa	E	**20**	B1
Leipzig	D	**41**	A8
Leiria	P	**24**	C2
Leirvåg	N	**50**	G1
Leirvik	N	**48**	C2
Leiston	GB	**9**	C11
Leixlip	IRL	**4**	G2
Leksand	S	**52**	F3
Le Lavandou	F	**19**	E7
Le Lignon	CH	**36**	E4
Le Locle	CH	**13**	G9
Lelystad	NL	**11**	C7
Le Mans	F	**15**	E9
Lemgo	D	**11**	D12
Lemmer	NL	**11**	B7
Lempäälä	FIN	**53**	E12
Lempdes	F	**17**	C10
Le Muy	F	**19**	D7
Lemvig	DK	**44**	D2
Lenart	SLO	**39**	F11
Lenauheim	RO	**77**	F9
Lendava	SLO	**76**	D1
Lendinara	I	**35**	D8
Lenggries	D	**37**	B11
Lenti	H	**76**	D1
Lentini	I	**30**	F6
Lentvaris	LT	**69**	F8
Leoben	A	**39**	D10
Léognan	F	**16**	E4
Leominster	GB	**8**	C5
León	E	**23**	D7
Leonberg	D	**13**	D12
Leonding	A	**39**	B9
Leonforte	I	**30**	F5
Leova	MD	**79**	E9
Le Palais-sur-Vienne	F	**17**	C7
Le Passage	F	**16**	G5
Lepe	E	**25**	K5
Le Petit-Quevilly	F	**15**	C10
Le Pian-Médoc	F	**16**	E3
Le Poinçonnet	F	**15**	H11
Le Poiré-sur-Vie	F	**16**	A2
Le Pont-de-Beauvoisin	F	**36**	G3
Le Pontet	F	**18**	C5
Leporano	I	**31**	C10
Le Puy-en-Velay	F	**17**	E11
Lequile	I	**31**	C11
Lercara Friddi	I	**30**	E3
Lerești	RO	**78**	G4
Lerici	I	**34**	F5
Lerida	E	**21**	E7
Lerum	S	**44**	A6
Lerwick	GB	**3**	C12
Les Arcs	F	**19**	D7
Les Borges Blanques	E	**21**	F8
Lescar	F	**20**	B6
Les Escaldes	AND	**21**	D9
Le Seu d'Urgell	E	**21**	D9
Les Herbiers	F	**15**	H7
Lesina	I	**33**	D10
Lesko	PL	**73**	E4
Leskovac	SRB	**82**	E3
Lesparre-Médoc	F	**16**	D3
Les Pavillons sous Bois	F	**12**	D2
Les Pennes-Mirabeau	F	**18**	D5
Les Ponts-de-Cé	F	**15**	G8
Les Sables-d'Olonne	F	**16**	B2
Leszno	PL	**70**	G6
Létavértes	H	**77**	C10
Lețcani	RO	**79**	C8
Le Teil	F	**17**	F12
Le Thillot	F	**13**	F9
Le Thor	F	**18**	C5
Le Touquet-Paris-Plage	F	**9**	G11
Letovice	CZ	**74**	E6
Le Tréport	F	**9**	H11
Letterkenny	IRL	**6**	E5
Leu	RO	**82**	C6
Leuze-en-Hainaut	B	**10**	G4
Levang	N	**54**	B5
Levanger	N	**54**	G4
Levanto	I	**34**	F5
Leven	GB	**3**	G7
Leverano	I	**31**	C11
Le-Verdon-sur-Mer	F	**16**	D3
Leverkusen	D	**11**	F9
Levice	SK	**75**	H9
Levico Terme	I	**35**	B8
Le Vigan	F	**17**	G10
Levoča	SK	**73**	F1
Levski	BG	**83**	D8
Lewes	GB	**9**	F9
Lewin Brzeski	PL	**75**	C8
Leyland	GB	**5**	F7
Leżajsk	PL	**73**	D4
Lezhë	AL	**86**	B2
Lézignan-Corbières	F	**18**	E1
L'Hospitalet de Llobregat	E	**21**	F10
Liberec	CZ	**41**	C12
Libourne	F	**16**	E4
Librazhd	AL	**86**	C3
Licata	I	**30**	G4
Lichfield	GB	**9**	B7
Lichtenfels	D	**40**	D6
Lida	BY	**69**	H8
Lidingö	S	**47**	C9
Lidköping	S	**46**	E4
Lidzbark	PL	**71**	D10
Lidzbark Warmiński	PL	**68**	G2
Liège	B	**11**	G7
Lieksa	FIN	**63**	G11
Lielvārde	LV	**66**	H6
Lienz	A	**39**	E7
Liepāja	LV	**68**	B3
Lier	B	**10**	F5
Liestal	CH	**13**	G10
Liești	RO	**79**	F8
Liezen	A	**39**	D9

Place	Country	Page	Grid
Lifford	IRL	6	E5
Liffré	F	14	E6
Lignano Sabbiadoro	I	35	C11
Ligny-en-Barrois	F	13	D7
Lilienthal	D	11	B12
Lilla Edet	S	46	E3
Lille	F	10	G3
Lillehammer	N	51	F7
Lillestrøm	N	46	B1
Lille Værløse	DK	44	E7
Lillhamra	S	51	E12
Lillholmsjö	S	55	G7
Limanowa	PL	73	E1
Limavady	GB	4	C2
Limay	F	12	C1
Limbaži	LV	66	F6
Limerick	IRL	7	L4
Limoges	F	17	C7
Limoux	F	21	C10
Linares	E	28	C6
Linaria	GR	87	G10
Lincoln	GB	5	G10
Lindau (Bodensee)	D	37	C9
Lindesberg	S	46	C6
Lindome	S	44	B6
Lindos	GR	88	G4
Lindsdal	S	45	C12
Lingen (Ems)	D	11	C9
Linguaglossa	I	30	E6
Linköping	S	46	E7
Linnich	D	11	F8
Linz	A	39	B9
Lioboml'	UA	73	B6
Lioni	I	30	B6
Lipany	SK	73	F2
Lipari	I	30	D6
Lipcani	MD	79	A7
Liphook	GB	9	F8
Lipjan	RKS	81	G12
Lipno	PL	71	E9
Lipova	RO	77	E10
Lipsko	PL	73	B3
Liptovský Mikuláš	SK	75	F11
Lisboa	P	24	F2
Lisburn	GB	4	D3
Lisieux	F	15	C9
Liskeard	GB	8	G3
L'Isle-Jourdain	F	16	H6
L'Isle-sur-la-Sorgue	F	18	C5
Liss	GB	9	F8
Liteni	RO	78	B7
Litija	SLO	39	G10
Litochoro	GR	87	E7
Litoměřice	CZ	41	C11
Litomyšl	CZ	74	D6
Litovel	CZ	75	E7
Littlehampton	GB	9	F8
Littleport	GB	9	C10
Littoinen	FIN	53	G11
Litvínov	CZ	41	C10
Livadeia	GR	88	B6
Līvāni	LV	69	C9
Liverpool	GB	5	G7
Livingston	GB	2	G6
Livorno	I	34	G6
Lizard	GB	8	H2
Lizzanello	I	31	C11
Lizzano	I	31	C10
Ljubljana	SLO	39	G9
Ljugarn	S	47	G10
Ljungby	S	45	C9
Ljungsbro	S	46	E6
Ljusdal	S	52	D4
Ljutomer	SLO	39	F11
Llagostera	E	21	E11
Llandrindod Wells	GB	8	C4
Llandudno	GB	4	G5
Llanelli	GB	8	D3
Llanes	E	23	B9
Llannon	GB	8	D3
Llantwit Major	GB	8	E4
Lleida	E	21	E7
Llerena	E	24	G7
Lliria	E	27	E10
Llodio	E	20	B1
Lloret de Mar	E	21	E11
Llucmajor	E	29	F9
Loano	I	19	C10
Löbau	D	41	B11
Łobez	PL	70	C4
Locarno	CH	34	B3
Lochaline	GB	2	F3
Lochboisdale	GB	2	E1
Lochem	NL	11	D8
Loches	F	15	G10
Loch Garman	IRL	7	L6
Lochgilphead	GB	2	G4
Lochmaddy	GB	2	D1
Łochów	PL	72	F3
Locri	I	31	G8
Löddeköpinge	S	45	E7
Lodève	F	17	G10
Łódź	PL	71	G9
Loftahammar	S	47	F8
Logatec	SLO	35	B12
Logroño	E	20	D2
Lohals	DK	44	F5
Lohja	FIN	64	G5
Lohne (Oldenburg)	D	11	C11
Loimaa	FIN	53	F11
Loja	E	28	E5
Lom	BG	82	C5
Lom	N	50	E5
Łomianki	PL	71	F11
Lomma	S	45	E7
Lomonosov	RUS	65	G10
Łomża	PL	72	D4
Lonato	I	34	C6
London	GB	9	E9
Londonderry	GB	4	D1
Long Eaton	GB	5	H9
Longford	IRL	7	H5
Longobucco	I	31	E9
Longueau	F	12	B2
Longué-Jumelles	F	15	G8
Longuenesse	F	10	G2
Longuyon	F	13	C7
Longwy	F	13	B7
Lonigo	I	35	C8
Löningen	D	11	C10
Lons-le-Saunier	F	36	D3
Lopătari	RO	79	G7
Lora del Río	E	25	J8
Lorca	E	29	D9
Loreto	I	35	G11
Lorient	F	14	F4
Lőrinci	H	77	B7
Loriol-sur-Drôme	F	18	B5
Los	S	52	D3
Los Barrios	E	25	M8
Los Corrales de Buelna	E	23	B10
Łosice	PL	72	F5
Los Palacios y Villafranca	E	25	K7
Los Santos de Maimona	E	24	G6
Lossiemouth	GB	2	D6
Lößnitz	D	41	C9
Los Yébenes	E	26	F4
Loudéac	F	14	E5
Loudun	F	15	G9
Loughborough	GB	5	H9
Loughton	GB	9	D9
Louhans	F	36	D2
Loulé	P	25	K4
Louny	CZ	41	C10
Lourdes	F	20	C6
Louth	GB	5	G10
Loutraki	GR	88	C6
Loutra Smokovou	GR	86	G6
Louviers	F	15	C10
Lovech	BG	83	E7
Loviisa	FIN	65	F7
Lovraeid	N	48	D3
Lovrin	RO	77	F8
Lowestoft	GB	9	C12
Łowicz	PL	71	F10
Loxstedt	D	11	A11
Loznica	SRB	81	C9
Lozovik	SRB	81	C12
Luanco	E	23	A7
Luarca	E	22	B6
Lubaczów	PL	73	D5
Lubań	PL	41	B12
Lubartów	PL	72	H5
Lubawa	PL	71	D10
Lübbecke	D	11	C11
Lübben	D	43	G10
Lübeck	D	42	C6
Lubin	PL	70	H5
Lublin	PL	73	B4
Lubliniec	PL	75	C9
Luboń	PL	70	F6
Lubsko	PL	43	G12
Lübz	D	43	D8
Lucan	IRL	4	G2
Lucca	I	34	F6
Lucé	F	12	E1
Lucena	E	28	D5
Lučenec	SK	75	G11
Lucera	I	33	D10
Lüchow	D	43	E7
Lucieni	RO	78	H5
Lucija	SLO	35	C11
Luckau	D	43	G10
Luckenwalde	D	43	F9
Luco dei Marsi	I	33	C7
Luçon	F	16	B3
Luc-sur-Mer	F	15	C8
Ludlow	GB	8	C5
Luduș	RO	78	E2
Ludvika	S	46	A6
Ludwigsburg	D	40	F4
Ludwigslust	D	43	D7
Ludza	LV	69	B11
Luga	RUS	67	D12
Lugano	CH	34	B4
Lugo	I	35	E9
Lugo	E	22	C4
Lugoj	RO	77	F10
Luik	B	11	G7
Luimneach	IRL	7	L4

Place	Country	Page	Grid
Luino	*I*	**34**	B3
Luizi Călugăra	*RO*	**79**	D7
Lukavac	*BIH*	**81**	C8
Lukovit	*BG*	**83**	E7
Łuków	*PL*	**72**	G4
Luleå	*S*	**56**	C4
Lüleburgaz	*TR*	**85**	B3
Lumbres	*F*	**9**	F12
Lumezzane	*I*	**34**	C6
Lumina	*RO*	**84**	C4
Lumparland	*FIN*	**47**	A12
Lunca	*RO*	**79**	B7
Lunca	*RO*	**83**	C8
Lunca de Jos	*RO*	**78**	D6
Luncavița	*RO*	**79**	G9
Lund	*S*	**45**	E8
Lüneburg	*D*	**42**	D6
Lunel	*F*	**17**	H11
Lunéville	*F*	**13**	D8
Lunguleţu	*RO*	**83**	B9
L'Union	*F*	**17**	H7
Lupeni	*RO*	**77**	G12
Lure	*F*	**13**	F8
Lurgan	*GB*	**4**	E2
Lu-Ruchheim	*D*	**13**	C11
Lusciano	*I*	**30**	B5
Lushnjë	*AL*	**86**	C2
Lustenau	*A*	**37**	C9
Lutherstadt Wittenberg	*D*	**43**	G9
Lütjenburg	*D*	**42**	B6
Luton	*GB*	**9**	D9
Luxembourg	*L*	**13**	B8
Luxeuil-les-Bains	*F*	**13**	F8
Luzern	*CH*	**13**	G11
Luzzi	*I*	**31**	E8
L'viv	*UA*	**73**	E6
Lwówek Śląski	*PL*	**74**	B5
Lyaskovets	*BG*	**83**	E9
Lycksele	*S*	**55**	E11
Lydney	*GB*	**8**	D6
Lymans'ke	*UA*	**79**	D12
Lymington	*GB*	**9**	F7
Lyneham	*GB*	**8**	E6
Lyon	*F*	**36**	F2
Lysekil	*S*	**46**	E2
Lyss	*CH*	**13**	G9
Lytham St Anne's	*GB*	**4**	F6
Lyubashivka	*UA*	**79**	B12
Lyubimets	*BG*	**83**	G10

M

Place	Country	Page	Grid
Maardu	*EST*	**66**	B6
Maaseik	*B*	**11**	F7
Maastricht	*NL*	**11**	F7
Mablethorpe	*GB*	**5**	G11
Macclesfield	*GB*	**5**	G8
Macea	*RO*	**77**	E9
Macerata	*I*	**35**	G11
Machecoul	*F*	**14**	H6
Măcin	*RO*	**79**	G9
Macomer	*I*	**32**	E2
Mâcon	*F*	**17**	B12
Madan	*BG*	**87**	B11
Maddaloni	*I*	**30**	A5
Made	*NL*	**10**	E6
Madona	*LV*	**67**	G7
Madrid	*E*	**23**	H10
Madridejos	*E*	**26**	F5
Mæl	*N*	**48**	C6
Mafra	*P*	**24**	E1
Magdeburg	*D*	**43**	F7
Magherafelt	*GB*	**4**	D2
Magione	*I*	**35**	G9
Maglaj	*BIH*	**81**	C7
Maglavit	*RO*	**82**	C5
Maglie	*I*	**31**	C11
Maglód	*H*	**76**	C6
Magura	*SRB*	**81**	G12
Măgurele	*RO*	**83**	B10
Mahmudia	*RO*	**79**	G11
Mahón	*E*	**29**	E12
Maia	*P*	**22**	F2
Măicănești	*RO*	**79**	G8
Maidenhead	*GB*	**9**	E8
Maidstone	*GB*	**9**	E10
Maieru	*RO*	**78**	C4
Mainburg	*D*	**38**	B5
Maintenon	*F*	**12**	D1
Mainz	*D*	**13**	A11
Maiolati Spontini	*I*	**35**	G11
Majadahonda	*E*	**23**	H10
Majdanpek	*SRB*	**82**	B3
Makarska	*HR*	**80**	E5
Makó	*H*	**77**	E8
Maków Mazowiecki	*PL*	**71**	E11
Maków Podhalański	*PL*	**75**	E11
Mala	*IRL*	**7**	M4
Malacky	*SK*	**75**	G7
Maladzyechna	*BY*	**69**	G10
Málaga	*E*	**28**	E5
Malagón	*E*	**26**	F4
Malahide	*IRL*	**4**	G3
Malalbergo	*I*	**35**	D8
Malaryta	*BY*	**72**	G6
Malbork	*PL*	**71**	C9
Malchin	*D*	**43**	C9
Malchow	*D*	**43**	D8
Măldăeni	*RO*	**83**	C8
Maldon	*GB*	**9**	D10
Malemort-sur-Corrèze	*F*	**17**	E7
Malente	*D*	**42**	B6
Malesherbes	*F*	**12**	E2
Mali Iđoš	*SRB*	**77**	F7
Mali Lošinj	*HR*	**80**	C1
Malines	*B*	**10**	F5
Malkara	*TR*	**85**	C3
Mallaig	*GB*	**2**	E3
Mallorca	*E*	**29**	F9
Mallow	*IRL*	**7**	M4
Malmberget	*S*	**60**	D3
Malmesbury	*GB*	**8**	E6
Malmö	*S*	**45**	F7
Malmslätt	*S*	**46**	E6
Malnaș	*RO*	**78**	E5
Måløy	*N*	**50**	D2
Malpica	*E*	**22**	B2
Malton	*GB*	**5**	E9
Malu Mare	*RO*	**82**	C6
Malung	*S*	**49**	A11
Mamers	*F*	**15**	E9
Mamonovo	*RUS*	**68**	F1
Mamuras	*AL*	**86**	B2
Manacor	*E*	**29**	F10
Mănăstirea	*RO*	**83**	C11
Mănăstirea Cașin	*RO*	**79**	E7
Mancha Real	*E*	**28**	C6
Manchester	*GB*	**5**	G7
Manciano	*I*	**32**	B4
Mandal	*N*	**48**	G4
Mandelieu-la-Napoule	*F*	**19**	D8
Mandello del Lario	*I*	**34**	B4
Mandra	*GR*	**89**	B7
Manduria	*I*	**31**	C10
Măneciu	*RO*	**78**	G6
Manerbio	*I*	**34**	C6
Mănești	*RO*	**78**	H5
Manfredonia	*I*	**33**	D11
Mangalia	*RO*	**84**	C4
Mangualde	*P*	**22**	G4
Maniago	*I*	**35**	B10
Manisa	*TR*	**85**	G3
Manlleu	*E*	**21**	E10
Mannheim	*D*	**13**	C11
Manningtree	*GB*	**9**	D11
Manno	*CH*	**34**	B4
Manoppello	*I*	**33**	C8
Manosque	*F*	**18**	D6
Manresa	*E*	**21**	E9
Mansfield	*GB*	**5**	G9
Mantes-la-Ville	*F*	**12**	D1
Mantova	*I*	**35**	D7
Mäntsälä	*FIN*	**64**	F6
Mänttä	*FIN*	**64**	C5
Mäntyluoto	*FIN*	**53**	E10
Manyas	*TR*	**85**	D4
Manzanares	*E*	**26**	G5
Manziana	*I*	**32**	C5
Maracena	*E*	**28**	D6
Mărăcineni	*RO*	**79**	G7
Maranello	*I*	**35**	E7
Marano di Napoli	*I*	**30**	B5
Mărășești	*RO*	**79**	F8
Maratea	*I*	**31**	D7
Marbella	*E*	**28**	F4
Marburg an der Lahn	*D*	**11**	G11
Marby	*S*	**51**	B12
Marcali	*H*	**76**	D3
March	*GB*	**9**	C9
Marche-en-Famenne	*B*	**11**	H7
Marchena	*E*	**25**	J8
Marchtrenk	*A*	**39**	C9
Marcianise	*I*	**30**	A5
Marciano della Chiana	*I*	**35**	G8
Marennes	*F*	**16**	C3
Margate	*GB*	**9**	E11
Margherita di Savoia	*I*	**33**	E11
Marghita	*RO*	**77**	C11
Marginea	*RO*	**78**	B5
Mărgineni	*RO*	**79**	D7
Mariánské Lázně	*CZ*	**41**	D8
Maribo	*DK*	**44**	G5
Maribor	*SLO*	**39**	F11
Mariehamn	*FIN*	**47**	A11
Marienberg	*D*	**41**	C9
Mariestad	*S*	**46**	D5
Marigliano	*I*	**30**	B5
Marignane	*F*	**18**	D5
Marijampolė	*LT*	**68**	F6
Marín	*E*	**22**	D2
Marina di Gioiosa Ionica	*I*	**31**	G8
Marineo	*I*	**30**	E3
Marinha Grande	*P*	**24**	C2
Marino	*I*	**32**	D5
Markdorf	*D*	**37**	B8
Market Deeping	*GB*	**9**	B9
Market Drayton	*GB*	**5**	H7
Market Harborough	*GB*	**9**	C8
Marki	*PL*	**71**	F11

Place	Country	Page	Grid
Markkleeberg	*D*	**41**	B8
Markopoulo	*GR*	**89**	C7
Marktoberdorf	*D*	**37**	B10
Marktredwitz	*D*	**41**	D8
Marl	*D*	**11**	E9
Marlborough	*GB*	**9**	E7
Marly	*CH*	**13**	H9
Marmande	*F*	**16**	F5
Marmaraereğlisi	*TR*	**85**	C4
Marmari	*GR*	**89**	B8
Marmolejo	*E*	**28**	C5
Marne	*D*	**42**	C4
Marne-la-Vallée	*F*	**12**	D3
Maromme	*F*	**15**	C10
Marousi	*GR*	**89**	B7
Marquise	*F*	**9**	F12
Marsala	*I*	**30**	E1
Mârşani	*RO*	**82**	C6
Marsberg	*D*	**11**	E12
Marsciano	*I*	**32**	A5
Marseillan	*F*	**18**	E2
Marseille	*F*	**18**	E5
Marsillargues	*F*	**17**	H11
Märsta	*S*	**47**	B9
Marstrand	*S*	**46**	F2
Martano	*I*	**31**	C12
Martfű	*H*	**77**	C8
Martigny	*CH*	**34**	B1
Martil	*MA*	**28**	H3
Martin	*SK*	**75**	F10
Martina Franca	*I*	**31**	B10
Martinsicuro	*I*	**33**	B8
Martorell	*E*	**21**	F10
Martos	*E*	**28**	C6
Maruggio	*I*	**31**	C10
Marvejols	*F*	**17**	F10
Maryport	*GB*	**4**	D6
Marzabotto	*I*	**35**	E7
Mascali	*I*	**30**	E6
Mascalucia	*I*	**30**	F6
Massa	*I*	**34**	F6
Massafra	*I*	**31**	B10
Massa Lombarda	*I*	**35**	E8
Massamagrell	*E*	**27**	F10
Massa Marittimo	*I*	**32**	A2
Massarosa	*I*	**34**	F6
Măstăcani	*RO*	**79**	F9
Matala	*GR*	**89**	G9
Mataró	*E*	**21**	F10
Mătăsari	*RO*	**82**	A5
Matca	*RO*	**79**	F8
Matelica	*I*	**35**	G10
Matera	*I*	**31**	B9
Mátészalka	*H*	**77**	B11
Matino	*I*	**31**	C11
Matlock	*GB*	**5**	G8
Mattersburg	*A*	**39**	C12
Mattinata	*I*	**33**	D11
Maubeuge	*F*	**10**	H5
Mauguio	*F*	**17**	H11
Mauléon	*F*	**15**	H7
Mauléon-Licharre	*F*	**20**	B5
Maurset	*N*	**48**	B4
Mavrodin	*RO*	**83**	C8
Mayen	*D*	**11**	G9
Mayenne	*F*	**15**	E8
Mazamet	*F*	**21**	B10
Mazara del Vallo	*I*	**30**	F2
Mazarrón	*E*	**29**	D10
Mažeikiai	*LT*	**68**	C4
Mazzarino	*I*	**30**	F4
Meadela	*P*	**22**	E2
Meaux	*F*	**12**	D3
Mechelen	*B*	**10**	F5
Medemblik	*NL*	**10**	C6
Medgidia	*RO*	**84**	C4
Mediaş	*RO*	**78**	E3
Medicina	*I*	**35**	E8
Medieşu Aurit	*RO*	**77**	B12
Medina del Campo	*E*	**23**	F8
Medina de Pomar	*E*	**23**	C11
Medina-Sidonia	*E*	**25**	M7
Medzilaborce	*SK*	**73**	F3
Megara	*GR*	**88**	B6
Mehadia	*RO*	**77**	H11
Meilen	*CH*	**13**	G11
Meinerzhagen	*D*	**11**	F10
Meiningen	*D*	**40**	C5
Meißen	*D*	**41**	B10
Mejorada del Campo	*E*	**23**	H11
Meldola	*I*	**35**	F9
Meldorf	*D*	**42**	B4
Melenci	*SRB*	**77**	F8
Melendugno	*I*	**31**	C12
Melfi	*I*	**31**	B7
Melicucco	*I*	**31**	G8
Melide	*E*	**22**	C3
Melilli	*I*	**30**	G6
Melissano	*I*	**31**	D11
Melito di Porto Salvo	*I*	**31**	H7
Melk	*A*	**39**	B10
Melksham	*GB*	**8**	E6
Melle	*F*	**16**	B4
Mellrichstadt	*D*	**40**	C5
Mělník	*CZ*	**41**	C11
Mels	*CH*	**37**	D8
Melton Mowbray	*GB*	**5**	H9
Melun	*F*	**12**	D3
Mélykút	*H*	**76**	E6
Memaliaj	*AL*	**86**	D2
Memmingen	*D*	**37**	B9
Mende	*F*	**17**	F10
Menemen	*TR*	**85**	G3
Menfi	*I*	**30**	F2
Mengeš	*SLO*	**39**	G9
Mengíbar	*E*	**28**	C6
Mennecy	*F*	**12**	D2
Mentana	*I*	**32**	C5
Menton	*F*	**19**	D9
Meppel	*NL*	**11**	C8
Meppen	*D*	**11**	C9
Mer	*F*	**12**	F1
Merag	*HR*	**80**	B1
Merano	*I*	**37**	D11
Mercato San Severino	*I*	**30**	B6
Mercato Saraceno	*I*	**35**	F9
Mercogliano	*I*	**30**	B6
Merei	*RO*	**79**	G7
Meriç	*TR*	**85**	B2
Merichas	*GR*	**89**	D8
Mérida	*E*	**24**	E6
Merseburg (Saale)	*D*	**41**	A7
Merthyr Tydfil	*GB*	**8**	D4
Méru	*F*	**12**	C2
Merzig	*D*	**13**	C8
Mesagne	*I*	**31**	B11
Mesimeri	*GR*	**87**	D7
Mesola	*I*	**35**	D9
Mesolongi	*GR*	**88**	B3
Mesoraca	*I*	**31**	E9
Messina	*I*	**31**	E7
Messini	*GR*	**88**	D4
Meta	*I*	**30**	B5
Metallostroy	*RUS*	**65**	H11
Metković	*HR*	**80**	F6
Metlika	*SLO*	**39**	H10
Metz	*F*	**13**	C8
Meximieux	*F*	**36**	F2
Meylan	*F*	**18**	A6
Mezdra	*BG*	**82**	E6
Mèze	*F*	**18**	D3
Mezőberény	*H*	**77**	D9
Mezőcsát	*H*	**77**	B9
Mezőhegyes	*H*	**77**	E9
Mezőkeresztes	*H*	**77**	B8
Mezőkovácsháza	*H*	**77**	E9
Mezőkövesd	*H*	**77**	B8
Mezőtúr	*H*	**77**	D8
Mezzolombardo	*I*	**35**	A7
Miajadas	*E*	**24**	E7
Miastko	*PL*	**70**	C6
Michalovce	*SK*	**73**	G3
Middelburg	*NL*	**10**	E4
Middelfart	*DK*	**44**	F3
Middelharnis	*NL*	**10**	E5
Middlesbrough	*GB*	**5**	D9
Middleton	*GB*	**5**	F7
Middlewich	*GB*	**5**	G7
Midhurst	*GB*	**9**	F8
Midleton	*IRL*	**7**	M4
Miðvágur	*FO*	**3**	B8
Miechów	*PL*	**75**	C11
Międzychód	*PL*	**70**	E5
Międzyrzec Podlaski	*PL*	**72**	G5
Międzyrzecz	*PL*	**70**	F4
Międzyzdroje	*PL*	**43**	C11
Mielec	*PL*	**73**	D2
Miercurea-Ciuc	*RO*	**78**	E5
Mieres	*E*	**23**	B7
Miesbach	*D*	**37**	B12
Migennes	*F*	**12**	F4
Migné-Auxances	*F*	**16**	B5
Miguelturra	*E*	**26**	G4
Mihăeşti	*RO*	**78**	G3
Mihăeşti	*RO*	**78**	G4
Mihăileşti	*RO*	**83**	B10
Mihail Kogălniceanu	*RO*	**84**	B4
Mihai Viteazu	*RO*	**78**	D2
Mijas	*E*	**28**	F4
Mikkeli	*FIN*	**65**	D8
Milan	*I*	**34**	C4
Milano	*I*	**34**	C4
Milas	*TR*	**88**	E3
Milazzo	*I*	**30**	D6
Milcovul	*RO*	**79**	F8
Mildenhall	*GB*	**9**	C10
Mileto	*I*	**31**	F8
Mílevsko	*CZ*	**41**	E11
Milford Haven	*GB*	**8**	D2
Milicz	*PL*	**70**	H6
Militello in Val di Catania	*I*	**30**	F5
Millau	*F*	**17**	G10
Millom	*GB*	**4**	E6
Milly-la-Forêt	*F*	**12**	E2
Milna	*HR*	**80**	E4
Milton Keynes	*GB*	**9**	D8
Mimizan	*F*	**16**	F2
Mimoň	*CZ*	**41**	C11
Minas de Riotinto	*E*	**25**	H6
Mindelheim	*D*	**37**	B10

Name	Country	Page	Grid
Minden	D	11	D12
Mindszent	H	77	D7
Minehead	GB	8	E4
Mineo	I	30	F5
Minervino Murge	I	31	A8
Minsk	BY	69	H11
Minturno	I	30	A4
Mira	I	35	C9
Mirabella Eclano	I	30	A6
Mirabella Imbaccari	I	30	F5
Miramas	F	18	D5
Miramont-de-Guyenne	F	16	F5
Miranda de Ebro	E	20	C1
Mirandela	P	22	F5
Mirandola	I	35	D7
Mircea Vodă	RO	84	C4
Mirceşti	RO	79	C7
Mirecourt	F	13	E8
Mireşu Mare	RO	77	C12
Miroslovești	RO	79	C7
Misano Adriatico	I	35	F10
Misilmeri	I	30	E3
Miskolc	H	73	H1
Mistelbach	A	39	B12
Misterbianco	I	30	F6
Mistretta	I	30	E5
Mitreni	RO	83	C11
Mitrovicë	RKS	81	F12
Mittersill	A	38	D6
Mittweida	D	41	B9
Mizhhir"ya	UA	73	G5
Mizil	RO	78	G6
Miziya	BG	82	D6
Mjölby	S	46	E6
Mjøndalen	N	49	C7
Mladá Boleslav	CZ	41	C12
Mladenovac	SRB	81	C11
Mława	PL	71	D10
Mnichovo Hradiště	CZ	41	C12
Moaña	E	22	D2
Moara Vlăsiei	RO	83	B10
Modena	I	35	E7
Modica	I	30	G5
Modra	SK	75	G7
Modriča	BIH	76	H4
Modugno	I	31	A9
Moers	D	11	E8
Mogilno	PL	71	E7
Moguer	E	25	K6
Mohács	H	76	F5
Mohelnice	CZ	75	E7
Moieciu	RO	78	G5
Moineşti	RO	78	E6
Mo i Rana	N	55	B7
Moirans	F	36	G3
Moisei	RO	78	B3
Moissac	F	16	G6
Mojkovac	MNE	81	F9
Mokrin	SRB	77	F8
Mol	SRB	77	F7
Mola di Bari	I	31	A9
Moldava nad Bodvou	SK	73	G2
Molde	N	50	C4
Moldova Nouă	RO	82	B2
Moldoviţa	RO	78	B5
Molėtai	LT	69	E8
Molfetta	I	31	A9
Molina de Segura	E	29	C10
Moliterno	I	31	C7
Mölle	S	44	D7
Mollerussa	E	21	E8
Mölln	D	42	C6
Mölndal	S	46	F3
Mölnlycke	S	44	A6
Molpe	FIN	53	B10
Momchilgrad	BG	87	B11
Monaghan	IRL	4	E2
Moncada	E	27	F10
Moncalieri	I	19	A9
Monchaltorf	CH	37	C7
Mondolfo	I	35	F10
Mondoñedo	E	22	B4
Mondovì	I	19	C10
Mondragone	I	30	A4
Monemvasia	GR	88	E6
Monesterio	E	25	H7
Monfalcone	I	35	B11
Monforte de Lemos	E	22	D4
Monifieth	GB	3	F7
Mońki	PL	72	D5
Monmouth	GB	8	D5
Monolithos	GR	88	G3
Monopoli	I	31	B10
Monor	H	76	C6
Monóvar	E	27	H9
Monreale	I	30	E3
Mons	B	10	G5
Monselice	I	35	C8
Monster	NL	10	D5
Monsummano Terme	I	35	F7
Montalbano Jonico	I	31	C9
Montalcino	I	32	A3
Montale	I	35	F7
Montalto di Castro	I	32	C4
Montalto Uffugo	I	31	E8
Montana	BG	82	D5
Montargis	F	12	F3
Montataire	F	12	C2
Montauban	F	17	G7
Montauroux	F	19	D8
Montbard	F	12	F5
Montbéliard	F	13	F9
Montbrison	F	17	D11
Montceau-les-Mines	F	17	B12
Montchanin	F	12	H5
Mont-de-Marsan	F	16	G4
Montdidier	F	12	B3
Montebello Ionico	I	31	H7
Monte-Carlo	MC	19	D9
Montechiarugolo	I	34	E6
Montefalco	I	32	B5
Montefiascone	I	32	B4
Montefrío	E	28	D5
Montegiorgio	I	35	H11
Montegranaro	I	35	G11
Montehermoso	E	24	C6
Monteiasi	I	31	C10
Montelepre	I	30	E3
Montelibretti	I	32	C6
Montélimar	F	18	B4
Montella	I	30	B6
Montellano	E	25	K8
Montelupo Fiorentino	I	35	F7
Montemor-o-Novo	P	24	F3
Montepulciano	I	32	A4
Monteriggioni	I	35	G7
Monteroni d'Arbia	I	35	G8
Monteroni di Lecce	I	31	C11
Monterotondo	I	32	C5
Monte San Giovanni Campano	I	33	D7
Montesano sulla Marcellana	I	31	C7
Monte San Savino	I	35	G8
Monte Sant'Angelo	I	33	D11
Montesarchio	I	30	A5
Montescaglioso	I	31	B9
Montesilvano	I	33	B8
Montespertoli	I	35	G7
Montevarchi	I	35	G8
Monthey	CH	36	E5
Montignoso	I	34	F6
Montijo	E	24	E6
Montilla	E	28	D4
Montivilliers	F	15	B9
Montluçon	F	17	B9
Montmélian	F	36	G4
Montmorillon	F	16	B6
Montorio al Vomano	I	33	B7
Montoro	E	28	C5
Montpellier	F	17	H11
Montpon-Ménestérol	F	16	E5
Montreuil-Juigné	F	15	F8
Montreux	CH	36	E5
Montrichard	F	15	G10
Montrond-les-Bains	F	17	D12
Montrose	GB	3	F7
Monts	F	15	G9
Mont-St-Aignan	F	15	C10
Monza	I	34	C4
Monzón	E	21	E7
Moorbad Lobenstein	D	41	C7
Moordorf (Südbrookmerland)	D	11	A9
Mór	H	76	C4
Mora	E	26	E4
Mora	S	51	F12
Morąg	PL	68	G1
Mórahalom	H	77	E7
Moraleja	E	24	C6
Morano Calabro	I	31	D8
Moratalla	E	29	B9
Moravská Třebová	CZ	74	E6
Moravské Budějovice	CZ	74	F5
Morbach	D	13	B9
Morbegno	I	34	B5
Morciano di Romagna	I	35	F10
Morcone	I	33	E9
Morecambe	GB	5	E7
Moreni	RO	78	H5
Morestel	F	36	F3
Morez	F	36	E4
Morges	CH	36	E4
Morlaix	F	14	D3
Moroeni	RO	78	G5
Morón de la Frontera	E	25	K8
Morpeth	GB	5	C8
Morshyn	UA	73	F6
Mortagne-au-Perche	F	15	D9
Mortagne-sur-Sèvre	F	15	G7
Morteau	F	13	G8
Mosbach	D	13	C12
Moscavide	P	24	F2
Mosina	PL	70	F6
Mosjøen	N	54	C6
Mosonmagyaróvár	H	76	B3
Moss	N	49	D8
Most	CZ	41	C10
Mostar	BIH	81	E7
Mosterhamn	N	48	C2
Móstoles	E	26	D4
Mostys'ka	UA	73	E5
Mota del Cuervo	E	26	F6

Motala	*S*	**46**	E6
Moţăţei	*RO*	**82**	C5
Motherwell	*GB*	**2**	H5
Motril	*E*	**28**	E6
Motru	*RO*	**82**	A5
Motta San Giovanni	*I*	**31**	G7
Mottola	*I*	**31**	B9
Mougins	*F*	**19**	D8
Moulins	*F*	**17**	B10
Moulins-les Metz	*F*	**13**	C8
Moura	*P*	**24**	G5
Mourenx	*F*	**20**	B5
Mouscron	*B*	**10**	G4
Moutier	*CH*	**13**	G9
Moûtiers	*F*	**36**	G4
Moyenmoutier	*F*	**13**	E9
Mozirje	*SLO*	**39**	F10
Mrągowo	*PL*	**68**	H3
Mrkonjić-Grad	*BIH*	**80**	C5
Mszana Dolna	*PL*	**75**	E11
Mszczonów	*PL*	**71**	G11
Much	*D*	**11**	F9
Mudanya	*TR*	**85**	D6
Mugeni	*RO*	**78**	E4
Muggia	*I*	**35**	C12
Mühlhausen (Thüringen)	*D*	**40**	B5
Muineachán	*IRL*	**4**	E2
Mukacheve	*UA*	**73**	G4
Mula	*E*	**29**	C10
Mulhouse	*F*	**13**	F9
Müllheim	*D*	**13**	F10
Mullingar	*IRL*	**4**	F1
Mullsjö	*S*	**46**	F5
Mulsanne	*F*	**15**	F9
Münchberg	*D*	**41**	D7
München	*D*	**38**	C5
Munchingen	*D*	**13**	D12
Mundolsheim	*F*	**13**	D10
Munich	*D*	**38**	C5
Munkebo	*DK*	**44**	F4
Münnerstadt	*D*	**40**	D5
Münsingen	*D*	**38**	B2
Münsingen	*CH*	**13**	H10
Munster	*F*	**13**	E9
Münster	*D*	**11**	D10
Münster	*D*	**42**	E5
Munteni	*RO*	**79**	F8
Muradiye	*TR*	**85**	G3
Muratlı	*TR*	**85**	B3
Murcia	*E*	**29**	C10
Muret	*F*	**21**	B9
Murgeni	*RO*	**79**	E9
Muriedas	*E*	**23**	B10
Murnau am Staffelsee	*D*	**37**	B11
Muro	*E*	**29**	F10
Muro Lucano	*I*	**31**	B7
Muros	*E*	**22**	C1
Murowana Goślina	*PL*	**70**	F6
Mûrs-Erigné	*F*	**15**	G8
Murska Sobota	*SLO*	**39**	F11
Mürzzuschlag	*A*	**39**	D11
Musselburgh	*GB*	**3**	G7
Musselkanaal	*NL*	**11**	B9
Mussidan	*F*	**16**	E5
Mussomeli	*I*	**30**	F4
Mustafakemalpaşa	*TR*	**85**	D5
Muxía	*E*	**22**	B1
Myadzyel	*BY*	**69**	F10
Mykolayiv	*UA*	**73**	E6
Mykonos	*GR*	**89**	D10
Myllykoski	*FIN*	**65**	F7
Myory	*BY*	**69**	D11
Myrina	*GR*	**87**	E11
Myślenice	*PL*	**75**	D11
Myślibórz	*PL*	**43**	E11
Myszków	*PL*	**75**	C10
Mytilini	*GR*	**85**	F2
N			
Naantali	*FIN*	**53**	G10
Naas	*IRL*	**4**	G2
Nabburg	*D*	**41**	E8
Náchod	*CZ*	**74**	C6
Nădlac	*RO*	**77**	E8
Nádudvar	*H*	**77**	C9
Næstved	*DK*	**44**	F6
Nafpaktos	*GR*	**88**	B4
Nafplio	*GR*	**88**	C6
Nagold	*D*	**13**	D11
Nagyatád	*H*	**76**	E3
Nagyecsed	*H*	**77**	B11
Nagyhalász	*H*	**73**	H3
Nagykálló	*H*	**77**	B10
Nagykanizsa	*H*	**76**	E2
Nagykáta	*H*	**77**	C7
Nagykőrös	*H*	**77**	C7
Nagyszénás	*H*	**77**	D8
Naintré	*F*	**16**	A5
Nairn	*GB*	**2**	D6
Nájera	*E*	**20**	D2
Nakło nad Notecią	*PL*	**71**	D7
Nakskov	*DK*	**44**	G5
Náměšť nad Oslavou	*CZ*	**74**	F6
Namsos	*N*	**54**	F4
Namur	*B*	**10**	G6
Namysłów	*PL*	**75**	B8
Nancy	*F*	**13**	D8
Nantes	*F*	**14**	G6
Nantwich	*GB*	**5**	G7
Naousa	*GR*	**86**	D6
Naples	*I*	**30**	B5
Napoli	*I*	**30**	B5
Narbonne	*F*	**18**	E2
Nardò	*I*	**31**	C11
Narni	*I*	**32**	B5
Naro	*I*	**30**	F4
Närpes	*FIN*	**53**	C10
Narva	*EST*	**67**	B10
Narvik	*N*	**57**	D5
Năsăud	*RO*	**78**	C3
Našice	*HR*	**76**	G4
Nasielsk	*PL*	**71**	F11
Naso	*I*	**30**	E5
Nässjö	*S*	**45**	A10
Nastola	*FIN*	**65**	E7
Naujoji Akmenė	*LT*	**68**	C5
Naumburg (Saale)	*D*	**41**	B7
Navalcarnero	*E*	**26**	D4
Navalmoral de la Mata	*E*	**24**	C8
Navalvillar de Pela	*E*	**24**	E8
Navan	*IRL*	**4**	F2
Navarcles	*E*	**21**	E10
Navàs	*E*	**21**	E9
Navia	*E*	**22**	B5
Năvodari	*RO*	**84**	B5
Naxos	*GR*	**89**	D10
Nazaré	*P*	**24**	D2
Nea Alikarnassos	*GR*	**89**	G10
Nea Artaki	*GR*	**89**	A7
Nea Filadelfeia	*GR*	**89**	B7
Nea Ionia	*GR*	**87**	F7
Nea Liosia	*GR*	**89**	B7
Nea Makri	*GR*	**89**	B7
Neapoli	*GR*	**88**	E6
Nea Styra	*GR*	**89**	B8
Neath	*GB*	**8**	D4
Neckartenzlingen	*D*	**38**	B2
Nedelino	*BG*	**87**	B11
Nedstrand	*N*	**48**	D2
Negotin	*SRB*	**82**	C4
Negotino	*MK*	**86**	B6
Negrești	*RO*	**79**	D8
Negrești-Oaș	*RO*	**78**	B1
Negru Vodă	*RO*	**84**	C4
Nehoiu	*RO*	**78**	G6
Neksø	*DK*	**45**	G10
Neman	*RUS*	**68**	E4
Nemenčinė	*LT*	**69**	F8
Nemours	*F*	**12**	E3
Nenagh	*IRL*	**7**	K4
Nepi	*I*	**32**	C5
Nérac	*F*	**16**	G5
Neratovice	*CZ*	**41**	D11
Nerja	*E*	**28**	E6
Nerva	*E*	**25**	H6
Nes	*N*	**49**	B7
Nesna	*N*	**54**	B5
Neston	*GB*	**4**	G6
Nettuno	*I*	**32**	D5
Neuageri	*CH*	**37**	C7
Neubrandenburg	*D*	**43**	C9
Neuburg an der Donau	*D*	**38**	A4
Neuchâtel	*CH*	**13**	H9
Neuenhaus	*D*	**11**	C9
Neuenkirchen	*D*	**42**	D5
Neufchâteau	*B*	**13**	B7
Neufchâteau	*F*	**13**	E7
Neufchâtel-en-Bray	*F*	**12**	B1
Neufchâtel-Hardelot	*F*	**9**	F12
Neuhof	*D*	**40**	C4
Neumarkt in der Oberpfalz	*D*	**41**	F7
Neumünster	*D*	**42**	B5
Neunkirchen	*A*	**39**	C11
Neunkirchen	*D*	**13**	C9
Neuruppin	*D*	**43**	E9
Neustadt an der Aisch	*D*	**40**	E6
Neustadt an der Weinstraße	*D*	**13**	C11
Neustrelitz	*D*	**43**	D9
Neutraubling	*D*	**41**	F8
Neuville-lès-Dieppe	*F*	**9**	H11
Neuwied	*D*	**11**	G10
Neviano	*I*	**31**	C11
New Alresford	*GB*	**9**	F8
Newark-on-Trent	*GB*	**5**	G9
Newbridge	*IRL*	**4**	G2
Newbury	*GB*	**9**	E7
Newcastle	*GB*	**4**	E3
Newcastle-under-Lyme	*GB*	**5**	G7
Newcastle upon Tyne	*GB*	**5**	D8
Newhaven	*GB*	**9**	F9
Newmarket	*GB*	**9**	C10
Newport	*GB*	**5**	H7
Newport	*GB*	**8**	E5
Newport	*GB*	**9**	F7
Newport Pagnell	*GB*	**9**	D8
Newquay	*GB*	**8**	G2
New Romney	*GB*	**9**	F11
New Ross	*IRL*	**7**	L6

Place	Country	Page	Grid
Newry	*GB*	**4**	E2
Newton Abbot	*GB*	**8**	G4
Newton Aycliffe	*GB*	**5**	D8
Newtown	*GB*	**8**	C4
Newtownabbey	*GB*	**4**	D3
Newtownards	*GB*	**4**	D3
Nicastro	*I*	**31**	F8
Nice	*F*	**19**	D9
Nichelino	*I*	**19**	A9
Nicolae Bălcescu	*RO*	**79**	E7
Nicolae Bălcescu	*RO*	**84**	B4
Nicolosi	*I*	**30**	F6
Nicoreşti	*RO*	**79**	F8
Nicosia	*I*	**30**	E5
Nicotera	*I*	**31**	F8
Niculiţel	*RO*	**79**	G10
Nidda	*D*	**11**	G12
Nidzica	*PL*	**71**	D10
Niebüll	*D*	**44**	G2
Niederbronn-les-Bains	*F*	**13**	D10
Nieder Reisbach	*D*	**41**	G8
Niemodlin	*PL*	**75**	C8
Nienburg (Saale)	*D*	**43**	G8
Nienburg (Weser)	*D*	**11**	C12
Niesky	*D*	**41**	B12
Nigrita	*GR*	**87**	C8
Níjar	*E*	**29**	E8
Nijmegen	*NL*	**11**	D7
Nijverdal	*NL*	**11**	C8
Nikel'	*RUS*	**59**	E11
Nikopol	*BG*	**83**	D8
Nikšić	*MNE*	**81**	F8
Nîmes	*F*	**17**	G12
Nimigea	*RO*	**78**	C3
Niort	*F*	**16**	B4
Niš	*SRB*	**82**	D3
Niscemi	*I*	**30**	G5
Nisko	*PL*	**73**	C3
Nisporeni	*MD*	**79**	C9
Nitra	*SK*	**75**	G8
Nittenau	*D*	**41**	F8
Nittendorf	*D*	**41**	F7
Nivala	*FIN*	**62**	F5
Nizza Monferrato	*I*	**19**	B10
Nocera Terinese	*I*	**31**	E8
Nocera Umbra	*I*	**32**	A6
Noci	*I*	**31**	B10
Nogent-le-Roi	*F*	**12**	D1
Nogent-le-Rotrou	*F*	**15**	E10
Noia	*E*	**22**	C2
Noicattaro	*I*	**31**	A9
Noirmoutier-en-l'Île	*F*	**14**	G5
Nokia	*FIN*	**53**	E12
Nomeland	*N*	**48**	D4
Nonancourt	*F*	**15**	D10
None	*I*	**19**	A9
Noordwijk-Binnen	*NL*	**10**	D5
Nora	*S*	**46**	C6
Norberg	*S*	**47**	B7
Nordborg	*DK*	**44**	G3
Norden	*D*	**42**	C2
Norderney	*D*	**42**	C2
Norderstedt	*D*	**42**	C5
Nordfjordeid	*N*	**50**	D2
Nordhausen	*D*	**40**	A6
Nordholz	*D*	**42**	C4
Nordhorn	*D*	**11**	C9
Nördlingen	*D*	**38**	A3
Noreikiškės	*LT*	**68**	F6
Norheimsund	*N*	**48**	B3
Nørresundby	*DK*	**44**	C4
Nørre Vorupør	*DK*	**44**	C2
Norrköping	*S*	**47**	E7
Norrtälje	*S*	**47**	B10
Northallerton	*GB*	**5**	E8
Northam	*GB*	**8**	F3
Northampton	*GB*	**9**	C8
North Berwick	*GB*	**3**	G7
Northeim	*D*	**42**	G5
North Walsham	*GB*	**9**	B11
Northwich	*GB*	**5**	G7
Norton	*GB*	**5**	E9
Nortorf	*D*	**42**	B5
Nort-sur-Erdre	*F*	**14**	G6
Norwich	*GB*	**9**	B11
Noto	*I*	**30**	G6
Notodden	*N*	**48**	D6
Notre-Dame-de-Gravenchon	*F*	**15**	C9
Nottingham	*GB*	**5**	H9
Nottuln	*D*	**11**	D9
Nouzonville	*F*	**12**	B6
Nová Baňa	*SK*	**75**	G9
Novaci	*RO*	**78**	G2
Nová Dubnica	*SK*	**75**	F9
Novafeltria	*I*	**35**	F9
Nova Gorica	*SLO*	**35**	B11
Nova Gradiška	*HR*	**76**	G3
Nova Pazova	*SRB*	**77**	H8
Novara	*I*	**34**	C3
Nova Siri	*I*	**31**	C9
Nova Varoš	*SRB*	**81**	E10
Nova Zagora	*BG*	**83**	F10
Novelda	*E*	**27**	H9
Novellara	*I*	**35**	D7
Nové Mesto nad Váhom	*SK*	**75**	G8
Nové Město na Moravé	*CZ*	**74**	E6
Nové Zámky	*SK*	**76**	B4
Novi Bečej	*SRB*	**77**	F7
Novi Iskŭr	*BG*	**82**	F5
Novi Kneževac	*SRB*	**77**	E7
Novi Ligure	*I*	**19**	B11
Novi Pazar	*BG*	**83**	D12
Novi Pazar	*SRB*	**81**	F11
Novi Sad	*SRB*	**77**	G7
Novi Travnik	*BIH*	**80**	D6
Novo Beograd	*SRB*	**81**	B11
Novo Mesto	*SLO*	**39**	G10
Novo Miloševo	*SRB*	**77**	F8
Novorzhev	*RUS*	**67**	G11
Novoselytsya	*UA*	**78**	A6
Novovolyns'k	*UA*	**73**	C6
Novoyavorivs'ke	*UA*	**73**	D5
Novska	*HR*	**76**	G2
Nový Bor	*CZ*	**41**	C11
Nový Bydžov	*CZ*	**74**	D5
Nový Jičín	*CZ*	**75**	E8
Novyy Rozdil	*UA*	**73**	E6
Nowa Dęba	*PL*	**73**	C3
Nowa Ruda	*PL*	**74**	C6
Nowa Sarzyna	*PL*	**73**	D4
Nowa Sól	*PL*	**70**	G5
Nowe	*PL*	**71**	C8
Nowe Miasto Lubawskie	*PL*	**71**	D9
Nowogard	*PL*	**43**	C12
Nowy Dwór Gdański	*PL*	**71**	B9
Nowy Dwór Mazowiecki	*PL*	**71**	F11
Nowy Sącz	*PL*	**73**	E1
Nowy Targ	*PL*	**75**	E11
Nowy Tomyśl	*PL*	**70**	F5
Noyon	*F*	**12**	B3
Nubledo	*E*	**23**	B7
Nuenen	*NL*	**11**	E7
Nuits-St-Georges	*F*	**12**	G6
Nules	*E*	**27**	E10
Nummela	*FIN*	**64**	G5
Nuneaton	*GB*	**9**	C7
Nunspeet	*NL*	**11**	C7
Nuoro	*I*	**32**	E3
Nurmes	*FIN*	**63**	G10
Nurmo	*FIN*	**53**	B11
Nürnberg	*D*	**40**	E6
Nusco	*I*	**30**	B6
Nuşfalău	*RO*	**77**	C12
Nybergsund	*N*	**51**	F10
Nyborg	*DK*	**44**	F5
Nyborg	*N*	**48**	B2
Nybro	*S*	**45**	C11
Nyby	*FIN*	**53**	B10
Nyergesújfalu	*H*	**76**	B5
Nyíradony	*H*	**77**	B10
Nyírbátor	*H*	**77**	B11
Nyíregyháza	*H*	**77**	B10
Nyírtelek	*H*	**77**	A10
Nykøbing	*DK*	**44**	G6
Nykøbing Mors	*DK*	**44**	C2
Nykøbing Sjælland	*DK*	**44**	E6
Nyköping	*S*	**47**	D8
Nykvarn	*S*	**47**	C9
Nymburk	*CZ*	**41**	D12
Nynäshamn	*S*	**47**	D9
Nyon	*CH*	**36**	E4
Nyons	*F*	**18**	C5
Nýřany	*CZ*	**41**	E9
Nýrsko	*CZ*	**41**	F9
Nysa	*PL*	**75**	C7

O

Place	Country	Page	Grid
Oadby	*GB*	**9**	B8
Oakham	*GB*	**9**	B8
Oban	*GB*	**2**	F4
O Barco	*E*	**22**	D5
Oberammergau	*D*	**37**	B11
Obernai	*F*	**13**	E10
Oberriet	*CH*	**37**	C9
Oberstdorf	*D*	**37**	C10
Obiliq	*RKS*	**81**	G12
Obrenovac	*SRB*	**81**	C11
Ocaña	*E*	**26**	E5
O Carballiño	*E*	**22**	D3
O Castelo	*E*	**22**	E2
Occhiobello	*I*	**35**	D8
Ochsenfurt	*D*	**40**	E5
Ocna Mureş	*RO*	**78**	E2
O Convento	*E*	**22**	D2
O Corgo	*E*	**22**	C4
Ócsa	*H*	**76**	C6
Odda	*N*	**48**	C3
Odder	*DK*	**44**	E4
Odense	*DK*	**44**	F4
Oderzo	*I*	**35**	B9
Odivelas	*P*	**24**	F2
Odobeşti	*RO*	**79**	F7
Odobeşti	*RO*	**83**	B9
Odorheiu Secuiesc	*RO*	**78**	E5
Odry	*CZ*	**75**	E8
Odžaci	*SRB*	**76**	F6
Oebisfelde	*D*	**43**	F7
Oelsnitz	*D*	**41**	C8

Place	Country	Page	Grid
Offenbach am Main	*D*	**11**	H11
Offenburg	*D*	**13**	E10
Ogre	*LV*	**66**	G5
Ogrezeni	*RO*	**83**	B9
Ogulin	*HR*	**80**	A2
Ohrid	*MK*	**86**	C4
Oia	*GR*	**89**	F10
Oituz	*RO*	**79**	E7
Okehampton	*GB*	**8**	F3
Øksfjord	*N*	**58**	C5
Olaine	*LV*	**66**	H5
Oława	*PL*	**75**	B7
Olbia	*I*	**32**	D3
Oldenburg	*D*	**11**	B11
Oldham	*GB*	**5**	F8
Olecko	*PL*	**68**	G5
Oleśnica	*PL*	**75**	B7
Olesno	*PL*	**75**	B9
Olevano Romano	*I*	**32**	D6
Olhão	*P*	**25**	K4
Oliva	*E*	**27**	G10
Oliva de la Frontera	*E*	**24**	G5
Oliveira de Azeméis	*P*	**22**	G2
Olivenza	*E*	**24**	F5
Olivet	*F*	**12**	F2
Olkusz	*PL*	**75**	D11
Ollioules	*F*	**18**	E6
Ollon	*CH*	**36**	E5
Olney	*GB*	**9**	C8
Olofsfors	*S*	**55**	G12
Olofström	*S*	**45**	D9
Olomouc	*CZ*	**75**	E7
Olonne-sur-Mer	*F*	**16**	B2
Oloron-Ste-Marie	*F*	**20**	B5
Olot	*E*	**21**	D10
Olsberg	*D*	**11**	E11
Ølstykke	*DK*	**44**	E6
Olsztyn	*PL*	**68**	H2
Olsztynek	*PL*	**68**	H2
Oltenița	*RO*	**83**	C11
Olula del Río	*E*	**29**	D8
Olvera	*E*	**28**	E3
Omagh	*GB*	**4**	D1
Omegna	*I*	**34**	B3
Omiš	*HR*	**80**	E5
Ommen	*NL*	**11**	C8
O Mosteiro	*E*	**22**	D2
Omurtag	*BG*	**83**	E10
Onchan	*GBM*	**4**	E5
Onda	*E*	**27**	E10
Ondarroa	*E*	**20**	B2
Onești	*RO*	**79**	E7
Onet-le-Château	*F*	**17**	F9
Ontinyent	*E*	**27**	G10
Onzain	*F*	**15**	F10
Oostende	*B*	**10**	F3
Oosterhout	*NL*	**10**	E6
Opalenica	*PL*	**70**	F5
Opatija	*HR*	**35**	C12
Opatów	*PL*	**73**	C2
Opava	*CZ*	**75**	D8
O Pedrouzo	*E*	**22**	C3
Opochka	*RUS*	**67**	H10
Opoczno	*PL*	**71**	H10
Opole	*PL*	**75**	C8
Opole Lubelskie	*PL*	**73**	B3
O Porriño	*E*	**22**	D2
Oppido Mamertina	*I*	**31**	G8
Oradea	*RO*	**77**	C10
Orange	*F*	**18**	C5
Oranienburg	*D*	**43**	E9
Orăștie	*RO*	**77**	F12
Orașu Nou	*RO*	**77**	B12
Oravița	*RO*	**77**	G10
Orbassano	*I*	**19**	A9
Orbeasca	*RO*	**83**	C9
Orbetello	*I*	**32**	B3
Orchomenos	*GR*	**88**	B6
Ordes	*E*	**22**	C3
O Real	*E*	**22**	B3
Orebić	*HR*	**80**	F5
Örebro	*S*	**46**	C6
Orense	*E*	**22**	D3
Orestiada	*GR*	**85**	B2
Orgiva	*E*	**28**	E6
Orhei	*MD*	**79**	C10
Oria	*I*	**31**	C10
Orihuela	*E*	**29**	C11
Orimattila	*FIN*	**64**	F6
Oristano	*I*	**32**	F2
Orivesi	*FIN*	**64**	D5
Orkanger	*N*	**51**	B7
Orlea	*RO*	**83**	D7
Orléans	*F*	**12**	F2
Ormes	*F*	**12**	C5
Ormož	*SLO*	**39**	F11
Ormskirk	*GB*	**5**	F7
Orneta	*PL*	**68**	G2
Örnsköldsvik	*S*	**53**	A7
Orosei	*I*	**32**	E4
Orosháza	*H*	**77**	D8
Oroszlány	*H*	**76**	C4
Orșova	*RO*	**82**	B4
Ørsta	*N*	**50**	D3
Orta Nova	*I*	**33**	E11
Orte	*I*	**32**	B5
Orthez	*F*	**20**	B5
Ortigueira	*E*	**22**	A3
Ortona	*I*	**33**	C8
Orvault	*F*	**14**	G6
Orvieto	*I*	**32**	B5
Oryakhovo	*BG*	**82**	D6
Orzinuovi	*I*	**34**	C5
Orzysz	*PL*	**68**	H4
Os	*N*	**51**	C8
Osby	*S*	**45**	D9
Oschatz	*D*	**41**	B9
Oschersleben (Bode)	*D*	**43**	F7
O Seixo	*E*	**22**	E2
Osen	*N*	**54**	F3
Osica de Sus	*RO*	**83**	C7
Osijek	*HR*	**76**	F5
Osimo	*I*	**35**	G11
Osipaonica	*SRB*	**81**	C12
Oskarshamn	*S*	**45**	B12
Oslo	*N*	**46**	B1
Osnabrück	*D*	**11**	D10
Osor	*HR*	**80**	C1
Oșorhei	*RO*	**77**	C11
Osøyri	*N*	**48**	B2
Oss	*NL*	**11**	E7
Ostend	*B*	**10**	F3
Osterburg (Altmark)	*D*	**43**	E8
Osterhofen	*D*	**39**	A7
Ostermundigen	*CH*	**13**	H10
Östersund	*S*	**51**	B12
Ostiglia	*I*	**35**	D7
Ostrava	*CZ*	**75**	D9
Ostróda	*PL*	**68**	H1
Ostrov	*CZ*	**41**	C9
Ostrov	*RO*	**83**	C12
Ostrov	*RUS*	**67**	F10
Ostroveni	*RO*	**82**	D6
Ostrowiec Świętokrzyski	*PL*	**73**	B2
Ostrów Mazowiecka	*PL*	**72**	E4
Ostrów Wielkopolski	*PL*	**71**	G7
Ostrzeszów	*PL*	**71**	H7
Ostuni	*I*	**31**	B10
Osuna	*E*	**28**	D4
Oswestry	*GB*	**4**	H6
Oświęcim	*PL*	**75**	D10
Oțelu Roșu	*RO*	**77**	F11
Otley	*GB*	**5**	F8
Otmuchów	*PL*	**75**	C7
Otočac	*HR*	**80**	B2
Otok	*HR*	**76**	G5
Otopeni	*RO*	**83**	B10
O Toural	*E*	**22**	D2
Otranto	*I*	**31**	C12
Ottaviano	*I*	**30**	B5
Ottenby	*S*	**45**	D12
Otterndorf	*D*	**42**	C4
Ouistreham	*F*	**15**	C8
Oulainen	*FIN*	**62**	E5
Oullins	*F*	**17**	C12
Oulu	*FIN*	**62**	D6
Oulunsalo	*FIN*	**62**	D6
Oundle	*GB*	**9**	C9
Oupeye	*B*	**11**	G7
Ouranoupoli	*GR*	**87**	D9
Ourense	*E*	**22**	D3
Outokumpu	*FIN*	**65**	B10
Outreau	*F*	**9**	F11
Ovada	*I*	**19**	B11
Ovar	*P*	**22**	G2
Överammer	*S*	**52**	A4
Ovidiu	*RO*	**84**	C4
Oviedo	*E*	**23**	B7
Oxelösund	*S*	**47**	D8
Oxford	*GB*	**9**	D7
Oxie	*S*	**45**	F8
Oxted	*GB*	**9**	E9
Oyonnax	*F*	**36**	E3
Ożarów	*PL*	**73**	C3
Özbaşı	*TR*	**88**	D3
Ózd	*H*	**73**	H1
Ozersk	*RUS*	**68**	F4
Ozieri	*I*	**32**	E2
Ozimek	*PL*	**75**	C9
Ozorków	*PL*	**71**	G9

P

Place	Country	Page	Grid
Pabianice	*PL*	**71**	G9
Pabradė	*LT*	**69**	E9
Paceco	*I*	**30**	E2
Pachino	*I*	**30**	G6
Pacy-sur-Eure	*F*	**12**	C1
Paczków	*PL*	**75**	C7
Paderborn	*D*	**11**	E11
Padeș	*RO*	**77**	G12
Padina	*RO*	**79**	H8
Padina	*SRB*	**77**	G8
Padinska Skela	*SRB*	**77**	H8
Padova	*I*	**35**	C8
Padrón	*E*	**22**	C2
Padsvillye	*BY*	**69**	E11
Padul	*E*	**28**	E6
Padula	*I*	**31**	C7

Place	Country	Page	Grid
Paide	*EST*	**67**	C7
Paignton	*GB*	**8**	G4
Paimio	*FIN*	**53**	G11
Paimpol	*F*	**14**	D4
Paisley	*GB*	**2**	H5
Pajęczno	*PL*	**75**	B10
Pakrac	*HR*	**76**	G2
Pakruojis	*LT*	**68**	C6
Paks	*H*	**76**	D5
Palafrugell	*E*	**18**	G2
Palagiano	*I*	**31**	B9
Palagonia	*I*	**30**	F5
Palaikastro	*GR*	**89**	G11
Palaiochora	*GR*	**89**	G7
Palaiokastritsa	*GR*	**86**	F2
Palamas	*GR*	**86**	F6
Palamós	*E*	**18**	H2
Palanga	*LT*	**68**	C3
Palas de Rei	*E*	**22**	C3
Palau	*I*	**32**	C3
Palavas-les-Flots	*F*	**17**	H11
Palazzolo Acreide	*I*	**30**	G6
Paldiski	*EST*	**66**	B5
Palencia	*E*	**23**	E9
Palermo	*I*	**30**	E3
Palestrina	*I*	**32**	D6
Palić	*SRB*	**77**	E7
Palma Campania	*I*	**30**	B5
Palma del Río	*E*	**28**	C3
Palma de Mallorca	*E*	**29**	F9
Palma di Montechiaro	*I*	**30**	G4
Palmi	*I*	**31**	G7
Palombara Sabina	*I*	**32**	C6
Păltinoasa	*RO*	**78**	B6
Pamiers	*F*	**21**	B9
Pamplona	*E*	**20**	C4
Panagyurishte	*BG*	**83**	F7
Panazol	*F*	**17**	C7
Pančevo	*SRB*	**77**	H8
Panciu	*RO*	**79**	F7
Pâncota	*RO*	**77**	E10
Pănet	*RO*	**78**	D3
Panevėžys	*LT*	**69**	D7
Pantelimon	*RO*	**83**	B10
Paola	*I*	**31**	E8
Pápa	*H*	**76**	C3
Papenburg	*D*	**11**	B10
Parabita	*I*	**31**	C11
Paraćin	*SRB*	**82**	C2
Paralia	*GR*	**88**	E6
Paralia Avdiron	*GR*	**87**	C11
Paralia Saranti	*GR*	**88**	B6
Paray-le-Monial	*F*	**17**	B11
Parchim	*D*	**43**	D8
Parczew	*PL*	**72**	G5
Pardubice	*CZ*	**74**	D5
Parempuyre	*F*	**16**	E3
Parets del Vallès	*E*	**21**	F10
Parga	*GR*	**86**	G3
Pargas	*FIN*	**53**	G11
Pargolovo	*RUS*	**65**	G11
Paris	*F*	**12**	D2
Pârjol	*RO*	**79**	D7
Parkano	*FIN*	**53**	D11
Parma	*I*	**34**	D6
Pärnu	*EST*	**66**	D5
Paroikia	*GR*	**89**	D9
Parsberg	*D*	**41**	F7
Pârscov	*RO*	**78**	G7
Partanna	*I*	**30**	E2
Parthenay	*F*	**16**	B4
Partinico	*I*	**30**	E3
Partizánske	*SK*	**75**	G9
Pașcani	*RO*	**79**	C7
Pasewalk	*D*	**43**	C10
Pasłęk	*PL*	**68**	G1
Passau	*D*	**39**	B8
Pastavy	*BY*	**69**	E10
Pasvalys	*LT*	**69**	C7
Pásztó	*H*	**77**	B7
Pătârlagele	*RO*	**78**	G6
Paterna	*E*	**27**	F10
Paternion	*A*	**39**	E8
Paternò	*I*	**30**	F6
Patos	*AL*	**86**	D2
Patra	*GR*	**88**	B4
Pattensen	*D*	**42**	F5
Patti	*I*	**30**	E6
Pau	*F*	**20**	B6
Pauillac	*F*	**16**	E3
Păunești	*RO*	**79**	E8
Pavia	*I*	**34**	C4
Pavilly	*F*	**15**	B10
Pavlikeni	*BG*	**83**	E9
Pavlovsk	*RUS*	**65**	H11
Pavullo nel Frignano	*I*	**35**	E7
Payerne	*CH*	**13**	H9
Pazardzhik	*BG*	**83**	G7
Pazin	*HR*	**35**	C12
Peal de Becerro	*E*	**29**	C7
Peccioli	*I*	**35**	G7
Pécel	*H*	**76**	C6
Pechea	*RO*	**79**	F9
Pechory	*RUS*	**67**	E9
Pecica	*RO*	**77**	E9
Pécs	*H*	**76**	E4
Pedro Muñoz	*E*	**26**	F6
Pedroso	*P*	**22**	G2
Peebles	*GB*	**4**	B6
Peer	*B*	**11**	F7
Pegnitz	*D*	**41**	E7
Pego	*E*	**27**	G10
Peiraias	*GR*	**89**	C7
Peitz	*D*	**43**	G11
Pejë	*RKS*	**81**	G11
Pelago	*I*	**35**	F8
Pelhřimov	*CZ*	**74**	E4
Pelplin	*PL*	**71**	C8
Pembroke	*GB*	**8**	D2
Pembroke Dock	*GB*	**8**	D2
Peñafiel	*E*	**23**	E10
Peñaranda de Bracamonte	*E*	**23**	G8
Peñarroya-Pueblonuevo	*E*	**24**	G8
Penarth	*GB*	**8**	E5
Peniche	*P*	**24**	D1
Penicuik	*GB*	**2**	H6
Peñíscola	*E*	**21**	H7
Penmarch	*F*	**14**	F2
Penne	*I*	**33**	B8
Penrith	*GB*	**5**	D7
Penzance	*GB*	**8**	G1
Penzberg	*D*	**37**	B11
Pëqin	*AL*	**86**	C2
Perama	*GR*	**89**	C7
Perechyn	*UA*	**73**	G4
Peretu	*RO*	**83**	C8
Perg	*A*	**39**	B9
Pergine Valsugana	*I*	**35**	B7
Pergola	*I*	**35**	G10
Periam	*RO*	**77**	E9
Périgueux	*F*	**16**	E6
Periș	*RO*	**83**	B10
Perișoru	*RO*	**83**	B12
Peristeri	*GR*	**89**	B7
Perleberg	*D*	**43**	D8
Përmet	*AL*	**86**	E3
Pernik	*BG*	**82**	F5
Péronnas	*F*	**36**	E2
Péronne	*F*	**12**	B3
Perpignan	*F*	**18**	F1
Perros-Guirec	*F*	**14**	D4
Pershore	*GB*	**8**	C6
Perstorp	*S*	**45**	D8
Perth	*GB*	**2**	G6
Pertuis	*F*	**18**	D6
Perugia	*I*	**35**	H9
Perushtitsa	*BG*	**83**	G7
Pervomaisc	*MD*	**79**	D12
Pesaro	*I*	**35**	F10
Pescara	*I*	**33**	B8
Pescia	*I*	**35**	F6
Peshkopi	*AL*	**86**	B3
Peshtera	*BG*	**83**	G7
Pesnica	*SLO*	**39**	F11
Pesochnyy	*RUS*	**65**	G11
Peso da Régua	*P*	**22**	F4
Pessac	*F*	**16**	E3
Peterborough	*GB*	**9**	C9
Peterhead	*GB*	**3**	D8
Peterlee	*GB*	**5**	D9
Petersfield	*GB*	**9**	F8
Petilia Policastro	*I*	**31**	E9
Petrești	*RO*	**83**	B9
Petrich	*BG*	**87**	B8
Petrila	*RO*	**78**	G1
Petrinja	*HR*	**76**	G1
Petrodvorets	*RUS*	**65**	H10
Petroșani	*RO*	**78**	G1
Petrovac	*SRB*	**82**	B2
Petrovaradin	*SRB*	**77**	G7
Peyrehorade	*F*	**16**	H3
Pézenas	*F*	**18**	D2
Pezinok	*SK*	**75**	H7
Pfaffenhoffen	*F*	**13**	D10
Pfarrkirchen	*D*	**39**	B7
Pforzheim	*D*	**13**	D11
Piacenza	*I*	**34**	D5
Piana degli Albanesi	*I*	**30**	E3
Pianella	*I*	**33**	C8
Pianoro	*I*	**35**	E8
Piaseczno	*PL*	**71**	G11
Piatra Neamț	*RO*	**78**	D6
Piatra Olt	*RO*	**83**	B7
Piazza Armerina	*I*	**30**	F5
Picassent	*E*	**27**	F10
Pickering	*GB*	**5**	E9
Piedimonte Matese	*I*	**33**	E8
Piedrabuena	*E*	**26**	G4
Piedras Blancas	*E*	**23**	B7
Pieksämäki	*FIN*	**65**	C8
Pieńsk	*PL*	**41**	B12
Piera	*E*	**21**	F9
Pierrelatte	*F*	**17**	F12
Piešťany	*SK*	**75**	G8
Pietarsaari	*FIN*	**56**	G5
Pietraperzia	*I*	**30**	F4
Pietrasanta	*I*	**34**	F6
Pihlava	*FIN*	**53**	E10
Piła	*PL*	**70**	D6
Pilis	*H*	**76**	C6

Place	Country	Page	Grid
Pilisszentiván	H	76	B5
Pilisvörösvár	H	76	B5
Pinarhisar	TR	84	H3
Pińczów	PL	73	C1
Pineda de Mar	E	21	E11
Pinerolo	I	19	B9
Pineto	I	33	B8
Pinkafeld	A	39	D11
Pinoso	E	27	H9
Pinos-Puente	E	28	D6
Pinto	E	26	D4
Piolenc	F	18	C4
Piombino	I	32	A2
Pionerskiy	RUS	68	E2
Piotrków Trybunalski	PL	71	H9
Pipirig	RO	78	C6
Piran	SLO	35	C11
Pirkkala	FIN	53	E12
Pirna	D	41	B10
Pirot	SRB	82	E4
Pisa	I	34	F6
Piscu	RO	79	F9
Piscu Vechi	RO	82	C5
Písek	CZ	41	E11
Pishchanka	UA	79	A10
Pisticci	I	31	C9
Pistoia	I	35	F7
Pisz	PL	68	H4
Piteå	S	56	C3
Pitești	RO	78	H4
Pithiviers	F	12	E2
Pitomača	HR	76	F3
Pizarra	E	28	E4
Pizzo	I	31	F8
Plaintel	F	14	E4
Plasencia	E	24	C7
Platanos	GR	89	F7
Plau	D	43	D8
Plauen	D	41	C8
Plenița	RO	82	C5
Plérin	F	14	D5
Pleszew	PL	71	G7
Pleven	BG	83	D7
Pljevlja	MNE	81	E9
Ploče	HR	80	F6
Płock	PL	71	F10
Ploemeur	F	14	F4
Ploërmel	F	14	F5
Ploiești	RO	78	H6
Plön	D	42	B6
Płońsk	PL	71	E10
Plopeni	RO	78	G6
Plopii-Slăvitești	RO	83	C7
Plopșoru	RO	78	H1
Plosca	RO	83	C8
Ploudalmézeau	F	14	D2
Ploufragan	F	14	E5
Plouguerneau	F	14	D2
Plouzané	F	14	E2
Plovdiv	BG	83	G8
Plungė	LT	68	C4
Pluvigner	F	14	F4
Plyeshchanitsy	BY	69	F11
Plymouth	GB	8	G3
Plzeň	CZ	41	E9
Pniewy	PL	70	F5
Pobiedziska	PL	70	F6
Pocking	D	39	B7
Pocklington	GB	5	F9
Podari	RO	82	C6
Podbořany	CZ	41	D10
Poddębice	PL	71	G9
Poděbrady	CZ	41	D12
Podgorica	MNE	81	G9
Podoleni	RO	79	D7
Podstrana	HR	80	E4
Podu Iloaiei	RO	79	C8
Podujevë	RKS	81	F12
Poduri	RO	78	E7
Podu Turcului	RO	79	E8
Poggiardo	I	31	C12
Poggibonsi	I	35	G7
Pogoanele	RO	79	H7
Pogradec	AL	86	C3
Poiana Lacului	RO	78	H4
Poiana Mare	RO	82	C5
Poiana Mărului	RO	78	F5
Poiana Teiului	RO	78	C6
Poieni	RO	77	D12
Poienile de Sub Munte	RO	78	B3
Poitiers	F	16	B5
Pokka	FIN	59	G8
Pola de Lena	E	23	B7
Pola de Siero	E	23	B7
Połaniec	PL	73	C2
Połczyn Zdrój	PL	70	C5
Polessk	RUS	68	F3
Polgár	H	77	B9
Polgárdi	H	76	C4
Poliçan	AL	86	D2
Police	PL	43	C11
Polichni	GR	87	D7
Polička	CZ	74	E6
Policoro	I	31	C9
Polignano a Mare	I	31	B10
Polistena	I	31	G8
Polkowice	PL	70	H5
Polla	I	31	B7
Pollença	E	29	E10
Pollenza	I	35	G11
Polski Trŭmbesh	BG	83	D9
Poltár	SK	75	G11
Põltsamaa	EST	67	D7
Polva	EST	67	E8
Polygyros	GR	87	D8
Polykastro	GR	87	C7
Pomarance	I	35	G7
Pombal	P	24	C3
Pomezia	I	32	D5
Pomorie	BG	84	F3
Pompei	I	30	B5
Ponferrada	E	22	D6
Poniatowa	PL	73	B3
Ponsacco	I	34	G6
Pont-à-Mousson	F	13	D8
Pontardawe	GB	8	D4
Pontarlier	F	13	H8
Pontassieve	I	35	F8
Pont-Audemer	F	15	C9
Pontcharra	F	36	G4
Pontchâteau	F	14	G6
Pont-du-Château	F	17	C10
Ponteareas	E	22	D2
Pontecagnano Faiano	I	30	B6
Pontecorvo	I	33	D7
Pontedera	I	34	G6
Ponteland	GB	5	C8
Ponte nelle Alpi	I	35	B9
Pontevedra	E	22	D2
Pontinia	I	32	D6
Pontivy	F	14	E4
Pont-l'Abbé	F	14	F2
Pontoise	F	12	C2
Pontremoli	I	34	E5
Pont-St-Esprit	F	17	F12
Pontypool	GB	8	D5
Pontypridd	GB	8	D4
Poole	GB	8	F6
Popești	RO	77	C11
Popești-Leordeni	RO	83	B10
Popoli	I	33	C7
Popovo	BG	83	D10
Poppi	I	35	F8
Poprad	SK	73	F1
Popricani	RO	79	C8
Porcuna	E	28	C5
Pordenone	I	35	B10
Poreč	HR	35	C11
Pori	FIN	53	E10
Porkhov	RUS	67	F12
Pornic	F	14	G6
Porozina	HR	80	B1
Porrentruy	CH	13	G9
Porsgrunn	N	49	D7
Portadown	GB	4	E2
Portalegre	P	24	E5
Port Askaig	GB	2	H3
Port Ellen	GB	2	H3
Portes-lès-Valence	F	18	B5
Portets	F	16	E4
Porthcawl	GB	8	E4
Portici	I	30	B5
Portimão	P	25	K3
Portishead	GB	8	E5
Port Láirge	IRL	7	M6
Portlaoise	IRL	7	K5
Portlethen	GB	3	E8
Portmarnock	IRL	4	G3
Portnahaven	GB	2	H2
Porto	P	22	F2
Porto Cervo	I	32	C3
Porto do Son	E	22	C1
Porto Empedocle	I	30	F3
Portoferraio	I	32	B2
Portogruaro	I	35	B10
Pörtom	FIN	53	B10
Porto Recanati	I	35	G11
Porto San Giorgio	I	35	H12
Porto Sant'Elpidio	I	35	G12
Portoscuso	I	32	G1
Porto Tolle	I	35	D9
Porto Torres	I	32	D1
Porto-Vecchio	F	19	G11
Portree	GB	2	D3
Portrush	GB	4	C2
Portsmouth	GB	9	F8
Portstewart	GB	4	C2
Port-St-Louis-du-Rhône	F	18	E5
Port Talbot	GB	8	E4
Portugalete	E	20	B1
Port-Vendres	F	18	F2
Porvoo	FIN	64	G6
Posada	E	23	B7
Posadas	E	28	C4
Pößneck	D	41	C7
Poșta Călnău	RO	79	G7
Postojna	SLO	35	B12
Potcoava	RO	83	B7
Potenza	I	31	B7
Potenza Picena	I	35	G11

Place	Country	Page	Grid
Potlogi	*RO*	**83**	B9
Potsdam	*D*	**43**	F9
Pottendorf	*A*	**39**	C12
Poulton-le-Fylde	*GB*	**5**	F7
Pouzauges	*F*	**15**	H7
Považská Bystrica	*SK*	**75**	F9
Póvoa de Varzim	*P*	**22**	F2
Poyrazcık	*TR*	**85**	F3
Požarevac	*SRB*	**81**	C12
Požega	*HR*	**76**	G3
Požega	*SRB*	**81**	D10
Poznań	*PL*	**70**	F6
Pozo Alcón	*E*	**29**	C7
Pozoblanco	*E*	**26**	H2
Pozuelo de Alarcón	*E*	**23**	H10
Pozzallo	*I*	**30**	G5
Pozzuoli	*I*	**30**	B5
Prabuty	*PL*	**71**	C9
Prachatice	*CZ*	**41**	F10
Prades	*F*	**21**	C10
Prado del Rey	*E*	**25**	L8
Prague	*CZ*	**41**	D11
Praha	*CZ*	**41**	D11
Praia a Mare	*I*	**31**	D7
Praia da Tocha	*P*	**24**	B2
Praid	*RO*	**78**	D4
Praszka	*PL*	**75**	B9
Prato	*I*	**35**	F7
Pravia	*E*	**22**	B6
Predappio	*I*	**35**	F9
Predeal	*RO*	**78**	F5
Preetz	*D*	**42**	B6
Preiļi	*LV*	**69**	C10
Prejmer	*RO*	**78**	F5
Preko	*HR*	**80**	D2
Premià de Mar	*E*	**21**	F10
Premnitz	*D*	**43**	E8
Prenzlau	*D*	**43**	D10
Přerov	*CZ*	**75**	E8
Preševo	*SRB*	**82**	G2
Presicce	*I*	**31**	D11
Prešov	*SK*	**73**	F2
Pressbaum	*A*	**39**	C11
Prestatyn	*GB*	**4**	G6
Přeštice	*CZ*	**41**	E9
Preston	*GB*	**5**	F7
Prestwick	*GB*	**4**	C4
Preutești	*RO*	**78**	C6
Preveza	*GR*	**86**	G4
Priboj	*SRB*	**81**	E9
Příbram	*CZ*	**41**	E10
Priego de Córdoba	*E*	**28**	D5
Prienai	*LT*	**68**	F6
Prievidza	*SK*	**75**	G9
Prijedor	*BIH*	**76**	H2
Prijepolje	*SRB*	**81**	E10
Prilep	*MK*	**86**	B5
Primorsk	*RUS*	**65**	G9
Priolo Gargallo	*I*	**30**	G6
Priozersk	*RUS*	**65**	E11
Prishtinë	*RKS*	**82**	F2
Priština	*RKS*	**82**	F2
Pritzwalk	*D*	**43**	D8
Privas	*F*	**17**	E12
Priverno	*I*	**32**	D6
Prizren	*RKS*	**81**	G11
Prizzi	*I*	**30**	E3
Prnjavor	*BIH*	**76**	H3
Probištip	*MK*	**82**	G3
Prokuplje	*SRB*	**82**	E2
Prostějov	*CZ*	**75**	E7
Proszowice	*PL*	**73**	D1
Provadiya	*BG*	**83**	E12
Provins	*F*	**12**	D4
Prudhoe	*GB*	**5**	D8
Prudnik	*PL*	**75**	C8
Prüm	*D*	**11**	H8
Prundeni	*RO*	**83**	B7
Prundu	*RO*	**83**	C10
Prundu Bârgăului	*RO*	**78**	C4
Pruszcz Gdański	*PL*	**71**	B8
Pruszków	*PL*	**71**	F11
Przasnysz	*PL*	**71**	E11
Przemków	*PL*	**70**	H5
Przemyśl	*PL*	**73**	E4
Przeworsk	*PL*	**73**	D4
Przysucha	*PL*	**71**	H11
Psachna	*GR*	**89**	A7
Psarades	*GR*	**86**	C4
Pskov	*RUS*	**67**	E10
Ptolemaïda	*GR*	**86**	D5
Ptuj	*SLO*	**39**	F11
Puchenii Mari	*RO*	**83**	A10
Puchheim	*D*	**38**	C5
Púchov	*SK*	**75**	F9
Pucioasa	*RO*	**78**	G5
Puck	*PL*	**71**	A8
Puçol	*E*	**27**	E10
Puente-Genil	*E*	**28**	D4
Puerto de Santa Maria	*E*	**25**	L7
Puertollano	*E*	**26**	G4
Puerto Lumbreras	*E*	**29**	D9
Puerto Real	*E*	**25**	L7
Pui	*RO*	**77**	F12
Puigcerdà	*E*	**21**	D10
Puig-reig	*E*	**21**	E9
Pula	*HR*	**35**	D12
Pula	*I*	**32**	H2
Puławy	*PL*	**72**	H4
Pulsano	*I*	**31**	C10
Pułtusk	*PL*	**71**	E11
Punta Umbría	*E*	**25**	K5
Purgstall an der Erlauf	*A*	**39**	C10
Pŭrvomay	*BG*	**83**	G8
Pushkin	*RUS*	**65**	H11
Pushkinskiye Gory	*RUS*	**67**	G11
Püspökladány	*H*	**77**	C9
Pustomyty	*UA*	**73**	E6
Puszczykowo	*PL*	**70**	F6
Pusztaszabolcs	*H*	**76**	C5
Putignano	*I*	**31**	B10
Putnok	*H*	**73**	H1
Puttgarden	*D*	**43**	A7
Pyle	*GB*	**8**	E4
Pyrgos	*GR*	**88**	C3
Pyrzyce	*PL*	**43**	D11
Pyskowice	*PL*	**75**	C9
Pytalovo	*RUS*	**67**	G10
Pythagoreio	*GR*	**88**	D2

Q

Place	Country	Page	Grid
Quakenbrück	*D*	**11**	C10
Qualiano	*I*	**30**	B5
Quarrata	*I*	**35**	F7
Quarteira	*P*	**25**	K3
Quartu Sant'Elena	*I*	**32**	G3
Quedlinburg	*D*	**43**	G7
Querfurt	*D*	**41**	A7
Quiberon	*F*	**14**	G4
Quiliano	*I*	**19**	C11
Quimper	*F*	**14**	F3
Quimperlé	*F*	**14**	F3
Quintana de la Serena	*E*	**24**	F8
Quintanar de la Orden	*E*	**26**	F5
Quiroga	*E*	**22**	D4

R

Place	Country	Page	Grid
Raahe	*FIN*	**56**	E6
Raalte	*NL*	**11**	C8
Rabastens	*F*	**17**	G7
Rabka	*PL*	**75**	E11
Răcăciuni	*RO*	**79**	E7
Racale	*I*	**31**	D11
Racalmuto	*I*	**30**	F4
Răcari	*RO*	**83**	B9
Racconigi	*I*	**19**	B9
Răchitoasa	*RO*	**79**	E8
Racibórz	*PL*	**75**	D9
Ráckeve	*H*	**76**	C5
Radashkovichy	*BY*	**69**	G11
Rădăuți	*RO*	**78**	B6
Radebeul	*D*	**41**	B10
Radenthein	*A*	**39**	E8
Radlje ob Dravi	*SLO*	**39**	F10
Radnevo	*BG*	**83**	G10
Radom	*PL*	**72**	H3
Radomir	*BG*	**82**	F5
Radomsko	*PL*	**75**	B10
Radovanu	*RO*	**83**	C11
Radoviš	*MK*	**82**	H4
Radovljica	*SLO*	**39**	F9
Radstock	*GB*	**8**	E6
Răducăneni	*RO*	**79**	D9
Radviliškis	*LT*	**68**	D6
Radymno	*PL*	**73**	D4
Radziejów	*PL*	**71**	E8
Radzyń Podlaski	*PL*	**72**	G5
Raffadali	*I*	**30**	F3
Ragunda	*S*	**52**	B4
Ragusa	*I*	**30**	G5
Rahden	*D*	**11**	C11
Rahovec	*RKS*	**81**	G11
Rain	*D*	**38**	B4
Raisio	*FIN*	**53**	G10
Rakamaz	*H*	**73**	H2
Rakhiv	*UA*	**78**	A3
Rakitovo	*BG*	**82**	G6
Rákóczifalva	*H*	**77**	C8
Rakovník	*CZ*	**41**	D10
Rakovski	*BG*	**83**	G8
Rakvere	*EST*	**67**	B8
Ramacca	*I*	**30**	F5
Rambervillers	*F*	**13**	E8
Rambouillet	*F*	**12**	D2
Râmnicu Sărat	*RO*	**79**	G7
Râmnicu Vâlcea	*RO*	**78**	G3
Ramonville-St-Agne	*F*	**17**	H7
Ramsey	*GBM*	**4**	E5
Ramsgate	*GB*	**9**	E11
Ramsjö	*S*	**52**	D3
Rånåsfoss	*N*	**46**	B2
Randazzo	*I*	**30**	E6
Randers	*DK*	**44**	D4
Randsjö	*S*	**51**	D11
Randsverk	*N*	**50**	E6
Rankweil	*A*	**37**	C9

Place	Country	Page	Grid
Raon-l'Étape	F	**13**	E9
Rapallo	I	**19**	C12
Rapla	EST	**66**	C6
Raseiniai	LT	**68**	E5
Råsele	S	**55**	F9
Răşinari	RO	**78**	F2
Raška	SRB	**81**	E11
Râşnov	RO	**78**	F5
Rätansbyn	S	**51**	C12
Ratekau	D	**42**	C6
Rathenow	D	**43**	E8
Rättvik	S	**52**	F3
Ratzeburg	D	**42**	C6
Raufoss	N	**49**	A8
Rauma	FIN	**53**	F10
Ravanusa	I	**30**	F4
Rava-Rus'ka	UA	**73**	D5
Ravenna	I	**35**	E9
Ravensburg	D	**37**	B9
Ravne na Koroškem	SLO	**39**	F10
Rawa Mazowiecka	PL	**71**	G10
Rawicz	PL	**70**	G6
Rayleigh	GB	**9**	E10
Razgrad	BG	**83**	D11
Razlog	BG	**82**	G5
Reading	GB	**9**	E8
Reboly	RUS	**63**	F11
Recanati	I	**35**	G11
Recaş	RO	**77**	F10
Recco	I	**19**	C12
Recea	RO	**78**	B2
Recke	D	**11**	C10
Reda	PL	**71**	B8
Redange	L	**13**	B7
Redcar	GB	**5**	D9
Redditch	GB	**8**	C6
Rediu	RO	**79**	C8
Rediu	RO	**79**	D7
Redon	F	**14**	F6
Redondela	E	**22**	D2
Redruth	GB	**8**	G2
Regalbuto	I	**30**	F5
Regen	D	**41**	F9
Regensburg	D	**41**	F8
Regenstauf	D	**41**	F8
Reggello	I	**35**	G8
Reggio di Calabria	I	**31**	G7
Reggio nell'Emilia	I	**34**	E6
Reghin	RO	**78**	D4
Reguengo	E	**22**	D2
Reguengos de Monsaraz	P	**24**	G4
Rehau	D	**41**	D8
Reichenbach	D	**41**	C8
Reichshoffen	F	**13**	D10
Reigate	GB	**9**	E9
Reignier	F	**36**	E4
Reims	F	**12**	C5
Reinosa	E	**23**	C10
Rellingen	D	**42**	C5
Remetea	RO	**78**	D5
Remiremont	F	**13**	E8
Remscheid	D	**11**	F9
Rena	N	**51**	F8
Rende	I	**31**	E8
Rendsburg	D	**42**	B5
Renedo	E	**23**	B10
Renens	CH	**36**	E4
Reni	UA	**79**	G9
Rennes	F	**14**	E6
Reposaari	FIN	**53**	E10
Requena	E	**27**	F9
Resen	MK	**86**	C4
Reşiţa	RO	**77**	G10
Rethel	F	**12**	B5
Rethymno	GR	**89**	G8
Reus	E	**21**	F8
Reuterstadt Stavenhagen	D	**43**	C9
Reutlingen	D	**38**	B1
Reutte	A	**37**	C10
Revel	F	**21**	B10
Revin	F	**12**	B6
Revúca	SK	**75**	G11
Reykjavík	IS	**6**	❐
Rezé	F	**14**	G6
Rēzekne	LV	**69**	B11
Rezina	MD	**79**	B11
Rheine	D	**11**	D10
Rheinsberg	D	**43**	D9
Rho	I	**34**	C4
Rhosllanerchrugog	GB	**4**	G6
Rhydaman	GB	**8**	D4
Rhyl	GB	**4**	G6
Ribadavia	E	**22**	D3
Ribadeo	E	**22**	B5
Ribadesella	E	**23**	B8
Ribe	DK	**44**	F2
Ribécourt-Dreslincourt	F	**12**	B3
Ribera	I	**30**	F3
Ribérac	F	**16**	D5
Ribnica	SLO	**39**	G9
Rîbniţa	MD	**79**	B11
Ribnitz-Damgarten	D	**43**	B8
Říčany	CZ	**41**	D11
Riccia	I	**33**	D9
Riccione	I	**35**	F10
Richmond	GB	**5**	E8
Ried im Innkreis	A	**39**	B8
Riesa	D	**41**	A9
Riesi	I	**30**	F4
Rieti	I	**32**	C6
Rīga	LV	**66**	G5
Rignano Flaminio	I	**32**	C5
Rignano sull'Arno	I	**35**	F8
Riihimäki	FIN	**64**	F5
Rijeka	HR	**80**	A1
Rijsel	F	**10**	G3
Rijssen	NL	**11**	C8
Rillieux-la-Pape	F	**36**	F2
Rimavská Sobota	SK	**75**	G11
Rimini	I	**35**	F10
Ringingen	D	**38**	B3
Ringkøbing	DK	**44**	E1
Ringsted	DK	**44**	F6
Ringwood	GB	**9**	F7
Riom	F	**17**	C10
Rio Maior	P	**24**	D2
Rionero in Vulture	I	**31**	B7
Ríos	E	**22**	E4
Rio Tinto	P	**22**	F2
Ripanj	SRB	**81**	C11
Ripi	I	**33**	D7
Ripley	GB	**5**	G8
Ripoll	E	**21**	D10
Ripon	GB	**5**	E8
Riposto	I	**30**	E6
Risca	GB	**8**	D5
Rîşcani	MD	**79**	B8
Risør	N	**48**	E6
Risskov	DK	**44**	D4
Riva del Garda	I	**35**	B7
Rivarolo Canavese	I	**34**	C2
Rives	F	**36**	G3
Rivesaltes	F	**18**	F1
Rivoli	I	**19**	A9
Rizziconi	I	**31**	G8
Roanne	F	**17**	C11
Roata de Jos	RO	**83**	B9
Röbel	D	**43**	D9
Rocca di Neto	I	**31**	E9
Rocca di Papa	I	**32**	D6
Roccastrada	I	**32**	A3
Roccella Ionica	I	**31**	G8
Rochdale	GB	**5**	F8
Rochefort	B	**10**	H6
Rochefort	F	**16**	C3
Rochlitz	D	**41**	B9
Rockenhausen	D	**13**	B10
Rødding	DK	**44**	F2
Rodel	GB	**2**	D2
Roden	NL	**11**	B8
Rodez	F	**17**	F9
Roding	D	**41**	F8
Rodna	RO	**78**	C4
Rodos	GR	**88**	G4
Rødovre	DK	**44**	E7
Roermond	NL	**11**	F7
Roeselare	B	**10**	F3
Rogatica	BIH	**81**	D9
Rogliano	I	**31**	E8
Rognac	F	**18**	D5
Rogoźno	PL	**70**	E6
Rohrbach in Oberösterreich	A	**39**	B8
Rokiškis	LT	**69**	C8
Rokycany	CZ	**41**	E10
Rollag	N	**48**	C6
Roma	I	**32**	D5
Roman	RO	**79**	D7
Romans-sur-Isère	F	**18**	A5
Rombas	F	**13**	C8
Rome	I	**32**	D5
Rometta	I	**30**	E6
Romford	GB	**9**	E9
Romilly-sur-Seine	F	**12**	D4
Romorantin-Lanthenay	F	**12**	G1
Romsey	GB	**9**	F7
Ronchamp	F	**13**	F8
Roncoferraro	I	**35**	D7
Ronda	E	**28**	E4
Rönnäng	S	**46**	F2
Rønne	DK	**45**	G10
Ronneby	S	**45**	D10
Ronnenberg	D	**42**	F5
Roosendaal	NL	**10**	E5
Ropczyce	PL	**73**	D3
Roquebrune-Cap-Martin	F	**19**	D9
Roquetas de Mar	E	**29**	E8
Roquevaire	F	**18**	E6
Rorschach	CH	**37**	C9
Rosarno	I	**31**	G8
Roscoff	F	**14**	D3
Roscommon	IRL	**7**	H4
Rosdorf	D	**40**	A4
Rosengarten	D	**42**	D5
Rosenheim	D	**38**	C6
Roses	E	**18**	G2
Roseţi	RO	**83**	C12
Roseto degli Abruzzi	I	**33**	B8
Roshchino	RUS	**65**	G10
Rosice	CZ	**74**	F6
Rosignano Marittimo	I	**34**	G6

Place	Country	Page	Grid
Roșiori de Vede	*RO*	**83**	C8
Roskilde	*DK*	**44**	E6
Roskovec	*AL*	**86**	D2
Rosolini	*I*	**30**	G6
Rosporden	*F*	**14**	F3
Rossano	*I*	**31**	D9
Roßlau	*D*	**43**	G8
Ross-on-Wye	*GB*	**8**	D6
Røssvassbukta	*N*	**55**	C6
Rostock	*D*	**43**	B8
Rot	*S*	**51**	F11
Rota	*E*	**25**	L6
Rotenburg (Wümme)	*D*	**11**	B12
Roth	*D*	**40**	F6
Rothenburg ob der Tauber	*D*	**40**	E5
Rotherham	*GB*	**5**	G9
Rothesay	*GB*	**2**	H4
Rothwell	*GB*	**5**	F8
Rottenmann	*A*	**39**	D9
Rotterdam	*NL*	**10**	D5
Rottweil	*D*	**13**	E11
Roubaix	*F*	**10**	G3
Rouen	*F*	**15**	C10
Roulers	*B*	**10**	F3
Rovaniemi	*FIN*	**61**	E8
Rovato	*I*	**34**	C5
Rovereto	*I*	**35**	B7
Rovigo	*I*	**35**	D8
Rovinari	*RO*	**78**	H1
Rovinj	*HR*	**35**	D11
Royal Wootton Bassett	*GB*	**8**	E6
Royan	*F*	**16**	D3
Roye	*F*	**12**	B3
Røyrvik	*N*	**54**	E6
Royston	*GB*	**9**	D9
Rožaje	*MNE*	**81**	F10
Rozavlea	*RO*	**78**	B3
Rozdil'na	*UA*	**79**	D12
Rožňava	*SK*	**73**	G1
Roznov	*RO*	**78**	D7
Rozzano	*I*	**34**	C4
Rubano	*I*	**35**	C8
Rucăr	*RO*	**78**	G4
Ruciane-Nida	*PL*	**68**	H3
Rudne	*UA*	**73**	E6
Rudnik nad Sadem	*PL*	**73**	C3
Rudolstadt	*D*	**41**	C7
Rudozem	*BG*	**87**	B10
Rudzyensk	*BY*	**69**	H11
Ruelle-sur-Touvre	*F*	**16**	D5
Ruffano	*I*	**31**	D11
Rufina	*I*	**35**	F8
Rugby	*GB*	**9**	C7
Rugeley	*GB*	**5**	H8
Ruginoasa	*RO*	**79**	C7
Ruma	*SRB*	**77**	G7
Rumburk	*CZ*	**41**	B11
Rumia	*PL*	**71**	B8
Rumilly	*F*	**36**	F3
Runcorn	*GB*	**5**	G7
Ruona	*FIN*	**53**	B12
Rupea	*RO*	**78**	E4
Rusănești	*RO*	**83**	C7
Ruse	*BG*	**83**	C10
Ruše	*SLO*	**39**	F11
Rushden	*GB*	**9**	C8
Ruski Krstur	*SRB*	**76**	F6
Russi	*I*	**35**	E9
Rute	*E*	**28**	D5
Rüthen	*D*	**11**	E11
Ruthin	*GB*	**4**	G6
Ruurlo	*NL*	**11**	D8
Ruvo di Puglia	*I*	**31**	A8
Ružomberok	*SK*	**75**	F10
Rybnik	*PL*	**75**	D9
Rychnov nad Kněžnou	*CZ*	**74**	D6
Ryde	*GB*	**9**	F8
Rydułtowy	*PL*	**75**	D9
Rygnestad	*N*	**48**	D4
Ryki	*PL*	**72**	G4
Rýmařov	*CZ*	**75**	D7
Rypin	*PL*	**71**	E9
Rysjedal	*N*	**50**	F2
Rzepin	*PL*	**43**	F11
Rzeszów	*PL*	**73**	D3

S

Place	Country	Page	Grid
Saalfeld	*D*	**41**	C7
Saalfelden am Steinernen Meer	*A*	**39**	D7
Saanen	*CH*	**36**	E5
Saarbrücken	*D*	**13**	C9
Saarenkylä	*FIN*	**61**	E8
Saarijärvi	*FIN*	**64**	B6
Saarlouis	*D*	**13**	C9
Šabac	*SRB*	**81**	B10
Sabadell	*E*	**21**	F10
Săbăoani	*RO*	**79**	C7
Sabaudia	*I*	**32**	E6
Sabiñánigo	*E*	**20**	D6
Sabinov	*SK*	**73**	F2
Sablé-sur-Sarthe	*F*	**15**	F8
Săcălășeni	*RO*	**78**	B2
Săcălaz	*RO*	**77**	F9
Săcele	*RO*	**78**	F5
Sacile	*I*	**35**	B10
Săcueni	*RO*	**77**	C11
Sadova	*RO*	**82**	C6
Sæby	*DK*	**44**	B4
Säffle	*S*	**46**	C4
Saffron Walden	*GB*	**9**	D10
Săgeata	*RO*	**79**	G7
Sagna	*RO*	**79**	D7
Sagunto	*E*	**27**	E10
Šahy	*SK*	**76**	A5
St-Affrique	*F*	**17**	G9
St-Aignan	*F*	**15**	G10
St-Alban-Leysse	*F*	**36**	G3
St Albans	*GB*	**9**	D9
St-Amand-Montrond	*F*	**12**	H3
St-Amarin	*F*	**13**	F9
St-André-de-Cubzac	*F*	**16**	E4
St Andrews	*GB*	**3**	G7
St Apollinaire	*F*	**12**	G6
St-Astier	*F*	**16**	E5
St-Aubin-lès-Elbeuf	*F*	**15**	C10
St Austell	*GB*	**8**	G2
St-Avé	*F*	**14**	F5
St-Avertin	*F*	**15**	G10
St-Avold	*F*	**13**	C9
St-Benoît	*F*	**16**	B5
St-Berthevin	*F*	**15**	E7
St Brelade	*GBJ*	**14**	C5
St-Brieuc	*F*	**14**	D5
St-Chamas	*F*	**18**	D5
St-Chamond	*F*	**17**	D12
St-Christol-lès-Alès	*F*	**17**	G11
St-Claude	*F*	**36**	E3
St Cloud	*F*	**12**	D2
St-Cyprien	*F*	**18**	F2
St-Cyr-sur-Loire	*F*	**15**	G9
St-Denis	*F*	**12**	D2
St-Dié	*F*	**13**	E9
St-Dizier	*F*	**12**	D6
St-Doulchard	*F*	**12**	G2
Ste-Adresse	*F*	**15**	B9
Ste-Livrade-sur-Lot	*F*	**16**	F5
St-Éloy-les-Mines	*F*	**17**	C9
Ste-Maxime	*F*	**19**	E8
Saintes	*F*	**16**	C3
St-Étienne	*F*	**17**	D12
St-Étienne-de-Montluc	*F*	**14**	G6
St-Florentin	*F*	**12**	E4
St-Florent-sur-Cher	*F*	**12**	H2
St-Flour	*F*	**17**	E10
St-Galmier	*F*	**17**	D12
St-Gaudens	*F*	**21**	B8
St-Georges-de-Didonne	*F*	**16**	D3
St-Germain	*F*	**12**	E5
St-Germain-du-Puy	*F*	**12**	G2
St-Gilles	*F*	**17**	H12
St-Gilles-Croix-de-Vie	*F*	**16**	B1
St-Girons	*F*	**21**	C8
St Helens	*GB*	**5**	G7
St Helier	*GBJ*	**14**	C5
St-Herblain	*F*	**14**	G6
St-Hilaire-de-Riez	*F*	**16**	A1
St-Hilaire-du-Harcouët	*F*	**15**	D7
St Ives	*GB*	**8**	G1
St Ives	*GB*	**9**	C9
St-Jacques-de-la-Lande	*F*	**14**	E6
St-Jean-d'Angély	*F*	**16**	C4
St Jean du Cardonnay	*F*	**15**	C10
St-Jean-de-Luz	*F*	**20**	B4
St-Jean-de-Monts	*F*	**14**	H6
St-Jean-de-Védas	*F*	**17**	H11
St-Jean-d'Illac	*F*	**16**	E3
St-Jorioz	*F*	**36**	F4
St-Junien	*F*	**16**	C6
St-Just-en-Chaussée	*F*	**12**	B2
St-Laurent-de-la-Salanque	*F*	**18**	F1
St-Laurent-du-Var	*F*	**19**	D8
St-Lô	*F*	**15**	C7
St-Lys	*F*	**17**	H6
St-Macaire	*F*	**16**	F4
St-Maixent-l'École	*F*	**16**	B4
St-Malo	*F*	**14**	D6
St-Marcel-lès-Valence	*F*	**18**	A5
St-Marcellin	*F*	**18**	A5
St Margaret's Hope	*GB*	**3**	E10
St Martens Latem	*B*	**10**	F4
St-Maurice-l'Exil	*F*	**17**	D12
St Maximin	*F*	**12**	C2
St-Maximin-la-Ste-Baume	*F*	**18**	D6
St-Médard-en-Jalles	*F*	**16**	E3
St-Mihiel	*F*	**13**	D7
St-Nazaire	*F*	**14**	G5
St Neots	*GB*	**9**	C9
St-Nicolas-de-Port	*F*	**13**	D8
St-Pair-sur-Mer	*F*	**14**	D6
St-Paul-lès-Dax	*F*	**16**	G3
St-Péray	*F*	**18**	A5
St Peter Port	*GBG*	**14**	C5
St Petersburg	*RUS*	**65**	G11
St-Philbert-de-Grand-Lieu	*F*	**14**	G6
St-Pierre-d'Oléron	*F*	**16**	C2
St-Pierre-en-Faucigny	*F*	**36**	F4
St-Pierre-lès-Elbeuf	*F*	**15**	C10

Place	Country	Page	Grid
St-Pierre-Montlimart	F	15	G7
St-Pol-de-Léon	F	14	D3
St Polten	A	39	B11
St-Pourçain-sur-Sioule	F	17	B10
St-Quentin	F	12	B4
St-Rambert-d'Albon	F	36	G2
St-Raphaël	F	19	D8
St-Renan	F	14	E2
St Sampson	GBG	14	C5
St Saviour	GBJ	14	C6
St-Sébastien-sur-Loire	F	14	G6
St-Tropez	F	19	E8
St-Vallier	F	17	B12
St-Vallier	F	18	A5
St-Victoret	F	18	D5
St-Yrieix-la-Perche	F	17	D7
Sajószentpéter	H	73	H1
Šakiai	LT	68	E5
Šaľa	SK	75	H8
Sala	S	47	B8
Sala Consilina	I	31	C7
Salamanca	E	23	G7
Salamina	GR	89	C7
Salas	E	22	B6
Salaspils	LV	66	G5
Salbris	F	12	G2
Šalčininkai	LT	69	G8
Saldus	LV	66	H3
Sale	GB	5	G7
Salemi	I	30	E2
Sälen	S	51	F11
Salerno	I	30	B6
Salford	GB	5	G7
Salgótarján	H	75	H11
Salice Salentino	I	31	C11
Salihli	TR	85	H5
Salisbury	GB	9	F7
Sălişte	RO	78	F2
Săliştea de Sus	RO	78	B3
Sallanches	F	36	F4
Sallent	E	21	E9
Salo	FIN	53	G12
Salò	I	34	C6
Salon-de-Provence	F	18	D5
Salonta	RO	77	D10
Salou	E	21	G8
Salsomaggiore Terme	I	34	D5
Salt	E	18	G1
Saltash	GB	8	G3
Saltcoats	GB	4	B4
Saltsjöbaden	S	47	C10
Saluzzo	I	19	B9
Salzburg	A	39	C7
Salzgitter	D	42	F6
Salzmünde	D	41	A7
Salzwedel	D	43	E7
Salzweg	D	39	B8
Samassi	I	32	G2
Sambir	UA	73	E5
Sambuca di Sicilia	I	30	F3
Sami	GR	88	B2
Samobor	HR	39	G11
Samokov	BG	82	F6
Šamorín	SK	76	A3
Samos	GR	88	D2
San Andrés del Rabanedo	E	23	C7
San Bartolomeo in Galdo	I	33	D9
San Benedetto del Tronto	I	33	A7
San Benedetto Po	I	35	D7
San Biago Platani	I	30	F3
San Casciano in Val di Pesa	I	35	G7
San Cataldo	I	30	F4
San Cipirello	I	30	E3
San Cipriano d'Aversa	I	30	B5
San Clemente	E	26	F6
Sâncrăieni	RO	78	E5
Sandanski	BG	87	B8
Sandbach	GB	5	G7
Sandefjord	N	49	D7
Sandhurst	GB	9	E8
Sandnes	N	48	E2
Sandnessjøen	N	54	B5
Sandomierz	PL	73	C3
Sândominic	RO	78	D5
San Donaci	I	31	C11
San Donà di Piave	I	35	C10
San Donato di Lecce	I	31	C11
Sándorfalva	H	77	E7
Sandown	GB	9	F8
Sandsele	S	55	D10
Sandstad	N	50	A6
Sandur	FO	3	B9
Sandvika	N	49	C8
Sandvika	N	54	G5
Sandviken	S	52	G4
Sandvikvåg	N	48	C2
Sandy	GB	9	C9
San Fele	I	31	B7
San Felice a Cancello	I	30	A5
San Felice Circeo	I	30	A3
San Ferdinando di Puglia	I	33	E11
San Fernando	E	25	M7
San Filippo del Mela	I	30	E6
San Gavino Monreale	I	32	G2
Sângeorgiu de Mureş	RO	78	D3
Sângeorgiu de Pădure	RO	78	E4
Sângeorz-Băi	RO	78	C3
Sangerhausen	D	41	A6
Săngeru	RO	78	G6
San Gimignano	I	35	G7
San Giorgio del Sannio	I	30	A6
San Giorgio Ionico	I	31	C10
San Giovanni Gemini	I	30	F3
San Giovanni in Fiore	I	31	E9
San Giovanni Rotondo	I	33	D11
San Giuliano Terme	I	34	F6
San Giuseppe Jato	I	30	E3
San Giuseppe Vesuviano	I	30	B5
San Giustino	I	35	G9
San Guiliano Milanese	I	34	C4
Sanislău	RO	77	B11
San Javier	E	29	C11
San Juan de Alicante	E	27	H10
Sankt Andrä	A	39	E10
Sankt Augustin	D	11	G9
Sankt Gallen	CH	37	C8
Sankt Moritz	CH	37	E9
Sankt-Peterburg	RUS	65	G11
Sankt Peter-Ording	D	42	B4
Sankt Pölten	A	39	B11
Sankt Veit an der Glan	A	39	E9
Sankt Wendel	D	13	C9
San Lazzaro di Savena	I	35	E8
San Lorenzo de El Escorial	E	23	H10
Sanlúcar de Barrameda	E	25	L6
San Lucido	I	31	E8
Sanluri	I	32	G2
San Marcello Pistoiese	I	35	F7
San Marco Argentano	I	31	D8
San Marco in Lamis	I	33	D10
San Marino	RMS	35	F9
Sânmartin	RO	77	C10
San Martín de la Vega	E	26	D5
San Martín de Valdeiglesias	E	23	H9
San Michele Salentino	I	31	B10
San Miniato	I	35	G7
Sannicandro di Bari	I	31	B9
Sannicandro Garganico	I	33	D10
Sannicola	I	31	C11
Sânnicolau Mare	RO	77	E8
Sanok	PL	73	E3
San Pancrazio Salentino	I	31	C11
San Paolo D'Argon	I	34	B5
San Paolo di Civitate	I	33	D10
San Pedro del Pinatar	E	29	C11
Sânpetru Mare	RO	77	E9
San Pietro Vernotico	I	31	C11
San Remo	I	19	D9
San Roque	E	22	D3
San Roque	E	25	M8
San Salvo	I	33	C9
San Sebastián de los Reyes	E	23	H10
Sansepolcro	I	35	G9
San Severo	I	33	D10
Sanski Most	BIH	80	B5
Santa Cataliña de Armada	E	22	C2
Santa Caterina Villarmosa	I	30	F4
Santa Croce Camerina	I	30	G5
Santa Cruz de Mudela	E	26	G5
Santaella	E	28	D4
Santa Eulalia del Río	E	29	G7
Santa Faz	E	27	H10
Santa Fé	E	28	E6
Sant'Agata di Militello	I	30	E5
Santa Giustina	I	35	B9
Santa Lucia del Mela	I	30	E6
Santa Margalida	E	29	F10
Santa Margarida de Montbui	E	21	F9
Santa Margherita di Belice	I	30	F2
Santa Margherita Ligure	I	19	C12
Santa Maria da Feira	P	22	G2
Santa María de Cayón	E	23	B10
Santa Marinella	I	32	C4
Sântana	RO	77	E10
Sant'Anastasia	I	30	B5
Sant'Anatolia di Narco	I	32	B6
Santander	E	23	B10
Sant'Angelo in Lizzola	I	35	F10
Sant'Angelo Lodigiano	I	34	C4
Santa Ninfa	I	30	E2
Sant'Antioco	I	32	H1
Sant Antoni de Portmany	E	29	G7
Santanyí	E	29	F10
Santa Pola	E	29	C11
Sant'Arcangelo	I	31	C8
Santarcangelo di Romagna	I	35	F9
Santarém	P	24	E3
Santa Teresa di Gallura	I	32	C3
Santa Teresa di Riva	I	30	E6
Santa Uxía de Ribeira	E	22	D2
Santa Venerina	I	30	F6
Sant Boi de Llobregat	E	21	F10
Sant Carles de la Ràpita	E	21	G7
Sant Celoni	E	21	E10
Sant Elia Fiumerapido	I	33	D7
Sant'Elpidio a Mare	I	35	G11
Santeramo in Colle	I	31	B9
Sant Feliu de Guíxols	E	18	H2
Santhià	I	34	C2
Santiago de Compostela	E	22	C2

S

Place	Country	Page	Grid
Santiago de la Espada	E	29	C8
Sant Joan de Vilatorrada	E	21	E9
Sant Josep de sa Talaia	E	29	G7
Sant Julià de Lòria	AND	21	D9
Santo André	P	25	H2
Santo Domingo de la Calzada	E	20	D1
Santomera	E	29	C10
Santoña	E	20	B1
Santo Stefano di Camastra	I	30	E5
Santo Stefano Quisquina	I	30	F3
Santo Stino di Livenza	I	35	B10
Santo Tirso	P	22	F2
Santurtzi	E	20	B1
San Vicente de Alcántara	E	24	D5
San Vicente del Raspeig	E	27	H10
San Vincenzo	I	34	H6
San Vito Chietino	I	33	C8
San Vito dei Normanni	I	31	B11
Sanxenxo	E	22	D2
São João da Madeira	P	22	G2
Sa Pobla	E	29	F10
Sapri	I	31	C7
Sarajevo	BIH	81	D8
Saran	F	12	F2
Sarandë	AL	86	E2
Sarata	UA	79	E12
Saray	TR	85	B4
Sárbogárd	H	76	D5
Sarentino	I	37	D11
Sarichioi	RO	79	H10
Sarıkemer	TR	88	D3
Sarıköy	TR	85	D4
Sarkad	H	77	D9
Şarköy	TR	85	C3
Sarlat-la-Canéda	F	17	E7
Şărmăşag	RO	77	C12
Sărmaşu	RO	78	D3
Sarnen	CH	13	H11
Sarno	I	30	B5
Saronno	I	34	C4
Sárospatak	H	73	H2
Sarpsborg	N	46	C2
Sarrebourg	F	13	D9
Sarreguemines	F	13	C9
Sarria	E	22	C4
Sarròch	I	32	H2
Saruhanlı	TR	85	G4
Sárvár	H	76	C2
Sarzana	I	34	F5
Sarzeau	F	14	F5
Săsciori	RO	78	F2
Sascut	RO	79	E8
Sassano	I	31	C7
Sassari	I	32	D2
Sassnitz	D	43	A10
Sassoferrato	I	35	G10
Sasso Marconi	I	35	E7
Sátoraljaújhely	H	73	H3
Satulung	RO	78	B1
Satu Mare	RO	77	B12
Sauda	N	48	C3
Saujon	F	16	D3
Saulgau	D	37	B9
Saumur	F	15	G8
Sausheim	F	13	F10
Sausset-les-Pins	F	18	E5
Sautron	F	14	G6
Sava	I	31	C10
Savaştepe	TR	85	F4
Savenay	F	14	G6
Săveni	RO	79	B7
Săveni	RO	83	B12
Saverne	F	13	D9
Savigliano	I	19	B9
Savignano sul Rubicone	I	35	F9
Săvineşti	RO	78	D6
Sävja	S	47	B9
Savona	I	19	C11
Savonlinna	FIN	65	D10
Sävsjö	S	45	B9
Sax	E	27	H9
Sazlı	TR	88	D3
Scaër	F	14	E3
Scalby	GB	5	E10
Scalea	I	31	D7
Scandicci	I	35	F7
Scanzano Jonico	I	31	C9
Scarborough	GB	5	E10
Scarperia	I	35	F8
Schaafheim	D	40	D3
Schaerbeek	B	10	F5
Schaffhausen	CH	13	F11
Schagen	NL	10	C6
Schärding	A	39	B8
Scheeßel	D	11	B12
Şcheia	RO	78	B6
Scheßlitz	D	40	D6
Schierling	D	38	A6
Schio	I	35	B8
Schleiz	D	41	C7
Schleswig	D	42	A5
Schleusingen	D	40	C6
Schlüchtern	D	40	C4
Schlüsselfeld	D	40	E6
Schmölln	D	41	B8
Schönebeck (Elbe)	D	43	F8
Schongau	D	37	B10
Schöningen	D	43	F7
Schopfheim	D	13	F10
Schöppenstedt	D	42	F6
Schotten	D	11	G12
Schramberg	D	13	E11
Schwaan	D	43	C8
Schwäbisch Gmünd	D	38	A2
Schwäbisch Hall	D	40	F4
Schwabmünchen	D	37	A10
Schwandorf	D	41	E8
Schwarzenbek	D	42	C6
Schwaz	A	37	C12
Schwedt an der Oder	D	43	D11
Schweinfurt	D	40	D5
Schwerin	D	43	C7
Schwyz	CH	13	G11
Sciacca	I	30	F2
Scicli	I	30	G5
Scilla	I	31	G7
Ścinawa	PL	70	H5
Scionzier	F	36	F4
Scobinţi	RO	79	C7
Scordia	I	30	F5
Scorniceşti	RO	83	B7
Scorrano	I	31	C12
Scunthorpe	GB	5	F9
Seaham	GB	5	D9
Seaton	GB	4	D6
Seaton	GB	8	F5
Seaton Delaval	GB	5	C8
Sebeş	RO	78	F2
Sebezh	RUS	69	C12
Sebiş	RO	77	E11
Sebnitz	D	41	B11
Seclin	F	10	G3
Sečovce	SK	73	G3
Secusigiu	RO	77	E9
Sedan	F	12	B6
Sedico	I	35	B9
Sedlčany	CZ	41	E11
Sędziszów Małopolski	PL	73	D3
Seeboden	A	39	E8
Seelow	D	43	E11
Seevetal	D	42	D5
Şegarcea	RO	82	C6
Segorbe	E	27	E10
Segovia	E	23	G10
Segré	F	15	F7
Şeica Mare	RO	78	E3
Seinäjoki	FIN	53	B11
Seini	RO	77	B12
Sejny	PL	68	G6
Selargius	I	32	G3
Selb	D	41	D8
Selby	GB	5	F9
Selendi	TR	85	G6
Selenicë	AL	86	D2
Sélestat	F	13	E10
Selimpaşa	TR	85	B5
Selkirk	GB	5	B7
Sellia Marina	I	31	F9
Selva	N	51	A7
Sénas	F	18	D5
Senec	SK	75	H8
Senftenberg	D	43	G10
Senica	SK	75	G7
Senigallia	I	35	F11
Senise	I	31	C8
Senj	HR	80	B2
Sens	F	12	E4
Senta	SRB	77	F7
Šentjur pri Celju	SLO	39	F10
Sępólno Krajeńskie	PL	71	D7
Septèmes-les-Vallons	F	18	D5
Septemvri	BG	83	G7
Seraing	B	11	G7
Seravezza	I	34	F6
Sereď	SK	75	H8
Seregno	I	34	C4
Sérignan	F	18	E2
Serino	I	30	B6
Serracapriola	I	33	D10
Serradifalco	I	30	F4
Serramanna	I	32	G2
Serramazzoni	I	35	E7
Serra San Bruno	I	31	F8
Serravalle	RMS	35	F9
Serrenti	I	32	G2
Serres	GR	87	C8
Sersale	I	31	E9
Sertolovo	RUS	65	G11
Serzedo	P	22	G2
Sessa Aurunca	I	30	A4
Sesto Fiorentino	I	35	F7
Sesto San Giovanni	I	34	C4
Sestri Levante	I	19	C12
Sestroretsk	RUS	65	G11
Sestu	I	32	G3
Sète	F	18	D3
Setúbal	P	24	F2
Sevenoaks	GB	9	E9
Sevilla	E	25	J7
Seville	E	25	J7

Place	Country	Page	Grid
Sevlievo	*BG*	**83**	E8
Sevnica	*SLO*	**39**	G10
Sevojno	*SRB*	**81**	D10
Sevrey	*F*	**36**	F4
Seynod	*F*	**36**	F4
Seysses	*F*	**21**	B9
Sežana	*SLO*	**35**	B12
Sézanne	*F*	**12**	D4
Sezze	*I*	**32**	D6
Sfântu Gheorghe	*RO*	**78**	F5
's-Gravenhage	*NL*	**10**	D5
's-Gravenzande	*NL*	**10**	D5
Shaftesbury	*GB*	**8**	F6
Shanklin	*GB*	**9**	F8
Sharkawshchyna	*BY*	**69**	E11
Shats'k	*UA*	**72**	H6
Shchyrets'	*UA*	**73**	E6
Sheerness	*GB*	**9**	E10
Sheffield	*GB*	**5**	G8
Shefford	*GB*	**9**	D9
Shepton Mallet	*GB*	**8**	E6
Sherborne	*GB*	**8**	F6
Sherburn in Elmet	*GB*	**5**	F9
Sheringham	*GB*	**5**	H12
's-Hertogenbosch	*NL*	**11**	E7
Shijak	*AL*	**86**	B2
Shkodër	*AL*	**81**	H9
Shrewsbury	*GB*	**8**	B5
Shtime	*RKS*	**81**	G12
Shumen	*BG*	**83**	E11
Shyryayeve	*UA*	**79**	C12
Siatista	*GR*	**86**	E5
Šiauliai	*LT*	**68**	C6
Šibenik	*HR*	**80**	D3
Sibiu	*RO*	**78**	F3
Sibo	*S*	**52**	E4
Siculeni	*RO*	**78**	E5
Šid	*SRB*	**76**	G6
Sidari	*GR*	**86**	F2
Siderno	*I*	**31**	G8
Sidirokastro	*GR*	**87**	C8
Sidmouth	*GB*	**8**	F5
Siedlce	*PL*	**72**	F4
Siegen	*D*	**11**	F10
Siegsdorf	*D*	**38**	C6
Siemiatycze	*PL*	**72**	F5
Siena	*I*	**35**	G8
Sieradz	*PL*	**71**	H8
Sieraków	*PL*	**70**	E5
Sierpc	*PL*	**71**	E9
Sierre	*CH*	**34**	A1
Sighetu Marmaţiei	*RO*	**78**	B2
Sighişoara	*RO*	**78**	E4
Sigmaringen	*D*	**37**	B8
Signa	*I*	**35**	F7
Sigüenza	*E*	**20**	G2
Sigulda	*LV*	**66**	G6
Siilinjärvi	*FIN*	**63**	H8
Siklós	*H*	**76**	F4
Šilalė	*LT*	**68**	D4
Silandro	*I*	**37**	D10
Silistra	*BG*	**83**	C12
Silivri	*TR*	**85**	B5
Silkeborg	*DK*	**44**	D3
Silla	*E*	**27**	F10
Sillamäe	*EST*	**67**	B9
Silleda	*E*	**22**	C3
Šilutė	*LT*	**68**	E3
Silvi	*I*	**33**	B8
Simeonovgrad	*BG*	**83**	G9
Simeria	*RO*	**77**	F12
Şimian	*RO*	**82**	B4
Simitli	*BG*	**82**	G5
Şimleu Silvaniei	*RO*	**77**	C12
Simmerath	*D*	**11**	G8
Simrishamn	*S*	**45**	F9
Sinaia	*RO*	**78**	G5
Sinalunga	*I*	**35**	G8
Sindelfingen	*D*	**40**	G3
Sındırgı	*TR*	**85**	F5
Sindos	*GR*	**87**	D7
Sines	*P*	**25**	H2
Sîngera	*MD*	**79**	D11
Sîngerei	*MD*	**79**	B9
Siniscola	*I*	**32**	E3
Sinj	*HR*	**80**	D5
Sinnai	*I*	**32**	G3
Sinnes	*N*	**48**	E3
Sintra	*P*	**24**	F1
Sint-Truiden	*B*	**10**	F6
Siófok	*H*	**76**	D4
Sion	*CH*	**34**	A1
Şipote	*RO*	**79**	C8
Sira	*N*	**48**	F3
Siracusa	*I*	**30**	G6
Siret	*RO*	**78**	B6
Şiria	*RO*	**77**	E10
Širvintos	*LT*	**69**	E8
Sisak	*HR*	**76**	G1
Şişeşti	*RO*	**78**	B2
Sisteron	*F*	**18**	C6
Siteia	*GR*	**89**	G11
Sitges	*E*	**21**	F9
Sittard	*NL*	**11**	F7
Sivac	*SRB*	**76**	F6
Siverskiy	*RUS*	**67**	B12
Six-Fours-les-Plages	*F*	**18**	E6
Sjenica	*SRB*	**81**	E10
Sjöbo	*S*	**45**	E8
Sjonbotn	*N*	**54**	B6
Skælsør	*DK*	**44**	F5
Skagen	*DK*	**44**	A4
Skala	*GR*	**89**	D12
Skalica	*SK*	**75**	F7
Skanderborg	*DK*	**44**	E3
Skanör med Falsterbo	*S*	**45**	F7
Skara	*S*	**46**	E4
Skarszewy	*PL*	**71**	C8
Skarżysko-Kamienna	*PL*	**73**	B1
Skawina	*PL*	**75**	D11
Skegness	*GB*	**5**	G11
Skei	*N*	**50**	E3
Skellefteå	*S*	**56**	E3
Skerries	*IRL*	**4**	F3
Ski	*N*	**46**	B1
Skiathos	*GR*	**87**	G8
Skidal'	*BY*	**72**	D7
Skien	*N*	**49**	D7
Skierniewice	*PL*	**71**	G10
Skipton	*GB*	**5**	F8
Skive	*DK*	**44**	D2
Skjærhalden	*N*	**46**	D1
Skjern	*DK*	**44**	E2
Skjervøy	*N*	**58**	D4
Škofja Loka	*SLO*	**39**	G9
Skoghall	*S*	**46**	C4
Skogmo	*N*	**54**	E4
Skole	*UA*	**73**	F5
Skopelos	*GR*	**87**	G9
Skopje	*MK*	**82**	G2
Skorovatn	*N*	**54**	E5
Skövde	*S*	**46**	E5
Skråmestø	*N*	**48**	B1
Skrunda	*LV*	**66**	H2
Skuodas	*LT*	**68**	C3
Skurup	*S*	**45**	F8
Skutskär	*S*	**52**	G5
Skwierzyna	*PL*	**70**	F4
Slagelse	*DK*	**44**	F5
Slangerup	*DK*	**44**	E6
Slănic	*RO*	**78**	G6
Slantsy	*RUS*	**67**	C10
Slaný	*CZ*	**41**	D10
Slatina	*HR*	**76**	F3
Slatina	*RO*	**78**	C6
Slatina	*RO*	**83**	B7
Slättberg	*S*	**51**	F12
Slavičín	*CZ*	**75**	F8
Slavonski Brod	*HR*	**76**	G4
Slavyanovo	*BG*	**83**	D8
Sławno	*PL*	**70**	B6
Sleaford	*GB*	**5**	H10
Sligeach	*IRL*	**6**	G4
Sligo	*IRL*	**6**	G4
Sliven	*BG*	**83**	F10
Slivnitsa	*BG*	**82**	E5
Slobozia	*MD*	**79**	D12
Slobozia	*RO*	**83**	B8
Slobozia	*RO*	**83**	B12
Slough	*GB*	**9**	E8
Sløvåg	*N*	**50**	G1
Slovenj Gradec	*SLO*	**39**	F10
Slovenska Bistrica	*SLO*	**39**	F11
Slovenske Konjice	*SLO*	**39**	F10
Słubice	*PL*	**43**	F11
Słupca	*PL*	**71**	F7
Słupsk	*PL*	**70**	B6
Smalyavichy	*BY*	**69**	G12
Smarhon'	*BY*	**69**	F10
Smederevo	*SRB*	**81**	C12
Smederevska Palanka	*SRB*	**81**	C12
Smedjebacken	*S*	**46**	A6
Smeeni	*RO*	**79**	G7
Śmigiel	*PL*	**70**	G6
Smilavichy	*BY*	**69**	H12
Smiltene	*LV*	**67**	F7
Smolyan	*BG*	**87**	B10
Smyadovo	*BG*	**83**	E11
Snagov	*RO*	**83**	B10
Sneek	*NL*	**11**	B7
Snina	*SK*	**73**	F3
Soběslav	*CZ*	**41**	F11
Sobra	*HR*	**80**	F6
Sobrance	*SK*	**73**	G3
Sochaczew	*PL*	**71**	F10
Socuéllamos	*E*	**26**	F6
Sodankylä	*FIN*	**61**	C8
Söderfors	*S*	**52**	G5
Söderhamn	*S*	**52**	E5
Söderköping	*S*	**47**	E7
Södertälje	*S*	**47**	C9
Södra Sandby	*S*	**45**	E8
Soest	*D*	**11**	E11
Sofades	*GR*	**86**	F6
Sofia	*BG*	**82**	F5
Sofiya	*BG*	**82**	F5
Sögel	*D*	**11**	B10
Søgne	*N*	**48**	G5
Soham	*GB*	**9**	C10
Soignies	*B*	**10**	G5

Place	Country	Page	Grid
Soissons	F	12	C4
Söke	TR	88	D3
Sokobanja	SRB	82	D3
Sokółka	PL	72	D6
Sokołow Podlaski	PL	72	F4
Solarino	I	30	G6
Şoldăneşti	MD	79	B10
Solec Kujawski	PL	71	E8
Soleto	I	31	C11
Solihull	GB	9	C7
Solin	HR	80	E4
Sollefteå	S	52	B5
Sollentuna	S	47	C9
Sóller	E	29	F9
Solofra	I	30	B6
Solothurn	CH	13	G10
Solsona	E	21	E9
Solt	H	76	D6
Soltau	D	42	E5
Soltvadkert	H	76	D6
Sölvesborg	S	45	E9
Soma	TR	85	F4
Sombor	SRB	76	F6
Şomcuţa Mare	RO	78	B1
Somero	FIN	53	G12
Sommacampagna	I	35	C7
Sommatino	I	30	F4
Sömmerda	D	40	B6
Sondalo	I	34	A6
Sønderborg	DK	44	G3
Sondershausen	D	40	A6
Sondrio	I	34	B5
Sonneberg	D	40	C6
Sonseca	E	26	E4
Son Servera	E	29	F10
Sonta	SRB	76	F6
Sonthofen	D	37	C10
Sopot	BG	83	F8
Sopot	PL	71	B8
Sopron	H	76	B2
Sora	I	33	D7
Sorgues	F	18	C5
Soria	E	20	E2
Soriano nel Cimino	I	32	B5
Sorø	DK	44	F6
Soroca	MD	79	A9
Sorrento	I	30	B5
Sorsele	S	55	C10
Sorso	I	32	D2
Sortavala	RUS	65	D11
Sortino	I	30	G6
Sosnovyy Bor	RUS	65	H10
Sosnowiec	PL	75	D10
Soto	E	22	B6
Sotrondio	E	23	B7
Soufli	GR	85	B1
Souk el Had el Rharbia	MA	28	H2
Souk-Khémis-des-Anjra	MA	28	H3
Souk Tleta Taghramet	MA	28	G3
Souppes-sur-Loing	F	12	E3
Soustons	F	16	G2
Southampton	GB	9	F7
Southend-on-Sea	GB	9	E10
Southport	GB	5	F6
South Queensferry	GB	2	G6
South Shields	GB	5	D8
Sovata	RO	78	D4
Soverato	I	31	F9
Sovetsk	RUS	68	E4
Sovetskiy	RUS	65	F9
Sovicille	I	35	G7
Soyaux	F	16	D5
Spadafora	I	30	D6
Spalding	GB	5	H10
Sparanise	I	30	A5
Sparti	GR	88	D5
Spata	GR	89	C7
Spello	I	32	A5
Spennymoor	GB	5	D8
Spetses	GR	88	D6
Spezzano Albanese	I	31	D8
Spiez	CH	36	D6
Spijkenisse	NL	10	D5
Spilamberto	I	35	E7
Spilimbergo	I	35	B10
Spinazzola	I	31	B8
Spinea	I	35	C9
Spinetoli	I	33	B7
Spišská Belá	SK	73	F1
Spišská Nová Ves	SK	73	F1
Spittal an der Drau	A	39	E8
Spjelkavik	N	50	C3
Split	HR	80	E4
Spoleto	I	32	B6
Spoltore	I	33	B8
Spremberg	D	43	G11
Springe	D	42	F5
Sprova	N	54	F4
Squinzano	I	31	C11
Srbobran	SRB	77	F7
Sredets	BG	83	F12
Srednogorie	BG	83	F7
Śrem	PL	70	G6
Sremčica	SRB	81	C11
Sremska Kamenica	SRB	77	G7
Sremska Mitrovica	SRB	77	H7
Sremski Karlovci	SRB	77	G7
Środa Wielkopolska	PL	70	F6
Srpska Crnja	SRB	77	F8
Stade	D	42	C5
Staden	B	10	F3
Stadskanaal	NL	11	B9
Staffanstorp	S	45	E8
Staffelstein	D	40	D6
Stafford	GB	5	H8
t-upon-Thames	GB	9	E8
Stalowa Wola	PL	73	C3
Stâlpeni	RO	78	G4
Stamboliyski	BG	83	G7
Stamford	GB	9	B9
Stănileşti	RO	79	D9
Stanišić	SRB	76	F6
Stanley	GB	5	D8
Stans	CH	13	H11
Staplehurst	GB	9	E10
Starachowice	PL	73	B2
Stará Ľubovňa	SK	73	F1
Stara Moravica	SRB	76	F6
Stara Pazova	SRB	77	H7
Stara Zagora	BG	83	F9
Stargard Szczeciński	PL	43	D12
Starogard Gdański	PL	71	C8
Starokozache	UA	79	E12
Staryy Sambir	UA	73	E4
Staßfurt	D	43	G7
Staszów	PL	73	C2
Stăuceni	MD	79	C10
Staudach im Allgau	D	38	D2
Stavang	N	50	E2
Stavanger	N	48	E2
Staveley	GB	5	G9
Stavsnäs	S	47	C10
Stebnyk	UA	73	F5
Steenwijk	NL	11	C8
Ştefan cel Mare	RO	79	E7
Ştefăneşti	RO	78	H4
Ştefăneşti	RO	79	B8
Ştefan Vodă	MD	79	D12
Ştei	RO	77	D11
Steinfurt	D	11	D9
Steinheim	D	11	D12
Steinkjer	N	54	F4
Stendal	D	43	E8
Stenløse	DK	44	E6
Stenungsund	S	46	F2
Šternberk	CZ	75	E7
Stes-Maries-de-la-Mer	F	18	D4
Stevenage	GB	9	D9
Steyerberg	D	11	C12
Steyr	A	39	C9
Stiens	NL	11	B7
Štip	MK	82	H3
Stirling	GB	2	G5
Stjørdalshalsen	N	51	A8
Stockach	D	13	F12
Stockerau	A	39	B12
Stockholm	S	47	C9
Stockport	GB	5	G8
Stockton-on-Tees	GB	5	D9
Stöde	S	52	C4
Stoke-on-Trent	GB	5	G8
Stolac	BIH	81	F7
Stolberg (Rheinland)	D	11	G8
Stollberg	D	41	C9
Stolzenau	D	11	C12
Stone	GB	5	H8
Stonehaven	GB	3	E8
Storby	FIN	47	A11
Støren	N	51	B7
Storkow	D	43	F10
Storlien	S	51	B9
Stornoway	GB	2	C2
Storozhynets'	UA	78	A5
Storrington	GB	9	F9
Storuman	S	55	D10
Storvreta	S	47	B9
Stourbridge	GB	8	C6
Stourport-on-Severn	GB	8	C6
Støvring	DK	44	C3
Stowmarket	GB	9	C11
Strabane	GB	4	D1
Straja	RO	78	B5
Strakonice	CZ	41	F10
Straldzha	BG	83	F11
Stralsund	D	43	B9
Strängnäs	S	47	C8
Stranraer	GB	4	D4
Strasbourg	F	13	D10
Strasburg	D	43	D10
Străşeni	MD	79	C10
Straßwalchen	A	39	C7
Stratford-upon-Avon	GB	9	C7
Strathaven	GB	2	H5
Straubing	D	38	A6
Straumen	N	59	B11
Strausberg	D	43	E10
Strážnice	CZ	75	F7
Street	GB	8	E5
Strehaia	RO	82	B5

Place	Country	Page	Grid
Strelcha	*BG*	**83**	F7
Stříbro	*CZ*	**41**	E9
Strommen	*N*	**46**	B1
Stromness	*GB*	**3**	E9
Strömstad	*S*	**46**	D2
Strömsund	*S*	**55**	G8
Strongoli	*I*	**31**	E9
Stropkov	*SK*	**73**	F3
Stroud	*GB*	**8**	D6
Struer	*DK*	**44**	D2
Struga	*MK*	**86**	C3
Strugi-Krasnyye	*RUS*	**67**	E11
Strumica	*MK*	**87**	B7
Stryn	*N*	**50**	D3
Stryy	*UA*	**73**	F6
Strzegom	*PL*	**74**	B6
Strzelce Krajeńskie	*PL*	**70**	E4
Strzelce Opolskie	*PL*	**75**	C9
Strzelin	*PL*	**75**	C7
Strzelno	*PL*	**71**	E8
Strzyżów	*PL*	**73**	E3
Studénka	*CZ*	**75**	E8
Stupava	*SK*	**75**	H7
Štúrovo	*SK*	**76**	B5
Stuttgart	*D*	**13**	D12
Suances	*E*	**23**	B10
Subiaco	*I*	**32**	C6
Subotica	*SRB*	**77**	E7
Suceava	*RO*	**78**	B6
Suchedniów	*PL*	**73**	B1
Suciu de Sus	*RO*	**78**	C2
Sudbury	*GB*	**9**	D10
Sudova Vyshnya	*UA*	**73**	E5
Sueca	*E*	**27**	F10
Süedinenie	*BG*	**83**	G7
Suhaia	*RO*	**83**	D8
Suharekë	*RKS*	**81**	G12
Suhl	*D*	**40**	C6
Sulechów	*PL*	**70**	G4
Sulęcin	*PL*	**70**	F4
Sulejów	*PL*	**71**	H10
Sulejówek	*PL*	**71**	F11
Sulingen	*D*	**11**	C12
Sully-sur-Loire	*F*	**12**	F2
Sulmona	*I*	**33**	C8
Sulzbach-Rosenberg	*D*	**41**	E7
Sumburgh	*GB*	**3**	C12
Sümeg	*H*	**76**	D3
Sumiswald	*CH*	**13**	G10
Šumperk	*CZ*	**75**	D7
Sundby	*DK*	**44**	C3
Sunde	*N*	**48**	C2
Sunderland	*GB*	**5**	D9
Sundsvall	*S*	**52**	C5
Sunnansjö	*S*	**46**	A6
Sunndalsøra	*N*	**50**	C5
Suolahti	*FIN*	**64**	B6
Supur	*RO*	**77**	C12
Surahammar	*S*	**47**	B7
Šurany	*SK*	**76**	A4
Surbo	*I*	**31**	C11
Surdulica	*SRB*	**82**	F3
Surgères	*F*	**16**	C3
Súria	*E*	**21**	E9
Surte	*S*	**44**	A6
Susa	*I*	**19**	A8
Sušice	*CZ*	**41**	F10
Susurluk	*TR*	**85**	E5
Susz	*PL*	**71**	C9
Sutton Coldfield	*GB*	**9**	C7

Place	Country	Page	Grid
Sutton in Ashfield	*GB*	**5**	G9
Suvorovo	*BG*	**83**	D12
Suwałki	*PL*	**68**	G5
Suzzara	*I*	**35**	D7
Svalyava	*UA*	**73**	G4
Svedala	*S*	**45**	F8
Sveg	*S*	**51**	D12
Švenčionėliai	*LT*	**69**	E9
Švenčionys	*LT*	**69**	E9
Svendborg	*DK*	**44**	G4
Svenes	*N*	**48**	E5
Svenstavik	*S*	**51**	C12
Sveti Nikole	*MK*	**82**	G3
Světlá nad Sázavou	*CZ*	**74**	E5
Svetlogorsk	*RUS*	**68**	E2
Svetlyy	*RUS*	**68**	F2
Svetogorsk	*RUS*	**65**	E9
Svidník	*SK*	**73**	F2
Svilajnac	*SRB*	**81**	C12
Svilengrad	*BG*	**83**	H10
Svishtov	*BG*	**83**	D9
Svislach	*BY*	**72**	E6
Svitavy	*CZ*	**74**	E6
Svoge	*BG*	**82**	E5
Svolvær	*N*	**57**	D3
Svrljig	*SRB*	**82**	D3
Swaffham	*GB*	**9**	B10
Swanage	*GB*	**8**	F6
Swanley	*GB*	**9**	E9
Swansea	*GB*	**8**	D4
Swarzędz	*PL*	**70**	F6
Świdnica	*PL*	**74**	B6
Świdnik	*PL*	**73**	B4
Świdwin	*PL*	**70**	C5
Świebodzice	*PL*	**74**	B6
Świebodzin	*PL*	**70**	F4
Świecie	*PL*	**71**	D8
Swindon	*GB*	**9**	E7
Świnoujście	*PL*	**43**	C11
Swords	*IRL*	**4**	G2
Syców	*PL*	**75**	A8
Syston	*GB*	**9**	B8
Szabadszállás	*H*	**76**	D6
Szamotuły	*PL*	**70**	E6
Szarvas	*H*	**77**	D8
Százhalombatta	*H*	**76**	C5
Szczebrzeszyn	*PL*	**73**	C4
Szczecin	*PL*	**43**	D11
Szczecinek	*PL*	**70**	C6
Szczytna	*PL*	**74**	C6
Szczytno	*PL*	**71**	D11
Szécsény	*H*	**75**	H11
Szeged	*H*	**77**	E7
Szeghalom	*H*	**77**	C9
Szegvár	*H*	**77**	D8
Székesfehérvár	*H*	**76**	C5
Szekszárd	*H*	**76**	E5
Szentendre	*H*	**76**	B6
Szentes	*H*	**77**	D8
Szentőrinc	*H*	**76**	E4
Szerencs	*H*	**73**	H2
Szigetszentmiklós	*H*	**76**	C6
Szigetvár	*H*	**76**	E3
Szikszó	*H*	**73**	H2
Szolnok	*H*	**77**	C7
Szombathely	*H*	**76**	C2
Szprotawa	*PL*	**70**	H4
Sztum	*PL*	**71**	C9
Szubin	*PL*	**71**	E7
Szydłowiec	*PL*	**73**	B1

T

Place	Country	Page	Grid
Taastrup	*DK*	**44**	E6
Tab	*H*	**76**	D4
Tábor	*CZ*	**41**	E11
Täby	*S*	**47**	C9
Tachov	*CZ*	**41**	E8
Tadcaster	*GB*	**5**	F9
Tafalla	*E*	**20**	D4
Taggia	*I*	**19**	D10
Taksony	*H*	**76**	C6
Talant	*F*	**12**	G6
Talavera de la Reina	*E*	**26**	E2
Talavera la Real	*E*	**24**	F6
Talayuela	*E*	**24**	C8
Talence	*F*	**16**	E3
Tälje	*S*	**52**	C3
Tallinn	*EST*	**66**	B6
Tălmaciu	*RO*	**78**	F3
Talmont-St-Hilaire	*F*	**16**	B2
Talsi	*LV*	**66**	G3
Tamási	*H*	**76**	D4
Tamași	*RO*	**79**	D7
Tampere	*FIN*	**53**	E12
Tamsweg	*A*	**39**	E8
Tamworth	*GB*	**9**	B7
Tanacu	*RO*	**79**	D9
Țăndărei	*RO*	**83**	B12
Tanger	*MA*	**25**	N7
Tangerhütte	*D*	**43**	F8
Tangermünde	*D*	**43**	E8
Tanna	*D*	**41**	C7
Țânțăreni	*RO*	**82**	B5
Taormina	*I*	**30**	E6
Tapa	*EST*	**67**	C7
Tápiószecső	*H*	**77**	C7
Tápiószele	*H*	**77**	C7
Tapolca	*H*	**76**	D3
Taraclia	*MD*	**79**	F10
Tarancón	*E*	**26**	E5
Taranto	*I*	**31**	C10
Tarare	*F*	**17**	C12
Tarazona	*E*	**20**	E3
Tarazona de la Mancha	*E*	**27**	F7
Tarbert	*GB*	**2**	C2
Tarbert	*GB*	**2**	G3
Tarbert	*GB*	**2**	H4
Tarbes	*F*	**21**	B6
Târgoviște	*RO*	**78**	H5
Târgu Bujor	*RO*	**79**	F9
Târgu Cărbunești	*RO*	**78**	H2
Târgu Frumos	*RO*	**79**	C7
Târgu Jiu	*RO*	**78**	G1
Târgu Lăpuș	*RO*	**78**	C2
Târgu Mureș	*RO*	**78**	D3
Târgu Neamț	*RO*	**78**	C6
Târgu Ocna	*RO*	**79**	E7
Târgu Secuiesc	*RO*	**78**	E6
Târgu Trotuș	*RO*	**79**	E7
Tarifa	*E*	**25**	N8
Tărlungeni	*RO*	**78**	F5
Târnăveni	*RO*	**78**	E3
Tarnobrzeg	*PL*	**73**	C3
Tarnos	*F*	**16**	H2
Târnova	*RO*	**77**	E10
Tarnów	*PL*	**73**	D2
Tarnowskie Góry	*PL*	**75**	C10
Tarquinia	*I*	**32**	C4

T

Place	Country	Page	Grid
Tarragona	*E*	**21**	F8
Tàrrega	*E*	**21**	E8
Tarrio	*E*	**22**	B3
Tårs	*DK*	**44**	G5
Tărtăşeşti	*RO*	**83**	B9
Tartu	*EST*	**67**	D8
Tarutyne	*UA*	**79**	E11
Tarvisio	*I*	**39**	F8
Tăşnad	*RO*	**77**	C11
Tát	*H*	**76**	B5
Tata	*H*	**76**	B4
Tatabánya	*H*	**76**	B5
Tătărani	*RO*	**78**	H4
Tatarbunary	*UA*	**79**	F12
Tauberbischofsheim	*D*	**40**	E4
Taucha	*D*	**41**	A8
Taunton	*GB*	**8**	F5
Tauragė	*LT*	**68**	E4
Taurianova	*I*	**31**	G8
Taurisano	*I*	**31**	D11
Tauste	*E*	**20**	E4
Tăuţii-Măgherăuş	*RO*	**78**	B2
Tavagnacco	*I*	**35**	B11
Tavankut	*SRB*	**76**	E6
Tavarnelle Val di Pesa	*I*	**35**	G7
Tavaux	*F*	**13**	G7
Tavernes de la Valldigna	*E*	**27**	G10
Taviano	*I*	**31**	D11
Tavira	*P*	**25**	K4
Tavistock	*GB*	**8**	G3
Tczew	*PL*	**71**	B8
Teaca	*RO*	**78**	D3
Teano	*I*	**30**	A4
Techirghiol	*RO*	**84**	C4
Tecuci	*RO*	**79**	F8
Tegelen	*NL*	**11**	E8
Téglás	*H*	**77**	B10
Teglio	*I*	**34**	B5
Teignmouth	*GB*	**8**	G4
Teiuş	*RO*	**78**	E2
Teixeiro	*E*	**22**	B3
Tekirdağ	*TR*	**85**	C3
Telč	*CZ*	**74**	F5
Telciu	*RO*	**78**	C3
Teleneşti	*MD*	**79**	B10
Telford	*GB*	**8**	B6
Telfs	*A*	**37**	C11
Telšiai	*LT*	**68**	C4
Temerin	*SRB*	**77**	G7
Tempio Pausania	*I*	**32**	D3
Templin	*D*	**43**	D10
Tenja	*HR*	**76**	G5
Tenterden	*GB*	**9**	F10
Tepelenë	*AL*	**86**	E2
Teplice	*CZ*	**41**	C10
Teramo	*I*	**33**	B7
Terespol	*PL*	**72**	G6
Tergnier	*F*	**12**	B4
Termini Imerese	*I*	**30**	E3
Termoli	*I*	**33**	C9
Terneuzen	*NL*	**10**	E4
Terni	*I*	**32**	B5
Ternitz	*A*	**39**	C11
Terracina	*I*	**32**	E6
Terråk	*N*	**54**	D5
Terralba	*I*	**32**	F2
Terranova da Sibari	*I*	**31**	D8
Terranuova Bracciolini	*I*	**35**	G8
Terrasini	*I*	**30**	E2
Terrassa	*E*	**21**	F10
Terrasson-Lavilledieu	*F*	**17**	E7
Teruel	*E*	**20**	H5
Tervel	*BG*	**83**	D12
Tešanj	*BIH*	**81**	C7
Teslić	*BIH*	**81**	C7
Tetbury	*GB*	**8**	D6
Teterow	*D*	**43**	C9
Teteven	*BG*	**83**	E7
Tétouan	*MA*	**28**	H3
Tetovo	*MK*	**82**	G1
Tewkesbury	*GB*	**8**	D6
Tezze sul Brenta	*I*	**35**	B8
Thame	*GB*	**9**	D8
Thaon-les-Vosges	*F*	**13**	E8
Thasos	*GR*	**87**	D10
Theix	*F*	**14**	F5
Thermo	*GR*	**88**	A4
Thessaloniki	*GR*	**87**	D7
Thetford	*GB*	**9**	C10
Thiers	*F*	**17**	C10
Thionville	*F*	**13**	C8
Thirsk	*GB*	**5**	E9
Thisted	*DK*	**44**	C2
Thiva	*GR*	**88**	B6
Thizy	*F*	**17**	C12
Thônes	*F*	**36**	F4
Thonon-les-Bains	*F*	**36**	E4
Thorne	*GB*	**5**	F9
Thornton	*GB*	**5**	F6
Thouaré-sur-Loire	*F*	**14**	G6
Thouars	*F*	**15**	H8
Thuir	*F*	**18**	F1
Thun	*CH*	**13**	H10
Thurles	*IRL*	**7**	L5
Thurso	*GB*	**2**	B6
Ţibana	*RO*	**79**	D8
Ţibăneşti	*RO*	**79**	D8
Tibro	*S*	**46**	E5
Ţicleni	*RO*	**78**	H1
Tidaholm	*S*	**46**	E5
Tiel	*NL*	**11**	D7
Tielt	*B*	**10**	F4
Tierp	*S*	**52**	G5
Ţifeşti	*RO*	**79**	F7
Ţigăneşti	*RO*	**83**	C9
Tighina	*MD*	**79**	D11
Tiha Bârgăului	*RO*	**78**	C4
Tikkurila	*FIN*	**64**	G6
Tilburg	*NL*	**10**	E6
Tilbury	*GB*	**9**	E10
Tileagd	*RO*	**77**	C11
Timişoara	*RO*	**77**	F9
Timrå	*S*	**52**	C5
Tinca	*RO*	**77**	D10
Tineo	*E*	**22**	B6
Tinnum	*D*	**44**	G1
Tinos	*GR*	**89**	C9
Tipperary	*IRL*	**7**	L4
Tiptree	*GB*	**9**	D10
Tiranë	*AL*	**86**	B2
Tirano	*I*	**34**	A6
Tiraspol	*MD*	**79**	D12
Tismana	*RO*	**77**	G12
Tiszaalpár	*H*	**77**	D7
Tiszacsege	*H*	**77**	B9
Tiszaföldvár	*H*	**77**	D8
Tiszafüred	*H*	**77**	B8
Tiszakécske	*H*	**77**	D7
Tiszalök	*H*	**77**	A9
Tiszalúc	*H*	**77**	A9
Tiszaújváros	*H*	**77**	B9
Tiszavasvári	*H*	**77**	B9
Titel	*SRB*	**77**	G8
Tito	*I*	**31**	B7
Titov Drvar	*BIH*	**80**	C4
Tittmoning	*D*	**39**	C7
Titu	*RO*	**83**	B9
Tivat	*MNE*	**81**	G8
Tiverton	*GB*	**8**	F4
Tivoli	*I*	**32**	C6
Tjeldstø	*N*	**48**	B1
Tjønnefoss	*N*	**48**	E5
Tjøtta	*N*	**54**	C5
Tlmače	*SK*	**75**	H9
Tłuszcz	*PL*	**71**	F12
Tobarra	*E*	**27**	H8
Tobermory	*GB*	**2**	F3
Todi	*I*	**32**	B5
Todireşti	*RO*	**79**	C7
Todireşti	*RO*	**79**	D8
Todmorden	*GB*	**5**	F8
Toft	*GB*	**3**	B12
Toijala	*FIN*	**64**	E4
Tokaj	*H*	**77**	A10
Tokod	*H*	**76**	B5
Toksovo	*RUS*	**65**	G11
Toledo	*E*	**26**	E4
Tolentino	*I*	**35**	G11
Tolmezzo	*I*	**39**	F7
Tolmin	*SLO*	**35**	B12
Tolna	*H*	**76**	E5
Tolosa	*E*	**20**	B3
Tomar	*P*	**24**	D3
Tomaszów Lubelski	*PL*	**73**	C5
Tomaszów Mazowiecki	*PL*	**71**	H10
Tomelilla	*S*	**45**	F9
Tomelloso	*E*	**26**	F5
Tomeşti	*RO*	**79**	C8
Tona	*E*	**21**	E10
Tonbridge	*GB*	**9**	E10
Tønder	*DK*	**44**	G2
Tonnay-Charente	*F*	**16**	C3
Tonneins	*F*	**16**	F5
Tonnerre	*F*	**12**	F5
Tønsberg	*N*	**49**	D7
Tonstad	*N*	**48**	E3
Topliţa	*RO*	**78**	D5
Topoľčany	*SK*	**75**	G9
Topoloveni	*RO*	**78**	H4
Topolovgrad	*BG*	**83**	G10
Topraisar	*RO*	**84**	C4
Torano Castello	*I*	**31**	E8
Torchiarolo	*I*	**31**	C11
Tordera	*E*	**21**	E11
Tordesillas	*E*	**23**	F8
Torekov	*S*	**45**	D7
Torelló	*E*	**21**	E10
Toreno	*E*	**22**	C6
Torgau	*D*	**43**	G9
Torgelow	*D*	**43**	C10
Torigni-sur-Vire	*F*	**15**	C7
Torino	*I*	**19**	A9
Toritto	*I*	**31**	B9
Torla	*E*	**20**	C6
Tornaľa	*SK*	**73**	G1
Tornio	*FIN*	**56**	B6
Toro	*E*	**23**	F8
Törökbálint	*H*	**76**	C5
Törökszentmiklós	*H*	**77**	C8
Torquay	*GB*	**8**	G4

Place	Country	Page	Grid
Torre Annunziata	*I*	**30**	B5
Torre del Greco	*I*	**30**	B5
Torredonjimeno	*E*	**28**	C6
Torrejón de Ardoz	*E*	**23**	H11
Torrelaguna	*E*	**23**	G11
Torrelavega	*E*	**23**	B10
Torremaggiore	*I*	**33**	D10
Torremolinos	*E*	**28**	F5
Torrent	*E*	**27**	F10
Torre-Pacheco	*E*	**29**	C11
Torre Santa Susanna	*I*	**31**	C11
Torres Novas	*P*	**24**	D3
Torres Vedras	*P*	**24**	E2
Torrevieja	*E*	**29**	C11
Torrijos	*E*	**26**	E3
Torrita di Siena	*I*	**35**	H8
Torroella de Montgrí	*E*	**18**	G2
Torrox	*E*	**28**	E6
Torsås	*S*	**45**	D11
Torshälla	*S*	**47**	C7
Tórshavn	*FO*	**3**	B9
Torslanda	*S*	**44**	A6
Tortolì	*I*	**32**	F3
Tortona	*I*	**19**	B11
Tortora	*I*	**31**	D7
Tortoreto	*I*	**33**	B8
Tortorici	*I*	**30**	E5
Tortosa	*E*	**21**	G7
Toruń	*PL*	**71**	E8
Tostedt	*D*	**42**	D5
Totana	*E*	**29**	C10
Tótkomlós	*H*	**77**	E8
Totnes	*GB*	**8**	G4
Totton	*GB*	**9**	F7
Toul	*F*	**13**	D7
Toulon	*F*	**18**	E6
Toulouges	*F*	**18**	F1
Toulouse	*F*	**17**	H7
Tourcoing	*F*	**10**	G3
Tourlaville	*F*	**14**	B6
Tournai	*B*	**10**	G4
Tournefeuille	*F*	**17**	H7
Tournon-sur-Rhône	*F*	**18**	A5
Tournus	*F*	**36**	E2
Tours	*F*	**15**	G9
Towcester	*GB*	**9**	C8
Trabotivište	*MK*	**82**	G4
Traian	*RO*	**79**	D7
Trakai	*LT*	**69**	F8
Tralee	*IRL*	**7**	M2
Trá Li	*IRL*	**7**	M2
Tramariglio	*I*	**32**	E1
Trá Mhór	*IRL*	**7**	M6
Tramore	*IRL*	**7**	M6
Tranås	*S*	**46**	F6
Tranbjerg	*DK*	**44**	E4
Trani	*I*	**31**	A8
Trapani	*I*	**30**	E2
Trasacco	*I*	**33**	C7
Traun	*A*	**39**	B9
Traunreut	*D*	**38**	C6
Traunstein	*D*	**38**	C6
Travnik	*BIH*	**80**	C6
Trbovlje	*SLO*	**39**	G10
Třebíč	*CZ*	**74**	F5
Trebinje	*BIH*	**81**	F7
Trebisacce	*I*	**31**	D9
Trebišov	*SK*	**73**	G3
Trebnje	*SLO*	**39**	G10
Třeboň	*CZ*	**41**	F11
Trebujena	*E*	**25**	L7
Trecastagni	*I*	**30**	F6
Trefynwy	*GB*	**8**	D5
Tréguier	*F*	**14**	D4
Trélazé	*F*	**15**	G8
Trelleborg	*S*	**45**	F8
Tremp	*E*	**21**	D8
Trenčín	*SK*	**75**	F8
Trento	*I*	**35**	B7
Treorchy	*GB*	**8**	D4
Trepuzzi	*I*	**31**	C11
Třešť	*CZ*	**74**	F5
Trets	*F*	**18**	D6
Treuchtlingen	*D*	**40**	F6
Trevi	*I*	**32**	B6
Treviglio	*I*	**34**	C5
Treviso	*I*	**35**	B9
Trévoux	*F*	**17**	C12
Trianta	*GR*	**88**	G4
Tricarico	*I*	**31**	B8
Tricase	*I*	**31**	D12
Trier	*D*	**13**	B8
Trieste	*I*	**35**	C12
Trifeşti	*RO*	**79**	D7
Triggiano	*I*	**31**	A9
Trignac	*F*	**14**	G5
Trigueros	*E*	**25**	J6
Trikala	*GR*	**86**	F5
Trim	*IRL*	**4**	F2
Třinec	*CZ*	**75**	E9
Tring	*GB*	**9**	D8
Trino	*I*	**19**	A10
Tripoli	*GR*	**88**	C5
Tritenii de Jos	*RO*	**78**	D2
Trittau	*D*	**42**	C6
Trivento	*I*	**33**	D9
Trnava	*SK*	**75**	G8
Trofa	*P*	**22**	F2
Trofaiach	*A*	**39**	D10
Trofors	*N*	**54**	C6
Trogir	*HR*	**80**	E4
Troia	*I*	**33**	E10
Troina	*I*	**30**	E5
Troisdorf	*D*	**11**	F9
Trollhättan	*S*	**46**	E3
Tromsdalen	*N*	**58**	D2
Tromsø	*N*	**58**	D2
Trondheim	*N*	**51**	A7
Troon	*GB*	**4**	B4
Tropea	*I*	**31**	F8
Trosa	*S*	**47**	D9
Trostberg	*D*	**38**	C6
Trouville-sur-Mer	*F*	**15**	C9
Trowbridge	*GB*	**8**	E6
Troyan	*BG*	**83**	E7
Troyes	*F*	**12**	E5
Trpanj	*HR*	**80**	F6
Trstená	*SK*	**75**	E11
Trstenik	*SRB*	**81**	E12
Trujillo	*E*	**24**	D7
Truro	*GB*	**8**	G2
Truşeşti	*RO*	**79**	B7
Truskavets'	*UA*	**73**	F5
Trŭstenik	*BG*	**83**	D7
Trutnov	*CZ*	**74**	C5
Tryavna	*BG*	**83**	E9
Trzcianka	*PL*	**70**	E5
Trzebiatów	*PL*	**70**	C4
Trzebnica	*PL*	**75**	A7
Trzemeszno	*PL*	**71**	F7
Tržič	*SLO*	**39**	F9
Tsebrykove	*UA*	**79**	C12
Tuam	*IRL*	**7**	H3
Tübingen	*D*	**13**	D12
Tubize	*B*	**10**	G5
Tuchola	*PL*	**71**	D7
Tuchów	*PL*	**73**	E2
Tudela	*E*	**20**	E4
Tudora	*RO*	**79**	B7
Tudor Vladimirescu	*RO*	**79**	F8
Tufeşti	*RO*	**79**	H9
Tui	*E*	**22**	E2
Tukums	*LV*	**66**	G4
Tulach Mhór	*IRL*	**7**	J5
Tulcea	*RO*	**79**	G10
Tullamore	*IRL*	**7**	J5
Tulle	*F*	**17**	D7
Tulnici	*RO*	**79**	F7
Tuluceşti	*RO*	**79**	F9
Tumba	*S*	**47**	C9
Tunbridge Wells, Royal	*GB*	**9**	E10
Tura	*H*	**77**	B6
Turceni	*RO*	**82**	B5
Turčianske Teplice	*SK*	**75**	F10
Turda	*RO*	**78**	D2
Turek	*PL*	**71**	G8
Turenki	*FIN*	**64**	E5
Tŭrgovishte	*BG*	**83**	E11
Turgutalp	*TR*	**85**	F4
Turgutlu	*TR*	**85**	H4
Türi	*EST*	**66**	C6
Turi	*I*	**31**	B9
Turin	*I*	**19**	A9
Turka	*UA*	**73**	F5
Túrkeve	*H*	**77**	C8
Turku	*FIN*	**53**	G11
Turnhout	*B*	**10**	E6
Turnov	*CZ*	**41**	C12
Turnu Măgurele	*RO*	**83**	D8
Tursi	*I*	**31**	C8
Turţ	*RO*	**77**	B12
Tuscania	*I*	**32**	B4
Tuszyn	*PL*	**71**	G9
Tutrakan	*BG*	**83**	C11
Tuttlingen	*D*	**13**	F12
Tuusula	*FIN*	**64**	F6
Tuve	*S*	**44**	A6
Tuzla	*BIH*	**81**	C8
Tuzla	*RO*	**84**	C5
Tveit	*N*	**48**	D3
Tvøroyri	*FO*	**3**	C9
Tvŭrditsa	*BG*	**83**	F9
Twardogóra	*PL*	**75**	A8
Twist	*D*	**11**	C9
Twistringen	*D*	**11**	B11
Tyachiv	*UA*	**78**	A2
Tychy	*PL*	**75**	D10
Tyfors	*S*	**46**	A5
Tynset	*N*	**51**	D8
Tyrnavos	*GR*	**86**	F6
Tysse	*N*	**48**	B2

U

Place	Country	Page	Grid
Úbeda	*E*	**29**	C7
Ubli	*HR*	**80**	F5
Ubrique	*E*	**25**	L8
Uchte	*D*	**11**	C12
Uckfield	*GB*	**9**	F9

U

Place	Country	Page	Grid
Uddevalla	*S*	**46**	E2
Udeşti	*RO*	**78**	B6
Udine	*I*	**35**	B11
Ueckermünde	*D*	**43**	C10
Uelzen	*D*	**42**	E6
Uetendorf	*CH*	**13**	H10
Uetersen	*D*	**42**	C5
Uetze	*D*	**42**	F6
Ugento	*I*	**31**	D11
Ugine	*F*	**36**	F4
Uherské Hradiště	*CZ*	**75**	F8
Uherský Brod	*CZ*	**75**	F8
Uig	*GB*	**2**	D2
Uithuizen	*NL*	**11**	A8
Újfehértó	*H*	**77**	B10
Újkígyós	*H*	**77**	D9
Újszász	*H*	**77**	C7
Ukmergė	*LT*	**69**	E7
Ulaş	*TR*	**85**	B4
Ulft	*NL*	**11**	D8
Ullånger	*S*	**52**	B6
Ullapool	*GB*	**2**	D4
Ulldecona	*E*	**21**	G7
Ulm	*D*	**38**	B3
Ulmeni	*RO*	**77**	C12
Ulmeni	*RO*	**83**	C11
Ulmu	*RO*	**79**	H8
Ulricehamn	*S*	**45**	A8
Ulsberg	*N*	**51**	C7
Ulsta	*GB*	**3**	B12
Ulucak	*TR*	**85**	G3
Ulverston	*GB*	**4**	E6
Umbertide	*I*	**35**	G9
Umbrăreşti	*RO*	**79**	F8
Umeå	*S*	**56**	F2
Umka	*SRB*	**81**	C11
Ungheni	*MD*	**79**	C9
Ungheni	*RO*	**78**	E3
Ungureni	*RO*	**79**	B7
Uničov	*CZ*	**75**	E7
Unirea	*RO*	**78**	E2
Unterägeri	*CH*	**37**	C7
Unterhaid b Bamburg	*D*	**40**	D6
Unterweitersdorf	*A*	**39**	B9
Uppingham	*GB*	**9**	C8
Upplands-Väsby	*S*	**47**	C9
Uppsala	*S*	**47**	B9
Urbania	*I*	**35**	G10
Urbino	*I*	**35**	F10
Urduña	*E*	**20**	C1
Urecheşti	*RO*	**79**	F7
Urganlı	*TR*	**85**	G4
Uricani	*RO*	**77**	G12
Urk	*NL*	**11**	C7
Urlaţi	*RO*	**78**	H6
Urziceni	*RO*	**83**	B11
Uskhodni	*BY*	**69**	G11
Uslar	*D*	**42**	G5
Ussel	*F*	**17**	D8
Ústí nad Labem	*CZ*	**41**	C10
Ústí nad Orlicí	*CZ*	**74**	D6
Ustka	*PL*	**45**	H12
Ustrzyki Dolne	*PL*	**73**	E4
Utbjoa	*N*	**48**	C2
Utena	*LT*	**69**	D9
Utiel	*E*	**27**	F9
Utrecht	*NL*	**10**	D6
Utrera	*E*	**25**	K7
Uttoxeter	*GB*	**5**	H8
Uusikaupunki	*FIN*	**53**	F10
Uxbridge	*GB*	**9**	E9
Uzès	*F*	**17**	G12
Uzhhorod	*UA*	**73**	G3
Užice	*SRB*	**81**	D10
Uzunköprü	*TR*	**85**	B2

V

Place	Country	Page	Grid
Vaasa	*FIN*	**53**	B10
Vác	*H*	**76**	B6
Văcăreşti	*RO*	**78**	H5
Vado Ligure	*I*	**19**	C11
Vadsø	*N*	**59**	D11
Vadstena	*S*	**46**	E6
Vadul lui Vodă	*MD*	**79**	C11
Vadu Moldovei	*RO*	**78**	C6
Vadu Paşii	*RO*	**79**	G7
Vaduz	*FL*	**37**	C9
Våg	*N*	**48**	D2
Våge	*N*	**48**	G4
Vagney	*F*	**13**	E9
Vågsodden	*N*	**54**	C5
Vágur	*FO*	**3**	C9
Vairano Patenora	*I*	**33**	E8
Vaison-la-Romaine	*F*	**18**	C5
Valandovo	*MK*	**87**	B7
Valašské Klobouky	*CZ*	**75**	F8
Valašské Meziříčí	*CZ*	**75**	E8
Valbo	*S*	**52**	G5
Valby	*DK*	**45**	E7
Valdagno	*I*	**35**	C8
Valdemoro	*E*	**26**	D4
Valdepeñas	*E*	**26**	G5
Valderice	*I*	**30**	E2
Valdobbiadene	*I*	**35**	B9
Vale	*GBG*	**14**	C5
Valea lui Mihai	*RO*	**77**	B11
Valea Râmnicului	*RO*	**79**	G7
Valea Seacă	*RO*	**79**	C7
Valea Stanciului	*RO*	**82**	C6
Valence	*F*	**16**	G6
Valence	*F*	**18**	A5
Valencia	*E*	**27**	F10
Valencia de Alcántara	*E*	**24**	D5
Văleni	*RO*	**79**	D9
Vălenii de Munte	*RO*	**78**	G6
Valenza	*I*	**19**	A11
Valga	*EST*	**67**	F7
Valguarnera Caropepe	*I*	**30**	F5
Valjevo	*SRB*	**81**	C10
Valka	*LV*	**67**	F7
Valkeakoski	*FIN*	**64**	E5
Valkenswaard	*NL*	**11**	E7
Valladolid	*E*	**23**	E9
Vallauris	*F*	**19**	D8
Vallentuna	*S*	**47**	C9
Valletta	*M*	**31**	□
Vallo della Lucania	*I*	**30**	C6
Valls	*E*	**21**	F8
Valmiera	*LV*	**66**	F6
Valmontone	*I*	**32**	D6
Valognes	*F*	**14**	B6
Valozhyn	*BY*	**69**	G10
Valpovo	*HR*	**76**	F5
Valréas	*F*	**18**	C5
Valu lui Traian	*RO*	**84**	C4
Valverde del Camino	*E*	**25**	J6
Vama	*RO*	**78**	B5
Vammala	*FIN*	**53**	E11
Vámospércs	*H*	**77**	B10
Vânatori	*RO*	**79**	F8
Vânătorii Mici	*RO*	**83**	B9
Vänersborg	*S*	**46**	E3
Vânju Mare	*RO*	**82**	B4
Vannes	*F*	**14**	F5
Vannvikan	*N*	**51**	A7
Vansbro	*S*	**49**	B12
Vantaa	*FIN*	**64**	G6
Varallo	*I*	**34**	B2
Varapayeva	*BY*	**69**	E11
Vărăşti	*RO*	**83**	C10
Varaždin	*HR*	**39**	F12
Varazze	*I*	**19**	C11
Varberg	*S*	**44**	B6
Varde	*DK*	**44**	E2
Vårdö	*FIN*	**53**	G8
Varel	*D*	**11**	A11
Varėna	*LT*	**69**	G7
Varennes-Vauzelles	*F*	**12**	G3
Vareš	*BIH*	**81**	D7
Varese	*I*	**34**	B3
Vargön	*S*	**46**	E3
Variaş	*RO*	**77**	E9
Varkaus	*FIN*	**65**	C8
Varna	*BG*	**84**	E3
Värnamo	*S*	**45**	B9
Varnsdorf	*CZ*	**41**	B11
Várpalota	*H*	**76**	C4
Vasa	*FIN*	**53**	B10
Vásárosnamény	*H*	**73**	H4
Vasilaţi	*RO*	**83**	C10
Vaslui	*RO*	**79**	D9
Västansjö	*S*	**55**	C7
Västerås	*S*	**47**	B8
Västerhaninge	*S*	**47**	C9
Västervik	*S*	**45**	A12
Vasto	*I*	**33**	C9
Vasvár	*H*	**76**	C2
Vatican City	*VAT*	**32**	C5
Vatra Dornei	*RO*	**78**	C5
Vauldalen	*N*	**51**	C9
Vauvert	*F*	**17**	H12
Växjö	*S*	**45**	C10
Veauche	*F*	**17**	D12
Vecchiano	*I*	**34**	F6
Vechta	*D*	**11**	C11
Vecsés	*H*	**76**	C6
Veda	*S*	**52**	B6
Vedea	*RO*	**83**	D9
Veendam	*NL*	**11**	B9
Veenendaal	*NL*	**11**	D7
Vegadeo	*E*	**22**	B5
Vegarshei	*N*	**48**	E6
Veghel	*NL*	**11**	E7
Veglie	*I*	**31**	C11
Veidholmen	*N*	**50**	A5
Vejen	*DK*	**44**	F3
Vejer de la Frontera	*E*	**25**	M7
Vejle	*DK*	**44**	E3
Vela Luka	*HR*	**80**	F5
Velen	*D*	**11**	D9
Velenje	*SLO*	**39**	F10
Veles	*MK*	**82**	H3
Vélez-Málaga	*E*	**28**	E5
Vélez-Rubio	*E*	**29**	D9
Velika Gorica	*HR*	**39**	G11
Velika Kladuša	*BIH*	**80**	B3
Velika Plana	*SRB*	**81**	C12
Veliki Preslav	*BG*	**83**	E11

Place	Country	Page	Grid
Velikiy Lyubin'	*UA*	**73**	E6
Veliko Tŭrnovo	*BG*	**83**	E9
Velingrad	*BG*	**82**	G6
Veľké Kapušany	*SK*	**73**	G3
Velké Meziříčí	*CZ*	**74**	E6
Veľký Krtíš	*SK*	**75**	H10
Veľký Meder	*SK*	**76**	B3
Velletri	*I*	**32**	D6
Vellinge	*S*	**45**	F7
Velyka Mykhaylivka	*UA*	**79**	C12
Velyki Mosty	*UA*	**73**	D6
Velykyy Bereznyy	*UA*	**73**	G4
Velykyy Bychkiv	*UA*	**78**	B2
Venafro	*I*	**33**	D8
Venaria	*I*	**19**	A9
Vence	*F*	**19**	D8
Vendargues	*F*	**17**	H11
Vendas Novas	*P*	**24**	F3
Vendôme	*F*	**15**	F10
Venelles	*F*	**18**	D6
Venezia	*I*	**35**	C9
Vénissieux	*F*	**36**	F2
Vennesla	*N*	**48**	F5
Vennesund	*N*	**54**	D4
Venosa	*I*	**31**	B7
Venta de Baños	*E*	**23**	E9
Ventimiglia	*I*	**19**	D9
Ventnor	*GB*	**9**	G7
Ventspils	*LV*	**66**	F2
Vera	*E*	**29**	D9
Verbania	*I*	**34**	B3
Vercelli	*I*	**34**	C3
Verdalsøra	*N*	**54**	G4
Verden (Aller)	*D*	**11**	B12
Verdun	*F*	**13**	C7
Vereşti	*RO*	**78**	B6
Vergato	*I*	**35**	E7
Vergèze	*F*	**17**	G12
Verín	*E*	**22**	E4
Verkhovyna	*UA*	**78**	A4
Verneşti	*RO*	**79**	G7
Verneuil-sur-Avre	*F*	**15**	D10
Vernier	*CH*	**36**	E4
Vernio	*I*	**35**	F7
Vernole	*I*	**31**	C12
Vernon	*F*	**12**	C1
Veroia	*GR*	**86**	D6
Veroli	*I*	**33**	D7
Verona	*I*	**35**	C7
Versailles	*F*	**12**	D2
Versoix	*CH*	**36**	E4
Vertou	*F*	**14**	G6
Verzuolo	*I*	**19**	B9
Veselí nad Lužnicí	*CZ*	**41**	F11
Veselí nad Moravou	*CZ*	**75**	F7
Vesoul	*F*	**13**	F8
Veszprém	*H*	**76**	C4
Vésztő	*H*	**77**	D9
Vetlanda	*S*	**45**	B10
Vetovo	*BG*	**83**	D10
Vetralla	*I*	**32**	C4
Vevey	*CH*	**36**	E5
Veyre-Monton	*F*	**17**	D10
Vezin le Coquet	*F*	**14**	E6
Viana do Bolo	*E*	**22**	D5
Viana do Castelo	*P*	**22**	E2
Viareggio	*I*	**34**	F6
Viarmes	*F*	**12**	C2
Viborg	*DK*	**44**	D3
Vibo Valentia	*I*	**31**	F8
Vic	*E*	**21**	E10
Vícar	*E*	**29**	E8
Vicchio	*I*	**35**	F8
Vicenza	*I*	**35**	C8
Vichy	*F*	**17**	C10
Vico del Gargano	*I*	**33**	D11
Vico Equense	*I*	**30**	B5
Vicovu de Sus	*RO*	**78**	B5
Victoria	*RO*	**78**	F4
Vidauban	*F*	**19**	D7
Videle	*RO*	**83**	C9
Vidin	*BG*	**82**	C4
Vidra	*RO*	**79**	F7
Vidra	*RO*	**83**	C10
Vidzy	*BY*	**69**	D10
Viechtach	*D*	**41**	F9
Vielsalm	*B*	**11**	H7
Vienna	*A*	**39**	C12
Vienne	*F*	**36**	G2
Viersen	*D*	**11**	F8
Vierzon	*F*	**12**	G2
Vieste	*I*	**33**	D11
Vietri sul Mare	*I*	**30**	B6
Vievis	*LT*	**69**	F8
Vigevano	*I*	**34**	C3
Vignola	*I*	**35**	E7
Vigo	*E*	**22**	D2
Viişoara	*RO*	**78**	D2
Vik	*N*	**48**	B2
Vikeså	*N*	**48**	E3
Vikna	*N*	**54**	E3
Viksmon	*S*	**52**	B5
Vila do Conde	*P*	**22**	F2
Vilafranca del Penedès	*E*	**21**	F9
Vila Franca de Xira	*P*	**24**	E2
Vilagarcía de Arousa	*E*	**22**	C2
Vilalba	*E*	**22**	B4
Vila Nova de Famalicão	*P*	**22**	F2
Vila Nova de Gaia	*P*	**22**	F2
Vila Nova de Ourém	*P*	**24**	D3
Vilanova i la Geltrú	*E*	**21**	F9
Vilar de Andorinho	*P*	**22**	F2
Vila Real	*P*	**22**	F4
Vila Real de Santo António	*P*	**25**	K5
Vilaseca de Solcina	*E*	**21**	F8
Vila Viçosa	*P*	**24**	F5
Vilches	*E*	**28**	B6
Vilhelmina	*S*	**55**	E9
Viljandi	*EST*	**67**	D7
Vilkaviškis	*LT*	**68**	F5
Villabate	*I*	**30**	E3
Villablino	*E*	**22**	C6
Villacañas	*E*	**26**	E5
Villa Carcina	*I*	**34**	C6
Villacarrillo	*E*	**29**	C7
Villa Castelli	*I*	**31**	B10
Villach	*A*	**39**	F8
Villacidro	*I*	**32**	G2
Villadossola	*I*	**34**	B2
Villafranca del Bierzo	*E*	**22**	C5
Villafranca de los Barros	*E*	**24**	F6
Villafranca Tirrena	*I*	**30**	D6
Villajoyosa-La Vila Joíosa	*E*	**27**	H10
Villa Literno	*I*	**30**	A4
Villamartín	*E*	**25**	L8
Villanueva de Córdoba	*E*	**28**	B4
Villanueva de la Serena	*E*	**24**	E7
Villanueva de los Infantes	*E*	**26**	G6
Villaputzu	*I*	**32**	G3
Villareal	*E*	**27**	E10
Villarosa	*I*	**30**	F4
Villarrobledo	*E*	**26**	F6
Villarrubia de los Ojos	*E*	**26**	F5
Villasana de Mena	*E*	**20**	B1
Villa San Giovanni	*I*	**31**	G7
Villasimius	*I*	**32**	G3
Villasor	*I*	**32**	G2
Villaverde del Río	*E*	**25**	J7
Villaviciosa	*E*	**23**	B7
Villefontaine	*F*	**36**	F2
Villefranche-de-Rouergue	*F*	**17**	F8
Villefranche-sur-Saône	*F*	**17**	C12
Villena	*E*	**27**	G9
Villeneuve-lès-Avignon	*F*	**18**	C5
Villeneuve-sur-Lot	*F*	**16**	F6
Villeneuve-sur-Yonne	*F*	**12**	E4
Villers-Cotterêts	*F*	**12**	C3
Villeurbanne	*F*	**36**	F2
Vilnius	*LT*	**69**	F8
Vilsbiburg	*D*	**38**	B6
Vilshofen	*D*	**39**	B7
Vilyeyka	*BY*	**69**	F10
Vimianzo	*E*	**22**	B1
Vimmerby	*S*	**45**	A11
Vimperk	*CZ*	**41**	F10
Vinaròs	*E*	**21**	H7
Vinci	*I*	**35**	F7
Vineuil	*F*	**15**	F10
Vinga	*RO*	**77**	E9
Vingåker	*S*	**47**	D7
Vinica	*MK*	**82**	G4
Vinje	*N*	**48**	A3
Vinjeøra	*N*	**50**	B6
Vinkovci	*HR*	**76**	G5
Vinstra	*N*	**51**	E7
Vinţu de Jos	*RO*	**78**	E1
Vipiteno	*I*	**37**	D11
Vire	*F*	**15**	D7
Viriat	*F*	**36**	E2
Virkkala	*FIN*	**64**	G5
Virovitica	*HR*	**76**	F3
Virrat	*FIN*	**53**	C12
Vis	*HR*	**33**	A11
Visaginas	*LT*	**69**	D10
Visby	*S*	**47**	F9
Višegrad	*BIH*	**81**	D9
Viseu	*P*	**22**	G3
Vişeu de Sus	*RO*	**78**	B3
Vişina	*RO*	**83**	B9
Visoko	*BIH*	**81**	D7
Visselhövede	*D*	**42**	E5
Viterbo	*I*	**32**	B5
Vitez	*BIH*	**81**	D6
Vitomiricë	*RKS*	**81**	G11
Vitoria-Gasteiz	*E*	**20**	C2
Vitré	*F*	**15**	E7
Vitrolles	*F*	**18**	D5
Vitry-le-François	*F*	**12**	D5
Vittel	*F*	**13**	E7
Vittoria	*I*	**30**	G5
Vittorio Veneto	*I*	**35**	B9
Viveiro	*E*	**22**	A4
Vize	*TR*	**84**	H3
Viziru	*RO*	**79**	G9
Vizzini	*I*	**30**	G5
Vlaardingen	*NL*	**10**	D5
Vladičin Han	*SRB*	**82**	F3
Vladimirescu	*RO*	**77**	E10
Vlăhiţa	*RO*	**78**	E5
Vlasenica	*BIH*	**81**	D8

V

Place	Country	Page	Grid
Vlašim	CZ	41	E12
Vlasotince	SRB	82	E3
Vlissingen	NL	10	E4
Vlorë	AL	86	D1
Vöcklabruck	A	39	C8
Vodice	HR	80	D3
Vodňany	CZ	41	F11
Voghera	I	19	A12
Vogošća	BIH	81	D7
Voikkaa	FIN	65	E7
Voinești	RO	78	G4
Voinești	RO	79	C8
Voiron	F	36	G3
Voitsberg	A	39	E10
Vojens	DK	44	F3
Volda	N	50	D3
Völkermarkt	A	39	F9
Volos	GR	87	F7
Volosovo	RUS	67	B11
Volovăț	RO	78	B5
Volovets'	UA	73	G5
Volterra	I	35	G7
Voluntari	RO	83	B10
Voranava	BY	69	G8
Vordingborg	DK	44	G6
Voreppe	F	36	G3
Vorona	RO	79	B7
Voru	EST	67	E8
Voss	N	48	A3
Voula	GR	89	C7
Voxna	S	52	E3
Vráble	SK	75	H9
Vranje	SRB	82	F3
Vranov nad Topľou	SK	73	G3
Vrapčište	MK	82	G1
Vratsa	BG	82	E6
Vrbas	SRB	77	F7
Vrbno pod Pradědem	CZ	75	D7
Vrbové	SK	75	G8
Vrchlabí	CZ	74	C5
Vreden	D	11	D9
Vrhnika	SLO	35	B12
Vrnjačka Banja	SRB	81	E12
Vroomshoop	NL	11	C8
Vršac	SRB	77	G9
Vsetín	CZ	75	E8
Vsevolozhsk	RUS	65	G11
Vukovar	HR	76	G6
Vulcan	RO	78	G1
Vulcănești	MD	79	F10
Vŭlchedrŭm	BG	82	D5
Vulturu	RO	79	F8
Vŭrshets	BG	82	E5
Vushtrri	RKS	81	F12
Vyalikaya Byerastavitsa	BY	72	D6
Vyborg	RUS	65	F9
Vyerkhnyadzvinsk	BY	69	D11
Vylkove	UA	79	G12
Vynnyky	UA	73	E6
Vynohradiv	UA	73	H5
Vyritsa	RUS	67	B12
Vyronas	GR	89	C7
Vyškov	CZ	75	F7
Vysoké Mýto	CZ	74	D6

W

Place	Country	Page	Grid
Wąbrzeźno	PL	71	D9
Wadebridge	GB	8	G2
Wadowice	PL	75	D11
Wągrowiec	PL	70	E6
Wakefield	GB	5	F8
Wałbrzych	PL	74	C6
Wałcz	PL	70	D5
Waldkirch	D	13	E10
Waldsassen	D	41	D8
Waldshut	D	13	F11
Wallasey	GB	4	G6
Walls	GB	3	C11
Walsall	GB	8	C6
Walsrode	D	42	E5
Walton on the Naze	GB	9	D11
Wangen im Allgäu	D	37	B9
Wantage	GB	9	E7
Wardenburg	D	11	B11
Ware	GB	9	D9
Waren	D	43	C9
Warka	PL	71	G11
Warminster	GB	8	E6
Warrenpoint	GB	4	E2
Warrington	GB	5	G7
Warsaw	PL	71	F11
Warszawa	PL	71	F11
Warwick	GB	9	C7
Washington	GB	5	D8
Wasilków	PL	72	D5
Wasselonne	F	13	D10
Wassenaar	NL	10	D5
Waterford	IRL	7	M6
Waterlooville	GB	9	F8
Watford	GB	9	D9
Wathlingen	D	42	E6
Watten	F	10	F2
Watton	GB	9	C10
Wattwil	CH	37	C8
Wedel (Holstein)	D	42	C5
Weener	D	11	B9
Weert	NL	11	F7
Wegberg	D	11	F8
Węgorzewo	PL	68	G4
Węgrów	PL	72	F4
Weiden in der Oberpfalz	D	41	E8
Weil am Rhein	D	13	F10
Weilburg	D	11	G11
Weilheim in Oberbayern	D	37	B11
Weimar	D	41	B7
Weinfelden	CH	38	D1
Weißenburg in Bayern	D	40	F6
Weißenfels	D	41	B7
Weißenhorn	D	37	A9
Weißwasser	D	43	G11
Weiz	A	39	D11
Wejherowo	PL	71	B8
Wellesbourne	GB	9	C7
Wellingborough	GB	9	C8
Wellington	GB	8	F5
Wells	GB	8	E5
Wels	A	39	C8
Welshpool	GB	8	B5
Wem	GB	5	H7
Wendelstein	D	40	E6
Wernigerode	D	42	G6
Wesel	D	11	E8
West Bromwich	GB	8	C6
Westende	B	10	F3
Westerland	D	44	G1
Westhill	GB	3	E8
West Kirby	GB	4	G6
Weston-super-Mare	GB	8	E5
Wetherby	GB	5	F9
Wetzlar	D	11	G11
Wevelgem	B	10	F3
Wexford	IRL	7	L6
Weybridge	GB	9	E9
Weymouth	GB	8	F6
Whitby	GB	5	E9
Whitchurch	GB	5	H7
Whitehaven	GB	4	D6
Whitley Bay	GB	5	C8
Whitstable	GB	9	E11
Wichelen	B	10	F5
Wick	GB	2	B7
Wicklow	IRL	4	H3
Widnes	GB	5	G7
Więcbork	PL	71	D7
Wieleń	PL	70	E5
Wieliczka	PL	75	D11
Wieluń	PL	75	B9
Wien	A	39	C12
Wiener Neustadt	A	39	C12
Wiesbaden	D	13	A11
Wiesmoor	D	11	A10
Wietze	D	42	E5
Wigan	GB	5	F7
Wigston	GB	9	C8
Wigton	GB	4	D6
Wijchen	NL	11	D7
Wil	CH	13	G12
Wilhelmshaven	D	11	A11
Wilmslow	GB	5	G7
Wimborne Minster	GB	8	F6
Wimereux	F	9	F12
Winchester	GB	9	F7
Windermere	GB	5	E7
Windsor	GB	9	E8
Winsen (Aller)	D	42	E5
Winsen (Luhe)	D	42	D6
Winterberg	D	11	F11
Winterthur	CH	13	F11
Winwick	GB	9	C9
Wisbech	GB	9	B9
Wishaw	GB	2	H5
Wisła	PL	75	E10
Wismar	D	43	C7
Witham	GB	9	D10
Withernsea	GB	5	F10
Witkowo	PL	71	F7
Witney	GB	9	D7
Wittenberge	D	43	E8
Wittenburg	D	43	C7
Wittingen	D	42	E6
Wittmund	D	42	C3
Wittstock	D	43	D8
Wivenhoe	GB	9	D11
Władysławowo	PL	71	A8
Włocławek	PL	71	E9
Włodawa	PL	72	H6
Włoszczowa	PL	75	B11
Woking	GB	9	E8
Wolbrom	PL	75	C11
Wołczyn	PL	75	B8
Wolfen	D	43	G8
Wolfenbüttel	D	42	F6
Wolfhagen	D	11	E12
Wolfratshausen	D	37	B11
Wolfsberg	A	39	E10
Wolfsburg	D	42	F6
Wolgast	D	43	B10
Wolin	PL	43	C11

Wołomin	*PL*	**71**	F11
Wołów	*PL*	**74**	A6
Wolsztyn	*PL*	**70**	F5
Wolvega	*NL*	**11**	B8
Wolverhampton	*GB*	**8**	C6
Woodbridge	*GB*	**9**	D11
Worb	*CH*	**13**	H10
Worcester	*GB*	**8**	C6
Wörgl	*A*	**38**	D6
Workington	*GB*	**4**	D6
Worksop	*GB*	**5**	G9
Wormerveer	*NL*	**10**	C6
Worms	*D*	**13**	B11
Worthing	*GB*	**9**	F9
Wrecsam	*GB*	**5**	G7
Wrexham	*GB*	**5**	G7
Wrocław	*PL*	**75**	B7
Wronki	*PL*	**70**	E5
Września	*PL*	**71**	F7
Wschowa	*PL*	**70**	G5
Wunsiedel	*D*	**41**	D8
Wunstorf	*D*	**11**	C12
Wuppertal	*D*	**11**	F9
Würzburg	*D*	**40**	E5
Wurzen	*D*	**41**	A9
Wyrzysk	*PL*	**70**	D6
Wysokie Mazowieckie	*PL*	**72**	E4
Wyszków	*PL*	**71**	F12

X

Xanthi	*GR*	**87**	C10
Xátiva	*E*	**27**	G10
Xinzo de Limia	*E*	**22**	E4
Xirivella	*E*	**27**	F10

Y

Yakoruda	*BG*	**82**	G6
Yambol	*BG*	**83**	F11
Yampil'	*UA*	**79**	A9
Yantarnyy	*RUS*	**68**	F1
Yarm	*GB*	**5**	D9
Yasinya	*UA*	**78**	A3
Yavoriv	*UA*	**73**	D5
Yaxley	*GB*	**9**	C9
Ybbs an der Donau	*A*	**39**	C10
Ydra	*GR*	**89**	D7
Y Drenewydd	*GB*	**8**	C4
Yecla	*E*	**27**	G9
Yenihisar	*TR*	**88**	E2
Yeovil	*GB*	**8**	F5
Yeste	*E*	**27**	H7
Y Fenni	*GB*	**8**	D5
Ylivieska	*FIN*	**62**	F5
Ylöjärvi	*FIN*	**53**	E12
York	*GB*	**5**	F9
Youghal	*IRL*	**7**	M5
Yssingeaux	*F*	**17**	E11
Ystad	*S*	**45**	F8
Ytterhogdal	*S*	**51**	D12
Yutz	*F*	**13**	C8
Yverdon	*CH*	**13**	H8
Yvetot	*F*	**15**	B10

Z

Zaandam	*NL*	**10**	C6
Ząbki	*PL*	**71**	F11
Ząbkowice Śląskie	*PL*	**75**	C7
Zábřeh	*CZ*	**75**	D7
Zabrze	*PL*	**75**	C9
Zadar	*HR*	**80**	D2
Zafferana Etnea	*I*	**30**	F6
Zafra	*E*	**24**	G6
Żagań	*PL*	**70**	G4
Žaglav	*HR*	**80**	D2
Zagon	*RO*	**78**	F6
Zagreb	*HR*	**39**	G11
Zaječar	*SRB*	**82**	C3
Zakopane	*PL*	**75**	F11
Zakros	*GR*	**89**	G11
Zakynthos	*GR*	**88**	C2
Zalaegerszeg	*H*	**76**	D2
Zalamea de la Serena	*E*	**24**	F8
Zalaszentgrót	*H*	**76**	D2
Zalău	*RO*	**77**	C12
Žalec	*SLO*	**39**	F10
Zambrów	*PL*	**72**	E4
Zamora	*E*	**23**	F7
Zamość	*PL*	**73**	C5
Zandvliet	*B*	**10**	E5
Zănești	*RO*	**79**	D7
Zapolyarnyy	*RUS*	**59**	E12
Zaprešić	*HR*	**39**	G11
Zaragoza	*E*	**20**	E5
Zarasai	*LT*	**69**	D9
Zărnești	*RO*	**78**	F5
Zărnești	*RO*	**79**	G7
Żary	*PL*	**70**	G4
Zas	*E*	**22**	C2
Zaslawye	*BY*	**69**	G11
Žatec	*CZ*	**41**	C10
Zavallya	*UA*	**79**	A12
Zavidoviči	*BIH*	**81**	C7
Zawadzkie	*PL*	**75**	C9
Zawiercie	*PL*	**75**	C10
Zduńska Wola	*PL*	**71**	H9
Zdzieszowice	*PL*	**75**	C9
Žednik	*SRB*	**77**	F7
Zehdenick	*D*	**43**	E10
Zeitz	*D*	**41**	B8
Zelenogorsk	*RUS*	**65**	G10
Zelenogradsk	*RUS*	**68**	E2
Želiezovce	*SK*	**76**	A5
Zella-Mehlis	*D*	**40**	C6
Zell am See	*A*	**39**	D7
Zelów	*PL*	**71**	H9
Zeltweg	*A*	**39**	E9
Zelzate	*B*	**10**	F4
Zemst	*B*	**10**	F5
Zemun	*SRB*	**81**	B11
Zenica	*BIH*	**81**	D7
Zerbst	*D*	**43**	G8
Zermatt	*CH*	**34**	B2
Zetea	*RO*	**78**	E5
Zeven	*D*	**11**	A12
Zevenbergen	*NL*	**10**	E6
Zeytinli	*TR*	**85**	E3
Zgierz	*PL*	**71**	G9
Zhabinka	*BY*	**72**	F6
Zhodzina	*BY*	**69**	G12
Zhovkva	*UA*	**73**	D6
Žiar nad Hronom	*SK*	**75**	G10
Ziębice	*PL*	**75**	C7
Zielona Góra	*PL*	**70**	G4
Zierikzee	*NL*	**10**	E5
Žigljen	*HR*	**80**	C2
Žilina	*SK*	**75**	F9
Zimnicea	*RO*	**83**	D9
Zirc	*H*	**76**	C4
Zirndorf	*D*	**40**	E6
Zittau	*D*	**41**	B12
Živinice	*BIH*	**81**	C8
Zlaté Moravce	*SK*	**75**	G9
Zlatna	*RO*	**77**	E12
Zlatograd	*BG*	**87**	B11
Zlín	*CZ*	**75**	F8
Złocieniec	*PL*	**70**	D5
Złotoryja	*PL*	**74**	B5
Złotów	*PL*	**70**	D6
Żmigród	*PL*	**70**	H6
Żnin	*PL*	**71**	E7
Znojmo	*CZ*	**74**	F6
Zoetermeer	*NL*	**10**	D5
Zografou	*GR*	**89**	C7
Zola Predosa	*I*	**35**	E7
Zorleni	*RO*	**79**	E9
Żory	*PL*	**75**	D9
Zossen	*D*	**43**	F10
Zrenjanin	*SRB*	**77**	G8
Zruč nad Sázavou	*CZ*	**41**	E12
Zschopau	*D*	**41**	C9
Zubia	*E*	**28**	E6
Zuera	*E*	**20**	E5
Zug	*CH*	**13**	G11
Zülpich	*D*	**11**	G8
Zulte	*B*	**10**	F4
Zumarraga	*E*	**20**	C3
Županja	*HR*	**76**	G5
Zürich	*CH*	**13**	G11
Żuromin	*PL*	**71**	E10
Zvolen	*SK*	**75**	G10
Zvoriștea	*RO*	**78**	B6
Zvornik	*BIH*	**81**	C9
Zwettl	*A*	**39**	B10
Zwickau	*D*	**41**	C8
Zwiesel	*D*	**41**	F9
Zwoleń	*PL*	**72**	H3
Zwolle	*NL*	**11**	C8
Żychlin	*PL*	**71**	F9
Żyrardów	*PL*	**71**	G10
Żywiec	*PL*	**75**	E10

Z

Ø

Øksfjord	*N*	**58**	C5
Ølstykke	*DK*	**44**	E6
Ørsta	*N*	**50**	D3

Å

Åbo	*FIN*	**53**	G11
Åby	*S*	**47**	D7
Åfjord	*N*	**54**	G3
Ågskaret	*N*	**57**	G2
Åhus	*S*	**45**	E9
Åkarp	*S*	**45**	E8
Åkersberga	*S*	**47**	C10
Åkerstrømmen	*N*	**51**	E8
Åkrehamn	*N*	**48**	D2
Ålesund	*N*	**50**	C3
Åmot	*N*	**48**	D5
Åmål	*S*	**46**	D3
Åndalsnes	*N*	**50**	C4
Åre	*S*	**51**	A10
Århus	*DK*	**44**	D4
Ås	*N*	**51**	B9
Åsele	*S*	**55**	F10
Åseral	*N*	**48**	E4
Åstorp	*S*	**45**	D7
Åtvidaberg	*S*	**47**	E7

Ä

Älmhult	*S*	**45**	D9
Älta	*S*	**47**	C9
Älvros	*S*	**51**	D12
Älvsbyn	*S*	**56**	C3
Ängelholm	*S*	**45**	D7
Äänekoski	*FIN*	**64**	B6

Ö

Örebro	*S*	**46**	C6
Örnsköldsvik	*S*	**53**	A7
Östersund	*S*	**51**	B12
Överammer	*S*	**52**	A4